Child Sexual Abuse

Child Sexual Abuse

A Primer for Treating Children, Adolescents, and Their Nonoffending Parents

SECOND EDITION ■

ESTHER DEBLINGER,

ANTHONY P. MANNARINO, AND

JUDITH A. COHEN

WITH

MELISSA K. RUNYON AND

ANNE H. HEFLIN

OXFORD
UNIVERSITY PRESS

OXFORD
UNIVERSITY PRESS

Oxford University Press is a department of the University of Oxford. It furthers the University's objective of excellence in research, scholarship, and education by publishing worldwide.

Oxford New York
Auckland Cape Town Dar es Salaam Hong Kong Karachi
Kuala Lumpur Madrid Melbourne Mexico City Nairobi
New Delhi Shanghai Taipei Toronto

With offices in
Argentina Austria Brazil Chile Czech Republic France Greece
Guatemala Hungary Italy Japan Poland Portugal Singapore
South Korea Switzerland Thailand Turkey Ukraine Vietnam

Oxford is a registered trademark of Oxford University Press in the UK and certain other countries.

Published in the United States of America by
Oxford University Press
198 Madison Avenue, New York, NY 10016

Library of Congress Cataloging-in-Publication Data
Deblinger, Esther, author.
[Treating sexually abused children and their nonoffending parents : a cognitive behavioral approach.]
Child sexual abuse : a primer for treating children, adolescents, and their nonoffending parents / Esther Deblinger, Anthony P. Mannarino, and Judith A. Cohen with Melissa K. Runyon and Anne H. Heflin. — Second edition.
p. ; cm.
Preceded by: Treating sexually abused children and their nonoffending parents : a cognitive behavioral approach / Esther Deblinger, Anne Hope Heflin. c1996.
Includes bibliographical references and index.
ISBN 978–0–19–935874–8 (alk. paper)
I. Mannarino, Anthony P., author. II. Cohen, Judith A., author.
III. Runyon, Melissa K., author. IV. Heflin, Anne Hope, author. V. Title.
[DNLM: 1. Child Abuse, Sexual. 2. Child Psychiatry—methods.
3. Adolescent Psychiatry—methods. 4. Parent-Child Relations.
5. Parents—psychology. WS 350]
RJ507.S49
618.92′858360651—dc23
2014044282

We would like to dedicate this book to survivors of child sexual abuse whose strength and courage have inspired our work and to our families with deepest gratitude for their unending love and support!

CONTENTS

FOREWORD

I am delighted to write the foreword for *Child Sexual Abuse: A Primer for Treating Children, Adolescents, and Their Nonoffending Parents*. When I wrote the foreword to the previous version back in 1996, we were still in the early stages of developing effective treatments for children and families impacted by child sexual abuse. We did know a fair amount about sexual abuse; a lot of knowledge had accumulated about prevalence, characteristics, risk factors, and impact. And there was an expanding number of treatment programs, many with a specific focus on sexual abuse. The book was significant because it was the first clinical resource based on empirical findings. The book reflected the results of the randomized trial that Esther Deblinger and colleagues had conducted. Now we had a tested and proven abuse-specific treatment.

Now, almost 20 years later, much has changed. Trauma-focused cognitive behavioral therapy (TF-CBT), the intervention that was developed as a result of Deblinger's as well as Cohen's and Mannarino's early studies has been refined and further tested by its developers, Esther Deblinger, Judy Cohen, and Tony Mannarino, and has become one of the most well-known and widely sought treatments for children affected by trauma. The model has been evaluated in numerous controlled trials, not just by the developers but all over the world. There have been studies in various countries in Europe showing similar positive results. It has also been tested with excellent outcomes in low-resource countries such as Zambia, Tanzania, Democratic Republic of Congo, and Cambodia. It works for both boys and girls, for multiple trauma types, children in foster care, children with complex trauma histories, children exposed to domestic violence, and more.

The TF-CBT story is remarkable. Part of it is the impressive amount of empirical support that has been amassed. It is on every list of evidence-based interventions. It has been identified as a highly cost-beneficial intervention. Adoption of a well-established evidence-based intervention has become increasingly important with policy shifts toward establishing preferences for evidence-based interventions. But the bigger story is that TF-CBT as an evidence-based intervention has been embraced to a degree that is exceptional for evidence-based interventions in routine clinical settings.

There are some important reasons why TF-CBT has been greeted differently relative to many other evidence-based interventions. Typically evidence-based interventions target a diagnosis or specific psychological conditions, whereas TF-CBT is designed to treat the impact of a traumatic event. A treatment that explicitly acknowledges the life experiences and context that lead to client difficulties resonates to a much greater degree within the community-based agencies where most children receive their mental health care. As a result, community clinicians are far more receptive to TF-CBT and see it as a likely fit for many of their clients whom they know have experienced child abuse and trauma.

Esther Deblinger and colleagues' original treatment study that was the basis for the earlier book had critical findings with regard to child and parent involvement in active therapy. It turned out that symptoms respond differentially based on who is involved in the therapy. For example, improvements in PTSD symptoms require direct involvement of the child in therapy, whereas active parental participation is likely necessary for improvements in trauma-related behavior problems. Since TF-CBT does not just address posttraumatic stress but also other trauma-specific impacts such as depression and trauma-related behavior problems, it is essential to have an intervention that contains both child and parent components.

This is another key aspect of TF-CBT that distinguishes it from many other evidence-based practices (EBPs). It addresses both internalizing and externalizing problems. Many of the proven treatments for the most common childhood conditions target either internalizing or externalizing problems. For example, CBTs for anxiety or depression in children do not contain parent components to address behavioral difficulties if present; whereas effective treatments for behavior problems typically do not directly address internal distress of the children but focus primarily on teaching parents new methods of responding to child misbehavior. TF-CBT as designed and tested is really a child and parent intervention that incorporates the evidence-based components for both internal distress and challenging behaviors.

This new book focuses on the application of TF-CBT with children, adolescents, and their nonoffending caregivers. It is a welcome addition to the clinical literature. Youth with a history of child sexual abuse are among the most commonly seen trauma survivors in clinical populations. As the authors point out, there are quite a few unique aspects of sexual abuse cases. For example, many children delay reporting because of concern about being believed or being blamed, which may lead to additional trauma-specific impacts that are far less common in children affected by other traumas. Parental support may be more at risk for being compromised due to the distress parents experience upon discovering that their child has been sexually abused. The sexual nature of the abuse creates complications all around, for the children, the caregivers, and others.

Like the earlier book, this one is chock-a-block with clinical examples illustrating the application of the various components of TF-CBT. The case examples provide specific guidance for clinicians in carrying out the treatment. They also convey the in-depth clinical knowledge and experience of the authors. There is no doubt that the authors have authentic life-based experience with this population and care deeply about helping youth and their families recover.

Child Sexual Abuse: A Primer for Treating Children, Adolescents, and Their Nonoffending Parents will be a valuable resource for clinicians. It brings alive how to deliver an evidence-based intervention in a supportive and flexible way that stays true to the model.

—Lucy Berliner
Director Harborview Center for Sexual Assault/Traumatic Stress
University of Washington

PREFACE AND ACKNOWLEDGMENTS

As this is a second edition that stemmed from work that began in the late 1980s, it is impossible to acknowledge all those whose support, creative ideas, and efforts have contributed to the work upon which this book is based. However, we would like to acknowledge at least some of the individuals whose encouragement and support made both the first and second editions of this book possible.

Ideas for the original book began percolating back in 1987, shortly after Dr. Susan McLeer offered the first author, Dr. Esther Deblinger, the position of co-director of the Child Sexual Abuse Diagnostic and Treatment Center at the Medical College of Pennsylvania. Dr. Deblinger cannot thank Dr. McLeer enough for being an outstanding mentor and believing in her ability to develop a clinical research service for children and their families impacted by child sexual abuse. Dr. Deblinger would also like to acknowledge Delmina Henry, Ph.D., and the late Helen Orvaschel, Ph.D., for their important early contributions, as well as Marc Atkins, Ph.D., and Caryn Lerman, Ph.D., for their early and ongoing support and friendship over the years. Fortuitously, Dr. Edna Foa, a renowned clinical researcher and faculty member, was actively engaged in treatment outcome research with adult rape victims at the Medical College of Pennsylvania at that time as well. She was also a great support and supervisor to the first author and has been an extraordinary colleague and a wonderful role model as a scientist practitioner par excellence for all three of the TF-CBT co-developers.

In 1989 Dr. Deblinger accepted Dr. Martin Finkel's offer to serve as the clinical director of a developing multidisciplinary center for the evaluation and treatment of suspected victims of child sexual abuse at the School of Osteopathic Medicine in Stratford, New Jersey. As a pediatrician, Dr. Finkel demonstrated tremendous commitment to not only healing the physical wounds of children impacted by child sexual abuse but also the psychological wounds. He was a great source of encouragement to Dr. Deblinger and she would like to express appreciation for his invaluable support, enthusiasm for research, and friendship over the past 25 years they have worked together. It should also be noted that the first edition of this book would not have been published without a great deal of encouragement from highly supportive colleagues including Jon Conte, Lucy

Berliner, Terry Hendrix, and of course, Anne Heflin, who was a co-author for the first as well as the second edition.

Concurrently, Drs. Anthony Mannarino and Judith Cohen were developing a very similar approach, first at the University of Pittsburgh School of Medicine/Western Psychiatric Institute and Clinic, and subsequently at Allegheny General Hospital. They are grateful for important collaborations with and support from Ellen Frank, Ph.D., the late Joaquim Puig-Antich, M.D., Trevor Price, M.D., and the late William Friedrich, Ph.D.

As the co-developers of TF-CBT, Drs. Deblinger, Mannarino, and Cohen would like to acknowledge the key role our statistical consultants have played in supporting the research that has been so critical to the success of the TF-CBT model. Robert Steer, Ed.D., has served as a statistics consultant and collaborator on many TF-CBT-related studies, and we are grateful for his expertise, insight, and dedication to this work. Satish Iyengar, Ph.D., has also provided statistical consultation for several of our studies, and we greatly appreciate his valuable contributions. It should be noted that research cannot be successful without the hard work and dedication of research coordinators who truly make it all happen. We have been extremely fortunate to have the assistance and support of outstanding research coordinators, including Allyson Maedel, M.A., Lori Galiano, M.A., Beth Cooper, M.S., Andrea Weiss, Ph.D., Michelle Gregor, M.S., Virginia Staron, M.A., Kraig Knudsen, Ph.D., Tiffany Tipton, M.A., and Suzanne Kodya, M.A.

Many other great colleagues have contributed to our clinical research efforts as co-investigators including Julie Lippmann, Psy.D., Lori Stauffer, Ph.D., Elisabeth Pollio, Ph.D., as well as Melissa Runyon, Ph.D., whose valuable contributions include serving as a co-author of this book. Additionally we acknowledge the important contributions of our colleagues Susan Padlo, LCSW, Carrie Seslow, LCSW, Tamra Greenberg, Ph.D., and Karen Stubenbort, Ph.D., in helping to refine clinical applications of TF-CBT and Krista Elston, LCSW, and Lori Malazich, LCSW for their dedication to our research projects. We are grateful to each of them for their support and significant contributions over the years. Many other members of our respective teams have importantly contributed as well including many research assistants, study clinicians, clinical supervisors, consultants, trainers, and researchers who have replicated our work both here in the United States as well as around the world. We would like to especially thank Ann Marie Kotlik for her outstanding administrative assistance over more than 25 years. A special thanks also goes to Jan Sands and Yolanda Virella for their invaluable administrative assistance. Finally, a great debt of gratitude is owed to Beth Cooper whose gentle nudging, incredible support, and expert editing every step of the way made it possible to complete the second edition of this book.

We would also like to acknowledge Julia Swope for her technical assistance with respect to the diagrams included in this book. The CSA handout (*Child Sexual Abuse Information [For Parents and Adolescents]*) is being reproduced with permission from Drs. Esther Deblinger and Julie Lippman. The *Self Care: Taking Care of Yourself and Your Child* and the *Positive Rituals and Routines* handouts are being reproduced with permission from Dr. Esther Deblinger. The *Behavior*

Contract handout is being reproduced with permission from Ms. Beth Cooper. The *Establishing House Rules* handout is being reproduced with permission from Dr. Leah Behl. The remaining parenting handouts are being reproduced with permission from Drs. Deblinger and Stauffer. The TF-CBT fidelity checklist is being reproduced with permission from Drs. Esther Deblinger, Judith Cohen, Anthony Mannarino, Laura Murray, and Ms. Carrie Epstein.

Today, we are very fortunate to continue to pursue our collaborative research and dissemination efforts in highly supportive work environments under the leadership of Thomas Cavalieri, D.O., at Rowan University School of Osteopathic Medicine, and Van Nickell, M.D., and Tony Farah, M.D., at Allegheny General Hospital respectively. This work requires these leaders to acknowledge and prioritize the needs of a vulnerable and often overlooked population of children, and we so greatly appreciate their leadership and commitment in this regard.

We also are indebted to the organizations that have supported and funded the development, evaluation, and dissemination of the TF-CBT model. These organizations include the National Center on Child Abuse and Neglect, the National Institute of Mental Health, the Eunice Shriver National Institute for Child Health and Human Development, the National Child Traumatic Stress Network (www.nctsn.org) which is funded by the Substance Abuse Mental Health Services Administration, the Foundation of UMDNJ, the Anne E. Casey Foundation, Staunton Farms Foundation, Rowan University Foundation, and the Robert Wood Johnson Foundation. We are particularly grateful to Malcolm Gordon, Ph.D., John Fairbanks, Ph.D., Bob Pynoos, M.D., and Lisa Amaya-Jackson, M.D., of the National Child Traumatic Stress Network as well as Ben Saunders, Ph.D., and Daniel Smith, Ph.D., at the Medical University of South Carolina and all of our colleagues associated with these organizations. Our collaborations with these individuals and organizations have led to the development of online TF-CBT training, as well as numerous other training projects and collaboratives that have made it possible for us to reach thousands of community-based therapists around the world.

It should also be said that from the very start, our greatest contributors have been the children and parents themselves; they have taught us so much about overcoming child sexual abuse and have been the motivating force behind our efforts. We have shared some of their experiences through dialogues and case examples, but we have significantly altered identifying information and characteristics to protect their right to confidentiality. We would, in fact, like to acknowledge all survivors of child sexual abuse, as it is their courage that inspires our work. Finally, we would like to express our deepest appreciation to our family members and dear friends who have provided unfailing support, have often been our most important teachers, and who have enriched our lives by helping us to balance the demands of this work with love, laughter, and fun.

Esther Deblinger, Ph.D.
Anthony Mannarino, Ph.D.
Judith Cohen, M.D.

Child Sexual Abuse

1

Introduction

Trauma-focused cognitive-behavioral therapy (TF-CBT) was originally developed to help children, adolescents, and nonoffending parents cope with the deleterious psychosocial impact of child sexual abuse (CSA; Cohen & Mannarino, 1992, 1994; Deblinger & Heflin, 1996). Although TF-CBT is currently implemented with children and adolescents who have experienced a wide array of traumatic experiences, CSA remains one of the most daunting and stigmatizing traumas for children and families to overcome. This book highlights the unique skills and special areas of sensitivity (e.g., unique parental reactions, sexuality related issues, medical, legal, and child protection considerations) that are particularly challenging when working with families facing the crisis CSA often precipitates. When it was initially developed over 25 years ago, TF-CBT, the first evidence-based practice designed specifically for this vulnerable population, was tied closely to the available empirical literature on the prevalence, impact, and dynamics of this widespread public health problem. Although this chapter is not an exhaustive review, it provides an update on the scientific research that continues to inform the practice, implementation, and dissemination of TF-CBT specifically with children and adolescents who have experienced sexual abuse.

DEFINITION: CHILD SEXUAL ABUSE

CSA has been defined in a variety of ways in the literature, with more narrow definitions limiting CSA to abuse involving physical contact such as fondling, oral-genital contact, and intercourse, and broader definitions including noncontact abuse such as voyeurism, exhibitionism, and exposure to adult sexual activities or pornography or online sexual victimization. Moreover, when discussing the sexual victimization of youth from a broad perspective, a wide array of terms may be used, including "sexual abuse," "sexual assault," "rape," "sexual harassment," "statutory sexual offenses," "sexual or pornography exposure by an adult," "date rape," "drug or alcohol facilitated sexual assault," and "online sexual harassment or solicitation" (Saunders & Adams, 2014). The federal Child Abuse, Domestic Violence, Adoption, and Family Services Act of 1992 defines sexual abuse as: "(A) the employment, use, persuasion, inducement, enticement, or coercion of any child to engage in, or assist any other person to engage in, any sexually explicit conduct or simulation of such conduct for the purpose of producing a visual depiction of such conduct; or (B) the rape, molestation, prostitution, or other form of sexual exploitation of children, or incest with children." CSA typically involves the sexual gratification of the offender, as well as both a power differential and a knowledge differential between the child and the offender (Child Welfare Information Gateway, 1993). A power differential refers to the fact that the offender often has greater power than the child in terms of physical strength and size, influence, or authority. A knowledge differential refers to the difference between the child and the offender in regard to an understanding of the sexual behavior (e.g., its illegality or inappropriateness) based on differences in age, developmental level, intelligence, social status, and/or other factors. Thus, current definitions of child sexual abuse typically include sexual victimization by adults and/or peers.

INCIDENCE AND PREVALENCE

CSA incidence and prevalence rates reported vary considerably likely due to the different definitions, as well as diverse sampling and assessment procedures used across investigations (Molnar, Buka, & Kessler, 2001). Furthermore, survey response rates across study samples may underestimate the true prevalence given the likelihood that study participants may not disclose sexually abusive experiences due to stigma, self-blame, embarrassment, confusion, and/or fears related to offender-imposed threats (Saunders & Adams, 2014; Wyatt, Loeb, Solis, Carmona, & Romero, 1999). In one large nationally representative, retrospective study of over 34,000 adults in the United States, Perez-Fuentes et al. (2013) found that just over 10% of participants reported an experience of CSA. Among those who reported a history of CSA, 75.2% were women.

Based on a review of the most methodologically rigorous studies using nationally representative samples in the United States, Saunders and Adams (2014) conservatively estimated that before they are 18 years of age approximately 1 out of 5 girls and 1 out of 20 boys experience sexual victimization involving physical contact. Moreover, these authors reported that the results of the National Survey of Children's Exposure to Violence II (Finkelhor, Turner, Shattuck, & Hamby, 2013) demonstrated lifetime prevalence rates for any type of sexual victimization reported by youth (ages 14 to 17) to be as high as 35% for females and 20% for males (Saunders & Adams, 2014).

Gender differences in the CSA prevalence rates cited above are found across studies and may reflect true differences and/or greater underestimations in males than in females. For example, it has been suggested that males may tend to be less likely to report CSA experiences due to greater stigma associated with male victimization especially by male offenders (Saunders & Adams, 2014). Similarly, girls from cultural groups that highly value virginity may be less likely to disclose, thereby artificially depressing the prevalence rates among certain subpopulations of females. Finally, it is important to note that a history of CSA is even more common in child and adolescent clinical populations than in nonclinical samples (Kumar, Steer, & Deblinger, 1996; Lanktree, Briere, & Zaidi, 1991; Rohsenow, Corbett, & Devine, 1988; Sansonnet-Hayden, Haley, Marriage, & Fine, 1987).

Although the above statistics reflect surveys conducted in the United States, CSA is an international problem that affects children of all ethnic, racial, and socioeconomic backgrounds (Finkelhor, 1994; Fleming, Mullen, Sibthorpe, & Bammer, 1999; Stoltenborgh, van IJzendoorn, Euser, & Bakermans-Kranenburg, 2011; Wyatt et al., 1999). In a recent meta-analysis of 331 studies examining CSA prevalence around the world, Stoltenborgh et al. (2011) found the CSA prevalence rates for males and females combined in nonclinical samples to be approximately 12%. The prevalence rate for females was higher (18%) than the prevalence rate for males (7.6%). Although epidemiological studies suggest that there may be some changes in the patterns of abuse, the problem remains highly prevalent worldwide (Finkelhor, Turner, Ormrod, & Hamby, 2009). Furthermore, it should be noted that youth with a history of CSA often have experienced more than one type of victimization. Indeed, Finkelhor, Ormrod, and Turner (2007a) reported that, among their sample of 2,030 children living in the United States, 86% of those who experienced sexual victimization also experienced another type of victimization.

It is encouraging to note that researchers gathering data from a variety of sources report that over the past 10 years there appears to be a decline in sexual abuse rates, particularly adult-on-child sexual abuse reports (Finkelhor & Jones, 2012). This decline may reflect increased law enforcement efforts, enhanced media attention to CSA, as well as greater efforts to educate adults and children about CSA and body safety strategies. It should be noted that this decline in prevalence may not be true for cases of child-on-child sexual abuse. In fact, a recent survey of child abuse physicians, working in the field for over 15 years, suggested that the rate of child-on-child sexual abuse referrals may have increased in the last 15 years (Finkel, DeLago, Deblinger, Runyon, & Cooper, 2014). The percentage of child-on-child sexual abuse cases in the treatment outcome research studies conducted by the authors has steadily increased since this research began. This increase in youth-initiated sexual abuse may reflect children's greater exposure to adult sexual activity through a variety of means including but not limited to pornography on the Internet (Finkel et al., 2014). In fact, the findings of a recent prevalence survey suggest that teens as opposed to adults are the offenders in a greater proportion of sexual assault cases (Saunders & Adams, 2014).

SHORT-TERM IMPACT

Children's reactions to the experience of sexual abuse vary widely. It is well documented that whereas some children who have experienced sexual abuse are asymptomatic, others experience severe and sometimes long-lasting psychiatric symptomatology (Bal, Crombez, De Bourdeaudhuij, & Van Oost, 2009; Beitchman et al., 1992; Browne & Finkelhor, 1986; Finkelhor, 1990; Kendall-Tackett, Williams, & Finkelhor, 1993). Indeed, individuals with a history of CSA are significantly more likely to develop a psychiatric disorder during their lifetime than are individuals without such a history (Molnar et al., 2001; Perez-Fuentes et al., 2013; Trickett, Noll, & Putnam, 2011). There is no specific constellation of symptoms associated with an experience of CSA. Rather, children with a history of sexual abuse may experience a wide range of sequalae.

Emotional difficulties commonly reported by children who have experienced sexual abuse include anxiety, depression, anger, guilt, and shame (Bal, Crombez, Van Oost, & De Bourdeaudhuij, 2003; Brent et al., 2004; Conte & Schuerman, 1987; Feiring, Coates, & Taska, 2001; Feiring & Taska, 2005; Mannarino & Cohen, 1996a; Perez-Fuentes et al., 2013; Trickett et al., 2011; Tufts New England Medical Center, Division of Child Psychiatry, 1984; Turner, Finkelhor, & Ormrod, 2006). Studies have also demonstrated that samples of children and young adults with a history of CSA have between 4 and 8 times the risk for incidences of self-harm and suicide attempts as compared to those who have not experienced sexual abuse in childhood (Brown, Cohen, Johnson, & Smailes, 1999; Trickett et al., 2011).

Behavioral problems exhibited by children with a history of sexual abuse include noncompliance, aggression, avoidant behaviors, truancy, and running away (Brent et al., 2004; Deblinger, McLeer, Atkins, Ralphe, & Foa, 1989; Feiring, Miller-Johnson, & Cleland, 2007; Mannarino & Cohen, 1996a; McLeer, Deblinger, Henry, & Orvaschel, 1992; Perez-Fuentes et al., 2013; Trickett et al., 2011). Research has also documented that age-inappropriate sexual behaviors are considerably more common in children with a history of sexual abuse as compared to those without such a history (Deblinger et al., 1989; Friedrich, Urquiza, & Beilke, 1986).

Cognitive symptoms are also not uncommon among children who have experienced sexual abuse. In fact, research has documented that a history of CSA increased children's risk of developing dissociative symptoms (Trickett et al., 2011), as well as negative cognitive beliefs that lead to distrust of others, feelings of self-blame, low self-esteem, feelings of shame (Deblinger & Runyon, 2005; Mannarino & Cohen, 1996a; Mannarino, Cohen, & Berman, 1994), and feelings of sexual dissatisfaction (Finkelhor, Hotaling, Lewis, & Smith, 1990).

Physiological symptoms sometimes experienced in the aftermath of CSA include headaches, stomachaches, startle reactions, and sleep disturbances (Adams-Tucker, 1981; Anderson, Bach, & Griffith, 1981; Perez-Fuentes et al., 2013; van der Kolk, 1988). Additionally, there is increasing evidence that CSA may be associated with long-term physiological changes including the development of obesity (Noll, Zeller, Trickett, & Putnam, 2007) and accelerated pubertal development (Trickett et al., 2011); while early trauma experiences in general have been associated with abnormalities or deficits in neurodevelopment (De Bellis & Kuchibhatla, 2006; Nadar, 2008), overactivation of the hypothalamic-pituitary-adrenal (HPA) system, and elevated levels of cortisol, which may result in enduring difficulties in managing stress that may predispose individuals to increased impulsivity, suicidal behavior, and impaired executive functioning, as well as negative health consequences (Nadar, 2008; Noll, 2008; Perez-Fuentes et al., 2013; Trickett et al., 2011). Finally, given the above described deleterious effects of CSA on the emotional, cognitive, behavioral, and physical functioning of its victims, it is not surprising that these children often experience academic and interpersonal difficulties. In fact, research has documented that this population of children is at risk for intellectual and academic problems as they have been shown to score lower than nonabused children on receptive language abilities, as well as fluid and crystallized abilities (Noll et al., 2010; Trickett et al., 2011). In addition, in the aftermath of CSA, children are at risk for interpersonal difficulties such as social withdrawal; being left out of desired peer groups; feeling different from peers; low social competence; sexual difficulties such as sexual anxiety, sexual aversion, and hypersexuality; teen pregnancy and motherhood; as well as revictimization (Boney-McCoy & Finkelhor, 1995; Cohen, Deblinger, Maedel, & Stauffer, 1999; Feiring, Simon, & Cleland, 2009; Mannarino & Cohen, 1996a; Noll, Trickett, & Putnam, 2000; Trickett et al., 2011).

LONG-TERM IMPACT

Adults who have a history of CSA continue to be at risk for psychiatric disorders (Fergusson, Boden, & Horwood, 2008; Noll, Trickett, Harris, & Putnam, 2009), though not all survivors show impairment in adulthood (Runtz & Schallow, 1997). In a study of more than 34,000 adults, Perez-Fuentes et al. (2013) found that a history of CSA was associated with a wide range of psychiatric disorders. More specifically, more than 55% of the sample who had been sexually abused reported a substance-use disorder at some point in their lives, over 55% reported an anxiety disorder at some point, over 49% reported a mood disorder, and over 14% acknowledged a suicide attempt at some point. The association between suicide attempts and CSA persisted even after controlling for the effects of comorbid psychiatric disorders. The increased risk of suicide attempts among adults who were sexually abused as children has been noted by numerous investigators (Fergusson et al., 2008; Gladstone et al., 2004; Nelson et al., 2002; Perez-Fuentes et al., 2013). Perez-Fuentes et al. (2013) suggested that the relationship difficulties that adult survivors often experience may contribute to feelings of isolation and stigma, which in turn may increase survivors' risk for suicidal behaviors.

Multiple studies have also found that adult survivors are at significantly greater risk for substance abuse problems than peers without a history of CSA (Cutajar et al., 2010; Fergusson et al., 2008; Fleming et al., 1999; Molnar et al., 2001; Nelson et al., 2002; Noll et al., 2009; Saunders, Kilpatrick, Hanson, Resnick, & Walker, 1999; Schraufnagel, Davis, George, & Norris, 2010). Saunders et al. (1999) suggested that adult survivors may use substances to self-medicate and to cope with their memories of childhood abuse. Similarly, many studies have documented the relationship between an experience of CSA and adult depression (Cutajar et al., 2010; Fergusson et al., 2008; Molnar et al., 2001; Nelson et al., 2002; Noll et al., 2009; Perez-Fuentes et al., 2013; Saunders et al., 1999). For example, in a study of 4,008 women completed by Saunders et al. (1999), adult survivors of child rape were almost twice as likely to have experienced major depression as nonvictims and were 3 times as likely to be currently depressed. Multiple studies have also demonstrated that anxiety disorders including phobias, panic disorder, and social anxiety disorder are more common among adult survivors of CSA than among their nonabused peers (Cutajar et al., 2010; Fergusson et al., 2008; Molnar et al., 2001; Nelson et al., 2002; Perez-Fuentes et al., 2013). Although less frequent, there are also findings linking an experience of CSA with the development of personality disorders (Cutajar et al., 2010; Fergusson et al., 2008). Fergusson et al. (2008) documented that the relationships between CSA and depression, anxiety disorders, substance-use disorders, and suicidal ideation and attempts persisted even when potentially confounding contextual factors were controlled, including low parental education; low socioeconomic status; family instability; parental alcoholism, drug use, and criminal offending; and low levels of parental care and affection.

Adult survivors of CSA are also at increased risk for interpersonal problems such as difficulties with interpersonal trust, relationship dissatisfaction, sexual difficulties, domestic violence, and sexual revictimization (Arata, 2002; DiLillo, 2001; Fleming et al., 1999; Nelson et al., 2002; Perez-Fuentes et al., 2013; Rumstein-McKean & Hunsley, 2001; Trickett et al., 2011). Saunders et al. (1999) reported that women with a CSA history were almost twice as likely to be divorced as their peers who did not have a history of CSA. Adult survivors of CSA are also at risk for achieving less academic and occupational success than nonabused peers, as they tend to have less education, are more likely to drop out of high school, and are more likely to be unemployed (Noll et al., 2009; Saunders et al., 1999). Furthermore, women sexually abused as children are at greater risk than nonabused women for a range of negative physiological outcomes resulting in greater health-care utilization, gynecological problems, preterm deliveries, and sleep problems (Sickel, Noll, Moore, Putnam, & Trickett, 2002; Trickett et al., 2011). Of particular concern are findings indicating that the negative effects of CSA may continue for generations, as the psychological, interpersonal, and physiological consequences of CSA may compromise adult functioning and parenting abilities, thus jeopardizing the development of the offspring of women who were sexually abused as children (Cavanaugh & Classen, 2009; DiLillo, 2001; DiLillo & Damashek, 2003; Kim, Trickett, & Putnam, 2010; Noll et al., 2009; Trickett et al., 2011). Studies have documented relationships between parental experiences of CSA and the development of psychiatric disorders in their offspring including mood disorders and suicidal behaviors (Brent et al., 2002; Brent et al., 2004), as well as increased likelihood of the offspring being born prematurely to a teenage mother and being involved in child protective services (Noll et al., 2009).

POSTTRAUMATIC STRESS DISORDER

Although children who have experienced CSA may exhibit a wide array of seemingly disparate symptoms as noted above, one of the most common and problematic constellation of symptoms falls within the category of posttraumatic stress disorder (PTSD; Cutajar et al., 2010; Deblinger et al., 1989; McLeer, Callaghan, Henry, & Wallen, 1994; McLeer, Deblinger, Atkins, Foa, & Ralphe, 1988; McLeer et al., 1992; Trickett et al., 2011). Studies have demonstrated percentages ranging from 20% to 43% of children with a history of CSA meeting full criteria for PTSD (Deblinger et al., 1989; McLeer et al., 1992; Ruggiero, McLeer, & Dixon, 2000), with significantly greater percentages of children exhibiting partial symptoms of PTSD. Additionally, studies have demonstrated that approximately one-third of adults sexually abused as children meet full criteria for PTSD in adulthood (Molnar et al., 2001; Saunders et al., 1999; Widom, 1999).

In the fifth edition of the Diagnostic and Statistical Manual of Mental Disorders (DSM-5; American Psychiatric Association [APA], 2013) a trauma is defined as: "Exposure to actual or threatened death, serious injury, or sexual violation" (APA 2013, p. 271). The explicit reference to a sexual violation is a change from the fourth edition (text revision) of the DSM (APA, 2000) and makes it clear that a sexual abuse experience constitutes a trauma that may result in PTSD. For the first time, in the fifth edition of the DSM, somewhat different criteria are provided for adults and youth older than 6 years of age as compared to children who are 6 years of age and under.

For youth who are older than 6 years of age and for adults, the DSM-5 specifies that the trauma may be directly experienced, personally witnessed, experienced indirectly through learning of a traumatic event that occurred to a close family member or friend, or experienced through "repeated or extreme exposure to aversive details of the traumatic event(s)" (APA, 2013, p. 271). The symptoms required for a diagnosis of PTSD, as delineated in DSM-5, are grouped in the following four categories:

1. Intrusion symptoms associated with the trauma demonstrated by at least one of the following: intrusive, distressing memories of the event, recurrent distressing dreams, dissociative reactions such as flashbacks, distress at exposure to reminders of the event, and marked physiological reactions to reminders of the event. Accommodations for the ways in which children may experience these symptoms are made as follows: the presence of distressing memories may be demonstrated through repetitive play focused on themes of the trauma; distressing dreams need not be overtly related to the trauma; and dissociative reactions may be demonstrated through trauma-specific play reenactment (APA, 2013).
2. Avoidance of internal and/or external stimuli associated with the trauma, including memories, thoughts, or feeling associated with the trauma or external reminders such as people, places, activities, and objects that arouse thoughts of the trauma (APA, 2013).

3. Negative changes in cognitions and mood after the trauma demonstrated by two or more of the following symptoms: inability to remember an important aspect of the trauma; persistent and exaggerated negative beliefs about oneself, others, or the world; a distorted sense of blame of self or others regarding the causes or consequences of the traumatic event; a persistently negative emotional state such as fear, anger, guilt, or shame; significantly diminished interest or participation in activities; feelings of detachment or estrangement from others; or a persistent inability to experience positive emotions (APA, 2013).
4. Changes in arousal and reactivity after the traumatic event, demonstrated by two or more of the following: irritability or aggression; reckless or self-destructive behavior; hypervigilance; an exaggerated startle response; concentration problems; or sleep disturbance (APA, 2013).

The symptoms must last for a minimum of one month and must cause significant disturbance in functioning.

The DSM-5 allows clinicians to use specifiers to indicate whether or not the individual is experiencing PTSD "with dissociative symptoms" that are categorized as consisting of symptoms of depersonalization or derealization. In addition, a specifier is provided for "delayed expression," for those individuals who do not meet full criteria until a minimum of six months after the trauma (APA, 2013, p. 272).

For children who are 6 years of age and younger, the trauma ("actual or threatened death, serious injury, or sexual violence" [APA, 2013, p. 272]) may be directly experienced, personally witnessed, or experienced indirectly through learning that the trauma occurred to a parent or caregiver. PTSD for young children requires symptoms from the same general categories identified above, with language altered and examples provided to reflect the different ways that young children may manifest those symptoms. For example, within the category of intrusive symptoms, it is noted that "spontaneous and intrusive memories may not necessarily appear distressing and may be expressed as play reenactment" (APA, 2013, p. 273). The categories of "Avoidance" and "Negative Alteration of Cognitions" are grouped together for these young children, with only one symptom being required in those two categories combined. There is less focus on a child's negative cognitions, as those are difficult to ascertain with a young child. Instead the focus is on behavioral symptoms that may be associated with negative cognitions such as, "markedly diminished interest or participation in significant activities, including constriction of play … [or] socially withdrawn behavior" (APA, 2013, p. 273). The symptoms described within the category of "alterations in arousal and reactivity associated with the traumatic event(s)" (APA, 2013, p. 273) are similar to those described for older children and adults; for example, increased irritability and angry outbursts, hypervigilance, an exaggerated startle response, concentration problems, and sleep disturbance. The requirements for duration, impaired functioning, and specifiers remain the same for this age group as for the older age group.

ABUSE-RELATED FACTORS: MODERATING EFFECTS

As previously noted, there is wide variability in children's responses to CSA, with some children responding with significant psychopathology and others exhibiting no discernible symptoms (Browne & Finkelhor, 1986; Finkelhor, 1990; Kendall-Tackett et al., 1993; Trickett et al., 2011). Thus, significant research efforts have been made to identity variables that may moderate the severity of symptomatology experienced by children and adults in the aftermath of CSA. Moderating variables were initially investigated in the areas of abuse-related factors, as information about those factors that are associated with significant psychopathology might help clinicians and researchers identify those children who are at greatest risk. The findings suggest that children exhibit significantly more symptomatology when abuse is perpetrated by a family member (Tremblay, Hebert, & Piche, 1999), particularly a father or father figure, as compared to a stranger (McLeer et al., 1988; Trickett et al., 2011; Trickett, Reiffman, Horowitz, & Putnam, 1997) although that relationship has not always been evident (Ruggiero et al., 2000).

Invasiveness of the abuse appears to be associated with severity of symptomatology, with penetration typically being associated with more negative outcomes (Cutajar et al., 2010; McLeer et al., 1988; Molnar et al., 2001; Nelson et al., 2002; Perez-Fuentes et al., 2013; Schraufnagel et al., 2010; Trickett et al., 1997). A number of studies have found a dose-response effect with frequency and duration of the abuse being associated with increased risk for psychopathology (Molnar et al., 2001; Perez-Fuentes et al., 2013; Reyes, 2008; Ruggiero et al., 2000; Trickett et al., 1997). The use of force or violence in the perpetration of CSA is also often associated with greater symptomatology (Trickett et al., 1997). Similarly, revictimization appears to result in greater risk for the development of more severe psychopathology (Perez-Fuentes et al., 2013). Poly-victimization, or the experience of multiple types of victimizations, is associated with greater symptomatology (Finkelhor et al., 2007a; Turner et al., 2006).

It should be noted that in examinations of all the above abuse-related factors, there have been some studies that did not document the expected relationships between abuse-related factors and child outcomes (Ruggiero et al., 2000; Trickett et al., 2011; Williams & Nelson-Gardell, 2012). Additionally, abuse-related factors are often correlated, making it difficult to determine which factors result in negative outcomes for children. For example, abuse perpetrated by a biological father has been associated with earlier onset and longer duration, whereas abuse by multiple perpetrators has been associated with the use of force or violence (Trickett et al., 2011). In their longitudinal study, Trickett et al. (2011) found that it was useful to identify subgroups of abuse victims through a hierarchical cluster analysis. They identified three subgroups: the first cluster experienced abuse involving physical violence over a relatively short period of time by multiple perpetrators (MP) who were not their biological fathers. The second group experienced abuse of relatively short duration, with infrequent violence, by a single perpetrator (SP) who was not the biological father but rather a father figure in about half the cases and another relative in the other half. The third group was characterized by abuse of long duration with minimal physical violence by the primary father, typically the biological father (BF). The BF subgroup experienced the most negative outcomes of the three groups. This study demonstrates the complexity of examining the relationships between abuse-related factors and resulting symptomatology.

It is important to note that the moderating factors discussed thus far are historical and unalterable. Psychosocial factors that are amenable to change and may mediate the impact of CSA are discussed in terms of their implications for treatment later in this chapter.

DYNAMICS OF CHILD SEXUAL ABUSE

The nature of the sexual activity pursued in CSA experiences varies significantly. Based on the data reported to law enforcement authorities, the National Incident-Based Reporting System indicated that for the year 2008, the types of sexual activities estimated to have been experienced by youth, ordered from most frequent to least frequent, are fondling, forcible rape, statutory rape, forcible sodomy, and sexual assault with an object (Finkelhor & Shattuck, 2012). Most children who are sexually abused experience multiple episodes of sexual abuse (Jonzon & Lindblad, 2004; Ruggiero et al., 2000; Saunders et al., 1999) as well as other types of victimization (Deblinger, Mannarino, Cohen, Runyon, & Steer, 2011; Finkelhor et al., 2007a).

The vast majority of sexual offenders are male (Finkelhor & Ormrod, 2000; McCloskey & Raphael, 2005). However, the results of a large scale adverse childhood experiences (ACE) study demonstrated that among adult survivors of CSA, 40% of the male survivors and 6% of the female survivors reported female perpetration of the abuse (Dube et al., 2005). In 90% of cases, CSA offenses are committed by individuals who are known to the youth (Finkelhor & Ormrod, 2000; Finkelhor & Shattuck, 2012; Saunders et al., 1999). While most often CSA is perpetrated by nonrelatives known to the child, studies have reported that approximately one-third of children are abused by family members (Finkelhor & Ormrod, 2000; Finkelhor & Shattuck, 2012; Wyatt et al., 1999). Most episodes of sexual abuse are perpetrated by adults, with juveniles responsible for at least one-third of sexual offenses (Finkelhor & Ormrod, 2000; Finkelhor & Shattuck, 2012). In many instances of abuse by an adolescent, the adolescent is an older sibling of the victimized child (Shaw, Lewis, Loeb, Rosado, & Rodriguez, 2000; Worling, 1995). It has been hypothesized that in many cases the older sibling may have developed sexually aggressive behaviors in the context of his or her own sexual abuse and directed those sexual acting-out behaviors toward accessible younger siblings (Worling, 1995). More recently, however, there is increasing concern among child abuse professionals that some children and adolescents may act out sexually with younger children following exposure to pornography on the Internet (Finkel et al., 2014). In other circumstances, adolescents may engage in sexual aggression in the context of dating relationships. Studies indicate that 15% to 77% of girls have been forced into sexual contact by a date, while 1% to 13% of girls have been forced by a date to have sex (Foshee et al., 2009).

Engagement in sexual abuse

Youth may be engaged in sexual abuse in a number of ways. Canter, Hughes, and Kirby (1998) identified three different styles of engagement used by offenders: aggressive engagement characterized by the use of threats, violence, and force; criminal-opportunist, which is often a one-time offense pursued at a time of opportunity; and intimate, which is characterized by the grooming process. Forty-five percent of the offenders studied engaged children through the grooming process. It is likely that the actual percentage of offenders who use a grooming process may be higher, as grooming behaviors may be used to minimize the likelihood of disclosure (Craven, Brown, & Gilchrist, 2006).

The term, "grooming," refers to a complex process through which an offender pursues a relationship with a child that may allow him to engage the child in sexual activities. A variety of possible steps in the grooming process have been described as follows: the potential offender may identify a vulnerable child; he then integrates himself into a situation through which he will have access to that child or to children in general; he develops an exclusive relationship with the child; and then he gradually sexualizes the relationship with the victim (Berliner & Conte, 1990; Craven et al., 2006). The sexualization of the relationship may occur through gradual violation of boundaries such as dressing or showering with the child and justification of sexual behavior in some way such as expressing his love and affection for the child (Craven et al., 2006). Physically, offenders often desensitize the child by engaging in nonsexual touching before gradually progressing to sexual touching on top of clothes and later moving to sexual touching under or without clothes (Berliner & Conte, 1990; Craven et al., 2006). The offender may use a variety of strategies to maintain the child's compliance and discourage disclosure. For example, the offender may offer bribes such as gifts or privileges, may make the child feel "special" through providing time or attention, or may threaten to withdraw love or attention if the abuse is disclosed (Berliner & Conte, 1990; Craven et al., 2006). In other instances, the offender may use threats of harm to the child or toward family members, make the child feel responsible for the abuse (Craven et al., 2006), or convince the child that negative outcomes will occur if the child discloses the abuse. The specific grooming process will vary significantly as offenders modify their strategies based upon the responses of the targeted child (Craven et al., 2006).

Disclosure of CSA

Given the process of grooming described above, it is not surprising that the sexual abuse experience is typically shrouded in secrecy. A variety of factors may discourage the child from talking about the abuse, including the stigma of sexual abuse, feelings of shame and guilt about the child's own participation, fear of the perpetrator, as well as anxiety regarding the reactions of others to the disclosure and the consequences of telling. Based on the findings of their qualitative study, McElvaney, Greene, and Hogan (2012) suggested that many youth actively withhold information about their abuse experiences. They may not want people to know what has happened, may deny the abuse when asked about it, and may have difficulty discussing the experiences even when they have decided to disclose. However, children may also have difficulty maintaining the secret and become ambivalent, torn between wanting and not wanting to tell. Children may experience significant psychological distress as a result of actively keeping the secret and eventually decide to confide in someone about the experience.

An intentional disclosure, as described above, has also been described as purposeful. Other patterns of disclosure described in the literature include emergent, accidental, and prompted or elicited disclosures; though not all disclosures fit neatly within these categories (Alaggia, 2004). Purposeful disclosures are made intentionally, typically to parents or other adults, siblings, or friends. The literature suggests that younger children are more likely to disclose to a parent or another adult, while older children are more likely to disclose to a peer (McElvaney et al., 2012). Emergent disclosures take place when a child intentionally gives verbal or behavioral hints that there is a problem, without explicitly providing details about the abuse (Alaggia, 2004). Children who disclose in this way may give partial information and wait to assess reactions before providing more details of their abuse (Gonzales, Waterman, Kelly, McCord, & Oliveri, 1993). Prompted or elicited disclosures typically occur during investigative interviews, psychotherapy, or in other supportive environments (Alaggia, 2004). Finally, accidental disclosures usually occur when a third party discovers the abuse by witnessing the abuse or through medical examinations (Alaggia, 2004). It has been noted that the process of disclosure is rarely linear and sequential (McElvaney et al., 2012). Rather, as suggested by Staller and Nelson-Gardell (2005), the disclosure is more accurately characterized as an ongoing process that is altered and informed by the child's experience at each point of disclosure and by the reactions of others.

Children often delay their disclosure of CSA (Hershkowitz, Lanes, & Lamb, 2007). Hershkowitz and colleagues found that 53% of children who made clear, credible disclosures of sexual abuse delayed their disclosures for periods ranging from one week to two years.

Goodman-Brown, Edelstein, Goodman, Jones, and Gordon (2003) found that children who were abused by a family member and feared negative consequences to others took longer to disclose as did children who felt responsible for the abuse. Other researchers have similarly suggested that children may delay disclosure based on desires to protect others from consequences such as family disruption, punishment, and negative emotions (Malloy, Brubacher, & Lamb, 2011).

It has been well documented that many children do not disclose CSA during childhood at all. Indeed, in retrospective studies of adults abused as children, 55% to 70% of adults reported that they did not disclose their abuse in childhood (Alaggia, 2004; Arata, 1998; Jonzon & Lindblad, 2004; London, Bruck, Ceci, & Shuman, 2005; London, Bruck, Wright, & Ceci, 2008; Roesler & Wind, 1994; Wyatt et al., 1999). In these studies, attempts have been made to identify whether abuse-related variables such as severity, identity of perpetrator, and threats by the perpetrator have been associated with likelihood of disclosure, but findings have been inconsistent (London et al., 2005; London et al., 2008). Recent research, however, has indicated that when children do disclose sexual abuse they are most likely to disclose to their mothers more than any other category of adults or peers (Malloy, Brubacher, & Lamb, 2013). Interestingly, other research findings suggest that offenders are most likely to be arrested when adolescents in particular disclose sexual abuse experiences to their mothers (Stein & Nofziger, 2008). Among studies of children who had not previously disclosed CSA, but whose abuse was categorized as likely based on other evidence, 43% to 49% of children disclosed the abuse during an investigative interview (London et al., 2005). Data suggests that males are less likely to disclose than females (Alaggia, 2004; DeVoe & Faller, 1999; Ghetti, Goodman, Eisen, Qin, & Davis, 2002; London et al., 2005) and more likely to delay disclosures, as many as 10 years longer than females (O'Leary & Barber, 2008). These differences may be due to expectations across cultures that men should be the aggressors. As a result, boys may be less likely than girls to disclose victimization experiences for fear that they will be viewed as weak and/or disgraced (Stoltenborgh et al., 2011).

The literature has also suggested that a significant percentage of children who initially disclosed CSA later recant their disclosures. London et al. (2005) identified problems with this literature, including the likelihood that some of the children who recant are actually correcting a previous false disclosure, though this occurrence appears to be rare, based on the clinical experience of the authors. In recent studies of children whose sexual abuse was substantiated, the percentage of children reported to recant their initial disclosures varied significantly, from 4% to 23% (Hershkowitz et al., 2007; London et al., 2008; Malloy, Lyon, & Quas, 2007). Malloy et al. (2007) reported the highest level of recantation (23%) and indicated that variables that predicted recantation included a lack of support from caregivers, abuse by a parent figure, and younger age of the child. These researchers suggest that children who recant may be responding to family pressure to deny abuse that has occurred.

Parental responses to disclosure

Historically, there has been confusion about the role of mothers in CSA, particularly in cases of incest. In the literature regarding incest published prior to 1975, mothers were often blamed for the sexual abuse, with suggestions that incest occurred because husbands could not obtain sexual satisfaction from their hostile, rejecting wives (Myers, Diedrich, Lee, Fincher, & Stern, 1999). In the 1980s and 1990s, a number of writers suggested that nonoffending mothers often failed to believe their children's disclosures of incestuous abuse and rejected or blamed their children (Elliott & Carnes, 2001; Summit, 1983). It was suggested that mothers often "colluded" in the abuse and thus facilitated it, either directly or indirectly (Crawford, 1999; Elliott & Carnes, 2001; Joyce, 1997). In contrast to these early theories, Elliott and Carnes (2001) reviewed a number of studies that found the majority of nonoffending mothers believe their children's allegations of both intrafamilial and extrafamilial sexual abuse (Deblinger, Hathaway, Lippmann, & Steer, 1993; Elliott & Briere, 1994; Heriot, 1996; Jinich & Litrownik, 1999; Leifer, Kilbane, & Grossman, 2001; Leifer, Shapiro, & Kassem, 1993; Lovett, 1995; Pellegrin & Wagner, 1990; Pierce & Pierce, 1985; Stauffer & Deblinger, 1996). However, it is important to acknowledge that only a minority of nonoffending mothers do not believe and/or take protective actions when faced with children's allegations of CSA (Elliott & Carnes, 2001; Pintello & Zuravin, 2001). There has been a limited amount of research investigating whether nonoffending fathers believe their children's disclosures.

It should also be noted that the findings of a qualitative study demonstrated that mothers coping with sexual abuse allegations often reported negative experiences with system interventions that left them feeling judged and/or unsupported (Plummer & Eastin, 2007). However, the mothers did cite individual police officers, child protection workers, attorneys, and (most often) therapists who listened and provided much-needed guidance and support (Plummer & Eastin, 2007). Although research seems to suggest important areas to address with parents in treatment, further research is needed to clarify factors that may strengthen initial and ongoing parental responses when children disclose experiences of sexual abuse.

SOCIAL SUPPORT

Though the history and circumstances of a child's experience of sexual abuse cannot be changed, psychosocial variables may be modifiable and thus may powerfully mediate children's post-abuse adjustment. One category of such modifiable variables that has been consistently linked to outcomes for children who have experienced sexual abuse is the degree of social support they have. In fact, studies have examined the mediating effects of social support received by children in the aftermath of sexual abuse in a variety of contexts. The quality of the parent-child relationship has been most carefully examined with findings repeatedly demonstrating more positive parent-child relationships are associated with lower levels of child symptoms (Hazzard, Celano, Gould, Lawry, & Webb, 1995; Spaccarelli & Kim, 1995). Support provided post-CSA disclosure has also been examined more specifically. Caregiver support following disclosure of CSA has consistently been identified as a protective factor that is associated with a reduced level of symptomatology post-abuse (Elliott & Carnes, 2001; Everson, Hunter, Runyon, Edelsohn, & Coulter, 1989; Feiring et al., 2001; Feiring, Taska, & Lewis, 1998a; Gries et al., 2000; Spaccarelli & Kim 1995; Williams & Nelson-Gardell, 2012). Indeed, in their review of this literature, Elliott and Carnes (2001) reported that a number of studies have found that parental support was more closely linked with positive adjustment after abuse than abuse-related factors (Cohen & Mannarino, 1996a; Fromuth, 1986; Johnson & Kenkel, 1991; Runtz & Schallow, 1997; Spaccarelli & Kim, 1995; Tremblay et al., 1999).

Other studies have examined interpersonal relationships more broadly and have similarly found that poor relationships appear to contribute to emotional distress (Whiffen & MacIntosh, 2005), while perceived social support from parents, peers, and teachers has been linked to reduced symptomatology (Tremblay et al., 1999). Several studies have more specifically examined the level of support received from a range of individuals when faced with the crisis of CSA and found that more positive crisis support was linked with less negative appraisals (Barker-Collo, Melnyk, & McDonald-Miszczak, 2000) and greater resilience (Rosenthal, Feiring, & Taska, 2003); and conversely that more negative social reactions were associated with increased posttraumatic symptomatology (Ullman & Filipas, 2001) and greater distress in adulthood (Roesler, 1994).

Another parental variable that has been examined in relation to children's post-abuse adjustment is level of parental distress. As has been described above, parental support for the child following disclosure of CSA is an important mediating factor in the child's response to the experience and potentially in the likelihood of recantation. There is considerable evidence that nonoffending parents experience significant levels of distress themselves following a child's disclosure of intrafamilial and extrafamilial sexual abuse (Davies, 1995; Deblinger et al., 1993; Deblinger, Steer, & Lippmann, 1999; Elliott & Carnes, 2001; Newberger, Gremy, Waternaux, & Newberger, 1993; Trickett et al., 2011). Several studies have documented that mothers who have a history of CSA themselves are at risk for greater distress than are mothers without a CSA history (Deblinger, Stauffer, & Landsberg, 1994; Hiebert-Murphy, 1998; Timmons-Mitchell, Chandler-Holtz, & Semple, 1996, 1997; Trickett et al., 2011). Moreover, research findings suggest that nonoffending parents' levels of emotional distress are related to children's levels of distress and psychological symptoms (Deblinger et al., 1999; Elliott & Carnes, 2001; Johnson & Kenkel, 1991; Mannarino & Cohen, 1996b). Much less attention has been given to the emotional reactions of nonoffending fathers, but limited data indicates that fathers also experience significant distress after their children's disclosure of CSA (Elliott & Carnes, 2001; Kelley, 1990; Manion et al., 1996). Unfortunately, the distress nonoffending parents experience may impair their ability to be supportive to their children. Because nonoffending parents have great potential to play a significant role in their children's recovery, the authors strongly encourage their involvement in treatment. Such treatment participation may address issues that have been associated with less-than-optimal parental responses in the aftermath of CSA. For example, treatment involvement may help parents with the loss of an intimate partner in cases of incest, the understanding and management of children's sexual behaviors, and increased levels of blame and doubt that parents appear to experience when the victim or offender is an adolescent (Pintello & Zuravin, 2001; Walsh, Cross, & Jones, 2012). In general, participation in treatment may not only help parents cope with their own personal distress but also may help them respond more supportively and effectively to their children's difficulties.

COPING STRATEGIES

Coping strategies have been explored with child and adult survivors of CSA with mixed findings. The findings regarding avoidant coping strategies appear to be most consistent. Although avoidant coping may temporarily be effective in reducing distress in the moment, the ongoing use of avoidant coping strategies has frequently been related to negative outcomes in the long term (Brand & Alexander, 2003; Canton-Cortes & Canton, 2010; Coffey, Leitenberg, Henning, Turner, & Bennett, 1996; Daigneault, Hebert, & Tourigny, 2006; Futa, Nash, Hansen, & Garbin, 2003; Leitenberg, Greenwald, & Cado, 1992; Marx & Sloan, 2002; Merrill, Thomsen, Sinclair, Gold, & Milner, 2001; Runtz & Schallow, 1997; Steel, Sanna, Hammond, Whipple, & Cross, 2004; Tremblay et al., 1999; Whiffen & MacIntosh, 2005; Wright, Crawford, & Sebastian, 2007). This relationship has not always been found across different types of symptoms (Bal et al., 2009; Chaffin, Wherry, & Dykman, 1997). Chaffin et al. (1997) also found that angry coping was associated with a wide range of behavioral and emotional problems based on teacher ratings, while internalized coping was associated with increased guilt and PTSD symptoms.

In another examination of how children and adolescents responded to their sexual abuse experiences, Simon, Feiring, and McElroy (2010) categorized the strategies these youth used to organize and make meaning of their experiences. They found that those youth categorized as absorbed (engrossed in abuse-related memories, affect, or cognition) were most symptomatic, while youth who demonstrated a constructive approach (an effortful processing of abuse stimuli) were least symptomatic. Avoidant youth (who avoid paying attention to abuse-related stimuli) exhibited symptoms at levels between those demonstrated by youth with absorbed and constructive approaches.

Some of the conflicting findings regarding coping strategies may result from the use of different operational definitions and assessment measures as well as different times of assessment in relation to the abuse. It is possible that different coping strategies may be differentially useful depending upon other variables such as the recency of the abuse and disclosure, whether the child is receiving social support and is participating in therapy, the child's other resiliency factors, and abuse related variables.

COGNITIVE APPRAISALS

Cognitive factors have also been investigated in relation to outcomes following CSA. Appraisals, or the victims' beliefs about how the CSA experience is threatening or may cause loss or harm, are one type of cognitive variable that has been explored (Bal et al., 2009). In fact, research has demonstrated that negative appraisals of the abuse have been associated with heightened symptomatology (Bal et al., 2009; Johnson & Kenkel, 1991; Spaccarelli, 1995) and have been found to account for a larger degree of variance in outcomes than abuse severity (Bal et al., 2009; Dunmore, Clark, & Ehlers, 2001).

Negative cognitions regarding abuse such as personal responsibility for negative events, feeling different from peers, low perceived credibility, and low levels of interpersonal trust have also been related to negative outcomes (Mannarino & Cohen, 1996a, 1996b). Abuse-related shame and self-blame attributions have consistently been related to negative outcomes such as PTSD symptoms, depressive symptoms, lower self-esteem, delinquency, sexual difficulties, and dating aggression over significant follow up periods (Feiring et al., 2007; Feiring et al., 2009; Feiring & Taska, 2005; Feiring, Taska, & Lewis, 1998b). In a number of studies, high levels of shame and a self-blaming attributional style have also accounted for more variance in abuse outcomes than abuse related variables (Feiring et al., 2009; Feiring et al., 1998b; Feiring, Taska, & Lewis, 2002; Whiffen & MacIntosh, 2005). In contrast, children's degree of hope and positive expectancy have been inversely linked with levels of symptoms post-abuse (Williams & Nelson-Gardell, 2012).

SUMMARY AND CONCLUSIONS

The available research documents the widespread prevalence, common dynamics, and the deleterious psychosocial impact of CSA on children and their families. In addition, research findings suggest that in the aftermath of victimization, children's levels of emotional distress and behavioral problems increase their vulnerability to revictimization (Cuevas, Finkelhor, Clifford, Ormrod, & Turner, 2010; Turner, Finkelhor, & Ormrod, 2010). Moreover, as noted above, there is mounting evidence that the accumulation of adverse childhood events of an abusive nature ultimately impacts not only emotional and social well-being but also brain development and overall physical health as well (Felitti et al., 1998; Nadar, 2008).

TF-CBT was originally designed to remediate the difficulties exhibited by children and their families in the aftermath of sexual abuse. Its development and implementation has been greatly influenced by the scientific literature outlined in this chapter, and it will continue to evolve as research advances. The empirical data on the prevalence, dynamics, and impact of CSA reported in this chapter is often provided to clients over the course of treatment, though it is shared in a more family friendly and developmentally appropriate manner. In addition, the structure and principles of TF-CBT reflect the findings of research on psychosocial factors that mediate the impact of CSA. Thus, it should not be surprising that nonoffending caregivers are actively engaged in the TF-CBT process and are encouraged to utilize effective coping and parenting skills to enhance parent-child communication and reduce behavioral difficulties. Furthermore, TF-CBT therapists, in collaboration with youth and their caregivers, encourage therapeutic processing of the sexual abuse and related traumatic stressors in a nonavoidant manner, with a focus on building strong coping skills, healthy relationships, and hopeful expectations for the future. Finally, by reducing behavioral and emotional difficulties and encouraging the development of personal safety skills, TF-CBT is designed to reduce children's risk of further victimization, while enhancing family recovery and growth.

2

Theory, Treatment Development, and Research

As noted earlier, trauma-focused cognitive-behavioral therapy (TF-CBT) was originally developed for use with children, adolescents, and nonoffending parents in the aftermath of child sexual abuse (CSA; Cohen & Mannarino, 1996a, 1998b; Deblinger & Heflin, 1996; Deblinger, Lippmann, & Steer, 1996; Deblinger, McLeer, & Henry, 1990). The model was designed to help caregivers and children cope with the many stressors associated with CSA with a particular focus on addressing posttraumatic stress disorder (PTSD) symptoms, generalized anxiety, depression, feelings of shame, as well as children's oppositional behaviors, age-inappropriate sexual behaviors, and/or other behavioral difficulties. Since then, the developers have adapted this model for children who have experienced a wide array of other traumas including exposure to domestic violence, traumatic loss, and widespread disasters (Cohen, Mannarino, & Deblinger, 2006). Moreover, while TF-CBT was originally designed to be delivered in individual therapy format in outpatient clinics, its effectiveness in group therapy settings has also been documented (Deblinger, Pollio, & Dorsey, 2015; Deblinger, Stauffer, & Steer, 2001; McMullen, O'Callaghan, Shannon, Black, & Eakin, 2013; O'Callaghan, McMullen, Shannon, Rafferty, & Black, 2013; Stauffer & Deblinger, 1996). More recently, TF-CBT has been used successfully with children and adolescents residing in foster care (Dorsey et al., 2014; Lyons, Weiner, & Scheider, 2006), those placed in residential treatment facilities (Cohen, Mannarino, & Navarro, 2012), as well as boy soldiers and girls who have been sexually exploited in the context of war (McMullen et al., 2013; O'Callaghan et al., 2013).

THEORY UNDERLYING THE DEVELOPMENT OF TRAUMA SYMPTOMS

TF-CBT integrates ideas and information from a variety of theoretical models, including family, empowerment, attachment, developmental neurobiology, and humanistic theories. Cognitive behavioral theory, however, provided the initial and primary foundation and rationale for the development of TF-CBT. Cognitive behavioral therapy is based on the central premise that cognitions, behaviors, emotions, and bodily sensations are highly interdependent. Thus, an intervention that specifically targets one of these areas of human functioning is expected to indirectly affect the other aspects of human functioning and adjustment. TF-CBT, in fact, integrates interventions that target behaviors, cognitions, emotions, and bodily sensations individually and in combination.

To conceptualize the etiology and treatment of psychological symptoms developed in the aftermath of sexually abusive experiences, the CBT theoretical model integrates learning theory particularly the influence of conditioning, contingencies, and models in the environment, with the impact of cognitive factors (Kendall, 1985). This model is used below to explain the development and maintenance of sexual abuse-related symptoms in children as well as the authors' conceptualization of the theoretical mechanisms underlying the efficacy of TF-CBT.

Observational learning

Modeling is an example of a simple learning process that can explain the development of both positive and negative behaviors in children. Children constantly imitate what they see and hear. Thus, through observational learning, children who have experienced CSA sometimes imitate verbalizations and behaviors exhibited by the perpetrators of their abuse. For example, the child may use foul language or engage in age-inappropriate sexual behaviors as a result of observing the offender. In other words, children's abuse-related behaviors may be simple reflections of the observational learning processes much like other more common behaviors children learn through observation.

Children's cognitive views and developing beliefs may also be significantly influenced by role models in their environment. Sex offenders may model dysfunctional attitudes regarding the abuse, sexuality, relationships, the trustworthiness of others, and so on. Even nonoffending, supportive parents may inadvertently contribute to the development of unhealthy views or beliefs. For example, when a well-meaning parent acts as though the sexual abuse is the worst thing that could ever have happened to the child, he/she may unintentionally encourage the child to adopt the same catastrophic view of the experience. In the aftermath of a sexual abuse disclosure, there are also many opportunities for children to learn positive coping behaviors by observing the responses of significant others. For example, if nonoffending parents discuss the sexual abuse in a calm, open, and direct manner, the child is likely to imitate that style in coping with his own thoughts, feelings, and concerns regarding the abuse. Indeed, as noted earlier, nonoffending parents may be children's most influential role models, though the distress they experience themselves may make it difficult for them to be at their best in the aftermath of CSA.

Respondent and instrumental conditioning

Another learning mechanism that may explain the development of children's abuse-related symptoms is referred to as two-factor theory. Two-factor learning theory suggests that fears are acquired through respondent conditioning and maintained through instrumental conditioning (Mowrer, 1939). According to respondent conditioning principles, when neutral stimuli are paired with unconditioned fear-evoking stimuli, the neutral stimuli alone begin to elicit fear responses. For example, for children who are sexually abused in the dark, darkness may be the previously neutral stimulus that is paired with the unconditional fear-evoking stimulus: the sexual abuse. As a result of the learned association between darkness and sexual abuse, a child's fear of being sexually abused in the dark may generalize to a fear of darkness.

When fear responses lead to avoidance of previously neutral stimuli, instrumental conditioning comes into play. Each time avoidance behavior occurs, it is negatively reinforced by a reduction in anxiety, thereby increasing the likelihood that the avoidance behavior will recur. To continue with the example provided above, children who learned to fear darkness as a result of the association between darkness and abuse now begin to avoid darkness to avoid experiencing the fear. Each time they successfully avoid the dark, they experience a reinforcing reduction in anxiety, which increases the likelihood of future attempts to avoid the dark. This association may then lead to problem behaviors including sleep refusal or insistence on sleeping with the lights on.

Recent revisions of the classical two-factor theory suggest other mechanisms for the development and maintenance of avoidance behavior. According to approach-withdrawal theory, avoidance may be maintained as a result of the positively reinforcing qualities of relaxation and/or other safety cues that follow avoidance behavior. Thus the children's avoidance of the dark is also positively reinforced by the sense of relief they experience upon successful avoidance, as well as by any other positive consequences such as increased parental attention in response to their verbalized fears of the dark. This increased attention sometimes takes the form of sleeping in the parents' bed, which can become reinforcing not only for its tendency to reduce anxiety but also because of the positive reinforcing feelings of closeness, warmth, safety, and attention.

Through the processes of generalization and higher order conditioning, a wider range of previously neutral stimuli may be paired with fear-evoking stimuli. Subsequently, previously neutral stimuli begin to elicit fear and avoidance responses. For example, the children described above initially may have feared only the darkness in their own bedrooms because that was where the abuse occurred. However, through generalization and higher order conditioning, they learned to fear darkness in general, across different settings. Such responses then become increasingly debilitating as the innocuous stimuli (e.g., darkness) that elicit troubling symptoms generalize from anxiety only when alone in the darkness of their bedroom, to anxiety in any dark room, to being extremely uneasy outside at night but not really understanding what is precipitating these symptoms of anxiety.

These conditioning principles provide a framework for understanding the development of posttrauma symptoms often exhibited by children who have experienced CSA. Many children experience feelings of fear, anxiety, pain, sadness, shame, and/or anger during the episodes of sexual abuse. Although they naturally associate these negative feelings with sexual abuse, some children, particularly those experiencing PTSD, generalize these feelings of distress from the actual experience of abuse to nonthreatening abuse-related cues such as darkness, men, being alone with one person, certain tones of voice, specific smells, bathrooms, enclosed spaces, getting undressed, etc. These cues are not in and of themselves dangerous, but because of their association with the abuse, they may trigger the emotions the children experienced during the abuse. Moreover, any cues that trigger CSA-related memories or thoughts may similarly come to be associated with anxiety, fear, anger, shame, and/or other distressing emotions experienced at the time of the abuse. Thus, in an effort to avoid these disturbing emotions, many children work hard to avoid specific abuse-related stimuli, while also actively avoiding thinking, talking, or being reminded of the abuse.

It should also be emphasized that many children use the same coping mechanisms that were seemingly adaptive in responding to sexually abusive experiences (e.g., dissociation, denial, numbing, and avoidance) to cope with innocuous abuse-related stimuli and/or other stressors in their day-to-day lives (e.g., peer pressure, test anxiety, parent-child conflict). Unfortunately, dissociative and avoidant coping strategies are not particularly successful when children apply them to the everyday stressors of child and adolescent development. In fact, relying on maladaptive strategies such as denial, avoidance, and/or dissociation to cope with abuse-related cues may inadvertently strengthen the inappropriate associations made between innocuous reminders of the abuse and psychological distress. For example, each time an innocuous abuse-related cue is avoided (e.g., darkness), a child experiences a reduction in distress and/or an increased feeling of safety that reinforces the avoidance behavior and strengthens the association between innocuous abuse reminders and emotional distress. Thus, although these coping mechanisms may have helped the child survive the abuse, their continued use once the abuse has ended may be maladaptive. Such continued avoidance may cause children to needlessly avoid innocuous situations, potentially preventing them from enjoying positive and important learning experiences. For example, children who feel anxious around and/or try to avoid dark-haired men or boys because their perpetrator had dark hair may be hindered from participating effectively in situations with other dark-haired males, such as teachers, coaches, neighbors, or peers. Furthermore, continued avoidance of abuse-related thoughts and memories may prevent these children from effectively processing and understanding their abusive experiences, potentially leaving them with misperceptions and inaccurate cognitive schemas related to the abuse. Furthermore, as noted earlier, there is evidence that both adult and child survivors of sexual abuse who use strategies of avoidance and suppression to cope with memories of CSA tend to be more symptomatic than those who rely on more active, constructive coping mechanisms (Leitenberg et al., 1992; Simon et al., 2010).

THEORETICAL MODELS UNDERLYING THE TF-CBT APPROACH

Prior empirical investigations have demonstrated the effectiveness of prolonged exposure in treating the symptoms experienced by adult PTSD sufferers (Fairbank & Keane, 1982; Foa, Rothbaum, Riggs, & Murdock, 1991). It seemed natural to build on the groundbreaking work of Dr. Edna Foa and her colleagues, whose work focused on the treatment of adult rape survivors. In fact, prolonged exposure seemed the treatment of choice for children experiencing PTSD symptoms in the aftermath of CSA. However, during early clinical trials with children, it quickly became evident that, unlike adult patients, children were often unwilling to subject themselves to anxiety-provoking stimuli for prolonged periods in exchange for the promise of long-term therapeutic benefits. In addition, many nonoffending parents expressed concern about the high levels of anxiety associated with immediate and prolonged exposure. Systematic desensitization, on the other hand, offered the advantage of using a gradual hierarchy of anxiety-provoking stimuli, which might be easier for children to tolerate. However, all the fears and anxieties children experience may not be apparent at the outset of therapy, and they may not fit neatly into a hierarchy. In addition, it is sometimes difficult to engage children, particularly young and/or developmentally delayed children, in the visualization and/or relaxation exercises required for systematic desensitization procedures.

To meet the needs of children, the first author and her colleagues at the Medical College of Pennsylvania combined elements of systematic desensitization and prolonged exposure in designing the intervention referred to as gradual exposure that essentially begins at the very start of treatment (Deblinger & Heflin, 1996; Deblinger et al., 1990). Like systematic desensitization, gradual exposure encourages children to confront feared stimuli, such as reminders, thoughts, and memories of the abuse, in a graduated fashion. Even though it can be helpful, a highly detailed hierarchy need not be constructed when developing a treatment plan for young children. It is important to assess the degree to which various stimuli or memories provoke anxious or avoidant responses and offer children choices for gradual exposure exercises, thereby ensuring that the process allows them to maintain control in choosing only slightly more anxiety provoking memories to review across sessions. Thus, the therapists may develop a more informal hierarchy as an overall plan that need not be shared with the child if it would provoke anticipatory anxiety. However, with some older children and adolescents, it may give them a greater sense of control if they collaborate in creating a general hierarchy in the middle stage of treatment when they are more confident in their ability to confront abuse-related memories and reminders. Initially, children will be encouraged to endure low-level anxiety-provoking stimuli before moving on to confront more distressing stimuli. For example, in the initial phase of therapy, psychoeducation about CSA may be shared in the abstract because that is less anxiety provoking than encouraging a discussion of the child's own abusive experience(s). Thus, the therapist may begin by engaging the child in discussions of factual information regarding sexual abuse such as prevalence, impact, reactions and dynamics of CSA. Then over time and during some coping skills training, the child may be asked to describe only her feelings related to the abusive experience and later during the trauma narrative component, the child may be asked to discuss the actual details of the least distressing of his or her own abusive experiences before moving on to discuss more anxiety-provoking memories in detail. As is the case with prolonged exposure, gradual exposure and processing exercises may be repeated until traumatic memories and innocuous stimuli in the environment no longer elicit maladaptive anxiety or avoidance.

With exposure to traumatic memories and/or different anxiety-provoking stimulus, it is expected that the child's anxiety level may increase somewhat. However, the increase in anxiety seems to reflect the increased anxiety the child experiences naturally upon exposure to abuse-related stimuli outside the therapy setting, rather than being a unique consequence of the therapeutic work. It is the experience of the authors that most children and their parents are able to tolerate this temporary increase in anxiety if it is explained in advance and they understand the long-term purpose of the work. Over time, the repeated exposures to abuse-related stimuli in a safe therapeutic setting will lead to a decrease in anxiety level. By the end of treatment, the child is expected to confront abuse reminders and discuss abuse-related memories without experiencing significant distress. Thus, gradual exposure aims to disrupt the maladaptive associations between innocuous abuse-related cues and the more extreme negative emotions that develop as a result of respondent conditioning. Moreover, when habituation occurs, new associations replace the old ones; that is, adaptive responses such as feelings of control, comfort, bravery, and/or pride become connected to previously anxiety-provoking memories, situations, thoughts, and/or discussion.

In addition to breaking the associations between innocuous abuse-related cues and distressing emotions, the connection needs to be disrupted between avoidance of innocuous abuse-related cues and positive or negative reinforcement. Repeated experiences with reduced anxiety as a result of avoidance behaviors strengthen avoidance and escape habits. Thus, it is very important for children to endure the anxiety-provoking thoughts and/or cues until anxiety decreases naturally without the child engaging in avoidance. In so doing, the child will learn that distress decreases without resorting to the use of escape strategies such as avoidance, dissociation, numbing, acting out, and so on, thereby resulting in decreased dependence on these maladaptive coping mechanisms. In addition, the child will learn that feelings of safety and mastery may be achieved in the face of memories, thoughts, and reminders of the abuse. Many parents also benefit from participating in gradual exposure exercises. At the start of therapy, many parents have less information than the investigator or caseworker about their child's abuse. Parents often experience high levels of anxiety when confronted with thoughts or reminders of their child's abusive experience and thus may seek to avoid those reminders as well. In exhibiting such avoidant behavior, parents model ineffective coping responses for their children. Thus, parents are encouraged to participate in gradual exposure exercises in order to become more comfortable with abuse-related stimuli, information, and discussion themselves, so that they can model more successful coping strategies for their children.

For many parents, the development of effective parenting and communication skills is central to their children's recovery particularly when acting-out behavior problems are exhibited by their children. Acting-out behaviors in children who have experienced sexual abuse may consist of angry outbursts that are sometimes associated with PTSD. They may also reflect behaviors learned over the course of the abuse that are being maintained through inadvertent reinforcement by parents and others.

In summary, the treatment approach described in this book includes educational, skill building, gradual exposure, and processing interventions designed to break the problematic associations children have made between negative feelings and abuse-related cues, such as memories and innocuous reminders. In that way, children become more comfortable confronting and making sense of abuse-related memories. Furthermore, this therapeutic work decreases children's reliance on maladaptive coping responses to innocuous abuse reminders such as avoidance and dissociative responses. TF-CBT also uses the modeling process described earlier as the therapist models ways to communicate about and cope effectively with troubling abuse-related thoughts, feelings, and reminders. In addition, the therapist coaches the nonoffending parent to model effective coping strategies for the child and to respond more effectively to abuse-related disclosures and behavior problems. More information about the TF-CBT PRACTICE components and the course of treatment from session to session is provided in the chapters that follow.

TF-CBT DEVELOPMENT AND RESEARCH

TF-CBT has its roots in scientific principles derived from general research in psychology as well as treatment outcome research. Many of the component interventions of TF-CBT were included in the model because of their demonstrated effectiveness with populations experiencing symptoms similar to those of children who have experienced sexual abuse. Moreover, as noted, early investigations found cognitive behavioral interventions to be effective in treating posttraumatic stress in adult sexual assault survivors (Foa, Rothbaum, & Ette, 1993; Foa et al., 1991). However, in the course of developing TF-CBT, it became evident that significant modifications were required to apply exposure based CBT interventions to children experiencing PTSD, including incorporating parent participation into the treatment model.

Dr. Deblinger and her colleagues and Drs. Cohen and Mannarino began conducting research studies to enhance the understanding of the therapeutic needs of children who experienced sexual abuse initially through independent studies at separate clinical research sites in the mid-1980s (Cohen & Mannarino, 1988; Deblinger et al., 1989; Mannarino & Cohen, 1986; Mannarino, Cohen, & Gregor, 1989; Mannarino, Cohen, Smith, & Moore-Motily, 1991; McLeer et al., 1988). A preliminary empirical evaluation of the model referred to today as TF-CBT examined the treatment response of children (ages 3 to 16 years) who were experiencing PTSD in the aftermath of CSA (Deblinger et al., 1990). The findings demonstrated no changes in children's symptomatology during a baseline period, but showed significant symptom improvements pre- to posttreatment. Although children's PTSD, depression, and behavioral symptoms improved significantly, at post treatment some children continued to remain in the mild depressive range. To better understand the impact of the parent and child interventions on specific symptom domains, Deblinger and colleagues next conducted a study examining the impact of the child and parent interventions separately and in combination. In this study, children and their nonoffending parents were randomly assigned to one of four treatment conditions: the full TF-CBT model including both the parent and child interventions; a child-only TF-CBT intervention; a parent-only TF-CBT intervention (in which parents were taught to serve as their child's therapeutic agent); or a community treatment comparison condition (Deblinger et al., 1996). The findings of this investigation documented that children assigned to conditions in which they actively participated in TF-CBT (i.e., child only or child/parent conditions) showed significantly greater reductions in PTSD symptoms as compared to children who were not active TF-CBT participants (i.e., parent-only or community comparison). In addition, parents assigned to conditions in which they actively participated in the implementation of TF-CBT (i.e., parent or child/parent conditions) showed significantly greater improvements in parenting practices, and their children exhibited significantly greater reductions in externalizing behavior problems as well as depression compared to conditions in which parents did not participate in TF-CBT (i.e., child-only or community comparison). Most importantly, the significant improvements found at posttreatment were sustained over a two-year follow-up period (Deblinger et al., 1999). This model was further evaluated for its efficacy in a group therapy format. Again, after demonstrating the benefits of TF-CBT in a group format through a preliminary pre-post investigation (Stauffer & Deblinger, 1996), Deblinger and colleagues conducted an additional randomized trial in which young children who had experienced CSA were randomly assigned along with their nonoffending parents to either a TF-CBT group program or education/support group program. The results of this investigation demonstrated that parents assigned to the TF-CBT group program experienced significantly greater improvements with respect to parental abuse-specific distress as compared to those assigned to the support group. Children assigned to the TF-CBT group program showed greater improvements with respect to body safety skills and knowledge as compared to those assigned to the educational/support groups (Deblinger et al., 2001).

During approximately this same time frame, Drs. Cohen and Mannarino began conducting treatment outcome investigations on an early version of TF-CBT as well. In fact, several studies were conducted examining the responses of preschool and school-age children to TF-CBT for CSA as compared to a nondirective supportive therapy condition. The findings in their initial study with preschool children (ages 3 to 6 years) demonstrated that children randomly assigned to TF-CBT showed significantly greater symptom improvements with respect to internalizing symptoms, as well as general behavior problems as compared to those children assigned to the nondirective supportive counseling condition (Cohen & Mannarino, 1996a). Moreover, from a clinical perspective, Cohen and Mannarino (1996a) found that TF-CBT was more effective than the alternative treatment condition in terms of helping children overcome potentially dangerous acting-out behaviors including sexually inappropriate behaviors toward others and was more efficacious in maintaining symptom reductions at the 1-year follow up assessment (Cohen & Mannarino, 1997). The findings of another investigation demonstrated that school-age children (ages 7 to 14 years) who were randomly assigned to TF-CBT in the aftermath of CSA exhibited significantly greater improvements with respect to depression, anxiety, sexual problems, and dissociation at the six-month follow-up as compared to children assigned to the nondirective supportive therapy condition (Cohen & Mannarino, 1998b; Cohen, Mannarino, & Knudsen, 2005). In addition, replicating their findings with preschoolers, the clinical findings of this investigation also suggested that TF-CBT seemed to be more effective than the nondirective therapy approach in addressing children's sexually inappropriate behaviors. Cohen, Mannarino, Perel, and Staron (2007) also conducted an independent study examining the potential benefits of psychiatric medication in addition to TF-CBT in addressing children's therapeutic needs in the aftermath of CSA. The findings indicated that with the exception of TF-CBT with sertraline medication being associated with significantly greater improvements in observed child global assessment ratings, TF-CBT with sertraline medication produced no significant benefits above and beyond TF-CBT alone with regard to PTSD, depression, anxiety, behavior problems, and all other clinical outcome measures. Although these findings should be interpreted with caution due to the small and unrepresentative nature of the study's sample, the authors conclude that the current evidence suggests that for most children with PTSD, including those with co-morbid depression, an initial trial of TF-CBT generally should be offered before combining trauma-focused therapy with medication.

The treatment approach described in this book reflects the integration of the developers' early independent treatment models (Cohen & Mannarino, 1993; Deblinger & Heflin, 1996), as well as the findings of TF-CBT treatment outcome research and the authors' clinical experiences to date. In fact, in the mid-1990s the authors conducted the first large-scale multisite collaborative investigation in which participants were randomly assigned to the integrated TF-CBT approach or a child centered therapy condition (CCT) across both clinical research sites (Cohen, Deblinger, Mannarino, & Steer, 2004). The findings of this investigation demonstrated significantly greater benefits of TF-CBT over the child-centered therapy condition in terms of the outcomes of both child and nonoffending parent. Children assigned to TF-CBT demonstrated significantly greater improvements with respect to PTSD, depression, abuse attributions, shame, behavior problems, and personal safety skills as compared to children assigned to the comparison treatment. The nonoffending parents assigned to TF-CBT also reported significantly greater improvements with respect to their own abuse-related distress, personal feelings of depression, parenting skills, and support levels as compared to those parents assigned to the comparison treatment condition (Cohen, Deblinger, et al., 2004). Furthermore, the findings of a follow-up investigation demonstrated that participant improvements across conditions were generally sustained over a one-year period, and children who experienced multiple traumas as well as comorbid depression exhibited poorer outcomes, but only in response to the child centered therapy (Deblinger, Mannarino, Cohen, & Steer, 2006).

Most recently, a dismantling study was conducted examining the impact of treatment length (eight versus 16 TF-CBT sessions) and the completion of a written narrative in the context of TF-CBT delivered to young children (ages 4 to 11 years) with a history of CSA (Deblinger et al., 2011). The results of this study suggested that a longer course of treatment (i.e., 16 sessions) and a greater focus on skill building appeared to be critical in helping parents enhance their parenting skills and children overcome externalizing behavior problems. The findings also documented the benefits of the TF-CBT trauma narrative component in most efficiently and efficaciously helping children overcome abuse-related fear and general anxiety in as little as eight TF-CBT sessions. Recently, Salloum and Overstreet (2012) conducted a similar study in which the results also suggested the value of trauma narration in addition to coping skills training particularly for highly distressed children. A follow-up to the dismantling investigation demonstrated that participants across all TF-CBT treatment conditions generally sustained their symptom improvements over a one-year posttreatment period (Mannarino, Cohen, Deblinger, Runyon, & Steer, 2012). The results also indicated that higher levels of internalizing and depressive symptomatology predicted the small minority of children (i.e., 11%) who continued to meet PTSD criteria at the one-year follow-up (Mannarino et al., 2012). From a clinical perspective, it is interesting to note that replicating earlier findings, many children assigned to the written narrative conditions reported that talking about the sexual abuse was the most helpful part of therapy (Deblinger et al., 2011; Deblinger, Mannarino, et al., 2006).

Over the years, many of the findings of the above-described studies have been replicated by other researchers that have documented the generalizability of the impact of TF-CBT with diverse populations of children and families impacted by CSA. Researchers in Australia, for example, randomly assigned children who had been sexually abused to one of three conditions: a parent and child TF-CBT condition, a child only TF-CBT condition, or a waiting list control condition. Not surprisingly, children assigned to the TF-CBT conditions exhibited greater improvements with respect to child-reported PTSD, fear and anxiety, as well as parent and clinician ratings of global functioning as compared to those children assigned to the waitlist control (King, Tonge, Mullen, et al., 2000). Interestingly, differences with respect to the child only and parent and child conditions emerged at the three-month follow-up, with children assigned to the parent and child TF-CBT condition exhibiting significantly less abuse-related fear than children assigned to the child only TF-CBT condition. The authors suggest that additional hypothesized differences between child only and parent and child TF-CBT may not have been detected due to the small sample size and the lack of focus in the parent and child condition on parenting skills training and the emotional impact of the sexual abuse on the parents.

Another recent randomized controlled trial conducted in the Democratic Republic of the Congo examined the efficacy of TF-CBT delivered in group format to girls who had experienced sexual exploitation, as well as numerous other traumas (O'Callaghan et al., 2013). In fact, the average number of childhood traumas experienced by this sample of girls was approximately 12 (as compared to an average of three to four traumas experienced by children in earlier TF-CBT trials). In addition to sexual abuse and war exposure, girls in this study experienced a severe lack of food or water, severe punishment or revenge, exposure to corpses, looting, fighting, attacks, and/or parental loss through death, divorce, and abandonment. Despite this, the results of this randomized controlled trial replicated the findings of other TF-CBT studies demonstrating that girls randomly assigned to a TF-CBT group exhibited significantly greater improvements with respect to trauma symptoms, depression, anxiety, conduct problems, and prosocial behaviors as compared to girls assigned to the wait list. Moreover, the positive changes observed in these domains of functioning at posttreatment were either maintained or further improved at the three-month follow-up assessments. Interestingly, these Congolese girls, including many who had never spoken about their trauma(s), reported that they valued the opportunity to talk about their traumatic experiences, much like children participating in previous TF-CBT trials in the United States (Deblinger et al., 2011; Deblinger, Mannarino, et al., 2006). In addition, it should be noted that the TF-CBT intervention provided in this context seemed to offer additional benefits due to its group format, including the opportunity to experience peer support from those with similar experiences (Deblinger et al., 2015).

Further clinical development of TF-CBT for children, adolescents, and nonoffending caregivers continues to be closely tied to the empirical literature based on the findings of an increasing number of treatment efficacy, effectiveness, and process studies conducted by the current authors as well as other researchers across the United States and the world (Cohen, Mannarino, & Knudsen, 2004; Cohen, Mannarino, & Staron, 2006; Murray, Familiar, et al., 2013; Murray et al., 2015; O'Donnell et al., 2014; Webb, Hayes, Grasso, Laurenceau, & Deblinger, 2014). These studies have continued to document the efficacy of TF-CBT in addressing CSA as well as a wide array of other childhood traumas including traumatic grief, abandonment, community violence, and other traumas. Several recent studies, in fact, have demonstrated the superior benefits of TF-CBT for children in foster care who often have experienced a wide array of traumas. More specifically, in a quasi-experimental study, Lyons et al. (2006) found that children who received TF-CBT as opposed to usual care not only exhibited significantly greater reductions in traumatic stress symptoms but were also one-tenth as likely to run away from the foster home and about half as likely to experience placement disruptions. This reduction in risk of running away from home and removal from foster homes is critically important given the associations found between placement disruptions and escalating emotional and behavioral problems in foster children (Chamberlain et al., 2006; Leathers, 2006). Moreover, it should be noted that a recent study documented the critical importance of engaging foster parents in the TF-CBT process. The results of this study documented that children and foster parents randomly assigned to TF-CBT with evidence based engagement procedures as opposed to TF-CBT without such procedures, were significantly less likely to drop out prematurely and significantly more likely to complete treatment (Dorsey et al., 2014). In another recent TF-CBT study, the results documented the superior benefits of a brief eight-session TF-CBT model delivered to children and their caregivers in shelters after exposure to domestic violence (Cohen, Mannarino, & Iyengar, 2011). In this context, children who received TF-CBT in comparison to usual care were significantly more likely to exhibit PTSD diagnostic remission and experienced fewer serious adverse events. The benefits of TF-CBT also have been documented with respect to addressing the psychosocial impact of widespread disasters such as 9/11 (CATS Consortium, 2010) and Hurricane Katrina (Jaycox et al., 2010). In addition, the results of another study conducted in the Democratic Republic of Congo demonstrated that TF-CBT provided in group format to boy soldiers (McMullen et al., 2013) produced significantly greater improvements in trauma symptoms, depression, conduct problems, as well as prosocial behaviors than did the wait-list control condition. Another randomized trial conducted in the Netherlands randomly assigned children to TF-CBT vs. Eye Movement Desensitization and Reprocessing (EMDR). The findings of this investigation documented that both interventions produced significant reductions in PTSD symptoms, however, only the children assigned to TF-CBT exhibited significant reductions in depression and hyperactive symptoms as well (Diehl, Opmeer, Boer, Mannarino, & Lindauer, 2015). Finally, a recently published randomized trial conducted in Norway (Jensen et al., 2014) replicated earlier TF-CBT findings and documented PTSD remission rates among the Norwegian participants (ages 10 to 18 years) that were almost identical to those found in the first multisite TF-CBT study conducted in the United States (Cohen, Deblinger, et al., 2004).

Table 2.1 provided here summarizes the samples, methods, and findings of the initial TF-CBT treatment outcome studies designed to address the therapeutic needs of children and their nonoffending caregivers in the aftermath of CSA as well as more recent TF-CBT studies that focus on other populations of youth impacted by diverse childhood traumas. The efficacy of TF-CBT in addressing other traumas, as described above, is important for the CSA population, given that research has demonstrated that children who have been sexually

Table 2.1. TF-CBT Outcome Studies with Children, Adolescents, and Nonoffending Caregivers Impacted by CSA

Study	Target Population	Country of Study	# of Sessions	Design	Treatment/ Control	Major Findings	Final Follow-Up
Deblinger, McLeer, & Henry, 1990	Children ages 3–16 years	U.S.	12	Pre-post	19 TF-CBT	Significant improvement in symptoms of anxiety, PTSD and depression as well as significant improvements in behavior problems	N/A
Cohen & Mannarino, 1996a	Children ages 3–6 years & their nonoffending parents	U.S.	12	Random assignment	39 TF-CBT 28 NST	Compared to NST condition, those in TF-CBT condition had significantly greater improvement in PTSD symptoms, internalizing symptoms, and sexual behavior problems	TF-CBT group was more efficacious than NST group in maintaining symptom reduction at 12 month follow up (Cohen & Mannarino, 1997)
Deblinger, Lippmann, & Steer, 1996	Children ages 7–13 years & their nonoffending mothers	U.S.	12	Random assignment	22 TF-CBT Parent Only 24 TF-CBT Child Only 22 TF-CBT Parent + Child 22 Community Control	Compared to conditions without child intervention, conditions with the TF-CBT child intervention had significantly greater reduction in PTSD symptoms. Compared to conditions without parent intervention, conditions with the TF-CBT parent intervention had greater reductions in children's externalizing behavior problems and depression and significantly greater improvements in parenting practices.	Improvements in PTSD symptoms, depression, and externalizing behavior problems were maintained over the two-year follow up period (Deblinger, Steer, & Lippmann, 1999)

(continued)

Table 2.1. Continued

Study	Target Population	Country of Study	# of Sessions	Design	Treatment/ Control	Major Findings	Final Follow-Up
Stauffer & Deblinger, 1996	Children ages 2–6 years & their nonoffending mothers	U.S.	11	Pre-post	19 TF-CBT	Significant decreases in children's sexualized behaviors and parental distress and significant improvements in parenting practices	Improvements maintained at 3-month follow-up
Cohen & Mannarino, 1998b	Children ages 7–14 years & their nonoffending parents	U.S.	12	Random assignment	30 TF-CBT 19 NST	Significantly greater improvement in depressive symptoms and social competence in TF-CBT condition at post-treatment compared to NST	Significantly greater improvement in PTSD and dissociative symptoms in TF-CBT condition at 12-month follow up (Cohen, Mannarino, & Knudsen, 2005)
King, Tonge, Mullen, et al., 2000	Children ages 5–17 years	Australia	20	Random assignment	12 TF-CBT Child 12 TF-CBT Family 12 WL	Significantly greater improvements across TF-CBT conditions in PTSD symptoms, fear, and anxiety as well as overall functioning compared to WL condition	Improvements were maintained at 12 week follow up. At follow-up, children assigned to the family CBT condition showed significantly greater improvement on abuse-related fear relative to those assigned to child only CBT.

Deblinger, Stauffer, & Steer, 2001	Children ages 2–8 years & their nonoffending mothers	U.S.	11	Random assignment	21 TF-CBT Group 23 Support Group	Compared to support group, TF-CBT group had significantly greater improvement in child-reported knowledge of body safety skills and significantly greater reductions in maternal abuse-related intrusive thoughts and negative parental emotional reactions to the abuse	Improvements maintained at 3-month follow-up. Mothers in support group showed significant reductions in emotional distress though they tended to obtain more additional help during follow-up compared to mothers in TF-CBT group.
Cohen, Deblinger, Mannarino, & Steer, 2004	Children ages 8 –14 years & their primary caregivers	U.S.	12	Random assignment	89 TF-CBT 91 CCT	Compared to CCT, TF-CBT condition had significantly greater reductions in children's PTSD and depressive symptoms, behavior problems, feelings of shame, and abuse-related attributions, as well as greater improvements in caregivers' depression, abuse-related distress, parenting practices, and parental support of the child	Compared to CCT condition, children in TF-CBT condition reported significantly fewer PTSD symptoms and feelings of shame at 6 and 12 month follow-up. Parents in TF-CBT condition reported less abuse-specific distress at 6 and 12 month follow-up (Deblinger, Mannarino, Cohen, & Steer, 2006)

(continued)

Table 2.1. Continued

Study	Target Population	Country of Study	# of Sessions	Design	Treatment/ Control	Major Findings	Final Follow-Up
Cohen, Mannarino, Perel, & Staron, 2007	Girls ages 10–17 years	U.S.	12	Random assignment	12 TF-CBT + sertraline 12 TF-CBT + placebo	Both conditions showed significant pre-post improvement on PTSD and other symptoms. No significant differences between conditions except on ratings of global functioning, which favored the TF-CBT plus sertraline group	N/A
Deblinger, Mannarino, Cohen, Runyon, & Steer, 2011	Children ages 4–11 years & their nonoffending caregivers	U.S.	8 or 16	Random assignment	40 TF-CBT 8 sessions no TN 39 TF-CBT 8 sessions with TN 35 TF-CBT 16 sessions no TN 44 TF-CBT 16 sessions with TN	Significant improvements reported across conditions on behavioral, emotional, and skill-based outcomes. 8 sessions with TN condition was significantly more efficient and effective in helping children overcome abuse-related fear and general anxiety as well as in helping parents overcome abuse-specific distress. 16 sessions no TN condition showed significantly greater improvements with respect to children's externalizing behavior problems and effective parenting practices.	Improvements reported at post-treatment were maintained at 6 and 12 month follow up; additional improvements on parental emotional distress and on child self-reported anxiety were reported at 12 month follow-up (Mannarino, Cohen, Deblinger, Runyon, & Steer, 2012)

Study	Target Population	Country of study	# of sessions	Design	Treatment/ Control	Major findings	Final Follow-Up
O'Callaghan, McMullen, Shannon, Rafferty, & Black, 2013	War-affected girls exposed to sexual exploitation and multiple traumas ages 12–17 years	Democratic Republic of Congo	15	Random assignment	24 group-based, culturally modified TF-CBT 28 WL	Significantly greater reductions in trauma symptoms and significant improvement in depression and anxiety symptoms, conduct problems, and prosocial behavior in TF-CBT group as compared to WL	N/A

Treatment Outcome Studies with Children, Adolescents, and Nonoffending Caregivers Impacted by Other Traumas

Study	Target Population	Country of study	# of sessions	Design	Treatment/ Control	Major findings	Final Follow-Up
Cohen, Mannarino, & Knudsen, 2004	Children ages 6–17 years & their primary caregivers; Trauma type = CTG	U.S.	16	Pre-post	22 TF-CBT-CTG	Significant reductions in children's behavioral problems & depressive, anxiety, PTSD, and CTG symptoms. Significant reductions in depressive and PTSD symptoms of parents	N/A
Cohen, Mannarino, & Staron, 2006	Children ages 6–17 years & their parents Trauma type = CTG	U.S.	12	Pre-post	39 TF-CBT-CTG	Significant reductions in children's behavioral problems and PTSD, CTG, anxiety, and depressive symptoms.	N/A

(continued)

Table 2.1. Continued

Study	Target Population	Country of Study	# of Sessions	Design	Treatment/ Control	Major Findings	Final Follow-Up
Lyons, Weiner, & Scheider, 2006	Children ages 0–21 years in foster care who experienced a moderate or severe trauma	U.S.	10	Quasi-experimental	69 TF-CBT 82 CPP 65 SPARCS 2218 TAU	Participants in all 3 EBP groups improved significantly in child and adolescent needs and strengths domains. As compared to TAU, youth who received TF-CBT achieved significantly greater gains on traumatic stress symptoms and behavioral/ emotional needs, were about one-tenth as likely to run away from placement, and about half as likely to have a disruption in placement.	N/A
CATS Consortium, 2010	Children ages 5 to 21 affected by the World Trade Center disaster on September 11th	U.S.	Trauma-specific CBT (TF-CBT for ages 5–12; Trauma and Grief Component Therapy for Adolescents for ages 13–21) 8 to 12 sessions Brief skills CBT 4 sessions	Quasi-experimental	239 trauma specific CBT 67 brief skills CBT	Both groups improved over time (trauma symptoms decreased). Although those who received TF-CBT began treatment with considerable family/environmental adversity and greater trauma-exposure than the brief skills CBT participants, the TF-CBT participants experienced significantly more clinical improvement moving from a probable diagnosis of PTSD to the mild range.	N/A

Jaycox et al., 2010	Fourth through eighth graders in New Orleans schools post Hurricane Katrina who reported PTSD symptoms Trauma type = hurricane exposures, vicarious traumas, and personal traumas	U.S.	TF-CBT 12 sessions CBITS 10 group sessions, 1–3 individual sessions	Random assignment	60 TF-CBT 58 CBITS	Significant reduction in PTSD symptoms of participants in both treatments	N/A
Cohen, Mannarino, & Iyengar, 2011	Children ages 7–14 years Trauma type = exposed to IPV	U.S.	8	Random assignment	64 TF-CBT 60 CCT (usual care)	TF-CBT participants in IPV shelter had significantly greater decreases in anxiety symptoms, hyperarousal and avoidance symptoms as compared to CCT	N/A
McMullen, O'Callaghan, Shannon, Black, & Eakin, 2013	Former child soldiers and other war affected boys ages 13–17 years	Democratic Republic of Congo	15	Random assignment	25 TF-CBT 25 WL	Compared to WL control, TF-CBT group had significantly greater reductions in posttraumatic stress, depressive, and anxiety symptoms, overall distress and conduct problems as well as significant increase in prosocial behaviors	Improvements maintained at 3-month follow up

(continued)

Table 2.1. Continued

Study	Target Population	Country of Study	# of Sessions	Design	Treatment/ Control	Major Findings	Final Follow-Up
Murray, Familiar, et al., 2013	Orphans and vulnerable children ages 5–18 years who experienced one or more traumatic events	Zambia	8–23 sessions (average = 11)	Pre-post	58 TF-CBT	Post-treatment assessment results showed significant reductions in trauma symptom severity and severity of shame symptoms.	N/A
Dorsey et al., 2014	Children in foster care ages 6–15 years and their foster parents Trauma type = multiple	U.S.	*M* = 15.0 for TF-CBT + engagement *M* = 12.3 TF-CBT	Random assignment	22 TF-CBT 25 TF-CBT + engagement	Significantly greater retention and completion rates among those who received engagement strategies compared to those who did not. Across treatments, all children displayed significant improvements in regard to clinical outcomes at post treatment.	Improvements maintained at 3-month follow up

Greer, Grasso, Cohen, & Webb, 2014	Children ages 7–18 years Trauma type = multiple	U.S.	Not reported	Quasi-experimental	90 TF-CBT 90 TAU	Over the course of a year, 2 times more money was spent on low-end mental health services for youth who received TF-CBT as compared to youth who received TAU and five times more money was spent on high-end mental health services for youth who received TAU as compared to youth who received TF-CBT	N/A
Jensen et al, 2014	Youth ages 10 to 18 years Trauma type = different traumas	Norway	12–15	Random assignment	79 TF-CBT 77 TAU	Compared to TAU group, TF-CBT group had significantly lower posttraumatic stress symptoms, depression, and general mental health symptoms as well as significantly greater improvements in functional impairment	N/A
O'Donnell et al., 2014	Children ages 7 to 13 years Trauma type = death of parent(s)	Tanzania	12 weekly sessions plus 3 individual visits	Pre-post	64 TF-CBT	Pre to post-treatment improvements in symptoms of grief, posttramatic stress, and depression as well as overall behavioural adjustment	Improvements maintained 3 and 12 months post-treatment

(continued)

Table 2.1. Continued

Study	Target Population	Country of Study	# of Sessions	Design	Treatment/ Control	Major Findings	Final Follow-Up
Webb, Hayes, Grasso, Laurenceau, & Deblinger, 2014	Youth ages 7 to 16 years with history of trauma and symptoms of PTSD Trauma type = different trauma	U.S.	$M = 10$	Pre-post	72 TF-CBT	Assessments at 3- and 6-months post intake indicate that participants showed a significant decrease in PTSD symptoms, as well as internalizing and externalizing problems.	Decreases in PTSD symptoms and internalizing and externalizing problems were maintained at the 9- and 12-month follow up assessments.
Diehl, Opmeer, Boer, Mannarino, & Lindauer, 2015	Children ages 8-18 years and their nonoffending parents Trauma type = different traumas	Netherlands	Maximum of 8 weekly sessions	Random assignment	25 EMDR 22 TF-CBT	Both conditions showed pre- to post-treatment reductions in symptoms of posttraumatic stress. Parents of children in TF-CBT condition only reported significant reductions in symptoms of depression and hyperactivity.	N/A
Murray et al., 2015	Children ages 8–18 years Trauma type = multiple	Zambia	10–16 sessions	Random assignment	131 TF-CBT 126 TAU	TF-CBT led to more positive outcomes than TAU	N/A

Note. TF-CBT, Trauma-Focused Cognitive Behavioral Therapy; PTSD, Posttraumatic Stress Disorder; NST, Nondirective Supportive Therapy; WL, Waitlist; CCT, Child Centered Therapy; TN, Trauma Narrative; CTG, Childhood Traumatic Grief; CPP, Child-Parent Psychotherapy; SPARCS, Structured Psychotherapy for Adolescents Responding to Chronic Stress; EMDR, Eye Movement Desensitization and Reprocessing; TAU, Therapy as Usual; CBITS, Cognitive-Behavioral Intervention for Trauma; IPV, Intimate Partner Violence; CCT, Child Centered Therapy.

abused frequently have experienced other childhood traumas as well including exposure to domestic violence, traumatic loss, and other diverse traumas (Finkelhor et al., 2007a). Although TF-CBT is not the only treatment approach with empirical documentation of its therapeutic efficacy with children who have experienced trauma, it does appear to have the strongest research track record (Jensen et al., 2014; Saunders, Berliner, & Hanson, 2004; Silverman et al., 2008). To date, there have been at least 25 empirical investigations of this model including 15 completed randomized controlled trials, with the largest proportion of those studies focusing specifically on children with a history of sexual abuse (Cohen, Deblinger, et al., 2004; Cohen & Mannarino, 1996a, 1998b; Deblinger et al., 1996; Deblinger et al., 2011; Deblinger et al., 2001; King, Tonge, Mullen, et al., 2000) (see Table 2.1). In addition, recent TF-CBT outcome research has not only replicated its efficacy with diverse community samples but has also established the cost-effectiveness of this short term model as compared to treatment as usual in the community (Greer, Grasso, Cohen, & Webb, 2014). Moreover, additional research is underway aimed at developing stepped care approaches to the delivery of TF-CBT to further reduce costs and enhance treatment accessibility, by more effectively matching treatment dose and intensity to children's needs (Salloum et al., 2014).

TF-CBT continues to evolve as a result of the ongoing research designed to enhance its overall implementation and effectiveness. However, to date, it should be noted that TF-CBT has been given the highest ratings for its efficacy and dissemination based on extensive reviews conducted by the U.S. Department of Health and Human Services (www.nrepp.samhsa.gov), the California Evidence Based Clearinghouse for Child Welfare (www.cebc4cw.org), and the Kaufman Best Practices Task Force Final Report (Chadwick Center for Children and Families, 2004). Finally, the results of a recent systematic review of evidence-based treatments for children exposed to maltreatment suggest that TF-CBT is the best-supported treatment and thus it is often recommended as the treatment of choice for this population (Leenarts, Diehle, Doreleijers, Jansma, & Lindauer, 2013).

3

Clinical Overview

Trauma-focused cognitive behavioral therapy (TF-CBT) is a short-term treatment model that is both structured and flexible in its format. To ensure that its implementation leads to the positive results found in the associated treatment outcome research, it is critical that clinicians generally adhere to the overriding principles of TF-CBT. In fact, research suggests that fidelity to the TF-CBT model is associated with more positive outcomes (Amaya-Jackson et al., 2012).

TREATMENT COURSE AND STRUCTURE

TF-CBT includes separate individual sessions with children and parents, as well as conjoint parent-child sessions as depicted in Figure 3.1. Although this book will focus primarily on the individual therapy format, TF-CBT has been successfully implemented with essentially the same structure in both individual and group formats in approximately 12 to 16 treatment sessions following the completion of a psychosocial assessment. However, in some clinical settings, TF-CBT may be implemented in as few as 8 sessions and in as many as 25 sessions, depending on the needs of the child and the complexity of the case. Treatment is generally longer when children have multiple diagnoses, complex trauma histories, when the family and/or legal circumstances are complicated, and when there is potential for family reunification with a sibling or parent who perpetrated the abuse. Moreover, in long-term treatment settings such as residential facilities, children and adolescents may continue to receive skill-building sessions and/or other general therapy after the TF-CBT components have been completed.

TF-CBT is conceptualized in three phases: the initial phase provides stabilization and skill building, the middle phase focuses on trauma narration and processing, and the final phase emphasizes trauma mastery, open parent-child communication, and safety skills training as a means of supporting the consolidation of skills in preparation for the completion of therapy. TF-CBT therapists typically divide treatment sessions into individual meetings with approximately equal time spent separately with the child and parent with increasing time

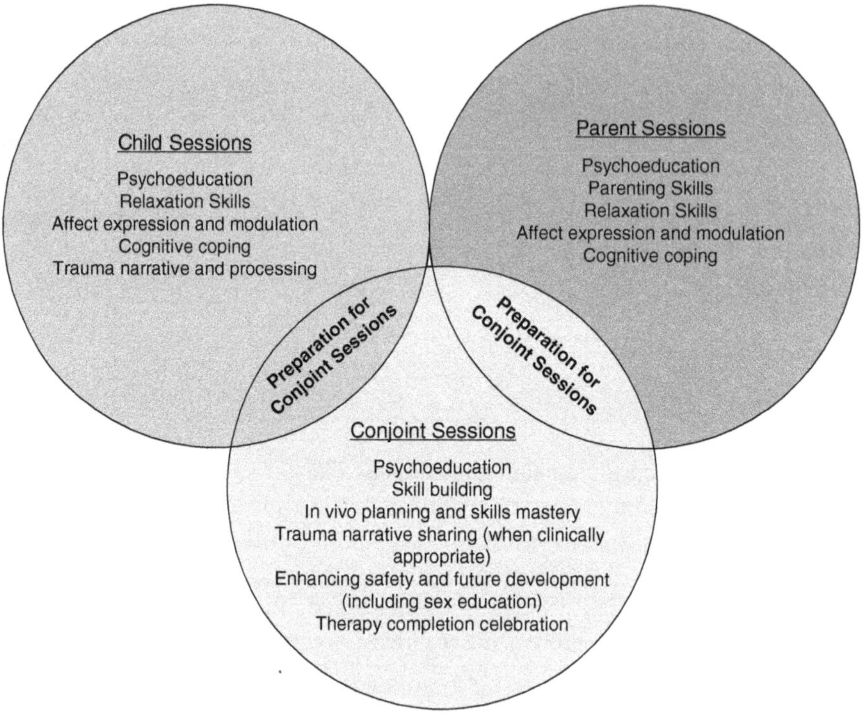

Figure 3.1 TF-CBT Model Overview.

devoted to conjoint sessions as needed over the course of treatment. However, the exact amount of time devoted to individual work with the child and parent as well as conjoint work may vary depending on the age of the child and the therapeutic needs of the family. Typically, more time is necessary with parents in individual parent and conjoint sessions when children are exhibiting significant behavior problems. However, therapists may devote more time to individual sessions with adolescents for skill building as compared to preschoolers, especially when the adolescent is exhibiting significant depressive or other internalizing symptoms. Conjoint parent-child sessions in which parents have an opportunity to practice behavior management and effective communication skills with their children should be initiated early in treatment when deemed clinically appropriate. Conjoint sessions in which parents have an opportunity to practice effective parenting skills are particularly important when children have acting-out or oppositional behavior problems including age-inappropriate sexual behaviors, noncompliance, and aggressive behaviors. During the trauma narration and processing phase of treatment, the goals of therapy begin to focus directly on more intensive exposure-based activities that focus on children's personal sexual abuse experiences. These activities generally include the development and processing of trauma narratives when appropriate but may also involve play, art, and other creative exercises that encourage the processing of thoughts and feelings related to the abuse. During this phase, parents and children often begin to show reduced symptomatology and improved coping skills. Parent and child readiness for the trauma-focused conjoint sessions is usually assessed and prepared for during the latter part of the middle phase, whereas the actual conjoint sessions are conducted during the final phase of treatment. When clinically appropriate, the therapist will begin preparing clients for the final phase of therapy, during which at least some of the therapy sessions are spent in conjoint meetings where sexual-abuse-specific information, skills, and narratives are shared and/or discussed with parents and children together. These conjoint therapy sessions are intended to provide the parent and child with skills for communicating about and processing the sexual abuse experience together so that they can continue the therapeutic process on their own after therapy ends. The final phase of therapy also provides an opportunity for families to review the educational information learned, practice the skills developed and fully process the traumatic experiences together as a family, while also learning additional skills individually and in conjoint sessions that will prepare them for the future (e.g., personal safety skills). This final phase is punctuated by the planning of a special graduation celebration that acknowledges the hard work of therapy, thereby reinforcing the strengths demonstrated by each family member.

Gradual exposure is a central concept underlying the treatment approach described in this book. From the first session, clients are exposed to discussions and general information regarding child sexual abuse (CSA). As treatment proceeds, both parents and children are gradually engaged in increasingly intensive trauma-related therapeutic activities that are designed to trigger specific memories and reminders of the experience of CSA in a safe, predictable environment. Although it is natural for children to experience distress and other emotions at the time of an abusive experience, PTSD develops when children experience conditioned emotional responses when confronted with abuse-related memories, thoughts, discussion, and other reminders. These distressing connections are often maintained long after the abuse has ended and may inadvertently be reinforced by adults who attempt to minimize the child's distress by shielding the child from abuse-related stimuli or discussions. Well-meaning parents often strengthen the association between abuse-related cues and emotional distress by avoiding abuse-related discussions, thereby signaling that the associated thoughts and memories are too horrible to openly confront and process (Lyons, 1987).

In the security of the therapeutic environment, gradual exposure, which occurs throughout the treatment components, slowly but repeatedly exposes children to abuse-related thoughts, discussions, and/or stimuli until anxiety or other forms of emotional distress decreases. With repeated exposure, children's emotional responses diminish through a process referred to as "habituation." When this occurs, relaxed or neutral responses become connected with previously feared abuse-related memories and/or discussion. The resulting overall reduction in emotional distress frees children to process their abusive experiences cognitively and affectively with the help of a therapist. Once children are more comfortable facing abuse-related memories, the TF-CBT therapist can help children understand more about what happened, correct any misconceptions they may have, and put the experience into perspective. Similarly, therapists may help children as well as their nonoffending caregivers process the experience affectively, as they are encouraged to sort out their feelings about the experience and about the perpetrator with the goal of achieving a greater sense of emotional equilibrium. Over the course of therapy, disturbing memories and related associations recede as new memories are formed reflecting the child's and families' strengths, improved communication, and closeness as they work through the TF-CBT process with the support and guidance of a skilled therapist.

THERAPIST QUALIFICATIONS AND ROLES

The effective implementation of TF-CBT requires significant clinical skill. Thus, it is recommended that TF-CBT clinicians have a minimum of a master's degree in a mental health field and are licensed or working toward a mental health degree and/or professional licensure under the required supervisory conditions in their state. Given the complexity of working with children who have been sexually abused, it is important for clinicians applying TF-CBT with this population to have up-to-date knowledge and understanding of the child abuse reporting laws and the investigatory and prosecutorial proceedings associated with child abuse investigations in their state. Moreover, clinicians should bear in mind that general comfort and experience working with children, adolescents, and their caregivers is critical to the successful implementation of TF-CBT. In addition to reviewing this book and/or other TF-CBT volumes (i.e., Cohen, Mannarino, & Deblinger, 2006; Cohen, Mannarino, & Deblinger, 2012), it is recommended that therapists take advantage of the free web-based TF-CBT introductory training accessed via www.musc.edu/tfcbt. When working with children who have experienced traumatic losses in addition to CSA, it can also be helpful to review the Child Traumatic Grief website at www.ctg.musc.edu. This free of charge web course describes an adaptation of TF-CBT for treating childhood traumatic grief. Both of these websites offer printable scripts, streaming video demonstrations, and links to additional resources. Finally, we also encourage participation in face to face TF-CBT training as well as obtaining consultation from an TF-CBT trainer when implementing this approach initially with clients.

TF-CBT clinician roles

The acronyms ARTS and CRAFTS (see below) are used to represent the important therapist roles and core values associated with implementing TF-CBT. Throughout the different therapy components, the therapist serves in many roles that are represented by the acronym ARTS: Active listener, Role model, Teacher, and Supportive coach.

Active listener

Engaging in active listening and offering general support is critically important given the crisis that families often face when they discover that their child has been sexually abused. Throughout the course of treatment, both children and caregivers benefit a great deal from feeling heard and validated. Thus, engaging in a therapeutic relationship that supports the open and honest sharing of thoughts and feelings is essential. Given the shameful feelings often associated with the experience of sexual abuse, active listening helps to validate the clients' thoughts and feelings throughout the course of treatment. In fact, the utilization of reflective listening is particularly important when clients share the details of their experiences as it conveys understanding, acceptance, and respect. By repeating back the thoughts, feelings, as well as specific words and terms clients use in describing abusive sexual acts, TF-CBT therapists contribute to the gradual exposure process and demonstrate their own comfort with using these terms and discussing the sexual abuse. Reflective listening seems to enhance clients' confidence in sharing the details of their experiences.

It should also be noted that there is evidence that the appropriate use of silence in therapy sessions may enhance client perceived support (Sharpley, 1997). Moreover, when sharing educational information or when asking Socratic questions later in treatment, research suggests that silence may provide clients a greater opportunity to internalize and process the information or questions posed, potentially increasing their responsiveness (Rowe, 1986). Silence may reinforce for clients that the therapist is comfortable waiting until they gain the strength needed to openly discuss sensitive and often anxiety provoking issues without explicitly stating such.

Throughout the course of TF-CBT, maintaining a careful balance between talking and listening is critical. The effective TF-CBT therapist incorporates active listening into structured sessions. Without such structure, the authors' experience suggests that caregivers in particular will often focus on and ruminate about their frustrations with the responses of the system and their desire for more severe penalties for the perpetrator. Though this is reasonable and understandable, research findings suggest that repeatedly focusing on issues that are beyond parental and therapist control (e.g., legal outcomes) may be associated with increased abuse-related parental distress (Deblinger et al., 2001). Thus, it may be best to acknowledge the limitations of the clinician's influence on legal/child protection proceedings while simultaneously emphasizing confidence in the parents' potential powerful influence on their child's adjustment. This emphasis is important given that research and the clinical experience of the authors suggest parental participation in the structured, active TF-CBT process results in significantly less parental distress posttreatment, as well as in positive outcomes for children (Cohen, Deblinger, et al., 2004; Deblinger et al., 1996; Deblinger et al., 2011). In the early stages of treatment, when working with a parent who is struggling with acceptance of the CSA allegations, reflective listening may be the most important intervention to establish feelings of trust and acceptance, while also encouraging the parent to maintain an open mind and collaborate with the therapist in working to bring clarity to the allegations and thereby optimally helping both parent and child.

Role model

Throughout the therapeutic process, the therapist serves as an important role model, particularly with respect to communication skills, positive coping behaviors regarding the abuse experience, and behavior management skills. Given that one of the treatment objectives is to have the child tolerate memories and discussions of the sexual abuse without significant distress, it is crucial that the therapist demonstrate calm, matter-of-fact discussions relating to CSA as well as related topics. The significance of the therapist's role in modeling effective communication is heightened by the fact that the child may not have had any other adult communicate in this way regarding the abuse.

Therapists should begin modeling open communication during the assessment and/or initial treatment session when they elicit, in a nonleading but supportive manner, a spontaneous narrative about the child's sexual abuse experience. In addition to demonstrating clear and open communication themselves, therapists should respond to children's disclosures with calm and empathic remarks. This is particularly important as highly emotional or overly concerned reactions to disclosures are likely to create anxiety in children, discouraging further disclosures. Therapists, therefore, are encouraged to process their own personal reactions to children's disclosures with supervisors and/or colleagues whenever necessary.

Although children will sometimes demonstrate considerable avoidance, anxiety, or embarrassment when abuse-related issues are raised, therapists should not allow such responses to alter their communication style. Thus, although a child may choose to whisper about the abuse, the therapist should respond in a clear and normal tone of voice. Similarly, therapists serve as role models for parents regarding ways to cope and communicate effectively with their children regarding the sexual abuse and healthy sexuality. Discussions of sex education provide another opportunity for therapists to model open and healthy communication. When discussing sex education, it is helpful to use humor and to discuss sexuality in positive ways to encourage openness and further communication. By pursuing therapeutic goals in a straightforward, systematic, calm, and open manner, therapists demonstrate that it is possible and appropriate to cope with abuse-related discussions in a calm, direct, and effective way.

Therapists will also serve as important models for parents in demonstrating behavior management skills. For example, it is important to demonstrate the importance of praise in interacting with others by acknowledging and praising nonoffending parents for generally supporting their children, as well as for specifically following through with practicing skill building at home. Therapists are also encouraged to model the behavior management skills in individual sessions in order to prepare parents to practice and utilize the skills at home and during conjoint parent-child sessions. In addition, therapists may look for opportunities to demonstrate effective behavior management skills during interactions with children that the parents can observe. For example, the therapist might demonstrate the effective use of positive attention by praising the child for waiting quietly while the parent is meeting with the therapist individually.

Therapists also serve as role models for healthy coping in other related areas. In general, therapists should model a view of the world that is both accurate and hopeful by talking about difficult issues in direct, honest, and optimistic terms. For example, from the start of treatment, therapists should convey, based on the wealth of TF-CBT research and their clinical experiences, the view that with parental support and effective counseling, children who have experienced sexual abuse can fully recover and lead happy, healthy, and productive lives.

Teacher

Therapists working with children and their families in the aftermath of CSA often serve as a valuable resource for important information. Providing basic information about the child protection, law enforcement, and medical examination procedures can be extraordinarily helpful. Such information can greatly help to calm clients' anxieties about interacting with unfamiliar systems and agencies (e.g., criminal justice, child protection, and victim witness organizations; Deblinger & Heflin, 1994). For many parents, contact with these agencies can be overwhelming, intimidating, and frustrating. Therapists should help by providing basic information about the agencies and their roles.

Families are also educated about the rationale and the strategies for implementing trauma-focused cognitive behavioral interventions. Rather than engaging clients in a mysterious process with the implied goal of emotional health, a TF-CBT therapist offers practical treatment rationales, clear and commonsensical therapy plans, and realistic expectations for outcomes. Thus, clients are in a better position to determine if the proposed interventions will suit their personal needs. This open and practical approach seems to be comforting to children and nonoffending parents whose abusive experiences have left them feeling betrayed and distrustful of others.

Finally, TF-CBT therapists offer important educational information to children and parents regarding CSA, coping skills, parenting skills, healthy sexuality, and personal safety. As providing education that will lead to significant changes is no easy task, therapists should utilize effective educational techniques. Strategies that make an educator effective such as planning lessons in advance and setting students up for success, will similarly influence the effectiveness of the TF-CBT therapist. Some examples of effective strategies are found in Box 3.1.

Supportive coach

Therapists also assume the function of coach whose role it is to inspire and motivate both parents and children to fully engage in the hard work of therapy. As coaches, therapists are responsible for planning and structuring the therapeutic activities and keeping clients focused. Occasionally, therapists may have to redirect clients who are discussing unrelated issues. Just as a coach might give a pep

Box 3.1

Strategies of Effective Educators/Therapists

The techniques that make educators effective can also be used by therapists. These include:

- Assessing the clients' baseline knowledge and/or skill level
- Sharing assessment data in the form of feedback
- Preparing adequately by planning the session in advance
- Respecting and tailoring the approach to the individual
- Stimulating clients to think rather than providing all of the answers
- Making the environment safe to take risks
- Pacing therapeutic exercises to set clients up for success
- Motivating clients to pay attention, collaborate, and practice skill building at home
- Offering charismatic, stimulating, and creative presentations
- Providing skills and information that have wide applicability to real-life situations
- Modeling and encouraging active participation in the learning process
- Simultaneously demonstrating predictability and flexibility

talk to an athlete, the therapist motivates clients by reminding them of treatment goals and applauding their efforts in working toward those goals. Indeed, it is important that the therapist draws the client's attention to any progress he or she is making (e.g., being able to discuss the abuse more comfortably). In addition, therapists motivate their clients by consistently reviewing client performance via review of practice done at home, skill rehearsal, and role-plays. When presenting the idea of practicing a skill in session with a role-play or behavior rehearsal, it helps to acknowledge that this is a standard practice of coaching and something that is done with all clients. Moreover, it reflects the belief that skill development requires practice and coaching, despite how artificial it might feel at first. Role-plays, in fact, can be valuable in every stage of treatment when clients are learning new skills, as well as when parents are preparing for conjoint sessions during which they will be openly discussing the sexual abuse and healthy sexuality with their children.

It may be most helpful to offer constructive feedback to both children and parents following role-plays in the form of a "compliment sandwich," such that specific praise that describes exactly what they did well is offered first, then specific constructive feedback is provided, followed by additional global praise that highlights the therapist's enthusiasm for working with them. By offering specific and global praise, the therapist is, in fact, modeling a parenting skill that is crucial to the implementation of the parenting component. Below is an example of how the therapist might use a compliment sandwich to provide constructive feedback after a client has practiced a skill in session.

Therapist: *Marissa, how did that breathing exercise feel?*
Marissa: *I felt sort of silly doing it.*
Therapist: *I think that it is pretty common to feel a little silly at first, and I really appreciate your honesty in sharing that with me. I also liked how you concentrated and counted each breath in and each breath out.* (specific praise) *That was really good. I'd like you to try it one more time and this time see if you can slow down a little and take a slower and deeper breath in. Breathe out more slowly as well.* (constructive suggestion)
Marissa: *Okay. I'll try.*
Therapist: *I really enjoy working with you Marissa.* (global praise) *Thanks for giving this another try.*

Supportive coaching such as in the above described exchange can be valuable throughout the course of therapy. Such coaching typically incorporates active practice as well as constructive feedback provided in the form of compliment sandwiches.

Core values—CRAFTS

In the context of addressing the psychosocial problems of children and their families facing the crisis of CSA, the TF-CBT approach adheres to the principles, ideas, and values summarized by the acronym CRAFTS, which stands for Components based, Respect for individual, family, religious, community, and cultural values, Adaptability, Family involvement, Therapeutic relationships, and Self-efficacy (Cohen, Mannarino, & Deblinger, 2006). These foundational TF-CBT concepts are summarized below.

Components based

"Components based" refers to the central TF-CBT therapy components that reflect a core set of educational, skill building, and processing interventions that target a wide array of psychological difficulties. The broad applicability of these component interventions is critical due to the diversity of symptomatic responses exhibited by children and their nonoffending parents in the aftermath of CSA. Moreover, the treatment components are not rigidly applied in a strict session by session manner but rather are designed to be tailored to the child's and family's specific needs with each component building on one another and integrated in a way that best meets the child's and family's particular therapeutic needs.

Respect for individual, family, religious, community, and cultural values

Respect for the clients' values is central to the effective implementation of TF-CBT. Because children of any racial, religious, or ethnic background may experience sexual abuse, the therapeutic interventions used need to be acceptable and effective with highly diverse families. Due to the active, directive, and structured nature of the approach, cognitive behavioral interventions not only appear to be effective but also seem to be preferred by minority groups including African Americans, Native Americans, Hispanics, and Asians (Paniagua, 2005). TF-CBT in particular has been well received and found to be effective with families of diverse cultures and backgrounds (Deblinger, Cohen, & Mannarino, 2012).

Adaptability

Flexibility and creativity on the part of the TF-CBT therapist is important. Because many children with a history of abuse experience difficulties to varying degrees and across different areas of functioning, it is important to individually tailor treatment strategies to the specific difficulties presented by the child and family. Moreover, the therapist may flexibly and creatively incorporate ideas and therapeutic activities that reflect clients' interests, coping styles, cultural backgrounds, and family values in order to optimally engage and motivate clients' collaboration in the design and implementation of the treatment plan.

Family involvement

The involvement of family members in the child's treatment significantly improves outcomes for children who have experienced sexual abuse (Cohen & Mannarino, 1996a; Deblinger et al., 1996). Thus, at the outset of TF-CBT, every effort should be made to engage and actively involve nonoffending caregivers in the TF-CBT process. The participation of a primary caregiver, whether the individual is a parent, foster parent, grandparent, or another adult caregiver, communicates to the child how committed the adult is to the child, and it allows the parent and child to develop skills for talking with one another about the abusive experience. Moreover, when a child discloses sexual abuse, all family members are affected and likely could benefit from some level of participation in treatment. This familial involvement may be particularly important for siblings in cases of intrafamilial sexual abuse as these children often grapple with dramatic changes in family structure and relationships. Parents are vital to the TF-CBT process, as their participation in a parallel treatment process is designed to provide them with the same coping skills that their children will be learning. This parallel treatment process for parents not only helps them cope but also assists them in serving as more effective coping role models for their children. Through a combination of parallel individual and conjoint parent-child sessions, parents overcome their own feelings of distress while they also learn to communicate effectively and respond optimally to their children's behavioral and emotional needs. Ultimately, parents develop enhanced skills for coping, parenting, and assisting their children in processing their traumatic experiences. In doing so, parents become therapeutic resources for their children so that healing and growth can continue after the final therapy session.

Therapeutic relationships

Therapeutic relationships are central to the effective implementation of TF-CBT, which requires the therapist and client to work collaboratively in designing interventions that can be used in sessions and at home. Such collaborative efforts are likely to encourage feelings of trust, acceptance, and empowerment among children and their nonoffending parents. In the aftermath of CSA, families may have little control over the investigative and prosecutorial processes associated with the sexual abuse, but the collaborative and empathic nature of the therapeutic relationship promotes a greater sense of control and trust that likely enhances clients' motivation to engage in the hard work of therapy.

Self-efficacy

Self-efficacy is encouraged throughout the TF-CBT process. Although TF-CBT is a short-term approach, it offers clients skills for coping with their current difficulties, as well as those that may arise in the future. Because the impact of sexual abuse may be felt by children through different stages of their lives, it is important to provide children and parents with skills that can be used not only during the course of therapy but also after therapy has ended. Moreover, given the evidence that a history of abuse increases one's vulnerability to future victimization (Boney-McCoy & Finkelhor, 1995; Finkelhor, Ormrod, & Turner, 2007b) and that the accumulation of traumas increases one's risk for physical and emotional difficulties (Felitti et al., 1998), it is imperative that treatment provide skills that will reduce children's future risk and enhance their confidence and resilience in response to the inevitable stressors of life.

THERAPY COMPONENTS

The TF-CBT treatment components are summarized by the easy-to-recall acronym, PRACTICE (Cohen, Mannarino, & Deblinger, 2006). The acronym is particularly apropos for this treatment model because what is learned in the context of TF-CBT requires *practice*, review, and implementation between sessions and after therapy ends. Clients receive educational information, learn new skills, and acquire new beliefs about themselves, their relationships, their experiences, and their future in the course of treatment. When healthier ways of thinking and newly acquired skills are *practiced*, long-term maintenance of clients' progress is increased. In addition, it is helpful for TF-CBT therapists to *practice what they preach*. By learning to utilize the skills emphasized in the context of TF-CBT themselves, TF-CBT therapists can more effectively model the skills for clients, while simultaneously getting a firsthand appreciation for the perseverance required to consistently implement these skills in real life. This experience allows therapists to connect and empathize with clients as they work to incorporate the skills and guidance offered into their day-to-day lives.

The PRACTICE acronym stands for Psychoeducation and parenting, Relaxation, Affective expression and modulation, Cognitive coping, Trauma narrative and processing, In vivo mastery, Conjoint sessions, and Enhancing safety and future development. The components are generally implemented in parallel but separate individual child and parent sessions with reviews of the educational material and skills learned occurring in conjoint parent-child sessions when possible. For ease of discussion, these components are described below as separate and distinct focuses of treatment, but in reality the components overlap, with work on one component contributing toward progress on another component. The treatment model should be viewed as fluid with work shifting from one component to another depending on the needs of the specific client.

The PRACTICE components described below build on one another with one step supporting the implementation of the next step and exposure to abuse-related memories gradually increasing throughout the process as depicted in Figure 3.2. The early sessions present clients with psychoeducation and skills designed to help them cope more effectively with the emotional distress generated by the sexual abuse experience. Although some gradual exposure to CSA reminders (e.g., psychoeducation) occurs during these early components, there is a more direct focus on the child's specific trauma reactions, feelings, thoughts, and experiences during the middle phase of treatment when clients are engaged in more intensive exposure-based activities including trauma narration and processing exercises. The final components are devoted to integrating all of the educational, skill-building, and processing experiences including in vivo mastery exercises when needed with both parents and children individually and in conjoint parent-child sessions, with the final sessions typically focused

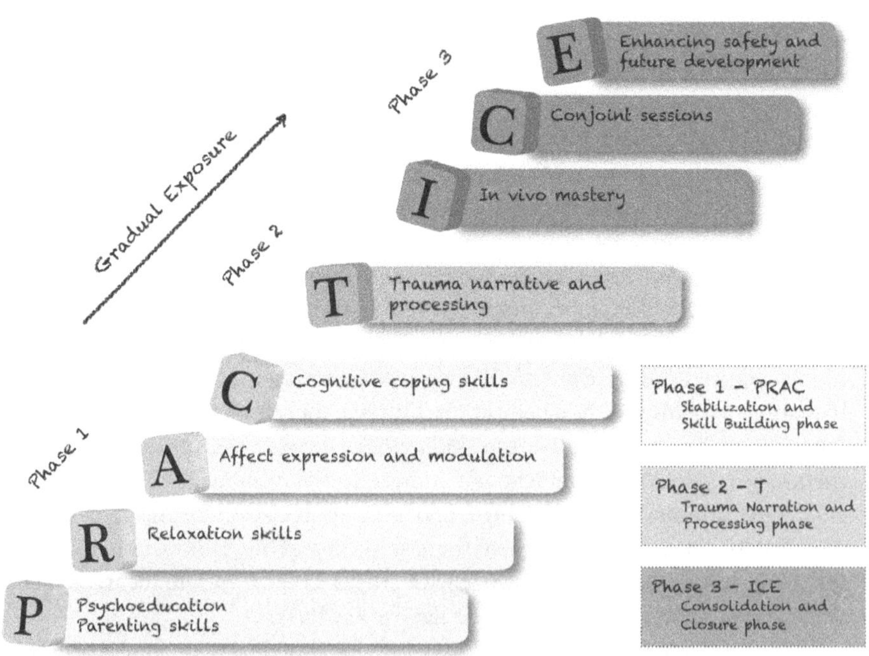

Figure 3.2 TF-CBT PRACTICE Components Overview.

on enhancing safety and future development. Specific activities associated with each of the PRACTICE components are described below, and suggestions are offered for planning an end-of-therapy celebration.

Psychoeducation

Both children and parents can benefit from education as knowledge can be highly empowering. Education may be provided at a variety of points in treatment but begins during the assessment and first session of treatment. From the start of treatment, it is important to provide information about the assessment findings and treatment procedures. Education regarding CSA is provided throughout treatment, including information about what sexual abuse is, why it occurs, who it affects, who the perpetrators are, how children feel when they have been abused, and why children sometimes do not disclose the abuse when it happens. It is also critical to discuss the impact of sexual abuse, highlighting the ways in which the child may have been affected in terms of his or her emotional, social, cognitive, physiological, and behavioral functioning. Most often education about CSA is provided gradually, beginning with some information provided at the start of treatment with increasingly detailed and personalized information offered as treatment progresses. Information regarding healthy sexuality is also an important part of treatment for children who have experienced sexual abuse, and it may be incorporated at different stages of treatment. Basic information such as the doctor's names for private parts may be taught early in treatment with more complex sex education most often being incorporated during the final enhancing safety component of treatment.

Parenting

Children can benefit immensely from the involvement of a loving adult in their treatment, whether that adult is a nonoffending parent, another relative such as a grandparent, or a foster parent. Parents participating in treatment learn specific skills to help them cope while also learning parenting skills to help them optimally respond to their children's emotional and behavioral needs in the aftermath of CSA. Over the course of treatment, parental participation speaks volumes in communicating their love and commitment to the child and, toward the end of treatment, helps the parent and child develop skills for talking with one another about the abusive experience. For parents whose children have responded to the sexual abuse experience with significant behavior problems, the therapist may focus considerable time on teaching behavior management skills to the parent. However, all parents can benefit from some parenting guidance in the aftermath of sexual abuse. Parents' reactions to their children's behaviors may significantly influence the improvement or exacerbation of children's abuse reactions. Well-meaning parents, for example, may model and reinforce avoidance behavior, believing that their children are better off forgetting about the abuse. Furthermore, parents may inadvertently reinforce abuse-related behavior problems by responding with increased or inappropriate attention. For example, children who begin talking excessively and inappropriately about sexual issues may continue such talk based on the attention it generates. TF-CBT addresses these negative behavior patterns by helping parents learn to model and reinforce effective coping responses in their children as well as learn to respond to children's abuse-related behavioral difficulties with effective behavior management skills.

Relaxation

During this component, children and parents learn to relax their bodies and their minds. Relaxation skills include deep breathing and muscle relaxation, as well as other activities that help calm the body and mind. Mindfulness skills may be taught to help clients purposefully attend to the present moment by learning to accept the natural flow of thoughts, feelings, and sensations without judgment and/or any corrective effort (Black, 2011). This practice has been associated with decreased stress-related symptoms (Carlson, Speca, Faris, & Patel, 2007; Davis & Hayes, 2011; Mackenzie, Carlson, Ekkekakis, Paskevich, & Culos-Reed, 2013) and may be particularly valuable for those clients who find themselves ruminating on the past and/or worrying habitually about the future (Davis & Hayes, 2011).

Affective expression and modulation

Affective or emotional expression skills and modulation are important in helping both children and parents effectively label, communicate, and manage their feelings about the abuse as well as other daily stressors. Initially, these skills help clients who are struggling with distressing emotions on a daily basis learn to acknowledge, label, and verbally express emotions, while also working collaboratively with the therapist to identify emotion modulation skills that will suit their coping styles and needs. Dysregulated parents and children will learn to effectively manage daily stress as well as trauma reminders in their environment so that some level of emotional stabilization can be achieved before proceeding to the more intensive trauma-focused work later in treatment. In addition, these skills will optimize the benefits of TF-CBT by enabling clients to not only acknowledge and describe feelings in the context of their trauma narrative but also to process feelings they experienced in response to sexually abusive experiences.

Cognitive coping

Cognitive coping skills training begins with an introduction to how thoughts, feelings, behaviors, and body sensations influence one another. Next, children, adolescents, and parents learn to catch automatic thoughts that fly by so quickly that clients are often not consciously aware of them. Initially, clients learn to identify and dispute generally dysfunctional or overly pessimistic thoughts, while replacing them with more accurate and helpful thoughts and coping responses. For example, a parent learns to dispute overgeneralized thoughts, such as "my child will be troubled by the sexual abuse for the rest of her life," by citing evidence that she has reason to be more optimistic about her child's future. These skills minimize distress clients may feel as a result of dysfunctional thoughts. Although parents' abuse-related cognitive coping work may start during this component, cognitive coping skills with children are generally taught and practiced with respect to more general distressing thoughts, then applied to the sexual abuse after the trauma narrative is completed and ready to be cognitively processed.

Trauma narrative and processing

As clients are able to identify and cope with difficult emotions more effectively and are able to acknowledge underlying automatic thoughts, they will be better prepared to engage in the next treatment component: the trauma narrative and processing component. This component combines elements of several cognitive-behavioral interventions designed to alleviate maladaptive fear, anxiety, and posttraumatic stress responses as well as depressive, pessimistic, and dysfunctional abuse-related thinking. Although gradual exposure begins at the outset of treatment with psychoeducation about CSA and continues with general references to the sexual abuse during the course of other coping skills components, the trauma narrative component encourages a more intensive examination of memories related to the sexual abuse and/or other traumas endured. When the child has completed much of the trauma narrative, the therapist can then support the child in examining the accuracy and helpfulness of abuse-related thoughts and developing beliefs revealed in the narrative. The overall objective is to identify and correct dysfunctional assumptions regarding self, relationships, sexuality, personal safety, and other related areas of concern that children may develop due to their sexual abuse. Parents participate in this component by reviewing the child's trauma narrative work in individual sessions with the support of the therapist. After processing their reactions to their children's narratives, therapists prepare parents in individual parent sessions to support their children's processing of these experiences through conjoint parent-child sessions later in treatment.

In vivo mastery

In vivo mastery or exposure is utilized when children avoid innocuous abuse reminders (e.g., safe playground, basement, or school environments) that are interfering with optimal individual and/or family functioning. This component is often not necessary as many avoidant behaviors decrease or disappear after the child and parent successfully work through the trauma narrative development and processing component. However, in some cases, in vivo exposure may need to be conducted earlier in treatment as in the case of a child's school refusal despite the perpetrator's discharge from the school setting. In other cases, the child's avoidance may persist even after successful narrative development and processing. In such instances, an in vivo graduated exposure plan may be devised to be implemented in collaboration with the parent in order to assist in helping the child regain her confidence in safe settings that have come to be feared due to associations with the sexual abuse (e.g., children's own bedrooms, basements, playgrounds, public bathrooms, etc.).

Conjoint parent-child sessions

Children and their caregivers benefit a great deal from carefully planned and structured conjoint parent-child sessions. These sessions are generally designed to provide opportunities for shared educational and skill-building experiences that lead to more trauma-focused conjoint sessions in which children share their trauma narratives or related products with their nonoffending caregivers who can then assist them in processing these experiences. When children exhibit significant behavior problems, conjoint sessions may begin earlier in treatment. This earlier initiation of conjoint sessions allows for a greater focus on the development and implementation of effective parenting and communication skills that may be practiced in individual parent sessions and implemented during conjoint sessions during which therapists observe and provide feedback.

Enhancing safety and future development

Personal safety skills training includes education regarding the continuum of "okay" touches versus "not okay" touches, the identification of inappropriate touches, and skills for responding effectively to inappropriate or confusing touches. This education is often introduced in individual child sessions and reviewed and practiced in conjoint parent-child sessions. Although body safety skills are generally taught and practiced toward the end of treatment, if the child is in an environment in which there is ongoing risk for sexual victimization as might be the case when a sibling who was abusive remains in the home, the skills may be taught earlier. Another important aspect of enhancing future development for children who have experienced sexual abuse involves the provision of healthy sexuality education. The therapist, in conjunction with the parent, should plan to provide developmentally appropriate sex education to the child, most often in the context of conjoint parent-child sessions. Given the evidence that children who have experienced sexual abuse may be at risk for developing sexual anxiety and difficulties (Cohen, 1995; Finkelhor, Hotaling, Lewis, & Smith, 1989), basic sex education should be combined with exercises that will help children explore and process their attitudes and feelings regarding sexuality.

THERAPY COMPLETION

As a short-term approach, the child's completion of TF-CBT should be anticipated from the start when the parent and child are informed of the time-limited nature of the therapy program. In fact, providing the approximate number of TF-CBT sessions initially helps parents and children to be hopeful that they will begin to feel better in a relatively short amount of time. The TF-CBT therapist is encouraged to confidently anticipate the child's therapy completion, mentioning it from time to time throughout treatment so that the parent and child can plan and look forward to celebrating their success in completing treatment. In fact, some children and caregivers enjoy planning a celebration that can include graduate caps and diplomas, as well as decorations, music, and other activities that encourage a festive atmosphere. This helps clients remember that therapy is much like a course with a beginning and end similar to the beginning and end of camp or the school year. This can be particularly helpful for children who as a result of their abusive experiences may be more sensitive to rejection. This sets up the therapist to be perceived more like a camp counselor or a teacher, helping children to accept and anticipate an end to the relationship potentially minimizing feelings of rejection. In addition, planning a therapy completion celebration as clients enter the third phase of treatment also helps children to view the end of therapy as a positive event that is associated with success. The final therapy session then can be enjoyed as a celebration of the child's and family's strengths and success in coping with the experience and aftermath of CSA.

SPECIAL TREATMENT CONSIDERATIONS

Therapists are generally encouraged to implement the TF-CBT PRACTICE components in the order and proportionality in which they are described above. However, it is important to balance fidelity to the model with flexibility when the therapist is addressing clinical challenges that require adjustments to the order of PRACTICE components and/or the proportionality of the TF-CBT treatment phases. Some examples in which there are special factors that must be considered when implementing TF-CBT include children with significant externalizing behavior problems, children with acute or ongoing safety issues, children with avoidant behaviors that interfere with daily functioning, and children who have experienced complex trauma.

Flexibility in sequencing of components

When children have significant externalizing behavior problems including sexual behavior problems, it is often important to include not only individual parenting skills sessions but also conjoint parent-child sessions early in TF-CBT treatment sessions as described earlier. During these conjoint parent-child sessions, the parent's attempts to practice effective communication and parenting strategies (e.g., praising the child for positive behaviors, utilizing differential attention, enforcing behavioral rules consistently without becoming overly emotional) may be observed, allowing the therapist to positively reinforce parenting skills and/or tweak them through subsequent modeling and practice during the parent's individual sessions. In addition, the therapist can individually prepare and then guide the parent and child during conjoint sessions in negotiating, establishing and later providing follow-up on behavior modification plans. Although guidance regarding the early implementation of behavior management skills is offered in the chapters that follow, additional information about applying TF-CBT for children with trauma and externalizing behavior problems is described elsewhere (Cohen, Berliner, & Mannarino, 2010).

Some children are at high risk for ongoing exposure to sexual abuse (e.g., those who were abused by a sibling who still lives at home or those whose perpetrator attends the same school). For these children, therapists should implement the "Enhancing Safety" component early in TF-CBT. Specifically, practicing developmentally appropriate personal safety skills and establishing a realistic safety plan (both typically done in collaboration with the parent) are critical early steps in treatment.

Children whose functioning is significantly impacted (e.g., those with school refusal, refusal to use a public bathroom or sleep in their own room) should begin in vivo mastery early in treatment (during the skills components of TF-CBT). This work should begin in conjunction with the child learning relaxation skills, which are important to pair with in vivo exposure activities; or during feeling identification exercises, during which the child can identify that he is afraid of going to school, using the bathroom, or sleeping in his own room. The therapist can then have the child develop a fear hierarchy ("fear ladder") and establish a schedule for in vivo exposure which the family and therapist will continue to work on while progressing through the other TF-CBT PRACTICE components. In vivo mastery of trauma stimuli that are interfering with daily functioning can take many weeks.

When early, chronic sexual abuse is perpetrated by a trusted attachment figure (often compounded by multiple other traumas) children may develop complex trauma (Cook et al., 2005). The process of establishing a trusting therapeutic relationship can trigger trauma reminders, requiring a longer initial engagement with these youth. Youth with complex trauma often also have severe affective and behavioral dysregulation that requires lengthier stabilization skills (Cohen, Mannarino, Kliethermes, & Murray, 2012). The proportionality of TF-CBT components typically needs to be adjusted when treating youth with complex trauma, such that about half of the treatment is spent on the initial skills-building components, with the second half of treatment spent on trauma narration and integration of skills. More information about applying TF-CBT for youth with complex trauma is described elsewhere (Cohen, Mannarino, Kliethermes, et al., 2012).

Parental participation complications

As noted in the introduction, the findings of numerous empirical investigations suggest that the ability of nonoffending parents to provide support following a child's disclosure of sexual abuse may be the most critical factor influencing the child's post-abuse psychological adjustment (Adams-Tucker, 1981; Conte & Schuerman, 1987; Everson et al., 1989). Nonoffending parents, however, do not always receive a great deal of support themselves. In fact, the professional community historically has not been sympathetic toward nonoffending mothers of children who have experienced sexual abuse. Rather, mothers, particularly those of incest victims, have been portrayed in the literature as collusive, denying, and indirectly responsible for the abuse of their children (Cormier, Kennedy, & Sangowicz, 1962; Sarles, 1975; Sgroi & Dana, 1982). Although the empirical evidence indicates that most mothers do not fit these negative stereotypes (Conte & Berliner, 1988; Deblinger et al., 1993; Sirles & Franke, 1989), it is likely that some parents may have encountered these harsh attitudes in their interactions with investigating professionals as well as others. In addition, many nonoffending parents may be unable to provide adequate support to their children due to their own emotional distress as well as their limited knowledge and skills in responding to abuse-related disclosures and difficulties. Early individual sessions with nonoffending parents, therefore, should be focused on providing support, as well as information and skills that will assist parents in coping with their own emotional reactions and their child's potential difficulties.

Shock, ambivalence, and/or disbelief concerning the CSA allegations

In the majority of cases, parents are adequately supportive of their child to be able to participate effectively, even if they are unsure initially of the veracity of the allegations or have questions about some of the details. When a child discloses sexual abuse, particularly when it concerns the parent's partner or another trusted family member, some members of the family (including the nonoffending parent) may experience considerable shock, ambivalence, and/or disbelief. This reaction should be viewed as a normal variation across a continuum of reactions to CSA allegations perpetrated by a trusted family or community member. It is not typically productive to try to convince such a caregiver of the veracity of the allegations as this may appear as if the therapist is aligning him/herself with the "system" and the investigating professionals rather than the parent. Rather, it is best to meet parents where they are in the process of attempting to cope with the crisis of discovering that their partner or another trusted/beloved individual sexually abused their child. Understanding the caregiver's perspective may best be accomplished by engaging in active reflective listening during the initial session(s). The therapist should validate the parent's feelings of disbelief by stating how difficult is for anyone to believe that someone you know, love, and trust could hurt your child. Moreover, it may be helpful to acknowledge that there are only two people who can be definitive about the veracity of the allegations—the child and the alleged offender. Thus, the therapist may ask the parent to maintain an open mind so information that may be helpful to the therapeutic process can be gathered together. It is important for the treating therapist to set reasonable goals for therapy (e.g., coping skill building) for the first phase of treatment given that a shift in ambivalent views regarding the allegations may be a gradual process and occur at different stages in therapy. Challenging nonoffending caregivers' attitudes is ill advised and frequently turns out to be unnecessary as parents' thoughts and feelings often change dramatically as they receive education about CSA and develop a greater understanding of the impact and circumstances of the sexual abuse. A positive change in attitude also may occur naturally as the interventions of child protective services and/or the legal system often create some distance and forced separation between the nonoffending parent and the alleged perpetrator. The therapist may gently encourage the parent to explore and discuss his or her feelings about the offender and about the parent's ability to trust and continue a relationship with that person. Over time, in conjunction with empathic listening and validation of feelings, the gentle use of Socratic questioning may assist the parent in examining her beliefs about the alleged sexual abuse. The TF-CBT therapist, however, should refrain from telling the parent what to believe but should work to ask questions and elicit information from the parent that would help her explore the possibility that the abuse may have occurred. Examples of good questions to be asked are: "Do you think there is any possibility that your daughter was sexually abused? Wow, it's so hard to imagine that someone you trust and love could have hurt your daughter, so what makes you think it didn't happen, and what makes you feel that maybe it did?" As time progresses and parents develop more effective coping skills, they may begin to realize that they are capable of coping with life without the offender. At that point, they are often better able to acknowledge that the abuse occurred and to offer the child the support he or she needs. In the context of therapy, it is best to empathize using a great deal of reflective listening. Nonoffending parents are often facing the greatest crisis of their life when they discover that their child has been sexually abused. Thus, it is most important to provide a forum where the parent can feel truly heard. For some nonoffending caregivers, the shift in their view concerning the allegations may not come until they begin to learn details about the abuse in the child's own words. Careful clinical judgment must be used concerning when and how to share abuse-related information provided by the child in this context. However, it is important to consider the sharing of the narrative, as some parents demonstrate a change of view when they learn more details about the abuse in the context of sharing portions of the child's narrative.

In sum, in order to foster a therapeutic relationship, it is important to maintain a supportive, nonjudgmental stance throughout therapy as nonoffending parents grapple with understanding allegations that naturally may seem impossible to imagine initially.

In relatively rare instances, nonoffending parents may be so overtly disbelieving and nonsupportive of the child that the child may be removed from their care by child protection. In those instances, it may not be possible or productive to have the parent participate in the child's treatment. Moreover, it may not be possible to obtain consent from either parent to proceed with treatment. In those cases, it is important to consult with child protective services and a legal advisor to determine how to proceed. In these instances, the nonoffending parent may be referred to her own therapist to work individually so that she can work through questions and feelings without judgment. As the case proceeds through the legal investigation, additional information may come to light that will be helpful to the nonoffending parent in making sense of the allegations. Thus, a long-term goal may be to initiate TF-CBT with the parent and child after the parent has made progress in becoming appropriately supportive of the child.

In situations in which it is not possible to involve a nonoffending parent, foster parent, or other custodial guardian, either because no such person is available or because he or she is not adequately supportive, the therapist may consider (with appropriate consents) the participation of alternative support persons such as a grandparent, adult sibling, or residential staff member. It may be particularly challenging to identify and/or involve a nonoffending parent when a child is placed in a residential treatment setting far from home and the parents are unable to participate. In such circumstances, a front-line staff member on the unit identified by the client can be asked to participate as a caregiver. This individual would be expected to maintain confidentiality with respect to the child's work during individual sessions and would actively participate in TF-CBT sessions as a caregiver would. This means that he/she would be encouraged to learn to reinforce all the skills the child is learning, while also preparing to help the child process the traumatic experiences during conjoint sessions in which the child may share the narrative. This and other TF-CBT modifications are encouraged based on our research and experience, which suggests that clients respond best to TF-CBT when the model is implemented with both fidelity and sufficient flexibility and creativity to meet the individual child's and family's therapeutic needs (Deblinger et al., 2012).

CULTURAL CONSIDERATIONS

Cultural factors are important to consider both in terms of how CSA might impact a child and her family, as well as how the family's culture and traditions can support the healing process and the implementation of TF-CBT. It is important to note that TF-CBT has been used with success across a wide range of cultures and countries around the world including Norway, Sweden, Germany, the Netherlands, Zambia, Tanzania, the Democratic Republic of Congo, Cambodia,

Japan, China, Israel, as well as in Latin American countries. TF-CBT researchers and clinicians (Murray & Skavenski, 2012) have reported that TF-CBT has been disseminated across some cultures and countries with little to no substantial modifications beyond the language adaptations required (e.g., western European countries). However, more significant TF-CBT cultural adaptations may be needed when working with families from cultural groups and/or countries where attitudes regarding mental health issues, counseling, and sexual abuse are highly distinct from those typically encountered. In fact, several authors have highlighted TF-CBT adaptations that may be made that incorporate helpful cultural and family traditions when implementing the skill-building and processing components (BigFoot & Schmidt, 2012; de Arrellano, Danielson & Felton, 2012).

Among the types of traumas that children experience, CSA may be most strongly associated with stigma and shame (Deblinger & Runyon, 2005). In large measure this is because many individuals erroneously conflate sexual abuse with sex. Taboos against sex during childhood are universal as are the value of virginity, but these taboos and values are more or less dominant among different cultural groups. Among cultural groups in which sexual taboos are particularly strong (for example, in cultures in which there is a very strong emphasis on the importance of girls' virginity), the negative impact of sexual abuse may be magnified for the child and/or the parents. Some examples may include the parent not allowing the child to talk about or report sexual abuse due to their fear that doing so will "shame" the family or "ruin" the girl's chances of being a good wife in the future. Although these parental responses may be well-intentioned toward the victimized child, they are likely to further stigmatize and shame the child, and to discourage disclosures of any sexual abuse that might occur in the future.

The family's cultural values can have a significant impact on how TF-CBT is implemented. For example, some cultures discourage or even prohibit adults from providing information about healthy sexuality to children (NCTSN, 2008). When treating a child from such a culture, it is critical for the therapist to work with the parents, and in some instances, with religious representatives, to obtain permission to address these topics. Most often therapists can do this most effectively through providing parents and other representatives with psychoeducation about the impact of sexual abuse and the value of providing specific information about healthy sexuality. Although to the authors' knowledge, no organized religions endorse the view that children with a history of sexual abuse are "damaged" or otherwise impure, some misguided members of such religions may express this view to the child and/or family. Recruiting the support of religious authorities may effectively counter such statements (Cohen, 1991). Therapists can address culturally based maladaptive cognitions such as "my daughter will never marry since she is not a virgin," by both exploring the likely negative impact of such beliefs on the parents and child (e.g., making the parents feel hopeless and the child act withdrawn, not care about her schoolwork or friends, etc.), and examining the possibly erroneous assumptions underlying these beliefs, as described in the dialogue in Box 3.2.

Box 3.2

Case Example: Addressing Parental Concerns about the Impact of Sexual Abuse on a Child's Virginity

Therapist: *What does it mean when you say she is no longer a virgin?*
Parent: *It means she is no longer pure.*
Therapist: *What does it mean to no longer be pure?*
Parent: *She is like an adult now, so she is not pure.*
Therapist: *But how do you know your daughter is no longer pure? What is different about her now?*
Parent: *She no longer has ... you know, she has been ... broken down there.*
Therapist: *You mean she no longer has an intact hymen?*
Parent: *Yes, that's right. She's been violated, and her husband would know on her wedding night that she is not pure.*
Therapist: *So it sounds like virginity is defined by a child having a few inches of skin called a hymen. Can you think of any situation where a girl might not have a hymen but hasn't had sexual intercourse or been violated in any way?*
Parent: *I guess a child could be injured in some way.*
Therapist: *That's true. In addition to that, did you know that 20 percent of girls are born without a hymen at all?*
Parent: *I didn't know that.*
Therapist: *And what if she were born without one? Or what if her hymen were accidentally broken, by using a tampon? Would she no longer be a virgin?*
Parent: *Of course not, that's not what I mean. I mean if it happened through the sex act.*
Therapist: *Ah, so now that we are talking about the sex act, let me understand what you mean by that. What has to happen to be the sex act?*
Parent (angry): *You are married—you know very well what is involved in the sex act.*
Therapist: *I may be confused, but are you talking about sexual intercourse?*
Parent: *Of course that is what I mean. Girls who are virgins have never had sexual intercourse.*
Therapist: *Please think very carefully about sexual intercourse. In sexual intercourse people decide they want to be involved with each other, they say yes, "I will have sex with you," and then they have sexual intercourse, right?*
Parent: *Sometimes it happens that way.*
Therapist: *How else does it happen?*
Parent: *Sometimes you are just swept away by passion.*
Therapist: *If you are swept away by passion are you still giving consent, that is, are you still agreeing to the act?*
Parent: *Yes, I guess so.*
Therapist: *Now think instead about a girl who never did those things, did not make a decision to be involved in sexual activity, did not agree to be involved in sexual activity, and who was not swept away in passion but instead was forced*

as part of an abusive, frightening, coercive act. Has she ever had sexual intercourse, or do we have a different word for that activity?

Parent: *I don't know. I think it's still sexual intercourse, isn't it?*

Therapist: *Let me ask you: if I hit you with a frying pan, you wouldn't call it cooking, would you?*

Parent: *Of course not. It would be violence, and I would probably sue you.*

Therapist: *So if someone violently abuses your daughter using his penis, why would you call it sexual intercourse? It is abuse.*

Parent: *I never thought of it like that. (Parent thinks) You're right ... hitting me with a frying pan isn't cooking because you're not using it the way it's meant to be used, you're using it for something else entirely. The man who abused my daughter was assaulting her, it had nothing to do with sex.*

Therapist: *How do you feel when you think about it that way?*

Parent: *I feel angry at the person who abused my daughter, but I feel better thinking that she really hasn't lost her virginity because it wasn't sex, it was an assault.*

After working through sensitive issues with parents, similar issues may be addressed with children and teenagers individually and later in conjoint sessions. After parents process these difficult issues themselves, it is often valuable to prepare them to explain to their teenager that virginity, for example, is something that is lovingly given to a spouse or partner and not violently taken away as described above.

Parenting attitudes and practices can be heavily influenced by cultural factors (e.g., race, ethnicity, gender, and religion) as well as the parents' upbringing and relationships with their parents. When providing parenting guidance it is often helpful to briefly inquire about the parents' childhood and relationships with their own parents, as well as to initiate discussions and demonstrate respect for families' cultural beliefs and traditions. The therapist is encouraged to work collaboratively with families to examine how new skills complement their beliefs, traditions, and home environment. This may help the therapist gain a greater understanding and appreciation for clients' current parenting approaches that may have been positively and/or negatively influenced by their own parents. In addition, inquiring about "sayings" that were frequently heard in childhood can provide some insight regarding parents' cognitive coping styles and tendencies as well. Faith and spirituality is one example of a cultural factor that can be identified as strengths for families and can help them cope with a traumatic experience like sexual abuse as well as a factor that may impact parenting style. For example, strong religious beliefs may also be associated with the common belief "spare the rod, spoil the child," a belief that may be associated with harsh parenting practices. In these instances, the therapist may praise the parent for wanting to discipline and guide the child while highlighting that the child needs this guidance and structure more than ever after experiencing a traumatic event. Simultaneously, the therapist collaborates with parents to find research that suggests that the true meaning of discipline in the Bible is to teach and guide just as the rod was used to guide the sheep. In another example, parents may believe that due to their cultural background their child may be less likely to be accepted by society and praised for their efforts, so the parents adapt "a tough love approach" in an effort to assist their child in coping with prejudices and biases that may be faced. The therapist can help the parents reframe the use of praise and positive parenting as a strategy to build the child's self-esteem and confidence, so the child is less vulnerable to negative influences outside the home and copes better with the negativity and biases that he/she may face throughout life.

DEVELOPMENTAL CONSIDERATIONS

The TF-CBT PRACTICE components should be modified to meet the needs of children and adolescents of all developmental levels. Generally speaking, when working with youth it is important to adjust one's language and questions to reflect the child's developmental level. For example, it helps to speak in shorter sentences with younger children and utilize terms that they naturally use such as "kids" rather than "children." Other adaptations include utilizing terms such as "okay" and "not okay" touches to refer to CSA when working with preschoolers. Older children and adolescents may understand the term "emotional abuse," but young children are able to understand feeling abuse as words that hurt your feelings when offered education about the topic. In addition, it is important to note that oftentimes young children may not perceive the abuse as serious or as negative as older children or adults who have a higher level of cognitive sophistication. Although it is important for professionals to convey that the sexually abusive behaviors were wrong or against the "rules," therapeutic and educational messages should not suggest that the perpetrator is a bad person or that their experiences were worse than children perceived them to be.

Repetition is critical to teaching new skills to youth, particularly young children. As such, TF-CBT involves introducing the respective components/skills by having the therapist model the skill, then having the child or adolescent practice or rehearse the skill. The therapist then provides feedback to help shape the behavior necessary to successfully perform the skill.

According to Weisz and Hawley (2002), therapists must vary levels of abstraction and cognitive sophistication when presenting skills to children and adolescents. The therapist must individualize the presentation of skills by assessing the level of abstraction that the youth will understand. Being too abstract with the presentation of educational information and/or skills may result in a lack of understanding on the client's behalf, while being too concrete may result in a lack of attention and engagement in the therapy process. It is generally helpful with children and adolescents to elicit as much information as possible from them about, for example, what CSA is or why it happens, before offering education or information. This inquiry provides the therapist an opportunity to further assess the developmental capacity of the child as well as to identify misconceptions the child may have, thus allowing the therapist to offer additional information that builds on what the child or adolescent knows without overwhelming him or her. In general, age appropriate games and activities that are fun are useful for introducing PRACTICE components to facilitate learning and decrease painful negative associations with the traumatic memories. In addition, the incorporation of developmentally appropriate games, books, and other activities helps to build rapport and enhance the therapeutic alliance while creating positive associations with the therapy experience. TF-CBT therapists often identify age appropriate or favorite games that may be played briefly at the end of the session as a reward for the hard work of therapy. In addition, TF-CBT therapists may transform almost any board game into an educational/exposure activity by incorporating question/answer cards that may be chosen and answered in order to move ahead. In the chapters that follow, suggestions are offered regarding how therapists may tailor the therapy components to the child's developmental stage.

SUMMARY

TF-CBT is a structured short-term treatment model designed for children, adolescents, and their nonoffending caregivers in the aftermath of trauma. The active participation of a primary caregiver is critically important, particularly if the child is exhibiting behavior problems; these behaviors are much more likely to improve with such involvement. In fact, primary caregiver involvement must be insisted upon when children exhibit aggressive, age-inappropriate, and/or sexually abusive behaviors, as these have the potential to escalate and ultimately cause harm to clients, as well as other children. However, when there are no significant behavioral difficulties and there seems to be no way to involve a caregiver, children and adolescents experiencing PTSD and other internalizing difficulties can benefit from TF-CBT even when they are seen without significant caregiver involvement (Deblinger et al., 1996). When a child does not exhibit behavior problems, it is equally important to include a supportive adult that could greatly contribute to the client's healing through their participation in TF-CBT (Deblinger et al., 1996; Dorsey et al., 2014). Additionally, recent research documents the association between caregivers' distress and their children's abuse disclosure (Runyon, Spandorfer, & Schroeder, 2014). As such, it is important to include the caregiver in the child's treatment to assist the caregiver in coping with personal distress and to enhance support of the child in order to promote optimal outcomes for the child.

The components of TF-CBT are implemented in three phases, with the gradual exposure process beginning in the initial phase and continuing throughout treatment. The introductory psychoeducational sessions for both the children and parents focus on building rapport, presenting assessment findings, treatment rationales, and basic information about CSA and its impact. The number of sessions devoted to each of the skill-building components varies so that the therapist may tailor the therapy to best meet the child's and parent's needs. Often, each component builds on the prior component, and several components may be reviewed and/or implemented in any one session. For example, in the middle phase of treatment, the first portion of a child session may be devoted to reviewing coping skills training, while the second portion of the session may be reserved for trauma narrative development and processing exercises with the final few minutes allotted for a fun ritual, a relaxation exercise, and discussion of practice done at home when indicated. Individual parent sessions parallel the child sessions in terms of involving graduated exposure to general and later more specific CSA-related information as well as coping skills training. In most cases, it is useful to provide coping skills training at the beginning of therapy in order to enhance the parents' ability to cope with both the stress of the immediate crisis and the emotions precipitated by the discovery that their child experienced sexual abuse. The development of effective coping skills will, in turn, increase the parents' capacity to respond most appropriately to their child. Parenting skills are also introduced to caregivers early on and throughout treatment. Parents are guided in the use of these skills in managing any abuse-related or nonabuse-related behavioral problems. As was true for the child treatment components, the amount of time devoted to each of the parent treatment components and the order in which they are presented should be based on the parents' needs as well as their child's particular symptom patterns. The final phase of therapy is reserved for trauma-focused conjoint parent-child work beginning with trauma education and skills review, the sharing of the trauma narrative when clinically appropriate, and sex education and personal safety skills training. This phase assists youth and their caregivers to integrate and consolidate the skills learned and healthy beliefs developed in preparation for ending therapy and moving forward in life. The end of therapy celebration is an opportunity for parents and children to reflect back on their therapy success and look forward to opportunities to continue to grow stronger and closer.

4

Setting the Stage for Treatment

Triage and Assessment

Factors that are important to consider prior to implementing trauma-focused cognitive-behavioral therapy (TF-CBT) are outlined in this chapter. It helps a great deal to review case histories and plan in advance to get treatment off to a good start. Such planning will encourage clients' trust in the treatment model as well as their confidence in the therapist.

CLIENTS FOR WHOM THIS TREATMENT APPROACH IS MOST APPROPRIATE

The treatment model as described has been and evaluated with children and adolescents ranging in age from 3 to 18 years. Given the wide range of abilities and difficulties experienced by children across this age range, it is important that the therapist adapt the treatment model to the developmental level of each child. Adaptations may include the therapist's style of communication and specific therapeutic activities. The authors believe this general treatment approach can also be used successfully with children who are developmentally delayed, as long as their cognitive functioning is, at minimum, on the 3-year-old level. Guidelines for implementing TF-CBT with children with developmental disabilities are provided elsewhere (Grosso, 2012).

Although TF-CBT has been successfully implemented with samples of children who have experienced a wide variety of traumatic events (i.e., sexual abuse, domestic violence, traumatic grief, and natural disasters), the primary focus of this book is TF-CBT's application to the child sexual abuse (CSA) population. In the aftermath of CSA, however, in some instances, the initiation of this treatment would be contraindicated and/or should be delayed until the child and/or family has achieved sufficiently emotional stability to benefit from TF-CBT. This includes cases in which the child and/or nonoffending parents are experiencing acute and/or chronic difficulties with respect to psychotic symptoms, active suicidal and/or homicidal intentions, and/or difficulties with other dangerous acting out behaviors (e.g., fire setting). Such difficulties typically warrant further evaluation and/or more intensive psychiatric attention (e.g., medication and/or hospitalization) to address those symptoms that would interfere with clients' active participation in treatment.

TF-CBT is an appropriate intervention for children and adolescents presenting with a wide range of sexual abuse experiences, both noncontact and contact sexual abuse. Sexual contact may involve physical contact such as kissing, fondling, oral, anal, or vaginal stimulation or penetration. Noncontact exposure includes exposure to pornographic materials, pornography of the child, exhibitionism, or having the child remove his/her clothes. TF-CBT is an appropriate treatment for children who present with single, multiple, or complex trauma histories. Though children who have experienced multiple traumas will not incorporate all the traumas in their narratives, representative traumas and/or themes that reflect the complex nature of their life experiences can be described and processed through their narrative work. As TF-CBT was designed to include nonoffending caregivers, it is not an appropriate treatment model if the participating caregiver was also the parent who sexually or physically abused the child.

INDEPENDENT DOCUMENTATION OF CHILD SEXUAL ABUSE BEFORE INITIATING TREATMENT

The use of TF-CBT with children who have experienced sexual abuse requires careful attention to factors that should be addressed prior to initiating treatment. In the United States and many other countries, there are requirements for professionals as well as others to report instances of suspected child abuse or neglect to the authorities. Thus, prior to initiating TF-CBT for CSA, it is important to report and/or verify the investigation and confirmation of any abuse experience(s) according to the requirements of the state or country in which the abuse took place. In order to make an appropriate child abuse report, one should be familiar with the relevant legal statutes and reporting laws in the state where a professional practices. Moreover, it helps to be familiar with the typical processes associated with child abuse investigations in one's home state as well.

In many areas of the United States, the investigation of CSA is a multidisciplinary process that may involve child protection, law enforcement, and/or other child abuse professionals (e.g., physicians, psychologists, social workers, etc.). It is not appropriate for the treating therapist to attempt to determine the credibility of the sexual abuse allegations, thus it is typically best to delay the initiation of TF-CBT for CSA until the initial investigation is complete and the allegations have been found to be credible by independent professionals.

With this population, in fact, it is important to obtain independent documentation of the sexual abuse by a professional other than the treating therapist prior to implementing TF-CBT. Independent documentation may be provided by the local child protection services (CPS) agency, law enforcement, the prosecutor's office, a medical provider, and/or a mental health provider other than the treating therapist. In cases that fall under the jurisdiction of CPS, an investigation of the sexual abuse allegations should be conducted to determine the credibility of the allegations prior to treatment. Most substantiated sexual abuse cases are appropriate for TF-CBT unless they exhibit some of the above described clinical contraindications. In some states, cases may not fall under CPS jurisdiction if the sexual abuse is perpetrated by an adult who is not in a caretaking role and/or if the child was sexually abused by another child or adolescent. Children who have been abused in these situations may be independently interviewed by law enforcement officials and/or other medical or mental health professionals. In the absence of a formal investigation by CPS, referrals may be appropriate for TF-CBT when independent professionals document the allegations of sexual abuse and report that the allegations are credible. The state entities or agencies (i.e., law enforcement, CPS, private agencies), for example, that handle child-on-child sexual abuse cases vary from state to state. In many states, child-on-child cases do not fall under the jurisdiction of CPS. In some instances, CPS will intervene with the case but do not substantiate the allegations because the child was not in a caretaking role. With respect to young children, TF-CBT may be appropriate even for the child who initiated the inappropriate sexual behavior if that child has a sexual abuse history and is engaging in sexually reactive behaviors. In cases of sibling abuse, prior to initiating treatment, it is important to ensure that the child who engaged in sexually abusive behavior is receiving appropriate treatment services and caregivers are appropriately supervising the children's interactions if they are residing in the same home and/or having visits with one another.

Given the legal and clinical ramifications of children's disclosures of sexual abuse, it is important to carefully document and maintain records of all child abuse reports made to the authorities, as well as other relevant information received or reports obtained that document the findings of child protection/law enforcement investigations and/or related psychosocial or medical examinations. If there is a need for therapeutic support prior to the completion of the CSA investigation and prior to the initiation of TF-CBT, therapy that provides nondirective support or more general coping skills training may be helpful. Information is provided below about child protection, law enforcement, and medical examination procedures that may occur in the context of a CSA investigation. Given that the focus of this book is on treatment, only limited information on the investigatory process is provided with the remainder of the chapter focusing on the treatment planning assessment that should be undertaken prior to the initiation of TF-CBT.

CHILD PROTECTION/LAW ENFORCEMENT CONSIDERATIONS

When treating children who have experienced sexual abuse, some involvement with child protection and/or law enforcement is likely. The CSA experience may be the family's first experience with these organizations, and it can be quite unnerving and intrusive. Thus, it may be helpful to the families to provide information regarding the clinician's role vis-à-vis child protection and law enforcement. For example, parents may erroneously believe that the therapist will be sharing personal treatment information with the investigating professionals. Thus, it will be important to highlight the confidential nature of client-therapist relationships, emphasizing the therapist's distinct and separate role from investigating professionals. These distinctions may be particularly important to highlight when treatment services are provided within the confines of a child advocacy center and/or child protection agency as therapists in those settings may be more likely to be perceived as working for the investigating agencies.

The degree of collaboration and cooperation between child protection and law enforcement professionals varies from one location to another. In communities with a child advocacy center, child protection, law enforcement, mental health, and medical professionals work closely together and often maintain offices within the same facility. Indeed, child advocacy centers are designed to minimize the stress of the CSA investigation by coordinating the efforts of the professionals involved so that the child does not undergo multiple, repetitive interviews and evaluation procedures. In communities without child advocacy centers, child protection and law enforcement professionals may still work cooperatively by going out together to interview the child and/or parents regarding the CSA allegations. In such instances, one professional may conduct the interview, while the other observes in order to avoid having the child undergo multiple investigative interviews. In other communities, child protection workers or law enforcement officials may initially work independently then involve the other professionals once it is determined that they will be needed. In some instances, the child will make a clear disclosure regarding the CSA experience in an initial interview with investigating professionals, and substantiation of the allegations may be made without delay. In those cases, TF-CBT typically can be initiated once that documentation and the investigation are completed. However, as was described in the first chapter, the disclosure process may not be linear. Rather, the child may make a tentative or partial disclosure while assessing the reaction of others. In other instances, although concerns have been raised regarding the possibility of CSA, the child may not disclose abuse to investigating professionals. When the credibility of the abuse allegations is unclear, the investigating child protection or law enforcement professionals may make a referral to a mental health practitioner to conduct an extended evaluation of the child. In those circumstances, it is not appropriate to initiate TF-CBT until the credibility of the allegations has been established.

As was described previously, it is recommended that if a mental health clinician participates in the investigation of the abuse allegations, that investigating professional should not be the person who provides psychotherapy. The American Psychological Association (2013) recommends that those roles be kept distinct for several reasons. If a clinician is involved in the investigation to determine the credibility of abuse allegations, then it can be expected that that clinician's report will need to be shared with other professionals involved in the investigation and potentially with the court. That expectation should be explained to the clients in advance. Although it may be appropriate to share that evaluation report prepared in the context of investigation, it is typically not appropriate to share information regarding the ongoing therapeutic process. It is important to maintain a clear distinction between mental health professionals that conduct evaluations designed to contribute to the investigative process and the treating therapist. Having one person conduct the evaluation to determine credibility of abuse allegations and another person provide psychotherapy helps to maintain the confidentiality of the child's therapy records. However, even when these recommendations have been followed, it is possible that the treating psychologist may receive a subpoena to provide information to the court. Although a subpoena should never be ignored, the treating clinician has an obligation to maintain the confidentiality of the child's psychotherapy records. Even when a court order is received, the clinician should consider a number of factors before releasing therapy records. Many states have "victim privilege" statutes that protect the confidential therapy communications between counselors and victims of violence. It is recommended that clinicians familiarize themselves with their state's specific statutes to protect the therapy records of victims of violent crime. In accordance with these statutes the clinician should not release client psychotherapy records in the absence of a court order, without first obtaining the written consent of the client's legal guardian and the client depending on state's age of consent. In fact, it is preferable not to release the records in response to a court order without first obtaining the legal guardian's and client's, when applicable, consent to release. In the presence or absence of a court order, if a family objects to the release of the child's confidential therapy records, the clinician may share information about the victim-counselor statute with the judge who may decide to do an in camera review of records and may determine that the records are not relevant and should not be released to the attorneys or others in the court. Given the complexity of these legal issues, it is often helpful for mental health clinicians to consult with an attorney who is knowledgeable about the relevant statutes when any type of release of records or court involvement is requested.

MEDICAL EXAMINATION

In the course of a CSA investigation, children are often referred for a medical examination. This examination can contribute significantly to the child protection and/or law enforcement investigation but also has great potential therapeutic value. In terms of the investigation, the medical examination may clarify the CSA allegations by providing information in the following categories "1-medical history/behaviors, 2-acute/healed ano-genital/extra-genital trauma, 3-pregnancy in adolescents, 4-sexually transmitted infections and 5-forensic evidence such as trace materials, seminal products" (Finkel, 2014). It should be noted that it is, in fact, quite rare for children who have experienced sexual abuse to present with acute physical findings such as those described in categories two through five. Thus, the medical diagnosis of CSA is most often made on the basis of a carefully obtained medical history. The medical diagnostic interview may elicit additional idiosyncratic details especially for those children who may be more inclined to disclose more about their sexual abuse experience(s) to a medical professional because of bodily concerns. In addition, it is critically important to identify the minority of children (approximately 5%) who do present with abuse-related physical findings in order to ensure that they receive proper medical care and timely treatment of any injuries or sexually transmitted infections contracted (Finkel, 2014).

Fortunately, most often the medical examination findings are quite reassuring to children and their caregivers as approximately 95% of children who have been sexually abused do not have acute injuries and/or sexually transmitted infections (Finkel, 2014). From a therapeutic standpoint, in the context of conducting a complete medical history and examination, a skilled medical professional conveys educational information that can be helpful to children and their caregivers. More specifically, the medical provider can most concretely and directly address the concerns and worries that some children, adolescents, and caregivers may have regarding the impact of the sexual abuse on children's bodies, future development, and sexual functioning. In fact, because of children's tendencies to think more concretely, a medical professional who examined the child may be in the best position to address bodily concerns as compared to mental health professionals who cannot conduct such physical examinations. Some examples of concerns that can be effectively addressed in the context of a medical examination might include an 8-year-old girl's concerns about developing breast cancer as a result of the offender putting his mouth on her breast and a 10-year-old boy's worry that he may have contracted the "dying disease" (i.e., AIDS; Finkel, 2014). When conducted in a skilled and child-sensitive manner, the medical examination can contribute significantly not only to the abuse investigation but also to the clients' psychosocial healing. When body image distortions or medical concerns persist and/or are revealed in the context of therapy, the TF-CBT clinician may utilize the medical report to provide helpful information and/or work collaboratively with the examining physician to address physical health concerns as part of the therapy process.

In summary, although a comprehensive description of forensic approaches designed to assess the credibility of CSA allegations is beyond the scope of this book, the above information may be valuable in providing a general understanding of the multidisciplinary processes involved in investigating CSA allegations. Readers seeking further information about the legal/investigative processes and/or medical examination procedures used in the context of investigations are referred to up to date comprehensive texts on these topics by Faller (2007), Lamb, Hershkowitz, Orbach, and Esplin (2008), and/or Finkel and Giardino (2009).

ENGAGEMENT IN THE ASSESSMENT AND TREATMENT PLANNING PROCESS

The components of a treatment planning assessment, as described below, occur after the findings of an investigation and/or other independent medical or psychological evaluation have established the credibility of the allegations. It is important to engage and motivate clients to actively participate in assessment and treatment at the initial point of contact, even before therapy begins. Research has repeatedly documented the need for and associated benefits of specific strategies designed to actively engage clients seeking therapy services for their children in public mental health settings. The use of strategies to engage clients is particularly important with respect to children who have endured victimization experiences as research suggests that most children who have experienced victimization do not receive counseling even when there is indication that they have been negatively impacted (Kopiec, Finkelhor, & Wolak, 2004). As parents are the most likely parties to seek mental health counseling for their children, it is most critical to actively engage caregivers and provide information about the efficacy of treatment designed for children who have experienced sexual abuse and/or other exposure to violence. Research on therapy attendance further suggests that children with internalizing disorders, such as the PTSD experienced by many CSA survivors, may be less likely to receive treatment than children exhibiting hyperactivity/impulsivity or other acting out disorders (McKay, Pennington, Lynn, & McCadam, 2001).

To address barriers to treatment, McKay and her colleagues have developed a number of empirically validated engagement strategies with positive results. Studies have shown that these engagement strategies have been associated with increases in treatment attendance and completion rates (McKay, Stoewe, McCadam, & Gonzales, 1998; Shivak & Sullivan, 1989). A recent study examined the impact of these engagement strategies in the context of implementing TF-CBT. In fact, Dorsey and colleagues (2014) found that while the use of active engagement methods combined with TF-CBT did not appear to improve clinical outcomes above and beyond standard TF-CBT, those participants assigned to the TF-CBT plus engagement strategies were significantly less likely to drop out of treatment prematurely, allowing them to complete a full course of treatment. Thus, there appears to be considerable value in encouraging the use of empirically validated strategies by intake staff, evaluators, as well as therapists to support and enhance client engagement, commitment, and receptivity to treatment. Strategies that may enhance client participation in both assessment and treatment include (1) brainstorming with parents to address potential concrete barriers including transportation difficulties, babysitting concerns for siblings, as well as scheduling conflicts, (2) establishing the need for and benefits of mental health care, (3) reviewing prior therapy experiences, (4) encouraging caregiver motivation for participation in treatment, (5) understanding whether the family has any stigma about receiving mental health services, and (6) establishing a collaborative working relationship. It should be noted that identifying and addressing the specific goals that the caregivers have for treatment will be important in enhancing their motivation and engagement. For example, if parents are most concerned about declining school performance and/or behavioral difficulties, these should be incorporated into the treatment plan. The above strategies should be utilized starting with the first point of contact with clients. Additional details regarding the implementation of these strategies are described in greater detail in the "Psychoeducation" chapter that describes the process of introducing parents and children to treatment later in this book.

Therapy environment

In establishing a therapeutic setting, clinicians should be aware that the physical environment may influence clients' feelings about participating in a psychosocial assessment and treatment. There is some empirical evidence that preschoolers interviewed by friendly individuals in warm, pleasant surroundings may be more accurate in their responses to questions than preschoolers who are interviewed by less friendly (stern) individuals in stark office environments (Goodman, Bottoms, Schwartz-Kenney, & Rudy, 1991). Thus, in designing a therapy setting, the following issues should be considered:

- The setting should establish a warm, welcoming atmosphere with appropriate seating and age-appropriate reading materials for children and their caregivers.
- The atmosphere should convey that the clinician likes and respects children, adolescents, and their parents (e.g., friendly, childlike wall hangings, other children's drawings).
- The waiting room should be secure and provide supervision for children who require such when their parents are being seen by the therapist.
- The setting should offer privacy with minimal distractions from external noise and interruptions.
- The setting should provide a sense of consistency and or predictability (e.g., the same office should be used each session, if possible).
- Most importantly, the setting should not be too stimulating or distracting for children due to an overabundance of toys or games.
- Therapists should maintain a small selection of toys and other materials that are not displayed but made available when appropriate so that children have choices for therapy activities without being overwhelmed. Some useful toys include paper, crayons, toy telephones, dolls, doll houses, puppets, a feelings chart depicting different emotions, therapy games, and computer applications.

Treatment planning assessment

Prior to initiating TF-CBT, a structured psychological assessment including demographic interviews and standardized measures should be conducted. The psychosocial assessment and its findings are critical to effective treatment planning. Indeed, treatment based on incomplete or out of date assessments may be misguided. Thus, the treatment planning assessment should generally be conducted within one month of the initiation of treatment. To develop a comprehensive case conceptualization, treatment recommendations and plans should stem from a thorough assessment that integrates information from a wide range of sources. A variety of assessment methods may be used, including observation; interviews with the child, nonoffending caregivers, and significant others; reports from social service agencies, teachers, and medical and mental health professionals; and standardized psychological measures. The treatment planning assessment represents an opportunity to encourage a collaborative approach with clients from the outset. Depending upon the organization's structure, these assessments may be conducted by the treating therapist or by someone in the organization other than the treating therapist. When the clinician conducting the assessment requests input and assistance from clients in collecting information that will result in a comprehensive and well-grounded assessment, clients often experience feelings of respect and appreciate the collaboration. During this process, it will be important to collect information concerning the clients' functioning in a variety of areas as these will have direct implications for treatment. The acronym CRAFTS is again used, this time to outline important areas of functioning to consider when assessing the impact of CSA on a child and his/her family (Cohen, Mannarino, & Deblinger, 2006). These potential areas of maladaptive functioning include the following:

Cognitive difficulties that may reflect dysfunctional thoughts about one's self, one's relationships with others as well as one's view of the world and the future.

Relationship problems with peers and/or family members potentially stemming from diminished self-worth, shame, and other interpersonal trust difficulties.

Affective difficulties due to a wide array of emotional reactions that can lead to emotional dysregulation in the aftermath of sexual abuse.

Family difficulties often reflecting heightened parental stress, parenting deficits and parent-child conflict due to heightened tension within the immediate and extended family.

Traumatic behavior problems reflecting both increased internalizing symptoms due to heightened fears and avoidance and increased externalizing symptoms including angry outbursts, oppositional behaviors, as well as age inappropriate sexual behaviors.

Somatic problems as a result of heightened arousal and increased vigilance that can lead to physical symptoms including muscle tension, headaches, stomachaches, and physiological panic symptoms.

It is useful to conduct an assessment of the child's psychological functioning prior to the initiation of and at the end of therapy. Given that the involvement of a supportive caregiver is a critical part of TF-CBT and of the child's recovery process, it is important to assess the emotional impact of the child's sexual abuse on the caregiver as well as the caregiver's interactions with the child. These variables may have an impact on the outcomes for the child (Cohen & Mannarino, 1996a, 1998a; Deblinger et al., 1996). Furthermore, caregivers may experience a host of emotional responses to their children's abuse that can interfere with their ability to appropriately respond to their child's postdisclosure needs (Banyard, Rozelle, & Englund, 2001; Esquilin, 1987). As such, TF-CBT focuses on assisting caregivers in coping optimally, so they can serve as a support to their children to promote optimal outcomes for children.

The initial purpose of the assessment prior to treatment, in conjunction with the information obtained from independent sources documenting the abuse, is to determine whether TF-CBT is an appropriate form of treatment for the child and her family. For instance, children who are actively suicidal, engaged in dangerous acting-out behaviors such as excessive drug or alcohol use, or are actively psychotic should receive other therapeutic interventions before participating in TF-CBT. If the caregiver accompanying the child to treatment is the perpetrator of the sexual abuse or some other form of maltreatment, such as physical abuse, TF-CBT would not be an appropriate treatment as it was developed primarily to work with the child or adolescent and nonoffending caregivers. It should be noted that caregivers are often struggling themselves to come to grips with the allegations of CSA and may demonstrate varying degrees of support to their children, as well as varying levels of effective parenting skills. This variability should be expected and may be addressed slowly over the course of treatment. Thus, it is important to note that one should not exclude parents from participating in the child's treatment because initially they are disbelieving or unsupportive, as this often changes considerably over time as parents feel understood and supported. The second purpose of the initial assessment is to identify areas of abuse-specific and/or general psychological impairment that should be targeted as a focus of therapy and to document symptom levels prior to initiating treatment.

Additional assessments may be useful during the course of treatment to assist the therapist in tracking treatment progress and symptoms that warrant additional intervention. Completing and reviewing scores on pre- and posttreatment measures toward the end of therapy can be empowering for the therapist, parent and child alike as therapy gains made over a short-term course of treatment can encourage feelings of pride and optimism for the future.

Background information

A semistructured interview may be conducted with both children and their parents to obtain relevant background history. The interviews include questions that allow for the collection of standard parent and child background information including developmental, family, academic, and social histories. In addition, detailed information about the child's sexual abuse experience, other trauma exposures (e.g., domestic violence, physical abuse, bullying, traumatic loss of loved ones, medical traumas, etc.) and general coping responses should be assessed. It is also useful to talk with parents about their personal childhood and adult trauma histories and their overall coping responses, as this information may have significant relevance to treatment planning.

The assessor should utilize standardized psychological measures whenever possible to assess the child's psychological functioning so that the child's level of symptomatology can be compared with that of other children of the same age and sex. Although parents and teachers often are the best source of information regarding externalizing symptoms, children themselves are usually the best reporters of internalizing symptoms. Thus, the assessor should consider administering self-report measures to the child, if he or she is old enough (i.e., chronologically and developmentally) to respond appropriately (i.e., 7 to 8 years of age and older), as well as measures completed by the caregivers about child behaviors. Although specific assessment measures to be administered may vary from case to case, the authors have found the measures described below to be helpful in assessing children's psychosocial functioning in the aftermath of CSA. It is recommended that at least one relevant standardized measure be utilized in assessing children's pre- to posttreatment progress, but offered here are a variety of measures from which to choose, some of which may be used in conjunction to measure distinct domains of functioning. Information on how to obtain these measures is provided in Appendix A.

Standardized child and caregiver assessment measures

CSA impacts many areas of functioning, and thus it is critical to conduct assessments that address a wide array of emotional and behavioral difficulties as well as strengths. Ideally, it is helpful to obtain pretreatment measures for both children and their caregivers so treatment progress can be objectively assessed for all participants in treatment.

Child assessment: posttraumatic stress symptoms

Among this population, it is important to obtain a thorough trauma history and to assess trauma-related symptoms. A trauma history may reveal whether or not a child has experienced additional CSA episodes as well as other traumatic events (i.e., domestic violence, physical abuse) that frequently occur concomitantly with CSA (Dong, Anda, Dube, Giles, & Felitti, 2003; Finkelhor et al., 2007a). As noted earlier, 86% of children with a history of CSA report other victimization experiences as well (Finkelhor et al., 2007a). It is important to assess trauma symptoms experienced by a child who has been sexually abused, given that sexual trauma is more likely to result in PTSD symptoms as compared to most other childhood traumas (Copeland, Keeler, Angold & Costello, 2007). Moreover, a majority of children referred for treatment in the immediate aftermath of CSA exhibit at least partial symptoms of PTSD with a significant proportion meeting full criteria for PTSD (McLeer et al., 1988). A critical part of TF-CBT is helping children to overcome trauma-related symptoms, manage trauma reminders, and effectively face and process traumatic memories.

While assessing PTSD symptoms, the assessors should carefully identify timeframes as to whether symptoms occurred prior to or after the sexual abuse and the specific context of the symptoms. The establishment of this temporal relationship is particularly important given the overlap of PTSD symptoms with symptoms of other psychiatric disorders, including Major Depressive Disorder (MDD), Attention Deficit Hyperactivity Disorder (ADHD), psychotic disorders, learning disorders, and so on. For instance, a child may report that he/she is no longer interested in playing with certain toys. This change could be related to a loss of interest associated with PTSD or anhedonia with depression. It could also reflect a normative change if the child reports upon further inquiry that he or she is "too old" to play with those particular toys. Attention and concentration difficulties are prominent in children with PTSD, ADHD, and MDD. In an example of attention problems related to PTSD, a parent may report that the child has difficulty attending and concentrating in school and that the child's grades have deteriorated since the sexual abuse occurred. The child then confirms that he or she has trouble attending because of thoughts of the sexual abuse. In another instance of attention problems, the parent may report that the child has difficulty attending and concentrating but that the child is waiting for a child study team evaluation to evaluate ADHD symptoms and that these symptoms have been present long before the sexual abuse occurred. Of course, children who have preexisting ADHD symptoms may be sexually abused and as a result have exacerbated attention, behavioral, and emotional symptoms as a result of the abuse as well. The assessor should also be careful to distinguish between true psychotic hallucinations or delusions and the flashbacks of abuse experiences that may be experienced as a symptom of PTSD. In the context of PTSD, these symptoms would not be viewed as a "true psychotic disorder," but as a PTSD-related symptom.

There are a number of measures and semistructured interviews available that measure PTSD symptoms and whether or not the child meets at least preliminary criteria for a diagnosis of PTSD. Though it is recommended that only one be used, two different PTSD measures for children are described here, including the UCLA PTSD Reaction Index for DSM-IV (PTSD-RI; Pynoos, Rodriguez, Steinberg, Stuber, & Frederick, 1998) and the Child PTSD Symptom Scale (CPSS; Foa, Johnson, Feeny, & Treadwell, 2001). One of these measures may be administered to assess the child's trauma history as well as the child's emotional response to the traumatic experience(s).

The UCLA PTSD-RI (Pynoos et al., 1998) is a diagnostic interview, consisting of 20 to 22 items (depending on the form) that assess trauma history and DSM-IV PTSD symptoms associated with the traumas in school-age children and adolescents. Symptoms are assessed from the perspective of multiple reporters as there are separate self-report forms for children and adolescents, as well as a parent-report form for the child/adolescent. The measure yields DSM-IV-TR PTSD diagnosis and provides a rating of the severity of the symptoms. The

PTSD-RI is easy to administer and score, is a widely used measure of PTSD, and has a DSM-V version now available.

The CPSS (Foa et al., 2001) consists of 26 items and is a self-report measure that assesses severity of PTSD symptoms and diagnostic criteria in children ages 8 to 18 years. It includes two event items, seven functional impairment items, and 17 symptom items, rated on a 4-point frequency scale (0 = "not at all" to 3 = "5 or more times a week"). The CPSS yields a total symptom severity scale score (ranging from 0 to 51), a total severity-of-impairment score (ranging from 0 to 7), and scores for each of the three PTSD symptom clusters. The CPSS is available free of charge and is also easily administered to both children and parents, but it should be administered after screening for traumatic experiences via an interview and/or a screening instrument like the Traumatic Events Screening Inventory (TESI-C; Ribbe, 1996) which is a 15-item structured interview designed to assess a wide array of potential traumatic incidents including sexual abuse and other forms of violence.

Children's Feelings of Shame

Shame, an emotional process related to children's perceptions about themselves, has been identified as an important factor explaining the variability in symptoms reported by children after an abusive experience (Brown & Kolko, 1999; Deblinger & Runyon, 2005; Feiring & Taska, 2005; Feiring et al., 1998b). According to the model proposed by Feiring, Taska, and Lewis (1996), following the experience of CSA, the likelihood of a child experiencing the negative self-evaluative emotion shame is related to abuse-specific attributions. Children with internal attributions for the CSA (e.g., "this happened because I am a bad person") are more likely to experience feelings of shame that contribute to children's post-abuse adjustment (e.g., depression and posttraumatic stress symptoms). Greater levels of shame appear to be associated with greater symptoms of psychological distress over the long term (Feiring et al., 1996). Given the relationship between shame and children's symptoms, it can be helpful to assess children's shame as a part of the treatment planning assessment. To the authors' knowledge, the Shame Questionnaire (Feiring & Taska, 2005) is the only available measure developed specifically to assess shame in children who have experienced CSA. There are eight items in this measure and each item is rated on a 3-point scale from zero to two: *not true, somewhat true, very true*, with higher numbers indicating greater agreement with the statements.

Child and Adolescent Sexual Behaviors

Given that a significant proportion of children who experience CSA exhibit inappropriate sexual behaviors (Deblinger et al., 1989; Friedrich et al., 1992), it is important to evaluate the presence of such behaviors. However, when working with caregivers it is critical to differentiate developmentally appropriate sexual behaviors from inappropriate sexual behaviors for children as well as adolescents. In fact, research suggests that many sexual behaviors are normative, though there are also adultlike sexual behaviors that may be suggestive of

across five scales: (1) emotional symptoms, (2) conduct problems, (3) hyperactivity/inattention, (4) peer relationship problems, and (5) prosocial behavior. To obtain reports from multiple informants, there are four versions of the SDQ available: separate parent/teacher reports for children ages 3 to 4 years, children ages 4 to 10 years, and children ages 11 to 17 years, as well as self-report for children ages 11 to 17 years. The SDQ may be obtained online free of charge at www.sdqinfo.com.

These measures may contribute to treatment planning through the identification of specific behaviors that the clinician may address through individualized parent training that is designed for the specific problematic behaviors identified. These measures also allow for the assessment of changes in children's behaviors over the course of therapy, thereby more objectively demonstrating therapeutic progress.

Caregiver assessment

Given the relationship between parental support and functioning and optimal outcomes for children's recovery (Elliott & Carnes, 2001; Yancey & Hansen, 2010), it is important to assess the parent's emotional responses to the child's sexual abuse. Research has shown that parents develop emotional distress in response to their children's sexual abuse (Runyon et al., 2014). TF-CBT teaches parents effective coping skills to assist them in coping with the abuse so they are available to support their children. By assessing the parent's emotional responses and identifying the parents' cognitive distortions, the therapist can more effectively address these distortions early in the therapeutic process.

The Parent Emotional Reaction Questionnaire (PERQ; Cohen & Mannarino, 1996b, 1996c) consists of 15 items designed to assess parental emotional reactions (i.e., fear, guilt, anger, and embarrassment) and cognitive distortions (i.e., "my child's life is ruined") to their child being sexually abused. Parents are asked to rate each item on a 5-point scale (e.g., 1 = never, 5 = always) to indicate the degree to which they experience that emotional response to their child's sexual abuse. A total score is derived by summing the values associated with the responses.

Parental Depression

Parental depression has been identified in the literature as one variable that can be extremely debilitating and diminishes the parent's ability to be available and supportive of the child (Elliott & Carnes, 2001). Research has documented that parents often report depressive symptoms after their children's disclosure of CSA (Runyon et al., 2014). The skill-building and cognitive processing components of TF-CBT are designed to assist parents in overcoming depressive symptoms. In fact, several TF-CBT outcome studies have demonstrated significant improvements in parental depression at post-treatment (Cohen, Deblinger, et al., 2004; Deblinger et al., 2011). The assessment of the severity of pretreatment parental depression is essential for triage as well as for treatment planning purposes. In rare cases, the assessment identifies a parental level of depression that requires a referral for individual therapy and/or crisis intervention because the assessment reveals suicidal intent or plans. In addition, the assessment of depressive symptomatology may guide the individual tailoring of parent interventions including the implementation of the TF-CBT coping skills and cognitive processing components.

The Beck Depression Inventory-Second Edition (BDI-II; Beck, Steer, & Brown, 1996) consists of 21 items and is the most widely used measure of depressive symptomatology in adults. Scores from 0 to 9 reflect normal levels of depression, scores from 10 to 18 represent mild depression, scores from 19 to 29 indicate moderate depression, and scores above 30 suggest severe depression.

Parenting Skills

As mentioned earlier, when faced with trauma even the most competent and well-meaning parents may respond to their children's behaviors and symptoms in a manner that contributes to and maintains their children's behavior problems, as well as their PTSD and depressive symptoms (Cohen, Mannarino, & Deblinger, 2006). In the aftermath of CSA, it is important for parents to enhance children's feelings of safety and security by serving as a positive role model and providing support, structure, and as much consistency and predictability in the home as possible. As such, it is important to assess parenting skills and to offer parenting-skills training to address any parenting deficits noted to produce optimal outcomes for children (Cohen, Mannarino, & Deblinger, 2006). These parenting skills may be tailored to address the specific behavior problems that parents report.

Two standardized measures that may be used to assess parenting skills are the Alabama Parenting Questionnaire (APQ; Frick, 1991) and the Parenting Practices Scale (PPS; Strayhorn & Weidman, 1988). The APQ has two forms, a parent-report and child report form. The APQ is a 35-item self-report measure that assesses five parenting constructs: parental involvement, positive parenting, poor monitoring/supervision, inconsistent discipline, and corporal punishment. Additional items assess discipline strategies other than corporal punishment. Respondents rate the frequency by which they or their parents engage in the parenting practices denoted by each item on a scale of 1 (never) to 5 (always). The APQ has strong evidence for reliability and validity.

The PPS (Strayhorn & Weidman, 1988) is a 35-item self-report measure completed by parents that assesses favorable and unfavorable parenting practices in three areas: (1) warmth/positive parenting, (2) consistency, and (3) punitive discipline. Respondents rate the frequency in which they engage in the parenting practices denoted by each item on a scale of 1 to 5. This measure has been used in several TF-CBT treatment outcome investigations (Cohen, Deblinger, et al., 2004; Deblinger et al., 1996; Deblinger et al., 2011).

Although the above list is not a comprehensive listing of psychological measures that can be utilized in the context of implementing TF-CBT, it does offer examples of critical domains of functioning that can be assessed via standardized measures with this population. The information obtained from the above described assessment process may be utilized in educating parents and motivating clients to collaborate and participate in treatment.

IMPORTANT CLINICAL NOTE AND SUMMARY

Finally, it should be noted that although the child may briefly acknowledge the sexual abuse during the trauma history and PTSD screening, the child's ability to provide a spontaneous narrative describing the abusive experience(s) is also an important aspect of assessment. The process of eliciting a baseline trauma narrative is described in the introductory treatment session (see Chapter 6). It has been the experience of the authors that when the assessment and treatment processes are conducted by different professionals at the same clinic, it may be best for the treating clinician (as opposed to the "intake" clinician conducting the assessment) to elicit a baseline trauma narrative in the introductory treatment sessions. The discussion of this baseline trauma narrative allows the therapist to establish rapport, acknowledge the abuse, and provide practice for the narrative activities in which the child will be engaged later in treatment.

In summary, prior to initiating treatment in cases of alleged CSA, therapists not only gather information from a variety of sources (e.g., child protection, law enforcement, and medical reports) but also assess children's psychological functioning through observation, interviews, and administration of standardized measures. Ultimately, in the initial conceptualization of a case, therapists integrate the information collected with their knowledge of psychopathology, developmental psychology, and the empirical data relating to CSA to develop an individually tailored TF-CBT treatment plan that will optimally address the child's therapy needs. For example, levels of depression, shame, and acting-out behaviors may determine the intensity and degree of focus on the particular coping skills that might be most helpful (e.g., relaxation, affect modulation, cognitive coping, anger management, and/or social skill building). In addition, given the critical role caregivers play in the child's recovery process, it is important to assess the emotional impact of the child's sexual abuse on the caregiver, as well as the caregiver's skills in interacting with the child. These caregiver variables may have a significant impact on outcomes for the child (Cohen & Mannarino, 1996a, 1998a; Deblinger et al., 1996). Furthermore, caregivers may experience a host of emotional responses to their children's abuse that can interfere with their ability to appropriately respond to their child's post-disclosure needs (Banyard et al., 2001; Esquilin, 1987). The findings of the overall assessment will help to establish the basis for developing a treatment plan that is not only tailored to meet the child's needs, but is also designed to help caregivers cope with their own emotional distress while simultaneously developing skills to optimally respond to their child's emotional and behavioral reactions. In summary, assessment findings will influence the sequence and amount of time devoted to each PRACTICE component, reflecting the importance of flexibility in planning treatment to address the presenting concerns while simultaneously maintaining overall fidelity to the TF-CBT model.

5

About This Treatment Guide

This component-by-component guide is designed to present trauma-focused cognitive-behavioral therapy (TF-CBT) as it has been implemented with families in the aftermath of child sexual abuse (CSA) with fidelity to the model as well as with flexibility and creativity. General guidance concerning the timing, length, and course of treatment, as well as the structure and tone of sessions is provided below. In addition, information about the use of informational handouts and specific terminology used in this guide is provided. The implementation of TF-CBT in group and other formats is addressed, and suggestions concerning TF-CBT implementation and additional training are offered.

LENGTH AND COURSE OF TREATMENT

There are many factors that determine the total length of treatment, as well as exactly what and how much a therapist covers in each session. Thus, each chapter outlines the delivery of the TF-CBT components and indicates the approximate number of sessions taken to cover the material that depending on the presenting complaints and the length of the session, may vary considerably. While TF-CBT has been shown to be effective in as little as eight sessions (Deblinger et al., 2011) and many children respond well in 12 to 18 sessions (Cohen, Deblinger, et al., 2004; Deblinger et al., 1996; Deblinger et al., 2011), there are some complex cases (complex and/or multiple traumas and children with severe behavior problems) that may require additional coping skills or parenting skills work, thereby extending treatment to as many as 25 sessions. In addition, therapists who are just learning the model may take a bit longer implementing each of the components. It is important, however, for therapists to strive to efficiently apply TF-CBT as they become more skilled in delivering the model as TF-CBT is not intended to encourage a focus on past trauma(s) for extended periods of time.

The PRACTICE components are implemented across three phases (e.g., stabilization and skill building; trauma narration and processing; and consolidation and closure [Cohen, Mannarino, Kliethermes, et al., 2012]) of treatment with each phase generally taking approximately one-third of the treatment. However, when children exhibit complex trauma reactions and/or severe comorbid difficulties, the initial phase focused on psychoeducation and the mastery of coping skills tends to be longer, resulting in almost half the sessions devoted to the first phase, with the second and third phases encompassing the other half of the sessions. With the exception of in vivo mastery, which is not always necessary, therapists should spend some time on each component as indicated in the guide that follows. It is important to note that parenting is first introduced as a part of the psychoeducation/parenting component, but it continues across all phases. In addition, all of the components build on one another and are integrated in their implementation and use throughout the course of treatment. The order of implementation of the TF-CBT components may change given particular clinical circumstances. For example, although the "Enhancing Safety" component generally is implemented toward the end of treatment, it can and should be moved up to the beginning of treatment for cases in which the child remains in a high-risk environment such as when there has been sibling abuse or domestic violence and there is ongoing contact with the individual or individuals who engaged in the abusive behavior. Youth with complex trauma by definition have experienced early interpersonal traumas in the context of attachment relationships. For many of these youth, initiating new relationships (e.g., therapy) serves as a trauma reminder of past attachment disruptions and produces a sense of danger for the youth. For these youth, providing the safety component at the start of treatment is often critical as well. Two other important adjustments in the sequence of implementing the PRACTICE components include engaging in conjoint sessions with a focus on parenting skills practice beginning in the stabilization and skill-building phase of treatment and implementing in vivo exposure in the stabilization and skill building phase of treatment when the child is struggling with school refusal. In general, although therapists are strongly encouraged to implement TF-CBT with fidelity to the overall principles, guidelines, structure, and content of the PRACTICE components, the treatment approach may be tailored to meet the needs of individual clients. Finally, therapists are encouraged to rely on general therapy skills (i.e., engaging, listening, praising, building on client strengths, behavior rehearsal, etc.), as well as their personal creativity to inspire and motivate clients to succeed.

THERAPY SESSION STRUCTURE AND TONE

The chapters that follow outline the implementation of each of the TF-CBT PRACTICE components with parents and children. Each chapter introduces the component, the implementation of the individual parent session, the individual child session, as well as an optional or recommended conjoint parent-child session. The order in which the parent and child sessions are conducted and presented vary as they naturally do in the implementation of TF-CBT depending on parent, child, and therapist preferences and needs. In general, the individual sessions reflect a parallel process such that the educational information and skill-building exercises presented to parents and children are similar, thereby helping the parent learn about, model, and reinforce what the child is learning. Each session follows more or less the same structure. Treatment sessions generally begin with a review of the prior session and/or clients' efforts to apply the skills learned in session at home. Therapy work at home is referred to as practice rather than homework, given the disdain many children have for doing homework. Next, sessions typically continue with psychoeducation, introduction to and practicing of a new skill in the stabilization and skill building phase and the consolidation and closure phase of treatment and/or the development or processing of the trauma narrative in the trauma narration and processing phase of treatment. Most sessions end with a skills practice assignment, preparation for a conjoint session when one is planned, and a brief end-of-session positive ritual. Conjoint sessions follow a similar format.

TF-CBT requires a constant balancing of reflective listening and empathizing, as well as effective modeling, teaching, coaching, and follow through with respect to each of the PRACTICE components. This structure can be a bit challenging and may require some preparation and practice especially for therapists who have previously been more nondirective in their approach. In addition, maintaining session structure can also be challenging with clients who prefer to use the sessions to vent their feelings and/or who had previous therapy experiences that were much less structured. In these instances, it is important to educate clients about how the therapy session will be structured. It may be helpful (though not required) for beginning therapists to write an outline for each session on a white board in order to help both the therapist and the client stay on topic and achieve the implementation goals. These goals may be accomplished in one or more sessions. However, it is important to note that the components build on one another (as depicted in figure 3.2 in Chapter 3) so that more than one component may be addressed in any one session based on the therapist's clinical judgment and client needs.

The TF-CBT therapist may respond to the traumatic experiences presented with sincere empathy, as well as a commitment to overcoming the associated negative effects. However, an overly serious tone need not be maintained throughout treatment. Rather, the therapist may encourage relationships with both caregivers and children that allow for serious discussions as well as humor, playfulness, enthusiasm, and optimism. In fact, research has documented that humor can positively affect feelings of hopefulness, as well as overall physical and emotional well-being (Davidson et al., 2005; Vilaythong, Arnau, Rosen, & Mascaro, 2003). In addition, being knowledgeable about popular expressions, music, apps, books, television shows, movies, etc., may also enhance therapeutic engagement with children and teens. The use of popular expressions with teens can often elicit a smile and possibly spark a discussion that can be relevant to the teen's experiences. For example, the expressions YOLO (i.e., you only live once), "hooking up" and/or LMAO (i.e., laughing my a** off) are popular teen expressions that may encourage discussions about peer pressure and may help clinicians connect with teens.

Handouts and other therapy resources

With regard to practice outside of sessions, therapists may use a variety of informational and parenting handouts provided in Appendix B of this book as well as others available online to facilitate the sharing of relevant educational information and the practicing of skills between sessions. The National Child Traumatic Stress Network's (NCTSN) Sexual Abuse Collaborative Workgroup has developed separate handouts to educate parents, school-aged children, and adolescents about CSA as well as other traumas. These handouts may be obtained at http://www.nctsnet.org/trauma-types. Descriptions of those relevant for working with children who have experienced sexual abuse are provided in Appendix B. These handouts may be utilized for practice purposes and then reviewed in session by the treating clinician in an interactive fashion to facilitate a discussion with the child, adolescent, and/or parent(s). The handouts also provide guidance for practice activities at home. In addition, there are a number of recommended therapeutic children's books and parenting books listed in the resource appendix (Appendix C) in this guide that are highly recommended for supporting the implementation of TF-CBT.

IMPORTANT NOTE

It is important for therapists to carefully review the chapters that follow, the handouts, and appendices, prior to implementing the model. There is also a specific chapter dedicated to treating children with sexual behavior problems toward the end of the book that should be read before engaging in work with such children. Given the safety issues that may be related to children who are engaging in sexual behaviors, especially when they are directed toward others, parent participation in treatment is especially important in these cases. In fact, it is imperative in these cases that the therapist begin addressing sexual behaviors immediately in the treatment process by helping the parent understand the nature of these behaviors, what types of sexual behaviors are developmentally appropriate, and how to respond appropriately to sexual behavior problems using effective parenting strategies (see Chapter 16 on sexual behavior problems).

TERMINOLOGY

The terms "child, children, or youth" are used throughout the book to refer to both children and adolescents. However, sensitivity to developmental differences is addressed through the presentation of therapy strategies designed specifically for young children and/or adolescents in many of the chapters. Throughout this book, the term "parent" or "caregiver" is utilized to refer to any nonoffending caregiver who is participating in treatment with the child. This may include, but is not limited to, biological, adoptive, and foster parents, as well as grandparents or other relatives who may be in the child's life in a caregiving role. The book frequently provides examples of working with one parent and one child, but TF-CBT often involves working with multiple parents and siblings. Siblings, however, typically have individual sessions with the therapist. Conversely, two nonoffending parents generally may be seen together. Foster parents are not typically seen with biological parents, and divorced parents are not seen together if their relationship is not amicable. Careful planning and clinical judgment is required in optimally arranging for how to schedule appointments when multiple caregivers (e.g., divorced parents, kinship or foster parents, etc.) are involved in the treatment. Although the child's primary caregiver (i.e., parent, foster parent, etc.) is the most common parental participant, it is important to emphasize that when that is not possible, the TF-CBT therapist may include another adult caregiver who is supportive of and involved in the ongoing care of the child. This could be another adult relative, mentor, long-term caseworker, and/or residential treatment staff member, if the clinician determines that this is clinically appropriate and the child and adults agree and provide the proper consent.

The pronouns "he" or "she" are used singularly throughout the book to refer to male and female parents and children. To enhance the readability of the chapters, the authors chose to avoid the use of the cumbersome "he/she," but vary the gender of the pronoun to highlight that the model is utilized with both males and females. Though nonoffending fathers may be strongly encouraged to participate in treatment as they can serve as powerful nonabusive male role models for children, female caregivers tend to be the more frequent participants and thus, the pronoun "she" is more frequently used when referring to the parent.

It should also be noted that the male pronoun is typically used when referring to offenders in this text because children are more often sexually abused by males as opposed to females. However, it should be noted that children are sometimes sexually abused by females including on occasion mothers, other female relatives, as well as older female peers. Thus, it is important to be sensitive to this possibility when screening for and/or treating children who have a history of sexual abuse.

The word practice is used throughout the book to refer to the treatment components of TF-CBT. In addition, as noted earlier, given children's distaste for homework, rather than using the word homework to refer to between session therapy assignments, skills and other therapy-related reading or activities are typically referred to as practice activities in this text.

For purposes of clarity, other terms commonly used in this treatment guide are defined in the glossary of terms (Appendix D) at the end of this book. Some examples of terms that can be found in the glossary include, but are not limited to, gradual exposure, complex trauma, subjective units of distress (SUDS), functional analyses, and compliment sandwiches.

GROUP AND OTHER TF-CBT IMPLEMENTATION FORMATS

Although this guide is generally written from the perspective of one therapist working with children and their nonoffending caregivers in the context of individual therapy, it can also be used to guide the delivery of TF-CBT in group therapy format. The efficacy of TF-CBT has been documented in the context of both individual as well as group therapy formats (Deblinger et al., 2015; Deblinger et al., 2001; McMullen et al., 2013; O'Callaghan et al., 2013; Stauffer & Deblinger, 1996). Group, in fact, can be quite healing given that this format provides a rare opportunity for children and their parents to meet others who are facing similar circumstances in the aftermath of CSA. Although there have been no direct comparisons of the differential impact of individual versus group TF-CBT implementation and both appear to be effective, there may be differential emphases that are worth considering when deciding whether to offer TF-CBT groups, as opposed to or in addition to individual TF-CBT services.

Provided below are considerations that are unique to providing TF-CBT in group format with additional details on group implementation available elsewhere (Deblinger et al., 2015). Confidentiality issues are addressed in the same way as in individual therapy, but it must be acknowledged that although group members are asked to maintain confidentiality, strict confidentiality cannot be guaranteed. Thus, some clients may prefer the greater privacy afforded by individual therapy. Conversely, TF-CBT groups provide children and parents with direct experience that they are not alone. Meeting and getting to know others who endured similar CSA experiences can be reassuring to children as well as parents. Furthermore, the group format allows for a great deal of creativity in terms of activities that can be interactive, engaging, and fun for both children and parents. However, therapists must be skilled in managing group dynamics and maintaining the group structure and agenda in order to ensure that everyone has an opportunity to actively participate in the educational and skill-building activities. With therapist guidance, parents, in particular, often learn a great deal from one another by sharing their efforts to implement the parenting and coping skills between sessions. In addition, with some direction, parents are often effective in validating other parents' feelings and disputing their unhelpful or inaccurate thoughts about the sexual abuse. Attention to praising and reinforcing children's prosocial behaviors and the development of group rules and consequences for breaking rules is important for the children's groups, especially groups that include children with sexual or acting out behavior problems.

Parent and child CSA groups are typically provided in parallel sessions with some time reserved at the end of each group session for conjoint parent-child time. Co-therapists for the children's groups are strongly recommended especially for larger groups of children (i.e., more than three children). Groups are generally designed for children of similar developmental stages but may include boys and girls and often include children who have experienced diverse forms of CSA. It is important to note that although children often share their narrative introductions and sometimes acknowledge the basic details of their abusive experiences in group (e.g., their relationship with the offender), they create and process their narratives individually with one of the co-therapists pulling them out of group for parts of several sessions. Similarly, the sharing of the narratives with parents is typically done in private, individual family sessions in the consolidation and closure phase of treatment with the different therapists leading separate families through this process. More details regarding the implementation of TF-CBT in group format can be found elsewhere (Deblinger et al., 2015).

Another way in which to implement TF-CBT involves having two therapists collaboratively work with the family—one works with the child while the other simultaneously works with the parent. When appropriate, both therapists work with parents and children in the conjoint parent-child sessions. This two-therapist approach has been used in busy clinical settings especially when there are no options for overseeing children in the waiting room when parents are being seen. This arrangement can be particularly advantageous for working with parents who themselves are struggling with significant traumatic stress reactions to the discovery that their child has been sexually abused; this is also an arrangement that can be good for those that need a great deal of parenting guidance.

TF-CBT TRAINING

Given the complexity of treating children who have experienced CSA, ongoing multidisciplinary training is recommended. In addition to reading this guide, other valuable professional resources are listed in Appendix E. Outlined below are general training recommendations.

1. Completion of TF-CBT*Web* which is accessible at http://tfcbt.musc.edu/ and is free of charge. This introductory web-based training on the principles and practices of the TF-CBT treatment model can be completed in about 10 to 12 hours, and it provides CE credits.
2. Attendance at a face-to-face introductory training of at least two days in duration with approved TF-CBT trainers. When possible, therapists are encouraged to participate in follow-up training or advanced training opportunities at local and national conferences as well.
3. Participation in twice-per-month consultation calls with an approved TF-CBT consultant over the course of at least six months. During the consultation period, clinicians should implement TF-CBT with several clients. This consultation is generally provided via small group supervision or phone consultation so that feedback on case specific

openly. Unlike traumas that involve death or widespread loss in which there are often traditional (e.g., funerals, memorials, etc.) or societal efforts to help individuals heal, there are typically no such traditions associated with helping individuals heal in the aftermath of sexual abuse. Thus, it is important in the initial phase of treatment to acknowledge the CSA experience openly while providing education and a forum for parents and children to openly ask questions and raise concerns. It should be noted, however, that children who develop PTSD symptoms may be less likely to talk about their CSA experiences until after gradual exposure as well as trauma narration and processing exercises have helped them to overcome their fears and avoidant tendencies.

The relaxation, affective, and cognitive skills learned in this phase of treatment will help children during the trauma narration and processing phase to more effectively cope with trauma reminders, while also enhancing their abilities to retrieve, share and process their feelings and thoughts related to the traumatic experiences. It should be noted that, as part of the gradual exposure process, general references to the child's experience of sexual abuse and other traumas (when applicable) are acknowledged from the start of treatment and increasingly incorporated into discussions, however, detailed discussions relating to children's actual experiences (aside from the brief discussions which take place during the assessment and baseline trauma narrative) typically do not occur until the trauma narration and processing phase of treatment.

PSYCHOEDUCATION AND PARENTING

The main objectives of the TF-CBT introductory psychoeducation sessions are to (1) engage and motivate clients' participation in treatment; (2) provide information about the assessment, treatment, and general clinic procedures; (3) begin psychoeducation about TF-CBT and CSA that will inspire hope, confidence, and an active commitment to the treatment process; (4) introduce the parent and child to the concept of trauma reminders and help them understand the child's response in a trauma framework; and (5) initiate therapy with a collaborative approach.

The opportunity to work with a child and family in the aftermath of CSA hinges in many instances on the parent's commitment to therapy. Thus, it is critical to engage the parent and establish a supportive, collaborative therapist-parent relationship. This may be achieved from the outset by (1) clearly presenting the assessment and treatment procedures, (2) addressing and overcoming any concrete obstacles to treatment in a collaborative, thoughtful manner; (3) identifying the concerns that parents are most worried about and incorporating these into the treatment plan; and (4) eliciting and discussing any perceptual barriers or negative therapy attitudes that would undermine therapy participation. Thus, after reviewing the assessment and treatment procedures, the therapist and parents should work to identify a certain time for weekly sessions that is both practical and consistent for all parties while attempting to avoid scheduling appointments that would interfere with the child's naptime, bedtime, mealtime, school hours, and/or favorite activity. The timing of the therapy sessions, in fact, may influence the client's attendance and level of active participation. Working with clients to identify the best time for sessions establishes an excellent precedent for collaborative problem solving. The therapist may address perceptual therapy barriers by eliciting information about both positive and negative prior therapy experiences and more general attitudes toward therapy. This type of collaborative problem solving and open communication should be continued throughout the course of treatment and may best be maintained by consistently communicating respect for the parent's opinions and knowledge regarding the child.

Although it is important to inspire client trust by appropriately demonstrating confidence in one's expertise with regard to CSA, TF-CBT, and the guidance being offered, it is also critical to acknowledge that parents are the experts on their children. Accessing parental knowledge and insight concerning the child's behavior in the context of collecting detailed information about parent-child interactions (i.e., behavioral functional analysis), for example, will be critical to developing effective treatment plans. Furthermore, the therapist should emphasize that the parent's role with the child is much more important than the therapist's role ever can or should be both by virtue of the amount of time the parent has with the child (i.e., much more than one hour a week) and by virtue of the significance of the parent-child relationship. When parents believe that their contributions are truly needed and valued, they are much more likely to actively participate in treatment. Parental participation in treatment can have a great influence on the child's responsiveness to therapy. It is, therefore, important to note that parents are typically seen before their children for the introductory treatment sessions to ensure that parents receive the assessment and treatment information they need to make an informed decision and commitment to the TF-CBT process.

The objectives for the child's initial treatment sessions should be similarly focused on building rapport and establishing a trusting therapeutic relationship while also providing information about the assessment and treatment plan. The therapist-child relationship should encourage a sense of acceptance, active collaboration, and open communication about CSA. During initial sessions, it helps to build rapport by inquiring about children's interests and favorite activities. Actively eliciting and using the child's interests and ideas for achieving therapy goals may encourage participation and a collaborative spirit. In addition, the child's interests may be utilized in establishing relaxing and rewarding end-of-session positive rituals. These brief positive rituals may not only motivate children to engage in the more emotionally challenging sessions, but can also help children learn how to regain their composure when distressed. During the introductory session with the child, the therapist may elicit both a neutral narrative about a favorite activity as well as a baseline trauma narrative about the CSA experience, thereby obtaining some information about the child's interests while also initiating open communication about the CSA experience(s).

PARENT SESSION(S)

Establish rapport, use evidence based engagement strategies and encourage optimism

TF-CBT is intended to be implemented in a flexible manner that also respects the fidelity of the model. It should be infused with the personal warmth, style, and skill that each individual therapist brings to the healing process. From the start, the therapist builds rapport by demonstrating a genuine interest in and understanding of the client's concerns, while simultaneously conveying confidence in the treatment approach and reviewing the proposed plan.

During the introductory sessions, it is particularly important that the therapist acknowledge the parents' efforts to support their child while simultaneously encouraging their commitment to treatment. This acknowledgement and encouragement may be conveyed in a variety of ways during the introductory sessions as well as during the sessions that follow. Recent research has documented the value of utilizing empirically validated engagement strategies that address both concrete as well as perceptual barriers to treatment to increase the likelihood of treatment participation (Dorsey et al., 2014; McKay & Bannon, 2004). For example, the therapist may enhance parental engagement by inquiring about and helping to resolve any concrete barriers to participation in treatment (e.g., scheduling sessions, oversight of siblings, transportation). In addition, research has documented that it may be most important for therapists to address perceptual and attitudinal barriers in terms of enhancing the likelihood of ongoing treatment participation (Dorsey et al., 2014; McKay et al., 1998). Perceptual barriers include prior negative experiences with treatment, stigma, and lack of confidence in the value of therapy as well as questions about the relevance of treatment in the context of the caregivers' greatest concerns regarding their child. Thus, it is helpful to inquire about previous therapy experiences, exploring similarities and differences between TF-CBT and prior therapy experiences being sure to highlight the differences between TF-CBT and less-than-satisfactory prior therapy experiences. Finally, research has also documented that in the aftermath of CSA, parental support and active parental participation in treatment greatly enhances a child's ability to fully recover (Cohen & Mannarino, 1996a, 1998a; Deblinger et al., 1996). Thus, when reviewing the structure of treatment and the impact of CSA, it is critical to emphasize the importance of parental participation in treatment. This can be done by posing the following question to parents:

Therapist: *What do you think is the most powerful factor influencing children's recovery from sexual abuse?*
Parent: *I don't know. Could it be how many times the child was abused?*

Therapist: *Actually, that may have some impact, but the most powerful factor in positively influencing a child's recovery from sexual abuse is something your child has in abundance.*
Parent: *Really? What is that?*
Therapist: *Support from a loving parent!*

It is also critical to maintain a generally optimistic attitude regarding the child's and family's recovery. Optimism is contagious and often self-fulfilling. If parents believe that their child has a bright future, it is much more likely that they will interpret the child's behavior in positive ways and notice and reinforce the child's strengths. Conversely, if parents anticipate that terrible things will befall the child because of the abuse, they will likely interpret behaviors and events negatively and notice the child's failings and weaknesses more frequently. Rather than just discussing a child's abuse-related symptoms, it is very important to highlight the child's strengths and acknowledge those things (e.g., assertiveness, open parent-child communication, etc.) that helped the child to disclose the abuse when the majority of children who have been sexually abused do not. This focus on strengths sets the stage for a positive working relationship and encourages optimistic expectations for the future.

Similarly, it helps to convey confidence in one's ability to help by linking the assessment findings to the proposed treatment plan and emphasizing the proven efficacy of TF-CBT. In fact, it is valuable to point out the depth of research supporting the effectiveness of this approach in helping children overcome traumatic experiences and related difficulties. To date, for example, there have been over 25 scientific investigations documenting the effectiveness of this treatment approach with the majority of those studies focused on helping children who have been sexually abused. This information can be very reassuring to many parents.

Review confidentiality issues

This process can be initiated by sharing any agency- and state-specific guidelines for handling child abuse reports and issues relating to confidentiality with parents. Although the standard limits of confidentiality with respect to making reports to authorities apply when providing TF-CBT, general guidelines in terms of sharing treatment information between the parents and children may be slightly different from other therapy approaches and should be carefully explained as described below.

Therapist: *If you have no other questions about our agency's expectations for therapy attendance, cancellations, and emergencies* (Include agency or practice specific expectations), *I would like to discuss how we handle issues of confidentiality. Would that be helpful?*
Parent: *Sure. Though I'm still not sure anyone can help my daughter cope with what she has been through.*

Therapist: *I hope you will feel differently by the end of this session. But first, let me explain how I will handle the confidential information you and your daughter will likely share in the context of therapy. In general, what you and your daughter share here will remain confidential. However, by law, therapists cannot maintain confidentiality regarding information that leads to concerns that you or your child might hurt yourself or others, or that a child has possibly experienced abuse or neglect that was not reported and documented already in our intake. This type of information cannot remain confidential because we are responsible to report it to authorities to ensure the safety of those involved. Do you have any questions about that?*

Parent: *No, my daughter's previous therapist reported the abuse, and that is how we were able to stop the abuse and then child protection referred us here.*

Therapist: *Okay. That's very good. I would also like to explain how confidentiality with respect to sharing information concerning your daughter's sessions with you is handled in the context of this type of therapy. As you know, sexual abuse is something that occurs in secrecy. And sometimes it goes on for a very long time because of the secrecy the offender demands of the child. We would like to minimize any feelings of secrecy in therapy here and promote open communication between you and your child. This means that we will explain to your daughter that we will be sharing with you some of what she shares in her individual sessions. We will explain that by doing so we will be able to help you be the best parent you can be—especially with regard to helping her cope with the sexual abuse experience.*

Parent: *My teenager may not be comfortable with you sharing what she says with me.*

Therapist: *Because your daughter is a bit older, I will explain that I will be careful to share in a way that will be helpful, but if there is ever something that she would prefer me not to share with you, as long as it is not something dangerous to her or others, I will respect that. But I must tell you my experience is that even teenagers deep down want more open communication with parents.*

It should be noted that in cases where children exhibit signs of complex trauma, they may be opposed to sharing any information with the caregiver. These children have typically had multiple traumatic experiences and have been hurt by individuals who were supposed to take care of them. Thus, trust is a major issue for many of these youth. Accordingly, it is important to give them control over what is shared with the caregiver. As they progress through TF-CBT, it is possible that their overall sense of trust will grow and that they may become more receptive to sharing with their caregiver.

Encourage caregivers to share reactions to CSA disclosure and their treatment goals

It is important to prepare well for the first treatment session by carefully reviewing both the assessment information obtained about the child as well as the parent. If it is the first meeting with the parents (i.e., another professional conducted the intake or initial assessment), the therapist should give the parents an opportunity to share a little about what precipitated them bringing their child to therapy and describe the goals they hope to achieve in therapy. In essence, this discussion is the beginning of gradual exposure for the parents in that when discussing what brought them to therapy, parents should be encouraged to share the feelings they experienced when they discovered their child had been sexually abused. The sharing of these emotions can be helpful, as these discussions help the clinician gain a better understanding of the parents' perceptions and affective responses. However, the discussions may reveal that parents are experiencing feelings that could be considered less than supportive of the child (e.g., ambivalence, anger toward the child, concern for the perpetrator, disbelief). As noted earlier, it has been the experience of the authors that even these seemingly nonsupportive feelings need to be validated and accepted. Taking a judgmental and/or confrontational stance tends to be counterproductive and may hinder the development of a collaborative therapeutic relationship. Indeed, parents who are actively confronted about their ambivalence concerning the allegations and/or their positive feelings toward the offender often respond with an entrenched position of support for the offender and may begin to view the therapist as aligning with the authorities rather than the parents. Moreover, confrontations frequently turn out to be unnecessary as parents' thoughts and feelings often change dramatically as they naturally develop a greater understanding of the circumstances of the sexual abuse within the context of therapy. It is important to remember that it is exceedingly difficult to believe that someone whom you loved and trusted has sexually abused a child. This realization typically requires that parents reconsider and reevaluate their previous beliefs and emotions about the perpetrator. In addition, it should be recognized that parental participation in treatment generally reflects their unstated desire to do the "right thing" on behalf of their child. For some parents, a painful acceptance of the abuse and a greater understanding of the child's reactions may occur as they themselves gain a greater understanding of CSA and as they develop feelings of strength as a result of the educational and skill-building components of treatment. With parents who are still in shock with respect to the allegations, it is best to not take a strong stance regarding the veracity of the allegations. Instead, clinicians should emphasize that with time and additional information, greater clarity concerning the allegations and greater feelings of strength in coping with the present circumstances often comes.

Conversely, some parents express intense anger toward the perpetrator and/or may be extraordinarily frustrated or dissatisfied with the response of child protection or law enforcement agencies. Given mental health clinicians' legal responsibility to report serious threats of harm (Widgery & Winterfield, 2013), it is important to assess the degree of anger expressed by parents and/or parental tendencies toward taking revenge. In some instances, it may be helpful for the clinician to consult with a lawyer to determine legal responsibility to report a serious threat that may bring harm to any individual including the perpetrator of the abuse. See pp. 243–248 in Chapter 9 on cognitive coping for more information about responding to parental anger and feelings of revenge that may need to be addressed early in treatment.

It should be noted that upon discovering that their child has been sexually abused, most parents are quite supportive of their children, although they may be experiencing a wide range of emotions including sadness, anxiety, guilt, as well as anger and shock. Although it is important to allow parents to share the full spectrum of their emotions regarding the child's abuse experience, it is best to avoid inadvertently encouraging parents to use the full session for sharing intense emotional reactions and details of the investigation. An exclusive focus on parents' emotional responses can easily happen given the intensity of the feelings that many parents experience. Research suggests that uncontrolled emotional venting typically does not help parents cope better in the long run (Deblinger et al., 2001), thus it is not helpful to allow parents to engage in such uncontrolled affective sharing. Rather, it is important to establish a focus for the session, allowing some time for parents to share about the circumstances of the sexual abuse, as well as their emotional reactions while structuring the remaining session time to ensure there is time for a review of the assessment findings and treatment plan as well as an opportunity to provide some psychoeducation that may allay some of the parents' concerns and inspire hope. By establishing some structure in the early part of treatment, the therapist is setting a precedent for the structure and collaborative nature of the sessions to follow.

In summary, it is helpful to encourage the sharing of the circumstances and feelings experienced when caregivers first learned of the abuse. In this context, it may be most important to utilize reflective listening to respond to the parents' sharing of distressing, angry, and/or ambivalent feelings for a portion of the session. In addition, it can be helpful to acknowledge how difficult it is to consider that the person who sexually abused the child may have been someone the parent trusted to care for the child. Moreover, it is important to explain assessment findings and carefully listen for and/or elicit the caregivers' expressed goals so that by the end of the session preliminary goals can be established that flow logically from the assessment findings and are consistent with both the caregivers' stated desires and the general goals of TF-CBT.

Review assessment findings

It is critically important to offer a verbal presentation of the evaluation findings to the nonoffending parents. The child should not be present during the therapist's presentation of evaluation findings to the parents, so that the therapist and parents can talk freely and openly regarding any symptoms the child is exhibiting. However, depending on the child's age, the therapist may choose to present evaluation findings to the child in a separate meeting (see child session below).

The presentation of the assessment findings is much broader than a psychiatric diagnosis. Therapists should present the assessment information that led to the evaluation findings and treatment recommendations in clear, jargon-free terms. For example, rather than reporting the child's scores on the UCLA PTSD Reaction Index for DSM-IV (PTSD-RI; Pynoos et al., 1998) or the Children's Depression Inventory 2nd Edition (CDI-2; Kovacs, 2011), the therapist might describe how the child was acknowledging feelings of significant anxiety, nightmares, difficulty concentrating, or sadness. The clinical meaning of the scores and diagnoses obtained should be shared as well as how the difficulties may stem from the sexually abusive experiences. Visual presentations such as the child behavior profile derived from the Child Behavior Checklist (CBCL; Achenbach & Rescorla, 2001) can be particularly helpful when presenting findings to parents as these can help parents understand their children may be functioning well within the normal range in some areas but not in others thereby highlighting strengths as well as areas of concern. The information and assessment findings concerning the parent's emotional adjustment should also be acknowledged. Most importantly, the assessment summary should emphasize the strengths seen in both the child and parents in terms of positive individual and relationship characteristics, effective coping skills, and healthy domains of functioning (e.g., maintaining friendships, passing grades, etc.) that encourage optimism and support a positive prognosis while simultaneously acknowledging the pain the abuse has caused. In turn, therapy recommendations should be presented as described below in terms of how they stem from the evaluation findings with an emphasis whenever possible on those salient factors (e.g., the presence of parental support as well as the child's strengths) that indicate that the child will respond well to therapy and overcome his current abuse-related difficulties.

Connect the child's current symptoms to traumas and trauma reminders

When linking the assessment findings to the treatment plan, it is critical to help parents understand the connection between CSA, trauma reminders, and the behavioral and/or emotional difficulties the child is exhibiting. Trauma reminders are cues that remind the child of trauma(s) endured and/or related experiences. These cues can be external (e.g., person, place, or thing, etc.) or internal (e.g., feeling, thought, body sensation, memory, etc.). Making the connection between the child's sexual abuse experience, trauma reminders, and the child's emotional and/or behavioral responses in the present can help parents more fully understand children's behavioral difficulties and how trauma-focused treatment will be helpful in addressing these problems. The rationale for trauma-focused treatment is described in the dialogue in Box 6.1 in which the therapist explains the link between the child's trauma reactions and the treatment approach. When parents understand that their children's behavior problems may be linked to the sexual abuse endured, they may experience greater compassion and respond more effectively. When children present with PTSD or complex trauma reactions, it can sometimes be helpful to explain that these

Box 6.1

Case Example: Treatment Rationale for Parents

The following dialogue shows how a therapist might present the treatment rationale to a parent by explaining how TF-CBT helps children effectively cope with sexual abuse-related memories and reminders over the course of treatment.

Therapist: *Child sexual abuse and the investigation that follows can be very stressful for a child and her entire family. Was it very stressful for you?*

Parent: *Stressful doesn't begin to describe it. More like devastating.*

Therapist: *You're right, stressful really doesn't begin to adequately describe what many families experience. And in response to the abuse and related experiences, children may have many different emotions. Often when children think about the abuse they experienced, they feel some of the same distressing emotions, such as fear, anger, sadness, or shame, which they may have felt at the time of the abuse. In fact, children may experience those same emotions whenever they are reminded of the abuse. Have you noticed anything like that?*

Parent: *I think I have.*

Therapist: *For example, a girl who was abused by a man with a beard may become frightened whenever she sees any man with a beard and start avoiding men with beards at school or in other settings. Can you think of any things that your daughter may be avoiding because they remind her of the sexual abuse?*

Parent: *Well, ever since the abuse started, Mary won't sleep in her room without a light on. I didn't understand why at first, but maybe it's because the abuse happened in the dark. And she really doesn't like to go on play dates anymore.*

Therapist: *I think you may be right. These are things that she may connect with the sexual abuse, given that it occurred at a friend's home at night. Those are not unusual fears for children to develop if they were abused under those circumstances. You can see that distressing memories of the abuse can be a problem for Mary, causing her to be upset and to avoid situations that may be perfectly safe now but remind her of the abuse. Over time, many children learn to avoid becoming upset by trying to avoid a number of things that remind them of the abuse, just as Mary tries to avoid becoming upset by avoiding the dark, something that makes her remember the abuse. Unfortunately, this may cause children to avoid harmless situations that might actually be positive. Do you think Mary is avoiding things that are interfering with her day-to-day activities? Or things she liked to do?*

Parent: *Well, I don't see the night light as much of a problem, but I do feel bad that she doesn't want to spend time with her friends anymore. That worries me a bit.*

Therapist: *You're right, Mary should not have to be afraid of the dark or be afraid to spend time at friends' homes because of this unfortunate experience she had. Avoiding things that remind her of the abuse can lead to other types of problems as well, so it is great that you see those issues now and want to address them.*

Parent: *Do you think Mary will have problems with relationships?*

Therapist: *The fact that Mary has a loving, supportive mom and that both of you are participating in counseling will greatly reduce her chances of developing any significant difficulties related to the abuse. We will work hard to uncover and address any disturbing thoughts or worries that may negatively affect your daughter now or in the future. In addition, we will work together to bring out Mary's strengths, while we identify and correct avoidant or other problematic behaviors so these won't interfere with her recovery.*

Parent: *I see. Can you help with problem behaviors she had before the abuse?*

Therapist: *Absolutely! The parenting principles you will be learning will help with all problem behaviors and will encourage healthy positive behaviors.*

Parent: *Are you sure she has to talk about the abuse?*

Therapist: *I realize some parents may feel uncomfortable with the discussion of sexual abuse themselves and may influence their child not to talk about it.*

Parent: *Oh gosh, I think I've done that myself. I told her not to worry about it, that it's all over now, and she doesn't ever have to think about it again.*

Therapist: *Many parents respond that way at first. After all, most parents never expected to have to handle a situation of child sexual abuse, and they haven't been trained in how to respond to such situations. That's why you're here, so that we can figure out together how we can best help Mary. Unfortunately, with highly traumatic events, ignoring disturbing memories and feelings doesn't make them go away. Avoidance of these distressing thoughts is understandable, but it simply does not work very well. In fact, attempts to forget traumatic experiences and avoid feelings may result in an increase in symptoms, such as posttraumatic stress symptoms. But we believe such symptoms can be prevented or corrected when children have caring supportive parents and effective counseling that encourages direct discussion of the traumatic experiences so that Mary can openly share any worries or questions she has. We've already talked about some symptoms that Mary seems to be currently experiencing because she is trying to avoid thinking about or being reminded of the abuse.*

Parent: *Like not wanting to go on play dates? And maybe having nightmares and problems concentrating at school?*

Therapist: *Exactly. It is unlikely that Mary will ever completely forget the abusive experience. Continuing to try to avoid thoughts of the experience takes a great deal of effort and will cause Mary to unnecessarily avoid potentially positive situations—like play dates. Because Mary probably will always have memories of the abuse, it is important that she become as comfortable as possible with facing those memories and talking about them.*

Parent: *Oh, I was hoping that she would be able to just forget about this eventually.*

Therapist: *I don't think that is very likely, particularly given that Mary is 10 years old. She probably will always remember something about what happened. In order to be more comfortable with her memories, she needs to be able to talk about the abuse and share her feelings. Did you think she would just forget what happened?*

Parent: *I guess I wished she would, but realistically I guess I know she won't.*

Therapist: *It is actually better for her to remember and understand what has happened so that she can learn to comprehend the abuse and think about it in ways*

and practice the techniques at home—and thus will not reap the benefits of the interventions. When presenting the treatment rationale, the therapist may enhance the parents' motivation to actively participate in therapy by:

- demonstrating knowledge and understanding of the experiences of the child and his nonoffending parents
- offering a clear, understandable conceptualization of the development of the child's abuse-related difficulties
- discussing the dangers of avoidance and minimization with respect to the long-term adjustment of the child
- describing the structure of treatment including the individual and conjoint sessions, the three phases, the expected course, and probable length of treatment
- demonstrating how the PRACTICE components will serve to ameliorate and prevent abuse-related difficulties in the future
- emphasizing the powerful role of nonoffending parents in terms of the child's postabuse adjustment.

General structure of treatment

The therapist should explain the structure and format of the treatment sessions. The structure of the sessions involves a parallel process in which the therapist initially works separately with parents and children in individual sessions during which parents and children spend approximately the same amount of time in session receiving similar developmentally appropriate psychoeducation and coping skills training. As therapy progresses, an increasing amount of time may be devoted to conjoint parent-child sessions, with those sessions possibly absorbing the majority of session time in the final phase of treatment. It should be explained to parents that by offering therapy in this manner, the information and skills provided not only help parents cope with and overcome their own abuse-related distress but also allow them to fully appreciate what their child is learning in therapy and help parents to serve as more effective coping role models for their children now and in the future.

Descriptions and rationales for parent, child, and conjoint sessions

When discussing the parent sessions, the therapist should explain that these sessions will provide parents with important information about CSA and skills that will assist them in coping with their own emotional reactions, as well as their child's emotional and behavioral responses to the abuse. Meeting with parents individually provides them a place to be vulnerable, shed tears, and/or continue to share their innermost fears and distress without concern for how this might impact their children. These individual parent sessions are designed to offer support, education, and coping skills, as well as parenting skills training. It may be emphasized that the parent is now and will ultimately be the child's most important therapeutic resource long after therapy ends. Thus, these individual sessions are critically important as they often help parents regain their emotional balance in the face of the crisis precipitated by the CSA disclosure or discovery, while developing greater confidence in their parenting skills. Many parents who have participated in TF-CBT describe the development of enhanced parenting and coping skills as the silver lining in the context of facing their child's CSA experience.

Rationales for the child's sessions should be provided to parents during the introductory sessions with more detailed rationales offered later in treatment as each PRACTICE component is introduced. It is particularly important not to overemphasize any single component initially as children can respond well to treatment without necessarily completing each and every component (Deblinger et al., 2011). For example, for some children there is no need to engage in in vivo exposure, while other children may not write a detailed trauma narrative that will be shared with the parent. Very young children may create drawings without a written narrative, and some older children may engage in gradual exposure-based activities (e.g., using art, drama, or other means of expressing thoughts and feelings about the abuse) that can be very therapeutic, but that do not involve the writing of a complete narrative. Thus, it is best not to emphasize the writing of a detailed trauma narrative at the start of treatment (Deblinger et al., 2011). It is best to describe TF-CBT to parents as a gradual process that will help their children develop coping skills that will assist them in managing their emotions in general, while also helping them with the sharing and processing of thoughts and feelings about their sexually abusive experiences. It should be indicated that therapy may be difficult for the child because the processing of sexually abusive experiences can be painful. However, suppressing abuse-related thoughts and memories could lead to problems in the long term, including problematic thought patterns and posttraumatic stress symptoms that could interfere with the child's healthy development over time.

It is critical to forewarn parents that they will need to encourage the child's continued attendance. It can be helpful to predict the course of treatment by mentioning that the child may at some point complain that the sessions are boring or distressing as therapy becomes increasingly focused on the child's most anxiety-provoking memories of abuse. However, it is important to emphasize that most children overcome this temporary resistance and successfully complete treatment with feelings of pride. If the child expresses such distress or avoidance at some point, this prediction may, in fact, give parents more confidence in the therapist as they recognize this response was anticipated.

Once parents express some level of comfort with the outlined treatment plan for their child, it is important to help the parents understand that they will also be gradually discussing CSA in therapy in much the same way as their child. Moreover, the treatment plan involves the parents learning coping skills, as well as parenting skills that they will be asked to practice in individual and conjoint sessions, and, most importantly, between sessions at home. The therapist should further explain that the healing process will be initiated with parents and children meeting mostly separately in individual sessions with the therapists, but in the future more time may be devoted to conjoint parent-child therapy sessions. These conjoint parent-child sessions represent opportunities for parents to practice the parenting skills they are learning while the therapist is available to them for feedback and coaching. In addition, it is during these sessions that the therapist can support parents in their efforts to be available to their children as effective therapeutic resources for discussing the sexual abuse or related issues once therapy ends. This is important given that abuse reminders and/or other sexual abuse related issues are likely to arise long after therapy ends. Thus, as parents become more comfortable with abuse-related discussion toward the end of treatment, parents will be encouraged to participate increasingly as "co-therapists" in conjoint trauma-focused sessions with the child when clinically appropriate.

Treatment course and length

It should be explained that there are essentially three phases of treatment, although there will be a focus on parenting and psychoeducation about CSA throughout the course of treatment. The first phase will focus on education and skills building, the second phase will focus more on processing the clients' personal experiences of sexual abuse, and the final phase will help clients integrate everything they have learned while preparing for conjoint parent-child sessions that will focus on open communication about CSA as well as personal safety.

When presenting the treatment plan, it is helpful to provide general expectations for the duration of therapy. Providing some indication of length of treatment may assure both the parent and child that the process is not endless and that there is a clear plan with a finite end. In most cases of CSA, treatment can be completed in 12 to 16 sessions. However, some children can complete treatment in as few as eight sessions, while children who have experienced multiple traumas and/or complex trauma may require as many as 25 sessions. Although it is not possible to provide an absolute termination date early in treatment, it is helpful to provide an estimate based upon the client's situation. It is important to work toward completing treatment in the estimated time frame. The therapist may offer an estimated duration for treatment, saying that shortly before the end of that period, the progress made in treatment will be assessed. The decision to terminate or continue in therapy may then be based on the assessment of the client's current psychosocial functioning, as well as other factors that might indicate a need for ongoing support (e.g., upcoming court involvement) or other referrals. When therapy is open ended, clients may feel a lack of control as they are more dependent on the therapist or other unknown factors to determine when the intervention will end. Parents may be more amenable to a short-term treatment commitment because it offers them a greater sense of clarity, closure, and accomplishment.

Cautionary note

There is no need to specifically discuss the trauma narrative and/or mention the sharing of the trauma narrative with parents at this introductory stage; this is not a requirement of therapy and will only occur if the child completes a written narrative and it is determined that the sharing of it with the parent is clinically appropriate. In some instances, it may be determined that the sharing of the narrative with a parent may be contraindicated due to parental emotional instability or other factors such as the child not agreeing to share it. As noted earlier, therapy can be successfully completed without the child specifically writing and/or sharing a trauma narrative about the CSA experience with the parent, as there are other ways to engage in gradual exposure to help children process their experiences (see alternatives to narrative development in Chapter 10). Thus, although it is appropriate to acknowledge that the child will be assisted in making sense of the trauma experiences endured, it is best not to specifically describe the writing or sharing of a narrative as trauma processing can and may take other forms depending on the needs and responsiveness of the child and his parents.

Provide psychoeducation about CSA

Although there is generally not sufficient time in the introductory treatment sessions to review all the facts about CSA, it is often useful to provide some basic information that may be comforting to parents. This information may be provided in an interactive manner by asking parents to guess the answers to some questions about CSA. Information that may be helpful to parents early in treatment includes: (1) the prevalence of CSA, (2) how often CSA goes undetected because of secrecy and threats, and (3) factors that promote recovery in the aftermath of abuse. Often families imagine that their child is alone in his or her experience of sexual abuse, and they are stunned to learn that prior research has suggested that more than 1 out of every 10 youngsters may experience CSA by the time they are 18 years of age, with that figure being closer to 1 in 5 for females (Finkelhor et al., 2013; Perez-Fuentes et al., 2013). These statistics may help parents understand that numerous other children are grappling with CSA experiences, and some of them unfortunately may not have the support of their families (like their child does) when they disclosed, while others may be continuing to experience CSA in silence. In fact, it is important to emphasize that the majority of individuals who have experienced CSA suffer in silence throughout their childhood and sometimes their adolescence as well. In fact, most survivors of CSA never tell anyone during childhood. Thus, their child is fortunate that the abuse came to light when it did. In fact, regardless of who the child told about the abuse, it may be helpful to give parents credit for instilling in their child the confidence and courage to do what most children who have been sexually abused are unable to do: tell someone about the abuse, even if it was a child protection worker after the CSA was witnessed or disclosed by someone else. Finally, it is critical to repeatedly emphasize that their child already has the single most important ingredient that predicts a positive recovery after CSA—a supportive parent or other adult. It should be added that if a therapist perceives that the parent is not very supportive, it is still important to focus on the parent's strengths including that she has brought the child to treatment. The parents' role in therapy will be critical not only in terms of providing general support but also in bringing out their children's strengths.

Introduce parenting with how children learn behaviors

It is important for the therapist to emphasize that parents cannot shield their children from all of life's difficulties, nor would they want to. In fact, an extremely overprotected child may not experience many significant childhood difficulties but may be fearful nonetheless due to lack of confidence in coping with problems. Moreover, such a child would be poorly prepared to deal with the struggles faced by most adults. Although no parent would want her child to experience sexual abuse, it is best to help the parent view the therapy experience as an opportunity to support the child's emotional and behavioral growth. When children are faced with difficult problems and have parents by their side to guide and support them each step of the way, they can feel confident in their ability to face life's challenges on their own in the future. Moreover, the parenting education that will be provided can help parents understand how children learn both abuse-related and nonabuse-related behaviors and most importantly how problematic behaviors can be unlearned while more adaptive behaviors are learned.

Children are constantly learning from the interactions they have with others, especially their parents. Children's behaviors, in fact, are most significantly influenced by their parents' current behaviors and responses. Without realizing it, parents are constantly teaching their children. Sometimes the teaching is deliberate (e.g., teaching a child to ride a bicycle); at other times, it may be inadvertent, as when they are demonstrating behaviors that the child is simply observing. Therapists may best help parents respond to their children's behavior problems effectively by offering a model for understanding how children learn both adaptive and maladaptive behaviors. This model will not only provide parents with an understanding of how sexual abuse–related behaviors were learned but will also offer them hope that these problematic behaviors can be unlearned and replaced with adaptive behaviors.

As a means of helping parents understand their child's abuse-related behavioral difficulties, the therapist may introduce the social learning model by describing three mechanisms of learning: association, consequences, and observation. It is important to emphasize that these three mechanisms explain not only the development of sexual abuse-related behaviors but also how children learn both positive and negative behaviors in general. Thus, when describing how each of these learning mechanisms works, it is useful to provide a handout (i.e., *How Children Learn Behaviors* in Appendix B) for parents to review, while also eliciting from them examples of both abuse-related and nonabuse-related behaviors their children have learned from their parents as well as others in their environments.

In essence the therapist should be prepared to help parents understand the development of some of the child's problem behaviors or symptoms revealed in the assessment by explaining how they likely developed from a social learning perspective. Posttraumatic stress symptoms, for example, may be explained using respondent (associations) and operant conditioning (consequences) principles, while sexual behavior problems may be best explained by describing the simple process of observation learning. (See handout in Appendix B for more detailed descriptions of how children learn behaviors). As always, it is best to engage in an interactive discussion when educating parents about these types of complex issues. Thus, it is useful to offer examples while encouraging parents to share examples that might demonstrate their understanding of the concepts as well, as shown in Box 6.2.

BOX 6.2

Case Example: Explaining How Children Learn Behavior

Therapist: *Observational learning is a process that goes on almost continuously in the lives of children. However, parents are often unaware of the degree to which their children are observing and imitating the behavior of important people in their lives. Describe to me a positive behavior your child learned from observing you.*

Parent: *That is a good question. Right now I don't see too many positive behaviors, but he does use an expression I use all the time: "take good care." The first time I heard him say it I almost had to laugh.*

Therapist: *That is a great example. Now I'm going to ask you a more difficult question. And it will require you to be really honest, because none of us are perfect. What kind of negative behaviors has your child learned from observing you?*

Parent: *I hate to admit it but that jumps right out at me. I have a bad temper at times, and I have messed up and cussed in front of my son. It wasn't until we got a note from the teacher about my son cussing that I realized I had to clean up my act.*

Therapist: *Thanks so much for your honesty. That is an excellent example and I must say not an uncommon example. Now your son learned that behavior by observing you and then he probably initially got positive consequences from engaging in that behavior. What kind of positive consequences do you think he received?*

Parent: *I don't know. He did get in trouble with the teacher. But the teacher did say that she reprimanded him in school but it continued so she felt she had to call us.*

Therapist: *Sometimes simple reprimands don't work because they inadvertently provide attention which can be positively reinforcing for children. Moreover, in this instance I would not be surprised if the other children were reacting to your son's cussing which provided further reinforcement for this behavior. So how did you handle this learned behavior?*

Parent: *He got some serious time out that day and it has apparently improved but we are still working on it and that includes me.*

Therapist: *Well, that is great. I can help you with that both in terms of supporting you to work on other ways of coping with frustration so you are not cussing in front of your son as well as looking carefully at the pattern of the behavior so* *we can reduce any inadvertent positive consequences he gets for cussing while increasing the negative consequences. Does that sound reasonable?*

Parent: *Sounds good to me.*

Therapist: *Unfortunately, Jeremiah has learned some problematic behaviors from observing the perpetrator of the abuse but the good news is he can unlearn those behaviors just the way he is learning not to cuss.*

Discussions such as the one illustrated above are intended to help parents recognize how natural it is for children to imitate what they observe. After realizing how readily children imitate behaviors, parents may find it less frightening to acknowledge that children who have experienced sexual abuse learn behaviors and language as a result of their observations during the abusive interactions. At this point, parents may be encouraged to identify behaviors that they think their child learned from observing the perpetrator of the abuse. Age-inappropriate or adultlike sexual behaviors such as a child asking another child to lick his or her private parts is likely something learned from the perpetrator of the abuse. Such behaviors should be addressed from early on in treatment. Thus, therapists should carefully review Chapter 16 on sexual behavior problems prior to initiating therapy with a child exhibiting age-inappropriate sexual behaviors.

It is also important to point out to parents that in addition to behaviors, children learn cognitive and affective coping styles through observation. Parents should therefore be reminded that they will be encouraged to work on their own coping skills so that they can model effective and optimistic coping responses for their children. In fact, it should be repeatedly emphasized to parents that perhaps the most powerful way they can positively influence their children's recovery is by exhibiting the behaviors they want to see in their child. Unfortunately, the adage, "Do as I say not as I do" simply doesn't work in terms of positively influencing children's behaviors. From preschoolers to adolescents, children are powerfully influenced by the behaviors they observe in their parents. As noted earlier, the handout *How Children Learn Behaviors* provides additional information about how children learn from observation as well as associations and consequences. This handout may be reviewed in session and/or as a practice assignment.

Practice activities assigned

Each week it will be important to end the session with enough time to carefully discuss what the child and parent will work on and practice between sessions; this is often as important as what occurs during the actual treatment session. It is also best not to encourage more practice exercises than the client is likely to be able to complete in the week. Thus, any practice should be individually tailored to clients so that it is not overwhelming or likely to be ignored. For example, while some parents appreciate reading handouts, others may be feeling too overwhelmed to read books or handouts. If that is the case, it may be best to encourage parents to read handouts, for example, while the clinician is in session with their child. In any case, it is often useful to end sessions with brief descriptions of the handouts provided and with encouragement for parents to feel free to ask any questions they have about information shared in session.

It is important to review the skill-building plan including the reading material that will summarize and expand on what was discussed in session. For the introductory sessions, therapists may use *Child Sexual Abuse Information* handout written for adolescents and caregivers and the *How Children Learn Behaviors* handouts that are provided in Appendix B. These handouts are written to both provide factual information about CSA and children's abuse-related difficulties while also encouraging optimism about children's natural resilience and responsiveness to treatment.

Ending the session on a positive note

It is important to end sessions with parents each week on a positive note. For these initial sessions, the TF-CBT therapist might explain how this approach to therapy helps children to replace the problematic behaviors and symptoms they have developed (through observation, association, or consequences) with healthy behaviors that will allow them to obtain attention, achieve feelings of control, and/or manage distress in more adaptive ways. Moreover, depending on the parents' receptivity to scientific information or research, the clinician should reemphasize that the therapy that they will be participating in has proven effectiveness based on numerous scientific studies. Furthermore, the clinician may highlight that this treatment approach has been found to be particularly effective in terms of helping children who have experienced sexual abuse overcome the very difficulties their child is presenting while also helping parents heal and gain greater confidence in their ability to cope and parent effectively.

CHILD SESSION(S)

Build rapport and optimism

The child's individual sessions initially focus on building rapport, obtaining some basic information (e.g., about school, friends, etc.), possibly conducting a baseline neutral and trauma narrative assessment, presenting assessment findings when developmentally appropriate, and reviewing the structure, rationales, and time frames for treatment. If there is remaining time, the clinician may provide some basic goals for treatment and briefly provide limited information about CSA and/or other traumas experienced by the child. Rapport building with children often involves engaging in a discussion that will elicit the child's favorite activities, subjects, hobbies, celebrities, TV shows, etc. Not only do children enjoy such conversations, but these discussions help to identify activities that may be incorporated into treatment and/or may be utilized as end-of-session positive rituals that may motivate children to do the hard work of therapy.

Review confidentiality

As with all clients, it is important to review the standard limitations of confidentiality concerning reports of child abuse and/or neglect and behaviors that are a danger to themselves or others. However, as noted above, one aspect of confidentiality specific to TF-CBT that should be reviewed with children reflects the objective of encouraging open communication between parents and children. This is particularly important with children who have been sexually abused given the secrecy often associated with CSA. Thus, in the context of TF-CBT, the therapist will emphasize that aside from the danger/abuse exceptions, information shared in therapy will remain private to the parent-child unit and will not be shared outside of the therapy environment. The therapist will create opportunities for open communication between the parent and child increasingly over time. More specifically, it should be explained that to create such openness the therapist will be sharing some of what the child shares in session with the parent(s) as well as some of what the parent shares with the child (with appropriate limits and careful clinical judgment). As mentioned previously, with youth who present with complex trauma who likely have significant issues with trust, the therapist should be clear with the child that she would only share with a caregiver what the child has shared if the child provides explicit consent. With these guidelines in place, children and teens may often agree to the sharing of information and this may increase as treatment progresses and trust increases thereby supporting the move towards increasingly open communication between parents and children.

Conduct baseline assessment including a neutral narrative and baseline trauma narrative

It may be helpful to obtain a baseline trauma narrative at the start of treatment to establish how much the child is able to share concerning the details of the sexual abuse as well as his related feelings. Before eliciting any information about the sexual abuse, however, it is helpful to first teach the child how to provide a narrative about a neutral or positive event using Sternberg and Lamb's (1997) narrative practice technique. In the context of initiating therapy, eliciting a narrative about a neutral or positive event serves several purposes (Cohen, Mannarino, & Deblinger, 2006). First, it provides children with an opportunity to practice sharing detailed accounts of personal experiences. Research suggests that this practice improves children's skills in sharing spontaneous narratives about traumas, sexual abuse in particular (Sternberg et al., 1997). More specifically, Sternberg et al. (1997) found that children who practiced how to provide a spontaneous narrative using a neutral or positive event in their lives, prior to their forensic interview regarding CSA allegations, provided CSA disclosures that were significantly more detailed and rich in content. Within the context of therapy, this procedure is used not only to enhance children's skills in providing detailed and rich accounts of sexual abuse but it is also designed to help children practice sharing emotions, cognitions, and bodily sensations. Moreover, the neutral narrative practice allows the therapist to assess skill levels in sharing this kind of information about personal experiences (Cohen, Mannarino, & Deblinger, 2006; Runyon & Deblinger, 2014). An additional purpose of this practice is to help the therapist assess the child's level of abuse-related avoidance, as well as the child's overall expressive language skills. By observing and comparing the details, feelings, thoughts, and sensations provided during the neutral narrative with those offered during the sexual abuse narrative, the therapist can assess children's skills in sharing details, thoughts, feelings, and sensations prior to the skill-building components. This information allows the therapist to set reasonable expectations for the child as it reflects the child's developmental capabilities in terms of expressing herself verbally and also provides information that may be valuable in planning the skills-building sessions. This knowledge may be particularly important for school-age children, as it is often difficult to approximate how much the child is capable of sharing. A child who provides a rich, detailed account of participation in a favorite activity, for example, has the ability to provide a similar account of his abusive experiences but may not provide those details in a trauma narrative as a result of PTSD-related avoidance. Conversely, if a child provides limited details for both the neutral and baseline CSA narratives, this may reflect developmental limitations that should be used to set reasonable expectations for the trauma narrative development planned for later in treatment. In addition to being a valuable assessment tool, eliciting a narrative about a child's favorite activity or hobby can be an excellent rapport builder. In Box 6.3, for example, the therapist elicits a positive narrative using the Sternberg and Lamb technique about a child's participation in his favorite activity, a baseball game (Sternberg et al., 1997).

It is important for therapists to not break the flow of children's words and to allow for natural pauses as children try to recall details (Cohen, Mannarino, & Deblinger, 2006; Runyon & Deblinger, 2014). If necessary, the therapist can use the prompts listed below to encourage children to expand on their narrative.

"What else?"
"Tell me a bit more."
"What happened next?"
"What did your parent say/do?"
"What did your teammates or coach say/do?"

However, research findings suggest that no more than about five minutes need be devoted to the neutral practice narrative described above; more time than that may lead to fatigue, thus undermining the potential benefits of the practice narrative in terms of increasing the number of details and richness offered during the baseline sexual abuse narrative (Holliday & Albon, 2004; Roberts, Lamb, & Sternberg, 2004).

helps me to understand what happened and why your mom thinks it's a good idea for both of you to meet with me. Thank you very much for sharing that. Now, let me tell you a little bit about what we will do together each session. Then you can ask me questions.

Child: *Okay.*

---

when eliciting an initial sexual abuse narrative so that children do not feel like you already know all about what happened. However, with some children, to get the child started there may be a need to ask increasingly focused questions based on the information available from the investigation or the child's previous disclosures (Saywitz, Lyon, & Goodman, 2011). Whenever possible it is better to avoid asking about a particular person or specific sexual act, as narratives tend to be much richer and more reflective of a child processing his memories when the child is providing spontaneous recollections. Thus, it is best to encourage children to tell everything, even little things they may think are not important (Saywitz et al., 2011).

The child's statement about what he told the police officer serves as a baseline trauma narrative and reflects how much detail about the abuse the child feels comfortable sharing at the start of treatment. It is important to accept and validate what the child has offered at this point and not use many additional prompts to elicit more detail at this stage. Some children may share very little detail and that's okay. In fact, most children are likely to offer many more details during the neutral (i.e., baseball) narrative as compared to the baseline sexual abuse narrative due to shame, embarrassment, guilt or fear (Saywitz et al., 2011). During the neutral and baseline trauma narratives, the therapist should carefully note the child's changing levels of anxiety and avoidance. If the child shared much less detail and/or emotions in the abuse narrative when compared to the neutral narrative, as in the above example, the therapist should develop a plan to address avoidance and limited emotional vocabulary over the course of therapy. Moreover, the information, what the child provided and what was omitted, will assist the therapist in developing the hierarchy of abuse-related stimuli for the gradual exposure process. For example, if based on the mother's report the abuse involved more invasive contact than touching, it is helpful plan to elicit narratives about more invasive abuse after the child has written chapters about the less-anxiety-provoking abusive interactions that involved only touching. In general, if the child becomes tearful during specific portions of the baseline trauma narrative, gives minimal responses to questions, and attempts to end the interview, the therapist should plan to pursue the gradual exposure process in the sessions that follow in carefully calibrated steps, beginning with topics that are only minimally anxiety provoking (i.e., narratives about positive, non-abusive encounters with the perpetrator). Conversely, if the child discloses with significant detail abusive experiences fairly easily, the therapist can expect that the gradual exposure process will move more rapidly.

For youth who present with complex trauma, it may be contraindicated for them to do a baseline trauma narrative as described above. These youth may have much greater issues with trust and avoidance, and thus, may be more likely to respond to such a suggestion with negativity and/or emotional distress which could interfere with effective therapeutic engagement. Thus, the eliciting of a baseline trauma narrative should be evaluated as to whether it would be therapeutically helpful and appropriate for each client.

During these introductory sessions, it is helpful to use a great deal of active listening to reflect back and validate what the child shares about himself as well as his experience of sexual abuse. This validation importantly demonstrates one's comfort with what is being shared and thus helps children to feel comfortable. At this stage, it is most important for children to feel accepted and validated for whatever they offer rather than pushing for additional abuse-related details. In fact, given that the child has not yet received coping skills training, no more than a relatively brief baseline trauma narrative or sometimes just an acknowledgement of the sexual abuse should be expected, especially if the child is exhibiting significant PTSD symptoms. The therapist should note the differences between the child's skills in sharing a neutral narrative versus the baseline trauma narrative as a reflection of the degree to which the child may be experiencing PTSD, avoidance symptoms, and/or feelings of shame.

Provide assessment findings (when developmentally appropriate)

Older children may have questions or concerns about what the therapist learned during the assessment process and may benefit from some explanation of the findings. An explanation of evaluation findings is less likely to be valuable for younger children. Any findings presented to the child must be described simply and concretely. Caution must be used to avoid overwhelming the child with too much information or with frightening information about emotional or behavioral problems. Typically, the findings can be summarized, with a focus on the child's symptoms. For example, the therapist might say:

> *Remember last week when you told me that thoughts about the abuse bother you, that you try not to think about the abuse, you stay away from things that remind you of it, and you have a lot more bad dreams than you used to? Well, it sounds like your thoughts and memories of the abuse are getting in your way and bothering you a lot. I know some things we can work on together so that those thoughts and feelings about the sexual abuse and even the bad dreams won't bother you so much. I have helped a lot of other children with just these kinds of difficulties after they experienced sexual abuse.*

Subsequently, the therapist might explain how the treatment plan will address those specific symptoms. With older children and teenagers, it is important to review specific symptoms reported as well, acknowledging that their symptoms are not unusual and that many other children or teens seen at the clinic report similar difficulties after experiencing sexual abuse. Moreover, it may be emphasized that the symptoms they have reported are not only common, but they are the very problems this therapy (i.e., TF-CBT) is designed to address.

Psychoeducation about trauma reminders and connection to trauma responses

As noted above, it is important in the introductory sessions to review the assessment findings and acknowledge children's reported difficulties. However, older youth also may benefit from understanding how their current difficulties are linked to the sexual abuse as well as other traumatic experiences. It can be helpful, for example, to review the specific symptoms reported by youth, including emotional, cognitive, behavioral, sexual, and/or relationship difficulties, while explaining how the trauma(s) endured may have contributed to the development of these difficulties. As described in the parent session above, the therapist may explain, in more simple and developmentally appropriate terms, how observations, associations and consequences experienced during abusive episodes may have contributed to the development of their reported emotional symptoms, cognitive confusion, and behavioral difficulties. Moreover, it is important to highlight several examples of how CSA-related memories and reminders in the environment may be linked to troubling emotional reactions in the present. This may be best achieved by eliciting from the client examples of emotionally disturbing trauma reminders that she may avoid or overreact to due to the distress such reminders cause.

Trauma reminders may be described as people, places, things, sounds, smells, feelings, sensations, and/or other cues that remind the youngster of past traumatic experiences. These cues can be experienced internally or externally. Internal cues might include memories, thoughts, feelings, and/or bodily sensations. External cues could include places, things, sounds, songs, words, smells, weather, situations, types of interactions (e.g., conflictual or sexual), specific people, and/or characteristics of people (e.g., older gray-haired men, adolescents acting cool). Sometimes youth respond to trauma reminders by reacting as if the trauma is happening all over again. However, often these trauma cues are not accurate signs or signals of impending trauma or danger. They may simply be innocuous or nondangerous reminders of bad things that happened in the past. Still, because of their associations with past traumas, these reminders may lead youth to experience extreme avoidant or severe emotional reactions and/or aggressive responses. A teen who has been sexually abused and continues to experience PTSD, for example, may respond to age-appropriate sexual interactions with extreme anxiety and/or aggression without fully understanding the connection between her reactions and the prior abusive experiences.

Though it should be emphasized that such reactions to trauma reminders are common and very reasonable (as it is natural to avoid and/or react to distressing reminders), it may be explained that such reactions have the potential to interfere with clients' desired life goals. During the course of therapy, children and teens will be helped to identify trauma reminders in their environment as well as those they may experience internally so they can better manage their reactions to such reminders. The therapist, however, need not overly focus on the importance of nonavoidance of innocuous trauma reminders as this will be addressed more gently through the gradual exposure process that ultimately helps youth habituate to such reminders, leading to less volatile reactions. At this stage of therapy, it is best to normalize and validate children's reactions to the sexual abuse and associated reminders, while helping them to gain a greater understanding of their symptoms, as well as the strength they have had in enduring the trauma(s) experienced and the ongoing distress and symptoms reported. Again, it is most important to offer hope by emphasizing how this specific therapy model is highly effective in helping children and teens overcome the very trauma-related difficulties reported, while also helping them to build on their strengths by working to gain knowledge and skills that will support their healing, growth, and happiness.

Provide basic overview of structure, rationales, objectives, and time frames for treatment

Treatment objectives and rationales should be presented to the child, albeit in an abbreviated and simpler fashion as compared to what was presented to the parents. For all but the youngest children, it is appropriate to outline the major components of the child's treatment plan (i.e., education regarding sexual abuse, coping skills training, drawing, writing, and other creative activities that will help them feel better) without putting undue emphasis on the trauma narrative. At the outset of treatment, while children need to know that the focus of treatment will be on coping with CSA, they need not know that there is any expectation to write a detailed narrative until it is time to begin that activity. Through the process of psychoeducation and gradual exposure, children are much more likely to be receptive to the idea of writing a trauma narrative when that session arrives than they will be at the outset of treatment when they may be much more symptomatic and avoidant. It is also very helpful for children to know that their parents are participating in therapy as well, so that they can learn about CSA and learn how to be the best parents they can be. Moreover, it may be helpful for some children to know that they will have some conjoint sessions with their parents to review and together practice the skills they are learning.

The dialogue provided in Box 6.5 illustrates the presentation of the treatment rationale to an 8-year-old girl. Note that the therapist attempts to be clear, simple, and interactive in her discussion with the child. It is important to note that portions of this treatment rationale often need to be repeated throughout the course of therapy as encouragement for the child to overcome her avoidance and continue the work of gradual exposure.

Box 6.5

Case Example: Treatment Rationale for Child

Therapist: *I'd like to tell you something about my plans for the work we will do together.*

Mary: *OK.*

Therapist: *First of all, I want to teach you what we know about sexual abuse.*

Mary: *Yuck!*

Therapist: *Yuck?*

Mary: *I hate talking about that.*

Therapist: *Well, I will do a lot of the talking about sexual abuse at first. Usually we feel better about things that we really understand. I'd like to teach you so much about child sexual abuse that you'll be an expert. Once you know all I have to teach you, I think you'll understand more about it and won't feel as confused or uncomfortable with the topic.*

Mary: *I guess that would be good.*

Therapist: *I would also like to teach you some ways to handle those confusing, distressing or yucky feelings you might have from time to time.*

Mary: *Like what?*

Therapist: *Well, sometimes when you're feeling nervous and upset, it helps to relax by making believe you're a wet noodle.* (Therapist demonstrates) *Then you don't feel so nervous.*

Mary: [laughing] *A wet noodle?*

Therapist: *Yeah, it seems like it would be pretty hard to be a nervous wet noodle, doesn't it?*

Mary: *Yeah. What else will we do?*

Therapist: *Remember how you told me that when you think about what your dad did, you get scared and upset?*

Mary: *Yeah, I just try not to ever think about it.*

Therapist: *Are you able to keep those thoughts out of your head all the time?*

Mary: *Well no, sometimes they pop in anyway, mostly when I'm doing my schoolwork and when I'm going to sleep. I try to forget about them though.*

Therapist: *Well, I don't want those thoughts to keep bothering you. If I had some kind of magic laser and could just zap them out of your brain so you could forget about them forever, we might try that. But we don't have a magic laser. I don't think that you can forget about them forever because you're too smart and too old to do that. The next best thing is to find a way for you to be more comfortable with being reminded about what happened.*

Mary: *How can I do that?*

Therapist: *In order to get more comfortable thinking about the abuse, we need to talk about it some, read about it or we could even play an educational game about sexual abuse so that you really get used to thinking about it.*

Mary: *You want me to think about it and talk about it?*

Therapist: *Yes, I want to talk about child sexual abuse with you. I know that may seem hard at first, but it will get easier and easier. It's like getting into a cold swimming pool. When you first stick your toe in a pool on a hot summer day, how does it feel?*

Mary: *Too cold—like ice.*

Therapist: *It is so cold, it might feel like an iceberg, right?*

Mary: *Yeah. I go in very slowly when it's really cold.*

Therapist: *Exactly. You might slowly get in up to your knees and you're still shivering. Once you get your tummy wet, you're starting to get used to it. And after a few minutes when you dunk your whole body in, how does the water usually feel?*

Mary: *Really good 'cause I love to swim.*

Therapist: *Sounds like you have done that.*

Mary: *Yeah, lots of times.*

Therapist: *Well, getting used to talking about the abuse is sort of like getting used to the cold water in a swimming pool. At first it seems hard to talk about, but every time we talk about it, it gets easier and easier until you're used to it.*

Mary: *I don't know. That sounds kind of hard.*

Therapist: *It may make you uncomfortable at first but it's the best way for you to get used to thinking about the abuse so that those memories of what happened won't pop into your head and bother you anymore. We can start by talking about and reading about child sexual abuse so you can become an expert.*

Mary: *Do we have to talk about it a lot?*

Therapist: *We will talk about it just enough so that talking about child sexual abuse won't upset you anymore; you'll just get bored with it! I'll try to find ways to make it more interesting and maybe even fun. We don't have to just talk. We can also draw pictures, play games, or even make up a play or songs to help teach other kids about child sexual abuse.*

Mary: *My teacher says I'm really good at drawing.*

Therapist: *Terrific! We can start with drawing then if you like.*

Mary: *Okay. That would be good.*

A developmentally appropriate overview of treatment should be provided to even the youngest children. In this overview, the therapist will explain that the focus of treatment will be on learning about and coping with the sexual abuse. The therapist may explain to a young child that the more one talks about the sexual abuse, the less scary it will be. Though children who have symptoms of PTSD often prefer not to focus on the trauma(s) experienced, it is the experience of the authors that acknowledging the sexual abuse focus from the start demonstrates comfort and confidence that therapy can be of help in coping with the impact of this experience on them and their family. It will be important to explain, however, that during the first phase of treatment the therapist and the client will be talking some about CSA but will also be playing games and engaging in activities that will help the child learn different skills for coping with all kinds of problems. Some fun examples of activities may be shared, explaining that as therapy goes along, the therapist will plan activities that will help them cope with their feelings and thoughts about the sexual abuse as well as other problems. With the youngest children, the focus and structure of treatment may be similarly acknowledged, but typically therapists will refer to the sexual abuse as experiencing "not okay" touches. Thus, the therapist might explain the following.

Therapist: *Each week when you come to therapy, we are going to have fun playing games, reading, talking, and even singing together if you like. Some of these activities are going to help us learn about different kinds of touches. One type of touch we will talk about happens when a grown up or older kid touches a younger child's private parts just because they want to, even though they know it is "not okay." This is the kind of touch you told me happened to you. We call this kind of touch a "not okay" touch. "Not okay" touches are against the rules and sometimes they hurt people's feelings and sometimes they hurt people's bodies. Can you think of any other "not okay" touches?*

Child: *Is hitting a "not okay" touch?*

Therapist: *Absolutely! Hitting, kicking, and biting other people are also "not okay" touches. So we will learn about all those kinds of "not okay" touches and we will also talk about many kinds of "okay" touches as well. Do you know what kinds of touches are okay?*

Child: *You mean like shaking hands or giving big hugs to people you love?*

Therapist: *Exactly. We will be talking a lot about what makes certain kinds of touches okay, while others are not okay.*

Treatment length

Children and adolescents often appreciate some information about the number of sessions they will be expected to attend and/or some estimate about when treatment will be completed. For some children, it can be quite motivating to count down the number of sessions. Of course, it is not wise to provide an absolute number of sessions as children more than adults will want to stick to that number; however, it is helpful to provide an estimate based upon the client's situation. The therapist may offer an estimated length of treatment by indicating an approximate number of sessions or that treatment will likely be completed by summer break or before school begins in the fall. Still, it is important to explain that progress made in treatment will be assessed and that the decision to end treatment will be carefully discussed and agreed upon with their parents to ensure that they have benefited as much as possible from treatment. Children also like to know that the therapy process is not endless. Thus, from the start it is useful for the therapist to set the expectation that the child will successfully complete treatment in a relatively short period of time and that there will be a party to celebrate therapy graduation at the end.

Psychoeducation about CSA

Children benefit a great deal from the therapist modeling nonavoidance and demonstrating general comfort with discussing issues related to CSA. Thus, as part of the introductory sessions, it can be helpful to begin by briefly sharing some basic information about the nature of CSA as well as its prevalence and impact. It is important for the therapist to get permission from parents, particularly of the younger children, to use the doctors' names for private parts (i.e., penis, vagina, breasts, and buttocks or bottom) in order to enhance the ease of communication about sexual abuse-related issues going forward. With younger children, it helps to use concrete examples and even dolls or stick figures to help children understand which parts of the bodies are private and what CSA is.

Children also seem to respond well to concrete evidence that they are not alone and that CSA happens to lots of children. Thus, it can be helpful for the therapist to point out de-identified drawings, books or other evidence of children that the therapist has worked with who have had similar experiences. With older children, one can share prevalence statistics (i.e., at least 1 out of 4 girls and 1 out of 6 boys experiences any kind of sexual victimization). The therapist may also explain that though most children do not talk about sexual abuse experiences, there are probably many other children in their school who have gone through very similar experiences. In addition, it can be helpful to share information about well-known individuals who have acknowledged a history of CSA. Such individuals include the TV talk show hosts Oprah Winfrey and Ellen DeGeneres, musicians Carlos Santana, Mary J. Blige, and Queen Latifah, actress Terri Hatcher, authors Antwone Fisher and Maya Angelou, NFL star Laveranues Coles, MLB player R. A. Dickey, and Olympic athletes Kayla Harrison and Kellie Wells. This can be particularly useful to share with youth to demonstrate the success people can have despite the experience of abuse in childhood (see case example in Box 6.6). Provided in Appendix B is the *Child Sexual Abuse Information* handout that provides additional helpful information for adolescents and their caregivers.

Box 6.6

Case Example: Avoidance Overcome with Oprah's Help

Early in the first author's career, she worked with an 8-year-old girl presenting with full blown PTSD who had experienced sexual abuse perpetrated by her stepfather. She was highly avoidant and refused to speak about the sexual abuse despite the fact that the offender had confessed. Session after session, she seemed disinterested in learning about CSA, but cooperated somewhat with the skill building activities. Halfway through treatment, her grandmother continued to report that the child remained oppositional and sullen at home. Despite gradual exposure and creative efforts to engage her in trauma narration, she objected to any discussion or writing about the sexual abuse until one day she entered therapy with a sudden change of heart. With her hand on her hip, she announced that Oprah Winfrey had been raped by her uncle when she was a little girl. She explained how Oprah talked about it on her TV show and suddenly the child showed a newfound readiness and willingness to not only talk about what she experienced, but she wanted to write a song about CSA that would help other kids. From this point on, the child made excellent progress in therapy and seemed to understand that the feelings of shame she had been experiencing did not belong to her or her fellow CSA survivor, Oprah. Rather she began to place the blame with her stepfather and seemed to show pride in talking openly about her experience and educating her grandmother about CSA. With Oprah's help, this child graduated therapy having overcome symptoms of PTSD, depression, and behavioral difficulties, and she taught the author about the value of sharing information about other CSA survivors who children look up to and admire.

Depending on the age of the child, the therapist may review some basic facts about CSA that will be reassuring. In this session, for example, it helps to emphasize that other children have experienced sexual abuse as well as some of the emotional difficulties the child is reporting. It is helpful to emphasize that symptoms reported are very common after an experience such as sexual abuse. Most importantly, it helps to highlight that the therapy program he will be participating in has helped many other kids overcome the same kinds of feelings and problems and that it will help the child to feel much better too.

Ending session on a positive note

Finally, it is important to end child sessions on a positive note. One can begin this by expressing admiration for the child's strengths and/or special talents that the parent may have shared. In addition, a brief discussion about favorite hobbies may be useful to identify brief but positive end-of-session rituals that can be planned for future sessions. Depending on their interests, some children, for example, may look forward to sharing a little about a soccer game or choir performance or might enjoy sharing jokes, riddles, musical pieces, and/or computer apps for a few minutes at the end of each session. Finally, children may be asked to be prepared to share ways in which they have showed strength in coping with the CSA, as well as examples of positive moments experienced during the week at next week's session.

CONJOINT SESSION(S) (OPTIONAL)

Conjoint sessions can be very helpful throughout treatment, though therapists should use their clinical judgment in determining their usefulness especially during the first two phases of treatment when their implementation very much depends on the presenting problems. With youth who exhibit significant behavior problems, conjoint sessions are more critical, as they provide important opportunities for therapists to coach parents and youth in the practicing of effective parenting and coping skills respectively. However, regardless of the implementation of formal conjoint sessions, therapists may learn a great deal about parents' and children's styles of interacting by taking note of their behaviors in the waiting room and at the beginning and end of treatment sessions.

Briefly review the treatment plan and elicit their agreement to participate

With parents and children together, the therapist may repeat the overall rationale for treatment, emphasizing one's confidence in the parents' and child's ability to work as a team. The therapist need not review the details of the treatment plan discussed with the parent and child individually. Typically, it should be emphasized that the initial sessions will be individual and focus on fun activities and skill building, and over time they will have more time together with the therapist. It also helps to highlight again the time-limited nature of therapy, with an estimate of the number of weekly sessions likely to be required (e.g., approximately 12 to 16 sessions) as a means of demonstrating confidence in the family's likelihood of successfully completed treatment in a concrete time frame.

Praise parent and child for their strength as well as participation in session

Moreover, this brief meeting is an opportunity for the therapist to model the importance of praise (i.e., an important parenting skill that will be introduced in the sessions that follow) by expressing specific praise to both the parent and child for their participation in session (e.g., "Thank you for your excellent questions"; "I really appreciated your openness in discussing the sexual abuse in session").

7

Relaxation Skills

Psychoeducation initiated in the introductory sessions continues with a focus on general education about child sexual abuse (CSA). For this reason, a basic information sheet about CSA for adolescents and their caregivers is included in Appendix B for use during this phase. In addition, there are many other valuable handouts related to specific CSA issues, as well as other traumas (e.g., domestic violence, physical abuse, traumatic grief), available through the NCTSN website (http://www.nctsnet.org/trauma-types), that are described in Appendix B. It is important to recognize that many children who have experienced sexual abuse have also experienced other forms of childhood trauma as was described previously. Thus, education about these other traumas is important as well. However, to avoid overwhelming clients with too many facts and figures that may not be important to their healing, therapists should carefully review available handouts and choose only a few over the course of treatment to be utilized as reading assignments when appropriate.

Therapists often ask how to provide psychoeducation for youth who have experienced multiple or complex trauma. For these youth, rather than providing discrete information about different types of traumas, it is usually more helpful for the therapist to conceptualize themes that unify the youth's repeated trauma experiences (Cohen, Mannarino, Kliethermes, et al., 2012).

Although the order of the presentation of the various coping skills (i.e., relaxation, affective modulation, and cognitive coping) is somewhat flexible, it has been the experience of the authors that relaxation training can be particularly helpful early on, in that these skills can help stabilize clients who are experiencing significant physiological arousal as well as feelings of anxiety. In addition to engaging parents in relaxation skills training, the therapist should focus considerable time on effective parenting skills. Given that children with a history of CSA are at risk for developing low self-esteem, internalizing symptoms, as well as externalizing behavior problems, a focus on parenting should be maintained throughout the course of treatment with parents of all children and adolescents—not just those exhibiting externalizing behavior difficulties. Parenting is without question challenging for all caregivers, but it is particularly difficult during times of stress like in the aftermath of a trauma such as sexual abuse. It therefore behooves therapists to simultaneously engage caregivers in the process of optimizing their parenting and coping skills to support their children's full recovery. Thus, in addition to parenting guidance, caregivers may benefit from encouragement to take care of themselves so they can serve as effective coping role models for their children (see *Self Care: Taking Care of Yourself and Your Child* handout in Appendix B).

PARENT SESSION(S)

Practice assignment review

It is important to briefly acknowledge whatever emotional and/or practical obstacles parents may have to overcome to get to session, while also providing specific praise for their attendance, commitment to ongoing therapy, and/or any related educational or skills practice activities the parent has engaged in between sessions. It is worth noting that for some parents the sessions may be so anxiety provoking that they may have a tendency to cancel or not show for their children's initial appointments. This may be particularly true for parents who are experiencing depressive or anxiety symptoms. Research has documented that a significant proportion of mothers experience clinical levels of distress in the aftermath of discovering that their child experienced sexual abuse (Deblinger et al., 1993; Kelley, 1990). Moreover, it has been found that these symptoms may interfere with their ability to optimally respond to their children's needs (Cohen & Mannarino, 1996c; Santa-Sosa, Steer, Deblinger, & Runyon, 2013). Thus, from the very start of treatment, it is paramount to emphasize the importance of following through with practicing coping and parenting skills between sessions. Moreover, coping or parenting practice assignments should be reviewed with the parent at the start of each session so that parents begin to anticipate this routine.

Given the limited time one has with parents each session, once in the private therapy office or space, the therapist might find that it helps to review the parents' efforts to practice skills at home and/or introduce the plan for the session. In this session, for example, the therapist might begin by inquiring about the caregivers' reactions to the *Child Sexual Abuse Information* and *How Children Learn Behaviors* handouts. If they have not followed through, then it is important to take some time to review obstacles and collaborate regarding how to overcome such obstacles in the future. If parents are unlikely to do much reading at home, it might be helpful for the parent to review whatever handouts or materials that may be relevant for their individual sessions while the therapist meets individually with the child.

Review how children learn by explaining the flight, fight, or freeze response

The dialogue in Box 7.1 provides an example of eliciting the parents' reactions to the handouts and explains the development of abuse-related behaviors and symptoms

Box 7.1

Case Example: Explaining Posttraumatic Stress to Caregivers

Therapist: *Tell me about your reactions to the handouts I provided to you last week.*

Caregiver: *Well, I started to read the one about child sexual abuse and I couldn't finish it because I don't like to think about what happened to my child ... but I read about how children learn behaviors and it was reassuring that my son can unlearn these behaviors that he has developed since the sexual abuse.*

Therapist: *So you read the* How Children Learn Behaviors *handout—that's terrific. And the* Child Sexual Abuse Information *handout you didn't finish. I understand why that was hard. We will take the discussion about child sexual abuse slowly and give you some coping skills to manage the naturally distressing feelings that you have when reminded of the sexual abuse.*

Caregiver: *That is good to hear because just talking about it now makes me want to cry.*

Therapist: *To be honest, in some ways that doesn't surprise me because that is a reflection of your love for your child and that love will help him heal. And crying is not necessarily a bad thing. It can be a great release and this is just the place to experience such a release, especially given the large supply of tissues I always have on hand here* (pointing to tissue box). *As we discussed last week, much of what we will do together is going to be directed to helping you cope so that you can start to feel better and in turn be in a better position to help your son. That's why this week I'm going to give you a handout called* Self-Care: Taking Care of Yourself and Your Child.

Caregiver: *I was hoping you would be the one to help my child.*

Therapist: *I have great confidence actually that I will help Ryan, but I can do that best in collaboration with you. Because you see, I have less than one hour a week with him, while you have many hours every week. So by learning about what I'm doing with Ryan, you can make a much greater impact on him. In fact, your influence will be important not only during the next 14 weeks or so, but the coping skills we will be practicing will be valuable for a lifetime for both you and your son. What do you think?*

Caregiver: *That sounds good to me.*

Therapist: *As I've mentioned before, each week I plan to share with you what I am working on with your child. In the early sessions, I will be teaching and practicing various coping skills with Ryan, and I would like to simultaneously work on these skills with you to help you feel better and to help you model these skills for your son. I realize this may be different from your previous experience in therapy.*

Caregiver: *Actually, I'm counting on this being different from my last therapy experience because Ryan is still having problems.*

Therapist: *Yes. We talked about how this will likely be very different. Can you remember some of the differences we talked about?*

Caregiver: *Well, you said that we wouldn't just be talking, but that my son and I would learn things and we would practice skills in session and then at home. It also sounded like it would be more active and fun for my son. So I do think this will be better but I am still so worried about him and how the sexual abuse has affected him.*

Therapist: *I really like how you remembered all those differences. And I thank you for your honesty in sharing how worried you are about how the sexual abuse has affected Ryan.*

Caregiver: *Yes. That's what I am worried about.*

Therapist: *Ryan is experiencing symptoms that are common for kids who have experienced sexual abuse. When individuals experience sexual abuse or other scary, confusing, or unexpected traumas, they react in ways that are different from the way we respond to everyday problems or events. We react in the same ways our prehistoric ancestors responded to severe danger or predators in the environment. We call this the fight or flight or freeze response, which refers to the automatic way our nervous system responds when there is a threat to our survival. When danger is signaled, in a spilt second our bodies respond with increased heart rate, rapid, shallow breathing, muscle tension, increased blood flow to our limbs, pupil dilation—all this happens to help us optimally respond to the threat. Usually these automatic physiological reactions of our (sympathetic) nervous system last only for the duration of the threat (which typically is relatively brief). This reaction might happen for example if someone cuts you off on the highway and you come close to having a car accident. Did that ever happen to you?*

Caregiver: *More than one time.*

Therapist: *Do you recall experiencing the rapid heartbeat and other physiological changes that help you to respond quickly to the danger, but then subside pretty quickly after the incident is over?*

Caregiver: *Yes.*

Therapist: *These physiological changes support different survival strategies that automatically kick in depending on the danger. The example of getting cut off on a highway might trigger an immediate flight response in which you quickly do what is necessary to get away from the car or danger. In response to other dangers, a fight response might be triggered. Then sometimes when nothing else seems likely to work, that survival instinct results in a freeze response in which playing dead or staying put seems like the best hope for survival. Many adults and children respond to an assault in all these ways. Some children and adults may try to flee or fight, but for many survivors their instinct leads them to stay put until the danger passes. Experts sometimes refer to these automatic survival responses as fight, flight, or freeze responses.*

Caregiver: *That makes sense—my son told the investigator that he tried to make believe he was sleeping sometimes and just let his uncle abuse him. But now that his uncle is in jail, why is my son still acting like he has to fight everyone?*

Therapist: *After some traumatic experiences, the physiological and emotional responses that occurred at the time of the traumas don't subside so quickly, even* *though the actual threat has passed. In fact, some adults and children continue to have these physical (such as that fight response) and emotional reactions in response to memories or reminders of the trauma. And sometimes when you have suffered significant trauma, you tend to be on guard and may tend to misperceive danger, even when there is no real danger anymore. This is due to associations that have been made in your mind between things that were present at the time of the abuse and the abuse itself.*

Caregiver: *Well, I guess my son had the freeze response, but now it seems like he is having this fight reaction to anyone he thinks might threaten him in any way.*

Therapist: *Actually, we'll talk more about this as therapy proceeds, but I have already gotten the sense from your son that he engaged in a variety of survival strategies including the fight, flight, and freeze responses, all of which ultimately helped him to survive the ordeal until he felt safe enough to tell. However, based on our assessment, it seems as if there are times when you and your son still experience some of those physiological symptoms because your bodies and minds may not yet be convinced you are out of danger. Are you still experiencing sudden intense physical symptoms out of the blue?*

Caregiver: *Definitely.*

Therapist: *What happens sometimes is that those ways of responding to real immediate threats get re-triggered by reminders of that event, even when there is no real threat to our physical safety anymore.*

Caregiver: *Yes that does happen to me when I drive by the area where I was mugged and even when I learned about the sexual abuse, I felt like I was being mugged—I had those physical feelings of terror come back to me and felt really angry and scared. So I mostly try to avoid that area and not think about the sexual abuse.*

Therapist: *Thank you for sharing that. It is similar for your son. Even though Ryan is now safe and has no contact with the person who sexually abused him, he seems to be avoiding reminders of the sexual abuse and does not want to talk about it. This is because the consequences he experiences when reminded of the abuse are negative in the form of physiological arousal and distress. But the truth is he is experiencing some of those physiological reactions and tendencies to fight or freeze when he is reminded of the abuse, even though he is not in real danger. And for you too—though the ongoing danger is no longer a realistic threat—it may not feel that way to you at times when some reminders trigger those feelings in you, so you probably try to avoid such reminders. But it is very difficult to do that because there are really reminders everywhere.*

Caregiver: *You're right—I still feel all keyed up at times like I did when I was mugged or when I just discovered the sexual abuse. And I get really down on myself because I'm so anxious and depressed. I'm not the kind of mother I want to be and I just feel so responsible for the abuse.*

Therapist: *We are going to tackle each one of those issues—the keyed-up feelings, the feelings of sadness and responsibility. We are going to work together step by step so that you can get back to feeling good again. And we are going to start with* *a very simple breathing exercise that will help you focus on the present. I will be practicing this exercise with your son as well so that you can both overcome the distressing feelings that were natural at one time but are now interfering with your well-being.*

Caregiver: *Really? Will he really be able to do this? He is very distractible you know.*

Therapist: *Like all children who have experienced posttraumatic stress, Ryan may be somewhat distractible, but I am confident he can do this. I will explain to him too that while it was healthy for the sexual abuse to signal danger and for the mind and the body to respond to that danger with increased heart rate, shallow breathing, and by preparing to fight, flee, or freeze, that is not necessary now because the memory or nondangerous reminder is essentially a false alarm. Unfortunately, responding to numerous false alarms can be exhausting and deplete you of energy that you need to engage in and enjoy everyday life. Are you feeling pretty wiped out these days?*

Caregiver: *Absolutely.*

Therapist: *That is likely because when reminded in anyway of the sexual abuse, your mind is automatically going back to these traumatic memories and acting as if these things are happening right now though they obviously are not. Unfortunately, when you are* not *being triggered by reminders of the past, the anxious mind loves to jump ahead and worry about the future. The way we can counteract those tendencies is to get fully focused on the present moment where it is much more comfortable.*

Caregiver: *Maybe you're right, I do think a lot about the sexual abuse, though it happened over a year ago now. And if I'm not thinking about that, I'm worried about my family's future.*

Therapist: *That is why we are going to work on focusing on the present moment. So I'd like to share some information with you about a practice called "mindfulness" that is designed to help children and adults to focus their attention on the present. Together we will practice a simple breathing exercise that will reinforce a present moment focus and help you cope with the keyed up, panicky feelings that, as you have said, seem to come out of the blue. Again, remember as you learn to cope more effectively, your son will likely learn these more effective ways of coping through observation. Do you have any other questions about the* How Children Learn Behaviors *handout?*

Caregiver: *Not right now.*

---

while also introducing the rationale for mindfulness and focused breathing to caregivers in the form of explaining the flight, fight, or freeze response.

As a means of helping parents understand their child's abuse-related behavioral difficulties, the therapist may introduce the social-learning model by reviewing the three mechanisms of learning: observation, association, and consequences. It is important to emphasize that these three mechanisms explain not only the development of sexual abuse-related behaviors but also how children learn both positive and negative behaviors in general. Thus, when describing how each of these learning mechanisms works, it is useful to provide a handout (i.e., *How Children Learn Behaviors*) for parents to review, while also eliciting from them examples of both abuse-related and nonabuse-related behaviors their children may have learned through these mechanisms.

Help parents practice focused breathing, mindfulness, and/or other relaxation exercises

The therapist may emphasize the importance of learning all the coping skills the child will be learning. This is so that the parents can model and reinforce those skills for the child but also so they will reap the emotional and physical benefits of effective coping as well. The therapist may then introduce and define the practice of focused breathing and/or the concept of mindfulness and other relaxation strategies. The practice of focused breathing can help many caregivers and children release physical tension and overcome physiological stress symptoms. The explanation of the benefits of focused breathing is shared by the therapist to inspire caregivers to begin to engage in and encourage their children to use deep breathing to manage stress as well.

Therapist: *When in stressful circumstances, it is not unusual for someone to say, "Breathe" or "take a deep breath." In fact, top coaches often remind athletes facing a stressful moment to breathe because it is not uncommon for individuals to hold their breath or engage in unhealthy shallow and/or rapid breathing when under stress. Thus, it can be extremely valuable for you and your child to learn to pay attention to your breathing patterns and engage in focused breathing when under stress. And the really good news is this is a coping skill you can use anytime and anywhere.*

For some clients, encouraging them to learn to take a few deep breaths can be surprisingly helpful when they are under stress or bothered by a traumatic reminder or memory. More distressed caregivers may be taught to combine focused breathing with the more complex practice of mindfulness so they can learn to let go of troubling thoughts about the past and/or worries about the future, thereby more fully relaxing their minds and bodies. This practice may be particularly valuable for caregivers who are experiencing significant emotional distress, as a review of recent mindfulness research has documented that engagement in mindfulness practices leads to decreases in rumination, anxiety and depressive symptoms, and increases in emotion regulation (Davis & Hayes, 2011; Hofmann, Sawyer, Witt, & Oh, 2010). The practice of mindfulness may be described to clients as described below.

Therapist: *In light of the difficulties you and your child have experienced, it would be easy to fall into focusing on the past or worrying about the impact of the sexual abuse on your child's future. However, doing that would only undermine your and your child's success in overcoming this experience. So I am going to encourage* *you (and possibly your child too) to engage in a practice known as mindfulness. Mindfulness means learning to be fully aware and engaged in the present moment. It will help you take better care of yourself. In fact, recent research has documented that learning to be fully engaged in the present moment is associated with decreases in depressive and anxious feelings as well as worrisome thoughts. One exercise we can practice to really focus on the present is noticing something that happens in the present that we usually ignore: our breathing.*

Below are some basics that can help therapists and clients begin practicing this highly effective coping skill and mindset. The authors recommend that therapists do additional reading on mindfulness to develop skills in engaging clients in this practice.

- Provide a comfortable chair and encourage the caregiver to sit with her eyes closed (if she would like) and her body in a relaxed position (i.e., uncrossed legs and arms).
- Count or choose a simple word (e.g., one, *ohm*, calm) that can be repeated with each exhalation and has a calming association or positive meaning for the caregiver.
- Encourage the caregiver to focus on her breath, inhaling and exhaling deeply and naturally, repeating the word or phrase with each exhalation.
- Ask the caregiver to focus on her breath but allow thoughts to come to mind naturally, observe them without judgment, and gently return her focus to her breath and the repetition of the chosen phrase or word.

After engaging in this practice, it is important to elicit the caregiver's feedback.

Therapist: *Tell me what that experience was like for you. Please describe how your body felt as well as the emotions and thoughts that came and went as you focused on your breathing.*

Review with the caregiver relaxation activities the child may learn that may similarly help the caregiver. When possible, it is helpful to identify practices that caregivers and children might enjoy together. Ultimately, it is most important to set caregivers and children up for success. Thus, over the next couple of sessions it is useful to identify relaxation activities that suit the particular clients in terms of their enthusiasm for the activity (e.g., focused breathing, yoga, mindfulness exercises, progressive muscle relaxation) and likelihood to follow through (e.g., favorite activity that helps them to relax their body and calm their mind).

Parenting introduced—Encouraging adaptive behaviors with positive rituals and praise

When parent training is initiated, the authors may suggest that parents begin reading a basic parent training book that is based on scientific principles that have been proven to be effective in encouraging adaptive psychosocial development in children and adolescents and healthy parent-child communication and relationships (see Appendix C for examples). The parenting skills reviewed in these books are typically derived from the social learning model, supported by empirical research, and applicable to children across diverse cultures. It is also important to note that parenting skills training should be as interactive as possible, with frequent questions tapping into the parents' knowledge about their children as well as collaborative efforts to tailor the parenting assignments to enhance the likelihood of its implementation. In addition, parenting skills training tends to be more effective when caregivers are asked to role-play and/or practice the parenting skills introduced during individual and/or conjoint sessions.

Increasing the quantity and quality of parent-child interactions

As noted before, a nurturing, positive parent-child relationship is important in supporting healing in the aftermath of sexual abuse and other traumas. Oftentimes during times of stress, such relationships become strained, as parents feel ill-equipped to manage the difficult and disturbing behaviors children sometimes exhibit as a result of their sexual abuse experiences. In fact, despite parents' best intentions, in the aftermath of CSA, parents' reactions to children's behavior problems may become more harsh and/or, due to feelings of guilt, more indulgent. Either way, these common parental reactions are likely to lead to increases in children's problem behaviors. Thus, it is critically important to support parents in terms of helping them cope while also guiding and enhancing their interactions with their children. This work often begins by encouraging parents to proactively create opportunities for daily positive interactions with their children.

Published studies of parent-child as well as teacher-child exchanges cite varying positive to negative interaction ratios associated with the maintenance of positive child adjustment ranging from 4 to 1 to 8 to 1 positive-to-negative interactions (e.g., Dumas, 1996; Latham, 1992; Wahler, Herring, & Edwards, 2001). In fact, it has been documented that increasing the positive-to-negative ratios of caregiver-child interactions can reduce the likelihood of disruptive child behaviors (Friman, Jones, Smith, Daly, & Larzelere, 1997). These findings suggest that attention to the tone and quality of parent-child interactions may be critical to minimizing the development of disruptive behaviors when children are at risk for developing such difficulties in the aftermath of CSA or other traumas. Thus, from the very start of trauma-focused cognitive-behavioral therapy (TF-CBT), the authors encourage therapists to support the revival and/or development of positive rituals, routines, and effective skills among parents and children that are likely to increase the ratio of positive to negative exchanges. This is a complex objective that requires therapists to help parents learn to encourage positive routines and provide global and specific praise as well as periodic constructive negative feedback in the context of warm, nurturing interactions. TF-CBT encourages the development of positive parent-child relations not solely from the perspective of teaching parenting skills but also by supporting the development of skills in children that will increase the likelihood that they will elicit positive reactions from parents as well as others.

Positive rituals and routines with children

One way to naturally increase positive parent-child interactions is to help parents identify rituals and routines that are positive in nature (see *Positive Rituals and Routines* handout in Appendix B). Predictable routines can be very comforting to children who have experienced sexual abuse because abuse experiences are often unpredictable and out of children's control. Positive routines and rituals especially enhance feelings of safety and security by restoring a sense of predictability in children's lives. When rituals are experienced daily or weekly at consistent times, children feel cared for and know what can be expected in terms of basic everyday activities such as morning routines, homework, meal time, and bedtime rituals. Proactively instituting pleasant rituals can, in fact, greatly increase children's compliance with even less-than-appealing activities such as homework and bedtime. It is well documented that children behave better and are comforted by environments that are structured and predictable. This process of increasing positive rituals may begin by sharing with parents the benefits of such rituals and asking if there are routines that have been disrupted and/or any rituals that they believe they could initiate on a weekly or preferably daily basis that would be beneficial to the child and family. Sometimes this leads to a return to routines that were in place before the crisis precipitated by the CSA, and/or it may result in the initiation of new positive rituals. It is best to brainstorm ideas for instituting or re-instituting positive rituals with parents. Some adaptive family routines that can be offered as examples include sitting down to dinner together and sharing positive events of the day, taking a walk together after homework is done, engaging in random acts of kindness, etc. In fact, multiple randomized trials have repeatedly documented that positive activities increase feelings of happiness among youth and adults (Layous, Chancellor, & Lyubomirsky, 2014; Sin & Lyubomirsky, 2009). Thus, caregivers may be encouraged to plan simple positive rituals that may include activities that encourage feelings of gratitude and/or acts of kindness as these types of activities have been associated with increased well-being and positive social connections (Layous et al., 2014). For example, some parents may participate more actively with their children in saying prayers together or counting blessings at bedtime or encouraging discussion about things family members are grateful for once a week at dinnertime. Other caregivers may plan family activities that are designed to help others such as participating in charity drives and/or engaging in simple random acts of kindness toward family members, friends, or neighbors. When parents model these types of behaviors, children are more likely to observe and imitate and generalize such prosocial behaviors beyond the family context, thereby enhancing their social interactions with others. In general, clinicians may collaborate with parents in identifying the type and timing of engaging in family rituals as parents and youth are more likely to engage in such activities on a regular basis if the planned positive rituals feel natural and consistent with the family's culture and values (Deci & Ryan, 2000).

With some parents it may help to emphasize how children's developing brains are positively influenced by nurturing, consistent parent-child interactions involving affection, touch, eye contact, and positive conversations during which parents both share and listen. Recent research, in fact, documented that parents, who share experiences or personal narratives about experiencing adversities and overcoming them, tend to have children who show greater resilience (Duke, Lazarus, & Fivush, 2008).

With young children there may be ample time for daily rituals to reinforce important habits and provide lots of opportunities for praise. However, as children get older, their schedules tend to get more complex, and they spend more time in group activities (e.g., sports, creative arts, and social activities) with peers, thus while brief daily rituals are encouraged with teens as well, parents may also consider engaging their teens in rituals that occur several times a week or on a weekly basis to reinforce the importance of family time and more extended parent-child interactions. Some parents establish specific activities with each of their children to ensure that they have opportunities to give each child undivided parental attention on a regular basis even if it is for a relatively limited amount of time. Such times ensure youth that if they need to share something troubling there are regular private times when they will have their parents' full attention. These shared parent-child rituals then become ideal times for parents to practice the positive parenting skills learned in the course of treatment (e.g., specific praise, reflective listening).

Positive parental attention

Some parents, especially when in throes of a crisis, may inadvertently attend to and get involved with their children more when children are engaging in negative as opposed to positive behaviors. This attention to negative behaviors sets up a pattern that can lead to increasing rather than decreasing behavioral difficulties. Thus, it is important for parents to learn to provide predictable positive attention to encourage children's positive behaviors rather than using negative parental attention in the form of begging, yelling, threatening, demanding, and/or physically punishing to discourage children's problem behaviors. The clinician should emphasize that such parenting strategies are, in fact, associated with maintaining and/or increasing children's behavioral difficulties. It is therefore useful to help parents become more aware of the power and benefits of positive parental attention in encouraging positive adaptive behaviors. When caregivers become aware of these problematic patterns of interacting with their children, they can begin to more consciously use positive attention and praise as tools to shape children's behaviors.

Parents often think of reinforcement for positive behaviors in terms of tangible items such as money and prizes which can be helpful as long as they are consistent with parental values. Tangible rewards, in fact, may be utilized in conjunction with a behavioral contract in which children engage in positive behaviors to earn an allowance or certain privileges. Such an approach can help children develop confidence in their ability to achieve specified goals through their positive behavior and hard work. Behavioral charts and contracts will be described in Chapter 9 and the *Behavior Contract* handout, respectively, as behavioral charts and concrete positive consequences can be useful to utilize with some families. Perhaps even more important than tangible consequences, however, are social consequences such as parental attention and involvement, as they are constantly being provided to children in one form or another by parents.

Most parents are not consciously aware of how powerful their attention can be in increasing children's positive behaviors and overall adjustment. Positive parental attention can be offered more consciously in the form of praise, which can be expressed in many different ways. Two forms of praise will be referred to throughout this manual: global and specific praise.

Global praise refers to parents' general expressions of adoration, love, respect, and care. This type of praise may be provided verbally (e.g., "I love you"; "I am so proud to be your parent") and/or through physical affection (e.g., hugs, kisses, high fives, etc.). Such praise is sometimes referred to as unconditional positive regard and it is important because it helps children to feel loved, secure, and important. Global praise or expressions of unconditional positive regard or love are also important to enhance feelings of security and counteract feelings of worthlessness or shame that are commonly experienced in the aftermath of abuse. Physical affection (e.g., goodnight kisses or hugs) may be a particularly important aspect of global praise to encourage parents to share with children who have experienced sexual abuse as it models touches that are appropriate and loving. Thus it behooves therapies to encourage parents' demonstrative sharing of all forms of global praise.

Specific praise helps children understand what kinds of behavior one wants to see by positively encouraging and specifically describing the desired behaviors when they are exhibited (e.g., "I really like how you took a deep breath when you were feeling frustrated"). Specific praise is important when children are learning new behaviors and when behavior change is necessary. Caregivers are encouraged to utilize specific praise to help support children's efforts to practice healthy coping behaviors and increase positive behaviors. Specific praise offered intermittently helps maintain positive behaviors that are developed.

Refocusing attention on positive behaviors

Due to the natural tendency for parents to focus on children's abuse-related symptoms and problems, it is often useful to begin behavior management training with a skill that requires parents to refocus their attention on more positive behaviors. It is in this context that the therapist can inquire about child strengths and/or positive parent-child interactions that occurred in the previous week, especially in relation to parenting skills practice activities that were recommended. Learning to effectively use specific praise or positive attention, for example, is an important skill for all parents, particularly for parents who rely heavily on negative methods (e.g., threats, scolding, spanking, evoking guilt) to influence their children's behaviors. In addition, when parents develop skills in using positive social attention, they often see immediate increases in positive child behaviors. Observation of these positive changes not only helps parents gain a greater awareness of their potential positive influence on their children, it also often inspires greater confidence in the treatment approach in general.

Many parents can benefit from learning to use positive attention and praise more effectively. Even parents who report that they give their children a great deal of positive attention may not be doing so in a way that leads to increases in positive behaviors. Some parents, in fact, give their children lots of attention in the form of global praise. Though there is no harm in being generally loving and supportive, such global attention may not help a child understand which specific behaviors are preferred or adaptive. Similarly, parents who are highly inconsistent in their delivery of attention and praise inadvertently create environments in which the contingencies are unclear and thus children remain unsure as to which behaviors will elicit parental attention and/or find that the most predictable attention is gained through negative behavior. Caregivers, in fact, may comment that their children know how to "push their buttons." This statement often reflects the fact that many youth behaviorally know how to predictably get negative attention but may not know how to consistently obtain predictable positive reactions from their parents. For these parents, training will be a process of learning the most effective ways and times to provide positive attention and specific praise so that their children really understand how to push "positive" parental buttons. Simultaneously, caregivers must learn to minimize their tendencies to provide negative attention to problematic behaviors.

Some parents are uncomfortable with the use of praise and may report that praise seems artificial and too simplistic to counteract the child's significant difficulties. For caregivers who insist that their parents used strict discipline to get them to behave and who may have received little praise themselves during childhood, learning to praise may be a difficult process that will require the therapist to validate and explore such parental feelings. With these parents, it is sometimes helpful for the therapist to inquire as to whether the parent might have had more confidence if they had received more words of praise as a child. Ultimately, however, therapists need to model and shape this parenting skill, ultimately asking caregivers to take a leap of faith in trying this important parenting skill.

Assessing parents' use of praise

To assess parents' current use of praise and positive attention, the therapist may ask parents to do one of the following exercises:

- List as many positive behaviors exhibited by the child as possible.
- Estimate the number of times they praised the child that day.
- Describe in as much detail as possible the last time they praised their child.

need some encouragement and feedback even for this simple role-play. Thus, the therapist should model praising by specifically describing the child's cooperative behaviors in his individual session. After the parent demonstrates some success in the role-play, the therapist can encourage her to praise the child in the waiting room or in the optional conjoint parent-child session described below. This role-play exercise allows the therapist to praise parents and provide them with constructive feedback before parents practice praising the agreed-upon child behavior at home. Therapists may also model effective praise for parents by themselves offering specific, purely positive, and highly enthusiastic praise for child behaviors exhibited in the waiting room or in session in the presence of the parent. The therapist also uses parallel process during TF-CBT by using these same praise strategies to reinforce parents' positive behaviors. For example, when the parent uses desired parenting strategies with the child, the therapist may review the interaction and praise the effective parenting behavior during the individual parent session.

Psychoeducation about CSA

Gradual exposure to CSA information continues during this early phase of treatment, as it is important to continue to raise issues related to the sexual abuse in each session until parents are comfortable and fully prepared to openly communicate with their child about CSA and possibly hear their child's narrative in the consolidation and closure phase of treatment. Thus, psychoeducation continues during this session with the objectives of providing additional information about CSA, while creating an environment in which parents feel comfortable sharing any CSA-related questions and/or concerns they may have. During this session it is important to review and elicit any questions that may have been stimulated by reading the *Child Sexual Abuse Information* handout. Although there may be times the therapist will be unable to answer parents' questions, it is important for the therapist to demonstrate a willingness to either pursue the answers on their behalf (e.g., by contacting the physician who examined the child in the aftermath of the abuse) and/or direct them to the person(s) that can assist them (e.g., a victim witness counselor associated with the prosecutor's or district attorney's office).

CSA information that is being provided to the child should also be shared with parents including information as basic as the doctor's terms for private parts (i.e., vagina, breasts, penis, and buttocks) that will be used and/or taught to their children. This information is important to discuss, as these terms will be new to some children and parents will occasionally object to their use. However, most parents are accepting of the use of these terms once they understand that the use of such terms not only helps children be clear about what they experienced but it may reduce their feelings of shame and enhance their ability to talk comfortably about the sexual abuse. Moreover, if children ever need to report a CSA threat or experience in the future they are much more likely to get the attention of authorities and proper protection when they use the correct terms. It can also be useful to demonstrate for parents how the child may play educational games in session by sharing some of the questions that will be reviewed in the context of an educational question and answer game with the child. It is empowering and confidence building to share and collaborate with parents in this way.

Psychoeducation about self-care for parents

It is also essential for parents to understand how the above relaxation and parenting skills exercises are tied to helping them and their children overcome an experience such as sexual abuse. Thus, it is important to explain that when emotional and/or behavioral problems develop, whatever the cause (i.e., sexual abuse, exposure to violence, or other stressors), if ignored, they can take on a life of their own and create further difficulties. However, when directly addressed, parents and children can learn skills that will not only help them manage the current difficulties but will be available to them as they face the ups and downs of life in the future. Most importantly, parents should be reminded that the most important thing they can do to help their child overcome the effects of CSA and/or other stressors is to be the model of coping that they would like to see in their child. For many parents, their child's well-being may be strong motivation for them to make adjustments in their coping and parenting approaches to optimize the child's recovery.

The therapist may introduce the handout *Self Care: Taking Care of Yourself and Your Child* explaining that the handout emphasizes the importance of parents taking care of themselves while simultaneously working to take care of their children's needs. This handout emphasizes the need for parents to practice the same healthy coping strategies their children will be learning. In addition, by reinstituting or creating positive routines and rituals that support healthy coping strategies, they will be more likely to maintain positive changes they are making in the future. Maintaining positive behavior change is difficult. Incorporating these positive behaviors into routines or daily habits enhances the likelihood of sustaining positive changes in the long run. Thus, during each session the clinician will teach parents the same coping skills that the child is learning. Parents are encouraged to develop structured routines that incorporate these skills into their lives to more effectively manage day-to-day stressors as well as the crisis of discovering that their child has been sexually abused. It is important to emphasize that when parents learn and practice these skills on a routine basis they will not only begin to feel better but also will be serving as excellent coping role models for their children, thereby supporting their children's healing and recovery.

Practice activities assigned: Self-care and parenting

Parents may be provided with handouts that will support the topics covered in their individual session(s). This may include an assignment to encourage their efforts toward self-care, as well as activities to support the implementation of effective parenting skills. The therapist may choose to provide the parent with written resources (e.g., handouts, parenting book, or Internet materials) about self-care, parenting (e.g., rituals and routines as well as praise), and/or other topics. The therapist may then review the basic information provided in the resource(s) with the parent and ask whether the parent has questions. Information about self-care is designed to encourage parents to focus on taking care of themselves in a variety of domains of functioning. This may mean reengaging in healthy routines for themselves and/or establishing special parent-child time that allows them to connect with their child in the context of a pleasant ritual. The practice assignments may be individually tailored to support the parents. The child and parents should be informed that they will be asked to report back on the agreed-upon activities or skills practiced.

The introduction of parenting skills often focuses on reestablishing positive rituals and/or the effective use of specific praise. Thus, it may be helpful to review information about the value of positive routines and rituals and/or implementing praise. Handouts are provided for those parents who might find such written materials helpful (see *Positive Rituals and Routines* and/or *PRAISE: The Power of Positive Attention* handouts in Appendix B). Parents typically do best when they identify one simple specific behavior that their child is exhibiting to some degree (e.g., helping clear the table) but they would like to see more often. This gives parents the opportunity to see praise work before they begin to apply the parenting strategies to encourage more complex positive behaviors. In addition, parents may be encouraged to specifically and purely positively praise their children when they see attempts at practicing the coping skills they are learning throughout treatment.

Prepare for conjoint parent-child session

If time allows, parents may be prepared for a brief conjoint session in which they will have the opportunity to practice their praise skills. This conjoint activity, however, should not be attempted if there is not sufficient time for preparation as many parents need coaching and preparation to effectively offer specific praise. In their individual session, parents should be coached to identify and praise a specific positive behavior that their child exhibited during the previous week. It is helpful if this behavior is one that can replace a problematic behavior about which parents are concerned, but it need not be during this first praise exercise. It is, however, important to avoid focusing on the problem behavior but rather to follow the praise guidelines discussed offering specific "purely positive" praise for an adaptive behavior. It is important to review with the parent and role-play this interaction, as parents do not necessarily know how to offer specific praise that will be productive. Simply reviewing exactly what the parent plans to say when offering specific praise to the child during the conjoint session provides an opportunity to help the parent be more specific in offering praise and less critical by avoiding negative tags that might undermine the praise. Many parents have a tendency to be negative even when they are trying to be positive (e.g., "I like how you cleaned your room, why don't you do that more often?"). However, with repeated practice and constructive feedback in individual and conjoint session, parents can improve their skills in using positive parental attention and praise to encourage adaptive behaviors in their children.

It also may be particularly important for children who have been sexually abused to experience global praise and learn to express and receive affection in healthy ways. However, it is important to be sensitive when encouraging exchanges of words or gestures of love as these may be closely tied to cultural norms. Many parents are comfortable following their specific praise with a simple expression of "I love you," or they may demonstrate this feeling with a hug or another similar expression of affection such as "I am so proud to be your mom." Other parents may feel awkward if it is not typical for them to express their feelings of love and affection in a verbal manner or in public. The motivation of those parents to express their unconditional love may increase once they understand how an experience such as sexual abuse can erode a child's feelings of worthiness. Thus, it can be helpful to encourage such interactions during some conjoint sessions as well as between sessions.

CHILD SESSION(S)

Children who have experienced sexual abuse and/or other traumas may feel anxious and unsure of what to expect in therapy. Thus, it is often helpful to begin the session by establishing the agenda with emphasis on the activities the child is most likely to enjoy including an end-of-session positive ritual they might look forward to after completing the less appealing therapy activities.

Introduce relaxation skills training

Early treatment may include a number of relaxation exercises that help children and/or adolescents learn to manage the physical and mental stress that they may feel on a daily basis. A variety of relaxation activities that can be fun and effective are described below. Therapists are encouraged to identify activities that they find particularly useful themselves, as well as those that may be best suited for their clients. It is not anticipated that clients will master the many different types of relaxation exercises described, rather it is best to identify a couple that are most likely to be implemented successfully by one's clients. The relaxation strategies described below are suggestions. However, therapists need to explore with children and adolescents what strategies may work best for them.

Mindfulness can also be introduced to children and adolescents as it can help them gain greater awareness of their feelings, thoughts, behaviors, and bodily sensations in the present moment. This information is valuable in developing many of the coping skills that will be learned throughout treatment and may help to optimize success during the narrative development and processing component. Mindfulness is designed to encourage a nonjudgmental focus and immersion in the present moment. This focus often helps children who have experienced trauma to gain a greater acceptance of what is and increases awareness of the relative calm experienced when one is fully focused on only the present moment. As noted earlier, mindfulness may be particularly helpful for children and caregivers who experience intrusive traumatic memories and/or worries about the implications of past trauma(s) on the future. Being stuck in the past or worried about the future often leads to mental and physical suffering. Mindfulness can help clients return their focus to the present moment.

In the context of TF-CBT, children may be encouraged to notice whatever feelings, thoughts, and sensations they experience in the present moment. Children should be reminded that this exercise encourages the acknowledging and accepting of whatever it is they are feeling, sensing, and thinking with no judgment. Although some of what is experienced during this exercise will be the troubling thoughts and feelings that brought them to therapy, when clients experience these thoughts and feelings in a comfortable, safe, and encouraging therapy environment, the current thoughts and feelings are likely to be less intense than they were at the time of the traumatic experiences. Noticing this difference in intensity is an important part of gradual exposure, leading children to be less avoidant of traumatic memories. TF-CBT, in fact, is designed to help children learn positive lessons from past experiences so they can then move on and live more fully and comfortably in the present.

Young children hardly need instruction in mindfulness as they often are naturally inclined to fully engage in the present moment. This may be the reason why some young children who have experienced sexual abuse are less distressed than their parents as they have little concern for the implications of their abuse on the future. However, young children do absorb the stress around them that may be generated by the distress exhibited by the concerned adults who are responding to the sexual abuse allegations, investigation, and other proceedings associated with CSA. Preschool children are acutely attuned to their parents' levels of distress but fortunately they are also often natural experts on mindfulness and relaxation. Young children are, in fact, frequently engaged in present moment activities such as when they fully immerse themselves in playing in the sand or the mud, finger painting with abandon, closely scrutinizing flowers or insects, or engaging in uninhibited imaginative play. Allowing for this type of play for a few minutes at the end of a session may not only be experienced as a reward for the hard work of therapy but can be a great stress reducer for children and can reinforce the value of present moment activity.

With older children and adolescents, mindfulness may best be introduced in the context of learning to respond to the fast pace and stress of our daily lives by slowing down, relaxing, and focusing on just "being" in the present moment. There are many wonderful ways of introducing mindfulness to children as well as adolescents through the use of books, CDs, DVDs, and computer applications.

Several educational tools for helping children practice mindfulness are included in the resource appendix (Appendix C).

The dialogue in Box 7.2 demonstrates how the TF-CBT therapist introduces mindfulness and highlights the present moment focus.

Focused breathing is an important relaxation skill that can benefit many children and parents. Moreover, it can be introduced in a manner that reinforces mindfulness concepts as well. As noted in the parent session, it helps to carefully set the stage for introducing this critical skill with the following steps:

- Provide a comfortable chair and encourage the child to sit with eyes closed (or open if preferable) and her body in a relaxed position (i.e., uncrossed legs and arms).
- Count or choose a simple word (e.g., one, "ohm", calm) that can be repeated with each exhalation and has a calming association or positive meaning for the child.
- Encourage the child to focus on breathing, inhaling and exhaling deeply and naturally, repeating the word or phrase with each exhalation.
- Explain that when thoughts enter the mind, the child should simply notice them and then gently refocus on the breath and the repetition of the chosen phrase or word.

Learning to practice simple deep breathing can enhance feelings of calm, which is particularly important given the physiological symptoms of anxiety that are often associated with PTSD that many children experience in the aftermath of sexual abuse. Moreover, learning to make the association between the act of taking a few deep breaths and the feelings of calm that such a simple act generates is often surprising to both children and their parents. Thus, it is important to not only teach clients to take notice of their breathing as this can help them to return to the present moment but also to notice how such deep breathing impacts their feelings and the tension levels in their bodies. This increased awareness can be achieved through a discussion about how they felt physically and emotionally after engaging in this simple breathing exercise.

Yoga is another activity that may be taught in combination with mindfulness as a means of engaging the body while simultaneously calming or quieting the mind. Practicing yoga and mindfulness can help children learn to be mindfully aware of their bodies while also gaining pride in the flexibility and balance they can achieve. Such exercises can encourage children to develop enhanced feelings of acceptance and pride in their bodies. This practice may be valuable for children who feel uncomfortable with their bodies due to their experience of sexual abuse. Yoga, in fact, may counteract negative body images and attitudes children may have developed as a result of the sexual abuse. Yoga activities for children, adolescents, and adults can be encouraged with simple practice poses in session. Yoga books and/or videos that therapists can lend or recommend for practice at home are included in the resources appendix (Appendix C). However, with the increasing popularity of yoga practice in the general population, there

Box 7.2

Case Example: Encouraging Present Moment Focus

Therapist: *As you know, we will be talking some about the things that happened to you in the past including the sexual abuse, but it is important to live life in the* present. *Why do you think that is?*

Child: *I'm not sure, but maybe because you can't do anything about the past.*

Therapist: *Exactly. Usually life is better if you are fully focused on the present instead of thinking about the past or worrying about the future.*

Child: *I try really hard not to think about the past but I do worry about the future a lot.*

Therapist: *A lot of people do that. Worrying about the future is actually a habit that many people have. But one thing we can learn to do is become more engaged in the present because usually what you fear in the future may be very unlikely to happen. Also, whatever is happening right in this moment is usually okay and not as bad as what you are worried about. Does that make sense to you?*

Child: *I guess. Right now I do feel okay but I worry about what is going to happen next.*

Therapist: *That does happen when you have been through a lot of difficult things and your mind and your body start to assume more bad things are coming. Sometimes without even realizing it, this can cause you to breathe really fast all the time or walk around with muscles that are all tensed up, sort of ready for the next bad thing to happen. This kind of breathing and muscle tension over time can cause you to feel pretty lousy. Do you ever feel lousy and you don't know why?*

Child: *Yeah. I feel nervous a lot. Sometimes I don't even know what I'm nervous about. And sometimes I get really bad headaches; my mom took me to see a doctor about them.*

Therapist: *Yes. Your mom was glad that your doctor gave your head an A+ for functioning just fine. It may be that the stress that you have been under was contributing to those headaches. And that is why we are going to practice focusing on the present because that will remind your body and your brain to stay in the present where things are okay. We can start by learning to focus on breathing because that really helps to focus the mind on something that is happening right in this moment. What do you think about that?*

Child: *My breathing?*

Therapist: *Usually we are completely unaware of breathing—this important and powerful thing our bodies do for us every day to keep us running smoothly. So what do you think about saluting this beautiful process, that we usually completely ignore, by taking some time today to notice our breathing?*

Child: *Okay. I'll try.*

Therapist: *Let's sit back and you can close your eyes or you can keep your eyes open and just focus on a picture on the wall.*

Child: *I'll look at your flower picture.*

Therapist: *Okay. Now let's sit together for just two minutes focusing on taking a full deep breath in through the nose and exhaling fully out through the mouth. Your thoughts might go in all different directions but see if you can bring your mind back to simply noticing your breaths as you inhale and exhale while you look at that pretty flower picture. I will let you know when two minutes are about to end.*

Child: *Seems kind of silly, but I'll try it.*

Therapist: *Great. And if your mind wanders away from your breath, gently bring your thoughts back to noticing your breaths by repeating the word "calm" after each exhalation.*

After engaging in this practice, it is important to elicit the child's feedback.

Therapist: *Tell me what that experience was like for you. Please describe how your body felt as well as the emotions and thoughts that came and went as you focused on your breathing.*

---

are numerous books, CDs, DVDs and computer applications to choose from that may be especially appealing to clients. Though clients' medical and/or physical limitations should be carefully considered, almost any child, adolescent, or caregiver can learn simple yoga positions that may be utilized in combination with mindfulness activities.

Progressive muscle relaxation, guided imagery, and other relaxation activities

Children who have experienced sexual abuse may carry a great deal of tension in their bodies. As a result of repeated and unpredictable experiences of sexual abuse, children may feel as if they do not have control over access to their bodies. This sense of a lack of control leads some children to experience a great deal of somatic stress that manifests itself in the form of muscular tension, headaches, stomachaches, and other stress-related symptoms that are often associated with PTSD and more generalized anxiety. Though it is important for parents to discuss physical symptoms and somatic complaints with their children's physicians, if there appears to be no underlying medical explanation, these symptoms may be highly responsive to relaxation exercises. These more active relaxation skills may give children a greater sense of control over the anxiety and physiological symptoms they may experience when traumatic memories are triggered or when confronted by abuse reminders in their environment.

Older children (i.e., those over 10 years of age) may be taught progressive relaxation including guided tension-releasing exercises. Some children may not have the attention span to work through all of the muscle groups in one session. Thus, the therapist may want to teach head, torso, and leg exercises separately or identify and focus on the most problematic muscle groups. For example, children who are prone to headaches may learn to focus on relaxing the muscles in their forehead, jaw, neck, and shoulders.

Some children, particularly younger ones, may be more responsive to image-induced relaxation. They may be taught to distinguish states of bodily tension and relaxation respectively by standing very straight and stiff like a "tin soldier or uncooked spaghetti" and collapsing into a chair like a "rag doll or wet noodle" (Deblinger & Heflin, 1996) or "pretending you're an elephant with a long, heavy trunk hanging to the ground" (Runyon, Basilio, Van Hasselt, & Hersen, 1998). It is important to have children notice the difference in their bodily sensations when they tense and relax. The child may then learn to elicit the "rag doll" feelings in the face of anxiety through personalized self-instructions such as relax, hang loose, lighten up, or calm down. Imagery can also be used to help children imagine that they are in a very relaxing and/or safe place. Young children sometimes describe their relaxing place as being in a cartoon or fantasy world or engaging in an activity they enjoy (i.e., playing in the park or riding a bike), while older adolescents may describe a beautiful scene such as a beach. Many children respond well to guided imagery that involves the use of DVDs, sounds of nature, music, or songs. For example, a simple song that children enjoy that encourages relaxing images, is "Row Row Row Your Boat." In addition to eliciting relaxing images, the lyrics—*row row row your boat gently down the stream, merrily merrily merrily merrily, life is but a dream*—reinforce the concept of acceptance in that they encourage the idea of going with the current rather than rowing upstream against it.

At this stage in therapy, children who have experienced sexual abuse may prefer not to do relaxation exercises with their eyes closed or lying down, as this may give rise to traumatic memories and feelings of vulnerability. Thus, it may be preferable to have children sit in a comfortable chair and to give them the choice of keeping their eyes open or closed when doing any of the mindfulness or relaxation exercises.

Appendix C provides information about some useful materials to facilitate the teaching of mindfulness, focused breathing, and/or relaxation skills as does the TF-CBT online training web site (www.musc.edu.tfcbt). TF-CBT*Web* contains some excellent examples of therapists presenting relaxation strategies to children of different ages that can be used to prepare for session or shared with children as a way of teaching them the skills.

Later in therapy, the therapist may also have the child use relaxation skills at the beginning of a challenging exposure or narrative development session that the child is anticipating with anxiety. Alternatively, relaxation skills may be used in a paradigm more similar to systematic desensitization, with a state of relaxation being induced and paired with a particularly anxiety provoking image of the abusive experience. Therapists should be aware of the possibility that children may use relaxation skills as a means of avoiding the gradual exposure work. Thus, it is preferable not to interrupt gradual exposure work to implement relaxation exercises except when there seems to be no other way of pursuing the work of gradual exposure.

Many children are able to tolerate narrative development and discussions of their abuse without active use of relaxation skills during the writing of the narrative as long as the increasingly anxiety-provoking memories are faced in a carefully paced, gradual manner. However, the presentation and review of relaxation skills early in treatment can help all children feel more confident in their ability to manage distressing bodily sensations in case they arise in or outside of session. Therapists are encouraged to present mindfulness, focused breathing, yoga, and/or other relaxation activities in ways that are fun and engaging for children. This can facilitate the development of positive attitudes toward therapy that may replace the feared negative associations between therapy and the aversive experience of recalling the abuse-related memories.

Psychoeducation about CSA and other relevant trauma(s) continued

Many children who have experienced sexual abuse exhibit generalized avoidance and distress in response to all abuse-related cues. However, this avoidance reduces their ability to obtain the needed information to effectively process their abusive experiences. Thus, it is important to provide psychoeducation about CSA. Children often seem to find it easier to talk about sexual abuse in the abstract than to talk about their personal experience of abuse. Thus, it is helpful to initiate and/or continue gradual exposure with additional information about CSA. This is important from the standpoint of helping children overcome avoidance but also because this gradual exposure may begin to naturally correct inaccurate or unhealthy beliefs that sometimes develop as a result of the abusive experiences and/or ideas conveyed by the offender. Engaging in an informal discussion, playing an educational game, or reading educational materials are useful ways to continue the gradual exposure process with children.

A game widely used in the context of TF-CBT is The *What Do You Know?* card game (Deblinger, Neubauer, Runyon, & Baker, 2006), which was developed to educate children about different types of abuse (i.e., physical abuse, sexual abuse, domestic violence) and body safety. With younger children, the clinician may create or use a limited set of cards that ask simple questions reflecting basic information about sexual abuse and/or other trauma(s). With older children and adolescents, the clinician may use more cards and can provide more detailed information about sexual abuse and other types of interpersonal violence as a significant proportion of children who have been sexually abused have experienced other forms of violence as well. The game also includes blank cards so personalized questions can be added for youth who appear more open and ready to begin discussing some of the more general aspects of their own sexual abuse experiences. There are many interesting ways to engage children in a fun psychoeducation question and answer game. Some therapists and children have used dice to determine who gets the potential to win points first (i.e., the person who throws the higher number on the dice can go first). Other therapists have used a game show format in which they will give points or stickers for effort (i.e., any attempt at answer the question), as well as for accurate answers so that the child can earn enough points to win a small prize.

To make psychoeducation activities appealing to youth of all ages, clinicians may use the *What Do You Know?* cards or develop their own set of index cards with CSA-related questions that can be used with any number of trademarked games (Runyon & Deblinger, 2014). For example, color-coded cards could be used with Twister by Hasbro so that each time a participant answers a question correctly she places her hand or foot on the respective color on the Twister mat and answers a general abuse-related question (e.g., "What is a 'not okay' touch?"; "How do children feel when they get a 'not okay' touch?"). A similar process can be followed by attaching small pieces of colored paper to the pieces of Jenga by Hasbro. When a participant pulls a piece with a particular color she takes a card with the corresponding color and answers a CSA question. The reverse can also be used so that after the player answers a question on a particular card, she removes a Jenga piece with the corresponding color. Any number of age-appropriate games can be turned into an educational game by encouraging children to answer a CSA or other trauma-related question in order to get a turn or move ahead on the game board. Such an approach allows the clinician to choose a game that is not only developmentally appropriate but one that may be particularly appealing to the client based on her interests. Some games that TF-CBT therapists have used to engage children of diverse ages and interests include Candyland, pick-up sticks, Barrel of Monkeys, checkers, The Game of Life, and Monopoly. It is also possible to use computer game applications as long as the focus remains on answering and discussing the abuse-related questions.

Some basic questions that are important to review early in treatment include: "What is CSA?" "What are some 'not okay' touches?" "How do children feel when they have been sexually abused?" and "Who sexually abuses children?" It is important to elicit answers from the children before providing answers to these and other questions. Children often have more information and a better understanding of sexual abuse than is realized by most adults. It can be encouraging to them to receive praise for the accurate information they have. In cases in which clients do not have accurate information, it is important to elicit their responses so their misconceptions can be identified. These misconceptions may be corrected by offering children more accurate general information or examples that may help them rethink their responses and come to more appropriate conclusions. For example, if a child believes that this happens only to girls, the therapist can point out the pictures in the office that were drawn by boys who experienced sexual abuse. In addition, the therapist might reinforce that CSA happens to a lot of children by asking how many children in the local school the child thinks may have experienced CSA and engaging in a discussion about that.

It is important to note that for some children, such as those exhibiting age-inappropriate sexual behaviors (see Chapter 16), education about the rules regarding "okay" and "not okay" touches are important to address at this stage of therapy, whereas for most children it is better to delay the full discussion about specific body safety responses and skills until after they have completed much of their narrative. This delay in educational discussions about body safety is important to minimize the risk of increasing a child's self-blame as some of these skills may not have been used by the child at the time of the abuse (e.g., saying no and getting away) due to confusion, fear, or a lack of understanding that what was happening was wrong. Thus, questions about body safety (e.g., "What could you do if anyone touches you with a 'not okay' touch?") are better reviewed during the final component after the child has written and processed her narrative.

Gradual exposure

The process of discussing this educational information regarding abuse allows the child to further reflect on her own experience of abuse without focusing on or sharing the specific details at this early stage of treatment. For example, when asking what is CSA or what is physical abuse, the therapist might list (i.e., on paper or a white board) the behaviors the child identified as abusive. Next, the therapist may personalize the exercise by asking the child to circle the types of abusive experiences she experienced herself. For example, the therapist might say, "Now, please circle the things that you experienced at the time of the sexual abuse."

This is an important opportunity to continue the gradual exposure process with gentle questions that naturally stem from the general and abstract discussion about CSA. Educational activities not only provide basic information about sexual abuse and/or other trauma(s) the child experienced but also contribute substantially to the gradual exposure process and prepare the child for the trauma narrative and cognitive processing that will occur later in treatment. Because children learn through repetition, these educational points may be expanded upon and reviewed throughout the course of therapy.

Though therapists are not encouraged to engage children in detailed discussions of their abusive experiences during this session, some acknowledgement of the child's experience of abuse is an important part of every session as it contributes to the gradual exposure process. Thus, though the focus in this session is on sharing the concept of mindfulness, teaching relaxation skills, and providing general education about CSA, it is appropriate and helpful to make reference to the child's experience of abuse and link the learned skills to how the skills will help in coping with the CSA. For example, therapists may inquire about trauma reminders in the child's environment and/or times the child thinks about or is reminded of the sexually abusive experience. If these reminders cause distress, the mindfulness and/or relaxation exercises can then be introduced as a means of responding to the tension and/or physiological symptoms the trauma reminders may trigger. If children deny any such reminders or intrusive thoughts, the skills may be encouraged as general tools for managing the stress everyone experiences in the context of daily life. It is important to note that eliciting information about trauma triggers in a child's environment not only furthers the gradual exposure process but may also be helpful later when working with the parent to identify and understand the factors that may be contributing to the child's behavioral difficulties.

Practice activities encouraged

Clients should be encouraged to practice their relaxation skills between sessions. Although it is preferable for children to be encouraged to practice their choice of relaxation exercises at home daily, if it seems unrealistic based on discussions with parents, the clinician might suggest a plan that requires the child to practice the exercises twice during the week at agreed upon times.

A child who has difficulty falling asleep due to associations between the sexual abuse and being in a bed may find it particularly useful to utilize relaxation and/or mindfulness strategies at bedtime. However, children should be instructed not to practice relaxation exercises exclusively as a prelude to sleeping as the goal is to help children achieve a conscious state of relaxation when they are awake and confronting fears. After children are consistently able to achieve a state of relaxation at these times, therapists may encourage them to use this skill in several different situations including bedtime.

Prepare for conjoint session

Prepare child to teach parent relaxation skill

During a conjoint session, the child can teach the parent a relaxation skill that was mastered in his individual session. It is important to assess the usefulness of this exercise and to prepare the child adequately. This conjoint session activity is not required and should only be undertaken if the child is likely to feel successful and have a positive interaction with the parent.

Prepare child for mutual exchange of praise

The mutual exchange of praise is a fun end-of-session activity for both parents and children. To prepare children for this exercise, it is helpful to encourage the child to identify and write down specific and global praise for the parent as sometimes children forget what they planned to say in the conjoint session. When global praise is explained to children, they are often more comfortable expressing their unconditional love in words and actions (e.g., "I love you," hugs, etc.) than parents, which breaks the ice for many parents. The therapist may elicit from the child several ideas for specific praise for the parent as well. Children may be encouraged to identify times when the parent has engaged in positive parenting activities such as rituals around bedtime or dinnertime (e.g., reading stories or cooking a meal together), helping with homework, listening, praising for a job well done, showing affection, and/or participating in or attending child activities that are more likely to support the development of positive parent-child interactions. Again, it is okay to steer children toward praise that acknowledges everyday healthy interactions as opposed to yearly events and/or pleasurable but unhealthy practices (e.g., going out for fast food and/or once a year events like vacation trips). Parents rarely receive specific praise from anyone for their daily parenting efforts. Thus, both parents and children genuinely seem to enjoy this conjoint activity.

Positive end-of-session rituals

At the end of children's individual sessions, it is important to reserve time for positive end-of-session rituals designed to help children decompress especially after discussing difficult trauma-related topics (i.e., the CSA education activity listed above) and/or sharing trauma memories. A child who enjoys art projects, for example, might enjoy creating a coping skills tool kit as described below. However, end-of-session activities need not be related to the session goals. Rather the main objective of such a ritual is to elicit feelings of relaxation and other positive emotions. Any brief activity or interaction that the child looks forward to can be very meaningful and motivating to some children. Given the limited session time, these rituals should not require much time. Some examples of brief rituals include eliciting brief updates on the child's soccer team's progress, checking out a new picture on the child's smart phone, exchanging riddles or jokes, sharing a piece of music, or engaging in a special way of shaking hands. Other fun mindfulness or relaxation activities that have been identified by the child can be used as rewarding end-of-session activities that not only reinforce the child's efforts and hard work during session but also provide further practice of these important skills at the end of a session.

Some TF-CBT therapists have found it useful to create an ongoing art project as a positive end-of-session ritual that incorporates what has been learned in treatment. A coping skills tool kit, for example, can take the form of an artistic poster project, an index box that is decorated, or a PowerPoint presentation. The index box, for example, will eventually include cards that describe the various coping skills learned. Thus, toward the end of each session, the child could create a new artistic card for the box that describes the coping skill learned. Thus, it is useful to elicit from the child the activities learned or naturally used that she finds most relaxing. In this way, the therapist can help the child create her very own coping tool kit. The "kit" or "list" will eventually include not only the relaxation activities learned and practiced during the session but other coping skills the child uses naturally or learns. The "kit" may start with the child's favorite relaxation activities, which later can be added to when the child begins to learn other affective modulation and cognitive coping strategies. Eventually it may be useful to help the child create her top five or ten coping favorites for the coping tool kit. For highly dysregulated children who may need grounding before engaging in more anxiety-provoking exposure-based therapy activities, it can be helpful to draw from this list of relaxation activities at the beginning of sessions.

CONJOINT SESSION(S)

In the stabilization and skill-building phase of treatment, conjoint parent-child sessions are optional, but they are recommended because they can be effective in enhancing the parent-child relationship. Conjoint sessions provide opportunities for children to demonstrate to their parents the coping skills they are learning, while parents have a chance to practice parenting skills (e.g., praise and active ignoring) as therapists observe and in turn provide constructive feedback.

Child teaches parent chosen relaxation skill learned in individual session

Conjoint session activities can provide fun opportunities for children to teach parents the skills they are learning. It helps to remind parents, however, to follow the guidelines for praise—focusing and praising only what the child is doing well—in the conjoint session. It may be helpful to predict for parents that children often exhibit some natural nervousness and noncompliance during these sessions which the therapist will redirect if necessary. Clinicians may remind parents that it is best to continue to focus on the child's positive behavior. After the child demonstrates the relaxation skill, for example, the parent may be prompted to offer specific, purely positive praise and/or the therapist may model such praise. If the therapist feels the parent is likely to be highly negative, there is no need to engage in this optional conjoint session this early in treatment.

Encourage practice activities at home

It is generally best to encourage practice activities at home that have been carefully reviewed and practiced in individual and/or conjoint session. Thus, practice assignments should be individually tailored to reflect what has been covered in session. For example, after having the child teach and/or practice the relaxation skills with the parent during the conjoint session, the therapist may help the parent and child agree on a plan to practice the relaxation skills at home. This plan should be developed collaboratively and should be one that is likely to be met with success. It should not be so ambitious that it will inadvertently increase conflict between the parent and child. Therefore, although parents should be encouraged to complete their parenting and coping skills practice so they can serve as effective role models, their role with respect to their child is to focus on "catching" their child using relaxation skills or managing stress effectively and offering specific praise. For children, practicing coping skills may be encouraged, but its completion will be addressed by the therapist rather than the parents. In fact, parents should be strongly discouraged from nagging, begging, cajoling, or yelling about their child's use of coping skills at home, as this will inadvertently reinforce noncompliance with therapy assignments. It may be emphasized to parents that practicing their own coping skills as much as possible, and "catching" their child doing well and offering specific praise, will not only bring out the best in their child but will also reduce their child's risk of developing any difficulties in the future.

Parent shares specific and/or global praise

This is a brief conjoint activity that may be helpful. During this exercise, parents may express both global praise and specific praise for a behavior that was identified with the help and guidance of the therapist. This exercise can be particularly helpful for parents whose children are experiencing behavior problems as such parents often need encouragement and constructive feedback on how to offer purely positive specific praise. Children with disruptive behavior problems often hear about what they are doing wrong, and parent-child interactions tend to be more negative. Thus, this activity provides parents with an opportunity to practice providing both specific and global praise to the child in an optimal fashion. The therapist assists in this process by not only encouraging the parent to prepare and practice their praise in the individual parent sessions (as described above) but also sets the stage for the parent to effectively provide praise. This may be done by directing the parent and child to sit next to one another, make eye contact, and for the parent to minimize attention to any distracting child behaviors while offering purely positive praise for an adaptive behavior the child engaged in during the prior week. It is also useful to encourage parents to take note of the child's reactions, which are often quite positive while also warning parents that children sometimes are taken by surprise and show disbelieving reactions (e.g., rolling of the eyes) that will lessen with time. However, it is important to discourage parents from linking specific praise with unconditional expressions of love as it is important for children to know that they are loved regardless of their specific positive or negative behaviors and/or their successes or failures.

Mutual exchange of praise

Time permitting, at some point, it can be quite healing to encourage a mutual exchange of praise between parent and child during a conjoint session. However, the child will need to be prepared in his individual session to share specific and/or global praise with his parent as described earlier in the mutual exchange of praise activity (see p. 160 of this chapter). Although with some families this *mutual exchange of praise* may initially feel artificial, with time, most parents and children look forward to this brief end-of-session positive ritual.

8

Affective Expression and Modulation Skills

Parents may continue to be seen before their children until they have gained trust in the therapist-client relationship, as well as the trauma-focused cognitive-behavioral therapy (TF-CBT) model. However, when parents and children feel comfortable (which often occurs by this component), children may be seen first, thus allowing therapists to incorporate information regarding what was accomplished with the child into the parent session. Not only is there flexibility regarding who is seen first (e.g., the parent is seen first if he or she wants to update the therapist on something that happened during the week), the order of engaging in the various practice activities in this component may vary as well. There is a great deal to cover in this component, and thus therapists are encouraged to use their own creativity to engage youth in learning and practicing affect expression and modulation skills. Similarly, creativity, compassion, and patience are also critical in finding ways to help parents practice the affect expression, modulation, and parenting skills in session and at home.

This chapter describes sessions that incorporate continued psychoeducation, parenting, and coping skills with an emphasis on promoting mastery of affective expression and modulation. Children who have experienced multiple, chronic, and/or complex trauma reactions may say they feel "nothing" (e.g., emotional numbing), may demonstrate their anger or anxiety in behaviors rather than words, and/or may have severe problems with emotional dysregulation. In some cases, expressing feelings may have been unsafe in these children's living circumstances, and it is critical for the therapist to ascertain whether doing so in the child's current living circumstances is safe before encouraging affective expression outside of therapy. In fact, there is some evidence that parents of children with anxiety disorders may model less emotional expressiveness and may discourage emotional expression in their children (Suveg, Zeman, Flannery-Schroeder, & Cassano, 2005). Thus, parallel work on affective expression and modulation with parents is crucial.

In general, it should be noted that some youth may test the therapist's trustworthiness at many points during treatment before revealing their most vulnerable feelings; thus, the focus on affective expression and regulation may continue for several sessions until these youth gain an enhanced ability to regulate their emotions. Most children, however, can achieve some level of affective expression and sufficient emotional regulation to move forward within several sessions. Achievement of optimal emotional regulation by the child is not required to move forward in TF-CBT treatment. As long as the youth shows some progress in emotional regulation capacity, it is important not to get stuck on this component. Thus, after several affective regulation sessions, even children who are "stably unstable" may continue to move forward with the model. "Stably unstable" refers to children or teens who may be in a state in which they exhibit some of their long-standing emotional and behavioral difficulties but are beginning to implement the coping skills they have learned and are not exhibiting extreme behavioral and/or emotional difficulties (i.e., suicidal behaviors and/or dangerous acting-out behaviors). Still, it is important to encourage the repeated practicing of newly learned affective expression and regulation to ensure that youth are internalizing these important coping skills.

Similarly, the critical parenting skills introduced in this component of TF-CBT often require repetition over several sessions before caregivers successfully and consistently implement them at home. Parents are also encouraged to learn and practice effective emotional expression and regulation, as they are their children's most critical role models in this regard. When there are minimal behavioral and emotional difficulties, children and parents may breeze through this component in one or two sessions, whereas others may continue to need a focus on additional affective regulation and/or parenting skills for several additional sessions. Thus, the number of sessions focused on this component may range from one to as many as five sessions.

CHILD SESSION(S)

The main objectives of the affective expression and modulation skills component for children are (1) developing and/or expanding their emotional vocabulary, (2) learning to recognize and share their own emotions with others, (3) accurately identifying and/or inquiring about emotions in others, and (4) learning to effectively manage their emotional distress.

Practice activities review

It is useful to begin by reviewing how the child did using the relaxation skills at home. The therapist should emphasize the value of utilizing the skills between sessions. By reviewing prior skills learned at the beginning of the session each week, children will anticipate the questions asked by the therapist and will be increasingly prepared to respond appropriately. This relatively brief check in on children's experiences in applying the skills they are learning is important in assessing progress. The clinician may inquire about any time the child utilized the relaxation skills learned in the previous session(s). If clients report that they did not utilize the skills, the therapist should inquire about times they may have benefited from utilizing the skills and explain that during this component they will learn other skills that may also help them with those difficult situations. This work will allow them to add to their "favorite" coping skills tool kit.

When reviewing the child's practice efforts, it is always important to utilize specific praise and selective attention to ensure that the focus is more on children's compliant and successful efforts than on their noncompliance with the planned practice. Selective or differential attention refers to minimizing the amount of attention (i.e., either positive or negative attention) given to problematic behaviors (e.g., noncompliance), while increasing attention to any small step toward the positive replacement behavior (e.g., some small level of compliance). For purposes of this guide, this process is referred to as selective attention as this may be a more meaningful term to parents. The use of selective attention by the therapist, as well as by parents is particularly important with children who have behavior problems and are accustomed to receiving more attention, albeit negative attention, for misbehavior and noncompliance than they are for positive, adaptive, and compliant behavior. Thus, when children do not practice the skills optimally as planned, it is best in these early sessions to identify and praise any efforts mentioned in terms of children's attempts to use effective coping skills at home. The therapist should then move quickly on to the planned session activities. Specific praise or other incentives for small steps toward fully implementing coping skills at home may be provided by the therapist as a way to shape more successful coping efforts in the future. This shaping process will be important over the course of TF-CBT as the progress seen in both children and parents tends to be incremental and builds on previously learned skills.

Help children develop and practice affective expression skills

A common first step in affective expression skills training is helping youth to develop and expand their emotional vocabulary. Typically, younger children will need more assistance in expanding their emotional vocabulary than older children. Often younger children know the words for the primary emotions (including happy, sad, mad, and scared), but they may not yet have the language to express other emotions they may have experienced, especially those resulting from the sexually abusive experience(s).

Even older children who are more informed about emotions may benefit from expanding their emotional vocabulary, while also working on emotional expression, particularly if they are uncomfortable or unaccustomed to discussing their feelings. In fact, children who have experienced sexual abuse often experience a wide range of distressing emotions, but they may not have the words to label those emotions nor the level of comfort needed to share their feelings with others.

Girls, for example, may be socialized to avoid acknowledging feelings of anger and might benefit from more education about expressing and managing anger (Suveg et al., 2008). And even more commonly, boys may need encouragement to label and share certain negative emotions, such as fear, that they are typically socialized to minimize (Suveg et al., 2008). The inability to acknowledge these natural emotions in the context of sexual abuse may leave boys vulnerable to ruminating on the more socially acceptable emotion of anger, which can lead to aggressive and/or destructive behaviors.

Therapists may initiate work on affective expression skills by first eliciting the feeling words children know and then helping to expand their emotional vocabulary with feelings books and fun activities. Developing and encouraging children to use their expanded vocabulary to express their emotions is important because this type of emotion socialization has been associated with better adjustment (Eisenberg, Cumberland, & Spinrad, 1998). Moreover, it has been documented that children with anxiety disorders, as well as their caregivers tend to express less negative and positive emotions (Suveg et al., 2005).

To informally assess the child's emotional vocabulary, the therapist can make a game out of asking the child to list as many general feelings as he can in a specified period of time (e.g., 30 seconds). To challenge older children and adolescents to expand their emotional vocabulary, the therapist can turn this activity into a playful competition during which the therapist and the teenager compete to write as many feeling words as possible in 30 to 60 seconds depending on the child's age. Another way to engage in this type of activity is to challenge youth to list as many feeling words as possible, noting that their caregivers will be doing the same in their separate session. Adolescents, in particular, may be less enthusiastic about these basic emotion skill-building exercises but when motivated by the concept of competing with their parents to list as many words as possible, the exercise may become more interesting and fun. Although teens often outperform their parents in terms of winning the "competition" (i.e., listing more words), therapists' and parents' lists often offer additional feeling words that can be helpful.

With children who share a limited list of emotions (e.g., happy, sad, mad, and scared), therapists may elicit or provide additional feeling words by using charts or picture books illustrating a variety of feelings (see Appendix C). "Feelings" charts or posters are widely available commercially (e.g., through Childswork/Childsplay, Inc.) and are valuable throughout the TF-CBT process, especially later in treatment during the trauma narrative to prompt children to share their feelings. "Feelings" word lists that children create themselves may be similarly utilized in the context of therapy.

The clinician may encourage young children and teens alike to draw simple faces that depict different feelings as a means of focusing on emotional expression. Most children can draw feeling faces that reflect different emotions. If the child seems to need examples or encouragement, the therapist can also participate in this exercise. In order to avoid using too much session time, other therapy discussions can occur while children draw, and/or they can continue to draw their feeling faces while the parents are being seen for their individual session. It can be fun for children to later share these drawings with their parents in a brief conjoint session (see the "Conjoint Session" section below).

During these emotional expression activities, it is useful for the TF-CBT therapist to suggest and/or incorporate feelings words that may be particularly relevant in terms of the impact of sexual abuse and the circumstances of the particular client (e.g., curious, ashamed, terrified, loved, excited, guilty, tingly, etc.). Many children and teens develop feelings of intense embarrassment and/or shame as result of the stigmatizing nature of child sexual abuse (CSA). Moreover, ongoing feelings of shame have been found to be significantly associated with poorer long-term adjustment among children who have experienced sexual abuse (Feiring & Taska, 2005; Feiring, Taska, & Chen, 2002). Though it can be useful for the TF-CBT therapist to suggest or incorporate additional potential abuse-related feelings into the activities or "lists" created in session, it can be valuable to encourage the child to identify feelings actually experienced in relation to the abuse as a gradual exposure activity later in session (see the gradual exposure section below). In general, these affective expression activities will assist children to label, acknowledge, and later (in the context of the trauma narrative development) explore and process distressing abuse-related feelings that they experienced and/or continue to experience.

Gradual exposure

Gradual exposure can be introduced following the general feelings expression exercises by engaging in an exercise or discussion that focuses on CSA in general and/or briefly references the child's personal experience with CSA or abuse reminders. This should not feel jarring or intense for children; so when a child is highly avoidant, it is best for the therapist to reiterate general information about how children might feel when they have experienced CSA. However, when possible it is helpful to gradually engage children in a more personal discussion; for example, by asking *them* to circle all the different feelings on the feelings poster or list that they think other children who have been sexually abused might experience. Once such feelings have been circled, the therapist can read them out loud and then ask the child which feelings the child experienced at the time of the abuse.

With less avoidant older children and teens, the therapist might say the following:

> *We've talked a lot about feelings. Tell me what feelings you had when you were sexually abused or how you felt when you told your mom about it. Kids usually have a lot of different feelings.*

The therapist can help a teenager generate a list of feelings experienced during the abuse, after the abuse, during the investigation, and/or currently when the teenager thinks about the abuse. Because sexual abuse often leads to seemingly contradictory feelings, it is important for the therapist and child to discuss confusing or mixed-up feelings. For example, sometimes children initially like the attention showered on them by the offender and they may have enjoyed some of the activities in which they were engaged. Children may genuinely care for or love the individual who engaged them in the abusive interactions. Thus validating positive feelings they may have had in relation to interactions with the offender prior to and during the abuse are important as well. Children's bodies may have responded to the sexual touches in a positive way. However, children may simultaneously or later begin to feel scared, angry, and/or confused by the sexually inappropriate actions of a person whom they cared for and trusted. The discussion of these positive and/or confusing feelings gradually exposes children to CSA-related memories without going into too much detail about the actual experiences. In fact, it is important to keep this discussion brief so that the child does not feel overwhelmed by emotions. Rather, this exercise can be used as an opportunity for the therapist to integrate and reinforce what has been learned about CSA by drawing parallels between the child's emotional experiences and what has been learned about the dynamics of CSA including "grooming" activities and how children respond to CSA with a wide range of different feelings.

Identifying emotions in self and others

After establishing and/or expanding the clients' emotional vocabulary, the therapist may focus on helping children identify emotions in themselves and others. It has been suggested that children who have experienced significant abuse may have difficulty getting in touch with their own emotions, as well as reading others' emotions. For example, some children may be hypersensitive to negative cues or facial expressions perceiving social threats where there are none (Stirling & Amaya-Jackson, 2008). This exercise may reveal difficulties in this area, thereby identifying an area in which more work may be required. With a young child the therapist might begin this work by saying the following:

> *When people are feeling happy or sad or mad, you can sometimes tell how they feel by the sound of their voices or the look on their faces. Have you seen someone who was very sad? How did he look? How could you tell that he was sad?*

The therapist should continue this discussion of physical and verbal cues regarding a variety of different emotions. The therapist may introduce an exercise in which the child can practice identifying how a person is feeling. This exercise can be conducted in a variety of ways. Younger children may learn to identify facial cues for emotions by first discussing how a person's face reveals the experienced emotions (e.g., eyes, mouth, brow, overall look, etc.). Then the child guesses which feelings the therapist is depicting when drawing a series of faces. Photographs, pictures, and puppets may also be used to identify and label emotions. Some children may enjoy reading a story about other children expressing their feelings. There are a number of books listed in the resource appendix (Appendix C) that are good choices for discussing feelings.

To help young children identify emotions in other people, the therapist may teach the phrase "look, listen, and ask" by explaining that the first steps in learning how someone else is feeling are to look at the person's face and listen to his voice and words. The therapist may inform the child that it is possible to misperceive someone else's emotions based only on those observations, so in order to be accurate in understanding another person's emotions one can also ask that person how he is feeling. The therapist may reinforce the lesson of "look, listen, and ask" by playing charades with the child. Each person can take turns acting out a scene that displays certain emotions. The observer then has to guess the feeling being depicted by looking, listening, guessing, and finally directly asking what feeling is being expressed. In this exercise, it is helpful to point out to the child that guesses are sometimes right and sometimes wrong and that it is impossible to read someone's mind and it often is difficult know what someone is feeling without asking.

It is important to also focus attention on children's awareness and identification of their own emotions. Although some children need assistance in getting in touch with their feelings, other children need to learn to notice, tolerate, and manage intense emotions. Children who have a tendency to suppress their feelings for fear of being overwhelmed may need encouragement to acknowledge feelings. Initially discussing less emotionally charged experiences (e.g., doing poorly on one test or being disappointed by a friend) may help these children to recall and acknowledge distressing emotions experienced in the past. This ability to face and express difficult emotions is particularly important for children who have developed sexual abuse-related PTSD symptoms. These children often fear being overwhelmed by emotions if they acknowledge the trauma(s) they experienced and/or the associated negative emotions no matter how mild the negative emotion may be. As a result, many children continue to exhibit emotional numbness and/or flat affect as they work to hold back the flood of emotions they fear.

Other children who have PTSD symptoms experience a great deal of affective dysregulation, often exhibiting emotional outbursts for no apparent reason. This over reactivity may be a result of reflexive reactions to cues in the environment that are reminders of the abuse. When children lack an understanding of the cues in the environment that trigger traumatic memories and related emotions, they may struggle more with affective dysregulation. These children may also be less likely to notice the subtle signs that they are becoming upset, thus their emotions may become intense before there is an opportunity to utilize any emotional regulation skills. Therefore, it is important to help children and adolescents learn about how certain things in the environment may remind them of their traumatic experiences and how these reminders may generate emotions that are similar to those they experienced at the time of the CSA. In addition, the therapist can help children learn about the subtle ways they can notice themselves becoming upset (i.e., body sensations) before the emotions become intense. For example, the therapist may ask a child or teen the following:

Therapist: *Sometimes we can tell that we are getting scared by how our body reacts to something that is happening in our environment. How does your body react when something scary happens?*
Charlene: *Usually my hands get sweaty when I'm scared or nervous.*
Therapist: *Thanks so much for sharing that. That's a very common physical response when people are nervous. How do you know that you're feeling sad?*
Charlene: *That's easy. I cry.*
Therapist: *That makes sense. Do you ever feel sad but you don't cry?*
Charlene: *I guess so. Sometimes my body just feels slowed down like I don't want to get out of bed.*
Therapist: *That's great to know. That is your body telling you "I'm sad." Just labeling the emotion reduces its hold on you and sharing those feelings with others can be very helpful too.*
Charlene: *I do tend to keep things in but when I talk to my friends I usually do feel a little better.*
Therapist: *It is good to be aware that when you talk to your friends, you feel better. It's also important to remember that feelings of sadness, like other negative emotions, are* not *permanent; they will diminish over time, and as you relax, participate in positive activities, laugh, and as time goes by, even the saddest feelings will diminish.*
Charlene: *You're right; there were times when I thought I would never be happy again and now there are some times when I feel pretty good.*

The therapist can enhance the child's awareness and identification of emotions by encouraging the child to discuss real and personal (although not necessarily abuse-related) situations that have led to a variety of different emotions. For example, the therapist might say:

Tell me about a time when you felt excited. What were you excited about? Could anyone else tell that you were excited?

A similar conversation might be pursued regarding a variety of other feelings such as mad, sad, scared, proud, worried, ashamed, confused, and so on. As noted earlier, confused feelings are particularly important to highlight in the context of expanding a child's feeling vocabulary, but at this early stage in treatment, it is best to keep the discussion about confusing feelings neutral unless the child links those feelings to the abuse. Thus, the therapist may ask the following:

Therapist: *Did you ever feel confused, like you're not sure how you should feel or like you have different feelings all at the same time?*
Charlene: *I sometimes feel confused about who my friends are. I have confused feelings about this one girl. I really like her and I also hate her for telling other kids about what happened.*

Therapist: *Yes. That can happen where you might really like someone like that girl but when the person does something that hurts you, you may have a negative feeling toward her at the same time. When you feel mixed up like that, it is hard to know what to do.*
Charlene: *I don't think there is anything you could do about a situation like that.*
Therapist: *One great thing you can do when you are feeling confused about anything is to talk to someone you trust. Who can you talk to about a confusing problem?*

Then the therapist may help the child generate a list of available people who typically help her to feel better. If this is not easy for the child, the therapist may point out therapy is ideal place to share feelings that are confusing.

The therapist should take time to actively listen, reflecting back and validating the child's experience of both positive and negative feelings. In the role of the helping professional, it is sometimes instinctive to jump in and offer advice when children share experiences that led to negative feelings, but it is preferable at this point to rely on reflective listening to validate the feelings shared. In addition, it is important to demonstrate that the simple act of sharing feelings, which may include the shedding of tears about unresolvable problems, can also be healing. Again, although most of the focus during this component is on nonabuse-related issues and feelings, it is appropriate for the therapist to make brief links to the CSA experience, thereby supporting the gradual exposure process.

During these exercises that focus on effective ways to acknowledge and express feelings, it is important to repeatedly emphasize that there are no right or wrong feelings, noting that all people experience positive and negative feelings throughout life. Initially, the therapist may elicit from the child how he expresses various emotions such as sadness, happiness, anger, fear, love, worry, and so on.

For younger children, it may be helpful to ask more specific and concrete questions such as "*When was the last time you felt sad? Did you share those feelings with anyone? Who?*"

Children may describe both adaptive and maladaptive ways of expressing different feelings. The therapist should encourage children who offer maladaptive ways of expressing feelings to share additional ways in which they responded when feeling sad. This is important because most children and adults utilize a host of strategies to express feelings, some of which are more adaptive than others. For example, if a child described coping with sadness by sitting alone and not talking to anyone, the therapist might respond as follows:

What other things do you do when you are feeling sad?
If you sit by yourself, without talking, how do you feel? Does that help you feel better?
What does make you feel happy/okay again?
What do you do to make other people feel better when they are sad?

It is important for children to understand that it is okay to feel sad, mad, scared, and so on. However, there are some ways of coping with feelings that are not okay, because they may intensify distressing feelings and/or put others in danger (e.g., anger leading to violent behavior).

> **Therapist:** *You know, everybody feels sad sometimes. But there are times when negative feelings last too long and become too painful to keep to yourself. And it does not help to hide those sad feelings because it does not make them go away. Instead it is better to express your feelings. There are many different and helpful ways to do that.*

The therapist should elicit from the child ideas about ways of expressing a variety of feelings, focusing on those emotions that are particularly relevant for that specific child. It is preferable for the therapist to elicit children's individual methods for sharing feelings. In that way, the therapist is more likely to hear about less effective (e.g., yelling and/or fighting), as well as more effective means of sharing emotions (e.g., talking out their problems and feelings with a best friend) children are using. In this way, the therapist can begin to build on and encourage the continued use of appropriate means of expressing emotions identified by the child before teaching new methods.

The therapist should emphasize that learning to use feeling words to express emotions is a big step forward for many clients and talking about these feelings with someone can be scary.

It may be useful to have the child draw a picture, write a paragraph, or talk about one person he can talk (or could potentially talk) to about problems. It helps to identify those individuals that help the child feel better, acknowledging that everyone has friends and/or relatives that are not good at helping others feel better so they may not be the best individuals with whom to share feelings. Role-plays can be used to allow children to act out how they could talk about specific feelings with someone in their life who is typically helpful. For teenagers, it is often useful to help them identify people in their lives that are good listeners and respond in ways that help them feel understood and less distressed.

Developmental considerations

With young children, the therapist can build on the exercise referred to earlier as "look, listen, and ask" during which children learned to identify feelings in others. The next exercise can help children to express their feelings to others. The training regarding appropriate expression of emotions for *young children* can be summarized by the phrase, "show and tell." Therapists should explain that children can most effectively cope with emotions by "showing" the emotions through appropriate behaviors and most importantly by using their words and "telling" other people how they are feeling. For young children in particular, this phrase "show and tell" may help them to remember the importance of sharing their feelings with "words," rather than just acting out their feelings which can sometimes get them in trouble (e.g., using their fists to show their anger).

Children who are struggling with the most intense emotions are oftentimes the ones who are the least likely to verbally share those emotions with others.

Thus, one of the most important skills to teach is the process of using the words that were listed and discussed early in session. It is important to acknowledge, however, that using these words may feel awkward at first. The best way to get comfortable and proficient at expressing one's emotions in a healthy way is to *practice.*

With *older children and teens*, it can be useful to do role-plays around real scenarios provided by the child in which the child practices expressing feelings in a way that is likely to be positively received. Practicing, "I statements" or "I expressions," can be helpful to older youth who struggle with interpersonal conflicts. This language is useful because the use of "I statements" often softens the way negative feelings are received by others.

Therapist: *Let's imagine that your Mom wasn't able to go to your game because she was on a business trip. What would you say to her if you were feeling really upset about that?*

Charles: *That has happened and I said to my mom, "Thanks a lot for missing my first and probably only shut out!"*

Therapist: *How did she respond when you said that?*

Charles: *I don't remember exactly but I know it probably made her mad.*

Therapist: *And then how did you feel when your mom got mad?*

Charles: *I think I said "Why do you have to travel so much?" And she said someone has to put food on the table . . . whatever that means... she says that a lot. We get mad at each other a lot.*

Therapist: *Well, let's see what would happen if you express your feelings in a different way. Let's do a role-play in which you share your mad feelings by using the feelings sentence on the board to express your feelings about your mom not getting to the game.*

I felt ___(feeling word) and ___(feeling word) when ___(event) happened

Charles: *This is stupid.* (Mutters under his breath)

Therapist: *Okay, so let's get this part of therapy over with quickly so we can make sure we have time for me to hear that new song you told me you have on your phone.*

Charles: *Okay. You're not gonna like it. I listen to it when I'm mad.*

Therapist: *That's okay. I'd like to hear what you listen to when you're mad. Now let's try this role-play as if you and I are actors and I am playing the part of your mom and you can look at the white board as our script...."Charles, I am sorry I missed your game."*

Charles: *I feel so mad and* (pause) *sad when . . . you don't come to my games* (under his breath) *because of your stupid job.*

Therapist: (deliberately ignores the "stupid job" comment) *You feel mad and sad when I miss your games. Thanks for sharing your feelings with me. I feel sad and mad too when I miss your games.*

Charles: *I don't think my mom would say that.*

Therapist: *Do you think she feels that way?*

Charles: *Maybe.*

Therapist: *Well your mom is learning all the same skills you are learning so that she can be as expressive as you. And we are going to do role-plays just like this with your mom so we will see how she responds when you share your feelings.*
Charles: *Okay. I bet she doesn't say that.*
Therapist: *Well, you did a great job sharing your feelings! Now let's practice sharing a positive feeling with your mom. Can you think of something that happened recently that made you feel good?*
I felt ___ *(feeling word)* and ___ *(feeling word)* when *(example)* ___

These role-plays and helpful "I statements" are important to practice as it can be quite difficult to express negative as well as tender positive emotions especially when the emotions are expressed directly to others. It is helpful for children to practice sharing positive feeling (e.g., "I really feel happy when you give me a hug.") to let others know how they feel in general, as well as when someone does something that is appreciated. In the case of negative emotions, by not accusing the other person of causing the emotion (e.g., "You make me so mad" versus "I feel mad when you say that I can't go out"), one increases the likelihood that the expressed feeling will be heard and validated rather than ignored and/or denied.

Expressing feelings assertively

During these role-plays, the therapist should not only help children practice verbally expressing themselves clearly, they should also take note of the child's body language in order to practice confident body language such as using a confident tone of voice, making eye contact, and sitting up or standing tall with shoulders back.

Children and teens who find themselves in frequent conflict with others may benefit a great deal from practicing the assertive communication of feelings with the additional step of making a request such that they learn to ask for whatever is wanted or needed in an appropriately assertive manner. Thus, in addition to practicing the *I feel . . . . when …* statements, children learn to include a request as demonstrated by the fill in the blanks and example below.

I felt ___ *(feeling word(s))*
When *(describe specific circumstance)* ___
Please, ___ *(express a specific, clear request phrased positively)*

For example, a child might practice saying, *I felt angry and lonely when you get home late from work.* The child may then be encouraged to practice adding a request such as, *Please call me when you are going to be late.*

When practicing the above, the child should also be coached to express such requests in an assertive, rather than a passive or aggressive manner (see below). Thus, it is important to take note of the child's tone of voice and body language.

Many children and teens, particularly those who have experienced victimization, can benefit a great deal from learning to communicate assertively. This education should also include learning about the differences between passive, assertive, and aggressive communication. Assertiveness skills training may be approached in a variety of ways depending on the child's developmental level. For example, young children may enjoy reading the book *The Mouse, Monster and Me: Assertiveness for Young People* by Pat Palmer (2011) in which the lead characters demonstrate passive, assertive, and aggressive ways of communicating. With some children, the therapist might describe or role-play with puppets or action figures different means of communicating feelings, while the child guesses which form of communication (passive, assertive, or aggressive) is being depicted. Ultimately, however, both children and teens benefit most from participating in behavior rehearsals that are tailored to their unique circumstances in which they have an opportunity to practice the sharing of feelings as well as assertively communicating their requests.

Aside from practicing the sharing of feelings in individual session, when clinically appropriate, the child should practice sharing feelings with the participating parent in conjoint sessions. However, it is important to carefully prepare parents to model, recognize, and effectively respond to their children's attempts to share both positive and negative feelings, even when the negative feelings are directed toward them. It therefore behooves therapists to role-play this skill in individual parent session using the actual feelings the child is likely to share (see conjoint session preparation for children and parents in this chapter). It should also be noted that therapists need to be culturally sensitive with respect to this issue because in some families, children expressing feelings, especially anger, directly to parents may not be acceptable. Therefore, therapists must understand the parents' perspective and find ways to balance feeling expression with familial cultural norms.

Help child develop and practice affective regulation skills

When children and teens are able to get in touch with and express their distressing feelings, they will be more able to effectively utilize their developing *coping skills tool kit*.

After the therapist praises the child for her efforts to share feelings appropriately, it is important to encourage the child to begin to focus on strategies people use for coping with negative or difficult emotions and problems. Children should be reminded that the relaxation exercises previously learned are important coping skills and that there are other coping skills that have been proven to be highly effective in coping with feelings of sadness, fear, and anger. The therapist should then have the child review the coping strategies list and identify additional strategies the child sometimes uses while also discussing strategies that may be most and least effective in helping people feel and do better. For example, there is some evidence that engaging in pleasurable social activities and/or participating in physical activities (e.g., sports, walking, biking, running, exercise, etc.) can effectively combat negative emotions (Blumenthal et al., 2007; Davidson et al., 2005; Layous et al., 2014; Nezlek & Derks, 2001; Ventis, Higbee, & Murdock, 2001; Vilaythong et al., 2003). Teens that have experienced sexual abuse may be particularly prone to depression and withdrawal. The therapist should therefore explore the impulse to withdraw when feeling down and educate teens about the value of identifying distracting, uplifting, aerobic, and/or other social activities that can help them cope with distressing feelings. Simple Socratic questions (e.g., "What do you think might happen if a depressed teenager began spending all his time alone in his room?") may be used to elicit strategies that tend to lead to more or less productive outcomes. It is important to elicit as many personal examples as possible of managing emotions using effective strategies that lead to positive long-term outcomes. With older teens it is helpful to distinguish between strategies that lead to short-term benefits but negative long-term outcomes and those that are beneficial both in the short term and long term (see examples of coping with anger below). Children sometimes have to draw from experiences that occurred prior to the sexual abuse when they were able to respond to stress more effectively (e.g., listening to music, talking things out, going for a run, etc.). These coping examples should be praised and built on, while those affective regulation strategies (i.e., tantruming, punching walls, yelling, hitting, cutting, running away, drinking, etc.) that may have felt good in the short run but do not lead to positive outcomes in the long run should be discussed using Socratic questioning. Once again, it is best to use Socratic questions, reflective listening, and collaborative problem solving to help the child or teen conclude that such strategies may not be the best choice to help her feel better in the long run.

Coping with anger effectively

When discussing emotional expression and modulation, it is often useful to spend some time discussing anger because it is not only a commonly experienced emotion in children who have experienced abuse but also because inappropriate expressions of anger can be particularly problematic. With a child who exhibits maladaptive responses to anger, the therapist may help the child learn about anger and ways of managing such feelings. Once a trusting therapeutic relationship has been established, it can be useful to elicit examples of times when the child became angry and managed those feelings well in addition to times when the child got into trouble for engaging in angry behaviors that were less than productive.

Although mental health professionals used to encourage the venting of anger through means such as hitting a pillow or a "bobo doll," research indicates that such exercises or prolonged discussions focused on anger maintain that emotional state and the unhealthy physiological responses associated with anger (Tavris, 1989). Though some believe that punching a pillow might momentarily feel good and seem to relieve a child's anger, such "venting" more often results in increased feelings of anger, increased blood pressure, and in some instances the generalization of aggressive behaviors to other environments in which such behavior is not condoned. When children mention such activities, it is important to preferably elicit and/or provide brief explanations as to why the suggested activity might not be best while praising the child for suggesting more effective emotion regulation skills and incorporating them into the *coping skills tool kit*. These more effective skills can then be practiced via role-plays designed to address and resolve distressing situations. In situations in which resolutions are not possible (e.g., it may not be possible to "right the wrong" the child experienced due to the abuse), therapists may encourage children to explore and express their anger through a variety of affective regulation activities that involve the expression of feelings through the use of creative arts. The therapist, for example, may encourage the child to write, sing, or draw a picture to communicate anger about an experience not related to the abuse so the child can notice the benefits of working through anger using creative expression. Such exercises also help children and teens gain insight into their feelings, potentially reducing tendencies toward aggressively acting out in anger or ruminating over the circumstances that caused the anger.

Some children may focus excessively on their anger as a means of distancing themselves from other more painful emotions. As noted, fear or sadness, for example, may be particularly difficult for boys to acknowledge because these emotions are less socially acceptable for boys to express (Suveg et al., 2008). Some boys may lack awareness of these emotions when they are experienced. Therapists should encourage such children to identify and express the full range of emotions they have experienced, explaining that anger is typically comprised of other underlying emotions.

Children can also be taught to manage anger and other distressing emotions more effectively through the use of the focused breathing and/or relaxation exercises learned previously. They may be encouraged to list other methods of managing troubling emotions that they have found to be successful in the past. These may include exercising, walking, running, dancing, painting, listening to music, playing an instrument, or distracting themselves with other positive activities. It is important for children and parents to understand that the objective is not to eliminate negative emotions but to prevent them from becoming all consuming and/or being expressed in ways that may be damaging to the child. Readers are referred to *Anger: The Misunderstood Emotion* (Tavris, 1989) for further information about the development, maintenance, and management of anger.

Fishing for feelings

When teaching means of expressing and/or managing emotions, it is helpful to incorporate fun, active games. In order to address a wide array of feelings, it can be useful to play what we have referred to as *Fishing for Feelings* (Baker, 2006). This simple game can be played in a variety of different ways to help children practice identifying emotions in others, expressing feelings, and/or coping with different types of feelings. One way involves having the child choose from pieces of crumpled papers that have a single feeling listed on them. Without telling the other person which feeling was chosen, the therapist and child take turns acting out the feeling and/or the strategy used to cope with it. This can be accomplished by either using words that exclude the chosen feeling word or without words at all. The other person (child or therapist) then must guess what feeling and/or coping strategy (e.g., focused breathing, problem solving, exercise, talking with a friend, etc.) the other person is depicting in the role-play. This game thus provides the child with an opportunity to see a strategy modeled by the therapist and/or allows the child to behaviorally rehearse the feeling and coping strategy in session. When the child demonstrates a coping strategy, the therapist has an opportunity to offer specific praise as well as constructive feedback when needed for the coping skills displayed by the child. In another version of this game, the child and/or the therapist chooses a feeling word from the hat and describes a situation in real life when the emotion was experienced and how she coped with it. It can sometimes be useful to give the child stickers or points for efforts and/or successes in identifying the emotions depicted by the therapist as well as for sharing times that the chosen feelings were experienced in real life. For many children, the stickers themselves serve as sufficient motivation to participate. Other children, however, may respond better if they are able to work for stickers/tokens that can be turned in for a small prize once they earn a sufficient number.

Introduce creative expression and arts activities to support affect regulation

Therapists can incorporate children's talents and interests as tools for helping youth manage difficult emotions. Many children enjoy drawing, playing an instrument, or engaging in sports and they may recognize that certain creative or recreational activities in and of themselves may be uplifting due to their calming effect and/or social nature. Other youth may enjoy listening to and/or creating songs or raps as a means of coping. It can be pointed out to both children and teenagers that many songs contain lyrics that include lots of different emotions as well as positive and negative coping strategies. Children can be challenged to identify songs that contain such lyrics in session or at home. It is interesting to note that thousands of songs were written during the Second World War to lift the morale of the nation and many (e.g., "This Land Is Your Land") continue to be sung today by people facing adversity as a means of coping (Winkler, 2013). Depending on the child's age, the therapist may offer examples of music and lyrics that may encourage positive feelings. For example, younger children may enjoy listening to and singing songs such as "Whistle While You Work" from *Cinderella* by Disney or "My Favorite Things" from *Sound of Music* by Rodgers and Hammerstein. To reinforce a child's expanded emotion vocabulary, the words to the song "When You're Happy and You Know It" can be altered to incorporate old and new emotion words. Older youth may be encouraged to identify uplifting songs they enjoy and/or the therapist might share examples of songs that inspire optimism such as "I Hope You Dance" by Lee Ann Womack, "Brave" by Sarah Barielles and Jack Antonoff, and "When You Believe" by Mariah Carey and Whitney Houston. Creative coping activities such as those described above can be particularly helpful when youth and their caregivers enjoy them together. Moreover, such activities can often be incorporated as positive rituals that families engage in on a regular basis or during typically stressful periods of the day (e.g., listening to uplifting music in the car or while preparing dinner after a long day at work or school).

Engage child in positive end-of-session ritual

Again, there are many simple positive end-of-session rituals in which children can be engaged. The therapist, for example, might suggest a fun and engaging method to create and/or expand the child's coping skills tool kit (e.g., using fancy/smelly magic markers or other arts and crafts materials to expand on their list or add additional decorated index cards to their coping skills index card box). It is useful to make the *coping skills tool kit* as accessible to the child as possible; thus, some teenagers might like to create coping skills apps or type their coping skills list into a computer or smart phone if they have one. Other children might enjoy briefly playing music, singing, or listening to one of the songs described above as a positive end-of-session ritual.

Practice activities encouraged

As always, it is important for therapists to suggest strategies for practicing skills between sessions that they are fairly confident the child will be able to complete with some level of success. Thus, the therapist may choose from among the variety of affective modulation activities listed below and/or create activities that flow from the focus of the child's individual session.

Enhancing affective expression and awareness practice

All children may practice using the feelings words they learned outside of therapy. More specifically, children may be encouraged to focus on sharing both positive as well as negative emotions with participating parents, using the feelings words and "I statement" expressions practiced in session. The therapist should inform clients that during the subsequent sessions they will be asked how their parents responded to their sharing of feelings. Thus, it will be important for them to pay attention to how their parents respond. In addition, children and teens that enjoy music may be encouraged to note lyrics that reflect the expression of emotions by the singer. It is important to note for clients that some songs can be mood lifters and other songs can lead one to feel more distressed. Children may be encouraged to keep track of how listening to various forms of music affects their mood. This can lead to a fun end-of-session activity in which the therapist and client briefly listen to mood lifting music together.

Enhancing affective modulation and other coping practice

Encourage the use of the *coping skills tool kit* including any of the relaxation and/or affective expression and modulation skills reviewed in session. It is best to agree on specific affect regulation skills that the child will be practicing during the week. It is likely that the more naturalistic the coping skill feels and the more details obtained in terms of when and how the child is likely to use the skills, the greater the child's commitment to following through will likely be (Deci & Ryan, 2000). In addition, the clinician should discuss the value of using the chosen affective regulation skills in general as well as specifically in relation to coping with sexual abuse reminders that trigger distress as a means of incorporating gradual exposure.

Prepare for conjoint session activities

If clinically appropriate, the child may be encouraged to share her list of feeling words and/or the *coping skills tool kit* in the conjoint parent-child session. As noted earlier, this can be particularly fun if the parent agreed to participate in a playful competition to see who could create the longest list of feelings words or coping strategies.

Affective expression conjoint activity

A more advanced conjoint activity that requires more time in terms of preparation and implementation involves having children share both positive and negative feelings using "I statements" with the parent. By standing in as the parent, the therapist can help the child practice through role-playing the sharing of nonabuse-related negative and positive feelings. Children are typically encouraged to share one nonabuse-related negative feeling and end the conjoint activity with the sharing of one positive feeling.

The sharing of feelings should be role-played with children so that therapists can anticipate what feelings the child will share in conjoint session with the parent. In fact, the therapist should elicit and write down exactly what the child is going to share including the negative nonabuse-related feeling (e.g., "I feel sad when I get a bad grade in school"), as well as the positive feeling that the child will share with the parent when prompted in conjoint session. The therapist can then fully prepare the parent to praise the sharing of feelings while also practicing reflective listening with the specific feelings statements the child is likely to share. The first time this conjoint activity is attempted, it is best to have the child just share the feeling without making a request as described in the above assertive communication section. This step allows parents to get used to their children sharing feelings while learning to praise and validate their children's feelings. More details on the parent preparation for this activity are provided below. As previously noted, it is best to steer children away from sharing highly charged emotions or sexual abuse related feelings with parents at this early stage of therapy.

All of these conjoint activities provide parents an opportunity to practice specific praise as well as reflective listening regarding their children's efforts to learn effective ways of expressing and managing their emotions.

Mutual exchange of praise

During this component, children can also be taught to use "I statements" to share positive feelings in the form of specific praise for their parents (e.g., "I feel happy when you give me a kiss goodnight"; "I feel loved when you come to my games"). This further reinforces the child's skills in sharing positive feelings in the activity referred to as *mutual exchange of praise* that can be incorporated into any conjoint parent-child session in the future. In fact, many children and parents come to look forward to this brief positive ritual at the end of the session even when there is not time for a lengthy conjoint parent-child session. Still, this conjoint activity does require preparation during parent and child individual sessions as many clients are not accustomed to sharing positive feelings in the form of purely positive praise. Thus, therapists are encouraged to help children and parents identify, tweak, and practice the praise they would like to offer so it is specific and free of negative tags.

PARENT SESSION(S)

Practice assignments review

The therapist might begin parent sessions during this component with a review of parents' efforts to engage in coping skills and parenting skills learned in previous sessions. This review of parents' practice efforts at home is designed to help parents improve their own personal coping (e.g., taking care of themselves) as well as their parenting skills (e.g., use of positive routines and/or specific praise). It is important for therapists to maintain careful progress notes on parents' commitments so that follow up can focus on inquiring about specific suggestions. These reviews would consistently include both coping and parenting skills efforts. During these sessions, for example, the therapist might review the parents' steps toward taking care of themselves as well as the use of positive rituals and/or specific praise in encouraging identified positive child behaviors as well as children's implementation of relaxation strategies (e.g., focusing breathing, mindfulness, etc.). A careful review of the parent's efforts to implement parenting skills including both positive and problematic parent-child interactions can be a very effective means of reviewing their skill acquisition. Described below is an effective approach to reviewing the antecedents, behaviors, and consequences (i.e., functional analysis) associated with parent-child interactions that allows for a careful review of the implementation of the positive parenting skills learned thus far.

Functional analysis reviews

It helps to emphasize to parents how important it is for the therapist to thoroughly understand what is happening at home in between sessions. It is during this time at home that the most healing and change occurs. This emphasis will help parents to understand and appreciate why they will be asked detailed questions from week to week, particularly about their interactions with their children. Moreover, the clinician may explain that the collection of information in this manner is referred to as functional analyses of behavior because the information obtained helps to identify what is motivating the child's behaviors. Thus, in collaboration with parents, the clinician may conduct functional analyses each week to examine the patterns of parent-child interactions in detail. This also allows the therapist to acknowledge parents for the effective implementation of the skills they are working on while also identifying areas in which more work is needed. Functional analyses are useful to help parents see the benefits of the positive parenting changes they are making while also obtaining information that will help to determine what parenting errors might be inadvertently reinforcing children's problem behaviors. Furthermore, functional analyses can reveal the subtle environmental factors that are contributing to the occurrence and maintenance of CSA-related symptoms and behaviors. Often parents are unaware of environmental factors that may be triggering children's CSA-related symptoms and they may not understand how they may be inadvertently reinforcing problematic behaviors with negative parental attention.

If parents were unable to follow through with the use of the coping and/or parenting skills discussed previously (e.g., relaxation and/or praise), a brief discussion of the obstacles should be pursued with an emphasis on collaborative problem solving to overcome barriers. The importance of follow through should be emphasized with the goals being to decrease parents' levels of stress, to support their children's healing, and to serve as effective role models. Finally, a helpful way to review parents' between session efforts is to include praise and constructive feedback delivered in the form of "compliment sandwiches," which may be more appropriately referred to as "constructive feedback on compliment toast" in that constructive feedback is best sandwiched between praise. This refers to first offering parents specific praise regarding something that they did well in the context of the parent-child interaction, then specific constructive feedback designed to improve the results of their parenting efforts, ending with additional specific or global praise. This format is important because many parents are highly sensitive to criticism in the area of parenting. This may be especially true of parents whose children were sexually abused, as they often are already berating and blaming themselves for their children's experience of abuse and associated difficulties. Thus, it is helpful to follow up any constructive feedback with additional specific or global praise (e.g., "These are simply tweaks that can help your child cooperate with you more. You are really a terrific parent.") Parents may also be asked to describe their efforts to implement relaxation skills with a similar focus on eliciting the details of their efforts as well as inquiring about their personal success in managing feelings of distress with these skills. It is also useful to inquire about whether their children observed them practicing relaxation skills and whether they observed their children using relaxation skills.

Describe children's affective expression and modulation activities

Once again, it is important to take some time to briefly highlight what the child is learning in his individual session. For example, it helps to explain that in individual sessions the child is learning to express feelings in words (i.e., affective expression) that will help to reduce his reliance on inappropriate behavioral means of expressing feelings (e.g., punching walls or hitting his brother). In addition, it is important to highlight the child's strengths and cooperative behavior thereby modeling for the parent specific praise of the child's efforts and positive behavior. Thus, the therapist might report something like the following:

> *Today, your son was able to create a very impressive list of feeling words and he practiced using them. I really liked how he put a lot of thought into developing role-plays about situations in which he might become frustrated or angry and he used those scenes to practice sharing feelings. This was an important step because research has demonstrated that children who are able to express their feelings using their words rather than their behaviors are much more likely to be emotionally adjusted not only in childhood but through adolescence and adulthood as well!*

As noted earlier, the therapist can begin by explaining that the child was motivated to engage in expanding his emotional vocabulary by developing a list of feeling words that would be longer than the one the parent developed. Thus, parents will be asked to take just a minute or so to participate in this playful competition in session by developing their own feelings words list, particularly if the child is excited about competing in this way.

Introduce affective expression and modulation skills for parental use

If the parent participates in developing a feelings list (as described above) for purposes of playfully competing with his child, the therapist may ask the parent to identify from the list the emotions he experienced upon learning about the allegations of abuse. This is a form of gradual exposure to abuse-related trauma reminders for the parent that may help to foster an open conversation about the impact of the child's disclosure on the parent. Aside from the victims themselves, there are probably no others who experience the trauma of CSA more than the nonoffending parents. Several studies have demonstrated that nonoffending parents suffer highly significant levels of psychological distress upon discovery that their child may have been sexually abused (Deblinger et al., 1993; Kelley, 1990). Unfortunately, however, parental emotional reactions are often not acknowledged or addressed by the professional community as the focus often tends to be on children's distress and difficulties. Therapists should begin the process of helping parents cope with their personal emotional reactions by encouraging them to explore and express the wide range of emotions they may be experiencing. Therapists, for example, might ask parents to describe how they felt at the time of the initial disclosure as well as how they currently feel when they are reminded of the child's abuse experience. This discussion gives parents an opportunity to explore and clarify their own feelings and it continues the gradual exposure process for parents.

Some parents may already have well-developed skills for identifying and expressing their emotions. Other parents may need considerable assistance in being able to sort out confusing and conflicted emotions. Such clarification of their emotions is important in enabling parents to respond to their children in well thought-out and effective ways and preventing parents from responding based on their own emotional distress.

These discussions of emotions allow therapists to validate parents' feelings by demonstrating acceptance of whatever they are expressing. By providing a safe forum for parents to express these intense feelings, the therapist may help parents manage their distress, thereby reducing the emotional contagion that may occur within families (Morris, Silk, Steinberg, Myers, & Robinson, 2007). Some parents may still be expressing feelings that could be considered unsupportive of the child (e.g., disbelief, anger toward the child, concern for the perpetrator). It has been the experience of the authors that even these "nonsupportive" feelings need to be acknowledged by the clinician. Moreover, in the context of therapy, it is best to empathize using reflective listening. A nonoffending parent often experiences a great deal of turmoil when she discovers that a beloved child has been sexually abused. It is therefore crucial to encourage the sharing of feelings, particularly those experienced when parents first learned of the abuse and to remain as neutral as possible, primarily utilizing reflective listening to respond to the parents' sharing of ambivalent feelings. Moreover, sometimes it is helpful to acknowledge how difficult it is to consider that someone you trusted and/or cared for sexually abused your child. It is not unreasonable for parents to find it difficult to believe that someone they knew and trusted for many years sexually abused the child. Thus, all the clinician can ask from parents is to continue to support the child by accompanying him to sessions while maintaining an open mind with regard to the allegations. It may be reinforced that in reality only the child and offender know exactly what happened but often with time and additional information clarity will come.

In addition, in the early stages of therapy, it is generally not appropriate for parents to share their abuse-related feelings with their children because the intensity and volatility of the emotions expressed may be quite troubling and may interfere with the children's ability to develop and express their own beliefs and emotions regarding the abuse and the offender. Thus, the therapist may encourage parents to carefully monitor and contain their expression of emotions regarding the abuse when in the presence of their children. Not only should parents be advised to avoid sharing their intense emotions directly with their children, they may also be encouraged to carefully monitor the sharing of emotions and related beliefs that the child might inadvertently overhear such as telephone conversations or discussions of the abuse with other people including law enforcement and child protection workers.

The therapist can encourage parents to share feelings in session and identify other adults with whom they can share their feelings regarding the sexual abuse without exposing their children to those conversations. Because sexual abuse is such a stigmatizing issue in this society, parents may be cautious about discussing this problem with others. That stance should be respected, though with some brainstorming, many parents can identify a support person who may help them to feel less alone in coping with this crisis. With parents who have difficulty expressing emotions appropriately in general, the therapist often needs to do more individual work with them on emotional expression and modulation skills so that such parents can become more effective models for their children.

During this component, it is important to review with parents the affective expression and regulation strategies that are being discussed with the child, so that they can begin to think about how they manage their emotions and whether or not their child is learning positive and/or negative coping strategies from them through observation and imitation. Children naturally learn to cope from observing their parents, so it makes sense to support the adaptive coping strategies in which both parents and children are most inclined to engage. Thus, therapists should take note of the families' typical coping styles, building on those familial coping strategies that are most effective, as well as most commonly used within their family and culture. Thus, some children and parents may be more inclined to talk through feelings as a means of coping while others may rely more on prayer and participation in religious and social activities for support and distraction.

It often helps parents to identify moments in which they felt less distressed in order to help them capture naturally effective coping strategies. These skills may include relaxation strategies (e.g., focused breathing, meditation, or mindfulness), the healthy sharing of feelings with friends as well as other healthy hobbies (e.g., gardening, playing music, etc.) and positive social activities of a variety of sorts that may help parents cope in times of stress. Parents may be encouraged to manage distressing emotions by continuing to work toward creating and/or reestablishing positive family rituals and routines. Parents can also be educated about coping strategies that have proven efficacy in enhancing affective regulation. Many parents are surprised to learn that routine exercise several times a week has been found to be more effective than antidepressant medication in reducing depression over the long term (Blumenthal et al., 2007). Thus, given the potentially negative side effects associated with the use of antidepressant medication with both adults and children, these affect regulation strategies should be encouraged.

As noted earlier, research suggests that positive activities, particularly those that encourage gratitude and/or generosity, may promote well-being by reducing the risk of loneliness and rumination on negative events (Layous et al., 2014).

Moreover, individuals that demonstrate an ability to use humor in the face of adverse life events also appear more able to effectively manage associated traumatic stress reactions and fully recover (Davidson et al., 2005; Nezlek & Derks, 2001; Ventis et al., 2001; Vilaythong et al., 2003). In fact, though humor must be judiciously used by clinicians in general, despite the serious nature of the trauma(s) experienced, TF-CBT sessions need not be devoid of laughter and humor. To the contrary, play and light hearted discussions help parents and children recognize that despite the trauma(s) experienced there can be laughter and light at the end of the tunnel.

Thus, it is useful to reserve session time each week to encourage parents to plan positive activities and help them connect their personal coping efforts to the child's coping and healing. It may be emphasized to parents that their efforts to take care of themselves and utilize effective emotional expression and modulation skills will be critical to support their child's healing. In fact, parents are children's most important teachers especially with regard to learning how to cope with life's biggest stressors. It is not unusual for parents to react to this information with concern as most parents do not cope optimally in the aftermath of discovering their child was sexually abused. Still, it is important to point out examples of the child imitating the parent's language and/or behavior to highlight how children learn so much through observation. Thus, parental willingness to participate in treatment with a focus on practicing more effective coping skills themselves will be of great benefit not only in helping them to feel better but also in helping their child learn important life lessons about facing and overcoming adversity. When parents and children learn and practice coping skills together, they gain individual feelings of strength while also developing greater feelings of closeness. Thus, it behooves the therapist to work with parents on developing and practicing the same affect expression and regulation skills that are being taught to the child. In this context, many parents who would not otherwise be interested in therapy or change are willing to do whatever it takes to help the child recover from the experience of sexual abuse. This seems to be particularly true for caregivers who themselves experienced significant adversity in childhood and hope to spare their child the trauma that they experienced. Finally, it is important to note that the parents' coping will not only be observed and imitated by their child, but the better parents feel emotionally, the more effectively they will be able to respond to the complex parenting issues precipitated by the impact of the sexual abuse.

Parenting skills continued with specific praise and reflective listening

As noted above, parents' personal coping as well as their parenting efforts should be addressed and supported each week. The therapist can also motivate parents to encourage children to share and manage their feelings in appropriate ways by shaping and praising children's attempts to do so in session and at home.

The therapist can also inquire about how parents might encourage their children to more frequently share their feelings about everyday events. If parents do not suggest it, the therapist might encourage parents to model the expression of feelings in developmentally appropriate ways such as the parent sharing feelings about work that the child could relate to (e.g., feeling frustrated that a task was taking a very long time to complete). It should be acknowledged that encouraging children to share their feelings can be challenging, but its importance should be highlighted by emphasizing that research documents that children and caregivers who are more emotionally expressive may be less likely to have psychosocial difficulties (Suveg et al., 2005). In fact, the therapist should emphasize that many children and families are not used to or comfortable sharing feelings. However, parents should be encouraged to persevere by occasionally posing open ended questions (e.g., "How are you feeling right now?"; "How did you feel today after taking that test?"), which may eventually prompt the sharing of feelings. Although this can be an excellent opportunity to specifically praise the child's sharing of feelings, parents should be forewarned that lack of responses to questions should not be met with disapproval as this is a skill that takes time to develop and one that the child will be working on in therapy.

Reflective listening

The therapist should emphasize to parents the value of using reflective listening in response to children sharing feelings and discussing positive experiences and events. When parents reflectively listen, children recognize that parents value what they are sharing. Thus, reflective listening can be as reinforcing as specific praise. When children share negative feelings or events, the objective of reflective listening is not to "correct" negative feelings. Rather, parents are asked to refrain from judging, problem solving, or over-sympathizing with negative feelings shared. In fact, it is extremely helpful for therapists to have parents practice validating children's negative feelings through role-plays in which they are asked to repeat back children's feelings with reflective listening and praising the sharing of feelings without attempting to fix the problem that caused the negative feelings. This may feel unnatural at first and will require discipline to simply reflect back what the child shares, but by so doing parents are much more likely to hear more from their child and reinforce the value of sharing feelings even regarding unresolvable problems.

Reflective listening and specific praise in the context of positive rituals and routines

As noted earlier, typical rituals and routines often get disrupted when a family faces a crisis. Building on earlier work related to positive rituals, it is important to remind parents that it is healing for children to have routine time with their parents on a consistent basis during which they can share feelings and thoughts. Thus, the clinician might encourage parents to reinstate and/or initiate special parent-child time on a routine basis during which the sharing of feelings can occur. The establishment of this parent-child time helps children know that there is a consistent time during which they can practice the affective expression skills they are learning in their individual sessions. It is important to emphasize that the tone and consistency of parent-child time may be more important than the actual duration of time. For example, giving the child truly undivided attention for just 10 minutes a day can help to maintain positive parent-child communication. The therapist can help the parent evaluate and improve the quantity, quality, and consistency of the time the parent currently spends in focused communication with the child by teaching and practicing reflective listening skills.

Setting aside a special time and place that the parent and child can "just share" on a predictable and consistent basis increases the opportunities for parents to practice their praise and reflective listening skills. Given the focus on teaching children to express their feelings in words, parents may be encouraged to use this time to specifically praise the sharing of feelings while also learning to reflectively listen. In addition, by consistently reserving a routine time when the parent will be reliably available to the child, the parent communicates the value she places on spending time with and listening to the child. This is an ideal time to express global praise (e.g., "I'm so lucky to be your mom.") as well which can enhance children's feelings of importance and security.

To help parents hone these seemingly basic but rather challenging listening skills, it is preferable to teach parents to begin practicing reflective or active listening skills when communicating with their child about positive activities in which the child is engaging. Giving one's full attention through active/reflective listening is as powerful as praising. Thus, it is important to teach parents to respond with reflective listening when children are sharing positive activities in which they have engaged as this parental attention reinforces those positive activities and associated behaviors.

Additionally, when children are troubled by confusing issues, it is particularly helpful for them to know that there is a predictable time when they will have their parents' undivided attention. When parents effectively engage in reflective listening during these times, children's feelings of security and comfort will increase because they feel heard and understood, regardless of whether they are sharing feelings about something positive or negative.

Parents may also be encouraged to use reflective listening when both children and adolescents are working through difficult problems with peers as well as other dilemmas. By listening and serving as a sounding board, parents are demonstrating confidence in their children's skills in resolving their own problems. It is surprising how often children alter their approaches to problems when they think them through out loud while their parents help them by simply repeating the child's feelings, the solutions the child is generating, as well as the possible outcomes for each proposed solution. The challenge for parents is controlling their desire to fix their children's problems. By not offering the "right" solution but rather allowing children to learn and discover the optimal solutions through their own thought processes and problem solving efforts, parents are reinforcing and encouraging the development of children's problem-solving skills that may enhance their general confidence.

Reflective listening requires parents to refrain from lecturing, debating, independent problem solving, or overreacting to children's expressed feelings. Rather reflective listening is a simple but powerful process of helping children to feel fully heard. This practice helps children gain greater confidence in their ability to acknowledge and share feelings with others. In fact, the sharing of feelings may be particularly helpful with chronic and/or unresolvable problems such as a history of sexual abuse, chronic illness, death of a loved one, and/or other losses. Detailed guidelines for practicing reflective listening (active listening) with children are provided in a handout (see *Reflective [Active] Listening* in Appendix B). Undivided parental attention is the hallmark of active listening, and it powerfully reinforces the adaptive behavior of sharing feelings. It is worth mentioning here that children and adolescents with complex trauma may be very slow to trust and reluctant to share feelings, particularly with caregivers. Reflective listening may well be successful with this particularly vulnerable group of children, but caregivers will need to be patient for their efforts to pay off.

Increasing parental use of selective attention

Children also need to learn that there are effective and ineffective ways of expressing and coping with emotions. For example, although children have every right to feel angry about the sexual abuse and other problems, they need to understand that hitting, yelling, and/or cursing at others are not effective ways of communicating their anger. Rather, they can be encouraged to express their negative emotions through respectful but assertive words, journaling, poetry, song, artwork, and so on. In general, parents should be reassured that their children will spend considerable time in individual child sessions learning to better express and manage negative emotions, but their commitment to model appropriate affective expression while also catching and praising their children's efforts to express feelings effectively will positively influence their child's likely use of these skills outside of therapy. Thus, this part of treatment will focus on educating parents about the power of their attention in encouraging adaptive child behaviors while minimizing the inadvertent reinforcement of problematic behaviors with negative parental attention. (See the *Selective Attention: Praise Plus Active Ignoring* handout in Appendix B).

As noted earlier, attention may be one of the most powerful consequences parents can use in influencing their children's behaviors. Children seek and enjoy attention. For some children, however, the most predictable way for them to get parental attention is to engage in negative behaviors, which parents often respond to with excited, angry, negative attention (e.g., yelling, lecturing, encounter discussions, etc.). This negative attention is unfortunate because the most powerful form of parental attention is neither positive nor negative attention: it is predictable attention. Children generally engage in those behaviors that most predictably elicit attention. Unfortunately, in some environments, children's negative behaviors as opposed to positive behaviors are more likely to gain adult and peer attention on a consistent basis.

Thus, children not only benefit from predictable positive routines but also seek predictable attention. In other words, children frequently engage in behaviors that will be most likely to achieve parental attention of any kind. If negative behaviors are more likely to predictably achieve parental attention (even if that attention is in the form of yelling), while positive behaviors may or may not get any attention at all, children will very likely continue to engage in negative behaviors. Thus, it is important to examine and correct patterns of parent-child interactions in which children are predictably and consistently getting lots of negative parental attention. An examination of parent-child interactions can be best achieved through functional analyses or a review of the ABCs (i.e., antecedents, behaviors and consequences) as described in Box 8.1.

Box 8.1

Case Example: Using the ABC Format to Analyze Behaviors

Since the sexual abuse, 5-year-old Jenny had become extremely clingy. Although she used to play independently, her mother reported that Jenny more recently has been unable to entertain herself even briefly. For example, Jenny constantly interrupted her mother while she was talking on the phone. The therapist first worked collaboratively with Mom to use the ABC format to analyze the behavior pattern by writing antecedents, behaviors, and consequences on a piece of paper, as follows:

Antecedents
Yesterday, Mother reported that she began talking on telephone as she often does after dinner in the evening.

Behaviors
Jenny began interrupting telephone conversation repeatedly; Jenny's behavior became increasingly whiny and loud with each interruption.

Consequences
Each time Jenny interrupted the phone conversation, mother got off the phone and spoke to her. Jenny responded initially by saying she is sorry and mom gave her a kiss and hug. After several more interruptions, Mother got increasingly frustrated and talked with her each time in a sterner manner. Mother finally stopped talking on telephone to scold Jenny, hanging up in frustration to discuss the situation with Jenny at length. During this discussion, mother asked Jenny if she was interrupting her on the phone because she was afraid to be alone because of what her uncle did to her. At that point, Jenny became tearful, and Mother hugged her.

After analyzing the behavior pattern, the mother was able to see that by stopping to scold Jenny and ultimately getting off the phone and talking with her at length, she was giving Jenny the consequences she desired, including parental attention and feelings of control, and thus the mother was inadvertently increasing the likelihood that her daughter would engage in this negative behavior again. Moreover, the mother realized that she did not proactively prepare Jenny to do something else while she was talking on the phone, nor did she give Jenny positive attention in the form of praise when Jenny did not interrupt her on the phone on other occasions. She was, in fact, ignoring the positive behavior and consistently and predictably attending to the negative child behavior. The clinician also reassured the mother that whether or not there was a link with the CSA in terms of the original cause of the behavior, the approach to addressing it would be the same. The parent would be encouraged to proactively set the stage for the child to occupy herself when mother makes a very brief phone call so that she could shape her daughter's independent play behavior slowly with lots of specific praise (with no negative tags) for playing on her own while her mother was on the phone. Over time, mother could begin increasing the time she is on the phone, still getting off periodically to praise her daughter's independent play and engaging her daughter in some one on one time (after the call) during which mother could practice praise and reflective listening.

While much of the focus up to this point has been on encouraging effective coping and positive behaviors in children, parents are often anxious to understand how they can effectively address the symptoms and negative behaviors they are seeing in their children (especially those that seem linked to the CSA). When conducting a functional analysis of a problematic child behavior as illustrated earlier, the therapist seeks to understand what is motivating the child's behavior as most behaviors are engaged in for good reasons. Parental attention is one of the most common factors to motivate children's behaviors. However, there are other needs that motivate children's behaviors as well, including the need for belonging, control, an escape from distress or pain, and the need just to feel good. All of these goals are reasonable; however, children's methods of attempting to achieve these goals are sometimes highly problematic. As noted above, functional analyses examine the patterns of parent-child interactions by reviewing the ABCs (i.e., the antecedents, behaviors, and consequences) associated with children's problem behaviors. Typically, the therapist asks numerous questions in order to elicit detailed examples of problematic parent-child interactions, but such an inquiry should begin with broad questions about what was happening before the problem behavior occurred (i.e., antecedents), what exactly the problem behavior was (i.e., to verify that the behavior is outside the norm), and what the consequences were for the child following the problem behavior. Once this information is obtained, a more detailed analysis of the parent-child exchanges that occurred is needed. This approach helps therapists to understand what is motivating the child's behaviors and allows for the individual tailoring of parenting methods to help the child learn to achieve the desired goal (i.e., attention, belonging, control, escape from distress, etc.) in more productive ways. When children exhibit significant behavior problems, the examination of the ABCs of problematic parent-child interactions helps clinicians to collaborate with parents. The dynamics of parent-child interactions may change dramatically in the aftermath of CSA due to the stress all family members may be experiencing. Through their behaviors, children may be expressing emotions they have never experienced before, and parents may begin engaging in more lenient and/or strict parenting approaches due to their guilt or concerns and/or fears about their children's well-being and safety. By examining what is happening prior to (antecedents) and following (consequences) the onset of children's behavior problems, parents can be given guidance about how they can proactively create environments or antecedent circumstances (e.g., instituting positive rituals or routines) that will reduce the likelihood of such problem behaviors, while also learning how to respond most appropriately when problem behaviors do occur (e.g., consequences) so that the child can learn to achieve the desired outcomes with more adaptive behaviors.

Parents whose children have been exhibiting escalating behavior problems will often express that they have tried everything. This statement may not be far from the truth but parents may have done so in a haphazard way that has reduced the predictability of their actions, thereby making it less likely for children's behaviors to improve. Not surprisingly, parents struggling with their children's behavior problems are often providing a great deal of predictable negative attention (e.g., encounter discussions following problem behaviors, begging, threatening, yelling, etc.) that inadvertently reinforces the problem behaviors. Furthermore, given their immersion in day to day crises, parents are often unable to identify what is motivating their children's behaviors, nor do they know what may reduce their children's behavior problems and/or what will serve to increase their children's positive behaviors.

The tendency to ignore children's positive appropriate behaviors may be exacerbated in the aftermath of a CSA discovery as well, when nonoffending parents may be preoccupied with the many pressing concerns raised by an abuse investigation (e.g., protection, shelter, separation, legal proceedings). This lack of consistent, positive attention may inadvertently lead children to act out in order to regain their parents' attention. Unfortunately, positive behaviors may not get attention from parents in a predictable and/or consistent manner especially when parents are under a great deal of stress. In fact, many parents today are preoccupied with numerous external stressors and use the time when children are engaged in positive behaviors to take care of business (e.g., chores, phone calls, and job related duties). As a result, parents may be inadvertently ignoring positive child behaviors and primarily attending to the child when she is acting out. Even when a parent does acknowledge a child's positive behavior with praise, often the parent's positive response is much less dramatic and less exciting than the intense emotional negative parental response the child receives following an inappropriate behavior. Thus, in some cases, the parents' pattern of responding to the child needs significant adjusting.

The sexual abuse may also lead some parents to become overly attentive to and protective of their children. Out of concern for their child's safety and well-being, some parents find themselves focusing on and inadvertently reinforcing their children's abuse-related fears, clinginess, and/or other problem behaviors. In fact, parents who are guilt ridden as a result of thinking that they "did not protect" their children from the sexual abuse may be particularly prone to inadvertently reinforcing fearful behaviors in their children with overprotective and reinforcing responses for these behaviors.

In general, it is not unusual for parents to be focused on their children's problem behaviors, particularly when they are seeking help for those problems. However, it is important to remind parents that sexual abuse does not completely transform children and eliminate all of their positive qualities. Their children's positive qualities may simply be overshadowed by increased problematic behaviors in the aftermath of the sexual abuse (e.g., increased clinginess, fearfulness, attention-seeking behaviors, angry behaviors). Thus, the initial focus of parenting is on skills that will help parents encourage positive behaviors through praise and reflective listening while minimizing problem behaviors through selective attention (i.e., minimizing attention to the negative behavior while increasing attention to the positive behavior).

Once parents begin to see increases in their children's positive behaviors as a result of their deliberate efforts to use specific and global praise, reflective listening, and proactive positive routines and rituals, parents will be ready to focus on reducing children's maladaptive behaviors. In order to gain parental confidence in the process, it helps to tackle relatively minor behavior problems first before taking on more serious difficulties. When parents experience some success in eliminating minor behavioral difficulties (e.g., whining, yelling, mild temper tantrums, angry outbursts), they will be motivated to apply the same principles and advanced skills to more difficult problems. While working to eliminate minor behavioral problems, it is also critical to help parents to identify those positive behaviors that can replace the mild problematic behaviors. Once those positive replacement behaviors are identified, parents can create positive rituals and use specific praise to increase those positive behaviors.

The application of selective attention to angry outbursts

The next few sections will outline the use of an important parenting skill, selective attention (also known as differential attention) as it applies to the treatment of angry outbursts or mild temper tantrums in children who have experienced abuse. The skills and principles discussed, however, are applicable to a wide range of behavioral difficulties exhibited by both children who have experienced abuse, as well as those who have not. Thus, it is important for the therapist to emphasize that the goal of this work is to provide parents with skills to effectively manage not only current behavior problems exhibited by the child but also any future behavior problems exhibited by any child in the family.

Many parents respond ineffectively to their children's angry outbursts. This may be particularly true of parents who believe that their child's anger is linked to the experience of sexual abuse. Understandably, parents of children who have experienced CSA may feel that their child's angry outbursts are justified given the abusive experience. Parents may believe that by throwing angry temper tantrums, the child is releasing pent-up emotions associated with the abuse. Not surprisingly, parents who link the angry outbursts to the abuse in these ways may find it difficult to discipline their child for this type of behavior.

Although the therapist may validate the parents' view that their child's angry outbursts may be linked to the abuse and thus are justifiable, it is important to stress that the child's current means of expressing anger is maladaptive. In fact it is likely that a child who exhibits repeated angry outbursts and temper tantrums will develop significant difficulties with respect to social interactions, family relationships, and school performance. Moreover, there is considerable evidence that those who cope with anger by lashing out may not only experience psychosocial and relationship difficulties but may also increase their risk of developing significant physical health problems (e.g., high blood pressure, cardiac difficulties, and other stress-related illnesses; Tavris, 1989; Williams et al., 2000).

In general, behavior that is violent in nature, even if it is symbolic, should not be encouraged. As noted earlier, there is no evidence that punching a pillow or a bobo doll reduces feelings of anger. In fact, the reverse appears to be true. When children are encouraged to act out their anger in these ways, these violent behaviors tend to increase and may generalize from hitting pillows to hitting walls to hitting other children. In light of this information, parents may be more receptive to teaching their children healthier methods of expressing anger while minimizing their children's reliance on dysfunctional means of expressing anger (e.g., tantrums, hitting). It is important to be clear from the start that the objective of therapy is not to suppress the child's anger. Rather, parents should be reminded that their child will be learning to label and express his negative emotions more effectively during individual sessions.

Careful functional analyses should be conducted to examine the parent-child interactions associated with the child's angry outbursts or temper tantrums. Such analyses will help the therapist to better understand the function or goals (i.e., attention, control, escape) motivating the child's problematic angry behaviors. This understanding will also help to determine positive replacement behaviors that will most effectively help the child achieve those goals in a more adaptive way.

Therapists should then encourage parents to model, shape, and reinforce appropriate means of achieving the identified goals or reinforce appropriate expressions of anger. Some parents will first need to learn more effective anger control and coping skills themselves before they can be effective models. Once parents are successful in expressing and managing their own anger effectively, they can be taught to use differential or selective attention to encourage the child's adaptive means of expressing anger while discouraging maladaptive means.

Positive reinforcement for appropriate expression of anger

The first step in teaching parents to use differential attention to shape appropriate expressions of anger is to teach parents to identify and reinforce children's attempts to express anger and other emotions in productive ways. This may mean encouraging their children to share their angry feelings in words. Interestingly, although a parent may be convinced that her child is constantly angry, that same parent may *never* have heard the child simply state, "I'm feeling really mad or frustrated because... ." In fact, parents who have their hands full coping with their children's acting out or angry behaviors often spend hours talking to their children about these maladaptive behaviors while more appropriate expressions of emotions are inadvertently ignored or given minimal attention. This pattern will need to be reversed such that children's appropriate verbal expressions of anger are reinforced before any discipline strategies (i.e., time out) for diminishing the angry outbursts can be effectively implemented.

Many children do not know how to express anger appropriately. With such children, the therapist in individual session and the parent at home will be teaching and reinforcing respectively a new repertoire of mechanisms for expressing and coping with anger as described earlier. The specific strategies children are working on in individual sessions should be reviewed with the parent, including talking about their feelings; using "I statements"; writing a letter, story, or song expressing their emotions; drawing a picture; problem solving; or engaging in activities such as exercising, relaxation, or breathing techniques. Parents should reinforce such appropriate behaviors by empathizing and offering purely positive, specific, and enthusiastic praise for healthy responses to anger-provoking situations. The key is not eliminating anger but rather helping parents to notice when their children are experiencing some level of frustration or anger as these are opportunities to support the child's efforts to manage this normal emotion more effectively.

In some cultures, it may not be acceptable for children to express anger in words to their caregivers. This might be viewed as a sign of disrespect. In these situations, therapists can explore with parents what their treatment goals are (e.g., adaptive behaviors at school) and mention how children verbally expressing anger directly to them might increase the likelihood of these goals being achieved. In other words, parents might be more accepting of children expressing anger in words if they understand that this might improve their behavior at school or at home. Also, role-plays with these parents might be quite important to help them respond more optimally to their children expressing anger with words, since this is something that may be new or unfamiliar for them.

Identifying consequences motivating maladaptive expressions of anger

Parents should be asked to examine the patterns associated with their child's maladaptive expressions of anger, using functional analyses or the ABCs approach described earlier. Starting with the most recent episode, it is useful to examine several episodes of angry outbursts so that the consequences the child achieves through these outbursts may be identified. As with any other behavior problem, it is important to determine what consequences were achieved by the outbursts. Understanding the particular factors motivating a child's behavior will help the parent and therapist identify an effective positive replacement behavior that will allow the child to achieve the desired consequences in more socially appropriate ways. Angry outbursts or tantrums are problematic child behaviors that may be motivated by several different types of consequences including escape from distress, attention, and/or feelings of control.

Escape from distress

For some children, for example, angry outbursts may achieve the consequence of escaping from situations in which they are generally fearful or specifically reminded of the sexual abuse (e.g., therapy sessions, going to bed, taking a bath). Such outbursts may be best addressed by encouraging children to develop other means of expressing negative feelings and/or coping with the anxiety associated with these reminders. Parents may, in fact, be reassured that the child is learning to do exactly that in his individual therapy sessions. In addition, children's participation in the gradual exposure and processing sessions may help them overcome the anxiety and abuse-related fears that may be underlying angry tantrums that are motivated by their desire to escape distress.

Attention

Some children may have angry outbursts that are initially triggered by an abuse reminder that is out of their awareness (i.e., PTSD symptoms) but the outbursts are now reinforced by parental attention. Parents of children who have experienced CSA may inadvertently reinforce angry outbursts by responding with a great deal of sympathetic attention in the form of "encounter discussions," comforting hugs, and so on. Other parents may become exasperated with the repetitiveness and the seemingly unprovoked nature of the angry outbursts and respond with a great deal of negative attention in the form of yelling or stern lectures. As noted earlier, attention, whether it is positive or negative, is reinforcing to children especially when the attention is provided by parents or other primary caregivers repeatedly. Children quickly learn which behaviors receive attention most predictably and they repeat those behaviors. Although children would not necessarily report that their parents' yelling is pleasing to them, their behavior patterns reveal that if negative attention (e.g., yelling) is more predictably achieved than positive attention, they will work for this negative attention by frequently throwing angry tantrums.

Control

A third consequence that may motivate angry outbursts are the feelings of control children may achieve from the outbursts. If the child is able to use the angry outburst to elicit a certain response from the parent (e.g., giving in to the child's request), the child may achieve a sense of control through the tantrum. Furthermore, if the parent responds to the child's outburst in a dramatic or highly emotional way, the parent may inadvertently encourage the child to feel he is in control because the parent appears out of control.

Parents may find it difficult to believe they are inadvertently encouraging tantrums or outbursts. It may be useful to acknowledge that scolding or yelling may be temporarily effective in stopping the outburst or tantrum for the moment.

However, it is important to help parents distinguish between parental responses that are temporarily useful versus those that are helpful in the long run. Thus, the therapist may point out that yelling does not stop children from repeating the behavior in the future. Therapists may help parents recognize this problem by asking parents if they find themselves yelling about the same problem behaviors over and over again. This pattern provides parents with evidence that their yelling is not working to eliminate the problem behavior in the long run. Yelling, in fact, often provides two consequences children are motivated to achieve: attention and control. Parental yelling also tends to be a powerful reinforcer because in many cases it is so predictable. Indeed, when a parent says, "My child really knows how to push my buttons," the parent is indicating that the child really knows how to predictably get negative attention from the parent. Unfortunately, this same child may not know how to predictably obtain positive parental attention with adaptive behaviors. Thus, it is extremely important to provide consistent and predictable attention for the desired adaptive behaviors that will replace the maladaptive ones.

Selective attention

The next step in reducing child behavior problems, in this case angry outbursts or temper tantrums, is to identify the positive replacement behavior that will be encouraged in the child. Selective or differential attention may then be used to reduce children's problem behaviors while increasing adaptive behaviors that can replace the angry behaviors in terms of predictably obtaining attention and/or feelings of control. Parents should be taught how to implement *active ignoring*, which requires parents to withdraw the reinforcing consequences that their child is experiencing following a temper tantrum or outburst by actively ignoring the outburst and simultaneously working hard to attend to the positive replacement behavior when it occurs. It is important to acknowledge that this process will be difficult, as it requires parents to break ingrained habits (e.g., yelling) and/or withdraw attention (e.g., comforting hugs) that they believe their child needs and deserves. Thus, the therapist will need to emphasize that by learning to actively ignore the child's maladaptive behaviors and praising a positive replacement behavior, parents will be teaching their children a more adaptive means of expressing their needs: this is extremely important for their long term well-being.

It is important to emphasize that active ignoring of mild problem behaviors will not work alone but should be used only in combination with positive reinforcement for the adaptive replacement behavior. In addition, parents should be warned that the targeted problem behavior often increases temporarily when active ignoring or selective attention is initiated. This temporary increase is often referred to as an *extinction burst.* It is important for parents to continue to actively ignore through the extinction burst to avoid inadvertently reinforcing a more exaggerated version of the original problem behavior. The potential for an extinction burst should be discussed in advance as parents may question the soundness of the therapeutic suggestions if they experience unexpected increases in their child's problem behaviors. In addition, active ignoring should not be attempted if parents believe the tantrum behavior has the potential to become violent or dangerous. In such cases, other intervention strategies such as time out combined with predictable positive consequences for positive replacement behaviors may be more appropriate. Guidelines for time out will be described in the chapter to follow.

Practice activities assigned

As noted earlier, practice assignments should be individually tailored to the child's and parent's needs. In addition, it is important that the practice assignments reflect what was covered in the session such that parents are well prepared to follow through at home.

Coping skills practice

It is important to remind parents that they will be encouraged to continue to engage in coping skills practices at home as they are their children's most important role models for coping. For example, parents may be encouraged to engage in and model:

- effective emotional expression skills (i.e., appropriately sharing feelings with other adults and/or sharing less intense nonabuse-related negative feelings [e.g., frustration, disappointment, happiness] as well as positive feelings with their children)
- effective affective modulation strategies and/or other personal coping rituals or routines (e.g., aerobic exercise, mindfulness practices, problem solving, etc.) in the presence of or in conjunction with their children.

Parenting skills practice

Listed below are parenting skills practice activities that therapists may encourage parents to engage in during the week depending on the specific activities covered in session as well as the child's therapeutic needs and difficulties.

- *Encourage children's expression of feelings.* Parents may be encouraged to continue to make time for positive parent-child time (i.e., positive rituals) and look for opportunities to provide children with positive reinforcement for sharing feelings appropriately at home. For example, parents may help *young children* further expand their emotional vocabulary and label their emotions by looking at faces in books and magazines and identifying the emotions the characters seem to be experiencing. Parents of *older children* may have more success modeling the sharing of appropriate feelings and engaging their teenagers in discussions about other teens' feelings concerning different situations as a way to begin to reinforce and model the value of sharing and discussing feelings, later inquiring about the child's own feelings with the open-ended questions (e.g., "How were you feeling today at school?") and reflective listening.

- *Reflective Listening.* Provide parents' with the *Reflective (Active) Listening* handout and encourage the practice of reflective listening and specific praise whenever the child shares positive activities and/or expresses feelings appropriately. If necessary, parents may pose open-ended questions (e.g., "How were you feeling after the soccer game today?") to initiate conversations or the sharing of feelings so that reflective listening can be practiced. It is important to prepare parents to work hard to control their instinct to offer commentary about their child's expressed feelings and/or "fix" their problems.
- *Selective attention.* Provide parents' with the *Selective Attention* handout and offer parents guidance to identify a mild problem behavior (i.e., a behavior that is not dangerous if it escalates some; see *Selective Attention: Praise Plus Active Ignoring* handout) that can be actively ignored while simultaneously specifically praising an agreed upon positive replacement behavior. It helps to record the specific problem behavior to be ignored, as well as the replacement behavior to be praised on the parenting handout and in the progress notes. It is critical that parents understand that generally ignoring all problem behaviors will not be effective and may, in fact, undermine a child's healing.

Some parents find it helpful to write down the details of the parent-child interactions so that they can be prepared the following week when their therapist elicits examples of parent-child interactions during the week. Such parents may be encouraged to use a journal to keep track of such details.

The selective attention parenting skills practice most often needs to be repeated over several sessions until parents build confidence and achieve some mastery of these skills.

Prepare for conjoint session

Reflective listening and specific praise skills may be practiced in preparation for a conjoint activity by engaging in role-plays in which the child first shares a negative feeling about a recent nonabuse-related problem and then shares positive feeling about a recent experience. The clinician may play the role of the child using the feelings the child indicated she would share during her preparation for conjoint session. In so doing, the therapist can prepare the parent for the actual feelings to be shared. In addition, when appropriate, the clinician may prepare for the possibility of the child exhibiting mild distracting behaviors if that is likely. Such a role-play can help the parent to simultaneously practice reflective listening, active ignoring of mild anxious or noncompliant behaviors, as well as specific praise for effective expression of feelings (i.e., selective attention).

Prepare for mutual exchange of praise activity

As in previous sessions, the clinician may encourage parents to share the specific praise and/or global praise they would like to give the child in conjoint session. At this stage in therapy, this is still important to review before the conjoint session as parents benefit from constructive feedback as they often continue to inadvertently offer praise that contains negative tags or is not purely positive. Surprisingly enough, praise does not come naturally to many parents especially in the aftermath of CSA when they are distressed themselves. It is important to emphasize for parents that while they may want to offer both specific and global praise during this exercise, these two forms of praise should not be repeatedly linked. Rather, it is important for children to experience expressions of love and affection (i.e., global praise) that are not linked to specific behaviors or achievements.

CONJOINT SESSION(S) (OPTIONAL)

Listed below are activities they can help parents and children practice the skills together. One or more of these activities may be engaged in depending on what was covered in their individual sessions.

Parent and child share their feelings and/or coping skills lists

This simple and quick activity provides the child an opportunity to share his successful efforts in individual session to identify feeling words and create a coping skills tool kit. In addition, the parent has an opportunity to demonstrate her commitment to encouraging the use of the words and skills reviewed on each of the lists through modeling and specific praise of the child's work.

Child teaches parent chosen affect modulation skill

As noted earlier, whenever possible the therapist should collaborate with the child in planning a conjoint activity. Thus, it is best for the child to choose from at least two possible affect regulation skills that can be taught or demonstrated for the parent in a brief conjoint activity. This activity can enhance the child's feelings of mastery while providing parents with the opportunity to practice active ignoring of minor problem behaviors (e.g., slumping in the chair, being oppositional, distractible, etc.), while praising adaptive behaviors and using reflective listening to demonstrate understanding of the skill the child is teaching.

Parent and child engage in reflective listening exercise

This activity may require a somewhat longer conjoint session (e.g., 10 to 15 minutes). During this activity, parents and children are encouraged to engage in the affective expression and reflective listening exercise described earlier. During this activity, the child is encouraged to use "I statements" to share a negative feeling about a recent nonabuse-related event and then a positive feeling about another recent experience. Parents may be supported in engaging in reflective listening, active ignoring, and specific praise in response to the child's sharing of these feelings. This conjoint activity should not be undertaken unless the parent has been prepared through role-plays as described in the individual parent session. However, even with such preparation the therapist may still need to jump in and gently refocus the session on active listening and specific praise for the sharing of feelings by modeling such skills if the parent begins to be defensive and/or engages in lecturing and/or problem solving in response to the child's sharing of negative feelings. The sharing of positive feelings should then follow more naturally. This practice allows the therapist an opportunity to observe parents' use of praise and reflective listening. Feedback in the form of compliment sandwiches can then be provided to parents in the individual parent session that follows.

Review practice activities encouraged

The therapist may also use conjoint session time to briefly review or ask children to review the skills they have agreed to practice between sessions. This can help at home so that parents can remember to model those skills themselves and offer praise whenever the child makes some efforts to use these coping skills at home. As always, it is important to remind parents to praise even the smallest steps toward using the more adaptive coping behaviors learned thus far.

Positive end-of-session ritual

To end the session on a positive note, parents and children may be encouraged to engage in the exchange of specific and/or global praise that they prepared for each other in their respective individual session. The therapist may also simply highlight the child's and parent's progress and/or briefly comment on something positive or exciting that parent or child shared.

9

Cognitive Coping Skills

This treatment component presents another critical coping skill to be taught prior to the initiation of the trauma narrative and processing component with the child. Cognitive coping skills help children as well as their parents get in touch with their thoughts. Some thoughts are so fleeting and/or automatic that they may be just out of one's awareness and require some effort to actively notice them. During this component, children and parents not only learn how to capture and examine their thoughts but also how thoughts can powerfully influence feelings, behaviors, and even physical well-being on a daily basis. With children, these skills are applied initially only to nonabuse-related thoughts and situations because it is important *not* to correct children's abuse-related thoughts until after they have revealed their innermost thoughts in the context of trauma narration. Challenging and/or correcting children's abuse-related thoughts prematurely can lead children to begin censoring what they share prior to revealing their most troubling thoughts and developing beliefs. However, through practice identifying, retrieving, and examining nonabuse-related thoughts, later during the development of the trauma narrative, children will likely be more successful in retrieving abuse-related thoughts and beliefs that may have developed during and after their experience of sexual abuse. In addition, learning to retrieve nonabuse-related thoughts may greatly enhance children's skills in catching and sharing abuse-related thoughts during trauma narration and later identifying and correcting abuse-related dysfunctional thoughts that may be underlying children's troubling ongoing behaviors and distressing emotions. However, with children, during this component the focus remains on cognitive coping skills as applied to nonabuse-related issues. In addition, with youth struggling with complex trauma and/or severe emotional dysregulation, a continued focus on integrating and building on the coping skills reviewed thus far is important. Thus, at the end of the child component, a discussion of the individual tailoring of the skill building components for children who experience comorbid difficulties and/or complex trauma is provided (Cohen, Mannarino, & Deblinger, 2012).

During this component, parents also learn to use cognitive coping skills to cope with nonabuse-related thoughts. However, parents may experience significant distress due to dysfunctional, inaccurate, and/or unproductive thoughts about the sexual abuse that are important for therapists to elicit and correct. Thus, unlike with the children, the therapist may help parents begin to apply these skills to both nonabuse- and abuse-related thoughts and feelings during this component. The amount of parent session time devoted to cognitive coping skills and/or behavior management skills should be determined based on the family's particular needs. When parental distress seems of greater concern than the child's behaviors, therapists may spend more time on parental coping as the parental distress may, in fact, ultimately undermine the child's behavioral adjustment. Conversely, the research of the authors suggests that a focus on ongoing behavior management training is important, as such appears to be critical to addressing the acting-out behavior problems that a significant proportion of youth exhibit in the aftermath of CSA (Cohen, Deblinger, et al., 2004; Deblinger et al., 1996; Deblinger et al., 2011). As noted earlier, many parents respond well to some combination of coping and parent skills training and do not need a separate therapist to help them cope with the impact of the CSA on their personal well-being. However, following this component, if a parent is continuing to experience emotional difficulties that seem to be unrelated to the impact of the sexual abuse or if the parent's personal difficulties are so severe that it is impossible to focus on the child's behavioral needs, the therapist may need to consider referring the parent to a therapist who will solely focus on the parent's own therapeutic needs. Parents, with whom a trusting therapeutic relationship has been established, typically view such a therapy referral as a reflection of one's caring and concern.

CHILD SESSION(S)

A session during this component might begin by simply inquiring about how the child is feeling. The feelings list the child developed and/or a feelings chart may help the child identify feelings. This activity provides a natural opportunity to praise the sharing of feelings.

Practice activities review

The trauma-focused cognitive-behavioral therapy (TF-CBT) therapist might review the at-home practice activities assigned during the prior session, bearing in mind that the overall goal is to encourage the active use of any of the relaxation, affective expression, and/or modulation skills learned in prior sessions. Although it is important to review the use of the skills learned and to demonstrate the therapist's interest and commitment to the work, there should be some focus on the use or potential use of these skills even if the child denies using any coping skills. When this occurs, it is best to help the child identify times she naturally used the skills being learned, as well as the outcomes of those experiences, while also reviewing times when the child could have benefited from using one or more of the skills. This work can best be accomplished by conducting a careful review or functional analyses of stressful situations experienced during the week that were resolved well and/or poorly. As always, even if the overall resolution of the stressor, conflict, or problem was less than optimal, it is important to identify some specific coping behaviors or attempts to praise. The therapist then may collaboratively problem solve and/or offer constructive feedback regarding things the child may have done differently, followed by praise, in the form of a "compliment sandwich."

Present cognitive coping skills and the cognitive triangle

Cognitive coping skills are valuable lifelong skills for children and adolescents. Though older children may more easily grasp these skills, even young children may be taught to see the connection between their thoughts and feelings, as well as their thoughts and behaviors. In fact, by slowing down the pace and offering many concrete examples, children as young as 4 years of age can understand how thoughts influence feelings. Older children and teens may be able to grasp the more complex interrelationships of thoughts, feelings, behaviors, and even bodily sensations. Readers interested in further information regarding the empirical development and use of these cognitive therapy techniques with children are referred to *The Optimistic Child* (Seligman, 2007).

Interrelationships of thoughts, feelings, and behaviors

The therapist may begin the cognitive coping component by defining and reviewing what is meant by thoughts, feelings, and behaviors. Defining thoughts and the relationships to feelings and behaviors can best be done by utilizing pictures, diagrams, or concrete anchors, such as explaining that thoughts are what our brain says to us inside our heads. Later, the therapist may present the interrelated nature of thoughts, feelings, behaviors and, when appropriate, bodily sensations in figures presented on a piece of paper or white board. The presentation of these concepts, however, should be carefully tailored to the child's developmental level and needs. With the youngest children, simple single arrow diagrams (see Figure 9.1) may help explain how thoughts affect feelings and how thoughts affect behaviors. Moreover, with children this young, repeated concrete examples of the influence of thoughts should be provided with Socratic questions used to verify a child's understanding of these important concepts (e.g., "How do you think a child would feel if he said to

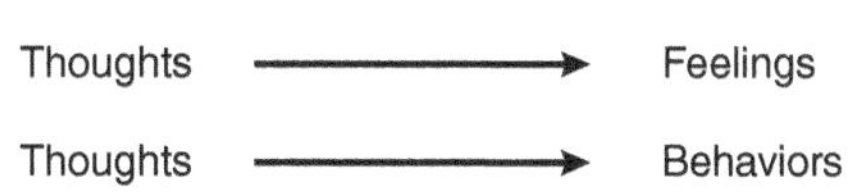

Figure 9.1 Cognitive Coping Arrows.

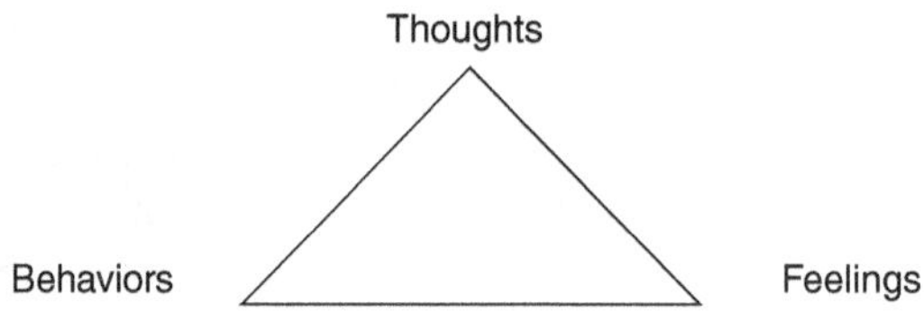

Figure 9.2 Cognitive Triangle.

himself, 'nobody likes me'? Do you think that is a good thing for a child to say to himself? What could that child say to himself to help him have more positive feelings?"). With older children, depending on their developmental sophistication and symptom presentation, the therapist may present the cognitive triangle (see Figure 9.2) or the coping diamond (see Figure 9.3) that can incorporate bodily sensations as well as thoughts, feelings, and behaviors. The cognitive triangle has been used quite effectively to help children who have experienced depression. The triangle not only demonstrates how dysfunctional thinking can lead to negative moods but also highlights how behaviors such as isolating oneself can reinforce dysfunctional thinking (e.g., "I am all alone in the world"), which may lead to negative emotions (e.g., sadness, loneliness), which in turn leads to the isolative behavior. The coping diamond is even more complex, but it can be particularly helpful with children who are experiencing physical manifestations of anxiety, depression, or PTSD. Reviewing with them how these symptoms are linked to their thoughts, feelings, and behaviors often helps clients feel less vulnerable and better able to manage somatic symptoms. When discussing these interrelationships and presenting examples, the therapist should draw one of these diagrams or figures on a piece of paper or preferably a white board so that the child can record some examples as the clinician helps the child to understand how these interrelationships work. In fact, it is often reassuring for parents to see the child's writing on the board as a demonstration of how much the child is learning in session. To explain how thoughts, feelings, and behavior can influence each other, a therapist might follow the method outlined in Box 9.1.

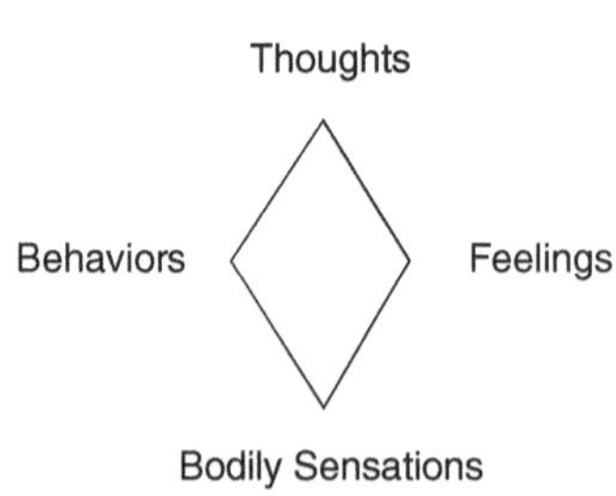

Figure 9.3 Coping Diamond.

Box 9.1

Case Example: Interrelationships between Thoughts, Feelings, and Behaviors

A therapist might begin discussing the interrelationships between thoughts, feelings, and behaviors with a general discussion:

Therapist: *I'd like for us to talk about how our thoughts can affect how we are feeling and then how both our thoughts and feelings may affect the way we act or behave. Let's start by talking about our thoughts. Our thoughts are the things we say to ourselves in our own heads. We all talk to ourselves all the time in our heads. Did you know that?*

Child: *I sort of thought I was the only crazy kid who did that.*

Therapist: *Nope. We all talk to ourselves—so I guess you're not crazy after all. Some of the things we say to ourselves are helpful or make us feel good while other things we say make us feel unhappy. For example, when we walk past a mirror, a person might look in the mirror and say something to herself. Let me give you an example. Two girls went shopping with their mom and bought a skirt for school. A girl passed a mirror in school and thought to herself, "I really like this new skirt, it looks really nice." How do you think those thoughts would make the girl feel?*

Child: *I guess she would feel happy or confident.*

Therapist: *I think you're right. She probably would feel happy, confident, and maybe even proud. Another girl who wore a new skirt to school might say, "My friends can probably tell that my mom picked out this skirt. I hate this skirt. It makes me look like a dork!" How do you think those thoughts would make that girl feel?*

Child: *That girl would probably feel embarrassed or mad that her mom made her wear that skirt.*

Therapist: *What if I told you both those girls were wearing the same skirt? You see, very often it is not a skirt or an experience that causes us to feel a certain way but it is what we say to ourselves about it that affects our feelings.*

The therapist might continue this work by providing hypothetical situations and asking the child to identify the emotions and the behaviors that can be generated by thoughts indicated in the situations, as follows:

> *Billy wasn't invited to a classmate's birthday party. Billy thinks, "I don't get invited to birthday parties. Nobody likes me." How do these thoughts make Billy feel? Then how does Billy behave toward other kids?*

The therapist might continue using Socratic questions to help the child understand the impact of thoughts on feelings and behaviors. As noted, the Socratic method refers to the use of carefully designed questions to help clients think through and correct their own dysfunctional thoughts. For example, after describing the above example, the therapist might ask the client, "*When Billy says to himself, 'Nobody likes me,' do you think it's true that nobody likes him? Not a single person? If he continues to think that nobody likes him, how do you suppose he will feel? And how will he act?*"

The therapist should be prepared to offer further relevant fictitious examples and this type of questioning until the child seems to have caught on to the cognitive triangle concept, particularly with respect to the influence thoughts have on our feelings and behaviors. As this work continues, the therapist may shift from having the child identify the emotions depicted in an example to having the child identify the thoughts underlying the emotions. For most children, identifying underlying thoughts may be more difficult than identifying emotions. The therapist should provide examples that describe the fictitious child's problem and her emotional reaction while asking the client to identify the thoughts that may have triggered the feelings. The following example requires the client to identify the underlying thoughts.

On Tuesday, Kathy's mother said they might go to the movies during the weekend, but on Saturday her mother says they are too busy with other activities to go. Kathy is really angry.

- *What might she be thinking to cause her to feel so angry?*
- *What else might she be saying to herself?*
- *What could she say to herself that would reduce her anger at her mother?*

DIFFERENT THOUGHTS RESULT IN DIFFERENT EMOTIONS

As the child begins to grasp the relationships between thoughts, feelings, and behaviors, the therapist should explain that to a large extent people determine their thoughts and thus ultimately their feelings. One can choose to think about a particular situation in positive, hopeful, or optimistic ways, and then those thoughts will generate positive feelings. It should also be explained sometimes one's thinking may become negative and this can lead to distressing emotions.

To illustrate that possibility, the therapist may provide the child with developmentally appropriate examples of how one can have different thoughts about the exact same problem, resulting in different emotions. An example is provided in Box 9.2. The therapist may use different examples to elicit from the child the various feelings that might result when someone thinks about a problem in different ways. Visual presentations of the cognitive triangle or cartoons of children with thought bubbles, triggering specific feelings (reflected in their hearts), and then leading to specific actions (as depicted by what the child's feet, hands, and/or mouth are doing) can help children grasp the impact of thoughts on feelings and behaviors. Different age-appropriate examples using paper and pencil or the whiteboard can be very helpful in teaching children these concepts.

BOX 9.2

Case Example: Different Thoughts Result in Different Emotions

The therapist might use the following story to help a child learn how different thoughts result in different emotions.

> *Jordan and Dennis are in the same fifth-grade class. They both failed their first math test of the year, each receiving a score of 55. When Jordan got his test back, he thought, "I must be the stupidest kid in the school. I failed this test, now I'll get an F in math on my report card and I'll end up flunking the fifth grade!" This kind of thinking made Jordan feel* [have the child fill in the blank]. *Based on how Jordan was thinking and feeling, how do you think he behaved after failing the test?*
>
> *Dennis received the same grade, but he had different thoughts about it. He thought, "Well, I didn't really study very hard because I went to my friend's party. Now I know what kind of tests Mrs. Smith gives and what I need to do to get ready for the next test. Next time I'm going to study more and I'm sure I will pull this grade up." These thoughts made Dennis feel* [have child fill in the blank]. *Based on how Dennis was thinking and feeling, how do you think he behaved after failing the test?*

After modeling the process for the child, the therapist may ask the child to work through an example, demonstrating how different thoughts about the same situation can result in different feelings. The therapist should continue practicing with the child until the child is consistently able to identify the positive (optimistic) or negative (pessimistic) thoughts that underlie different feelings in various examples. Again, the therapist can explain to the child that there are many different ways to think about the same problem. Furthermore, the therapist may say the following:

> *When we think about a problem in a way that leads to okay or good feelings, we call those thoughts positive, hopeful, or optimistic thoughts. When we think about a problem in ways that lead to bad feelings, we call those thoughts negative, unhelpful, or pessimistic thoughts. In addition, sometimes negative thoughts are inaccurate. Correcting those thoughts can help us feel better.*

Identify and practice disputing negative thoughts

Once the child understands how it is possible to think about the same situation in different ways, the therapist should begin to teach the child how one can change negative, unhelpful thoughts to more optimistic or hopeful thoughts that result in more positive emotions and behaviors.

The therapist should emphasize that negative thoughts are not necessarily true or permanent (no matter how much one believes them). In fact, sometimes people's thoughts are completely inaccurate, but because they believe them to be true, they may feel very sad or scared of something that is highly unlikely to happen (e.g., in Jordan's case, failing the fifth grade). Sometimes getting more accurate information can help change one's negative thoughts. In turn when our thoughts become less negative due to more hopeful information, one is likely to feel better. The therapist may further explain that the process of changing thoughts and emotions is a skill that must be practiced to be used effectively. Furthermore, the change in thoughts and emotions often does not occur quickly and completely, particularly if the problematic thoughts and emotions are ones that have been experienced on a repeated basis. However, with practice it is possible to change both the thoughts and feelings that have been distressing. Using fictitious examples, the therapist can teach the child to formulate positive replacement thoughts to substitute for negative, dysfunctional thoughts. An example of this process is provided in Box 9.3.

Applying the model to the child's own negative thoughts

Once the child has a good grasp of the concepts presented, the therapist may encourage him to dispute his own negative (although not abused-related) thoughts, replacing them with more positive, hopeful thoughts. When encouraged to do so, some children can challenge their negative thoughts quite readily.

The therapist may begin teaching the child the process of disputing negative thoughts initially using relatively minor difficulties and then more significant current but nonabuse-related difficulties. During this phase of treatment, it helps to have children practice becoming more aware of their own automatic thoughts on a daily basis, working to identify those thoughts to determine if their day to day thoughts are helpful or hurtful, and to replace hurtful thoughts with ones that are more helpful. Because thoughts are often automatic, habitual, and/or fleeting in nature, helping children bring their thoughts to awareness sometimes requires considerable practice.

By helping children to develop their skills in identifying and acknowledging thoughts in general, they may be more likely to successfully retrieve thoughts they may have had at the time of the abuse when the child begins to develop a trauma narrative. These skills, in fact, will become critical during the next phase of treatment in the context of processing sexual abuse–related memories. However, to minimize the development of anticipatory anxiety in the child, there is no need to discuss this objective until the session in which the child will actually begin the narrative. Still, on occasion, the child may spontaneously offer an example of an abuse-related thought that causes distress. If the thought raised appears to be interfering significantly with the child's current functioning, it may be useful to provide child sexual abuse (CSA) educational information that contradicts the thought and possibly helps the child cope. As noted previously, more in depth processing of thoughts and feelings is best postponed until the child has shared the details of the sexual abuse experiences during the development of the trauma

Box 9.3

Case Example: Disputing Negative Thoughts

The therapist might help a child learn about disputing negative thoughts, by telling the following story:

> *Jasmine was the first student through the lunch line and sat down at a table in the corner. When her friends Kathy and Nicole came through the line, they sat at another table. Jasmine thinks, "They don't like me anymore. Nobody likes me. I'm the least popular girl at school." Those thoughts cause Jasmine to feel sad and hurt. How can she replace those negative thoughts with more optimistic thoughts that will help her feel better?*

If the child has difficulty generating a positive replacement thought, the therapist might ask the following:

Therapist: *How do you think those thoughts made Jasmine feel?*
Child: *Sad and maybe a little angry.*
Therapist: *And if Jasmine was thinking that and feeling sad and angry, what do you think she might do?*
Child: *Maybe she would just go to the bathroom and cry or go over to them and yell at them.*
Therapist: *Are there some different things Jasmine could have said to herself about why her friends sat at a different table?*
Child: *I don't know.*
Therapist: *Do you think it is possible that Jasmine's friends just didn't see her?*
Child: *Sure, that's possible.*
Therapist: *So what would be a better thing for Jasmine to say to herself that would not be so upsetting?*
Child: *Maybe she could say, "They must not have seen me over here. I am sort of hard to notice in this corner."*
Therapist: *Exactly. And how do you think she would feel if she said that to herself?*
Child: *Normal. Not sad or anything.*
Therapist: *Normal, not sad. And what do you think she might do then, if she thought that and just felt okay about it?*
Child: *She might just go over and sit with them.*
Therapist: *I think you're right. And then how might she feel?*
Child: *Happy and just glad she has some friends to eat lunch with.*

The therapist should continue having the child generate replacement thoughts for fictitious examples until the child is adept at that process.

narrative. This sequence is important because if the therapist begins to challenge abuse-related thoughts prematurely, children may sometimes report thoughts in their trauma narrative that they think they "should" have had, rather than revealing the actual thoughts and feelings they had at the time of the abuse that may be underlying their PTSD symptomatology.

The therapist may show the child how cognitive coping skills can be used to cope with a current problem she is having, as illustrated in Box 9.4.

Box 9.4

Case Example: Disputing Current Pessimistic Thinking

Therapist: *Jessica, would you like to see how cognitive coping could help you with a problem with a friend or family member?*

Jessica: *Sure, I have arguments with my friends sometimes and it gets me really down.*

Therapist: *Okay. Tell me about a recent time you had a conflict with a friend.*

Jessica: *Well, yesterday my best friend didn't sit next to me on the bus.*

Therapist: *Okay. Tell me exactly what happened from the moment you got on the bus yesterday.*

Jessica: *Well. I walked onto the bus and my best friend was sitting next to a boy and she was laughing about something with him.*

Therapist: *Okay. When you saw this, what did you say to yourself?*

Jessica: *I guess first I said, "Where am I supposed to sit?"*

Therapist: *And how did you answer that question to yourself?*

Jessica: *I thought to myself, "There is nowhere to sit."*

Therapist: *You said to yourself, "There is nowhere to sit"; okay, what other thoughts went through your mind?*

Jessica: *I'm not sure what you mean.*

Therapist: *Usually we talk so fast to ourselves that it is hard to catch all the thoughts. So I would like you to slow down and see if you can catch some other things you said to yourself at that moment.*

Jessica: *You mean like: "They're probably laughing about me. I hate my life."*

Therapist: *Exactly. And how did those things make you feel?*

Jessica: *I felt really mad and sad.*

Therapist: *How did those upsetting thoughts and feelings influence your behavior?*

Jessica: *What do you mean?*

Therapist: *When you were thinking, "There's nowhere to sit. And they're laughing about me and I hate my life," and you were feeling sad and mad, what did you do?*

Jessica: *I sat down in the back of the bus by myself.*

Therapist: *How did you feel then?*

Jessica: *Still mad and sad and lonely too.*

Therapist: *Now thinking back, do you think those thoughts were true? For example, it sounds like there was some place else to sit, right? And were they laughing about you?*

Jessica: *There were places to sit, you're right—and they could have been laughing about a bunch of different things.*

Therapist: *Now here's a really important question. Do you hate your whole entire life? Every minute of it? Everything about your life?*

Jessica: *I guess I don't really hate my whole entire life—just some things that happened—not what happened on the bus. That was nothing really. We are still best friends. I guess mostly it's the sexual abuse I hate.*

Therapist: *Thank you for sharing with me that you hate that the sexual abuse happened. And that is very natural. That thought about hating sexual abuse may make you feel sad, but it is accurate and very reasonable. We are going to talk more about the sexual abuse so even that thought won't cause you as much distress anymore. But when you think that you hate your whole life that is much broader. How does that thought make you feel?*

Jessica: *Really, really sad and mad too.*

Therapist: *Exactly. So what might be a better thing to say to yourself when you are in a situation like this in the future, such as when someone else is sitting with your friend on the bus? What do you think you could have said to yourself that would have not made you feel so sad and mad?*

Jessica: *I could have thought my friend really likes that boy.* (long pause)

Therapist: *Great. Your friend really likes that boy. What else could you say to yourself?*

Jessica: *She must be really excited that he sat down next to her and she forgot about me for the moment.*

Therapist: *How do you think you would have felt if you said that to yourself?*

Jessica: *Maybe excited to talk to my friend after the bus ride.*

Therapist: *And then with that thought and feeling in mind, what do you think you would have done?*

Jessica: *Probably just sat with some other friends and moved to sit with my friend when that boy got off the bus.*

Therapist: *So do you think the bus ride would have felt and been different if you had changed your thought to something like that?*

Jessica: *Yeah, I guess so.*

Therapist: *Fantastic. You really did a great job examining and correcting thoughts that were not helpful. I really am impressed with how you pick up these skills so quickly.*

Jessica: *Thanks.*

Children who are younger or developmentally delayed may have difficulty comprehending the abstract process of identifying and disputing dysfunctional thoughts. However, these children are often still capable of understanding the basic connection between thoughts and feelings. For example, when asked, "How do you think you would feel if you kept saying to yourself, 'I am so dumb'?" even very young children generally understand that this thought would make them feel sad. After teaching children about that basic connection, it is helpful for the clinician to help the child recognize that sometimes people say things to themselves that are really not true and that if they replace those thoughts with nicer, kinder, and even more accurate thoughts they usually feel much better. Next, the therapist may teach a series of positive self-statements that can replace their clients' most common dysfunctional thoughts. These self-statements should be tailored to the child's particular difficulties. Thus, for example, a child who seems to have a poor self-image might be encouraged to say, "I am special because ___" or "I am just as good as other kids." A child who seems to be withdrawn and/or fearful might learn to say, "Trying new things can be fun," or "I can be very brave sometimes." Other positive self-statements specific to abuse-related fears and worries may be introduced after the trauma narrative and processing component is completed. Thus, suggestions for those are discussed in greater detail in the chapters that follow. However, all children may be introduced to the concept of self-praise at this stage of therapy.

Even children who were struggling with significant difficulties at the start of treatment can begin to acknowledge some personal strengths. Thus, the therapist may help children identify things that they can praise themselves for by simply asking questions which children are anticipated to answer in a positive manner. For example, based on information the parent has provided, the therapist might ask the following:

- *Tell me about something that happened yesterday that made you feel good.*
- *What can you say to yourself about how you have helped your brother lately?*
- *What have you done in therapy sessions that you feel good about?*
- *What is something that you learned recently that you are proud of?*
- *Let's list things you can say to yourself that will lead to positive feelings.*

Gradual exposure

Although the focus of therapy at this point is not yet on developing the trauma narrative, it is still important to continue the gradual exposure process by making some reference to the sexual abuse in every session including during this component. Thus, when initiating a discussion about positive self-statements, the therapist might ask, "What can you say to yourself about the sexual abuse that would lead to a positive feeling?" Some children and teens will respond with, "I'm proud of myself for telling or for learning about child sexual abuse." However, if the child is unable to identify a positive abuse-related self-statement, the TF-CBT therapist could offer an example that is consistent with the child's experience (i.e., "I was really brave when I talked to the police officer about the sexual abuse").

Children's learning and retention of new skills such as cognitive coping and optimistic or positive thinking may be greatly enhanced through the use of behavioral rehearsal. Thus, rather than relying on only verbal instruction to encourage children to be aware of their thinking (i.e., the way they talk to themselves), children may be engaged in role-plays in which they are encouraged to incorporate optimistic thinking or positive self-statements into the scenes (e.g., "I can speak up for myself"; "I can do this!") as frequently as possible. The therapist may assist children in transferring these skills from the therapy office to real situations by reenacting interactions that they have, in fact, experienced or anticipate experiencing. Through role-plays, children can also learn to distinguish when positive self-statements such as, "I can handle this" may be more appropriately said to themselves or out loud.

There are also some wonderful children's books and songs that encourage positive self-talk. Some examples of children's books that encourage optimistic thinking include *The Little Engine That Could* (Piper, 2012), *The Can Do Duck* (Ducktor Morty, 2005), *Somebody Loves You Mr. Hatch* (Spinelli, 1996), and *The Hyena Who Lost Her Laugh* (Lamb-Shapiro, 2001). As noted in the previous chapter, music and songs can also be valuable coping tools. Some songs that encourage positive self-talk include "Roar" by Katy Perry and "Hero" by Mariah Carey. In addition, it sometimes helps to encourage children to develop positive personal mantras such as "I can do it" or the currently popular phrase "Keep calm and carry on."

Mid-treatment assessment

By this stage of treatment, it may be useful to conduct a mid-treatment evaluation of treatment progress. The therapist can do this using formal (e.g., standardized parent report and/or child self-report measures) or informal assessment strategies (e.g., assessment of PTSD symptoms based on observation and interview). This mid-treatment assessment can help to identify the amount of progress the child has made thus far and enable the therapist to individually tailor the amount of time spent on the skill-building components, as well as future components to the child's needs. When working with children who are anticipated to move shortly or experience a change in placement, it is helpful to know that recent research has documented that many children make significant progress completing only the psychoeducation and skill-building components when gradual exposure is incorporated into those components (Deblinger et al., 2011). However, if no such placement changes are anticipated, and the assessment documents progress with respect to coping skills mastery, clients are typically ready to move into the next phase of treatment that focuses on trauma narrative development and processing. Even children who exhibited fairly significant affect dysregulation at the start of treatment can achieve a level of stability that the authors have referred to as "*stably unstable*" that may allow them to move forward with the trauma narrative component with the support of their parents and therapist while simultaneously engaging in ongoing development of the basic coping skills already reviewed. If the therapist determines that it is clinically reasonable to move forward in treatment, it is important to carefully re-assess progress with these children, while tailoring the sessions and the skill building activities to specifically meet their particular therapeutic needs. Similarly, in some cases with children who continue to exhibit relatively mild behavior problems, the therapist may continue on with the trauma narrative component (described in the next chapter), while their parents devote additional time and sessions to sharpening their parenting and communication skills designed to support the child's continued behavioral progress.

Individual tailoring of coping skills implementation

Due to the severity of their ongoing emotional and behavioral difficulties, some children and adolescents may need additional time and/or sessions for coping skills training prior to initiating the trauma narrative development and processing component. Although with many children the number of sessions devoted to the three phases of treatment, (i.e., stabilization and skill building; trauma narration and processing; consolidation and closure phases) are equivalent, for some clients with complex trauma, proportionately more time needs to be devoted to the first phase emphasizing the stabilization and skill building phase (e.g., half of the number of total sessions; Cohen, Mannarino, Kliethermes, et al., 2012). As described earlier, complex trauma involves ongoing interpersonal trauma with attachment disruption in early childhood that leads to significant dysregulation in multiple areas of functioning including emotional, behavioral, cognitive, physiological and/or interpersonal functioning. For more detailed information and guidance regarding the assessment of youth with complex trauma and guidelines on how to implement TF-CBT with this population, readers are referred to more extensive publications listed in the reference section (Cohen, Mannarino, Kliethermes, et al., 2012; Cook, Blaustein, Spinazzola & van der Kolk, 2003; Kliethermes & Wamser, 2012). However, recent research suggests that children who develop these types of severe reactions will respond to TF-CBT when the sessions and components are individually tailored to address their particular skills deficits, dysfunctional beliefs, and problematic behavior patterns (Deblinger et al., 2011; Mannarino et al., 2012). These more severe trauma responses often reflect children's dysfunctional efforts to protect themselves from future abuse and/or manage the overwhelming emotions associated with the multiple traumas experienced. To protect themselves, some children actively withdraw from interpersonal interactions (which can lead to depression and other difficulties), whereas other children strike out to proactively protect themselves (which can lead to aggressive behavior patterns and resulting consequences). It is with these youth that the TF-CBT therapist may need to extend the stabilization and skill-building phase from the typical 4 to 6 sessions to 8 to 12 sessions prior to moving on to the trauma narration and processing phase of treatment. Additional coping skills, such as problem solving and social/assertiveness skill building may be important for youth who are struggling with interpersonal conflicts. More resources are provided in Appendix C for training in these skills and further suggestions on implementing these skills with children are provided in Chapter 14. Most critically, the therapist must understand that since these youths' core trauma involves attachment disruption, they may experience close relationships (e.g., therapist-client relationship) as trauma reminders and trusting a new person such as a therapist is experienced as risky. Thus, the therapist who is treating youth with complex trauma often experiences frequent testing, questioning the therapist's trustworthiness, as well as the challenges described in detail elsewhere (Cohen, Mannarino, Kliethermes, et al., 2012).

In sum, careful assessment and clinical judgment should be used to determine the focus of additional skill-building sessions with children, adolescents, and their parents. Numerous coping skills activities have been outlined in the prior chapters; however, it is important for the therapist to identify the skills that the child, teen, and parent(s) are most likely to naturally utilize and most likely to receive family as well as other environmental support for implementing in real life. Moreover, the therapist should motivate the between-session practice of these skills by reviewing in great detail how, when, and where children plan to practice the skills in order to enhance their commitment.

Practice activities encouraged

The therapist might encourage the inclusion of cognitive coping skills in children's coping skills tool kit. Additionally, the therapist may review and encourage the use of the child's favorite coping skills from the tool kit as well as personalized positive self-statements during the week. The therapist may review the automatic thought records (see *Identifying and Challenging Your Problematic Thoughts* handout in Appendix B) with older children and teens and encourage them to catch, record, and replace distressing thoughts with more productive, accurate, optimistic thoughts whenever possible during the week. For purposes of completing this task, it is useful to introduce the concept of subjective units of distress (SUDS) scores. These scores help therapists and children monitor the degree to which their cognitive coping efforts are positively influencing their distress levels. SUDS are typically based on a scale of one to five with five being the highest level of distress and one indicating no distress at all. This scale can be presented as a fear thermometer with the high temperatures depicting more distress or a series of faces depicting more or less distress. SUDS scores are also used during the trauma narrative and processing component to monitor children's distress levels.

Prepare for conjoint session activities

Cognitive coping

Time permitting, the child may prepare to present what he is learning about cognitive coping to the parent(s), using the cognitive coping diagrams described above and created on paper or on the board. As part of this presentation, the child may be encouraged to share an example of how cognitive coping could help him to think about a real situation in a healthier or more positive way. In addition, the therapist may help the child demonstrate the concept of the cognitive triangle in a conjoint parent-child session by providing an example of talking to oneself in a positive way (i.e., something positive that the child may say to himself that makes the child feel better). Parents may also be asked to share a prepared example (see parent conjoint session preparation) of talking to themselves in encouraging ways as well in response to a challenging (but nonabuse-related situation). This can be valuable given the recent research finding suggesting that children whose parents share personal experiences of overcoming adversity tend to be more resilient (Duke et al., 2008).

Mutual exchange of praise

By this stage of therapy if the child continues to have difficulty identifying parent behaviors to praise, the therapist might elicit positive activities the parent has been working on and has previously reported to the therapist (e.g., *Some examples of what you can praise are small things that your parent does like simply listening to you when you shared something nice or giving you affection in some way. You can also praise a parent-child activity that you enjoy*). If possible it is helpful to steer the child toward acknowledging and praising a specific positive parenting behavior (e.g., "I like when Mom and I take a walk together"; "I like when my dad tells me I'm doing a good job on my homework") that the parent is working on in therapy. Surprisingly, children are often more naturally skilled at offering purely positive, specific praise with enthusiasm than parents are if given just a nudge in that direction. However, practice may also help children to avoid negative tags as well when praising their parents in conjoint session. It also helps to steer children away from praising their parents for getting them video games, fast food, etc., or taking them to Disney, by encouraging children to praise everyday parent behaviors that don't cost anything.

PARENT SESSION(S)

There are many new concepts to introduce during this component of treatment, both in terms of coping skills and parenting practices. Thus, it is likely that this will require more than one session, particularly for parents who will need continued practice with respect to cognitively processing dysfunctional thoughts, as well as with respect to the learning and practicing of effective parenting skills. Again, however, some parents will require more or less focus on all these skills depending on their presenting complaints, symptoms, and desired goals.

Practice assignments review: Parenting skills

The therapist may inquire about parents' successes, as well as challenges in following through with the skills learned from the prior week. It is important to acknowledge the importance of the parents' efforts to both practice positive parenting skills, as well as the effective coping skills that both they and their children are learning. The therapist might start by reviewing the parenting skills work if the child is exhibiting significant behavior problems; whereas, the coping skills assignment may be reviewed first if there is greater concern about parental distress or depression.

Parenting skills functional analysis review

In beginning a review of parenting practices, the therapist may inquire as follows:

> *It would really help me if you could tell me what happened yesterday when you tried to encourage your child to get his homework done. Please share as much detail as possible. Let's start with what was happening before you started to encourage him to do his homework and then describe the interaction when you asked him to get his homework started. I want to know not only what you and he said and did but also what you were thinking and feeling before, during, and after the interactions around his homework.*

If the parent does not provide details, the therapist may prompt the parent to provide increasingly more details including if possible the parent's thoughts, feelings, and actions in response to the youth's behaviors (e.g., using the ABC format).

It is most important to highlight what the parent did right in his attempts to shape the child's behavior using specific praise, active listening, and/or differential attention with the child before offering constructive feedback (i.e., using a "compliment sandwich"). When parents deny observing any positive child behaviors, the therapist should remind them that the focus in this review is on both parent behavior and child behavior. So it is still worth examining interactions in which the child exhibited a partially positive behavior from the standpoint of antecedents, behaviors, and consequences. In such cases, the therapist may spend more time on antecedents to identify ways the parent could proactively set the stage to increase the likelihood of the desired behavior occurring.

More specifically, the clinician should elicit information about the antecedents, behaviors, and consequences (i.e., ABCs) in relation to the positive replacement and/or the problematic behaviors that have been identified during the assessment and early treatment sessions. As noted earlier, this functional analysis will allow the therapist to not only better understand the child's motivation for engaging in problem behaviors but will also help identify parenting behaviors that should be acknowledged and praised, as well as areas for constructive feedback. Before offering specific feedback on how parents can enhance their efforts, it is often helpful to emphasize how lucky their children are to have parents who are dedicated to doing everything, including "tweaking" their parenting approaches to ensure that their child recovers optimally from the sexual abuse.

The benefits of routines and rituals in creating circumstances (i.e., antecedents) that increase the likelihood of positive behaviors can also be reviewed. This is a good time to inquire about, acknowledge, and praise parents' efforts to initiate new positive routines and/or the return to comforting rituals that were in place prior to the disclosure of abuse. Given the potential for children who have experienced CSA to develop feelings of shame and insecurity, it is important to explore with parents the value of creating nurturing routines to enhance children's feelings of general confidence and security. Parents whose children are acting out a great deal may find this challenging, as their negative thoughts and feelings may be interfering with their ability to be warm and nurturing to their children. With these parents, starting the session with cognitive coping exercises described later in this chapter may be particularly valuable. Again, there is great flexibility in the implementation of this model. As always, the therapist may use her clinical judgment in determining the order of topics and number of sessions devoted to the various parenting and coping skills topics listed in this chapter.

Parenting skills continued with effective instructions, family rules, time out, and work chores

It should be emphasized that parenting skills build on one another, and it is important to have parents follow through on the early positive parenting practices at home before moving on to discuss the use of negative consequences for problem behaviors. To reinforce the importance of creating and enhancing positive interactions with their children, it is useful to remind parents of the optimal ratios between positive and negative interactions (i.e., at least four positive parent-child interactions to every one negative interaction). This is critical given the research that documents the importance of positive activities and interactions promoting healthy relationships (Layous et al., 2014). Parents may be encouraged to increase their positive interactions by planning positive routines, rituals, and activities and noticing and specifically praising small positive behaviors (i.e., shaping), using selective attention and practicing active listening. Parents may be encouraged to use these skills particularly in response to children reporting positive interactions, sharing anything learned in school, and/or appropriately sharing feelings or concerns.

It must be repeated that in the crisis of facing CSA and related disruptions in family life, it may feel unnatural to create and/or focus on positives, so this process may go more slowly for some families as compared to others. In fact, when children have significant behavior problems, it may be particularly difficult for parents to break out of a negative cycle and shift attention from negative to positive behaviors. Thus, the therapist may need to gently but repeatedly remind parents that the problem behaviors may be attributable at least in part to the sexual abuse as well as other trauma(s) but treatment and most importantly their efforts will be the keys to helping their child overcome these experiences and associated behavioral difficulties. Still, parents whose children have significant behavioral difficulties will need to work at creating positive interactions. For example, parents should be encouraged to create opportunities for positive interactions and avoid the tendency to nag about problem behaviors, while simultaneously shaping positive behaviors with specific praise that is devoid of inadvertent negative tags.

For some children, praise, reflective listening, and parents' effective use of selective attention produces dramatic improvements in children's behaviors sometimes helping children to return to pre-abuse behavioral functioning relatively quickly. Still, sexual abuse can significantly undermine children's emotional and behavioral functioning. In fact, as noted earlier, in the aftermath of CSA, children may engage in problematic behaviors to manage their heightened needs for attention and control as well as to escape from or cope with cues in the environment that frequently trigger symptoms of posttraumatic stress. Thus, it is important to continue to strengthen parenting skills, particularly with respect to encouraging effective parental communication skills that will support children's understanding of and ability to comply with behavioral expectations and house rules.

Thus, the parenting focus in this session may turn to the importance of clear communication, effective instructions, and explicit rules as described below. Although selective attention is a powerful parenting tool, there are many problem behaviors for which it is neither effective nor appropriate to actively ignore the problem behavior. For example, as indicated earlier, active ignoring should not be used with problem behaviors that have the potential to escalate into dangerous behaviors during the extinction burst (e.g., "not okay" touches, breaking things, etc.). Nor should active ignoring be used with noncompliance as such a response may only serve to reinforce noncompliant behavior.

In general, in the aftermath of a trauma such as sexual abuse, children not only appreciate positive rituals and routines as emphasized in an earlier session but also benefit from clear-cut expectations regarding what behaviors are acceptable and unacceptable. This type of communication creates an environment that is structured and predictable, which is particularly important for children who have experienced the unpredictable impact of abuse. This information can best be conveyed to children in the form of clear instructions and a limited number of basic house rules.

Giving effective instructions

Learning to give effective instructions may be particularly important for parents whose children are exhibiting a great deal of noncompliance. In the aftermath of CSA, in an effort to regain control over their lives, children sometimes exhibit increased rates of noncompliant behaviors. During the course of the sexual abuse, offenders often use guilt, bribes, threats, and/or physical force to maintain control over their victims. As a result, children who have experienced abuse often feel the offenders have greatly restricted their ability to make independent decisions about how and with whom they spend their time, and they may have felt a lack of control over access to their own bodies. The unpredictability of the sexual abuse often leaves children feeling helpless and fearful of experiencing such a lack of control again. Thus, after disclosing the abuse, many children experience a sudden surge in their ability and desire to exert control to ensure that no one limits their control in this way again. For some children, this need is expressed in the form of increased demanding and/or noncompliant behavior.

It is important for parents to recognize that this increase in noncompliant behavior may be natural and expected, given the newfound feelings of freedom children may want to exercise and/or anger they may be feeling in the aftermath of disclosing abuse. Thus, parents may be encouraged to offer their children more opportunities to make *choices* and to engage in independent behaviors in order to encourage adaptive means of experiencing feelings of control. When children experience chronic feelings of helplessness, they are at increased risk for developing both physical and emotional difficulties throughout their lives. However, when children regain some feelings of control they can manage stress more effectively. Thus, it is critically important to encourage adaptive coping behaviors that provide children with developmentally appropriate levels of control that may replace problematic coping responses and behaviors. Such an approach is far superior to trying to eliminate problem behaviors with repeated threats and harsh punishments. Thus, as noted above, it is important to identify and encourage acceptable, independent behaviors. However, it is not healthy or reasonable for children to believe that they can be in complete control all the time. Although children's abilities to influence personal life events grows as they get older, even when they are adults they will have only limited control over many aspects of their lives. Thus, it is important for parents to help their children identify when it is appropriate to assert control and express their independence and when it is necessary for them to accept certain limits and/or comply with instructions. In order to help children distinguish between those situations where they may or may not be able to make their own decisions, parents must develop skill and clarity in communicating with their children.

The effectiveness of parental communication styles, particularly with respect to their methods of giving their children instructions, may also be assessed using functional analyses conducted using the ABC (i.e., antecedents, behaviors, consequences) format. Parents may be encouraged to describe in as much detail as possible the last time or two they gave their children instructions by sharing with the therapist the antecedents (i.e., what was happening before the parental request), behavioral responses to the parental instruction (e.g., children's behavioral responses to their requests), and consequences (i.e., what happened after the child's response to the parental request). These examples are likely to reveal some instances in which parents were successful and others in which they were unsuccessful in gaining their children's cooperation.

Practice giving effective instructions role-play

After providing educational information regarding effective instructions (see *Encourage Cooperation with Effective Instructions* handout), the therapist may first demonstrate giving an effective instruction and then describe and act out the parent-child scenario (while taking on the role of the child) that would compel the parent to give an instruction. The parent can then role-play giving an instruction, while the therapist responds as the child might. When the parent inadvertently makes one of the errors discussed, the therapist, acting as the child, may respond negatively (e.g., taking advantage of the parent who gives instructions in the form of a question). As always, when critiquing the role-play, the therapist should offer positive feedback as well as some suggestions for improvement using the "compliment sandwich" format. Parents may be encouraged to the review the effective instructions handout in Appendix B. Using the guidelines in the handout parents may critique their own role-play performance and identify areas for improvement in terms of their personal styles of communicating instructions.

Introducing house rules

Many families have unspoken rules that children and adolescents follow. These may include talking respectfully to parents and siblings, going to bed at a particular time each night, behaving well in school, and following through each day with homework. In families that are functioning well, children follow these expectations primarily because the family environment is generally nurturing, the expectations are made clear by parents, and there are positive, natural, social, and sometimes tangible consequences when children comply with these unspoken rules. The parenting focus up until this point has been on increasing positive interactions between parents and children through the use of praise, positive rituals, selective attention, and reflective listening. However, with children with significant ongoing behavior problems, it is important for parents to communicate their behavioral expectations to their children, as well as the consequences for positive and negative behaviors. Thus, in addition to learning to give clearer instructions, parents can help their children overcome behavior problems by discussing house rules more explicitly. Caregivers may need some guidance in learning to collaborate with their children when developing a limited number (e.g., three to five) of positively worded house rules. An excessive number of rules often cannot be remembered by young children and may fail to highlight parents' most important priorities.

Behavior charts and contracts

Behavior change is not easy to accomplish with many parents and/or children, thus, it sometimes helps for the therapist to encourage the development of house rules or positive behavior chart or contract that can be reviewed. A contract formalizes an agreement between the child and parent and the positive consequences that will be achieved when the behavior or job is successfully completed. (See *Behavior Contract* in Appendix B.) A behavior chart and/or house rules list may also serve as excellent reminders and/or prompts for both parent and child behavior change (see *Establishing House Rules* handout in Appendix B). It is worth noting that children and adolescents may feel a greater buy in and willingness to abide by rules if they have contributed their ideas to both the rules and the positive and negative consequences for following and breaking the rules respectively. A few simple house rules and/or behavioral expectations can help children feel more comfortable and secure. Children may earn points for following the rules and engaging in the positive behaviors listed. With young children, it is best if the points lead to prizes or stickers every day, whereas older children can accumulate points that may lead to more significant prizes or even to an allowance that is given once a week. The prizes/rewards must be reasonable for the parent to provide on an ongoing basis, so the prizes must be within the parents' budget as well as within their control. Positive consequences for following rules and consistent negative consequences for breaking the rules can enhance the predictability of the family environment, thereby supporting the healing of children whose abusive experiences were often unpredictable and highly anxiety provoking. Thus, the therapist should help the parent and child agree on and create a poster or chart that lists the positively stated house rules or clearly defined behavioral expectations. A calendar or chart can then be used to keep track of the child's success. Ideally, the agreed-upon house rules or behavior charts should incorporate the positive behaviors that will replace children's problematic behaviors. Positively stated rules and behavior charts can support parents' efforts to give their children more effective instructions and positive reinforcement in the form of praise, stickers (e.g., on a simple calendar), and tangible rewards (e.g., weekly allowance for success in exhibiting positive behaviors, completing homework, chores, etc.). When displayed prominently, these charts can serve as excellent reminders for children, but even more importantly for parents to follow through with specific praise and appropriate positive consequences to increase their children's cooperative and adaptive behaviors. If rules have not been in place, children may initially reject such structure, but such negative reactions may be selectively ignored, while praising any positive contributions to the process.

Negative consequences for problem behaviors

As noted earlier, positive parenting changes are not always sufficient to reverse negative behaviors that have become ingrained over time. Thus, some negative behaviors, especially those that should not be ignored, require collaborative therapist-parent efforts to understand the factors motivating the behaviors (using functional analyses), while also developing appropriate procedures that involve effective mild negative consequences for the problematic behaviors and positive consequences for the identified positive replacement behaviors. In collaboration with the therapist, parents and children should agree on what behaviors will not be tolerated and/or what the consequences will be for both following and not following the rules.

Described below are negative consequences that have been repeatedly found to be effective in reducing behavior problems when implemented in an effective and consistent manner. When parents indicate that they have tried "time out" and it has not been helpful, this is usually an indication that the time out procedure was not implemented correctly or consistently and/or it was the wrong choice of negative consequences for the particular problem behavior. Thus, it is best to conduct careful reviews of their attempts to use time out following the ABC format for conducting functional analyses in order to examine the factors that may be motivating the problem behavior. In addition, it is important to identify what the parents may have done right and what they may have inadvertently done that undermined the success of the time out intervention.

Some parents, however, find it difficult to use negative consequences consistently after discovering that their child was sexually abused. For some parents, this may stem from a belief that their child has endured enough punishment already. For others, feelings of guilt or responsibility for the abuse may interfere with their ability to set limits and administer negative consequences effectively. In the aftermath of sexual abuse, other parents become highly restrictive and even harsh in terms of punishing any remotely risk taking behaviors in an effort to protect their child from any further abuse or misfortune. These issues as well as general attitudes regarding punishment should be explored before proceeding to collaborate on a discipline plan involving time out or other negative consequences.

Time out

Time out from positive reinforcement is a procedure that is extremely effective for noncompliant behavior, as well as for other problem behaviors that cannot be actively ignored. However, in order for it to be effective, it must be combined with the positive parenting practices discussed thus far. Time out involves removing the child from an environment where reinforcement is available. Thus, this disciplinary procedure works best if the child's ability to obtain positive attention and reinforcement in a predictable manner is well established in the environment. Time out essentially involves placing the child in a designated place where no attention, gratification, or reinforcing consequences may be obtained. Time out is given for a short period of time contingent upon the occurrence of a specified problem behavior. In fact, the number of minutes recommended for time out generally corresponds to the child's age. For example, a 4-year-old would be expected to do no more than four minutes in time out. It is preferable to use time out initially with one repetitive problem behavior that has been identified in advance so that the child is able to quickly learn that she will receive positive consequences for the positive replacement behavior and negative consequences for the specific problem behavior.

Because it may be difficult for some parents to use even mild forms of punishment, it is often useful to review the advantages of using time out as opposed to other discipline practices. This review is particularly important for parents who continue to rely on less effective forms of discipline such as nagging, scolding, yelling, criticizing, and/or spanking. Parents who otherwise have abandoned discipline may end up resorting to spanking out of frustration as their children's behavior problems escalate. Thus, it is important to establish early on the value of incorporating both positive and mild negative consequences into their repertoire of parenting practices as well as the dangers of relying on corporal punishment.

Box 9.5 provides an overview of the reasons for using time out.

Box 9.5

Advantages of Time Out

The time out procedure

- may be presented as a method to teach children to remember the rules
- provides a response to a problem behavior that may be implemented immediately
- requires only a brief amount of a parent's time and minimal monitoring
- does not require parents to think of a punishment when they are upset
- does not require any expression of negative emotion or criticism
- does not model aggressive behavior as is the case with physical punishment techniques
- does not negatively affect children's self-esteem as does the repeated use of criticism
- is more effective than punishments that are longer and seem more severe
- research has repeatedly documented its effectiveness when implemented correctly.

Teaching parents the steps for using time out

Once parents understand and have accepted the concept of time out, the therapist may review the *Time Out Guidelines* handout (provided in Appendix B) that outlines the steps for implementing the procedure. Time out is useful for stopping behavior, not for starting behavior. Parents can use it when a child disobeys a command, but the behavior they will influence is the disobeying, not the positive behavior in which they had wanted the child to engage. For example, if a child verbally refuses to put on her coat, the parent could place the child in time out, saying, "Time out for not following my instructions to put on your coat." To get the child to put on a coat more often when it is time to go outdoors, parents need to specifically praise the child for putting on her coat on a consistent basis initially and then intermittently praise this behavior later.

Work chores and other mild negative consequences for older children and adolescents

Although time out is an appropriate and effective discipline practice for children 10 years of age and younger, when children reach about 11 years of age it is important to consider other possible consequences for engaging in problematic behavior. Negative behavioral consequences commonly recommended for use with teens include loss of privileges (e.g., loss of television, use of car for one evening), time out for prized possessions (e.g., cell phone, iPad, etc.), and work chores (Patterson & Forgatch, 2005). These are negative consequences that teens can learn from relatively quickly without experiencing feelings of humiliation or extreme anger.

In general, Patterson and Forgatch (2005) suggest punishments that

- are small and limited in duration work better than those that are big and/or lengthy
- can be administered right away are better than delayed punishments
- are consistently applied are better than empty threats
- are administered in the context of nurturing, reinforcing environments work better.

When negative consequences are administered that are physical, too harsh, or severe in duration (e.g., grounding for three months), teens experience such extreme emotions that they learn little from the experience and learn to lie and cover up their mistakes for fear of enduring the pain, humiliation, or extreme restrictions associated with more severe punishments. Moreover, the milder negative consequences suggested have been found to be more effective and they can be used repeatedly as problematic behaviors are generally not eliminated in one trial but often require repeated experiences with negative consequences (and positive consequences for the replacement behaviors) before teens overcome negative behavioral patterns.

The therapist may discuss with parents the various options for negative consequences (i.e., loss of privileges or prized possessions or work chores) as it is important for parents to feel comfortable with the approach so that they will follow through each and every time rules are broken or the identified problem behaviors occur. Teens should of course not be expected to behave perfectly as all youth make mistakes, misplace things, test limits to some degree, and experience some emotionality related to the common trials and tribulations of adolescence. However, once parents establish basic rules and expectations (particularly with respect to repeated problem behaviors), it will be important for parents to follow through with the agreed-upon mild, time-limited negative consequences. Thus, it is important to create a discipline plan that is practical, reasonable, effective, and most likely to be consistently implemented by the parent(s).

The work chore approach may be new to parents, but it can be highly effective if parents and children agree to the approach. Work chores are household chores that can be completed in a brief period of time (about 5 minutes). Parents may give an older child or teen a work chore to complete as a negative consequence for an inappropriate behavior. A list of work chores, however, should be agreed upon in advance that include chores that can typically be completed in about 5 minutes, such as sweeping the porch, organizing two shelves in the linen closet, cleaning the kitchen sink, vacuuming the car, cleaning the inside or outside of the car, vacuuming one room, etc. Much like time out, when a teen engages in a problem behavior, the parent should remind the teen of the work chore consequence without yelling or encounter discussions with the clear expectation that noncompliance with the required work chore will lead to a loss of privileges. Many teens will test the new approach by initially refusing to do a 5 minute work chore. It is therefore important for parents to have back up plans that involve an additional chore or the loss of privileges. Though it is not appropriate for parents to withhold basic necessities (e.g., food, basic clothing), common privileges that may be withdrawn are ones many teens take for granted including cell phones, iPads, laptops, televisions, shopping, and/or driving privileges. Once again, parents should use privileges that they have control over and when privileges such as these are withdrawn because of misbehavior, the loss should be for a brief period of time but should occur each time the problem behavior (e.g., noncompliance or a broken curfew) happens. Most importantly, parents should be reminded that it may be difficult to maintain their cool when engaged in a conflict, but doing so by using focused breathing or taking a cool down before addressing the problem is perhaps the most critical parenting skill. By addressing the problem as calmly as possible, parents are modeling important coping skills for managing stress and demonstrating their commitment to the agreed upon discipline plan. Such predictability is in the long run comforting to youth. Thus, focused breathing and other affect regulation skills are important to practice with parents particularly in the context of preparing them for disciplinary interactions with their children.

In sum, whatever mild negative consequence the parent and youth agree on for particular problem behaviors, it is important for the parent to present the rules and/or behavioral expectations in positive terms. Moreover, therapists may remind parents to provide repeated encouragement for positive behaviors in the form of praise, active involvement, reflective listening, and general enthusiasm for the many small steps it takes for youngsters to achieve good grades (e.g., completing homework daily), practice athletics or musical instruments, and develop positive friendships. Given that CSA can undermine children's trust in others, the importance of parents encouraging and supporting children's positive peer relationships cannot be emphasized enough. In addition, parents should be clear about negative consequences in a firm but warm, compassionate manner. Thus, it is often helpful for the parent to practice the presentation of the discipline plan with the therapist so that the parent can gain some confidence in her ability to be simultaneously firm and nurturing. Parents, for example, may be coached to highlight (1) their desire and/or commitment to help the child heal from the sexual abuse and other trauma(s) endured and (2) their belief that the rules and the negative consequences agreed upon will support that goal by helping the child to remember rules that encourage healthy, positive behaviors. For example, a parent whose child is having difficulty following instructions might say, "You know that we've been arguing with each other more than either of us would like. Some of your anger may be due to the sexual abuse, but it does not help for us to argue so much. I don't want to fight anymore. It is not good for you or for me. So to help you remember to follow my instructions, I'm going to be giving you work chores when you forget and you yell or talk disrespectfully to me. The work chores will be tasks that can be completed pretty quickly, in about 5 minutes or so. I have created a list of such chores, but you can add to this list as well." It is important to present this approach with confidence to parents. Thus, it can be useful to review the description of the work chores approach in more detail in *Parents and Adolescents Living Together, Part 1: The Basics* by Patterson and Forgatch (2005).

Important reminder

As noted above, parents often have success in helping their children overcome behavior problems using specific praise, positive rituals, reflective listening, selective attention, and other effective parenting practices. However, it cannot be overstated how important it is to impress upon parents the value of modeling positive behaviors and effective coping responses for their children. As noted earlier, parents are often unaware of how much children imitate them, and thus they may express concern about behaviors that they are, in fact, inadvertently modeling for their children (e.g., yelling, sarcasm, cursing, lying). Thus, these problematic parent behaviors are very important to gently point out and address as parent behavior change is critical before positive child behavior change is likely to occur.

Practice assignments review: Coping skills

It is important to review, acknowledge, and praise parents' efforts to model and utilize the coping skills learned in previous sessions. Parents are likely to gravitate to the types of coping skills that suit their style and personality best. Thus, it is important to highlight the positive, productive relaxation and affective regulation strategies utilized between sessions, so that their continued use can be encouraged. In addition, it continues to be critical to identify times when parents were less successful in utilizing effective coping skills so that the therapist can support parents in identifying methods or creating circumstances that will increase their chances of successfully using the coping skills learned effectively.

Cognitive coping with parents

After acknowledging and praising parents' efforts to utilize parenting and coping skills learned thus far, the therapist can introduce cognitive coping that may be presented as a highly effective means of addressing distressing abuse-related and nonabuse-related thoughts and feelings. In the aftermath of CSA, many parents engage in coping methods that can be particularly ineffective, such as ruminating on negative circumstances that cannot necessarily be changed (e.g., the child being sexually abused or delaying disclosure for a long period of time; the offender getting a light sentence). In the cognitive coping component with parents, pessimistic or maladaptive parental coping styles may be explored both in terms of their impact on the parent as well as the impact pessimistic thinking may ultimately have on the child's abuse recovery and developing coping style.

The therapist may explain the cognitive triangle (or the cognitive coping diamond when appropriate) to parents, explaining that the child is learning about the relationships between thoughts, feelings, and behaviors as well. Then, it is valuable to inquire about a recent time when the parent found herself reminded of the sexual abuse and/or distressed about its impact on the child and family.

When the parent identifies such a time, the therapist should elicit feelings experienced and then as many thoughts as the parent can recall. This exercise is important to do slowly and carefully, patiently waiting and encouraging parents to share their innermost thoughts (including the most socially undesirable thoughts) that are causing them the most distress. Thus, it is important to wait out the silences as parents retrieve and share such thoughts.

The example in Box 9.6 illustrates how a therapist might introduce the concept of cognitive coping skills training to a parent. Note that the therapist highlights the important role nonoffending parents play in influencing the adjustment of their children.

Interrelationships between thoughts, feelings, and behaviors

The therapist may present the interaction between thoughts, feelings, and behaviors visually by presenting the cognitive triangle (illustrated in Figure 9.2 on page 208). Subsequently, the therapist can begin teaching the parent how thoughts can influence feelings and behaviors both negatively and positively by using examples such as this one.

Therapist: *I'd like to describe an example that illustrates how two women may respond to the exact same situation in very different ways because they think about the situation differently. These women are at a party when each notices someone looking at them.*

First Woman:
Thoughts: *Why is that person staring at me? I must look really weird; I just don't fit in here.*
Feelings: *Sad, embarrassed, lonely.*
Behavior: *Leaves the party alone.*

Therapist: *Another woman I'll describe is faced with the same situation, but thinks differently about it.*

Second Woman:
Thoughts: *Why is that person staring at me? I think that he is interested in meeting me.*
Feelings: *Excited, curious.*
Behavior: *Walks over and strikes up a conversation.*

Therapist: *As you can see, the two people in the above example had different thoughts about the situation and consequently responded with different emotions and behaviors. In fact, your style of thinking can dramatically influence your feelings and behaviors.*

At this point, the therapist might ask the parent to identify a minor personal problem and trace the parent's own interactive thoughts, feelings, and behaviors.

BOX 9.6

Case Example: Introducing Cognitive Coping Skills

Therapist: *Both parents and children experience lots of different emotions and difficulties following an experience of child sexual abuse. We've talked about how you felt angry, sad, and even guilty about Katie's sexual abuse experience. Just as I will do with Katie, I am going to ask you to share not only your feelings, but also how you have been thinking about the sexual abuse and the domestic violence you experienced because both your feelings and thoughts influence your overall coping and adjustment. We'll continue to discuss your feelings, but during this session I am going to really encourage you to share the thoughts that underlie some of your most distressing feelings. Learning to cope better with your distressing feelings and thoughts will help you feel better and will in turn help you serve as an even more effective coping model for Katie.*

Mother: *I am trying to do that, but I often feel like I am failing.*

Therapist: *As you know, there is a great deal of research that demonstrates that children learn coping strategies from their parents. Thus, if we can help you cope more effectively, it is likely that Katie will observe you and will learn to cope more successfully with problems and stressors that she faces now and in the future.*

Mother: *I don't know if I can be a good model for Katie.*

Therapist: *I have no doubt that you can, but it is natural for you to have some feelings of depression having not only discovered that your child was sexually abused but also having to face the fact that the person who abused her was your husband. That is a lot to cope with at one time.*

Mother: *I just feel like my life has been turned upside down. So I brought Katie to you so you could help, because I just am no role model right now.*

Therapist: *Certainly, I hope I can be a good role model for Katie as well. In fact, today I taught Katie about the same cognitive coping skills I will be reviewing with you. But your ability to influence Katie is much greater than mine is. You are a much more powerful model, both because your relationship is so important to her and because you have much more time with her than I ever will.*

Mother: *I see. I guess I can try, but I'm not sure how I should show her to handle this situation.*

Therapist: *You and I will be working together to help you develop skills for being the most effective role model possible and these skills will help you combat the feelings of depression that you are experiencing. I'm sure that as we work together, you'll learn how to cope effectively with this experience and with other difficulties as well. We will be talking mostly about your emotional and coping responses to the discovery of Katie's sexual abuse experience, but I believe the coping methods I will be teaching you will also help you with other difficulties. The coping model we will be discussing is based on the belief that your thoughts, feelings, and behaviors all influence one another.*

After the parent is able to successfully identify the links between her thoughts, feelings, and behaviors with respect to a nonabuse-related problem, the therapist should help the parent apply this model to the parent's thoughts and feelings regarding the child's abusive experience. It is important to acknowledge that we all have frequent conversations with ourselves, but it may be difficult to bring these internal dialogues into our awareness. Therapists can help parents do this by asking them to describe the situation they were in when they experienced the identified emotions. This description may trigger the recollection of the parent's thoughts at that time.

Therapist: *Now I'd like to use this cognitive coping model to examine your thoughts and emotions regarding your child's sexual abuse experience. To help you cope with your child's experience of sexual abuse, we are going to work backward from your emotional reactions to the thoughts that may be underlying those reactions. So let's first identify a time recently when you found yourself feeling distressed about the sexual abuse or a related circumstance. When was the last time you found yourself feeling very distressed about your child's experience of sexual abuse?*

Mother: *Just last night.*

Therapist: *Okay tell me where you were last night and what happened to trigger those feelings.*

Mother: *I was home. It was after dinner and I was sitting in my living room by myself when something on TV reminded me of all of this.*

Therapist: *Okay, first, let's list all the emotions you were having at the time.*

Mother: *Well, mostly, I felt mad, but I also started to feel sad and scared for myself and my daughter.*

Therapist: *Okay—I am going to write that down—so you were feeling mad and sad and scared too. Thank you for sharing that. Frequently both parents and children experience lots of different emotions in response to abusive experiences. In fact, parents often report experiencing seemingly opposite emotions at the same time.*

Mother: *That is definitely me.*

Therapist: *Although there are no emotions that are wrong, some may be so troubling that they interfere with both your daily functioning and the healing process for you and your child.*

Mother: *I worry about that, but I guess that is why I'm here.*

Therapist: *Exactly, and so we are going to work together to help you cope with those feelings. And one way to do that is to examine the thoughts that underlie your most distressing feelings. So, I want you to catch the thoughts that you had last night and again I'm going to write them down if that's okay—so speak slowly and tell me everything you were saying to yourself last night when you were thinking about the abuse and feeling mad and sad and scared.*

The therapist should patiently elicit thoughts underlying the distressing emotions as described above and/or with additional open-ended questions (e.g.,

"What were you saying to yourself when you were feeling that way?"), while silently waiting as the parent retrieves thought memories. The parent's feelings and thoughts may be recorded on a sheet of paper or on a white board.

Disputing dysfunctional thoughts

As the parent continues the work of identifying underlying thoughts, the therapist should emphasize that some of these thoughts may be accurate and functional, whereas others may be dysfunctional. There are two general types of dysfunctional thoughts the therapist should help the parent learn to dispute or replace: thoughts that are inaccurate and thoughts that are nonproductive (regardless of whether or not they are accurate).

Inaccurate thoughts

Thoughts that are inaccurate may be most effectively disputed by providing the parent with accurate information. Parents typically lack accurate information regarding CSA and can benefit from being reminded of the facts regarding prevalence, identities of perpetrators and the children affected, the secretive nature of sexual abuse, ways sex offenders engage children and prevent them from disclosing, and children's responses to sexual abuse. It is not unusual for parents to initially avoid reading the provided educational materials regarding CSA, so this is a time to review that material again. At this point in the therapeutic process, parents may be more comfortable reading additional information about CSA that may be relevant to their situation (see *Child Sexual Abuse Information* handout as well as other handouts at www.NCTSN.org). This information may be provided to parents during sessions, or parents may be asked to read written materials in the waiting room or at home. Subsequently, the therapist can refer to that information in disputing inaccurate and distressing thoughts. For example, the mother of a sexually abused boy may experience unpleasant and unnecessary anxiety because she believes that when boys are sexually abused they grow up to be sex offenders. The therapist can help to reduce that mother's distress by providing her with the accurate information that the vast majority of children who are sexually abused never abuse others and do not become offenders. The therapist should help the mother practice replacing the thoughts, "My son, Nicholas, has been sexually abused and now he is going to be a sex offender himself," with the more accurate and positive thought, "Most children who have experienced sexual abuse never abuse anyone else. Nick is getting help in coping with his abuse so there is no reason to believe he'll abuse anyone else."

Nonproductive thoughts

The second category of dysfunctional thoughts covers thoughts that are nonproductive, regardless of their accuracy. For example, a parent who is preoccupied with anger toward the perpetrator may experience repeated thoughts such as, "He sexually abused my child and broke our family apart. He is the scum of the earth." Although the parent's anger may be justified, some of these thoughts are accurate but not helpful. In such a case, it is not appropriate to attempt to dispute the parent's thoughts; rather the therapist should empathize with the parent's emotions and then shift to helping the parent redirect her thoughts in a more productive way. It may be helpful to explain that although the parent's anger is completely understandable and justified, it is difficult to be happy and satisfied with life while focused on anger. Reminding the parent that the joint goal of the therapist and the parent is to help the child be happy and well adjusted, the therapist will help the parent refocus on how the parent can best help the child adjust after this experience. An example of such a replacement thought is, "I'm not going to waste time thinking about Ray anymore. I'm going to focus on helping Sammy by getting her to counseling each week and doing the practice activities the therapist gives us. And most of all, I'm not going to let the sexual abuse stop us from having a good relationship going forward."

Pessimistic thinking

Many nonproductive thoughts are characterized by a negative style of thinking called pessimistic thinking. It is clear that many distressing emotions are driven by highly negative or pessimistic thoughts. In fact, research suggests that pessimistic coping styles not only lead to negative emotions but are frequently associated with poor physical health and low achievement (Seligman, 2006). Parents who are receptive to additional reading may be referred to *Learned Optimism*, by Martin E. P. Seligman (2006) or another self-help book based on cognitive behavioral principles. Seligman (2006) presents the concept of cognitive coping in a readable and interesting format. Therapists may also find it helpful to use this book as a guide to presenting the coping material. Seligman identifies three qualities that often characterize pessimistic thoughts about problems. These characteristics include viewing the problem as permanent, pervasive, and/or personal. Although problems are often thought of this way, most problems are actually changeable rather than permanent, specific rather than pervasive in their impact, and their occurrence is related to non-personal rather than personal factors.

Therapists may assist parents in examining their thoughts to determine if they tend to reflect any of these pessimistic qualities. When identifying negative thought characteristics, it is important that the therapist's comments not sound critical but empathic in pointing out that the parent's thoughts are in fact more harsh and negative than they need to be. The parent, in fact, deserves more kindness and comforting than the parent is giving herself. Interestingly, when people learn to be kinder and more positive to themselves, this tendency is likely to generalize to how they think about and treat others including their children.

Socrative method: common areas of distress and dysfunctional thinking

When pursuing cognitive coping skills training with parents, the therapist should focus on the specific areas of emotional distress identified by the parent as described above in the therapist-parent dialogue. The first step involves patiently eliciting as many thoughts as possible. As noted earlier, this means allowing for pauses and silence as parents retrieve the thoughts associated with distressing feelings. Research, in fact, has documented that such silences during therapy sessions are perceived as supportive by clients (Sharpley, 1997). Thus, it is important for therapists to encourage parents to do the work of retrieving or, later, challenging their own dysfunctional thoughts before assisting them.

Although the types of emotions experienced will vary from parent to parent, some of the more common areas of distress and dysfunctional thinking are identified below. The dialogues highlight therapists' efforts to elicit and challenge dysfunctional thoughts that may be underlying parental distress. It is often helpful for new TF-CBT therapists to first generate healthy thoughts that will specifically replace the identified problematic thoughts (in their own mind or using the relevant form in Appendix F) in order to effectively formulate Socratic questions that when posed will lead parents to those or similar healthy replacement thoughts. When possible, therapists should not simply give parents replacement thoughts but rather help parents process their own dysfunctional thoughts through the elicitation of healthier thoughts via Socratic questioning. Such questions should be designed to lead parents to answers that refute and/or replace problematic thoughts with more optimistic or productive thoughts. In fact, it is best not to ask Socratic questions to which one does not know how the client is likely to answer. Rather therapists are encouraged to pose Socratic questions that they are confident parents can answer in a productive way based on prior experiences with their children, psychoeducation discussions, or reading materials provided to parents. The use of reflective listening and silences during Socratic questioning further supports parents' efforts to process dysfunctional thoughts and integrate healthier ways of thinking. While the focus of this book is on CSA, it is important to remember that many children who have been sexually abused have experienced other trauma(s) as well, so the information provided should be relevant to all the specific trauma(s) experienced by the child and the parent. Interestingly, in the aftermath of trauma, parents often report very similar distressing thoughts—the most common of which are described below.

Responsibility/guilt

Some parents may feel guilty for not preventing or recognizing the sexual abuse. Parents whose children were abused by a family member or someone well known to the family may be especially vulnerable to distressing feelings of responsibility. After eliciting from parents the thoughts that are underlying their feelings of guilt or sadness, the therapist may help parents dispute their dysfunctional thoughts by (1) providing educational information and (2) utilizing Socratic questions to help parents replace their dysfunctional thoughts with more accurate and/or productive thoughts. This can help parents depersonalize the problem, thereby diminishing inappropriate feelings of responsibility and/or guilt. The dialogue addresses common thoughts related to feelings of parental guilt.

Therapist: *You mentioned that you often feel guilty about the sexual abuse. Can you take me back to a time recently when you found yourself feeling very upset? I am interested in what you say to yourself when you experience feelings of guilt and self blame. Please speak slowly so I can write down your thoughts.*

Parent: *It was just this morning. I was thinking there is something wrong with me that this would happen to my child. I don't know any other child that this has happened to. I should have known my ex could do this.*

Therapist: *Thank you for sharing. Let's review these thoughts for their accuracy and their helpfulness. Do you remember what percent of girls experience sexual abuse by the time they are 18 years of age?*

Parent: *Was it almost 1 out of every 4 girls may be sexually abused?*

Therapist: *That is right! So do you think there is something wrong with twenty five percent of moms?*

Parent: *There can't be something wrong with all their moms, but there certainly is something wrong with people who sexually abuse children. Why couldn't I see that this guy was an abuser?*

Therapist: *Do you think I can identify a sex offender without witnessing the sexual abuse?*

Parent: *I don't know.*

Therapist: *I could not identify a sex offender even if I spent time talking to the person or knew the person quite well. Do you think you could tell if a person is a sex offender?*

Parent: *I guess not.*

Therapist: *Even a child sexual abuse expert could not pick a sexual offender out of a group. Remember sex offenders are generally not "dirty old men" or strangers. There is nothing about their public behavior or appearance that distinguishes them. So, what could you say to yourself when you find yourself feeling guilty?*

Parent: (long pause) *Even experts can't identify sex offenders just by looking at or knowing them. So maybe, I am not a fool, just a mom who loves her child.*

Therapist: *That is absolutely true; even experts cannot identify sex offenders and you are a very loving mom.*

Parent: *But I should have been looking out more for my daughter. I should have been able to tell by her behavior.*

Therapist: *You did notice that she was experiencing some stress, didn't you?*

Parent: *Yes, her grades were dropping a little. So I encouraged the guidance counselor to talk to her.*

Therapist: *We can't tell from a child's behavior that they are being sexually abused, but you did notice that something was wrong and you did something about it. What are you doing that is so important to helping her academically as well as emotionally?*

Parent: *I guess I brought her to see you and you are teaching my child to cope with the sexual abuse.*

Therapist: *Exactly, together we are helping her to learn to cope with the sexual abuse and other problems she may face. So what can you say to yourself when you are feeling down and blaming yourself for the abuse?*

Parent: *I guess I can remind myself that I have been a good parent and I am helping my daughter now.*

The educational information presented to a particular client should be tailored so that replacement thoughts can be generated that specifically address the areas of cognitive distortion that are creating distress. Even after reviewing educational information, it is helpful to ask Socratic questions that will encourage parents to apply the information to their own child's circumstances so that they process and internalize a healthier way of thinking.

In addition to helping parents generate replacement thoughts as a means of coping with dysfunctional feelings of guilt and responsibility, therapists may engage parents in role-plays designed to allow them to rehearse a more effective cognitive style.

Sample best friend role-play exercise

To help parents who seem to have difficulty getting in touch with their feelings, the therapist may encourage parents to try a "best friend" role-play. In this role-play, the therapist should play the parent, while the parent is asked to be a good friend who uses her compassion and knowledge about CSA to convince the guilt-ridden parent that she is not responsible for her son's abuse. In playing the parent, the therapist should express the client's previously shared guilt-ridden thoughts, while also using the Socratic method to help the "friend" evaluate the accuracy and productiveness of these thoughts. Though the therapist is essentially playing the role of the client, the "best friend" role-play is most effective when it encourages the client to get emotional in her efforts to help her "best friend" feel better. Thus, it is important to initially resist the client's help and ask Socratic questions before accepting the client's suggestions as to why the thoughts are inaccurate or unproductive.

Anxiety/Distrust

Some parents may experience an enormous amount of anxiety about their child's safety and well-being in the aftermath of discovering that he was sexually abused. Such emotions, though natural, can lead parents to severely overprotect their children. In fact, parents experiencing significant anxiety and distrust may become so overprotective and potentially indulgent that the child's ability to develop a healthy sense of self and independence may be compromised. Parents may use some of the coping skills discussed earlier to manage their anxiety, but ultimately it may be most important to elicit and replace the thoughts that underlie their ongoing fears and distrust. In addition to helping parents generate replacement thoughts as a means of coping with dysfunctional thoughts, therapists may engage parents in role plays designed to allow them to rehearse a more effective cognitive style.

Sample role reversal role-play exercise

To help parents to overcome dysfunctional thinking, the therapist may encourage parents to try a "role reversal" role play. In this role-play, the therapist should play the parent, while the parent is asked to be therapist who uses empathy and knowledge about CSA to help the distressed parent with her anxiety and/or overprotectiveness. In playing the parent, the therapist should express the client's previously shared anxiety-provoking thoughts, while also using the Socratic method to help the "client" evaluate the accuracy and productiveness of these thoughts. Though the therapist is essentially playing the role of the client, this role-play is most effective when it encourages the real client to work hard to help the "client" feel less distressed and more confident. Thus, it is important for the therapist to use Socratic questions before accepting the real client's initial educational and therapeutic suggestions.

Therapist: *I wonder if we could try a role play in which I play your friend and you play my therapist. Sometimes we are better at helping others with distressing thoughts than we are at managing our own distressing thoughts and feelings. So, how about I share with you some distressing or dysfunctional thoughts? Then maybe with all that you have learned about sexual abuse you can help me feel better so I can best help my child.*

Parent: *Okay, I'll give it a try. I always wanted to be a therapist.*

Therapist: *So I am going to share some thoughts I have heard from you as well as other parents whose children have experienced sexual abuse. In this role-play, you are my therapist and you are giving me advice concerning my child who was sexually abused. Can I call you Dr. Wilson, just for this role-play?*

Parent: *Okay.*

Therapist: *Dr. Wilson, I really feel like I can never trust anyone again with my son. No one is trustworthy.*

Parent: *It is hard to find trustworthy people.*

Therapist: *I cannot allow my son to be around anyone who might abuse him again. So, do you think I should avoid extracurricular activities and using babysitters until my son is grown, Dr. Wilson?*

Parent: *Well, maybe that wouldn't hurt. I understand how you feel.*

Therapist: *So, Dr. Wilson, you think it is dangerous to leave children with babysitters or let them engage in activities led by young adult counselors?*

Parent: *No, I didn't say that. Most babysitters and counselors are not abusive.*

Therapist: *What should I do then? How can I protect my son from any kind of abuse from anyone?*

Parent: (long pause) *Well, you can't actually do that–no one can. You can't keep him away from all young adults, and it would not be good for your son to be afraid of all people.*

Therapist: *No. I don't want him going through life thinking he can't trust anyone. What can I do to protect him?*

Parent: *I will help you teach your child coping skills so if something bad happens he will know how to cope and he will be able to say NO, get away, and tell you so you can help. My child did that, and he is doing well now.*

Therapist: *Really, he is doing well now? The truth is that I am doing all I can to help him learn how to manage stressful experiences with other people and not accept any kind of abuse. Dr. Wilson, honestly do you think I am a lousy mom because this happened?*

Parent: *You are a good mother. You gave your son the strength to tell, and you are supporting him now.*

Therapist: *Why was it difficult for me to detect the sexual abuse? Why did my son keep this a secret for so long?*

Parent: *Offenders often threaten children not to tell. So even though you talked to him about telling if anyone hurt or touched him, he was scared. The secretive nature of sexual abuse makes it difficult to detect and to prevent. Most children never tell and the fact that your son was able to tell when he did was because you did something right!*

Therapist: *Wow! That really helps me feel better to think about it that way, Dr. Wilson. I guess no matter what I did (short of locking my son in his room), no matter how good a parent I try to be, I cannot ensure that my child would never be hurt or even sexually abused again. But is there anything I can do to prepare my son for the future?*

Parent: (long pause) *That is a hard question, but I think you can prepare him by getting him therapy like you are so he can cope with whatever difficulties happen in life.*

Sadness

Many parents struggle with feelings of sadness and grief regarding their child's sexual abuse experience. Although those feelings are understandable and expected, some parents experience such overwhelming grief that their displays of emotion negatively affect their children. When working with such parents, the therapist may motivate them to examine and strengthen their coping responses for the child's sake. The therapist may explain that if the parent's response to the sexual abuse communicates that a catastrophe has occurred, the child may assume that what happened to her is something so bad that she will never get over it. Many parents experience sadness that is exacerbated by underlying thoughts that are inaccurate or dysfunctional. In a dialogue such as the one in Box 9.7, a therapist might help a depressed parent work through the process of

---

Box 9.7

Case Example: Helping a Depressed Parent Deal with Pessimistic Thoughts

Therapist: *For the last couple of weeks, we've talked about how depressed you get when you think about your son having been sexually abused.*

Mother: *Sometimes I get so down about it I can't snap myself out of it.*

Therapist: *Well, let's talk about the last time you were feeling this way. I'm going to write down the thoughts you were having. Start by telling me briefly what was happening the last time you were feeling this way.*

Mother: *It was just today. My son was acting really sassy. John is only 8, but sometimes he acts like he's 16. I just thought to myself, my son's childhood has been stolen. He has real problems now.*

Therapist: ... *"My son's childhood has been stolen. He has real problems now." What else were you saying to yourself?*

Mother: *I was thinking that this is the worst thing that could have ever happened to him. It's going to ruin his life. Just like my experience with sexual abuse ruined my life.* (long pause)

Therapist:... *you were thinking "This is the worst thing that could have ever happened to him. It's going to ruin his life. Just like my experience of sexual abuse ruined my life." Please continue—did you have some other thoughts?*

Mother: *I thought this is all my fault. What kind of mother am I?* (long pause)

Therapist: *(continues writing) And when you thought, "What kind of mother am I?" How did you answer that question?*

Mother: (tearfully) *I'm a bad mother who wasn't there for her child. But I did say to myself I am really trying to be there for him now and I am not going to let my child go through this alone.*

Therapist: (therapist offers tissues) *So you said to yourself... "I'm a bad mother who wasn't there for her child. I am really trying to be there for him now and I am not going to let him go through this alone." Okay, some of those thoughts would lead anyone to feel depressed. Let's see if we can use some of the cognitive coping strategies we've been talking about to look at how accurate some of those thoughts are. First, you said your son's childhood was stolen. Let's step back and examine that thought—do you think it's accurate?*

Mother: *Yes, it's true!*

Therapist: *He hasn't enjoyed any aspects of his childhood?*

Mother: *Well,* (long pause) *he's had lots of friends that he's enjoyed doing lots of different activities with. And he's always been very close to me and his father—we've had a lot of fun vacations. But with his cousin sexually abusing him all that time, he couldn't have really enjoyed life.*

Therapist: *Did he understand that what his cousin was doing was wrong?*

Mother: *No, I guess not at first. After he did, though, it took him a while to tell.*

Therapist: *How long?*

Mother: *A few months.*

Therapist: *Then maybe he did enjoy all those important childhood relationships and activities.*

Mother: *Maybe you're right.*

Therapist: *You also said that John has some problems as a result of the sexual abuse. I guess that's a pretty accurate thought, but if you didn't recognize that he had problems, you wouldn't be here getting him the help he needs.*

Mother: *Exactly.*

Therapist: *But what about some of these other thoughts, like, "This is the worst thing that could have ever happened to him." Are you sure there's nothing else that could have been worse?*

Mother: *You mean like getting hit by a car or something more permanent? I guess that would be worse. And he could have kept this to himself for a longer period of time and maybe he could have even been infected with HIV.*

Therapist: *Maybe when you have these negative thoughts, you could remind yourself that although John has some problems as a result of the abuse, they are not necessarily permanent problems. In fact, I have great confidence that your son will overcome these difficulties with your help and counseling.*

Mother: *That makes sense. But I still worry that he's going to have all the problems that I had as a result of my sexual abuse.*

Therapist: *Well, let's list the ways in which the experience of sexual abuse and what happened when he told have been different for him as compared to you.*

Mother: *Well, I guess for starters I believed him right away and I never even told because I thought no one would believe me.*

Therapist: *That is a great thought for you to repeat to yourself when you have some of these distressing thoughts. Remind yourself that you didn't tell as a child, but your son told you.*

Mother: *That is true. I could try to remind myself of that.*

Therapist: *Another important and more positive and accurate thought you had was that you are doing something now. You are not going to let your child go through this alone. That is an accurate and helpful thought. Let's list the things that you are doing that are helping your son recover from the sexual abuse that you unfortunately did not experience as a child.*

Mother: *Okay.*

Therapist: *Do you think there might be things on that list that will reflect that fact that you are not only NOT a bad mother, but that you are actually a very good, loving, and devoted mom?*

Mother: *Okay. I see where you are going with this. Do I still have to write the list?*

Therapist: *Absolutely.*

The above dialogue continues with the therapist helping the mother acknowledge that her experience of sexual abuse at the hands of her father was in certain respects more severe in nature and longer lasting. Additionally, as a child, she did not get the support that she and her husband are providing for her son, John. Also, the mother was able to acknowledge that she never received any kind of counseling and had a great deal of difficulty coping with the experience on her own. Next, the therapist should remind the mother that the contents of her thoughts may be causing her to feel even worse about the sexual abuse than is necessary. Thus, it will be helpful to continue working to identify inaccurate and excessively negative thoughts and replace them with more positive and accurate thoughts. In the case of the above mother, it can be useful to have her list the qualities she believes a good mother has and then inquire as to whether she exhibits any of those qualities, listing specifically those qualities that classify her as not only a good mother, but a devoted mother who is committed to getting her son the best help available.

identifying, evaluating, and disputing inaccurate or overly pessimistic thoughts about a child's experience of sexual abuse.

Anger

Parents may experience anger at a variety of people involved in the abusive situation. For example, parents may be angry with the child for having participated in the abusive activities or for not telling sooner. In addition to the guilt described previously, some parents may feel angry with themselves for not preventing the abuse or for not helping the child to tell sooner. Most significantly, parents often feel angry with the perpetrator. The therapist may explain that all these experiences of anger are normal and are signs that a parent cares. The therapist may further explain that it would be of greater concern if a parent was not having any strong feelings about what happened.

Anger at the Child or the Parent

When working with parents who are experiencing anger at the child for participating in the abusive sexual activity or at themselves for not preventing it, the therapist may encourage the parents to identify ways in which they believe the child was engaged in the abuse. Using the list in Box 9.8, the therapist should help parents identify and list those vulnerabilities most applicable to their child's specific experiences. The parent might generate the list and the therapist can provide additional methods that the parent may not have previously considered. Then the therapist can use that information as illustrated below to help parents dispute the thoughts that are generating anger.

Parent: *I don't know why my child did not just hit him or come home. We've talked about how to handle situations like this.*

Therapist: *When you are thinking this way, how do you feel?*

Parent: *Just so frustrated and angry. Why did she let this happen?*

Therapist: *Let's discuss this because it doesn't help your daughter for you to hold on to feelings of anger and frustration. Unfortunately, even when parents educate their children like you did, children find it very difficult to respond effectively and get away. Do you know why that might be?*

Parent: *Well, I guess there are many reasons.*

Therapist: *Exactly. I would like you to take a little time to think this through and list all the different ways children are engaged in abusive sexual interactions and reasons they don't tell.*

Parent: *Should I write them down?*

Therapist: *Sure. Take your time.*

Parent: (writing) *This is hard, I didn't expect to come up with so many.*

Therapist: *Fantastic. So which of these do you think were your daughter's reasons?*

Parent: *Well, the biggest reasons for my child were that the offender was her cousin and she trusted him and loved him. And she didn't want him to get in trouble.*

Therapist: *Yes, that does make it much harder for children to say no and tell.*

BOX 9.8

Some Ways Perpetrators Engage Children

- The offender took advantage of my child's natural curiosity about sexuality.
- The offender encouraged my child to think that the activity was okay by presenting it as a game.
- The offender maintained my child's cooperation by making her feel good physically and emotionally.
- The offender took advantage of the fact that my child believed the sexual activity was an appropriate expression of affection or love.
- The offender took advantage of my child's eagerness to please an adult (particularly applicable when the perpetrator is a father, teacher, good family friend, etc.).
- The offender took advantage of my child's natural responsiveness to authority.
- The offender used my child's fears, threatening her with repeated abuse, as well as physical injury to her and to me.

Parent: *I'm so angry at myself too because I told her about "stranger danger" but I didn't mention that even a relative could abuse her. If only I had done a better job educating her.*
Therapist: *While you're right the "stranger danger" warning is not the best way to educate children about sexual abuse, it was great that you talked to her about sexual abuse in general.*
Parent: *Do you think that helped her disclose?*
Therapist: *Absolutely! I think you did quite a good job educating her. So good that she was able to disclose!*

When working with parents who are angry with the child for not disclosing sooner or at themselves for not having elicited an earlier disclosure from the child, the therapist may explain that in the child's mind, there may be many, many reasons not to tell, and relatively few good reasons to tell. Then the therapist may encourage the parent to list reasons children may not tell. If it is necessary, the therapist may assist the parent in generating that list of reasons by using the information in Box 9.9. In most cases, the therapist may point out that the child did eventually disclose, despite all of these reasons not to tell. The therapist may encourage the parent to use the generated list of reasons for not telling to practice disputing her thoughts that are anger producing. An example of that process follows.

Therapist: *Remember, most children never ever tell about sexual abuse. And we talked about some of the reasons why your child may have found it hard to tell at first, but now let's review all those things that gave your child the courage to tell when most children don't ever tell about sexual abuse.*

Parent: *Just speaking this way may be frightening to Andy. It's not going to help him if I hurt the offender and I end up in jail myself. I'm going to concentrate on getting Andy the counseling he needs.*

When working with a parent who is discussing plans for revenge, the therapist should carefully assess the parent's intent and his development of a true plan. Depending on the laws of the state, the therapist may have a legal obligation to inform both law enforcement officials and the intended victim if the parent acknowledges intent to actually harm the perpetrator. The therapist should learn the relevant state laws regarding a therapist's "duty to warn" an intended victim of a crime (Widgery & Winterfield, 2013). If the therapist is bound by such a law, she should inform all parents of that obligation when discussing the limits of confidentiality (e.g., homicidal and/or suicidal intent) at the initiation of therapy and should again remind them of this obligation when issues of revenge and anger are raised in the course of therapy.

Often parents focus excessively on their anger, although they are not actively formulating a plan for revenge. Such parents also may be encouraged to think through the consequences of their anger in terms of its impact on their child. The therapist may ask questions such as the following:

How does your daughter feel when she sees you so angry and upset?
How does your anger help your son cope with this experience?

If a parent does not seem to recognize how significantly his or her anger influences the child, the therapist might discuss the information in Box 9.10, which describes a number of ways that children may be influenced by their parents' angry reactions to an incident of abuse.

Here's one example of how a therapist might help a parent replace anger-producing thoughts.

Parent: *I'm just so angry at my father for doing this to Sharon. Now we have to talk to Child Protective Services and the Prosecutor's Office and come to counseling while nothing seems to be happening to him!*

Therapist: *Continuing to focus on how unfair the situation is not helping Sharon or you. And I'm afraid it is just causing you more distress. What can you do or say to yourself that would be more helpful?*

Parent: *Maybe I could concentrate more on how I can best help Sharon cope with this.*

Therapist: *That is a great idea. Do you think that would have more of an impact on her recovery than what happens to the offender?*

Parent: *I guess.*

Therapist: *I am confident that it will. There doesn't seem to be any relationship between legal system outcomes and children's recovery. What do you think most helps children recover fully from sexual abuse?*

Box 9.10

How Excessive Parental Anger Affects Children

- If children see their parents lose control and become overwhelmed with anger whenever the subject of the abuse comes up, the children may learn to avoid discussing the abuse in order to avoid making their parents angry.
- Young children tend to feel that they are the center of the world and that they cause what happens around them. If a child sees his parents get extremely upset or angry about something that has happened to them, the child may think, "Look how upset Mommy and Daddy are. I must have done something very bad."
- Children have difficulty recognizing that they have been coerced, manipulated, or bribed into taking part in the sexual activities. Thus, they may feel as blameworthy as the perpetrator for their participation.
- Children tend to imitate parental responses. Thus, if a parent exhibits extreme anger regarding the situation, the child may similarly react with apparent anger, potentially masking other emotions he may be experiencing and acting on the anger.
- Children who are consistently exposed to parental anger will learn to focus exclusively on an anger response potentially leading to problematic aggressive behaviors.

Confusion

Many parents of children who have experienced sexual abuse as well as other interpersonal violence report feeling confused and frustrated. They often want answers to questions such as, Why did this happen? and Why would anyone violate a child? Parents are likely to continue experiencing negative emotions as they ruminate over these questions and/or generate answers that are inaccurate or dysfunctional. Therapists can help parents break a cycle of unproductive rumination by providing some basic information, such as the material found in Box 9.11. The therapist can help parents to replace confusing and/or depressing thoughts by using this information to formulate Socratic questions that will help to challenge the dysfunctional, repetitive aspects of their thinking.

Parent: *I don't know why my husband did this. Maybe if I had been a more responsive sexual partner.*

Therapist: *Do you think most people who have marital difficulties solve those problems by sexually abusing a child?*

Parent: *Maybe not.*

Therapist: *Do you think spouses can change someone who is inclined toward sexually abusing children?*

Box 9.11

Information about Why CSA Occurs

- There is no one, simple explanation for why sexual abuse occurs.
- Some sex offenders have been sexually abused, physically abused, and/or neglected as children.
- Some sex offenders have problems with alcohol or drug abuse.
- Some sex offenders have experienced a great deal of social isolation and alienation and have interpersonal problems relating to adults.
- Some sex offenders are exclusively sexually attracted to children.
- Some sex offenders have problems with power, authority, and/or impulse control.
- Regardless of the problems that may have contributed to his or her abusive behavior, the responsibility for sexual abuse rests squarely on the shoulders of the sex offender.

Parent: *I guess not.*
Therapist: *With whom does the responsibility for this behavior fall?*
Parent: *My husband.*
Therapist: *Absolutely. What do you think he should have done given his problems?*
Parent: *Maybe he should have gotten some help for his drinking and his anger about his own abuse. Besides, even if he was dissatisfied with our sex life, he didn't have to sexually abuse our child.*
Therapist: *Yes. So what can you concentrate your energy on that will be more productive for you and your child?*

The amount of time needed to pursue cognitive coping and other coping skills with parents may vary dramatically from one parent to another, depending on the parent's level of distress when confronted with thoughts of the sexual abuse. However, some cognitive coping work is critical with all parents to elicit underlying thoughts that may impact their interactions with their children at home and in conjoint trauma-focused sessions later in treatment.

Parents who have a personal history of CSA may experience greater feelings of facing this crisis alone (Deblinger et al., 1994) and require considerable cognitive coping and affective regulation before their distress diminishes enough that they can effectively discuss the abuse with their children. Although the authors do not encourage parents to focus a great deal on their own history of abuse, it is important to acknowledge that personal abusive experiences may make it more difficult for some parents to cope. At the same time, however, it should be emphasized that many parents who are survivors themselves can be excellent sources of support to their children. However, if parents appear to have symptoms that stem from their own history of abuse, it may be useful to share that observation and to offer a referral for adult survivor counseling now or after their child has completed treatment. By this stage of treatment, a trusting therapist-client relationship may be sufficiently established such that the parent may be willing to accept a referral for additional personal therapy if recommended. The therapist, for example, might point out that the parent deserves the opportunity to work through his or her abuse experience just as much as the child does.

Practice activities assigned

Practice for parents should flow from whatever was covered in session. However, the therapist should be careful not to overwhelm parents with too many practice assignments, but rather recommend between session practice that will likely be met with some success. Thus, if there is not sufficient time to fully explain and practice the new skill set, it is best to delay its implementation until the following session when more time is allotted for practice and role-plays. Below are a several possible areas for practice that may be introduced and practiced at home depending on what is covered in the parent session during this component.

Cognitive coping skills practice

Parents should be encouraged to practice their cognitive coping skills at home. They may be asked to keep a list of any distressing emotions they have experienced regarding the abuse, the thoughts underlying those distressing emotions, and the replacement thoughts they used to dispute the dysfunctional thoughts. These thoughts and emotions may be recorded in a journal or automatic thought record provided (see Appendix B for the automatic thoughts record included in the *Identifying and Challenging Your Problematic Thoughts* handout). The therapist can then review the parents' thought record or journal to monitor the client's success in disputing dysfunctional thoughts and to offer suggestions for improving those skills.

Parenting skills practice

Relevant parenting practices (see effective instructions, time out and work chore assignments below) might also be given using a handout that is briefly reviewed and provided to the parent to take home and read. Parents can be reminded that the parenting skills learned must continue to be practiced in order to encourage and maintain children's positive adjustment and development. At this stage of treatment, if parents have successfully implemented the positive parenting practices discussed in previous sessions, it is appropriate to provide one parenting handout to help parents begin to implement another important parenting practice such as giving effective instructions, creating house rules/behavior charts or, the time out implementation guidelines.

Effective instructions practice

In addition to continuing their work with specific praise, reflective listening, and selective attention, parents may be provided with a handout (see Appendix B) and asked to do the following to practice giving effective instructions at home:

- Examine the frequency and quality of the instructions they give their children.
- Give children effective instructions to do things parents think they would like to do (e.g., "Billy, please sit down and draw a picture with me").
- Offer specific praise immediately following children's efforts to comply (e.g., "Billy, I really liked how you followed my instructions to sit down and draw a picture with me").
- Practice encouraging compliance to instructions through gentle physical contact. For example, when a child repeatedly wanders off in a store, rather than yelling at him or her not to wander away, the parent may be encouraged to draw the child close and take his or her hand. Thus, the parent may create an opportunity to praise compliance by stating that the parent really appreciates the child staying with the parent and that the parent enjoys holding hands with the child.
- Engage the child in conversation or identify ways the child can immediately help (e.g., "Please get the ketchup on that shelf"), and whenever the child does comply provide lots of positive reinforcement by offering specific praise and positive attention.
- Always look for small compliant behaviors to praise even it is simply responding to your questions in conversations (e.g., "I really like talking with you and hearing your ideas").
- Follow the guidelines for effective, specific PRAISE!

Parents are shaping compliant behavior by starting with instructions with which children are likely to comply. It is then easier in the future for parents to move on to giving children instructions that are less appealing. Still, it is important for parents to be positive, warm, yet firm when giving instructions, while highlighting the potential benefits of complying with the instructions (i.e., a positive consequence that will follow their compliance) such as *after you finish your homework we can watch a TV show together.*

Time out or work chore introduction and implementation practice

Parents may be reminded of the importance of offering purely positive, specific, and enthusiastic praise for the positive behavior that has been identified as a replacement for the problem behavior. Simultaneously, the parents should eliminate any reinforcing consequences (e.g., yelling, lectures) that the child has been receiving for the target problem behavior. Parents may present or review the time out procedure with their child, emphasizing that initially it will be used for only one behavior. The identified problem behavior, however, may be a class of behaviors such as not following parents' instructions. Well-adjusted children do not comply and/or cooperate 100% of the time. In fact, research suggests that most nonclinic children comply only 60% to 80% of the time (Forehand, 1977). Thus, it is helpful for parents to communicate clearly when noncompliance is not an option and time out will follow if they don't comply. Some parents make this clear by using their child's full name including their middle name. Other parents start to count (e.g., to 3 or 5) as a signal that children must follow their instructions quickly. Finally, some children report that they recognize a parental tone of voice or a look that signals to them that their parents expect immediate responsiveness. However, when such a signal is not used by parents or clearly recognized by the children, it is helpful to have parents and children agree on a signal that indicates that if they do not comply with a parent request, they will be expected to take a time out. It is important that the parents be clear and specific in defining the problem behavior for the child. For example, if the target behavior is not following parental instructions, the parent should explain to the child, "Whenever I say to you, 'I'm giving you an instruction now or I begin to count,' that is a signal that you need to follow the instruction or we will use time out to help you remember that rule the next time." Parents may then implement time out, making every effort to follow the steps outlined in the time out handout (see Appendix B).

Prepare for conjoint session

Conjoint sessions following the activities typically engaged in during this component should be designed to provide opportunities for successful practice of parenting and coping skills learned. Thus, after reviewing the conjoint session goals agreed upon (see below conjoint session activity options), it can be helpful to have parents role-play any conjoint session activity planned. In general, it is always helpful for parents to prepare and share the specific and/or global praise they plan to share in the conjoint session, as some parents continue to need help adjusting their praise to eliminate negative tags and/or be more specific in what they are praising for quite some time before they begin offering specific praise optimally. Some parents are also not accustomed to sharing feelings of love and pride (i.e., global praise), but encouraging such expressions can go a long way in enhancing parent-child relationships. Specific and global praise exercises may be implemented at the end of different conjoint sessions as a positive end-of-session ritual.

CONJOINT SESSION(S)

Again, these conjoint activities, though optional, may be particularly important when children have behavior problems and parents would benefit from observed practice of the parenting skills. In fact, regardless of the conjoint activity chosen for implementation, the parent(s) may be prepared in advance and coached to focus on what the child is doing right, while practicing relevant parenting skills (e.g., selective attention, specific praise, reflective listening). Given time constraints, the therapist should determine the most pressing needs of the parent and child and choose from among the below-described alternative conjoint activities. However, it is important to note that conjoint session activities should not be implemented without prior preparation particularly with the parent to enhance the likelihood of success.

Encourage child to teach parent(s) about cognitive coping

If the child is continuing to experience significant depressive, angry, and/or anxious feelings and would benefit from parental support with regard to the use of cognitive coping skills, the conjoint session might focus on reviewing those skills. After the child presents what he learned about cognitive coping by drawing or using a diagram and/or presenting real life examples, the parent should be coached to reflectively listen and praise the child's efforts. As has been noted previously, it is easy for children to get silly or less than cooperative during conjoint activities so these sessions present excellent opportunities for therapists to model and for parents to practice using praise and selective attention to help the child stay focused on discussing cognitive coping. Parents are also encouraged to demonstrate their understanding of cognitive coping by offering examples, as well as successful coping experiences that they prepared with the help of the therapist. In fact, the therapist should encourage both parents and children to share positive self-statements as these may be beneficial for both the child and parent(s) as often pessimism and negative self-talk can be quite contagious in families.

Assist parent and child to collaboratively develop a behavior or family rules chart

If the child is exhibiting acting-out behavior problems, it may be best to use the conjoint session time to engage in family problem solving in order to develop a house rules list or a relevant behavior chart. Such a review should also be carefully planned with the parent with a focus on highlighting the positive replacement behaviors that were identified through functional analyses. Parents and children together should agree on the positive consequences for displaying the positive behaviors or fulfilling the behavioral expectations. However, this too should be carefully discussed in advance so parents do not agree to positive consequences that they are not prepared to offer. In addition, the therapist should help the parent think through in advance possible negative consequences (e.g., no points, missed allowance, time out, work chores) for problem behaviors. Parents may review and discuss such consequences at home with therapist preparation and/or in a conjoint session. Additional conjoint activities from which to choose are listed below.

Encourage parent and child to review and/or practice coping skills learned

It can be helpful to point out to clients that they have now learned coping skills that can help them manage stress that affects their bodies, feelings, and/or thoughts. Older children and adults can be asked to describe which coping skills are most likely to help them in each of those areas. They may each be asked to report on times during the previous week when they were able to use different coping skills effectively. The parent and child may also be encouraged to engage in role-plays demonstrating how they can use various coping skills such as relaxation, affect expression and regulation, as well as cognitive coping to respond effectively to different hypothetical situations that the therapist may pose. In addition, to summarize the work they have done so far, during the conjoint session children can share their coping skills tool kit project with parents including the cognitive coping skills and/or personalized positive self-statements they may have added to their top 5 or 10 coping skills favorites list. Parents and the child should be encouraged to recognize that the coping skills they are learning may help them cope effectively with all kinds of life difficulties, in addition to the distress or difficulties associated with the abuse and/or trauma(s) endured and the trauma reminders experienced.

Brief skills practice reminder

Careful assessment and clinical judgment should be used to determine the focus of ongoing skill-building practice with children, adolescents, and their parents. Although all parents and children should be encouraged to learn about cognitive coping, as well as the other coping skills (e.g., relaxation and affect regulation skills) outlined in the prior chapters, practice should be designed individually to meet the needs of particular clients. At this stage of treatment, it is important for the therapist to begin to identify the skills that the child, teen, and parent(s) are most likely to naturally utilize and most likely to receive family, as well as other environmental support for implementing in real life. These are the coping and parenting skills assignments that should be repeatedly practiced throughout the remainder of treatment so that they become natural habits for healthy coping that children and parents will maintain after therapy ends.

End-of-session positive ritual

As the family prepares to move into the trauma narration and processing phase of treatment, it is particularly important to identify and engage in end-of-session positive rituals that the parent and child find relaxing and enjoyable. The mutual exchange of praise is one such activity some parents and children seem to greatly enjoy when they are prepared in advance for the activity.

10

Trauma Narrative Development Part I

Initiating the Trauma Narration and Processing Phase of Treatment

The trauma narration and processing phase of trauma-focused cognitive-behavioral therapy (TF-CBT) includes the trauma narrative development and processing component. The introduction of this component should not feel jarring or sudden. As noted earlier, both children and parents are engaged in a gradual exposure process that gently encourages them to think and talk about sexual abuse from the start of treatment. This began during the initial treatment sessions by encouraging the child to talk about child sexual abuse (CSA) in general terms with limited but consistent and increasing references to the child's personal CSA experience(s) throughout the initial stabilization and skill-building phase of treatment. Thus, when beginning the trauma narrative, children should not feel as if they are suddenly scaling a cliff; rather due to prior gradual exposure, the process should feel more like climbing a gentle hill that represents only slightly more challenging therapy goals each step of the way. In fact, during this phase, children are generally well prepared to focus more specifically on the sexual abuse endured and/or other related experiences. The development of the trauma narrative, in particular, assists the child in disconnecting the associations frequently made between emotional distress and sexual abuse–related memories, thoughts, discussion, and other reminders. Caregivers who attempt to minimize children's distress in the aftermath of sexual abuse by shielding them from abuse-related stimuli or discussion often inadvertently reinforce avoidance and related distress and confusion. In fact, although well-meaning, parents may strengthen the association between abuse-related memories and emotional distress by avoiding abuse-related discussion, thereby signaling that abuse-related thoughts and memories are too horrible to confront and process openly (Lyons, 1987). Although parents and children are still not encouraged to initiate discussions about the abuse outside of therapy, parents during this phase may be informed that they may use reflective listening when and if their children share thoughts or feelings about the abuse. In addition, parents should be informed that children will begin to explore abuse-related emotions and experiences more actively and directly during individual sessions, while they simultaneously continue to practice their coping skills. During this treatment phase, it is important to remind parents that children may temporarily complain about therapy and/or express a desire not to attend session given that children may experience some increased feelings of distress. However, with continued encouragement the vast majority of children overcome these feelings and begin to feel a great deal of pride in their ability to talk about, write about, or even create art or music reflecting their CSA experiences. Working through sexual abuse memories in an active, structured, and time-limited fashion is consistent with the constructive coping strategies that researchers have found to be associated with greater long-term abuse resolution and decreased trauma-related symptoms in children with a history of CSA (Simon et al., 2010).

TRAUMA NARRATIVE DEVELOPMENT AND PROCESSING COMPONENT: PART I

During individual sessions, children progressively develop their trauma narratives in a manner that repeatedly helps them to master their traumatic responses to abuse-related memories, thoughts, discussion, and/or emotions until anxiety or other forms of emotional distress decrease. During the narrative development, children's emotional responses diminish through a process referred to as habituation. When this occurs, relaxed or neutral responses become connected with previously feared CSA-related memories and/or discussion. As children experience an overall reduction in emotional distress, they often begin to reveal more of their most troubling sexual abuse–related memories, thoughts, and questions.

Children who have experienced sexual abuse and/or other stigmatizing abuse experiences often have little information to understand their abuse. As a result, thoughts about the abuse, especially at the time these experiences were occurring, may be confused, inaccurate, and/or dysfunctional. It is therefore essential to help children become aware of and share their abuse-related feelings and thoughts in the course of developing their narrative. Once children have completed their narrative, therapists can help them use what they have learned about CSA, as well as cognitive coping skills to identify and alter inaccurate or unhelpful thoughts. By closely examining their abusive experiences, children often gain confidence in their abilities to face difficult life experiences. Although some processing of abuse-related memories naturally occurs throughout the course of therapy, the more formal review, identification, and processing of thoughts and emotions occurs once the narrative is complete. During trauma narrative development sessions, the therapist should encourage the child to review the developing narrative with the goal of incorporating additional memories of CSA, other trauma(s), and related experiences. With those children who have experienced multiple and/or complex trauma, the therapist should help the child to identify overarching trauma themes (e.g., "The people who should have protected me hurt me"; "Everyone I ever trusted left me", etc.) that may underlie their current difficulties. Once the trauma narrative is complete, the therapist can engage the child in processing that helps to reinforce healthy functional thoughts and feelings while simultaneously encouraging the child to identify and correct inaccurate, dysfunctional thoughts. During the processing of the trauma narrative (described in the following chapter), misconceptions clients may have had about themselves, the world, and their relationships with others can be corrected and replaced with more optimistic, adaptive beliefs that may be incorporated into a final summary chapter.

During this phase of treatment, therapists simultaneously work with caregivers to help them to continue to cope with their own emotional reactions to the disclosure of the sexual abuse. Therapists should use their clinical judgment in determining the most appropriate timing for sharing additional knowledge about the sexual abuse with parents. For example, the sharing of abuse-related details during this phase with some parents might undermine their focus on effective parenting. Such parents may be better served if their individual sessions continue to focus on the development of effective coping and parenting skills. In fact, the premature sharing of sexual abuse–related details with parents who are still struggling with feelings of guilt and anxiety may undermine their development of a more consistent and effective parenting approach. Thus, although the relationships between the sexual abuse and the child's problem behaviors should be acknowledged and processed, it is important to help parents simultaneously maintain their focus on enhancing the parent-child relationship with positive rituals, routines, and praise, while implementing effective parenting skills, including clearly expressed expectations and firmly implemented limits and negative consequences for problem behaviors. Some parents may benefit emotionally from learning about some of the strengths their child displayed in response to the abuse.

CHILD SESSION(S)

Although this component intensifies the focus on trauma narrative development, it is important to continue to build on and integrate the psychoeducation and coping skills training previously covered. In addition, the therapist should maintain and model a positive, open, and encouraging attitude demonstrating confidence in the child's ability to openly share the abuse experiences.

Practice activities review

Reviewing the child's use of coping skills practice between sessions is especially important to continue during this phase of treatment particularly with children and teenagers who are struggling with affective dysregulation. Developing the trauma narrative will have an almost immediate positive impact for many children, whereas others may experience transient and mild return of symptoms that had previously remitted (e.g., mild increase in irritability or abuse-related nightmares). This may be especially true for children who have been highly avoidant and are openly facing the details and related thoughts and feelings about the sexual abuse for the first time. Even these children typically experience only mild and transient symptoms. For example, a child may have one or two nightmares during the first week or two of starting the trauma narrative but will not likely return to the previous level of having several nightmares nightly. Throughout the process of developing the child's trauma narrative, the therapist should focus on the child's positive steps in mastering abuse memories.

With many youth, it helps to identify stimuli in the environment that may trigger negative thoughts and emotional distress due to their associations with the experience of sexual abuse. This is intended to help children better understand their reactions. Thus, while children will still be held accountable for unacceptable behaviors, this new understanding of their reactions may help them to anticipate difficulties and proactively prepare to use more productive coping responses. With children who are not highly dysregulated, the therapist may still inquire about the use of the coping skills discussed, while continuing to provide praise and encouragement for what they are learning, absorbing, and implementing whatever the level of follow through. It is also useful to help children who have had fewer opportunities to practice the coping skills during the week to imagine situations in which the various coping skills would be valuable.

Initiate trauma narrative development with the child

Although the trauma narrative development component may appear to be a relatively straightforward procedure, it can be difficult for some therapists to implement. Typically, a mental health professional's objective is to help individuals feel better. However, discussing and/or writing a narrative about highly traumatic experiences can be challenging and anxiety-provoking for some children. Many children must be encouraged to endure some distress during the process before reaching the goal of feeling better. As a child begins to show signs of distress, the therapist's natural instinct may be to back off or to give the child a break for several sessions. Clearly, this is an empathic response; however, it is counterproductive for the gradual exposure process. By backing off, the therapist is inadvertently reinforcing and modeling avoidant behavior. Thus, it is important for the therapist to be aware of the natural tendency to avoid encouraging the child to discuss distressing abuse-related issues. When the child begins to exhibit some distress during the course of gradual exposure, the therapist should view this as progress and continue to gradually move forward, demonstrating confidence that the child will be capable of successfully getting through the process despite some anxiety or tears. It is important to remember that the child's ability to endure, survive, and disclose sexual abuse already reflects a great deal of strength. It may help to remind clients that the strength they had in enduring and disclosing the sexual abuse will serve them well as they confront any fears or stressors they may face in therapy or in the future.

Preparing for trauma narrative development

During the course of the assessment and initial stages of therapy, the therapist should be gathering information regarding the child's sexual abuse experiences as well as the level of avoidance. This information regarding the child's pattern of avoidance and anxiety will guide the trauma narrative development plan for the child and also reveal important areas for review during processing. Moreover, this information will help the therapist organize the treatment sessions such that encouragement may be offered to write or talk about the less anxiety-provoking memories first with continued narrative development focusing on increasingly difficult memories and stimuli over the course of treatment. For example, during the evaluation, the therapist may find that the child easily described the last incident of abuse but only hesitatingly told about other episodes that happened while on vacations with extended family members years earlier.

During earlier sessions, the therapist has identified children's play preferences (e.g., drawing, doll playing, and puppeteering), observed children's skills for coping, and assessed their overall attention, concentration, memory, and verbal skills during the baseline narrative practice exercises. This information will be useful in planning the narrative development sessions, particularly in terms of offering appealing choices for developing the narrative and having reasonable expectations for the level of details.

Although it is important to provide parents and children with a general rationale for creating a narrative about the sexual abuse, in most cases it is not necessary or useful to describe the specific items on the therapist's tentative exposure hierarchy (i.e., narrative chapters list) to a young or highly avoidant child. Such details may heighten the child's anxiety, impede the gathering of additional details regarding the abusive experiences, and may not reflect the actual content of the narrative as it unfolds. Moreover, the specifics of the trauma narrative process may change in response to the child's initial reactions to creating it. Conversely, it can be beneficial to involve less avoidant children in the development of a general hierarchy for different parts of the narrative as that involvement may afford the child a greater sense of control and collaboration. This may be done by creating a tentative list of chapters or in essence a table of contents for the narrative.

As noted earlier, the rationale for the narrative development may best be explained to more avoidant children during the session in which the planned activity will take place. Generally, children do not need to be informed far in advance that they will be writing in detail about their abusive experiences as this may be upsetting and inadvertently encourage anxiety and avoidance. However, during the session in which the trauma narrative is introduced and initiated, the therapist should emphasize that the child's hard work will pay off because it will help the child to feel better and not feel as much distress when confronted with reminders of the abuse in the future.

Offering rationale for trauma narrative development

To help clients understand the potential value of directly discussing and/or writing about the abuse, therapists often use the analogy involving a physical cut or injury. Below the therapist describes what happens if one ignores a severe cut as opposed to gently cleaning and tending to the wound.

Therapist: *What do you think would happen if you got a really bad cut and you just ignored it? You just went out and played maybe even got dirt in the cut.*
Client: *It might get infected I guess.*
Therapist: *Exactly. When you ignore a cut, it has the potential to get infected and maybe even leave a scar. Have you ever seen an infected cut?*
Client: *Yes, it turns red, and sometimes stuff oozes out of it.*
Therapist: *That's right. The cut gets worse and hurts more. Sexual abuse is similar to an infected cut. If you try to forget it or ignore what happened, the memories can sometimes become more troubling and confusing. You may have more nightmares or feel more scared and more thoughts of it may pop into your head. But, if you gradually face those memories, it's like gently cleaning a wound. In the long run you'll feel better and you are much less likely to be left with a scar. Do you know what I mean by that?*
Client: *Maybe if you face it now, you won't have a scar or like problems later.*
Therapist: *Yes. That's exactly what I mean. If you deal with the sexual abuse now, you will feel better and be healthier later.*

Some children avoid and/or suppress abuse-related memories and thoughts so successfully that they initially have difficulty acknowledging worries or problems associated with the abuse. With such a child, it may be helpful to explain in the following way:

Therapist: *Sometimes we don't know that something bothers us, but it stays in our memory and causes us problems in the future. That is why it is very important to talk about your feelings and thoughts about the abuse now so that we can prevent them from becoming worries or problems later on. You can let me know how you are feeling over the course of the session by using the feelings thermometer.*

Some avoidant children may be motivated by the idea of helping other children. In such instances, the therapist might discuss this in the following way:

Therapist: *Offenders work hard to keep children silent, but writing a narrative about what happened is way of standing up to the offender. In some ways, a narrative will not only help you to share all your thoughts and feelings about it, but you may also help me to better understand about child sexual abuse so that I can better* *help other children who have been sexually abused who can't express themselves as well as you can!*

Building on psychoeducation about CSA

As noted earlier, children often seem to find it easier to talk about sexual abuse in the abstract than to talk about their personal experience of sexual abuse. Thus, it is helpful to begin the session by discussing more general questions and answers regarding sexual abuse. Similarly, children often find it comforting to learn about and discuss celebrities who have experienced sexual abuse and have gone on to lead successful lives (see Chapter 6 for examples of well-known survivors). Such discussions serve as lower-level exposure exercises that provide an opportunity to reinforce what children have learned thus far about CSA thereby enhancing their confidence and reducing their avoidance

Some advanced questions that might be discussed include:

Who sexually abuses children?
Why does sexual abuse happen?
Why don't children tell?

It is important to elicit answers from the children before providing answers to these and other questions. By this stage of therapy, children often have more information and a better understanding of sexual abuse than is realized. Thus, to them it can be encouraging to receive affirmation of their thoughts and beliefs when responding to questions.

Many children benefit a great deal from reading a published story about CSA (see Appendix C for such books) immediately before introducing the concept of writing their own book. In fact, reading such a story occasionally stimulates children to "spontaneously" express interest in writing a book about CSA based on their experiences. Either way, reading such stories often reinforces for children that there are many other children who have experienced sexual abuse, and it provides the therapist with a natural way to introduce children to the idea of writing their own book or narrative.

Gradual exposure

The therapist may interrupt the reading of a published children's book periodically to pose questions and initiate dialogue about the book and about the children's thoughts and feelings related to their own abusive experiences. For example, after reading an account of a child being sexually abused, the therapist might pause and ask the client how she believes the child in the book is feeling and how the client felt at a similar point in his abusive experiences. At other points, the therapist might ask the child how the abusive experience described in the book is similar or dissimilar to the child's own experience.

There are a number of picture books as well as other books cited in the resource list that are helpful to read with clients at this stage of therapy. The picture books recommended do not contain explicit descriptions of sexually abusive interactions nor do they focus on prevention as neither would be appropriate for use at this stage in the gradual exposure process. Although there are several chapter books on the list, the authors suggest only individual chapters with a minimal sexual abuse details be shared with teenagers, as these books can be distressing and overwhelming if read in their entirety by teens at this stage of therapy. If possible, it is helpful to select one book or chapter to read in which the main character is similar to the client, as often children relate better to the story if there are shared personal and abuse-related characteristics. Reading such a book often provides a natural transition to introducing the trauma narrative component (see therapist introduction below).

Transitioning from general CSA discussion to trauma narrative development work

One approach to introducing the idea of writing a narrative is presented in the dialogue below. The therapist in the dialogue refers to the book, *Please Tell*, which is a particularly useful picture book written by a child who experienced sexual abuse (Jessie, 1991).

Therapist: *What did you think of that book,* Please Tell?

Child: *It was okay.*

Therapist: *You mentioned that you had some feelings when you were sexually abused that were similar to the girl in the book.*

Child: *Yes, but what happened to me was different.*

Therapist: *How was it different?*

Child: *I'm older and it was my dad, not my uncle, who did something to me.*

Therapist: *That's true. You are a little older than the girl who wrote that book, and I was thinking that you could probably write a much better book about what happened to you. It could help children who have had sexual abuse experiences similar to yours.*

Child: *I'm not sure I want to.*

Therapist: *I think it would not only be great for you to write a book because it would help to get through the therapy process faster, but it could also help me to better understand what happened and then I would be better able to help other kids.*

Child: *Do you really think it could help others?*

Therapist: *Absolutely. It is important for me to understand what the offender did and said so that when I see other children who are not as brave in talking about it as you are I would have a better idea of what they may have gone through.*

Child: *Could I draw pictures too for the book?*

Therapist: *I think pictures are a great idea!*

At this stage of therapy, in response to earlier gradual exposure experiences, many children feel ready to write or preferably dictate their personal trauma narrative describing their abusive experiences. However, it often helps for children to write an introduction about themselves and/or their family to put the traumatic experience in context before writing about the abuse. Moreover, for some children additional narrative practice in the form of describing a positive or neutral experience incorporating feelings, thoughts, and sensations may enhance their understanding of and confidence in writing their trauma narrative. As noted in the engagement chapter, with avoidant children this type of narrative practice may not only enhance children's confidence in spontaneously sharing their experiences but also may increase the level of details children offer when sharing their experiences of sexual abuse (Sternberg et al., 1997). Thus, it sometimes helps for the child to write a first chapter that describes herself and/or a recent positive experience (e.g., playing a favorite sport) including thoughts and feelings before encouraging the child to write about an abusive experience.

Overview of trauma narrative development sessions

During narrative sessions, therapists should work in a structured manner to aid children in not only recounting their experiences but also in getting in touch with associated thoughts, feelings, and sensations. It is generally best for the therapist and child to collaborate on the specific plan for each narrative development session. The writing of a trauma narrative is an effective mode of gradual exposure, as it provides the therapist with a concrete document to review and build on each session. Young children should not be encouraged to actually write the narrative themselves given the amount of time it takes many children to write. Rather young children, as well as older children and adolescents, may be encouraged to describe their experiences as the therapist writes or types their trauma accounts on paper or on the computer respectively.

During the initial narrative session, the child might be encouraged to choose a narrative title, as well as the mode of creating the narrative (e.g., writing, typing, or dictating as the therapist writes or types, or other narrative strategies to be discussed later). Then, it is important to actually engage in writing at least one trauma-focused chapter so that the child can experience some success. It is important to assess how the child felt before, during, and after writing the trauma-focused chapter. Most children report experiencing the most anxiety anticipating writing the chapter; some report anxiety during the writing of it, followed by relief after completing the chapter. The therapist should emphasize the value of sharing thoughts and feelings and remind the child that she will experience greater relief the more she writes and talks about the abuse. This reduces the risk that children will experience anxiety in anticipating future sessions when they will be sharing more about their abuse experiences. And this emphasis also reinforces the purpose of recounting traumatic memories: feeling better.

With some children and adolescents, particularly those who are avoidant, it also can be useful to utilize a fear thermometer or another subjective unit of distress scale (i.e., SUDS) to enhance feelings of control during narrative development sessions. Such scales can help children communicate their feelings at the beginning of the session, during the narrative development, and again at the end of the session. By using such a measure, the therapist can also review the progress made during the session and solicit information about the degree to which the child's distress has decreased in response to abuse memories and/or reminders over time. The therapist may use a "distress faces" rating scale or fear thermometer with younger children and/or encourage older children to report SUDS scores with a simple numbers scale (e.g., 1 = no distress; 5 = highest level of distress possible). Many children who have experienced sexual abuse have a need to maintain control due to the vulnerability and loss of control they experienced at the time of the abuse. Extremely avoidant children may be reassured if they reach a level of stress on the SUDS or distress faces rating scale that seems intolerable they can temporarily stop recounting the details of the abuse. The therapist would then help them practice coping skills to manage the associated distress. Once this distress has decreased, the youth can return to the narrative. In most cases, it is not necessary to discontinue the narrative because youth are given a sense of control over the process. Offering choices during narrative development sessions can also help children experience greater feelings of control and mastery. Thus, it is helpful to offer the child an opportunity to choose between two proposed exposure or narrative development activities or chapter topics each session. For example, after the child has completed an introduction or narrative practice chapter, the therapist can offer a choice between two possible chapters to write next, asking the child the following:

> *Today, I would like you to write a chapter about either the last time your cousin sexually abused you or telling your mom about the abuse.*

The TF-CBT therapist does not turn over complete control, as in a strictly nondirective approach, but rather offers choices and incorporates children's creative suggestions for developing the trauma narrative and/or engaging in other gradual exposure activities. Through the agreed-upon gradual exposure activity, the child is encouraged to share abuse-related memories while recounting the sensations, thoughts, and feelings experienced. The therapist may need to repeatedly remind the child that it is better to share feelings and let feelings show than to keep them bottled up inside. In fact, some increase in visible anxiety and/or tears is not uncommon during the trauma narrative development and may be validated with the sharing of tissues or other acknowledgment. During all trauma narrative sessions, exposure should continue until some anxiety reduction is evident (i.e., the child reports feeling no more than a little upset). If insufficient reduction of anxiety is evident even after a positive end-of-session activity is introduced, the therapist may introduce coping strategies such as relaxation, cognitive coping statements, or images that deal successfully with the feared situation or distress. Every effort, however, should be made to prevent the child from using avoidant or dissociative coping mechanisms prior to, during, or after exposure sessions. Rather, the child and therapist should plan together to end the exposure portion of the session, leaving time for a positive activity rather than aborting narrative development and the session due to distress. During these sessions, children are simultaneously learning to face their emotional fears by engaging in writing and/or discussions that may trigger distress, while also learning to manage the distress and actively disengage when appropriate (e.g., toward the end of the session). If anxiety has been decreasing within and across exposure sessions, the therapist should call that to the child's attention by making comments about the child's skills in managing the distress such as the following:

You are doing fine; it is okay to talk through your tears.
You are doing great, stay with the memory, but slow down a little so I can type every word.
I like how you are using your coping skills as you are working on this chapter.
Keep taking those deep breaths and tell me about what you were thinking and feeling then.
I want you to notice that you are much less upset than you were in the beginning of the session.
I can see you became more relaxed and comfortable the more we talked about the sexual abuse.
I am so proud of you for telling me about the time involving anal sex.

Some children may prefer to write about their experiences in journal, letter, or poetic form. Both younger and older children may find it helpful to draw pictures of their abusive experiences to incorporate into or stimulate the development of their narratives. This may be extremely helpful for children with developmental delays who need something concrete to stimulate the verbal development of a narrative about the abuse.

Each narrative development or exposure session should include time to review the child's work before moving on to the next chapter or ending the session. In other words, after the initial sharing of an abusive episode, the therapist should slowly read back what was shared, pausing at places where the child might add additional details, as well as additional thoughts, feelings, and sensations. At the end of the session, the therapist should review the progress made during the session and may observe and/or elicit information about the degree to which the child's distress has decreased.

Throughout all of the narrative sessions, children should be encouraged to share everything they can about what happened and what they were feeling, thinking, and sensing at that time. Box 10.1 provides a sample hierarchy of topics for the narrative with a child who experienced multiple episodes of sexual abuse and other trauma. Such a hierarchy may be created together with the child as a useful guide, but it need not be rigidly adhered to, as information gathered during the course of therapy may alter or add further steps to the development of the narrative and/or order in which chapters are written. As noted earlier, with highly avoidant and young children, therapists may write their own tentative hierarchy that need not be shared with the child. With such children, offering two suggestions (from the therapist's tentative hierarchy) for the writing of the

Box 10.1

Sample Gradual Exposure Hierarchy

1. Basic information about the child and family
2. Nonabusive interactions with the offender
3. The first episode of abuse or "grooming" incidents
4. Other abusive episodes (associated with events such as holidays, birthdays, etc.)
5. The most recent abusive or traumatic experience
6. The disclosure and resulting investigation and/or medical exam
7. The most disturbing or embarrassing abusive episodes
8. Final summary chapter: the counseling experience, what has been learned, who helped, and future expectations

next chapter may be sufficient to encourage children's collaboration and feelings of mastery.

The child may be engaged in narrative development by drawing (and describing what is happening in the pictures), dictating (as the therapist writes or types the child's words), or writing about the chapters listed in whatever order is most comfortable. Thus, based on the child's choices, the writing of chapters may be chronological or may begin with the least anxiety-provoking memory, with the later chapters reflecting the more anxiety-provoking memories. Helping the child create a clear, organized narrative appears to be important to long-term healing. In fact, recent research suggests that adolescents and young adults who are able to recount their CSA experiences in a coherent manner using the past tense, but with a present perspective, exhibit significantly better emotional adjustment as compared to those whose narratives reflect chaotic or avoidant efforts to reflect on their experiences (Simon et al., 2010). The chapters outlined above represent a common order in which the chapters may be written, but sometimes children find it easier to write their narrative in reverse chronological order as they may find it less anxiety-provoking to write about the last episode of abuse or when they had the courage to tell. In fact, as noted, giving children a choice as to what memory (or chapter) they would like to write about may not only enhance their feelings of control but may also reveal which experiences are associated with more anxiety, as children usually choose to write about the least anxiety-provoking experiences first.

The narrative development, in fact, involves repeated reviews of these chapters (i.e., initially in individual sessions and later in conjoint sessions if clinically indicated) that ultimately lead to the diminishing of avoidant and overwhelming negative emotional responses. In fact, through repeated narrative development, abuse-related memories and reminders are disconnected from the associated distress, allowing the child to effectively store the abusive experiences in conscious memory with greater clarity, perspective, and coherence.

Some children may respond to the narrative development work with flat affect rather than with heightened emotional distress. Such children may be avoiding the emotions associated with the actual abuse due to the extreme intensity and painfulness of those emotions. Helping children to understand and allow themselves the freedom to cry and/or (at the minimum) acknowledge the intensity of the emotions experienced at the time of the abuse will be a step forward. The therapist may also emphasize that in the safety and security of the therapeutic environment those emotions may be triggered, but they will very likely be less intense, and the client now has the skills to cope with them and to return to a more relaxed state. The goal of trauma narrative development with such children is to help them recount, confront, and become comfortable sharing the emotions and thoughts they experienced at the time of the abuse, as well as the emotions that are generated by abuse-related thoughts and other reminders in the present. The importance of eliciting a coherent and emotion-focused narrative is critical given the accumulating evidence suggesting that trauma narratives that demonstrate greater coherence, as well as more emotion words, are associated with healthier posttrauma adjustments (Mundorf & Paivio, 2011; Simon et al., 2010). In addition, regardless of the order in which children write their narrative chapters, it is helpful to assist them in organizing the chapters chronologically before processing the chapters as described in the next section. Organizing the chapters moves children toward creating coherent, more adaptive ways of storing traumatic memories.

Introducing the Writing of the First Chapter about the Sexual Abuse

The therapist might engage a child in this work with the following instructions:

> *To help you write a chapter about your experience of sexual abuse, I am going to ask you to share everything you can about the first time or the last time you were sexually abused including what happened, what you were feeling and thinking, and how your body was reacting. I will ask you to describe the experience as clearly as you can with as much detail as possible. As you share the details of what happened, I will write down what you are sharing, so it is important that you speak slowly. Again, I would like you to share with me not only everything that happened but also what you were feeling, what your body was sensing, and what you were saying to yourself.*

The child should then be asked to choose which abuse-related memory she would like to concentrate on and asked to describe it. The therapist may pose some specific questions initially to help the child return to the scene of the abuse. The "first pass" or first recounting of an abusive experience may contain limited details and relatively few thoughts and feelings. That is okay because the next step is reading it back so that the child can add additional details, thoughts, and feelings during the review or "second pass." To elicit the first account the therapist might say the following:

I really like the title and introduction of your book. Now I would like you to write the first chapter and describe everything you can about the very first time your pop-pop gave you a "not okay" touch. Maybe you can tell me where you were when that happened. Describe the room you were in and what it looked like. Was it daytime or night time, light or dark?

After the child has shared some basic information, the therapist might continue as follows.

As you describe what happened in the bathroom when your pop-pop gave you a "not okay" touch, I'd like you to share exactly what happened, including what Pop-pop did and said, what you did and said. Describe how your body felt, what you were thinking, and how you were feeling inside.

It is important to encourage, as much as possible, a spontaneous recounting of the sexually abusive experience(s) without repeated or fast-paced questioning. Too many intellectual or tangential questions can actually interfere with the recollection experience and distract the child from the memory that is the focus.

As noted earlier, silence has been found to be perceived by clients as quite supportive. Thus, during the child's recounting of the abuse, the therapist's silence and patience, in fact, can be therapeutic and can help children to reveal experiences that they have been struggling with alone for a long time. Therefore, only basic questions such as the ones outlined below should be asked as necessary to assist the child in recounting the abuse experience once the child begins to spontaneously recount his experience.

What were you feeling?
What was your body sensing?
What happened next?
What were you thinking (or saying to yourself) then?

Reviewing the initial narrative account

After an initial recounting of an abusive episode, the child often experiences some relief and reduction in distress. Depending on the degree of avoidance and distress experienced, children may provide a continuum of events, thoughts, feelings, and sensations during the initial account. Regardless of the degree of detail in the first pass, the therapist should acknowledge the child's hard work in sharing the initial account. During the session in which the chapter was written, the therapist can explain that she will slowly read the narrative back pausing at times, when needed, to inquire about additional thoughts, feelings, and/or sensations the child may have experienced at that time. This is regarded as the "second pass" during which the child is encouraged to stay with the memory so that she can correct any inaccuracies recorded. Most importantly, by reviewing the child's initial account, the therapist provides additional exposure, as well as an opportunity for the child to recall more, thereby adding additional richness to the narrative. While the child is sharing additional details of the sexual abuse, the therapist may note feelings and thoughts that seem dysfunctional but should *not* disrupt the gradual exposure process to dispute thoughts until the entire narrative is complete. Therapists sometimes feel compelled to correct dysfunctional thoughts in this early stage of narrative development but doing so can lead the child to begin self-correcting and ultimately not share her deepest, most troubling thoughts and concerns.

Children's written narratives may include chapters that describe the abusive episode(s), the disclosure and investigation process, the medical examination, as well as more positive experiences, such as how a friend tried to help after the client told about the abuse, how the medical doctor said something kind or funny, and/or how the cousin's mother did not yell at them when she found her son sexually abusing the client. It may also be helpful for children to acknowledge experiences in which the perpetrator of the abuse did some things that were nice. This may be especially important when the child is struggling with ambivalent feelings about an abusive father with whom he may have had many other positive interactions or experiences. In addition, in cases in which there was long-standing and/or multiple types of abuse, the client may write separate chapters about important positive events (e.g., sports or school achievements or special experiences with good friends) that happened in the context of a chronic series of sexually abusive or other traumatic experiences. These narrative pieces may reflect children's strengths, as well as times when others (e.g., teachers, friends, parents) were kind and/or helpful. These types of experiences may help children internalize positive images of themselves and their relationships with others. Moreover, including positive interactions with others may allow children to make sense of their sexually abusive experiences in context by providing a more complete picture of their lives around the time of the traumatic experiences. In sum, such positive memories highlight a child's ability to survive, engage in healthy relationships, and thrive despite their abusive experiences.

As always, the session should not end until the child's anxiety level has diminished, which often occurs naturally with the introduction of positive end-of-session activities. However, if necessary, coping skills may be employed to help the child regain his composure. Engaging the child in a fun, positive ritual is of value during every session, but this may be particularly important following a trauma narrative session. A positive ritual that elicits laughter or relaxation highlights for the child the important life lesson that one can talk about highly distressing past events while maintaining the ability to return to the present moment and more comfortable and even positive feelings with relative ease. In fact, research documents that maintaining a sense of humor in the face of adverse events is a quality that is associated with more positive adjustment (Davidson et al., 2005; Vilaythong et al., 2003).

Additional guidelines for narrative development

Caution must always be used not to move beyond the child's memories of the abuse. The therapist should not suggest details or memories that the child has not provided. The therapist should encourage the sharing of real experiences and not include fantasy in the trauma narrative. In an effort to gain mastery over their abusive experience, young children sometimes end their description of an abusive experience with a statement about an aggressive act, such as "then I threw him out the window." To help children remain as reality-based as possible, sometimes it is useful to gently pose a question or offer reminders such as the following:

Is that what really happened, or is that what you would like to have done?
Let's make sure we include only what really happened in this book.
Another time we can write a make believe book where the kid has super powers and strength like that.

Some children will seek to avoid distressing issues with fantasy play. The therapist should be prepared to gently direct the child's attention back to the gradual exposure process. For example, when asking a child to describe a distressing memory of sexual abuse, the therapist should help the child focus on that specific abusive episode allowing any associated anxiety to increase and decrease naturally without aborting the discussion suddenly. The therapist may do this by reflecting back the child's verbal description of the sexual abuse and by asking open-ended questions to elicit further thoughts, feelings, and sensations. Again, the objective is not to interrogate the child about the episode but rather to assist the child in facing the traumatic memory as fully as possible while enduring the associated emotions and sensations. Although children may experience increased anxiety during these sessions, they generally recognize that they do not experience the overwhelming fear or distress they experienced during the abuse. This can be very reassuring.

Children who experienced multiple episodes of abuse may have difficulty remembering specific details clearly because they tend to merge the episodes in their memory. In such a case, a child may describe the abuse in general ways, such as "He always took me in his bedroom, and then he would rub my private with his hand." Such a generalized discussion may not help the child to reexperience the emotions associated with specific episodes. Thus, the therapist might help the child move beyond such generalized discussions by focusing on specific episodes such as the first and last episodes of abuse; episodes associated with specific occasions such as holidays, birthdays, trips, visitors in the home, or school events; or episodes in which different types of sexual contact were pursued. In cases involving multiple episodes, it is not realistic to expect the child to remember specific details of all the episodes. In determining whether or not to continue to pursue gradual exposure regarding specific memories, the critical question is whether or not there remain memories that are distressing to the child and/or memories that continue to trigger posttraumatic stress symptoms. When possible, such memories should be identified, described, and processed until they no longer have the capacity to cause significant distress or avoidance. Also, there are often common themes that cut across multiple episodes that can be identified and later processed.

As many children who have experienced sexual abuse have endured other forms of violence or victimization, it is important to incorporate different types of traumas in the narrative when indicated. There is considerable evidence that the accumulation of traumatic childhood experiences causes the most harm to an individual's emotional, mental, social, and physical development (Felitti et al., 1998). The recounting, exploring and sharing of some of these distinct traumatic experiences may reveal the pattern of dysfunctional thinking that may be developing and the themes that will need to be processed. This will be particularly important when working with children who have experienced complex trauma, as there may be underlying, core trauma themes (e.g., "I can't trust anyone"; "I am damaged; that's why nobody wants me") that connect the many different traumas (Cohen, Mannarino, Kliethermes, et al., 2012; Kliethermes & Wamser, 2012).

Developmental considerations

The extent to which the child will have clear, specific, detailed memories of the abuse will depend on a number of factors, including the child's age, the length of time since the abuse occurred, and the number of episodes of abuse. For example, preschool children should not be expected to recount as many specific details of their abusive experiences as older children. In fact, repeatedly questioning very young children regarding the same issue may cause the child to feel confused or less confident. Thus, therapists working with preschool children should be careful not to push a child to provide details beyond those that the child readily recalls. Typically, the gradual exposure work will take less time with very young children than with older children as there will be fewer details to discuss and/or write about.

Depending on children's developmental and verbal capacities, as well as the extent of their sexual abuse experiences, children's narratives may range from one page with several paragraphs representing separate chapters, to narratives that include several pages for each chapter incorporating as many as three to ten chapters. Most narratives, however, are somewhere in between and may be a few pages long. In general, it is important to limit the trauma narrative work to no more than approximately one-third of the total number of therapy sessions. Limiting the focus on recounting past events can help children avoid ruminating on the past, which is a tendency that can inadvertently contribute to depression and anxiety.

Other modes of trauma narrative development

Although the majority of children are receptive to writing, dictating, and/or discussing their abusive experiences, alternative modes of narrative development can be useful in eliciting children's cooperation, particularly when working with highly avoidant children. Creating a therapeutic environment that incorporates fun and gives children a sense of control enhances engagement. However, it is important to limit the therapy materials to those toys and props that may encourage play and/or talk around abuse-related issues, as other toys may distract children from the narrative work.

Reenactment using dolls, play and/or other creative arts

Although children of all ages may be capable of dictating a narrative, dolls and puppets can be helpful. Young children may be asked to reenact their abusive experiences with dolls or puppets by assigning different individuals in their life to selected dolls or puppets. If the child has trouble understanding the instructions, the therapist can briefly initiate the narrative play by recreating the scene for the child on the basis of concrete information provided by the child about where and when the abuse happened. The therapist should encourage the child to reenact real-life experiences and should avoid using the words "pretend" or "make-believe," as these words may encourage fantasy play. The therapist's objective is to encourage the use of creative props (e.g., dolls) to assist the child in describing and/or demonstrating the abusive interactions actually experienced. This method may be particularly useful for younger children, who think concretely, do not demonstrate good articulation skills, and cannot tolerate lengthy discussions. Here is how a therapist might introduce this exercise:

> *Jennifer, you told me a little about what happened with your cousin Louis. And I understand that you don't want to write a book about it. So I thought you could show me exactly what happened using dolls that I have. You may have dolls at home that you pretend with, but my dolls are not for playing make-believe games, Jennifer. We use these dolls so children can show me exactly what happened to them. This doll can be Louis, and this can be the Jennifer doll. With these dolls, you can show me everything that happened that first time. And as you are showing me, I would like for you to tell me how you were feeling and even what you were saying to yourself when Louis touched your vagina.*

Older children may prefer to describe their abusive experiences using other creative outlets such as drawing, painting, and/or sharing their thoughts and experiences in the form of a poem or song. Though more creative than simple written narratives, these techniques still allow children to document abusive experiences with a tangible creation that they are proud of and that may be shared with participating caregivers. With these children it may be useful to share examples of how famous musicians, artists, poets, and writers incorporate their personal traumatic experiences in their work which not only helps them heal from these experiences but often helps others who have experienced similar traumas feel less alone.

In some cases, it is possible to motivate even the most highly avoidant children by appealing to their compassion for other children who may have experienced sexual abuse as well. Although this may not be possible in all settings, the authors have received written consent from both the parent and the child to share anonymous versions of children's artwork, poems, and other creative works to educate children and adults in the community about childhood trauma. The sharing of such creative works may motivate more avoidant children to more readily communicate their thoughts and feelings about their abusive experiences. Many children experience a sense of pride and accomplishment in being able to help other children, and this can be a powerful motivator for them. Of course, the therapist should always obtain parental permission before talking with the child about the possibility of sharing even anonymous poems, songs, prose, or artwork with others. In addition, the therapist should obtain appropriate written consents from the child and caregiver and be careful to ensure that all identifying information has been altered on any products that will be shared with other people.

Therapists may also share some of the empathic remarks below that validate what children are expressing or exhibiting in response to the exposure process.

It is good to share feelings.
It is okay to cry.
Sometimes children feel shaky when talking about upsetting things. That's okay.
Every time we talk about the abuse it will get a little easier.
Facing those memories is hard work but you can do it.
The more you share your feelings, the better you will feel in the long run.

When working with a child who is highly avoidant and resistant to gradual exposure efforts, the therapist should focus on maintaining a working relationship with the child while continuing to work on gradual exposure in one form or another. In the example in Box 10.2, the therapist successfully kept the therapeutic focus on gradual exposure while maintaining a positive working relationship with the child by respecting his wish to not discuss another abusive episode. Sometimes it may be necessary to take a detour in the gradual exposure process to focus on different aspects of the abusive experience. Such a detour is not problematic as long as the child is not allowed to avoid all exposure to thoughts and memories of the abuse.

However, when the child seems avoidant of discussing any aspect of the abusive experience(s), it may help to explore the child's thoughts. These thoughts may be contributing to the emotional distress that underlies the avoidant behavior. For example, a child who thinks, "He (i.e., the offender) told me he knows what I'm doing even when he's not there. And he doesn't want me to talk about it," may be too anxious to discuss the abusive experience initially. In this instance, utilizing the cognitive coping skills to help the child dispute these thoughts may reduce the child's distress and allow the child to write and process the trauma narrative. Some questions that the therapist might pose to help a child challenge those thoughts include the following:

Why do you think, he (the offender) told you that?
Do you think he would say anything to keep you from talking about the abuse?
What else did he say to keep you from telling?
When you were little did you believe all the things he told you?

time to enjoyable activities at the end of the narrative sessions helps children experience feelings of mastery and it helps them regain their composure if any level of distress was experienced.

Practice activities encouraged

The therapist may continue to encourage the use of coping skills in response to the everyday stressors children face. In addition, it is useful to encourage a continued focus on noticing and identifying children's use of coping skills in response to trauma reminders. Once children have completed some of their narrative, therapists may also encourage children to notice their changing and hopefully improving reactions toward trauma reminders if this has been observed in session or by parents at home.

Prepare for conjoint session

Time permitting, children may be prepared to participate in an end-of-session positive ritual with their parents, thereby continuing to provide opportunities for positive parent-child interactions in which parents can practice effective parenting skills. After trauma narrative development sessions, there may be limited time to engage in lengthy conjoint activities; however, children may find it reassuring to engage in a simple mutual exchange of praise with their parent(s) and/or other brief but fun activities that are unrelated to the abuse.

PARENT SESSION(S)

Skills training with parents should continue as children move into the trauma narrative component. Some parents need a great deal more work on affective regulation and cognitive coping, whereas others may benefit most from a continued focus on parenting skills, especially those with children exhibiting ongoing behavior problems. It is important to continue parenting skills training given the recent research findings suggesting that when therapists focus attention on parent skill building, parents are more likely to show parenting practice improvements which are associated with greater improvements in children's behavior problems (Deblinger et al., 2011).

Although it is important to keep parents apprised of their children's progress and movement into the trauma narration and processing phase, it may be wise in some circumstances to delay the parents' review of their children's narrative, as their feelings of guilt and compassion concerning the abuse may undermine their ability to appropriately follow through with effective disciplinary strategies. In fact, some parents may be inclined to be somewhat lax regarding rules and discipline due to guilt feelings and sympathy for the child as a result of the sexual abuse experiences. However, this can inadvertently undermine children's behavioral progress. Thus, it is important to maintain parents' focus on their coping and parenting skills development and implementation during this phase of treatment. Again, when children are experiencing behavior problems, it may be best to maintain the parents' focus on developing effective parenting skills until the final third of treatment when they can be prepared for the sharing of the completed narrative. However, therapists should use their clinical judgment in determining what, if any, information from the child's narrative may be appropriate to share with parents. In general, the trauma narrative should not be shared with the parent until the therapist has confidence that the parent can cope with the information effectively and the sharing of the narrative is deemed to be in the child's best interest. Determining the clinical appropriateness and the timing of sharing the child's narrative with the parent is discussed in the chapter on trauma processing to follow.

Practice assignment review: Parenting and coping skills

Consistent amounts of time should continue to be devoted to reviewing the child's progress outside of sessions. Once again, this should be individually tailored depending on the family's needs with appropriate focus on caregiver coping, as well as parenting skills when necessary. In fact, functional analyses may be conducted to review parent-child interactions when parents are struggling with ongoing behavior problems. This can be valuable in reinforcing and shaping parents' implementation of the behavior management skills learned in the first phase of treatment.

Treatment rationales for narrative development and parenting

When children initiate their narratives, parents should be encouraged to support their children's active participation in treatment despite the fact that some children may resist this work initially. Parents may be reminded that many children show some increased avoidance during this phase, but the research of the authors has documented that in the end most children report that talking about and writing about the sexual abuse is the most helpful part of therapy (Deblinger et al., 2011). Given the potentially negative impact of chronic PTSD and confusing dysfunctional beliefs relating to the sexual abuse, it is important that parents know to encourage their children's participation even if the children do not feel a need for therapy or complain of anxiety or even boredom with the discussion of the abuse.

Therapist: *Today, Tommy and I began talking in more detail about his sexually abusive experiences and we will likely continue to do that for the next few sessions. So far, he seems to be fairly comfortable talking and even writing some* *about his experiences, but he may complain about this focus when we start discussing the more distressing aspects of his experience of sexual abuse. This sometimes happens because as Tommy confronts more difficult memories, he may fear being overwhelmed by negative emotions like those he naturally experienced at the time of the abuse.*

Mother: *I hate for him to have to talk about that jerk and what he went through. Are you sure this is going to be helpful? He seems to be doing better already.*

Therapist: *I agree he is doing much better and I attribute a great deal of that to your support. But it is important for him to actively cope with this experience by facing it now and being able to share with me any troubling thoughts and questions he has.*

Mother: *It happened so many times. Will he have to talk about every incident?*

Therapist: *No, we won't be talking about every incident, but we will most likely talk about a few of the incidents. He may initially fear being overwhelmed by his own emotions when he shares these memories, but over time the distressing emotions that come up will lessen. Believe it or not, many children's fears are replaced with feelings of pride about their ability to talk about and/or write about the sexual abuse. In fact, children often gain feelings of strength as they face traumatic memories that they have avoided until now.*

Mother: *I don't know. Tommy said the one thing he didn't want to do is to talk about what happened.*

Therapist: *Well, of course, I can't force him to do that, but he has already begun to share some of his thoughts and feelings about the abuse and I will present him with different ways to process these experiences so he feels in control. The main objective is to ensure that any confused feelings or discomfort he has with himself and the abusive experiences be addressed now, so that he doesn't hold on to anger, fear, or shame that could cause problems in the future. Also, by sharing these memories, many children are able to begin to ask the questions that are troubling them, and they begin to understand that the abusive experience is not a reflection of who they are but rather something that happened to them.*

Mother: *If you can get him to talk about it that is fine with me. Good luck. You may be doing most of the talking.*

Therapist: *Okay. He may not talk a lot, but I am confident he will get a lot out of this next phase of treatment. Still, it will be important for you to continue your efforts in the parenting realm, with praise, especially in terms of encouraging the positive behaviors we discussed while simultaneously being firm about the consequences we agreed on when he misbehaves.*

Mother: *That is going to be hard. Sometimes I feel so sorry for him and that I let him down.*

Therapist: *We will talk more about your feelings of letting him down. But please know that an important way you can show him your love and support is with clear and consistent communication of your expectations, which means effusively acknowledging the positives with praise and other positive consequences but also using effective instructions and following through with the agreed-upon* *negative consequences when he messes up as all kids do. What do you think about your ability to do that?*

Mother: *I will try.*

Therapist: *What will be the hardest part of trying?*

Mother: *Putting him in time out. It feels so heartless to do that to him right now when you are having him talk about the sexual abuse.*

Therapist: *I think of using time out effectively as a very loving thing to do. Can you imagine what makes time out a loving thing to do?*

Mother: *I guess it's better than yelling at him and it may ultimately keep him from developing behaviors that may cause him problems in school.*

Therapist: *Exactly. Though it will require a great deal of effort on your part, it is very loving to help him in this way. In fact, there is research that indicates that the yelling and threats lead to more anxiety in kids which time out does not do. In fact, it takes a lot more effort to thoughtfully use time out in combination with creating very positive experiences of "time in" than it does to yell or repeatedly correct his behaviors. Can you give me some examples of how you have been creating more positive "time in" experiences?*

Mother: *You mean like spending time with him before he goes to bed? That has been really nice, and I am amazed that he really wants to do that even though I stopped reading stories to him years ago. He seems to just love shooting the breeze with me and he certainly appreciates the praise I give him when he tells me about the positive things that he's doing in school.*

Therapist: *That's great.*

Mother: *I guess he's not too old for a goodnight kiss, too. But I'm not sure time out has worked better than yelling for me. It feels like I have tried every kind of discipline and nothing works.*

Therapist: *Well, it is best not to keep trying different things, because if you remember children do best in very predictable environments. As you use time out consistently we will examine whether or not it seems to be working based on whether the whining and angry outbursts are decreasing. I want you to begin thinking about using time out consistently and correctly as one of the most loving things you can do.*

Mother: *I wish he would think of it that way. But it would be good for me to think of it that way.*

Therapist: *It is important that you don't go back to yelling and letting him get away with more during this period. That will actually undermine his progress—so this is exactly the time to be loving and warm but also firm in your follow through. Because as I have mentioned, when going through difficult times, children benefit from predictable consequences for both positive and negative behaviors. Though they would never admit to this, children prefer to have clear limits for their behavior.*

When the focus is on children's behavior problems and discipline practices, parents may feel they are neglecting their child's emotional recovery. It is at these times that it will be important to emphasize the importance of parents' efforts to help their children get back on track behaviorally so that the sexual abuse does not derail their success in school, with friends, and in life going forward. At the same time, it may be reassuring to remind parents of the important work the therapist is doing with the child. Thus, at this stage of treatment with parents, it may be helpful to review the major reasons for pursuing gradual exposure and the narrative development work as demonstrated above. Again, it is important that parents understand the purpose of the therapeutic work, so that they can collaborate with the therapist as partners in the process of therapy. Some parents may be resistant to discussing the sexual abuse themselves for a variety of reasons. In some cases, parents are anxious about managing the distress such discussions may produce. With such parents, the therapist may emphasize the fact that their children will likely have ongoing memories of the abuse and thus they will need to find ways to become more comfortable with thoughts and discussion about the abuse so that they can be available and responsive to their children's questions and needs as they get older. Children's understanding of sexuality and CSA will change as they develop and may lead to new questions particularly when children enter adolescence.

In addition, the therapist again may stress the unique opportunity that parents have, by virtue of their relationship with the child, to positively influence how the child responds to the abusive experience. It is important that the therapist continue to identify whatever the parent's specific concerns are, especially those triggered by the additional information they have learned about sexual abuse over the course of treatment. With most parents, it is appropriate for the therapist to continue to emphasize the value of parental participating in treatment in terms of supporting the child's full emotional and behavioral recovery. Moreover, given the increasing presence of CSA in the news, the widespread prevalence of the problem and the potential impact of CSA on a child's understanding of healthy sexuality, parents' participation in treatment now will help them to be prepared to have the ability to openly communicate about these issues with their children when they are faced with sexual abuse reminders or issues related to healthy sexuality in the future.

Additional parenting skills introduced as needed

In the context of therapy, when parents raise particular issues and problems, it is important to use these opportunities to elicit from them the parenting principles they can apply to achieve the outcome desired. By approaching problems in this way, their skills are more likely to generalize so that caregivers will be able to apply the parenting skills to challenges faced after therapy ends.

Alternative negative consequences

There are many situations in which negative consequences, other than time out or work chores, may be used effectively. For example, if an inappropriate behavior occurs that cannot be ignored but that has not been identified as a target behavior for time out, then alternative negative consequences may be used. As is true with time out, negative consequences should be applied as soon as possible following the inappropriate behavior and should be limited in duration (typically lasting no longer than a day at most). Many parents have the misimpression that grounding children for lengthy periods of time will be more effective in eliminating the behavior problem and keep the child safe. Parents should be reminded that negative consequences should be administered as a means to change behaviors, not as punishment delivered with anger and resentment. Moreover, research suggests that time limited consequences are more effective in reducing behavior problems. Very lengthy negative consequences increase the likelihood that children will focus on their anger and resentment rather than changing their behaviors. Rather, reasonable negative consequences (e.g., relatively brief loss of privileges) when applied in a dispassionate manner as a means of teaching can be effective. In fact, parents are generally more effective in administering negative consequences when they are calm and when they can administer the negative consequences with as few words as possible. When parents get into long diatribes explaining the consequences, they end up reinforcing the negative behavior with parental attention. Several types of effective negative consequences are described in the section that follows.

Natural consequences

Natural consequences are those consequences the child would experience naturally following a problem behavior, without the parent needing to artificially create or impose the consequences. For example, the natural consequence of a child not eating dinner is that the child will be hungry late in the evening. Well-meaning parents often protect their child from experiencing the natural consequences of behavior, thus inadvertently preventing the child from learning why that behavior is not appropriate or effective. Many times, simply allowing the child to experience the natural consequence of his behavior is sufficient to change the problem behavior. An example of a natural consequence might be requiring a child to walk to school if dawdling in the morning causes him to miss the bus. Interestingly, this is a natural consequence that parents might hesitate to implement out of concern for the child's safety and/or fear that he will miss important work in school. However, assuming that the child is old enough and the neighborhood is reasonably safe, such a consequence has great potential to correct the behavior very quickly if the child doesn't like to walk. Conversely, there are times when it is not appropriate or possible to allow the child to experience natural consequences. For example, the natural consequence for running into the street after a ball is that the child may be hit by a car or truck. Obviously, the child cannot be allowed to experience that natural consequence. Thus, the parent must be encouraged to consider other types of consequences, as described below.

Logical consequences

When it is not possible to use natural consequences, parents should be encouraged to use logical consequences; that is, negative consequences that are logically linked to the problem behavior. For example, if a boy rides his bicycle outside the area permitted by his parents, a logical consequence would be to prohibit him from riding his bike for the rest of the day (or the next day, if the problem behavior occurs late in the day). Logical consequences can be described as punishment that fits the crime. (See the *Using Positive and Negative Consequences* handout in Appendix B).

Loss of privileges

Parents may use loss of privileges as consequences in situations in which natural and logical consequences are not possible or appropriate. Privileges that can be considered for loss include using a cell phone, watching television, listening to music, riding a bike, participating in extracurricular or social activities, using the computer, and so on. Typically, parents should be encouraged to take away only one privilege and to take it away for a limited period of time, for example, one evening or one day. Also, as noted in an earlier chapter, if the child or teen refuses to take time out or do a work chore when instructed to do so, the parent may take away any and/or all privileges until the child completes the time out or work chore appropriately (Patterson & Forgatch, 2005). Nowadays, with the widespread use of cell phones, tablets, and laptops, parents can physically remove these items essentially creating a technology time out as a negative consequence for older children and teens. Again, it is critically important for parents to stay focused on the objective of bringing out the best behavior in their child by following through with effective parenting skills at home, while also consistently attending to positive behaviors and participating in treatment sessions.

Continue cognitive processing with parents

Gradual exposure work with parents may continue with a review of their cognitive coping efforts during the week. Many parents have dysfunctional thoughts that need to be addressed and disputed repeatedly before parents come to adopt more functional beliefs and optimistic views with regard to the child's future. During this component, it is also appropriate to further explore through more personalized discussions what parents already know about the details of what the child experienced. Gradual exposure to abuse-related discussions with parents can be useful in reducing the parent's own level of emotional distress and avoidance regarding the abuse. As has been described previously, many parents experience a great deal of distress themselves upon learning of their child's sexual abuse experience. Parents who are highly distressed may be less available to assist their children because they are overwhelmed with their own distress. Gradual exposure that continues to incorporate CSA psychoeducation and cognitive processing can help to reduce the level of emotional distress experienced by parents, thereby increasing their availability to their child.

Parents' gradual exposure work will ultimately enable them to model for their child how thoughts and discussions of the abuse can be tolerated without significant distress and need not be avoided. Early in treatment, many parents may choose to avoid abuse-related thoughts and discussion as a means of avoiding the associated emotional distress. The avoidance of such discussions with their children is appropriate early in treatment, but it is important for parents to begin to get comfortable talking about the abuse in their individual parent sessions. This will allow parents to eventually model nonavoidant active coping for their children in conjoint sessions both in the final phase of treatment and after therapy ends. This is important because research has demonstrated that active coping is associated with more positive emotional adjustment in the aftermath of childhood abuse (Mundorf & Paivio, 2011; Simon et al., 2010). Moreover, the therapist's progress in helping the child effectively confront and process the abusive experiences will be compromised as long as parents are exhibiting significant distress and avoidance in response to abuse reminders. Such parental distress and avoidance may inadvertently convey to the child that what she experienced is so abhorrent that her parents cannot handle thinking or speaking about the abuse. Children may observe these negative parental reactions and internalize them as negative reflections on them. In fact, there is considerable evidence that negative reactions of others can significantly impair children's ability to recover from sexual abuse (Simon et al., 2010). In contrast, the child's recovery may be enhanced if, with the therapist's help, the parents learn to model a pattern of actively coping with memories and reminders of the abuse. Thus, parents' gradual exposure and cognitive processing work with the therapist should continue until parents can demonstrate and model nonavoidance and more active coping efforts for their child at home as well as during trauma-focused conjoint sessions in the final phase of treatment.

Prepare for conjoint session

As has been continuously emphasized, TF-CBT should be implemented with the specific needs of the individual child and family in mind. Thus, if brief conjoint sessions with the parent have been valuable in the practicing and implementation of parenting skills, these conjoint sessions can continue through the trauma narration and processing phase of therapy. However, for some families given the limited session time, conjoint sessions need not occur during this phase, although parents should be strongly encouraged to continue to offer words of encouragement to their children for their hard work in therapy and openness in sharing their thoughts and feelings with the therapist.

CONJOINT SESSION(S) (OPTIONAL)

Given the initiation of the trauma narrative during the child's individual session, there may be little time for an extended conjoint session. Thus, this optional conjoint session may be used to briefly review positive progress in therapy and at home, offer brief skills practice reminders, while also encouraging the mutual exchange of praise.

Mutual exchange of praise

The mutual exchange of praise is a positive end-of-session ritual that may help parents continue to practice specific and global praise and is interestingly something that youth often look forward to despite the sometimes anxiety-provoking aspects of this middle phase of therapy. During this conjoint session, it can be particularly helpful for parents to express their pride in the child's strength in coping with the sexual abuse and participating in therapy as well as offering specific praise regarding positive behaviors the child is exhibiting at home. Similarly, children may be encouraged to identify any specific positive changes they are seeing in their parents at home. The exchange of global praise, which may include expressions of love in words or through physical affection (e.g., high fives and/or hugs), is also often helpful in encouraging positive parent-child interactions.

11

Trauma Narrative Development and Processing Part II

The trauma narrative and processing component achieves two important objectives. First, as described in the previous chapter, it helps children face and acknowledge the feelings, sensations, and thoughts experienced during and after traumatic experiences in the context of a safe, therapeutic environment. This allows children to create new emotional associations such that traumatic memories that were previously avoided and/or associated with highly negative emotions become associated with feelings of calm, comfort, and even pride in recognition of their survival and strength. This chapter will describe the next important step, which involves cognitive processing of the narrative. During the development and later the processing of the trauma narrative, the TF-CBT therapist may identify children's inaccurate and/or unproductive thoughts that may have developed at the time of their abusive experiences and may underlie problematic symptoms and behaviors. Dysfunctional thoughts may characterize the sexual abuse in terms that are overly permanent, pervasive, and/or personalized, reflecting a developing pessimistic style of thinking (Seligman, 2006).

Children are naturally concrete and egocentric and when trying to make sense of why a problem occurred, it is not uncommon for children to come to highly dysfunctional conclusions. For example, they may believe something about them caused the problem (personal). They may think most people cannot be trusted (pervasive) and/or as a result of repeated abusive experiences, they may conclude that life is not worth living (permanent). The development of these types of beliefs can be particularly problematic when the problem is a highly stigmatizing one such as child sexual abuse (CSA) or exposure to domestic violence. Most children will not openly discuss these experiences with others, thereby reducing the likelihood that they will receive corrective feedback. Thus, the processing of the trauma narrative provides a critical opportunity for children to share these difficult and confusing experiences, as well as their innermost thoughts and feelings about them. In so doing, they will have the chance to gain a healthier understanding of the abusive experiences, thereby allowing them to come to adaptive conclusions. In turn, these healthier ways of thinking about CSA and other traumas will help children to feel better about themselves, their relationships with others, as well as their expectations for the future.

Successful cognitive processing of the abuse experience may be a crucial factor in children's postabuse adjustment. After experiencing abuse, many children try to make sense of what happened to them. Providing general psychoeducation about CSA and other traumas helps children to begin cognitive processing early in treatment. Some children respond well to psychoeducation alone; as they begin to recognize that CSA happens to many other children and that adults who offend are responsible for their behavior, these children feel less shame and self-blame even early in treatment. However, most children benefit from additional cognitive processing as part of the trauma narrative work. This is particularly true of children with high initial levels of fear or anxiety (Deblinger et al., 2011). Including thoughts and feelings during the narrative development is often therapeutic in and of itself, but cognitively processing the narrative adds another layer of healing by helping the child to identify, explore, clarify, and correct dysfunctional thoughts and beliefs that may have developed in response to abusive experiences. Thoughts and feelings about the sexual abuse and its aftermath may significantly influence a child's developing self-image and cognitive coping style.

The child's cognitive schema for understanding the trauma, in fact, may become a template for cognitively processing problems and stressors in the future. Thus, particularly for children who have experienced multiple, complex traumas, it is helpful to identify conceptual themes revealed by the youth's thoughts and developing beliefs that may explain the ongoing behavioral and emotional difficulties. Recent research suggests that it may be particularly important to look for themes that reflect overgeneralizations, as these may be associated with PTSD, as well as internalizing and externalizing symptoms (Ready et al., 2014). For example, a girl who believes she "deserved" the abuse because she was bad may later believe she deserves any subsequent poor or abusive treatment; therefore, she may be more likely to accept and/or tolerate abusive behaviors in other relationships. A boy whose sexual abuse leaves him with the feeling and belief that he is pleasing to others only when he is sexual may engage in sexually inappropriate and risky behavior. Another teen may conclude that she was sexually abused because she is a bad kid and may act out in angry ways that reflect her internalized aggressive self-concept. Other possible themes that may be reflected in children's narratives include cognitive distortions related to repeated experiences of rejection and loss. Such experiences can leave children fearing all relationships because of their association with suffering. Given the potential negative outcomes of these dysfunctional beliefs and behavioral patterns, it is important to identify and correct such cognitive distortions as early as possible. In fact, recent research suggests that reductions in such overgeneralized beliefs and increases in more adaptive thinking may not only result in reduced PTSD and internalizing symptoms over the course of treatment, but may also have implications for reducing the risk of longer term difficulties with externalizing behaviors (Ready et al., 2014).

CHILD SESSION(S)

Cognitive processing helps children to explore and correct maladaptive beliefs that may have developed as a result of the child's abuse or other traumatic experiences. The TF-CBT therapist may prepare to engage the child in cognitive processing by carefully reviewing (between sessions) the child's narrative and/or other notes or materials that reveal potential areas of maladaptive thinking. It is useful to identify examples of the child's adaptive as well as maladaptive thoughts that were included in the trauma narrative. A form is included in Appendix F (see *Processing Dysfunctional Thoughts* therapist form) that therapists may choose to use to list the dysfunctional thoughts identified in the child's narrative. This form also provides a place to formulate and record adaptive replacement thoughts, as well as a place to list a series of Socratic questions that may be helpful in encouraging children to think about their experiences in a more flexible manner thereby encouraging them to consider more adaptive ways of viewing their reactions to the sexual abuse as well as other trauma(s). Described in Box 11.1 are examples of dysfunctional thoughts that children who have experienced sexual abuse commonly report, as well as guidance for therapists in developing Socratic questions to challenge maladaptive cognitions. Over time, it is anticipated that children will learn to replace maladaptive thoughts with healthier ways of thinking about themselves, their experiences, their relationships, and their expectations for the future.

Practice activities review

As always, though the focus of sessions during this component may be on the processing of the trauma experience(s), it is still critically important to encourage and review the use of effective coping skills between sessions. The TF-CBT therapist may demonstrate interest in children's successful implementation of the coping skills learned by eliciting, discussing, and praising those successes. However, it is also important to reserve time when needed to examine stressors that clients were unable to respond to in an optimal fashion. Such coping crises often provide opportunities to use Socratic questioning, reflective listening, and collaborative problem solving (see problem-solving skills examples listed in Chapter 14) to help children and parents think through how they could use what they have learned thus far in therapy to manage whatever difficulty or conflict they are facing. However, in order to avoid having crises of the week (COWs) interfere with the progress of therapy, it is sometimes best to follow through with the planned therapy activity of cognitive processing first, while reserving time at the end of the session to address the crisis.

Initiating the processing of the trauma experience(s)

The trauma narrative and the processing of the trauma experience(s) are both part of the same component of TF-CBT. Indeed this component is not completed until children have processed their distorted and/or unhelpful thoughts and have added a contextualization section to the narrative (e.g., "How have I changed because of therapy?" "What would I tell other children who have been sexually abused?" etc.)

When children have experienced chronic CSA or multiple traumas, it is not possible or productive to encourage the recounting of all their traumatic experiences in narrative format. In fact, such an approach is not only unrealistic but it may encourage rumination that may lead to unproductive coping and increased symptomatology. It is helpful to encourage the sharing of the first, the last, and at least one middle episode of CSA as children's reactions to these episodes tend to differ from a cognitive and emotional standpoint. In addition, it can be helpful to incorporate other traumatic incidents that may have been unique in some way. Ultimately, it is most important to encourage and provide opportunities for the child to share the most embarrassing or distressing memories. Thus, after the child has written most of the agreed-upon narrative chapters, before moving on to cognitive processing it may help to pose the question below in order to enhance the likelihood that the most distressing traumatic experiences have been revealed.

Therapist: *Leslie, I have been so impressed with how much you have opened up about your experiences with sexual abuse. You have done a great job sharing all of your thoughts and feelings. But before we move on, I would like to encourage you to write one more chapter or share one more abusive or traumatic experience that you thought you would never ever tell anyone about. This would be a great time to get that off your chest.*

Although not all children will respond to the above query, it is worth posing the question because some children do respond by sharing something that they have been struggling with—perhaps something they have not shared with the therapist before. For those who report that they have nothing additional to share, it is important to accept such a response with the proviso that they can always share additional experiences if they chose to in the future.

Once it has been agreed that the narrative is almost complete (with the exception of the final summary chapter), children may be encouraged to slowly re-read the narrative with the objective of processing thoughts and feelings. Of course, all children's feelings and thoughts ought to be initially accepted and validated as normal responses to traumatic circumstances. In addition, after validating children's feelings and thoughts, the therapist may support children in identifying thoughts that were helpful and adaptive. In fact, it is valuable to highlight those times when the child demonstrated courage, as well as times when others were helpful and kind (e.g., in the context of disclosing and overcoming the impact of the sexual abuse). In fact, when processing the trauma(s) with the child, it helps to balance the focus on identifying and correcting inaccurate and/or dysfunctional thoughts with the identification and praise of healthy thoughts that may be contained in the narrative as well.

At this stage of therapy, some children may recognize that at the time of the abuse they had some thoughts that were inaccurate. For example, some children may have believed things that the offender said (e.g., "Your mom won't believe you" or "Daddies are supposed to show their daughters how to have sex") but now understand their inaccuracy. The therapist, however, may need to help children identify problematic thoughts that are less obvious and both inaccurate thoughts and accurate thoughts that are not helpful. Initially, the TF-CBT therapist can use Socratic questioning to help children replace these dysfunctional, sexual abuse–related thoughts with more accurate and/or optimistic thoughts. Some therapists find it useful to have children incorporate these accurate and/or more optimistic thoughts into the body of the narrative (contextualization as described above), by inserting sentences such as:

I used to think that but now I know ...
I realize now ...
Now that I am older I understand that he said that because ...
Now I know ...

Box 11.1 is an example of a therapist helping a child process the trauma by reading a chapter and identifying both helpful and unhelpful thoughts. The therapist uses Socratic questioning to help a child think through the accuracy of dysfunctional abuse-related thoughts. Through this process the child is encouraged

---

Box 11.1

Case Example: Socratic Questioning Used to Dispute Dysfunctional Thoughts

Therapist: *Tommy, I really like how you wrote and read that chapter. It helped me to really understand how confusing it was for you when your coach sexually abused you. Can you identify thoughts in that chapter that were accurate and helpful?*

Tommy: *Well, it was accurate when I thought, "What is he doing? It doesn't seem right for a grown man to want to play with my dick. I should tell my mom."*

Therapist: *It does seem like you were listening to your gut there and thinking this doesn't seem right. That was a helpful thought.*

Tommy: *But then I didn't tell my mom right away.*

Therapist: *Were you encouraging yourself to tell?*

Tommy: *Yes.*

Therapist: *So then I would say it was good that you were saying that to yourself.*

Tommy: *But then I wrote, "I was thinking I should stop him! I should not let him do this to me. I felt scared and chicken to say anything at all. I thought I am really dumb."*

Therapist: *Tommy, let's look at each one of those sentences. I am glad you wrote them because they express what you were feeling then, but let's see if you were*

being too hard on yourself. First, you wrote "I was thinking I should stop him." Think about this for a minute. I'm going to draw a stick figure here. Let's say that is you. Now we'll draw a stick figure of your coach. How big should I make him?

Tommy: *Up to here.*

Therapist: *So, who is the bigger of you two?*

Tommy: *The coach was much bigger.*

Therapist: *Who would you guess is stronger?*

Tommy: *Well, the coach, of course. I'm just 10 and he's about 30-something.*

Therapist: *So how often do you think a 10-year-old who is this big can stop a man who is 30-something from doing something he really wants to do?*

Tommy: *Not very often.*

Therapist: *Now, you said you felt scared and chicken to say anything at all. Based on what we have read about sexual abuse, do you think that most kids would be scared and not speak up?*

Tommy: *Well, we read about how most kids are scared and most kids never tell.*

Therapist: *Exactly—so you felt like most kids do. And I think you probably could not have stopped him right then. So what did you do later that was really smart and took a great deal of courage on your part?*

Tommy: *I didn't do anything to stop him but I did tell.*

Therapist: *Is he going to abuse anyone now?*

Tommy: *No!*

Therapist: *Why not?*

Tommy: *I guess I did stop him from doing that. He got arrested because I told what happened.*

Therapist: *That's right. What is really important is that you stopped him from abusing you again or anyone else by telling when you felt safe to do that. What gave you the courage to do that?*

Tommy: *Well I started to think that he might do this to my little brother so I told my mom.*

Therapist: *Great. Well let's add something to your narrative about that.*

Tommy: *I can write after "I felt dumb because I didn't know what to do" but I figured it out and when I felt safe and got the courage up and I told my mom which was pretty smart I guess.*

Therapist: *There's no guessing about that. I think it was very brave and very smart to tell when you did.*

Tommy: *Okay—do you want me to cross out "I guess"?*

Therapist: *Yes I think so, what do you think?*

Tommy: *Okay.*

Therapist: *You're doing great job writing and reading your book about the sexual abuse.*

Tommy: *Thanks.*

to process and correct inaccurate thinking while incorporating more helpful thoughts into the final narrative.

Another approach to disputing dysfunctional thoughts is to record the corrections on a separate piece of paper and incorporate them into a final contextualization chapter that highlights what was learned in treatment including corrective thoughts that are more adaptive and helpful. This allows children who prefer not to change the original narrative as it is a reflection of their past experience, while simultaneously creating a final chapter that reflects their current way of thinking about the abuse.

Cognitive strategies such as disputing dysfunctional thoughts may be used with younger and older children during the processing component as depicted in the above example. However, sometimes to help very young children make sense of these experiences, it may be best to combine simple Socratic questions to correct dysfunctional thoughts with the provision of healthy replacement thoughts (see below). Common Socratic questions might include:

Does CSA happen to a lot of kids?
How do most children feel when they have been sexually abused?
Why don't most children tell about sexual abuse?
What gave you the courage to tell when you did?

As noted above, if younger children are not able to respond to the Socratic questioning, they may be encouraged to use positive self-statements to replace their negative abuse-related thoughts. Specific and global positive self-statements that can be helpful for young children include:

Sexual abuse happens to lots of kids.
I can solve problems.
I am brave for telling.
I have courage.
I am important.
I didn't do anything to make the sexual abuse happen.
My cousin was wrong for giving me not okay touches.
I wrote a really good book about the sexual abuse.
It took a lot of courage to tell about the abuse.
My parents are proud of me.

Whenever possible, self-statements may be tailored to the child's particular circumstances and concerns. With older children, it is preferable to elicit statements such as these using the Socratic method (i.e., questioning designed to elicit certain responses). As noted earlier, this approach allows children to do the work of therapy and learn a process of thinking that will help them counteract negative thoughts in the future. For example, the therapist could engage the client in a dialogue such as the one below to elicit some positive self-statements:

Therapist: *I know when the abuse was happening you thought your parents would be mad at you. Who were your parents really mad at?*

Jaime: *My cousin.*

Therapist: *That's right. Your parents were mad at your cousin. Can you tell me why?*

Jaime: *Because my cousin did it even though he knew it was wrong.*

Therapist: *Exactly. Your cousin gave you not okay touches even though he knew it was wrong. So how do your parents feel about you telling?*

Jaime: *I guess they are proud of me.*

Therapist: *They are proud. And how do you feel about you?*

Jaime: *I feel okay.*

Therapist: *Okay. So for next week, when you are reminded of the not okay touches, I want you to say to yourself, "I am brave for telling!" Most kids never ever tell because they are so scared. You were really brave.*

Jaime: *I was brave?*

Therapist: *What do you think?*

Jaime: *I miss my cousin, but . . . I am brave for telling.*

Therapist: *I understand that you miss your cousin. And I agree that it was very brave of you to tell!*

Identify themes or areas of maladaptive cognitions

Some of the more common areas of maladaptive cognitions that may be identified and addressed in therapy with children who have experienced sexual abuse and/or other trauma(s) are described in the sections that follow. Also provided are ideas for challenging dysfunctional thinking in those areas. For children who have experienced multiple or complex traumas, it is particularly important to use the historical information received, as well as the narrative to identify unifying themes that may underlie their troubling thoughts and behavior patterns. For example, when early childhood trauma(s) have been perpetrated by caregivers (e.g., physical abuse or domestic violence) and/or resulted in disrupted caregiver-child relationships (e.g., sexual abuse by a parent, parental substance abuse and/or incarceration, foster placement due to neglect), many youth begin to live with the assumption that others cannot be trusted. This theme may be reinforced repeatedly as the child interprets the impact of daily stressors and trauma(s) through a highly distrusting lens.

Children may also have a confused or distorted understanding of why they were abused. In fact, inaccurate explanations for the abuse may have been encouraged and reinforced by the offender in very concrete ways (i.e., "I abused you because you are too sexy") and thus can be challenging for children to process. Thus, it is important that the therapist addresses the issues of responsibility for and distorted explanations for the sexual abuse while also acknowledging the child's often confused feelings toward the offender. Many children experience confusion, both cognitively and affectively, regarding the causes of the abuse, not only who is responsible for it but also regarding their feelings about the offender. With youth who have experienced multiple or complex traumas, it is important to incorporate diverse traumas experienced for which there may be confusion about the cause. Given children's natural tendencies toward concrete, egocentric thinking, it is not surprising that many youth hold themselves responsible for all kinds of traumatic events.

Responsibility for the abuse

Many children inappropriately attribute responsibility for the abuse either to themselves or to another person such as a nonoffending parent. It is important that questions and confusion about abuse responsibility be explored and clarified so that the child does not continue to attribute responsibility inappropriately. As children repeatedly blame themselves for bad things and take little credit for positive events, they naturally become increasingly pessimistic in their thinking about themselves and their future. Thus, it is important to make clear that sexual abuse is always the offender's responsibility and not the child's. In fact, the therapist might state that even if a child asks an older person to do something sexual, it is the older person's responsibility to say no and set the limits. It may also help children to understand that adults and/or older teens are held responsible for abuse regardless of the child's behavior because the older person is expected to be more knowledgeable and more mature and has more options and resources than children (Berliner & Wheeler, 1987). A "responsibility pie" can be used to assess children's feelings with regard to the degree of responsibility assigned to the offender versus others by presenting a circle and asking the child to indicate how much of the pie represents the offender's responsibility for the abuse while also creating slices of the pie that reflect the degree of responsibility others share. Changes in the pie breakdown may reflect changing cognitions as youngsters come to understand the degree to which the offender engaged in grooming and other coercive efforts to gain the child's cooperation and silence.

The simple message of "it's not your fault" ought not to be repeated to all children without respect for their individual situation and circumstances. Indiscriminately repeating such messages, in fact, may be confusing to children who never considered themselves responsible in the first place. Furthermore, when working with children who inaccurately assume some responsibility for the abuse, a general message of "it's not your fault" is not likely to address each child's specific areas of concern. It is more helpful to elicit children's thoughts about responsibility for the abuse so that any idiosyncratic dysfunctional thoughts can be addressed. Another approach might involve indicating that some children might think it is their fault that the sexual abuse happened and then asking the child what she would tell those children. Such a question may reveal children's dysfunctional and/or functional thoughts about self-blame in addition to those that are depicted in their narratives. Sometimes children include thoughts in the form of questions in their narratives. Below is an example of a paragraph from a narrative that incorporates several dysfunctional thoughts including a question that likely reflects the child's ongoing feelings of self-blame.

I was feeling nervous and thinking when is my mom coming home. Then I put my mouth on his penis and he pushed my head up and down. Then I saw sticky stuff come out of his penis and it got on me. He said go get yourself cleaned up. I thought, "Why did I do that? Why did I put his penis in my mouth?"

To assist the child in cognitively processing the above paragraph, the therapist might ask the child to examine the section where she asked herself the questions, "*Why did I do that? Why did I put his penis in my mouth?*" The therapist might suggest that the child list all the reasons that she or any child in that circumstance would do that. Next, the therapist can utilize continued Socratic questioning to help the child cognitively process those questions/thoughts.

Therapist: *Wow. This a long list—so there were a lot of reasons that you put your mouth on your dad's penis. First, you wrote he told you to do that. Have you been taught to listen to adults when they tell you to do something?*

Child: *Yes. But I never expected for him to ask me to do that.*

Therapist: *It's very hard to know how to respond to something that is unexpected like that. You also said you put his penis in your mouth because you were scared and you didn't want to get hurt and you didn't want him to get mad and you didn't want him to get in trouble and you wanted to make him happy. Now looking back, do you think that most scared 8-year-old girls would do exactly what you did for all those reasons too?*

Child: *I guess so, if they didn't know what else to do.*

Therapist: *Exactly. Do you think most children would know exactly what to do if their father asked them to do something like that?*

Child: *Nooo!*

Therapist: *Now remember we discussed what it means to be brave.*

Child: *Yes. You said it was like being strong even though you're scared or something like that—right?*

Therapist: *Good job. That's exactly what it means. And how did it make you feel when your father asked you to do that?*

Child: *Really scared, but I just did it because I thought I had to.*

Therapist: *So you were scared in facing that difficult situation. Do you think you were brave in that situation too?*

Child: *I guess so.*

Therapist: *Why?*

Child: *Because I stayed strong, did what he said, and when I thought it was safe to tell, I told. Even though it took me a long time?*

Therapist: *It can sometimes take time to build up the courage to be brave! You did stay strong and tell when you thought it was safe. I think that was incredibly brave. I think even if you hadn't told when you did, you were still brave just to get through that night.*

Child: *Thanks.*

Many children who feel responsible for the sexual abuse develop feelings of shame or guilt that can be long lasting if not addressed. Some children develop feelings of shame because of the misguided belief that the abuse happened because there is *something wrong* with them. Other children may experience feelings of guilt and believe they deserved to be abused because of *something they did*. Researchers have suggested that both shame (Feiring & Taska, 2005) and guilt (Morrow, 1991) have been associated with negative outcomes for youth. Feelings of shame, in particular, are often deep rooted in explanations such as "He abused me because I am bad" or "I deserved the abuse because I am a slut." When children feel shame and believe that the abuse happened because there is something wrong with them, research suggests that they are much more likely to develop long-term difficulties (Feiring & Taska, 2005). Examples of guilt-ridden distortions include "I was abused because I dressed too sexy" and "I was abused because I flirted with my uncle." Similar to shame, research suggests that adolescents who attribute the abuse to something they did as opposed to attributing the abuse to external factors are more likely to experience depression and low self-esteem (Morrow, 1991). Moreover, such guilt ridden thoughts can lead to self-destructive behaviors such as overeating or engaging in anorexic behavior to avoid looking too "sexy." These types of responses can result in an ongoing pattern of interpreting negative events in a highly personalized and over generalized manner. Thus, given the negative impact such beliefs can have on a child's developing self-image, it is particularly important to elicit and correct any such personalized distortions whether they are revealed in the narrative or other processing exercises. These feelings greatly lessen as children begin to understand the prevalence and dynamics of CSA and recognize the limitations of their control and place full responsibility for the CSA on the offender.

The literature suggests, however, that some recognition of personal behaviors that may have contributed to the occurrence of trauma may positively influence the recovery process (Janoff-Bulman, 1985). For example, if a girl was abused while at a neighbor's home her parents had forbidden her to visit, she may understandably feel responsible for having broken her parents' rule. To simply tell her, "It's not your fault," will not address her concerns regarding her violation of the rule and may increase her confusion. Instead, it may help children to identify the control they did exert or could have exerted to influence the abusive situation while also acknowledging the limits of their control. Thus, in the example given above, the therapist might help the girl acknowledge that she made a mistake in visiting that home without permission while explaining that her mistake did not give the perpetrator the right to sexually abuse her. In other words, children may *regret* some behaviors that increased the likelihood of abuse, but they are still not *responsible* for the abuse. Though it is important to reinforce the benefit of following rules, it is also helpful to normalize the fact that many adolescents do break rules, and sometimes that increases their risk of finding themselves in dangerous situations. For example, it is well documented that drinking and/or engaging in other drug use increases one's risk of being sexually assaulted (e.g., Abbey, 2002). However, during processing of the abuse it is important to emphasize that the offender's abusive behavior is against the law and unacceptable regardless of the rule(s) broken by the child or teen. It is also important to acknowledge that there are some steps children and adults can take to reduce their chances of being assaulted. In fact, after the trauma processing is completed, children learn and practice personal safety skills (see Chapter 14) that may lessen their feelings of vulnerability and reduce their risk of re-victimization.

Explanations for the Abuse

While discussing responsibility for the abuse, the therapist can elicit the child's explanation for why the offender abused the child. The child's explanation should be explored before offering a "professional" explanation. This gives the therapist an opportunity to applaud and encourage the child's efforts to process the experience. Moreover, some children may have developed explanations that are accurate and more age appropriate than the explanation the therapist offers. Other children's explanations may contain dysfunctional thoughts that can be identified and addressed in treatment. Many children may carry with them and internalize the distorted explanations provided by the offenders themselves. As noted above, some offenders encourage children to view the abuse as sex education or as an act of love. Other offenders blame their behavior on the nonoffending parent for not satisfying their sexual needs. By offering such an explanation to a child, the offender may set up a dynamic that allows the abusive relationship to thrive, while the child's anger is inappropriately directed toward the unsuspecting nonoffending parent. It is important to correct this distortion in order to encourage more positive and open communication between the child and the nonoffending parent.

There is some evidence that posttrauma adjustment is more positive when the survivor's search for meaning leads to a greater understanding or mastery over the traumatic event (Silver, Boon, & Stones, 1983). Thus, if children offer no explanation or a dysfunctional explanation, the therapist can provide an age-appropriate explanation for the offender's behaviors. A simple explanation that conforms to what is currently known about offenders is preferable. Berliner and Wheeler (1987) suggest the following explanation:

> *He [the offender] has a problem; he wants to be sexual with children, something that most grownups don't want. And he tells himself it's okay to do it even though he knows it is wrong (p. 428).*

These authors discourage the use of explanations suggesting that the offender is sick, confused, or misguided, as these explanations may diminish the intentionality of the behavior and may encourage children to feel too much sympathy for the offender, as well as guilt for feeling angry or upset about the abuse.

Feelings Toward the Offender

When the perpetrator is a parent or other family member, children may experience a great deal of confusion with regard to their feelings toward this person, as well as pain concerning that person's feelings toward them. Children may ask, "Will my father ever love me again?" "Did my Aunt do this because she hated me?" or "If my cousin is so bad, why do I still love him?" Therapists can respond to these questions by helping children separate their feelings about the abuse and the offender's abusive behavior from other feelings they have toward the offender. Below is an example of a dialogue that a therapist might have to help a teenager come to the conclusion that it is okay for her to love her father but not to accept or like his abusive behavior.

Therapist: *I noticed in this chapter about telling your mom, you wrote, "I thought I would hate my father for abusing me, but I still love him. That felt weird because my mother kept screaming I hate him! I hate him!"*

Marissa: *Yeah, I sort of want to hate him, but I just can't. We had so much fun together and I miss that. But I feel weird saying I still love him.*

Therapist: *Whatever feelings you have are okay. So it sounds like your dad has good qualities too and you enjoyed the times when your dad treated you nicely and you had fun together.*

Marissa: *I think so.*

Therapist: *But there were other things that he did like making you touch his penis that you didn't like?*

Marissa: *It was confusing though because when I was little he told me he was teaching me what to do with my husband—so even though I didn't much like it, I still loved him then.*

Therapist: *I understand. So you loved him, but you didn't exactly like what he was doing or you weren't sure if you liked it?*

Marissa: *Yes. I wasn't sure at first. When I got a little older and I realized that what he was doing was really wrong—I got mad and I didn't want to even be near him, but I couldn't tell because I didn't want him to get in trouble or anything.*

Therapist: *That makes sense to me because although you were angry with your dad about the abuse, you loved him and didn't want him in trouble. What do you think your mother loved about your dad when she married him?*

Marissa: (long pause) *Maybe what I loved—how fun he can be even though he is a little crazy too.*

Therapist: *Do you think it is okay for your mom to be really mad at him and have feelings of hate toward him for what he did to you?*

Marissa: *Oh yeah. I get that. I just don't get me, why I still love him and she doesn't.*

Therapist: *Can you accept that she doesn't feel the same way you do because of what he did to you? And perhaps because she loves you so much, it is hard to love someone who hurt you.*

Marissa: *Yes.*

Therapist: *So maybe now that your mom has learned a lot about child sexual abuse and the very difficult feelings children experience, she can accept that you have both loving and angry feelings toward your dad.*

Marissa: *I don't think my mom could accept that because she doesn't love any part of him.*

Therapist: *Is it possible that your mother loves the part of him that gave her you?*
Marissa: *I don't know . . . maybe.*

Given the many characteristics that a child may share with a familial offender due to genetically inherited traits, it is important to help the child distinguish between the offender's overall character and his abusive behavior. In fact, the therapist may discourage tendencies to place people in good or evil categories by keeping the focus on specific behaviors and how some behaviors simply cannot be tolerated. When children get stuck in good versus evil thinking, such tendencies can ultimately lead them to place themselves in one or the other category (both of which can be troubling). Thus, the TF-CBT therapist may help the child to focus on specific problematic and unacceptable behaviors, as distinguished from pervasive character flaws, by posing questions such as the following:

What did your father do that was wrong?
What did your father do that indicates that he knew his behavior was wrong?
Are there other things that your father has done that were right or good?
Tell me about positive qualities that you share with your father.
Tell me about negative behaviors that your father exhibited that you did not like.

It is important to remain consistent in the message that although the perpetrator may have done things that are not okay, his character may not be all bad. Being excessively negative about a loved offender may be confusing to a child who has seen positive aspects of the offender's character, and it may also alienate the child from the therapist. In addition, as noted above, when the offender is a parent or sibling, children may recognize that they share some similar characteristics and wonder if that is the way they will be viewed as well. Conversely, the therapist must be clear in communicating that the perpetrator's abusive behavior was wrong and should not be tolerated or imitated. Moreover, the perpetrator, in fact, may need to experience negative consequences as a result of the abusive behavior as severe as jail or juvenile detention.

As mentioned previously, young children may have difficulty identifying and disputing their own thoughts regarding responsibility and explanations for the abuse. Thus, the therapist might provide self-statements or encourage them to repeat their own more adaptive conclusions. Below are some examples.

My cousin made the abuse happen—not me.
He did it even though he knew it was wrong.
All people make mistakes sometimes.
My cousin told a lie to get me to keep it a secret.
Most people don't give kids not okay touches.
Adults should know better.
I can still love my father even though he did something very wrong.
When it happened I was confused and I didn't know what to do.
Sexual abuse can happen to anyone.

I am brave for telling about the abuse.
Children don't tell for many reasons.

Social reactions

Children's perceptions of others' reactions to the discovery or disclosure of the abuse is another important area to explore during cognitive processing. There is considerable evidence that the reactions of nonoffending family members powerfully influence post-abuse adjustment (Conte & Schuerman, 1987; Everson et al., 1989; Tufts New England Medical Center, 1984). Thus, it is important to elicit and review children's observations and perceptions of others' reactions in the narrative. Unfortunately, many children are exposed to highly emotional reactions including extreme upset, disbelief, anger (or mixed reactions) when they disclose sexual abuse. Children's interpretations of these reactions may significantly influence their understanding of the abuse, their self-image, and their ability to trust others. Moreover, these perceptions of others' reactions can change when children are encouraged to flexibly explore different explanations for the perceived reactions of others. Thus, it is important to carefully process the child's chapter about disclosing the abuse.

A child, for example, may initially perceive a parent's negative emotional reactions to mean that the abuse was much worse than she realized. Such a child may develop permanent or pervasive thoughts about the potential impact of the abuse that may be both distressing and dysfunctional. For example, a child may interpret Mom's extreme distress to mean that the abuse caused permanent bodily damage or destroyed the entire family. Other children may be so shaken by initially disbelieving responses that they may begin to question the reality of their own experience or they may be tempted to make false recantations.

Children's perceptions of others' reactions may also influence their thoughts about themselves. Young children may be particularly prone to believing that angry or upset feelings exhibited by others are directed at them. These over personalized thoughts may lead children to experience increased guilt and diminished self-worth.

Socratic questioning or cognitive processing exercises can be used to help children process thoughts and feelings about the reactions of others and to reconsider their initial interpretations of others' reactions. In addition, children may be encouraged to assess the accuracy of their perceptions regarding others' responses and feelings toward them. Again, rather than offering evidence that contradicts children's dysfunctional thoughts, it is preferable for TF-CBT therapists to use questions and exaggerated statements about thoughts to elicit evidence from the children themselves.

Children's perceptions of others' reactions to the disclosure of CSA may also influence their ability to achieve an adaptive balance between trust and mistrust of others. For example, a child who is sexually abused by one parent and not supported by the other may be particularly prone to developing a pervasive mistrust of others. Such a child may have difficulty trusting or depending on anyone. Although this reaction may seem reasonable, it is highly dysfunctional in terms of developing healthier relationships in the future. Thus, it is important to elicit, process, and help children correct maladaptive thoughts such as "No one can be trusted; people will desert you when you're in trouble; people you love will betray you." The therapist may help the child identify other relationship experiences that did not lead to abuse or betrayal as well as other more helpful reactions to their disclosure of the sexual abuse. With some children this can be challenging as they may have had many abusive relationship experiences. Still, more positive trusting relationships both in the past and the present can usually be identified (e.g., teacher, current foster parent, sibling, TF-CBT therapist, etc.) sometimes with the help of a nonoffending caregiver. It can be powerful to turn the child's attention to noticing and acknowledging positive interactions with a family member, a friend, or even one professional in the immediate aftermath of sexual abuse. Further exploration of the qualities of the individuals with whom children have had positive experiences may help them to be more able to identify trustworthy individuals in the future.

Children who have been sexually abused sometimes generalize their negative expectations and distrust of others to other interpersonal situations. Thus, it is important to explore how children interpret others' emotional, behavioral, and interpersonal reactions toward them. Box 11.2 has an example of a TF-CBT therapist using Socratic questions to assist a child with disputing

---

Box 11.2

Case Example: Disputing Dysfunctional Thoughts Regarding Others' Responses

Therapist: *Janine, in this chapter you wrote about what happened in the days after the trial. It is really a good chapter. It really helped me understand how challenging that time was for you and your mom. I would like to review that chapter today and identify thoughts that you think helped you to cope and any thoughts that you may now realize are not all that accurate or helpful. Would you like to read the chapter or shall I read it out loud?*

Janine: *I can read it.... Chapter Five: After the Sentencing*

When we found out my dad's sentence, my mom seemed really sad. When she got off the phone with the prosecutor, she said he is going to get 10 years for what he did. She looked really upset and sad and ran into her bedroom. I thought to myself why isn't she happy? I went into my room. I figured she didn't want to see my face. I was thinking that I ruined my mom's life and my life too. We'll never be happy again. My dad shouldn't have sexually abused me like that. That is why he has to go to jail.

Therapist: *That was powerful what you wrote there. I think it is very healthy that you thought and wrote "My dad shouldn't have sexually abused me like that. That is why he has to go to jail." That is exactly right—he is going to jail because of his behavior. He broke the law when he sexually abused you.*

Janine: *Thanks.*

Therapist: *Though those thoughts are very accurate and helpful, I'm not sure about some of the other thoughts you were having at that time. Do you still think your mom didn't want to see your face? Or could there be another reason she went into her room?*

Janine: *I don't know.* (long pause) *Maybe she didn't want me to see her upset.*

Therapist: *That makes a lot of sense to me. And you know we can ask her why she went into her room that night if you like later in a conjoint session. What about you ruining your mom's life and yours too?*

Janine: *Well, if I didn't tell none of this would have happened.*

Therapist: *None of it. What about the sexual abuse?*

Janine: *Well the sexual abuse would have happened, but my father would not be in jail.*

Therapist: *And how would you be doing if your father wasn't in jail?*

Janine: *Probably terrible because he might have kept abusing me and maybe my little sister and brother too.*

Therapist: *And do you think that your mother would have liked that better?*

Janine: (long pause) *I get what you're trying to tell me that my dad ruined our lives.*

Therapist: *Well what do you think? Are you responsible or is your dad responsible for causing all the difficulties then and now?*

Janine: *Definitely not me. He did it and he should have known better.*

Therapist: *It is great that you are clear about who caused the abuse and the difficulties you have had since then. And I think your dad made things very difficult, but I'm not sure that your lives have been ruined. Have your lives been totally ruined?*

Janine: *I don't know.*

Therapist: *Well it seems to me that you and your mom have gotten stronger and closer and some good things have happened for you recently. So let me ask you another important question. Did your dad ruin your entire lives or are there still some good things happening in your lives?*

Janine: *Well, maybe not our entire lives. We are alive. He didn't kill us like he threatened.*

Therapist: *So convince me now that he did not succeed in ruining your lives. Let's write a list of all the things happening in your lives now that are positive.*

Janine: *I don't know if I can write a list for my mom, but I have a few good things for my list.*

Therapist: *Let's start with those, and maybe we can ask your mom to add to this list later.*

Janine: *Okay.*

---

dysfunctional beliefs about her mother's emotional distress when she disclosed the sexual abuse.

Processing is planned for this stage of therapy because it is important for the therapist to know the child, nonoffending caregiver, and the circumstances of the abuse in order to formulate effective Socratic questions that will lead to more helpful and functional thinking as demonstrated above. Again, the *Processing Dysfunctional Thoughts* therapist form, provided in Appendix F can assist therapists in listing maladaptive thoughts identified, possible positive replacement thoughts, and then a series of Socratic questions that may help the therapist elicit those positive replacement thoughts from the child. In general, it is better to ask clients Socratic questions that the therapist knows the answers to, thereby increasing the likelihood that children will respond with healthy, more functional thoughts. For example, the therapist should be aware that there are some positive things happening in the child's life before asking if there are any good things happening.

The following are some examples of maladaptive thoughts, possible helpful replacement thoughts, as well as a series of Socratic questions highlighted in bold that a therapist might use to elicit those more functional, adaptive thoughts. Multiple Socratic questions should lead to and reinforce adaptive replacement thoughts ultimately provided by the child in the form of answers to those questions.

Dysfunctional thoughts:
I never should have told about the abuse. My mom got so upset. And no one believed me.
Replacement thoughts:
I am glad I told. People are proud of me for telling. Now I am safe.
Socratic questions:
Who is proud of you for telling about the abuse?
You are. My mom, my grandmom (anyone else?), and you said all the people that interviewed me were impressed that I told all the details. I guess many people are proud of me for telling about the abuse. I was brave to tell about the abuse.
Why do you think your mom got upset when you told about the abuse at first?
At first, maybe my mom was shocked and maybe she was upset because she cares about me and my dad. Sometimes my mom cries, but she is glad I told about the abuse.
Why do you think some people didn't believe your father could have sexually abused you?
Some of my dad's relatives still can't imagine that he would ever do anything wrong. So I guess they still don't understand that someone could do a lot of good things but also do this very wrong thing.
Do you think people who did not believe you when you told about your father knew much about sexual abuse?
Maybe not so much. They didn't understand about sexual abuse happening to so many kids. Maybe some of my relatives learned about it, and they believe me now.

Dysfunctional thoughts:
This happened because I am a loser. I can't trust anyone anymore.

Replacement thoughts:
I am actually good at solving problems, and I have succeeded in many things. There are people I can trust.
Socratic questions:
Do you think this happens to a lot of children?
Well. You told me that it happens to a lot of children. But it helps to see other kids in the waiting room; that's how I know what you said about it happening to a lot of other kids is the truth.
Do you think they are all losers?
I guess not. They seem like nice kids.
Do you think there are some people who were sexually abused as children and grew up to be successful?
Well, you showed me that list of famous people, but maybe I could check that out by looking some of them up.
Do you think that most adults sexually abuse children?
Some do, but there are many more people who don't abuse children.
So how do you know if someone is going to sexually abuse a child?
You don't know for sure. You can't tell by looking at someone. But most people don't do that.
So how do you know who to trust?
When you get to know someone you slowly decide if they are okay or not. If someone is mean or tries to make you keep creepy secrets then that tells you to get away from that person and tell someone about it.

Using role-plays in cognitive processing

In addition to the use of educational information and Socratic questioning to dispute dysfunctional thoughts and feelings, role-plays may be used. Role-plays are particularly useful when children seem to understand the inaccuracy of their dysfunctional thoughts intellectually but are not convinced emotionally. These role-plays are called best-friend or therapist-client role-plays.

Best-friend or therapist-client role-play

In a best-friend or therapist-client role-play (similar to "Mr. Puppet game" described by Seligman [2006]), children are asked to imagine that their best friend or client was sexually abused and is having certain negative thoughts. In the role-play, it is important for the therapist to make the child work hard cognitively and emotionally to dispute the dysfunctional thoughts. The therapist may do this by realistically playing a child similar to the client who is still struggling with problematic beliefs about self, relationships with others, and/or the world. The child plays the role of the therapist or best friend who is trying to help a client or friend (played by the therapist, puppet, empty chair, etc.) who was sexually abused. In this context, children often become more animated and may work harder to convincingly explain why the friend's negative thoughts are not true. When using the best-friend role-play to help the child dispute dysfunctional abuse-related thoughts, it can be particularly helpful to incorporate dysfunctional thoughts that the client revealed early in therapy and/or in the course of developing the narrative. With younger children, it helps to use a puppet, thereby reinforcing the message that this is an exercise or game and not the therapist's real thoughts or feelings. These types of role-plays may be particularly beneficial for children and adolescents who have depressive and/or pessimistic tendencies.

The example provided in Box 11.3 illustrates how the therapist might introduce and pursue a best-friend role-play with a 10-year-old boy named Luis who seemed to be stuck on the belief that if others found out about the CSA they would think he was disgusting.

Box 11.3

Case Example: Role Reversal Role-Play

Therapist: *We've been working together for a while now, and you've done an excellent job learning about child sexual abuse. And you have written a terrific book.*

Luis: *How many more sessions do we have?*

Therapist: *Actually, we don't have that many more sessions together. So, I thought we could do something sort of fun today so that you can show off how much you have learned. You know when you first wrote your narrative you shared some things that you were saying to yourself at the time of the abuse that were pretty mean. In fact, if you had a best friend who was sexually abused, I don't think you would say those things to him and if you were a therapist I'm sure you wouldn't say those things to your clients. So what I would like to do is a role-play in which I will play you. Then I will share with you some of the things you seemed to say to yourself sometimes. And I would like you to be my therapist and try to help me feel better. You can use all the information you learned in counseling so far to convince me that some of the thoughts I have are not correct.*

Luis: *Well, I don't know… Could I sit in your seat if I'm going to be the therapist?*

Therapist: *Sure. Let's give it a try. I think you'll be great!*

Luis: *Okay.*

Therapist: *Okay, I'll be you and you be Dr. D. My problem is similar to something you were struggling with at first. I'm afraid if anyone found out about the sexual abuse they might think I did something wrong and that I was disgusting. Do you remember thinking that?*

Luis: *Yeah.*

Therapist: *So now you are going to be the therapist and help me with that. Okay?*

Luis: *I guess, but this is so dumb.*

Therapist: *Okay, let's switch seats.* (Playing a client): *Hey, Dr. D. can we talk about something?*

Luis (in role of the therapist): *Yeah, what's going on kid?*

Therapist (playing a client): *Remember when I told you what happened with me and our neighbor, Wayne, how he touched me and stuff?*

Luis (as the therapist): *Yeah, that was abuse!*

Therapist (playing a child client): *Well, I had to tell so many people about it-a police officer, a child protection person, and this counselor who keeps bugging me to talk about it.*

Luis: (smiles) *Yeah, she's a real pain.*

Therapist: *I just don't want to talk about it. I'm really afraid it's going to get out. Do you think the counselor or the officer will tell anybody?*

Luis: *I don't think they are allowed to—they're supposed to keep this stuff, what do you call it, confidential.*

Therapist: *Yeah, I think you're right. The counselor did say something about that. But still if one kid finds out, then everyone in the whole school will be talking about it. Don't you think everyone will think I'm disgusting?*

Luis: *Maybe if they knew what he did, but just don't tell them.*

Therapist: *Well you know what he did- do you think I'm disgusting?*

Luis: *Well, I don't think you're disgusting.*

Therapist: *That's good but you're a therapist; what do you think other kids might think?*

Luis: *(pause) I don't know, but I know some kids who like you a lot. And I think they are the kind of kids who would stick up for you, because they like you.*

Therapist: *What do they like about me?*

Luis: *Well, you are a nice kid. And you are pretty good at sports.*

Therapist: *So how does all that help?*

Luis: *It helps because kids like to be friends with other nice kids.* (Pause) *and they would want you to be on your team 'cause you are pretty quick.*

Therapist: *Well thanks! That makes me feel good. But don't you think the kids would just keep talking about the sexual abuse thing. Do you think they have anything more important to talk about?*

Luis: *I think they have a lot of other things to talk about.*

Therapist: *Like what?*

Luis: *Like sports and video games.*

Therapist: *Okay I get it. But what if they do talk about it a little?*

Luis: *If one kid finds out, he may talk about it with a couple of kids for a little bit.*

Therapist: *Wouldn't they think I'm disgusting?*

Luis: *I think they'll think Wayne's the disgusting one.*

Therapist: *You really think so? Maybe you're right, but it will still bother me to think that anyone is talking about it.*

Luis: (long pause) *They may talk about it a little, they might even have some questions about it. But they're not going to keep talking about it all the time.*

Therapist: *Are you sure? Do you think they have other things to talk about?*

Luis: *Yeah! The kids probably have much better things to talk about.*

Therapist: *Like what?*

Luis: *Well, right now the playoffs and boys like to talk about girls.*

Therapist: *So you think they have better things to talk about. Yeah. I guess you're right. That helps me feel a lot better. Thanks!*

Elicit questions to ask parents to enhance processing

Therapists may encourage children to share concerns by consistently asking at the end of each processing session if they have any questions or worries. Consequently, children begin to anticipate that they will have an opportunity to ask questions each session, and it may give them the needed time to build their courage to ask embarrassing or troubling questions about sexual acts, legal issues, or parental responses. Some of these questions may be addressed in individual sessions by the therapist, while others may need to be responded to in conjoint session with parents (e.g., "Were you upset with me when I told you about the sexual abuse, Mom?" "Are you still mad at me?" "Will people be able to tell that I was sexually abused?"). Children are encouraged to develop a list of questions that they may want to pose to their parents during conjoint parent-child sessions. The TF-CBT therapist can then share these questions with the parent in the individual sessions so that the parents can prepare therapeutic responses with the support of the therapist.

Brianna: *Sometimes I still wonder how my mother feels about me. My brother should not have sexually abused me, but my mom got so mad when I told. I think she must still be mad at me for getting my brother in trouble. Maybe she hates me. She really didn't want my brother to have to go to juvenile detention.*

Therapist: *Remember how we talked about how thoughts can influence how we feel? How do you feel when you say to yourself, "My mother is still mad at me. Maybe she hates me."?*

Brianna: *I feel really sad. Sometimes I want to cry.*

Therapist: *I'm not surprised that you feel really sad when you say that to yourself. That would make anyone feel pretty down. But I think some of these thoughts may not be accurate. I've written them all on the board. Can you identify thoughts that are accurate and then pick out the thoughts that might not be all that accurate and tell me why?*

Brianna: *Well, it is true that my brother should not have sexually abused me.*

Therapist: *You're right. That thought is very accurate and healthy too. What about the others?*

Brianna: *I'm not sure if my mother is really mad at me. Sometimes I wonder if she hates me for getting my brother in trouble. I don't know.*

Therapist: *Okay. Let's examine the accuracy of those thoughts. What evidence is there that your mom is really mad at you?*

Brianna: *Well, she got really mad when I told. And she never talks to me about the sexual abuse. She doesn't want anyone to know about it.*

Therapist: *Other than being mad at you, can you think of other reasons why she may not talk about the sexual abuse or tell others about it?*

Brianna: (long pause) *Maybe she's uncomfortable talking about it like I was at the beginning of therapy. And maybe she thinks other people won't understand about sexual abuse.*

Therapist: *Those reasons sound like good possibilities. Now is there any evidence that your mother doesn't hate you, but that your mother is proud of you and loves you?*

Brianna: *Well, she comes here with me and praises me every time. She loves to come to my school activities. But I still wonder about some of the things she said when I first told.*

Therapist: *I think those are all great examples of how your mother shows you that she is proud of you and loves you. But let's come up with a few questions we can ask your mom that might help you understand her reactions better when you first told. Okay?*

Brianna: *Okay. Could I ask her who was she more mad at me or my brother? And maybe I could ask her if she is still mad.*

Therapist: *Those are two great questions. And I have one more question for you. You had the thought that you got your brother in trouble. Who really got your brother in trouble?*

Brianna: *Well, I told on him.*

Therapist: *But who did the behavior that caused the trouble in the first place?*

Brianna: *My brother?*

Therapist: *If your brother never sexually abused you, would he be in detention now?*

Brianna: *I guess not.*

Therapist: *So your brother did what?*

Brianna: *He sexually abused me . . .*

Therapist: *Yes, and who got him in trouble?*

Brianna: *He got himself in trouble.*

Therapist: *You got it! Your brother got himself in trouble.*

Writing a final summary chapter: timing and content

A final summary trauma narrative chapter may be written at any point in the final phase of treatment after the traumatic experience(s) has been processed. However, trauma education and additional processing may continue through the final phase of treatment with in vivo, sex education, and safety skills training, as well as conjoint trauma-focused sessions that may lead children to develop important productive beliefs about themselves and others, as well as positive expectations for the future. Thus, the child may choose to add additional thoughts or ideas to a final summary chapter at any point before sharing the narrative with the parent and/or before finishing therapy.

Research has revealed characteristics of healthy or constructive narratives that are associated with greater abuse resolution and decreased symptomatology (Horowitz, 1986; Janoff-Bulman, 1985; Simon et al., 2010). Healthy narrative characteristics seem to include the ability to coherently acknowledge what happened, the sharing of vulnerable, as well as strong feelings, reflections, or insights on what has been learned from a present perspective, and optimistic expectations for the future. As a final assessment of the client's progress and success in processing the abusive experiences, it helps to encourage the writing of a final narrative chapter that summarizes what has been experienced and learned about the self, the world, relationships with others, and expectations for the future. Again the authors often refer to this final chapter as *contextualization*. In addition to closure, the final chapter will also simultaneously summarize the experience and the child's feelings and thoughts then and now, while expressing optimistic expectations for the future. A summary chapter may be particularly important for children who have written longer multichapter narratives. It is important for children not to view this as another full-fledged narrative but rather as a brief summary reflecting what they have learned and their processing of the abusive experiences. A final summary chapter can also be valuable with cases in which a parent's emotional instability precludes the sharing of the full narrative. In those instances, it can be beneficial to have the child share only the final chapter with the parent. The below outline is therefore designed to assist the child in creating such a final chapter that provides closure.

- Introduce self and/or family that participated in treatment.
- Describe the sexual abuse and/or other trauma(s) briefly.
- Describe primary feelings and thoughts at the time of the abuse.
- Describe positive interactions they have had with others since the abuse.
- Describe what was learned about CSA.
- Describe how their feelings and thoughts may have changed after counseling.
- Describe how their participating parents helped them cope.
- Include what they would like other children to know about CSA.
- Describe their positive expectations for the future.

Below is an example of a final summary chapter.

My name is Destiny and my mom and I came to counseling to see Dr. Jan after my pop pop sexually abused me. Grand Pop hurt me many times and I felt sad and scared. It used to be hard for me to talk about. Now I know that I have nothing to be ashamed of because I didn't do anything wrong. At first, I was afraid to tell my mom. It was her dad. I feel proud now that I had the courage to tell about the sexual abuse. When I told my mom, she looked confused and called my dad because she said she wanted me to be safe. Dad called the police. Since then, my counselor has given me a lot of support and helped me see that I am brave and strong. Most people who know about the abuse say I'm brave and strong. My grandmother doesn't understand about how child sexual abuse happens so she is still confused about it. I have learned a lot in counseling that I'd like to share with other kids. Like you are not alone. Sexual abuse happens to a lot of kids. Sexual abuse is never the kid's fault. It is always the bigger person's fault, kid or adult, because they know better than to do sex with a kid and that it's against the law. If someone sexually abuses you, please tell someone so you can get help like I did. I want to go to grow up to be a counselor so I can help other kids. Right now, I'm excited to go to Disney World with my dad. Even though they don't live together, my mom and dad love me. My mom came to therapy with me every time, and she gives me lots of hugs and helps me when I need it. We learned a lot in therapy about feelings and praise and sexual abuse. I love my mom, and I love me.

Practice activities encouraged: Cognitive processing

As noted earlier, coping skills practice may continue to be encouraged throughout this component. The therapist may help children identify those coping strategies from the coping skills tool kit that are the most successful for them. In addition, with children who have experienced complex trauma and continue to struggle with affect dysregulation and/or sensitivity to trauma reminders in the environment, daily journaling and/or thought records may help them capture what they are saying to themselves when they are feeling distressed and/or when reminded of the abuse (see *Identifying and Challenging Your Problematic Thoughts* handout in Appendix B). Clients can then go back and identify dysfunctional, inaccurate, and/or unproductive abuse-related thoughts and replace them with more functional, adaptive thoughts on their own. These thoughts records can then be reviewed in session when the therapist can help clients expand on their efforts at home to practice more flexible, adaptive, and optimistic thinking.

PARENT SESSION(S)

During the parallel parent individual sessions, although caregivers do not typically develop a trauma narrative, they participate in gradual exposure through active and direct discussions about the child's sexual abuse and/or other traumatic experiences. These discussions may be enhanced by the therapist's growing knowledge and understanding of the child's experiences through the trauma narrative development process. Given the sensitivity of the issue of CSA, parents rarely have others with whom they feel comfortable discussing the details of the CSA-related experiences. Moreover, unlike almost any other problem a child might have, nonoffending parents often feel they are in the dark with respect to their child's sexual abuse experience. In fact, it is not unusual for children to share more details about their abusive experiences with caseworkers, law enforcement officials, and/or medical doctors than with their parents. However, nonoffending caregivers may be the only ones available to children in the long run to address their abuse-related concerns and questions. Moreover, children may be most likely to shed their feelings of shame when they are ultimately able to experience the proud response or embrace of a parent after sharing the most disturbing details of their abuse in conjoint session in the final stage of treatment. Thus, at this stage, it is important to assess the parents' capability of participating in such sessions by engaging them in gradual exposure during individual parent sessions.

In this middle phase of treatment (the trauma narration and processing phase), it is important to continue to engage parents in more personalized discussions of CSA, which may include sharing additional details that have come to light over the course of therapy. These personalized discussions about the child's abusive experiences will continue with accompanying cognitive processing until the parents' abuse-related avoidance and associated emotional distress begins to diminish as well.

Practice assignments review

This component is a particularly important one in which to review parents' coping in relation to the sexual abuse, as well as their progress with respect to parent-child interactions at home. As always, when reviewing coping and parenting skill utilization, the emphasis should be on identifying and shaping positive skill implementation with constructive feedback in the form of compliment sandwiches (as described in Chapter 8 and the glossary of terms). During this component, it is particularly important to begin to assess parents' progress in order to determine their readiness for trauma-focused conjoint sessions.

Assess parents' readiness for reviewing child's completed narrative

From the start of therapy, the therapist continuously assesses parental progress and emotional stability in order to individually tailor and update the overall treatment plan. The assessment of parental progress is critical at this stage in determining the clinical appropriateness of sharing the child's narrative in the parent's individual sessions, as well as in future conjoint parent-child sessions. Thus, if parents are still unable to demonstrate an ability to manage their emotions and cope with abuse-related reminders in their environment as well as in session, the sharing of additional abuse-related information may need to be delayed until such improved coping is evident or it may be contraindicated in some circumstances.

Cautionary note

It is important to carefully evaluate the degree to which details of the abuse and/or the child's narrative are appropriate to share with caregivers, as there are some clinical circumstances in which such sharing may be not be appropriate. For example, the child's trauma narrative may inadvertently heighten distress and/or symptoms in parents who themselves have untreated PTSD as a result of trauma(s) they experienced in childhood. Conversely, many parents who have their own history of sexual abuse prove to be excellent sources of support for their children and find it helpful to read the child's narrative. However, parents who have a significant history of mental health, substance abuse, and/or anger problems may have greater difficulty coping with the abuse-specific details, and for them it may not be clinically appropriate to share the narrative. Thus, in general, it is important for the therapist to use careful clinical judgment in determining the clinical appropriateness, optimal timing, and/or benefits of sharing the child's narrative with the parent. With many parents there seems to be considerable benefit to sharing the narrative, but such sharing is not essential for the child to have a successful therapy experience. These individual parent sessions are, therefore, used to assess the therapeutic benefits of discussing the details of the abuse and/or the value of sharing of the child's narrative with the parent first in individual sessions and then (if deemed appropriate) in conjoint session(s) with the child in the final phase of treatment (the consolidation and closure phase). For example, it may not be therapeutically beneficial to share the child's completed narrative in either individual session or conjoint session with a parent who continues to be emotionally overwhelmed when minimal abuse details are shared during individual parent sessions over the course of treatment.

During this component, it can be useful to further explore the abuse details the parents have become aware of whether through their discussions with the caseworker and/or the detective or via spontaneous comments made by the child since the start of treatment. Though parents are not encouraged to discuss the abuse outside of therapy with the child, it is useful to inquire about spontaneous abuse-related conversations that parents and children may have had at home to assess parents' knowledge and reactions to these discussions. In addition, for purposes of assessment and planning, the therapist may gradually share with the parent some of what the child has shared to assess the parent's emotional reactions. To counter parental distress and dysfunctional thinking, it is helpful to highlight information about the child's progress in treatment as well. This assessment and processing is important to do to determine the clinical appropriateness of sharing the child's actual narrative with the parent.

The initial assessment of parental readiness will consist of the therapist's evaluation of the parent's emotional reactions to all discussions of the child's sexual abuse and related traumatic experiences over the course of treatment. Observed parental emotional reactions should be considered in terms of evaluating parents' abilities to respond therapeutically to open parent-child communication about the sexual abuse. It is anticipated that early on in therapy many parents will naturally react to CSA-related discussions with some degree of emotional distress. However, it is expected that over the course of the gradual exposure process, the development of coping skills will help the parent manage abuse-related distress more effectively. As parents make progress in emotionally coping with the abuse, it will become important to begin to assess their potential readiness for reviewing the child's trauma narrative.

When assessing parental readiness for such, it is important that the therapist talk with parents about any specific anxieties or concerns they may have about hearing the CSA details. Some parents may feel they are not emotionally capable of hearing the details of the child's sexual abuse experiences. Having parents discuss their worries allows the therapist to deal with those concerns directly. With some parents it can be helpful to gradually provide information (related to the child's experiences) without sharing the complete narrative to help the parents assess their own emotional preparedness.

With many parents, it may be preferable to share the narrative after it has been processed with the child and includes healthy adaptive thoughts that temper the more distressing aspects of the narrative. Sharing unprocessed trauma narratives may unnecessarily heighten parental concerns. In fact, it may be helpful to encourage the child to incorporate what she has learned in each of the narrative chapters. This can be helpful to the child, as well as for the parents as they are reading the narrative. For example, when a child writes about the offender saying that mom doesn't love her, the child can correct that in the narrative, as described above, by writing "*Now I know* that my mom really didn't know what he was doing, and she does love me and is proud of me for telling." Though it is natural for parents to show some level of distress, their ability to maintain a level of composure and focus on the child's needs will help to determine whether sharing even a fully processed narrative in a conjoint parent-child session would be helpful or therapeutic for the child and parent. If the sharing of the narrative is determined to be clinically appropriate, the initial sharing of details and then the sharing of the processed narrative in individual parent session is critical. This individual session serves as an important part of the gradual exposure process and will help to prepare parents if it is determined that it would be of clinical value to have the child share the processed trauma narrative later in conjoint sessions with the parent.

When clinically indicated, review with parents completed narrative

Once it has been clinically determined that the parent is emotionally stable enough and prepared to review the child's narrative, the therapist may offer to read the narrative out loud or have the parents read it themselves in individual sessions. As the child's trauma narrative is reviewed, the therapist may encourage the parent to share all the emotions, thoughts, as well as questions that the child's account evokes. Thus, it is important for the therapist to be prepared for the expression of sometimes intense parental emotions, including anger as well as sadness in the form of tears. Having parents verbally share the feelings and thoughts that are precipitated by the narrative will assist them in fully exploring their own reactions to the child's experience of sexual abuse. In this way, the parent can work through any dysfunctional thoughts or beliefs that may interfere with her own coping and parenting efforts.

It is important that parents be engaged in cognitive processing of their thoughts and feelings regarding the narrative. In other words, parents need to clarify their emotional responses to the abuse while identifying and disputing any dysfunctional thoughts triggered by the reading of the narrative. (This processing work has largely been described in the section on cognitive coping skills training for parents.) Sometimes the sharing of the narrative elicits additional parental thoughts and feelings that need to be processed further. It can be disconcerting for children to see parents come out of their individual session extremely distressed. Thus, it is important to time the sharing of the narrative with parents well so that parents have time and support to both process what they have read and regain their composure prior to the end of a session.

If the child has written a lengthy narrative describing multiple episodes of abuse, the sharing of the narrative may require more time. In cases where the child's narrative is brief, as is often true with preschoolers, the gradual exposure process with the parent is likely to be much shorter. The therapist may judge when the work of gradual exposure is completed by observations of the parent's emotional response or by the parent's reported subjective units of distress (i.e., SUDS) scores before and after the sharing of narrative or other abuse-related information. Parents should be able to discuss the abusive episodes without significant distress prior to encouraging them to participate in conjoint sessions in which the narrative is reviewed and/or specific details of the abusive experiences are discussed with the child.

Prepare questions for parent(s) to ask child

After reviewing the child's narrative, parents may be encouraged to ask questions. It is important for the therapist to review the questions parents have and identify those questions that can be answered without the involvement of the child, as well as those that would be best posed to the child. Getting answers to their abuse-related questions directly from their children may help some parents more effectively process the sexual abuse themselves and develop adaptive ways of thinking about it. For example, rather than thinking there is something they did wrong that caused their child to be sexually abused, parents may be able to shift their dysfunctional thinking with the help of the therapist and perhaps the child.

Some questions such as "Why did the offender tell my child I wanted him to teach my child about sex?" can be processed with a parent by sharing that offenders often use that tactic as part of the grooming process. A review of the methods offenders' use to groom children and maintain their silence, in general, can help parents understand why CSA of hundreds of children can go undetected sometimes for many years. In addition, it can be helpful to ask the parent to brainstorm all the reasons offenders might use that particular lie to engage children in age-inappropriate sexual interactions. While looking at the different reasons listed, parents may begin to see how vulnerable all children are. In addition, the therapist can encourage more adaptive thinking by asking parents to consider what skills and personal characteristics have helped their child cope thus far with this experience despite all the lies the offender may have told.

Many parents also ask why the child did not tell right away. In fact, it is not uncommon for parents to have already questioned their children about this asking at the time of the disclosure, "Why didn't you tell me sooner?" When posed this way, this question can be guilt provoking for the child. Other parents may never have asked the question directly but may continue to be haunted by it. When parents feel a need to ask their children such a question, the therapist can help them to get the answers they need in a more therapeutic manner. In such instances, the therapist can encourage the parent to think about how the question could be asked in a less guilt-provoking manner. Once a therapeutic question such as the one below is formulated, the therapist might ask the parent to practice posing the question to the child in a role-play prior to the conjoint session.

> *I learned in therapy that most children never, ever have the courage to tell about sexual abuse like you did. You were so brave! And I also learned that there are a lot of different reasons why children don't tell. I wonder what your reasons were for not telling at first and then I'd really like to know all the things that gave you the courage to tell when you did.*

Sharing children's questions with parents

During this component, if clinically indicated, the TF-CBT therapist may begin to share children's questions with their parents. When answered by parents, these questions can also greatly assist children in processing their thoughts and feelings in a productive way. For example, many children wonder if their parents' emotional responses in the aftermath of their disclosure reflected anger toward them. This is important to process, as it can hinder the healing of the parent-child relationship, which may be quite impaired especially if the sexual abuse was perpetrated by the nonoffending parent's partner. In such cases, offenders often deliberately engage in behaviors and lies to disrupt a child's relationship with the parent in order to minimize the likelihood that the child will tell the parent about the abusive interactions.

With support and guidance from the therapist, parents can prepare answers to these questions that will be shared and discussed during trauma-focused conjoint sessions. Children's questions may be guilt provoking for some parents and may reflect children's concrete thinking (e.g., "Why did you make me visit grandpa?" "Where is Daddy now?" "Why did you hire that babysitter when I told you I didn't want you to go out?"). Thus, during individual sessions with parents, it is important to help parents use cognitive coping skills to manage the distressing feelings generated by children's questions, while gaining feelings of mastery as they prepare answers that will be healing and therapeutic for their children. Although it is important for parents to respond as honestly as possible to their children's questions, therapists can help parents respond in ways that will support the healing process. This means parents may need to acknowledge even difficult thoughts and feelings (e.g., "Initially I couldn't believe what you were saying was true, but now I know …"), while simultaneously emphasizing what they have learned about CSA (e.g., grooming and secrecy) that has altered the way they feel and think about the abuse disclosure now (e.g., pride, understanding, love, etc.). Since these discussions can be difficult, it is best to role-play with parents exactly what they would like to say. This provides an opportunity to give feedback to optimize parents' responses to children's challenging questions.

Therapist: *So one question that your child would like to ask you during the conjoint session is why you yelled at him when he told you about Grandpa touching his penis. He continues to wonder if you were and maybe even still are mad at him.*

Parent: *I really wasn't mad—just sort of hysterical. I don't know why he keeps saying that.*

Therapist: *Children do repeat themselves a lot, especially when they are struggling with something they are confused about. That is why patience is one of the most challenging and critical parenting skills. Another reason he may be stuck on this question is because his Grandpa told him you would be mad if he told. So it is actually a good thing that he keeps asking until he is convinced that you are not mad at him.*

Parent: *But I really wasn't mad at him.*

Therapist: *I understand that you weren't mad at him. But do you think you were mad?*

Parent: *I guess, but I was mostly shocked and so upset.*

Therapist: *That makes sense, but his perception of your emotion may not have accurately reflected what you felt inside. Since he perceived your reaction as a mad reaction, he seems to need reassurance of some kind as this is something he continues to worry about. What do you think you could say to him so he feels that you understand how he felt, while also correcting the inaccurate way he continues to think about it?*

Parent: *Well, maybe I could explain that I probably looked really mad because I was so shocked and had so many different emotions at the same time.*

Therapist: *That is terrific because we have talked about mixed emotions. Then, maybe you could share the emotions you had, emphasizing that you weren't angry with him, but you were angry at his grandfather who is responsible for the sexual abuse.*

Parent: *Okay, I can say that without role-playing it.*

Therapist: *I'd feel better and more confident going in to conjoint session if we role-played. I have noticed that you go in more focused and confident when we role-play. Let's give it a shot.*

Parent: *Alright.*

Practice activities assigned

During this component, as parents learn more about the abuse their children experienced they may be inclined to be more lax with discipline out of sympathy. Unfortunately, this can undermine children's progress. Thus, it is important during this phase to encourage parenting skills practice at home. Particular attention should be focused on parents' efforts to follow through on the use of praise, selective attention, effective instructions, and/or the use of positive consequences and negative consequences in relation to children's responses to family rules. It is most important to remind parents that clinical experience and research document that children flourish in family environments in which there is structure and limits imposed in the context of warm nurturing relationships and environments. Thus, it is important for parents to continue to engage in positive, nurturing rituals and follow through with both the positive and negative consequences established for children's behaviors in a predictable way.

By this stage in therapy, it is important to begin to talk to parents about therapy eventually coming to an end. This means that although their children have made significant progress, continued improvement and maintenance of their children's positive behaviors will require parents' continued efforts. Thus, the most significant way parents can contribute to their children's continued healthy adjustment is to model healthy coping behaviors including facing and managing their own feelings about the CSA. In this regard, it is helpful to encourage not only the implementation of effective parenting skills but also to provide support to parents to take care of themselves by making habits of the coping skills and rituals that have worked for them so that they can serve as effective coping skills role models for their children.

CONJOINT SESSION(S)

There again may or may not be time for conjoint sessions during this component. However, when possible it is useful to engage in brief end-of-session positive rituals with parents and children together (e.g., the ritual of exchanging mutual praise and/or reviewing the child's progress in treatment or at home). To reinforce the importance of ongoing attention to positive adaptive behaviors, the therapist may engage the parent and child in a simple positive ritual (e.g., talking briefly about extra-curricular activities) or a brief conjoint session that is designed to acknowledge the child's success in achieving stickers or other incentives related to positive behavior contracts or charts he is completing at home. For youth who have experienced complex trauma, an ongoing focus on practicing the coping skills is very important. Thus, encouraging, reviewing, and practicing such skills with youth and parents together in conjoint sessions is advisable.

12

In Vivo Mastery Component

Initiating the Consolidation and Closure Phase

Following the completion of the trauma narration and processing phase, children move into the final phase of therapy, which focuses on skill consolidation in preparation for the end of treatment. This phase includes three important components: in vivo mastery of overgeneralized trauma reminders, conjoint trauma-focused parent-child sessions, and enhancing safety and future development.

One of the first steps in this phase again involves the informal or formal assessment of progress, as well as identifying remaining behavioral difficulties particularly those that may continue to interfere with day-to-day functioning. Due to their participation in gradual exposure and trauma narration and processing, many children no longer exhibit significant fears and have overcome most trauma-related avoidance behaviors by this stage. Moreover, as a result of parenting efforts, children's psychological difficulties generally show significant reductions by this phase. However, some children may continue to display avoidance behaviors that may be problematic and/or if gone untreated may become problematic due to overgeneralization, potentially interfering with their healthy emotional and social development. For those children, the in vivo mastery of trauma reminders or cues is critical. In collaboration with clients, the therapist typically designs in vivo sessions to help children, often with the support of their caregivers, plan to take steps between sessions to face overgeneralized fears or avoidance of trauma reminders in the external environment (e.g., people, places, and things that are innocuous trauma reminders).

Another important component in this phase involves the implementation of trauma-focused conjoint sessions that focus on encouraging open parent-child communication about child sexual abuse (CSA) and other trauma(s), as well as the child directly sharing the trauma narrative with the parent when clinically appropriate. This component allows for the gradual transfer of the supportive role with regard to CSA from the therapist to the caregiver. As indicated in previous chapters, early brief conjoint sessions may focus on practicing general coping and parenting skills. These later conjoint trauma-focused sessions are important, however, for preparing parents and children to engage in healthy open communication directly about CSA, as well as other sensitive trauma-related issues now and after therapy ends.

The final enhancing safety component encourages the review, practicing, and development of skills that will enhance the child's safety and future development. With children who have experienced CSA, this component not only focuses on personal safety skills training but also often incorporates education with respect to healthy sexuality. Finally, the therapist begins to prepare clients for the end of treatment, focusing on the review and practicing of skills as well as the planning of an end-of-therapy celebration.

IN VIVO MASTERY COMPONENT

When children progress through the trauma narrative and processing component, they often gain confidence and experience less anxiety in day-to-day situations. Indeed, as children demonstrate greater strength with respect to facing their traumatic memories in session, there tends to be a natural diminishing of abuse-related avoidance and fearful behaviors outside of therapy. The therapist may encourage this reduction of avoidance over time by reminding children and their parents that they need not avoid nondangerous abuse reminders at home or in the community (e.g., safe places that remind the child of where the abuse took place; male teachers that remind the child of the offender). It is particularly important to encourage parents to be aware of overprotective tendencies they may have developed since the abuse that may inadvertently reinforce children's overgeneralized fears and avoidant behaviors. The therapist can praise and highlight even small steps toward facing rather than avoiding innocuous abuse-related reminders. In addition, children's development and implementation of coping skills further supports their abilities to face trauma reminders and more general life stressors. Thus, systematic in vivo exposure or mastery interventions may not be necessary for many children who have experienced sexual abuse.

Some abuse-related avoidant behaviors, however, may persist even after the child has completed the trauma narrative and processing work. These problematic avoidant behaviors may disrupt children's achievement of important developmental milestones and may interfere with the child's ability to fully engage in positive social activities. During this phase of therapy, it is therefore important to assess the presence of ongoing abuse-related fears and avoidant behaviors that may interfere with the child's healthy development.

Normative versus problematic fears

The presence of fear and/or avoidant behaviors alone are not necessarily indicative of a need for in vivo exposure interventions. In fact, many fears across childhood and adolescence are highly prevalent and transient in nature. Nighttime fears, for example, are experienced by nearly two thirds of children and adolescents in the general population with concerns about home invasion and/or intruders being the most commonly reported nighttime fear overall (Gordon, King, Gullone, Muris, & Ollendick, 2007). These fears like others tend to diminish over time and are more common in younger rather than older youth (Gordon et al., 2007). It is also helpful for parents to understand the developmental changes typically seen in relation to normative fears in order to reduce parental tendencies to associate such fears with CSA as such associations may lead parents to overattend to and inadvertently reinforce fearful behaviors.

Normative fears in infancy, for example, are typically associated with immediate environmental experiences such as loud noises and loss of support. Possibly as a reflection of their cognitive maturation, children begin to experience normative anticipatory anxieties that include fears of strangers, heights, and separation anxiety as they approach their first birthday (Gullone, 2000). Later during the preschool years, fears of animals, darkness, and being alone typically begin to emerge (Gullone, 2000). When children reach approximately 6 years of age, these earlier fears diminish and children show tendencies to develop fears of the supernatural, as well as fears of criticism and bodily injury (Gullone, 2000). During adolescence, however, the most common fears tend to be more abstract and global including fears of failure, school, social evaluation, and death (Lane & Gullone, 1999). The content and pattern of normative fears change over the course of child and adolescent development in a systematic way that has been repeatedly documented. Moreover, as noted earlier, normative fears are typically transient and diminish over time as children develop and mature. However, parental over-reactions to normative fears due to misplaced concerns that they are associated with the sexual abuse may inadvertently reinforce them leading to exaggerated and more persistent avoidance and/or fearful behaviors. Thus, it is important to evaluate the intensity, duration and disruptive nature of fearful and avoidant behaviors in determining the need for intervention. In some cases, parents may benefit from some basic psycheducation about the prevalence and generally transient nature of normative fears exhibited by their children, whereas other children's fear and avoidance may warrant the development of an in vivo exposure intervention.

It is also important to determine whether abuse-related fears exhibited by clients are truly associated with innocuous stimuli or rather reflect a healthy fear response to a real danger or threat. For example, a child may fear walking to school because he was bullied or assaulted while walking to school. If the juvenile offender resides in the neighborhood and continues to be threatening, an in vivo paradigm would not be appropriate. Instead a safety plan would be the most helpful intervention.

As noted above, in vivo exposure is most often used when avoidant behaviors of innocuous trauma reminders have not naturally diminished in response to the general gradual exposure process, including the trauma narrative development and processing component. Though not all children display ongoing avoidant behaviors that interfere with their functioning, those that do will need preparation for facing abuse reminders in their day-to-day lives. For these children, the therapist can develop an in vivo treatment plan in collaboration with parents and children. Because parental involvement in the implementation of an in vivo treatment plan is critical to success, it is important to present the in vivo treatment rationale and plan to parents first in order to assess and obtain their commitment prior to engaging the child.

Timing

Although in vivo work is often done after processing the trauma narrative, there are some avoidant behaviors that may be best addressed earlier in treatment. In general, the timing of the implementation of in vivo plan should be informed by careful clinical assessments and judgments that are specific to the child's particular circumstances. However, since avoidant behaviors such as school refusal and sleep-related behavior problems have the potential to greatly disrupt day-to-day functioning and become more difficult to treat the longer they are reinforced, therapists should consider introducing in vivo exposure plans for these behaviors earlier in treatment. Indeed in vivo exposure may be the first trauma-focused cognitive-behavioral therapy (TF-CBT) treatment component for some children. More details concerning the implementation of in vivo plans specific to school refusal and problematic sleep behaviors are provided at the end of this chapter. Regardless of when the in vivo exposure work is pursued, the following guidelines should be applicable.

PARENT SESSION(S)

Parents play a critical role in in vivo mastery, especially when the mastery or exposure activities require practice outside of the office. Thus, it is crucial that the therapist work with the parents to enlist their involvement in the in vivo process. In addition, some avoidant behaviors (e.g., school refusal) require the involvement of other caregivers in the child's life, as well as other professionals including teachers, guidance counselors, coaches, etc.

Explain the rationale and process of in vivo mastery

The therapist may offer the parents a rationale for the in vivo process that describes how the child's continued pattern of avoidance unnecessarily constricts the child's life, limiting opportunities for new experiences that offer important learning and socialization opportunities. Furthermore, the therapist can explain that although the avoidance developed naturally in the context of the child's sexual abuse experience, now that those abusive experiences have ended, avoidance of nondangerous reminders of the abuse no longer serves a functional purpose.

The therapist, for example, might explain the treatment rationale by saying the following:

Therapist: *You have done a great job in encouraging your daughter Mary to participate in therapy and process her sexual abuse experience. And she is really doing great with that. But you've also described some situations that she continues to avoid unnecessarily. For example, you mentioned that she still avoids social situations especially going over to her friends' homes to play because her sexual abuse occurred at a friend's house.*

Parent: *Yes, but to be honest, I prefer it that way because I never want anything like this to happen again.*

Therapist: *I understand, and of course she should not go to the home where the offender lives. But there seem to be times that she is missing out on social experiences and having fun with her friends. This kind of avoidance may actually make Mary and you feel safer now, but in the long run if Mary continues to generalize fear of certain social situations, it may interfere with her social development and create more problems for her in the future.*

Parent: *Like what kind of problems?*

Therapist: *If Mary never leaves your side, she may have increasing difficulty participating in typical social activities and school trips, which will just increase her anxiety about these types of things. Eventually social fears can interfere with her interest in something like going away to camp or dating. And it also will have an impact on your ability to have a life of your own.*

Parent: *Well, that does seem to be true. She does seem like she is attached to my hip lately. She used to be a very friendly kid, but maybe that is why this happened.*

Therapist: *Let's do some cognitive coping right now. Do you think all kids who are friendly are sexually abused?*

Parent: *Probably not.*

Therapist: *And do you think you can keep her away from people to such an extent that she will never be at risk of being hurt in anyway?*

Parent: *I guess not. But does she have to sleep over?*

Therapist: *No. Let's start by seeing if we can make a plan that encourages her just to spend more time with friends at her home and then later at their homes.*

Parent: *Okay, but it's not going to be easy—she is not interested in play dates at all. How will we get her to do that?*

Therapist: *We need to develop a plan to help her gradually approach those social situations that make her anxious. It is important that you be involved in this process, as much of this work will be done with your help outside of therapy. Role-plays, in sessions though, will help Mary approach these anxiety-provoking situations in a gradual way using coping skills, so that she doesn't feel overwhelmed.*

Parent: *I have to admit this may be as scary for me as it will be for her.*

Therapist: *I understand that and I will support you and we'll do some cognitive coping together. Also, as part of this process, I will work with Mary on personal safety skills. Though these skills can't prevent sexual abuse from ever happening, they may reduce her risk of such victimization and the skills will help Mary feel more confident in responding to any situations in which she feels uncomfortable.*
Parent: *If you can do all that, I'm up for it too.*

Examine parent-child interactions around avoidant behaviors

After presenting the rationale for in vivo mastery, the therapist can engage parents in the identification of the situations that the child continues to avoid. In discussing those situations, the therapist may engage the parent in conducting a functional analysis to explore what may be motivating and maintaining the problematic avoidance behaviors, as well as examining the thoughts and feelings that may be underlying the parent's reactions to the child's fearful and/or avoidance. Such a detailed review of parent-child interactions associated with the avoidant behavior should help parents examine their responses to the child's avoidance. Often, well-intentioned parents inadvertently reward the child's avoidant behaviors in their desire to spare the child any additional anxiety or distress. The unfortunate outcome of that reinforcement is that the avoidant behaviors are strengthened. Thus, the therapist can help the parents identify inadvertent reinforcement they have been providing for the child's avoidance and consider alternative responses that provide reinforcement for approach or adaptive behaviors.

Encourage parental participation in implementing in vivo plans

After identifying problematic avoidant and/or fearful behaviors and the patterns associated with them, the therapist may begin to collaborate with the parent on the development of an in vivo plan. This often begins with a discussion that leads to the creation of a loose hierarchy of anxiety-provoking situations for the child's in vivo mastery work. The therapist may then coach the parents to provide reinforcement for the child's efforts in each stage of the plan. To continue with the example provided above regarding a child who avoids playing at her friends' homes, the therapist may help the parents to consider whether they have provided inadvertent reinforcement for those avoidant behaviors such as saying, "It is okay if you don't want to go, why don't we find a movie to watch together?" The parents can be encouraged to replace the reinforcement for avoidance with active praise for each effort the child makes in playing with friends. Those efforts might begin with the child having a friend over to play, eventually progressing to having the client and her mother visit at the friend's house. This can be an important step for parents who feel that it is important for them to get to know the family the child is visiting, especially if the abuse occurred when the child was with a family the parents did not know. However, it is important to remind parents that one cannot predict or identify sex offenders by looking at them or even knowing the person well, as sometimes seemingly successful and socially adept individuals engage in sexually abusive behavior toward children in a highly secretive manner. Thus, the best parents can do on behalf of their children is to avoid potentially risky situations (e.g., homes where there are known problems with abuse, violence, drugs, or troubled older teens). More importantly, parents with the support of the therapist may arm their children with knowledge and skills to respond to problematic situations as best as possible. Thus, for this type of avoidant behavior, personal safety skills (as described in Chapter 14) are important to teach prior to encouraging the child to play independently at the friend's house. Although this does not guarantee that the child will avoid any type of harm or victimization, it establishes that both the parent and therapist believe that the child has the needed skills to respond, which is an important confidence builder for all children. Once the necessary skills are practiced and the plan is agreed upon, a gradual approach may be implemented. Thus, for example, the child may be encouraged to play at a specific friend's home for a limited period of time, progressing to longer periods of time at that friend's home, and eventually expanding to playing at other friends' homes. At each step, the parents should praise the child for her increased efforts to play with friends and encourage her to use the coping skills that she has learned in therapy to help in managing anxiety when necessary.

The therapist may encourage skill-building practice exercises that parents and children may engage in together at home. With some parents, a great deal of preparation work must occur in advance to ensure that parents are convinced that the in vivo goals are worthy ones. Parents may inadvertently undermine the in vivo plan due to their own anxiety or ambivalence about the goals. Thus, it is very important to review with parents the thoughts and feelings that may be keeping them from encouraging their children to engage in nonavoidant behaviors. Parents, for example, may be encouraged to use the information they have learned about CSA and their cognitive coping skills to counter thoughts that may lead them to encourage avoidance.

Below is an example of discussion between the therapist and parent in which the therapist initiates a discussion aimed at identifying and examining possible instances in which the parentis inadvertently reinforcing the child's avoidant behaviors due to the parent's own fears and dysfunctional beliefs.

Therapist: *Angel mentioned that since the abuse occurred she hasn't gone on the school bus, even though the driver who sexually abused her is no longer driving the bus.*

Parent: *I can't bear to think that this could happen again. I'd rather just drive her to school.*

Therapist: *Do you intend to do that until she graduates high school?*

Parent: *I hadn't thought about that.*

Therapist: *The reason I ask is because Angel mentioned that she was concerned that she wasn't sure she wanted to go on the upcoming class trip, but it's okay because you wouldn't let her go on a bus anyway.*

Parent: *Well, I didn't say I wouldn't let her go, if she really wants to go.*

Therapist: *I think your daughter is looking to you to help her figure out if it is safe to do things like go on the bus or on school trips. And it seems that she is coming to the conclusion that it is not safe which can lead her to be increasingly fearful and avoidant of many situations.*

Parent: *Well, I don't want that for her.*

Therapist: *So let's look at your interactions with your daughter around this issue of the class trip and maybe we can figure out how it is that she is coming to the conclusion that you would prefer that she doesn't go. Lots of times parents convey things to kids that they really don't intend to.*

Parent: *I guess I may be doing that especially since I am worried about something like this happening again.*

Practice activities assigned

After conducting a functional analysis, the therapist may collaborate with parents in developing skill-building practice activities in which they create opportunities for the child to naturally engage in nonavoidant behaviors that the parent can then praise and/or reward in other ways (e.g., stickers, special activity rewards, etc.). With some families, it can be helpful to carefully develop a behavioral contract that will help guide the implementation of an in vivo mastery plan. In the above example, the therapist guided the parent through cognitive coping exercises that helped her to conclude that in the long run it would be important for her child to gain the confidence to ride on buses again.

CHILD SESSION(S)

Many children will be anxious and sometimes resistant about the possibility of participating in in vivo mastery activities. With very young children such discussions may not be necessary, since the parent will initiate much of the in vivo work at home with the therapist's guidance. However, with older children and teens, it will be important to present a sound rationale for in vivo exposure work. Children avoid anxiety provoking situations because their avoidant behaviors often produce short-term reductions in their anxiety. Of course, those avoidant behaviors typically do not serve the child well in the long term as they restrict the child's life and opportunities for new experiences and growth.

Explain the rationale and process of in vivo exposure

Young children may have difficulty trading the short-term goal of anxiety relief for the long-term goal of increased opportunities for new experiences and development. Children are naturally more interested in the here and now than they are in long-term therapeutic benefits. Thus, it is useful for the therapist to present a sound rationale that is meaningful for the child, linking the exposure work to increased opportunities that would be rewarding for the child now. For example, a child who avoids all contact with unfamiliar men may be missing opportunities to participate in youth sports because she is anxious and avoidant about contact with male coaches. The therapist in that situation might explain the value of facing and overcoming specific fears by engaging the child in Socratic questioning as depicted below.

Therapist: *I can understand that you continue to have some anxiety about meeting men you don't already know based on your experience of being sexually abused. What have you learned that might help you participate in soccer now that the abusive coach is no longer at school?*

Child: *I don't know. A lot of kids did get abused by that coach.*

Therapist: *But that coach is no longer at the school. Do all coaches sexually abuse kids?*

Child: *No I guess not.*

Therapist: *How do you know that?*

Child: *Well, I think you said that most adults don't sexually abuse children.*

Therapist: *That's true. And how else do you know that all coaches do not sexually abuse kids?*

Child: *I guess because I had other coaches that didn't do that.*

Therapist: *Exactly. So the chances are the new coach won't do anything like that. But who could you talk to about anyone (adult or child) who makes you feel uncomfortable at any time?*

Child: *My parents and you I guess.*

Therapist: *Sure, you could talk to your parents and call me even after you are done coming to therapy. Now, remind me why you enjoyed playing soccer before the sexual abuse happened.*

Child: *It was fun to run around and get goals. And it was just fun hanging out with my friends.*

Therapist: *It would be unfortunate for you to miss out on the chance to play soccer and enjoy all of that fun because you still worry about sexual abuse happening. So with the help of your grandmom, I'd like to help you to figure out a way you can overcome these worries and get back to playing soccer.*

Identifying situations that continue to trigger anxiety and/or are avoided

In developing a plan for in vivo mastery, the therapist can begin by working with both the child and the parent to identify situations that the child is avoiding or refusing due to irrational fears. Some fears may be directly linked to the sexual abuse, whereas others may be fears that are typically transient when experienced in childhood, but have become more intense and persistent due to a variety of factors associated with the aftermath of CSA. These factors include the presence of posttraumatic stress symptoms that may have increased the child's susceptibility to overgeneralized and enduring fears and inadvertent reinforcement of fearful behaviors by well intentioned parents as noted in the introduction to this chapter on *determining the need for in vivo mastery.*

As noted above, the therapist may look for behaviors that reflect small steps toward decreased avoidance, offering specific praise and thereby actively shaping nonavoidant behaviors. In this way, the therapist is modeling the importance of recognizing any progress, no matter how small, toward overcoming avoidant tendencies.

In conjunction with the child and the parents, the therapist also attempts to identify day-to-day situations in which the child continues to experience anxiety and subsequently attempts to avoid situations. The therapist, for example, may inquire about possible fears as follows.

Therapist: *You have made so much progress since the start of therapy. You have faced your fears of talking about the sexual abuse, and you even wrote a magnificent book about the abuse. But sometimes when kids have been abused they have other fears. Can you think of anything else that you have started to avoid since the abuse?*

Child: *Not really.*

Therapist: *What about anything that reminds you of the abuse? For example, do you avoid being around people or doing things that remind you of the abuse?*

Child: *Well I don't like taking showers anymore because of what happened in the shower, and I don't like being around boys at all anymore.*

Therapist: *I appreciate you sharing that with me. So let's talk about what would change if you stopped avoiding showers and being around boys.*

The in vivo plan may be developed based on information obtained from the child, the parents, as well as from therapist observations. Examples of common avoidant behaviors that may be addressed by an in vivo plan at this stage of therapy include fears of social situations, showering, darkness, sleeping alone, playing in the basement, participating in sports, after-school activities, playing at friends' homes, and meeting unfamiliar individuals who resemble the offender.

Develop a tentative hierarchy of in vivo mastery steps

In planning for in vivo mastery, the therapist may roughly organize the work into a series of hierarchical steps involving exposure to stimuli that evoke progressively increasing levels of anxiety. For a child who avoids the dark, for example, an in vivo hierarchy of exposure experiences might look like the following:

- 3 minutes of near darkness in the therapist's office (with lights turned off)
- 5 minutes of near darkness in the therapist's office (with lights turned off)
- 5 minutes of near darkness (with just a nightlight) in her bedroom with her mother

- 5 minutes in her bedroom alone with just the nightlight
- 5 minutes in her bedroom alone without the nightlight
- 10 minutes in her bedroom alone without the nightlight
- 15 minutes in her bedroom alone without the nightlight

Clinicians may use their clinical judgment and observations of the child's anxiety to assess whether it would be productive or nonproductive to engage the child in the development of the entire hierarchy. Although some children may benefit from the sense of control gained by assisting in the development of that hierarchy, other children may experience the anticipation of the in vivo exposure steps as highly anxiety provoking. For them it may be preferable to present two choices for taking the next step rather than formulating and presenting the complete hierarchy. Thus, in vivo mastery work may be implemented in a similar manner as gradual exposure in the context of the narrative with choices for each step. With most children, the gradual approach and the child's success in facing each increasingly difficult in vivo exposure step sufficiently prepares the child for the next step. Other children may benefit from the use of active coping skills when preparing to face innocuous trauma reminders.

Review coping methods child has mastered

For some children it may be helpful to pair in vivo exposures with the use of coping skills (e.g., focused breathing, progressive muscle relaxation, affect modulation, and cognitive coping skills) to manage distressing feelings and anxiety-provoking thoughts. At this point, the therapist can review the relevant skills with the child and encourage the child to use those skills when approaching anxiety provoking situations if necessary. However, the most powerful aspect of in vivo exposure will be helping children notice that nothing bad happens when they face their fears.

In cases in which the in vivo plan may increase children's exposure to individuals who pose a risk to their safety (e.g., a teenager who sexually abused the child at school; others who are angry and/or disbelieving of the child's disclosure), it is best to encourage the learning and practicing of personal safety skills prior to implementing the in vivo plan (see "Enhancing Safety and Development," Chapter 14). However, such personal safety skills training should not be presented to parents or children as providing assurance that the child will never experience any kind of victimization again. Instead, the training can be presented as providing greater comfort and confidence that the child will be more skilled in averting and/or telling about abuse, bullying, or other traumatic experiences should they occur.

Begin in-session implementation of in vivo plan

Some in vivo exposure can be conducted in the clinician's office. Using the example of a child who has anxiety and avoidance regarding the dark, the below dialogue describes how an initial in vivo mastery exercise can be conducted in the office.

Therapist: *I understand that you are afraid of the dark, even in places that are really pretty safe. I would like to help you feel more comfortable in the dark as this is important for you to be able to feel safe at night and even in your own bedroom. We're going to start by practicing being in the dark in my office. We've already talked about what a safe place this is and that the darkness doesn't make it unsafe. So we just have to help you get rid of the anxiety that is left over from when you did have a reason to feel afraid of the dark in your bedroom because that is where you were sexually abused. But what caused the abuse in that situation? Was it the darkness?*

Child: *No. I guess not.*

Therapist: *Then what, or maybe I should say who, caused the abuse to happen?*

Child: *My cousin, I guess. She did it in the car where it was light too.*

Therapist: *Exactly. So it isn't anything about darkness that causes abuse. And in order to practice getting comfortable in the dark, I'm going to ask you to turn off the light in this office in a few minutes. While we sit in the dark, we can tell jokes, listen to music, practice focused breathing, or just sit quietly; it is your choice. You might want to choose from the activities we have enjoyed together in session before. After a little while, I will ask you to turn on the light, and we will talk about how you felt and what you were thinking. So tell me, what activity would you like to do together while the light is off?*

Another example is the situation in which an in vivo exposure activity is arranged in session for a child who is anxious and avoidant of meeting unfamiliar men. The therapist might introduce the in vivo work as follows:

> *In order to help you get more comfortable meeting men that are new to you, I've arranged to have one of our doctors, who is a man, drop in to meet us. He works here with me, helping children who have had difficult experiences. I'll call him and he'll stop in for a few minutes to meet you in my office. I'll be here with you as well. Before he comes in, let's do some of the relaxation exercises that you enjoyed doing with your mom in earlier conjoint sessions.*

In that way, the therapist can arrange for a relatively low-level anxiety provoking in vivo exercises in the office.

Plan in vivo exposure implementation between sessions

Although some in vivo work may be done in the office, most in vivo exposure exercises will need to be conducted at home. It is crucial to successfully engage parents and/or other adults (e.g., front line residential staff, teachers, coaches, etc.) in planning and participating in between session exposure exercises, as children often need coaching at home or at school to follow through with such plans.

When planning in vivo exercises, a careful evaluation of the child's level of anxiety and avoidance is necessary. Thus, SUDS scores may be particularly helpful to utilize during these exercises to gauge the child's progress in facing anxiety provoking situations and overcoming fears. The goal of an in vivo exercise is to give the child a success experience in approaching a previously avoided situation. Thus, a careful plan is needed to optimize the likelihood of a successful experience. If the chosen exercise is too anxiety provoking, and the child avoids doing the exercise, the child's pattern of avoidance will be reinforced again by the reduction in his anxiety. Thus, if in doubt as to the child's ability to fully comply with exposure to the anxiety-provoking situation, it would be preferable to step down the hierarchy to a less anxiety-provoking exercise rather than risk the child not being able to successfully complete the exercise. When possible, it can be very helpful to initiate in vivo exposure with therapist guidance in session as described with the darkness example.

CONJOINT SESSION(S)

For some avoidant behaviors such as sleep refusal exhibited by young children, the parent may implement the in vivo plan at home based on plans carefully developed in the individual parent session with no need for conjoint session preparation. Other in vivo plans, particularly with older children, are best planned in collaboration with both parents and children together in both individual and conjoint preparation sessions. See Box 12.1 for an in vivo case example.

While some children may overcome their avoidant behavior in a relatively brief time (e.g., one week), others may require a focus on the gradual in vivo steps to be accomplished each week over the course of several individual and conjoint sessions. Thus, conjoint sessions may vary in length depending on whether they are designed to actually initiate the in vivo plan or to review and encourage further steps in the plan.

Plan in vivo practice steps for between sessions

The focus of conjoint in vivo sessions is on working together with the child and parents in a cooperative manner to review and plan for in vivo exposure steps to be taken between sessions. Based on information collected over the course of the assessment and treatment, the therapist may develop tentative plans for in vivo exercises but be flexible in changing those plans based on feedback from the child and the parents. Again, the goal in planning in vivo steps is to provide the child and parent with success experiences that build confidence and enable the child to continue to engage in increasingly nonavoidant behaviors. Thus, it is preferable to err on the side of encouraging in vivo experiences that the child can

Box 12.1

Case Example: A Teen Who Wore Numerous Layers of Clothes to Sleep as well as to School

A teenager who was sexually abused by her stepfather got into the habit of wearing several layers of clothes to bed in an effort to protect herself from future sexual abuse. In fact, on some occasions this seemed to deter the stepfather's efforts. After the abuse was witnessed by a brother and the stepfather was arrested, the teenager continued to wear several layers of clothes to bed as well as to school. With the help of the therapist, the child and nonoffending parent developed a series of hierarchical steps that would be taken toward the goal of wearing a nightgown or pajamas to bed and just one layer of clothing to school. When the teenager became uncooperative with the in vivo plan, the mother began purchasing nice clothes and nightgowns in an effort to reinforce the daughter for engaging in the planned in vivo steps (i.e., wearing one less layer each day). Unfortunately, the mother provided the clothing items prematurely and the teenager began wearing the new items over other layers of clothing and continued to refuse to cooperate with the original plan. In addition, the mother began resorting to begging and rationalizing with her daughter.

During the session that followed, after conducting a careful functional analysis, the therapist explained to the mother that she was inadvertently reinforcing the avoidant behavior (of wearing all those layers) by giving her daughter lots of attention (in the form of discussing and debating with her daughter) and additional clothes, even though she was continuing to engage in the avoidant behavior. Ultimately, the therapist explained that her daughter would likely give up the layers when she learned by experience (not by her mom telling her) that nothing bad would happen when she wore just one layer of clothing. Since the teenager had not yet participated in narrative development and processing, the therapist suggested that the specific in vivo plan not be the focus of treatment just yet. Though the mother agreed to this plan, between sessions she created just the motivation she thought her daughter needed to discover on her own that nothing bad would happen if she wore fewer layers of clothing. Mother decided to turn up the heat in the home so slowly and gradually that it was not noticeable to her daughter. Without any discussion, the slight adjustment in heat encouraged her daughter to spontaneously wear one less layer of clothing on her own. Each time she wore fewer layers, the mother praised her and pointed out how nice she looked and how nothing bad seemed to happen in school or at night. This creative approach conceived by the mother in this case highlights the most important factor in helping children overcome innocuous fears, which is ultimately discovering that nothing bad happens when the feared situation is faced.

tolerate comfortably, rather than requesting that the child do something that is overwhelming, as this is likely to result in avoidance that is then reinforced by the reduction in anxiety that it produces. Accordingly, it is best not to encourage the in vivo work until it appears that the parent is committed to fully following it, understanding that the child is likely to demonstrate some level of resistance and/or distress.

In some instances, an older child or teen may work closely with the therapist in the individual child session to develop in vivo plans. However, the child may be encouraged to review and present the in vivo plans to the parent in the conjoint session. This provides an opportunity for the child to experience feelings of mastery.

Acknowledge and praise child's nonavoidance and progress

Conjoint parent-child sessions during this component also focus on providing praise for the child's in vivo efforts in session and at home. It is important to remember that parents may have some hesitation to praise fearless behaviors. Thus, it is important to review with parents the importance of engaging in the behavior that they are encouraging in the child while also utilizing specific praise and selective attention to encourage nonavoidant behavior. In addition, it is often useful for parents to prepare and practice offering purely positive, specific praise in conjoint sessions, as this will be critically important to do at home in response to in vivo steps taken. For many families, using a calendar or chart to acknowledge successes in overcoming fears and engaging in nonavoidant behaviors can be helpful. Recording and providing stickers for such behaviors can help parents provide the consistent positive attention and small rewards that reinforce and maintain nonavoidant behaviors.

Engage in end-of-session positive ritual

The therapist in collaboration with the parent may plan an end-of-session positive ritual that can be incorporated into a celebration or acknowledgement of each step the child takes toward facing the feared situations or circumstances delineated in the in vivo plan. The child's progress may be documented on a calendar or chart so that the child can track his progress and look forward to earning stickers or points toward earning a small prize, a special privilege (i.e., later curfew), or a special activity to be enjoyed with the parent.

SLEEP AVOIDANCE AND SCHOOL REFUSAL DIFFICULTIES

As noted earlier, children experiencing PTSD often exhibit avoidance reactions that may generalize to people, places, and things that are associated with the traumatic experience(s) but in and of themselves are not dangerous (e.g., sleeping alone and going to school). Moreover, children's fears may be reinforced as the avoidance behaviors frequently continue to reduce distress. In fact, as children's avoidance becomes more frequent and serious, the associated fears lead to increasingly restricted activities. Thus, it is very important to identify and address children's fears and avoidant behaviors given their potential to interfere with day-to-day functioning as well as healthy social and emotional development.

Two commonly encountered situations that arouse anxiety and often lead to avoidance for children who have been sexually abused include sleeping in their bedrooms alone and attending school. Avoidance associated with sleeping and/or school can be particularly problematic and require thoughtful in vivo exposure plans. In vivo with respect to addressing sleep difficulties can sometimes be delayed until after the narrative and processing components as such problems sometimes spontaneously remit in response to children's progress in treatment. However, school refusal is important to assess and address as early as possible in treatment in order to reduce the negative effects of missing school.

Sleep difficulties

Children who have experienced sexual abuse often experience sleeping difficulties such as bedtime refusal or bedtime stalling, refusing to sleep alone or in the dark, frequent nighttime awakenings, and repetitive nightmares. Dahl (1996) theorized that sleep and vigilance are antithetical (Keller & El-Sheikh, 2011). Children who have been abused may respond with increased vigilance to environmental threats that hinder sleep. Of course, many nonabused children experience sleep difficulties as well. Indeed, researchers report that approximately 25% to 30% of young children experience problems getting to sleep or awakening during the night (Kuhn & Weidinger, 2000; Liu, Liu, Owens, & Kaplan, 2005). Thus, sleep problems exhibited by children who have been abused cannot automatically be attributed to their abuse experiences. However, children with a sexual abuse history are at increased risk for developing ongoing sleep problems. Additionally, parents of children who have been sexually abused may have particular difficulty deciding how to appropriately respond to sleep problems based on their anxiety about how to help the child cope with the abuse experience. Several excellent texts provide guidance and assistance in determining the origin and optimal response to children's sleeping difficulties (Ferber, 2006; Owens & Mindell, 2005).

The first step in addressing these difficulties is to carefully assess the child's sleep problems in terms of nature, duration, and relationship to the sexual abuse. Sexual abuse experiences may be linked with sleep problems in a variety of ways. Children who have been abused often experience a reduction in emotional security or security about family relationships. A reduced sense of security, in turn, has been associated with increased sleep problems (Keller & El-Sheikh, 2011). Increased sleep problems exhibited by a child who has been sexually abused may also be the result of a specific negative association between the abuse and the sleeping situation. For example, a child who was abused in the dark may learn to fear sleeping in the dark. Similarly, a child awakened from sleep by a sexual abuse experience may link the abusive experience with sleep. Even without such a direct association, a child with a sexual abuse history may experience increased anxiety at night regarding concerns about the abuse, such as threats made by the perpetrator. For example, if a perpetrator threatened to harm the child or his family, the child may anxiously ruminate about those thoughts at bedtime when not occupied by other activities. The child may then attempt to avoid the anxiety associated with those thoughts by avoiding sleeping alone.

Many children who experience anxiety at bedtime will develop the habit of sleeping with a nonoffending parent. Some families do not mind having children sleep in their parents' beds, and those shared sleeping arrangements may provide comfort and temporarily reduce the children's anxiety. However, in many instances, having the children share the parents' bed may ultimately create further problems as the children and parents may experience disrupted sleep and children may not develop a healthy and increased comfort with autonomy and independence. If children's anxiety about sleep appears to be the result of a negative association between sleep and abuse-related cues/memories, the association needs to be broken in order to enable children to sleep independently once again.

Helping the avoidant child learn to sleep alone

Over the course of TF-CBT, several components may be useful in helping the child learn to sleep alone without significant anxiety. Initially, the therapist and parents can engage in psychoeducation, relaxation, and affective modulation strategies that can be applied to sleeping difficulties early in treatment. In addition, both the therapist and the parent may engage the child in cognitive coping exercises focused on disputing the anxiety-provoking thoughts. For example, a child who fears sleeping alone may be thinking, "What if it happens again? What if he's coming back to touch me again?" The therapist and the parents can help the child to dispute that thought with a more accurate thought such as, "He's in jail now, he can't hurt me" or "My mom and the police know what happened, and they won't let him near me anymore."

Even when the above strategies are used, some children continue to avoid sleeping alone or in the dark because of the reinforcing benefits of sleeping in their parents' beds. Unfortunately, avoidance of sleeping alone prevents children from learning that their fears are unnecessary. In such cases, children must learn to break through the maladaptive associations between anxiety and sleeping alone by changing their actual sleep experiences and related behaviors. In other words, the child needs to have experiences of sleeping alone without any negative consequences in order to learn and truly believe that he can sleep alone without risk.

In order to break the association between anxiety and sleep, the therapist may encourage the parents to assist the child in a process that combines the principles of behavior management with in vivo exposure (Meltzer, 2010; Taylor &

Box 12.2

Case Example: In vivo mastery for sleep problems

John is a 6-year-old boy who was sexually abused by a neighbor. The neighbor threatened John that if he ever mentioned the abuse to anyone, he would be hurt or even killed. After the abuse began, John started experiencing sleep problems. Because of his strong resistance to going to bed, John's parents began allowing him to sleep in their bed. When they eventually learned of the abuse, they continued the policy, the thinking being that they should provide comfort and support for John. A year later, the perpetrator had been arrested and incarcerated. However, John still refused to sleep alone. His parents were no longer certain how to best respond to this problem.

Upon hearing of this difficulty, the therapist first helped John identify the thoughts underlying his feelings of anxiety. John was able to say quite clearly that he was afraid that the perpetrator would get him if he were alone in his room. In collaboration with John, the therapist identified helpful statements that John could practice saying to himself to replace the anxiety-provoking thoughts he often had at night. With practice, John began to replace the thought, "He'll get me if I'm alone," with the thought, "He's in jail and he can't hurt me again." Although John reported that he felt better when he said that, he still refused to sleep alone.

Subsequently the therapist began working with the parents to formulate a strategy for helping John learn to sleep in his own bed. The therapist explained to the parents that John had to actually fall asleep in his own bed in order to learn that there was nothing to fear from sleeping alone. Although his parents expressed concern about John becoming overly distraught, they were willing to commit to the treatment plan because they had both had been suffering numerous sleepless nights as a result of John's insistence on sleeping with them. They implemented the following plan.

The first night, they explained that they and John would sleep better if they slept in their own beds. They stated that they wanted to help John be a big boy and learn to sleep in his own room, and they were sure he would do a great job. They went on to say that they were so confident of his success that they had bought him a matchbox car (which he loved) that he would receive in the morning if he slept in his bed all night. Then they left the room, saying that they would be back to check on him in a few minutes. As they left, John began crying (as the therapist had predicted), but his parents remained calm and firm and left the room. John's mother, listening carefully, returned a few minutes later when John was briefly quiet, and she praised John for staying in his bed and said she would return in a few more minutes. As she left, John began crying louder; however, after a few minutes, his crying became somewhat quieter. In 10 minutes or so (again, when John was relatively quiet), John's mother returned to praise John for trying to relax in bed. John pleaded with her not to leave. She simply said she was really proud of him for staying in his bed and then she left, saying she would return shortly. Again, John increased his crying as she left and continued to cry during the next 15-minute interval. At the end of that time period, his mother returned again to praise John. John sobbed loudly as she left. After about 10 minutes the sound of his crying diminished until it was no longer audible. When his mother went to check on him after about 20 minutes, John had fallen asleep. The next morning, John's parents praised him extravagantly and proudly presented him with his matchbox car. The same process was followed for the next three nights. Each night John cried for briefer time periods and fell asleep more quickly. Simultaneously, his parents lengthened the time intervals between their return trips to his room. By the end of the fourth night, John fell asleep before his parents returned for the first check-in. The next morning, John's parents made a special celebration surprise at breakfast to acknowledge John's success in sleeping in his own bed all night. They continued to praise him each morning for some time after that and John continued to sleep alone successfully.

---

nightmares which may be associated with normal developmental stressors, if a child experiences frequent, repetitive nightmares, the nightmares may reflect more significant psychological stress or emotional distress. For a child who has a history of sexual abuse, repetitive nightmares may represent the child's unsuccessful efforts to resolve confusing and frightening abuse experiences. When these awakenings occur, it is best for parents to briefly acknowledge the bad dream, gently encourage a return to sleep, and if necessary repeat a brief bedtime ritual (e.g., a song or prayer) to help the child relax and return to sleep. In addition, when children experience repetitive nightmares, it is important to assist the child in confronting and processing the memories and thoughts associated with the abuse experience in a therapeutic setting. However, parents should be warned that children who have been avoiding abuse-related thoughts and memories may initially experience some increase in nightmares and other symptoms when they first begin confronting those memories in therapy. Parents may be warned about the possibility of such mild exacerbations of symptoms so that they are not alarmed if symptoms initially seem to worsen. As children make progress in confronting their abuse related thoughts and memories through the gradual exposure process, it is expected that nightmares will diminish. In addition, it can be helpful to educate children about nightmares so that they can understand that bad dreams often reflect fears and unresolved problems.

Sleep terrors

In other instances, children's nighttime awakenings occur as a result of sleep terrors as opposed to nightmares. Sleep terrors in children, characterized by extended periods of crying, moaning, thrashing, screaming, and even hallucinating in the first few hours of non-REM sleep, are often upsetting to parents as they may understandably be misinterpreted as extreme reactions to the trauma of sexual abuse. These episodes, however, are believed to reflect the normal maturation of a child's sleep stages rather than physical or emotional problems, and they typically remit spontaneously with time. Thus, parents may be encouraged to help children get sufficient sleep by establishing effective bedtime expectations and routines and to carefully supervise the child during such episodes to avoid any inadvertent accidents. Discussions of these sleep terror episodes with a knowledgeable pediatrician can also be quite reassuring to parents.

School refusal

Another area of problematic functioning that may be treated through an in vivo exposure plan is school refusal. It is important that school refusal behavior be addressed as quickly as possible, given the academic and social costs involved in missing school (Beidas, Crawley, Mychailyszyn, Comer, & Kendall, 2010). Addressing school refusal in the context of treatment for CSA is particularly important, given the stigmatizing effects of sexual abuse which can be further compounded by extended periods at home during which children's feelings of shame and aloneness may be reinforced by social isolation.

The first step in responding to a child's school refusal is to assess the etiological and maintaining factors involved in the school refusal behaviors. If the child is experiencing aversive situations at school that are either related or unrelated to the abuse such as bullying, peer rejection, academic challenges, or difficulties with teachers, those problems can be addressed. Other instances of school refusal may be due to oppositional behaviors that developed in response to the abuse. When children ultimately disclose abuse, they often want to maintain control and may do so by engaging in demanding and oppositional behavior. This behavior may develop into school refusal, which is then reinforced by the rewarding consequences children may experience when they avoid school and stay home. For example, children may refuse to attend school initially due to distress associated with the abuse, but they quickly begin to enjoy the added benefits of staying home, which may include watching TV, playing videogames, or spending time with friends or parents (Kearney, 2008a, 2008b). In such cases, it may be useful to develop a contingency contract that provides rewards for school attendance and reduces incentives for nonattendance (Kearney, 2008a). However, in many instances, school refusal reflects a combination of children wanting control and feeling increasingly anxious about returning to school. When this is the case and/or the school refusal is primarily motivated by anxiety, an in vivo exposure plan may be needed.

Among children who have a sexual abuse history and who are exhibiting anxiety-based school refusal, a minority of them may have experienced sexual abuse at school or were abused by an offender who is present at school such as a staff member or older peer. In those instances, the child may have specific learned associations between the experiences of abuse and the school environment that may result in anxiety regarding school attendance. If the offender is no longer present in the school setting, and there is no real physical or psychological danger to the child in that setting, then in vivo exposure to the school environment is likely to be appropriate. However, in less-typical circumstances, if the offender is still present in that setting or if the school community is divided in terms of their beliefs about the allegations, then it may be appropriate to carefully consider with the parents and child whether an alternative school placement would be a more appropriate solution than returning to the original school. More commonly, children who have been sexually abused may resist attending school due to heightened levels of general anxiety subsequent to abuse, even when the abuse was not directly associated with the school setting. It is not unusual for children who exhibit anxiety-based school refusal to also exhibit other manifestations of anxiety as well as depression (Egger, Costello, & Angold, 2003; Kearney & Albano, 2004; McShane, Walter, & Rey, 2001). Children who have a heightened level of anxiety as a result of sexual abuse may seek the comfort and security of staying at home with a nonoffending parent. Though school refusal may begin in an effort to avoid anxiety, it is often maintained by reinforcing consequences. Parents who are attempting to help the child by providing nurturance and attention may inadvertently be reinforcing the child's anxiety and school refusal behavior.

The therapist may introduce the in vivo plan by offering a review of the psychoeducation that has been previously provided regarding anxiety and its somatic components, as well as the cycle of avoidance. Then coping strategies used to manage the somatic symptoms such as relaxation training and focused breathing may be reviewed. Cognitive coping skills may be encouraged to identify and modify cognitions that may be contributing to anxiety about going to school. If the school refusal is associated with specific fears, those fears can be addressed via a variety coping skills exercises (Beidas et al., 2010).

Next a gradual in vivo mastery plan can be developed based on a loose hierarchy of anxiety-provoking stimuli and avoidance patterns (Kearney, 2008a). The therapist may work with the child and the parents to identify the level of anxiety that is associated with various activities pursued during the school day. Those activities can be sequenced in the in vivo hierarchy in order of the potential to evoke increasing levels of anxiety. For example, for a child with a sexual abuse history, it might be that being present for routine classes evokes mild levels of anxiety, but attending physical education class in which the students are required to change clothes provokes greater anxiety. In such a case, the in vivo plan might begin with attendance in typical academic classes, allowing the child to master her anxiety associated with those classes before moving up the hierarchy to attendance in physical education classes. For many children, it may be helpful to begin the in vivo mastery program by planning for the child to attend school for a limited portion of the day and gradually but consistently increase the time spent in attendance each day. For example, a child with severe anxiety might begin in vivo exposure by spending an hour meeting with the school counselor. The next day could include meeting with the counselor and attending one period of classes and gradually extending the period of attendance. It is most important that the child be consistently and progressively exposed to the school context

(Beidas et al., 2010). The child's efforts to participate in the gradual exposure plan by attending school for longer and longer periods of time can be rewarded by parents and teachers. For example, a child might receive stickers or tokens for attendance that can be used toward a larger prize over time. Or, with older children, perhaps they can be rewarded with a special celebration or extra time with friends or watching videos, etc. The child can also be encouraged to offer self-reinforcement as well including encouraging self-talk and praise (Kearney, 2008a).

Significant attention should be given to enlisting the parents' cooperation and participation in the in vivo mastery work. Parents will need to commit to waking up the child, encouraging the child to get ready, and facilitating transportation to school while minimizing their attention and reactions to the child's protests. They can be encouraged to provide lavish verbal praise and reinforcement for any small cooperative efforts the child makes toward attendance. Additionally, it is important that parents be educated about the need to eliminate reinforcement of the school refusal behaviors by making time spent at home during the school day as similar to school as possible (Beidas et al., 2010). The time at home should not include preferred activities such as sleeping late, playing with younger siblings, watching TV, or eating favorite foods. Finally, it is important that the therapist consult with teachers or other school staff members to make the child's attendance at school as positively reinforcing as possible. The therapist may assist by collaborating with the parent and school personnel to create a hierarchy of steps that are likely to lead to successful school experiences. Thus, returning to school when there is a class the child enjoys or a fellow student that the child feels comfortable with can be incorporated into the initial in vivo plan. The use of these cognitive behavioral strategies involving an in vivo exposure plan have been supported across a variety of clinical trials (Barnes, Bauza, & Treiber, 2003; Beidas et al., 2010; Doobay, 2008; Heyne et al., 2002: Kearney, 2008b; King & Bernstein, 2001; King, Tonge, Heyne, & Ollendick, 2000). For additional information and detailed treatment plans for complex cases of school refusal, readers are referred to an excellent treatment guide written by Chris Kearney (2008a).

13

Conjoint Trauma-Focused Sessions

It is important for the trauma-focused cognitive-behavioral therapy (TF-CBT) therapist to assess each family member's progress and readiness in their individual sessions before initiating trauma-focused conjoint sessions, particularly in terms of the child directly sharing the trauma narrative with the parent. By this stage of therapy, many children and parents are well prepared to discuss child sexual abuse (CSA) openly in conjoint trauma-focused sessions. However, it can be considerably more challenging to openly discuss the child's actual CSA experience. Thus, it is important to carefully plan and prepare parents and children for such discussions during their individual sessions. Trauma-focused conjoint sessions continue the gradual exposure process and may begin with a review of educational information about CSA before engaging parents and children in discussions about the child's actual abusive experiences and/or reviewing the child's narrative.

As noted earlier, however, for some families sharing the trauma narrative during conjoint parent-child sessions would not be therapeutic for either the child or parent. For example, if despite multiple individual parent sessions using gradual exposure and processing the parent still sobs uncontrollably when hearing the child's narrative alone with the therapist, it would likely be highly distressing and counter-therapeutic for the child to share the narrative directly with this parent in a conjoint session. Thus, again, it is important for the therapist *not* to emphasize the sharing of the narrative with the parent or child during earlier TF-CBT sessions until it is determined that it would be clinically appropriate. The goal is for parents and children to feel successful in completing therapy regardless of whether or not the child directly shares the narrative with the parent in conjoint trauma-focused sessions.

Outlined below are factors that are important to consider when determining the clinical appropriateness of sharing the child's trauma narrative with the parent in conjoint sessions. It is important to emphasize that whether or not the narrative is reviewed in a conjoint session with the parent and child together, conjoint sessions can provide an opportunity for the parent to serve as a positive role model for the child, particularly in terms of modeling healthy coping and communication skills while simultaneously demonstrating pride in the child's response to treatment overall.

PARENT SESSION(S)

Parents are often children's most important role models, due to both the nature of the parent-child relationship and the amount of time parents spend with their children. However, even the most well-meaning parents may have initially responded to the child's disclosure of sexual abuse in a manner that frightened the child, discouraged further discussion of the abuse, and/or encouraged avoidance of such discussions. The conjoint trauma-focused sessions offer parents an opportunity to respond in more helpful ways, modeling more effective coping strategies for the child. Thus, whether or not the child shares the full narrative directly with the parent during the conjoint sessions, the therapist can carefully plan trauma-focused conjoint sessions to maximize the positive influence of parents. Parents can model several effective coping strategies for the child. For example, parents may teach the child by example how it is possible to discuss CSA and other sensitive issues calmly without avoidance or extreme distress and with a focus on optimistic expectations for the child's future.

Practice assignments review: Coping and parenting

During this final phase of treatment (the consolidation and closure phase), it is increasingly important to check in with parents regarding their efforts to practice the parenting and coping skills at home. As therapy nears its end, it is important to encourage parents to establish routines that will help them to internalize effective coping skills and adopt optimal parenting approaches. When reviewing parents' interactions with their children at home, the therapist may identify, praise, and encourage those parenting changes that are most likely to become routine, thereby fostering the maintenance of children's ongoing positive adjustment.

Assess parents' readiness for trauma-focused conjoint sessions

The determination of when to initiate trauma-focused conjoint sessions depends on the ongoing assessment of both parent and child progress, including their emotional readiness and responsiveness to treatment. This assessment is ongoing but is particularly important during the trauma narration and processing phase of treatment described in previous chapters. It is crucial that the parent be ready, both in terms of emotional state and level of skills, before initiating these trauma-focused conjoint sessions. A parent who is not emotionally ready or is not adequately prepared may inadvertently undermine the child's therapeutic progress. For example, if a child who has been progressing nicely in gradual exposure during individual sessions observes a parent break down and sob dramatically during the initial conjoint session, the child may be discouraged from any further open CSA discussion. Moreover, the child may feel responsible for the parent's extreme distress. Thus, throughout the course of treatment, during individual parent sessions, the therapist should carefully monitor the parent's progress in an attempt to determine parental readiness for openly discussing sexual abuse with the child. Moreover, as described in Chapter 11, the parent should have several opportunities to hear and process the child's narrative alone with the therapist before hearing it in the child's presence. This helps to ensure that the parent has effectively processed personal maladaptive cognitions about the child's CSA and is well prepared to support the child's therapeutic progress.

Some parents may be unable to participate effectively or respond appropriately to their children's narratives during conjoint sessions due to their own psychological distress or emotional instability related to unresolved and severe personal traumatic experiences, such as CSA. In such cases, it may be preferable to forgo directly sharing the child's trauma narrative during conjoint sessions rather than risk highly counterproductive parent-child interactions relating to the abuse. In situations where it appears to be clinically contraindicated to share the child's full trauma narrative, conjoint trauma-focused sessions might include playing a game about CSA in general, having the child share only the final narrative chapter, and/or reviewing some of the questions or concerns the child or parent raised after careful preparation for such a discussion in separate individual sessions. Such conjoint trauma-focused sessions can be highly therapeutic even without the sharing of the full narrative during the conjoint session.

For most parents, however, once it has been determined that the sharing of the narrative in conjoint session with the child would be therapeutic, additional parental preparation for such should be provided. Below are guidelines for preparing parents for the review of the child's narrative during conjoint child-parent sessions. As noted in earlier chapters, prior to engaging in such trauma focused sessions, the therapist should encourage a review of coping strategies that may help parents manage their emotional reactions to hearing the child read the narrative and guidance should be offered to parents about providing effective therapeutic support to the child.

Conjoint trauma-focused sessions may be initiated with a focus on general information about CSA, later moving on to discussing the details of the sexual abuse or reviewing the child's trauma narrative. Fidelity to TF-CBT in terms of the overall model and principles is important. However, the model is designed to be flexible, as TF-CBT sessions should be individually tailored to accommodate the family's clinical circumstances, thereby optimizing outcomes. Thus, the order of the topics to be discussed in conjoint trauma-focused sessions such as CSA education and trauma narrative, as well as personal safety and sex education (see chapter on enhancing safety component to follow) may vary depending on the needs of specific clients in terms of what parents and children are most comfortable with.

Preparing parents for the review of the trauma narrative in conjoint session

In addition to assessing and supporting parents' emotional readiness, it is important to assess and support the parent's ability to take an active and supportive role in these sessions. Typically, this ability will develop concurrently with the emotional readiness just discussed. Parents must move beyond their own emotional response to the abuse to be able to access what they can say that will be most helpful and supportive to the child. As was noted previously, it should be recognized that evidence indicates that parents who have a history of sexual abuse themselves tend to feel more alone when confronted with their child's abuse experience (Deblinger et al., 1993). Thus, therapists working with such parents may want to allow them more time and preparatory work before initiating conjoint trauma-focused sessions. With appropriate preparation and support, these parents, however, can be highly empathic and can serve as excellent therapeutic resources for their children.

Provide parents with rationale for trauma-focused conjoint sessions

The conjoint trauma-focused sessions are important, as they provide an opportunity for the parent and child to learn to communicate openly regarding CSA and/or other trauma(s). It may be explained that it is helpful for parents to participate in such sessions, so the parent and child can practice discussing the abuse in the context of the therapy. Moreover, after therapy ends, these sessions will help parents and children to feel more confident in their abilities to communicate about sexual abuse and related issues when needed far into the future (e.g., abuse reminders in the environment and/or on TV; criminal court proceedings; release of offender from prison). Moreover, the conjoint parent-child sessions allow children to discover that it is okay to share this experience with the parent and reinforces the important belief that others (as modeled by the parent) will continue to admire, respect, and care for them despite knowing about the sexual abuse and/or other traumatic experiences. Also, since children's abuse-related thoughts, feelings, and questions may change over the course of their development, it can be valuable for the child to openly discuss the sexual abuse with the parent rather than just with the therapist.

While CSA is not likely to be a frequent topic of discussion after therapy ends, the trauma-focused conjoint sessions allow parents to demonstrate to their children that they are comfortable discussing sensitive issues and answering or obtaining the answers to difficult questions that may arise as children mature.

Additional key points to emphasize in presenting the rationale for the conjoint trauma-focused session activities to parents are as follows. The conjoint sessions offer the parent an opportunity to serve as a positive role model, demonstrating how to cope effectively with the sexual abuse experience. The sessions can facilitate communication between the parent and the child regarding the sexual abuse and/or other trauma(s), providing an opportunity for the clarification of any points of confusion or misunderstanding. Finally, during conjoint sessions, the parent can assume a more active role in helping the child process the abuse experience, developing patterns that will allow the therapeutic process to continue long after formal therapy is over. Adolescence, for example, is a time when youngsters may have new questions about the sexual abuse as well as sexuality in general. Moreover, these sessions prepare parents and children to communicate openly about abuse-related concerns (e.g., the offender's release from prison) and/or symptom relapses that may occur in the future.

Prepare parents for conjoint trauma-focused session activities

Parents may be introduced to the experience of general conjoint parent-child sessions earlier in treatment, when the therapist initiated such sessions around neutral coping skills practice. By engaging in some skills-based conjoint parent-child sessions early in treatment, the therapist has an opportunity to observe general parent-child interactions providing guidance to parents on communication and parenting skills. In addition, these earlier conjoint sessions help parents and children become comfortable with the idea of participating in conjoint sessions. However, as the time approaches to actually begin conjoint trauma-focused sessions, the therapist should begin some more specific preparatory work with the parent and child. Some parents may need more sessions to prepare, whereas others can begin participation in conjoint trauma-focused sessions with somewhat less practice. However, as noted, it is critical for the therapist to review important CSA education points as well as the child's trauma narrative in individual sessions before reviewing this material in conjoint session with the child.

Prepare the parent for general CSA related discussion with the child

After presenting the above rationales, the therapist should prepare the parent for how to most effectively respond to the child during the conjoint trauma-focused sessions. These conjoint sessions allow parents to practice effective communication skills regarding the CSA experience (e.g., active listening, specific praise) under the tutelage of the therapist. As the trauma-focused conjoint sessions continue and the parents' skills progress, the therapists may assume a more passive role, allowing the parents to take a leadership role in openly discussing CSA and related issues. During this component, parents learn to apply the skills they have learned (e.g., selective attention, reflective listening) in the context of communicating with their child about the sexual abuse and related therapeutic

their highly emotional reactions that they prefer not to have the child read the narrative in conjoint session. In such circumstances, with the parent's support, the therapist may report to the child that the parent read the narrative and was proud of the child's strength and ability to write a book about the sexual abuse. With some of these parents, it may also be possible for the child to read just the final summary chapter to the parent if that would be less emotionally distressing.

Prepare parent to respond to child's narrative via role-plays

It has been the experience of the authors that most parents are emotionally capable of participating in a conjoint session in which children read the narrative aloud to them. However, some parents have particular worries about reviewing and discussing the narrative with the child such as fear that the child is angry with the parent for "allowing" the abuse to occur and/or concerns about becoming tearful during the conjoint sessions. These fears are often best addressed via role-plays in which the therapist plays the child raising the issues about which the parent is most concerned. Role-plays provide parents with opportunities to practice their coping skills and their responses to the child's narrative thereby enhancing their preparedness for the conjoint session. In such role-plays, the therapist may assume the role of the child reading the narrative, while the parent can practice reflective listening by repeating a little bit of what was heard after each chapter the child reads. In fact, it is often helpful to encourage the parent to repeat those sections of the chapter that include language and/or information about which the child is most likely to be concerned. By repeating back some of the more difficult passages, the parent concretely demonstrates comfort, pride, and love for the child despite what the child has shared. In addition, by reflecting back some of what was written, the parent demonstrates that he not only heard the disturbing details, but he is comfortable talking about them. During such role-plays, the parent may also practice sharing specific praise regarding the child's skills and efforts in writing about what happened. This may take the form of having the parent take the time to prepare what he would like to say. For example:

> *I am so impressed with the work you put into drawing the pictures.*
> *I really like how you shared all your feelings about the sexual abuse.*
> *Thank you for sharing with me exactly what happened.*
> *I can see what courage it took to tell, I am so proud of you.*
> *You are a wonderful writer.*

In preparation for this conjoint session, some parents find it helpful to write down what they would like to say to their child. Occasionally, parents will write a letter to express their feelings. Such a letter can be particularly helpful when the parent had an extreme reaction to the child's initial disclosure or when the parent desires to address specific dysfunctional beliefs the child may have developed.

Preparing to answer children's CSA-related questions and concerns

During this component, the therapist may also review and help the parent to answer the child's questions related to the parent's reaction to the child's disclosure and/or any other concerns the child may have. Sometimes the child's experience of disclosing the sexual abuse can be as traumatic as the abuse itself. This can occur if the person to whom the child disclosed had an intense emotional reaction that the child negatively interpreted and/or the disclosure led to violent fights and/or arrests that were shocking or distressing to the child. This is important for the child to process with the parent in conjoint session so that the child can overcome any feelings of self-blame. Once again, preparation is often the key to successful trauma-focused conjoint sessions. Thus, having a parent prepare what he could say to alleviate a child's guilt or concerns about the parent's initial reactions allows the parent to get constructive feedback from the therapist, while also practicing managing emotions in the context of discussing CSA related incidents. For example, a parent's initial instinct might be to explain to the child that he wasn't upset at all when the child disclosed, he was really glad that the child told. If this doesn't reflect what the child observed and described in the narrative, the therapist should point out this discrepancy and help the parent say something that validates the child's feelings and observations, while still alleviating the child's feelings of self-blame. The below dialogue demonstrates how the therapist might coach the parent to come up with something more validating and therapeutic to say to the child about the parent's emotional reaction.

Therapist (playing the role of the child): *Mom, I wanted to know if you were upset with me when I told you about the sexual abuse.*

Parent: *I wasn't upset at all when you told about the sexual abuse, I was really proud of you for telling.*

Therapist: *I think you are on the right track in terms of clearly using the terms sexual abuse to describe what your child told you and I love your expression of pride in your child telling. However, from her observations she thought you were quite upset and children are sometimes more observant and sensitive to parental emotions than we realize. So it's great to say you are so proud of her for telling, but maybe it would be best to acknowledge whatever emotion you recall having, but help her understand that she was not the cause of those emotions, the offender was.*

Parent: *You mean something like . . . when you told me about the abuse, I was really surprised and upset that you went through that. But most of all, I was upset with Uncle Marvin for abusing you. I wasn't upset with you at all. In fact, though I may have not expressed it then, I was really proud of you for telling.*

Therapist: *Exactly. That would be terrific!*

It may be useful for some parents to have them assume the role of the child while the therapist assumes the parent's role and demonstrates alternative means of giving support and answering children's complex questions. Subsequently, as the parent grows more confident, the parent can retain his own role with the therapist playing the role of the child. This allows the parent to gain practice helping the child not only process the questions the child raises in relation to the sexual abuse but also may be of value in preparing the parent to address difficult questions and issues in a validating way as they arise in the future. For other parents, the therapist may from the start assume the role of the child as the parent answers the child's question as in the above dialogue.

Asking nonthreatening, open-ended questions

Another area of communication to rehearse with parents is asking nonthreatening, open-ended questions that might encourage discussion of the sexual abuse. Together the therapist and parent can brainstorm a list of questions. For example, the parent might ask the child additional questions about what she was thinking or feeling when specific episodes of abuse occurred. Or the parent might ask questions regarding specific details, such as what the offender said before or after the abusive interactions occurred. The parent should be cautioned against asking too many questions or questions that the child may interpret as criticism. For example, the parent should be discouraged from asking questions such as "Why didn't you tell me earlier what was happening?" or "Why didn't you scream for help when he touched you?" In fact, it is quite common for parents to wonder why children did not tell them right away. Thus, the therapist might help the parent formulate a related question in a noncritical way.

Therapist: *There are lots of reasons children don't tell about abuse. Many children never ever tell. Please share with your dad, some of the reasons kids never tell about sexual abuse.*

Therapist (playing the role of child): *Some kids are scared that the person who did it will hurt them if they tell. Some kids are just plain embarrassed to tell. And sometimes they think they will get in trouble too because the person who did it told them that!*

Therapist: *Great job Jason. Were any of those the reasons you didn't tell at first?*

Therapist (playing the role of child): *Yeah, well my uncle said we would both go to jail. And I was really scared of him too.*

Therapist: *Dad, what do you think about Jason telling you about the sexual abuse?*

Parent: *I'm so proud that you did tell even though it must have been very scary. So tell us what gave you the courage to tell when you did.*

Therapist (playing the role of child): *I just started to think he must be lying about me going to jail. I was still scared that he'd hurt me, but I just couldn't take it anymore. I wanted the sexual abuse to stop.*

Parent: *Jason, thank you for helping me understand everything by writing the book and explaining about how scary it was. Now I really understand what kept you from telling at first and how much courage it took to tell.*

The therapist may also prepare the parent to discuss any points of confusion or concern related to the parent-child relationship that the child raised during individual sessions. The therapist can then assist the parent in developing a plan of how to respond to the child's specific questions. Examples of these concerns include worry that a parent is unable to cope with hearing about the abuse and/or concern that a parent is angry that the child is responsible for the abuse. Children may also have questions or issues that they want to address with the parent such as feeling angry with the parent for not being aware of or stopping the abuse. Such issues can be addressed effectively in conjoint sessions if the therapist prepares the child and parent during individual sessions. This can be a therapeutic exchange that can help to heal the parent-child relationship that may have been damaged by the abuse and/or the misinformation the child received from the offender. In some cases, a parent may choose to write a letter to the child to express his feelings and optimally address certain issues. In addition, it is particularly important to plan positive end-of-session rituals to encourage positive associations with these important parent-child exchanges.

It is helpful to prepare the parent to take the lead in initiating praise at the end of the conjoint sessions. The parent should be asked to think carefully about how she would like to praise the child after the trauma-focused conjoint activity. During this component, the child demonstrates what she has been learning and doing in therapy, and thus it is a natural time for the parent to offer specific praise to the child relating to therapy progress and accomplishments.

Practice activities assigned: Skills practice and open CSA communication

By this stage of therapy, it helps to discuss the importance of continuing to maintain open communication about the sexual abuse after therapy ends. Parents should continue to practice the coping and parenting skills at home and also may be instructed to take note of sexual abuse or other trauma reminders that occur naturally during the week. When a reminder comes up, it may be useful for the parent to take note of the child's reactions and comment on the reminder in some way. For example, if a news report comes on relating to sexual abuse or other violence, the parent may ask the child what she thinks about the news report and/or what she would want to say to the child affected by the abuse. Most importantly, this is the time to emphasize the importance of maintaining after therapy ends the effective coping and parenting skills caregivers have been practicing. In fact, some therapists and parents work collaboratively to design creative reminders (e.g., refrigerator magnets, family rule signs, inspiring pictures or messages) that reinforce and/or help parents to maintain the new more effective parenting habits developed.

CHILD SESSION(S)

Although over the course of therapy, many children are able to share with the therapist the details of their abusive experiences, those same children may be quite anxious about discussing the CSA and/or other traumatic experiences with parents. Trauma-focused conjoint sessions are therefore designed to help children and parents openly communicate about such experiences. Conjoint trauma-focused sessions lead to further reductions in children's symptoms and concerns. The principles of gradual exposure are followed during these sessions such that children are prepared for and engaged in less anxiety- provoking general discussions of CSA prior to more anxiety-provoking personal CSA discussions and/or sharing of the narrative with parent(s). Furthermore, during these sessions, children are often able to share their questions and concerns, thereby clarifying points of confusion or misunderstandings that may exist between children and their nonoffending parents.

Assess children's readiness for trauma-focused conjoint sessions

The assessment of the child's readiness for conjoint trauma-focused sessions includes an examination of the issues similar to those outlined in the assessment of parental readiness. The therapist may assess the child's progress and responsiveness to gradual exposure throughout treatment. Typically, children should have (1) demonstrated improvement in terms of emotional and behavioral symptoms, (2) discussed the general issue of CSA with the therapist with relatively little distress, and (3) completed the trauma narrative before engaging in trauma-focused discussions and the sharing of the narrative with parents. When children continue to have significant behavioral difficulties and conflict with parents, the therapist may still consider the sharing of the completed trauma narrative with parents, as it may enhance parental compassion for what the child has endured. The therapist who decides to go forward with conjoint sessions in this situation should carefully prepare and collaborate with the parents and child about specific goals and activities that are most likely to encourage positive interactions. In some cases, the child sharing the trauma narrative may help parents to have a greater appreciation for generalized trauma reminders that may at times lead the child to become behaviorally or emotionally dysregulated. However, it is important to emphasize that parents can most effectively assist children in overcoming behavioral difficulties by consistently and effectively implementing the parenting strategies learned regardless of the origin of the behavioral difficulties.

Provide child with rationale for trauma-focused conjoint activities

In the individual child session immediately preceding the trauma-focused conjoint session, the therapist may explain the benefits of generally discussing and sharing what has been learned about CSA with the parent. This focus on discussing sexual abuse in the abstract with parents is an important gradual exposure step toward talking more openly about the child's own experience. Through these abstract CSA information activities, children generally learn that they and their caregivers are more comfortable talking together about the general issue of CSA than was anticipated.

When presenting the rationale for these general CSA discussions with parent(s) to the child, it is important for the therapist to emphasize that the conjoint sessions will provide an opportunity for the parent and child to become closer as they learn about and discuss CSA together. Some children may be proud to share with a parent their knowledge about CSA and/or a general CSA creative product (e.g., drawings or poems about CSA) they have worked on in therapy. Other children may be encouraged to participate with their parents in general CSA discussions by reminding them that the parent(s) has also been attending sessions and learning about CSA and is excited and prepared to participate in the planned educational games or activities. It is best to present two options for general CSA discussion activities rather than asking a yes or no question as to whether the child would like to participate in any single activity with the parent. When presented as a yes or no question, children may be more likely to say "no" as a result of ongoing avoidance and/or concern that such an activity would be upsetting to the parent. Again, it is important to present the planned activity in a positive, self-assured manner emphasizing that the conjoint activity will be worthwhile and even fun.

Prepare child for general trauma-focused conjoint activities

Once it has been determined that the parents' participation in a general discussion of CSA would be beneficial, it may only be necessary to share brief developmentally appropriate introductions and rationales such as the ones below to the child to invite participation in an educational game with the parent.

For younger children, it is best to keep it short and simple. For example:

> *We are going to have your dad join us so that you can show him what you have been learning. In fact, your dad is really excited about playing the What Do You Know? card game so that he can show you how much he has learned about CSA too.*

With older children, it is useful to provide more details about the activities that will occur in conjoint trauma-focused sessions with a similar focus on playing a fun game highlighting the competitive aspects of the game and the opportunity to compete with their parents and perhaps win.

Providing rationale for sharing the trauma narrative

After the child has had a successful experience talking with the parent about CSA in the abstract and/or participating in a game such as the one described above, the therapist may then discuss sharing the trauma narrative with the parent(s) if it has been determined to be clinically appropriate. The therapist may explain that it is important that there not be any remaining secrets that can build walls between the child and parent. Moreover, it can be reassuring to the child to be reminded that the parent has been learning about what happened to the child in individual parent sessions, and thus the parent is highly prepared and/or looking forward to these conjoint sessions. Furthermore, the therapist may emphasize that the parent loves the child and wants to provide support.

If the child has experienced confusion or discomfort in her relationship with parent around the issue of the CSA, the therapist can also identify the conjoint sessions as an opportunity to clarify that confusion. Finally, the therapist may discuss with the child that the conjoint sessions allow the parent and child to become accustomed to discussing difficult issues such as the sexual abuse so they can continue to openly communicate at home on their own about other important issues in the future.

In order to prepare to address children's concerns and questions, the therapist may carefully review the narrative asking children prior to the conjoint parent-child session about instances during or after the abuse when they may have had some questions that could be addressed or clarified by the parent. These questions may be written down for the parent to review prior to a planned conjoint session so that the therapist can assist the parent in preparing therapeutic responses for the child. Many children are given misinformation by the offenders that create tension between the nonoffending parent and the child (e.g., your mom doesn't care about you; your mom would be mad at you if you told, etc.). Thus, the conjoint session during which the child asks the parent clarification questions provides a natural opportunity to correct such misperceptions.

Prepare child for sharing of trauma narrative or other products

After successfully engaging the child in general trauma-focused activities with the parent (e.g., *What Do You Know?* card game Deblinger, Neubauer, et al., 2006), it is important to determine the clinical appropriateness of sharing the narrative in conjoint session, while simultaneously assessing family readiness for such sharing. With some children, it is not in their best interest to share the narrative with their parent(s). With the appropriate consents, these children are sometimes able to share their narrative with another individual such as a staff member at their residential facility or another caregiver. And some children will complete therapy successfully sharing the narrative only with their therapist.

However, in most cases, the child will have created a written narrative and/or another product (e.g., drawings, poems, songs, and/or a final chapter) that reflects her thoughts and feelings about the abuse experience(s) that can be shared with a nonoffending parent or caregiver. In some cases, the therapist may identify parts of the narrative and/or other creative products that may be appropriate to share based on the assessment of both the child and parent.

Regardless of what is being shared, the therapist should prepare the child for the conjoint sessions by collaboratively planning the sessions and/or engaging the child in preparatory role-plays. It is important to note, however, that discussions and/or role-plays about sharing specific trauma-related work should only occur with the child during the session in which there is time to follow through with sharing that particular piece of work with the parent whether it is the narrative or other product (e.g., poem, etc.). Otherwise, the child may experience anticipatory worries about sharing the trauma narrative or related product during the week and may become avoidant and ultimately uncooperative for fear it will upset the parent.

In preparing children to share their trauma-related work, it is important to emphasize that the therapist is confident that the parent is not only fully prepared to hear the narrative, but the parent is proud and excited to review the child's work. Role-plays for those children who feel particularly anxious about how their parents may respond to the narrative can be helpful. Similarly, the therapist may encourage the child to rehearse discussions of any concerning or confusing issues with the parent. Although fairly anxious children may benefit from role-plays devoted to preparing for conjoint sessions, other children may not need such specific preparatory work before initiating the trauma-focused conjoint sessions especially if they are excited to share their narrative and/or other creative products developed in the course of treatment.

CONJOINT SESSION(S)

The goals of the trauma-focused conjoint sessions include encouraging open communication between parents and children regarding general information about sexual abuse and/or other traumas, as well as more personal discussions about sexual abuse or other traumatic experiences. The objectives include further reducing anxiety and avoidance associated with such abuse-related memories and reminders. The number of trauma-focused conjoint sessions varies depending on the clinical circumstances, as well as the length of the narrative. However, each trauma-focused conjoint session generally follows brief (5- to 15-minute) individual preparation sessions with parents and children.

The order of the topics or activities included in trauma-focused conjoint sessions can be determined based on the needs, interests, and comfort level of both children and parents. The initial conjoint sessions, however, should be based on the individual assessment and preparation sessions described above and follow the principles of gradual exposure with the less anxiety provoking activities preceding those that may be associated with more anxiety.

Encourage general CSA discussion

The initial trauma-focused conjoint session should not be overwhelmingly anxiety provoking for either the parent or child. The first of the trauma-focused conjoint sessions may include general CSA related discussions in the form of question and answer games (e.g., *What Do You Know?* card game; Deblinger, Neubauer, et al., 2006), news or talk show role-plays about CSA, and/or the sharing of artistic educational products (i.e., drawings, poems, etc.) about CSA or related trauma(s) created during individual sessions. Engaging in such activities provides a relatively easy way to begin gradual exposure to open CSA discussion in conjoint sessions; it provides some structure for the session, allows the child to share information learned and/or artistic work created and gives the parent an opportunity to provide lots of support and praise for the child's efforts.

Many children and parents seem comfortable discussing CSA in general in the context of a therapeutic game and/or activity. This may be done in a variety of ways including a simple question and answer game format as exemplified by the *What Do You Know?* card game (Deblinger, Neubauer, et al., 2006). This game consists of a series of questions about CSA, physical abuse, as well as exposure to domestic violence. However, blank cards are included for therapists to create questions about other traumas as well. When playing this game it is best to carefully select or create a subset of questions (e.g., 5 to 15 questions) that are appropriate to the child's age and personal experiences including at least some questions that the child is highly likely to address with confidence and accurate responses. The therapist may also select questions about areas of continuing concern to be explored which allows for healthy adaptive responses and ideas to be further reinforced by the parent and therapist.

Another parent-child activity that may be implemented during an initial trauma-focused conjoint session allows the child to assume the role of a law enforcement professional at a news conference reporting on a case of CSA. During this activity the parent and therapist can pretend to be reporters asking questions about CSA in general, as well as about the specific case in the news. Another variation of this activity involves having the child pretend to be an adult sharing the experience of CSA on a talk show. The therapist and/or the parent can then assume the roles of different people who are calling in to the show with questions about CSA and/or for advice regarding their own or their children's sexual abuse experiences. The therapist may write questions in advance outlining the specific concerns of the different individuals calling in for advice. The questions should reflect the CSA information reviewed and/or concerns that have been voiced by the child in therapy. In responding to the concerns, the child demonstrates mastery of CSA information and how effectively she has been able to address the issues in her own life.

These general CSA discussion activities are the springboard for achieving the goal of increased communication regarding the child's personal experiences of sexual abuse. Thus, some references to the child's personal experiences of sexual abuse during such activities are an important part of the gradual exposure process. It is helpful to ask some questions during these games or activities that touch on the more personal details. Gradual exposure during the news or talk show activity, for example, might include a question to the guest survivor about who sexually abused him and what he did, said, or felt in response to the abuse. The questions in the *What Do You Know?* card game (Deblinger, Neubauer, et al., 2006) also lend themselves to personalization such that after answering the question, "How do children feel when they have been sexually abused?" the therapist might ask, "Did you have any of those feelings?" In addition, the parent may prepare comments and ask questions about the child's creative product that might encourage the spontaneous sharing of thoughts and feelings about the sexual abuse. For example, if a teen shared a drawing or poster created about CSA, the parent might be encouraged to ask the teen what she would want other teenagers to learn about CSA if she could create a public service announcement that went along with the artistic images.

Encourage sharing of trauma narrative, when clinically appropriate

In some cases, children are so proud of the trauma narrative they created in individual sessions and parents are so well prepared that it is natural to share the narrative next or immediately following more general CSA discussion or parent-child activities in a conjoint session. In other situations, the prior activities reveal that discussing the sexual abuse experience continues to be highly anxiety provoking and may be contraindicated and/or delayed until the parent and child have achieved some greater comfort by discussing other issues such as sex education or personal safety skills, which are described in the next chapter. In this case, it may be appropriate initially to have the parent and child read the sexual education materials together.

Sharing the narrative can be presented to parents and children as a triumph over the offender's attempts to keep the child silent. The therapist can acknowledge that disclosing the sexual abuse, writing a narrative, and sharing it are heroic acts on the part of the child that defy the offender's attempts to keep the abuse a secret. In addition to providing a positive introduction, the therapist may give the child a choice as to how he would like to share the trauma narrative, thereby helping the child manage his anxiety by choosing the approach that feels most comfortable as well as enhancing the child's feelings of control. For example, the therapist can offer the child the choice of who (the child or the therapist) will read the narrative out loud to the parent. If a child who is not a strong reader chooses to read the narrative, the therapist and child can take turns reading the narrative chapters. Regardless of who reads the narrative, the parent may be encouraged to make eye contact with the child and address reflective listening remarks and praise directly to the child. Below is an example of how the therapist might introduce the reading of the narrative.

Therapist: *Mom is excited to for you to read the book you wrote so she can really understand what you went through including all your thoughts and feelings. Would you like me to read it out loud, or would you like to read it?*

Carmela: *I'll just read it.*

Therapist: *Okay, great. I want you to read loudly and slowly so that we can hear every word. After each chapter, I would like you to take a break so that your mom can reflect on what she heard and ask questions or just offer comments.*

Carmela: *Should I start now?*

Therapist: *Yes. Start by sharing that beautiful title page that you created and then you can read the first chapter.*

Carmela: *Should I read the title?*

Therapist: *Absolutely and the author's name too.*

Carmela: *Sexual Abuse Happened to Me and I'm Okay by Carmela*

Therapist: *What do you think about the title, Mom?*

Mom: *I like it—right away you know what this book is about sexual abuse and that Carmela is okay!*

Therapist: *I agree it is a great title! Carmela, go ahead and read the first chapter for us.*

Carmela: *You ready mom?* (Mom shakes her head yes) *Chapter 1- My name is Carmela. I am 9 years old. I like to play video games. This year I have a pretty cool teacher, but I still don't like school much. I live with my mom and my sister who bugs me. I visit my dad on the weekends. I have a cool family. This book is about sexual abuse. And about other things too.*

Therapist: *Nice job reading that first chapter Carmela. What did you think Mom?*

Mom: *Carmela, I like how you wrote about what you like to do and about your family and that the book is about sexual abuse and other things.*

Carmela: *Thanks Mom. Should I read the next chapter?*

Mom: *Sure.*

Carmela: *Chapter 2—The First Time the Sexual Abuse Happened! This chapter is all about the sexual abuse. Are you sure you want to hear this mom?*

Mom: (after a pause) *Yes, I do want to hear it.*

Carmela: *You sure?*

Therapist: *Carmela, Mom knows a lot about the sexual abuse that happened, and she is proud of you and has been looking forward to hearing what you wrote about it especially your thoughts and feelings.*

Mom: *Yes. I am really proud of you for writing about it Carmela.*

Carmela: *Okay, here goes. I was watching TV. Then the babysitter Joe came. I was glad to see him. I thought we might play video games again. After Mom left Joe said he had some videos he could show me—he said they were really for big girls* *and boys. I said, cool! Then he put on the videos and there were naked people touching each other's private parts. Joe asked me to touch him like that. I was very surprised. I wanted to say no—are you nuts? But the words didn't come out. I felt scared, weird, and sad. He put my hand on his penis and rubbed it up and down until stuff came out. It was sticky stuff. Then he got up and went to the bathroom. When he came out he said I couldn't tell or we'd both get in big trouble. I felt curious, scared, and confused. I was saying to myself, please come home mom.*

Therapist: *I like how you read that nice and slowly Carmela. What do you think Mom?*

Mom: *I think you did a really good job describing how Joe made you rub his penis and how you felt scared, weird, and sad. And I understand why you were thinking, come home soon, Mom.*

Therapist: *I think you really summarized that chapter well, mom. Carmela, let's read chapter 3 now.*

Carmela: *Okay.*

Encourage conjoint processing and correction of distortions

As noted earlier, another focus of the conjoint sessions should be to address any specific points of confusion or concern. Both the parent and child should be prepared in their separate individual sessions to address those issues. The conjoint sessions can be particularly helpful in addressing specific problems within the parent-child relationship. One common issue is the anger some children experience toward the nonoffending parent for not being aware of and/or not stopping the abuse. In order to resolve that anger effectively, children often need to verbalize their feelings as well as the beliefs underlying the anger. For example, a child who is angry at her nonoffending mother may be able to explain that she is angry because, "I told you I didn't want to stay at home alone with Joe, that he wasn't nice to me, but you made me anyway." With further questioning, it may become clear that the child believes her comments should have been adequate to communicate to her mother that she was being abused. It is important that the child's inaccurate belief (that her mother knew about the abuse) be corrected (if this did not occur adequately during the trauma narrative and processing) and that her anger be processed effectively in order to prevent the possibility of long-term difficulties in the mother-child relationship.

The mother may help the child to replace her inaccurate and anger-producing thoughts by describing the mother's thoughts and understanding of the situation at the time the child made the initial disclosure. For example, the mother might explain that she genuinely did not understand what was happening at the time and that she is sorry she was not able to intervene then. Furthermore, the child can be helped to recognize that the mother did intervene to stop the abuse and protect the child once she understood that the child was being abused.

In other cases, the child's perception may be accurate; she did disclose clearly, but the mother failed to respond in an appropriately protective way. In these situations, perhaps the mother was in strong denial because of the possible repercussions of the abuse for her family. During the earlier treatment sessions, hopefully such a parent would have made some headway in regard to coming to terms with what actually happened. But this is not always true. Accordingly, the therapist will have to be careful in determining whether the parent can communicate in a clinically appropriate manner about the abuse with the child during a conjoint session. If indeed the parent has made progress in acknowledging that she did not respond appropriately, the therapist should help her prepare to explain to the child why she responded to the child's disclosure as she did and to apologize for failing to protect the child. For example, the mother might explain:

> *Samantha, I'm so sorry. I know you told me that John was hurting your bottom, and I should have really listened and helped you. I just couldn't believe that I could have married a man who would abuse my daughter. It was easier for me to believe that it was an accident or that you were confused about what happened. I made a mistake, a big mistake, but I understand now and I want to do whatever I can to help you get through this.*

The statement above by the mother is just the beginning of a more extended conversation that can help to heal the relationship. The case example in Box 13.1 illustrates how conjoint parent-child sessions might be used to effectively clarify and process a point of confusion or concern in the parent-child relationship.

As demonstrated above, the processing of the sexual abuse continues throughout the conjoint sessions by helping children to both resolve remaining questions and integrate what has been learned into their understanding and beliefs about the impact of the CSA on themselves, their families, their relationships with others, and their future. With the support of their therapist and parent(s), older children and teens are encouraged to view the abusive experiences in the context of many life experiences from which they can learn and grow. In fact, some teens that have experienced complex or multiple traumas create trauma/life narratives and/or timelines that incorporate the CSA as well as other trauma(s). It can be beneficial for the therapist and/or parent to assist teens in incorporating positive events into such narratives or timelines, particularly including instances in which others supported them. This is important given that research suggests that children's resilience is positively influenced by supportive relationships with others, as well as knowledge of successful family experiences in overcoming adversities (Duke et al., 2008). Finally, lessons learned and positive expectations for the future are often highlighted in the child's last narrative chapter that is reviewed with parent(s) during these conjoint sessions, thereby reinforcing the consolidation of traumatic memories in the context of hopeful expectations for the future.

Box 13.1

Case Example

A 16-year-old teenager believed that her mother was probably angry at her because the offender, a popular teacher in school, repeatedly told her that her mother (a teacher at the same school) would be mad at her because the teen "seduced" him. Although the therapist attempted to deal with this erroneous belief through cognitive coping skills, the girl seemed to need reassurance from her mother that in fact she is not angry with her daughter. After spending part of the conjoint session engaged in gradual exposure exercises, the therapist encourages the daughter, Tracey, to raise this issue. The mother has been prepared through prior role-plays with the therapist to effectively respond to her daughter's concern.

Therapist: *Tracey, I think there was something else we agreed that you would talk about with your mother tonight.*

Tracey: *Do you mean now? Do I have to?*

Therapist: *I think that the only way for you to feel okay about all of this is to discuss it. You know your mom really wants to help you, but she can't if you don't share your worries with her.*

Mother: *Tracey, I hope you can talk to me about whatever is bothering you. I'd really like to help.*

Tracey: *I guess I was just wondering if you were mad at me. I mean, I know you said you weren't. But Mr. B said that I started everything by wearing short shorts and skirts to school and stuff; he said that I made him do it. And he said that if you knew that I seduced him like that, you'd be really mad at me.*

Mother: *You know I am not mad at you.*

Tracey: *But he told me that you would be mad because he would lose his job and you would too. So that part is true.*

Mother: *Oh, Tracey, I'm not mad at you and I didn't lose my job, I quit my job because I will feeling very low myself.*

Tracey: (silence, head down)

Therapist: *Tracey, it is okay to share with mom how you thought she felt when she quit.*

Tracey: (long pause) *When you first quit your job, you seemed really mad and you wouldn't talk to me about it. And I know you didn't want to quit and you were crying a lot. And I never saw you cry before.*

Mother: *You know Tracey, I tried my best to hide my feelings, but I didn't do a very good job of that and now I'm glad because as we both learned it is better to share your feelings when you are going through something very hard.*

Tracey: *I guess that is why we came here.*

Mother: *That is exactly why. I needed someone to talk to about all this and so did you.*

Tracey: *But I still think that you had to quit your job because of me and now we don't have much money and it's hard to find a job. I thought maybe he was right—you think I seduced him and this whole mess is my fault.*

Mother: *Well, I was very upset, but really because there were other teachers and staff at school that didn't seem to understand and you know it was hard when others didn't initially believe that Mr. B could sexually abuse a student.*

Therapist: *Mom, what did you hear Tracey say about what she thought you were feeling after you quit your job?*

Mother: *Tracey, you are right you saw me feeling mad and sad and scared all at the same time. Because I didn't know how I could stay at that school and still support you and your brothers. But I was upset about how the school handled it and what Mr. B did. It was very confusing for me and eventually I felt I couldn't stay there and I wanted to do everything I could to help you.*

Therapist: *Tracey, can you share with your mom how you were feeling when mom quit and maybe how you are feeling now?*

Tracey: *When you first quit, you seemed so mad and you were not talking to me at all, so I felt really alone. Now, I feel less alone, but I still worry that you blame me for losing your job.*

Mother: *I don't know what to say.* (Mom tearing up)

Therapist: *Mom, maybe first if you could reflect what you heard Tracey share.*

Mother: *Tracey, it seems like when I quit my job, I wasn't talking to you about all of that and you thought I was mad at you and you felt really alone.*

Therapist: *Did Mom hear you correctly?*

Tracey: *Yeah. Are you still mad?*

Mother: *I'm still mad at Mr. B, but I'm not mad at you. I understand that no matter what you wore or did, it is against the law for a teacher to do what he did to you. And it makes me angry that he made you even think that any of this could be your fault. Nothing that happened was your fault.*

Therapist: *Your mom is exactly right nothing that happened is your fault Tracey. A teacher should not respond in a sexual manner no matter what his student does even if she dances naked in front of him. Do you understand that Tracey?*

Tracey: *I think so.*

Mother: *And Tracey, I'm glad I quit my job—it led to getting us help. I love teaching and one day I'll do it again.*

Tracey: (Begins crying) *You are really not mad at me?*

Mother: (Embraces Tracey) *No, honey, I'm not mad at you at all. I'm so glad that you were able to tell me what you were worried about.* (Mother starts to cry) *Oh dear, I didn't want to cry.*

Therapist: *Sometimes crying is a good thing. It can make us feel much better. Is the crying helping both of you feel better?*

Mother: *I know I feel better and I'm proud of how we are coping with this together.*

Tracey: *Me too.*

Practice activities encouraged: Open communication about CSA or related issues

Once the family is in the final phase of therapy, it is an appropriate time to begin to explore how they might continue to maintain open lines of communication about CSA and/or other related issues after therapy ends. The therapist, in fact, may provide parents with a handout that may spark ideas about how they might encourage such open communication at home.

Engage in end-of-session positive ritual

Given the intense emotions sometimes associated with trauma-focused conjoint sessions, it is particularly valuable to plan end-of-session positive rituals. It should be noted, however, that the sharing of the narrative sometimes leads to emotions that are quite positive, thereby setting the stage for a therapeutic exchange of specific and global praise. As has been noted, however, this exercise tends to go most smoothly if parents and children prepare what they want to say in advance especially in relation to remarks about the sharing of the narrative and/or the experience of coping with the sexual abuse and/or other trauma(s) together.

CONJOINT TRAUMA-FOCUSED SESSIONS WITH SIBLINGS

In a number of different types of situations, it is helpful to include siblings in some of the conjoint sessions. Sessions involving siblings are particularly important if the siblings were victims of the abuse, the siblings were aware of the abuse as it was ongoing, or the siblings have been significantly affected by the identified client's abusive experience in some way. When deciding whether or not to include siblings in conjoint sessions, the therapist should carefully assess the purpose(s) of such work. Also, including siblings in conjoint sessions should not occur if the child who has been abused is opposed to this idea. One common goal is to improve communication and increase understanding of the sexual abuse experience among all family members. For example, younger siblings are sometimes not told why the perpetrator, who was a family member, had to leave the home. The therapist may help the parent and the child who directly experienced CSA decide how to share that information with the sibling. The authors believe that in most cases, it is best to be as honest as possible and for siblings to be informed of the basic information about the sexual abuse. It is not necessary nor appropriate to give siblings many explicit details of what happened during the sexual abuse. Moreover, providing such information could compromise the confidentiality and privacy that rightfully belongs to the client and which has facilitated her participating and disclosing in treatment. However, it will be important to provide some general education about sexual abuse to siblings. By fostering open communication among all family members, the therapist can help the family to lift the veil of secrecy that was created within the family by the abuse. In families in which multiple siblings were abused, the siblings may never communicate clearly with each other about their experience without some therapeutic intervention.

Another reason to include siblings is to correct misconceptions or misunderstandings the siblings may have. For example, if a father who is the perpetrator has left the home, siblings who were not abused may blame the child who was abused for somehow making Daddy so angry that he left. In an attempt to avoid long-term conflict between the siblings, it is important to clarify what actually precipitated the father leaving the home. In other situations, the nonabused siblings sometimes feel inappropriately guilty about the abuse because they failed to protect the sibling, they failed to stop the abuse, or because they were not abused themselves. Again, those siblings need to be educated about the dynamics of sexual abuse and the reality of this particular situation in order to alleviate their feelings of guilt. Therapists should be aware, though, that siblings may not readily believe that a parent figure has abused their brother or sister, particularly if they now have limited or no contact with this parent because of the abuse allegations.

Whenever siblings are included, the therapist should be clear that the siblings' participation in the conjoint sessions will not substitute for their participation in individual therapy themselves. Thus, a sibling who is experiencing significant distress should see a therapist individually. Oftentimes, therapist availability and practical matters dictate whether siblings are seen by the same or different therapists. Depending on the clinical circumstances, siblings can have successful therapy experiences when seen by the same or different therapists as long as each child has individual time with the therapist and private conjoint time with a parent or caregiver. When siblings are receiving TF-CBT from different therapists, conjoint family sessions that include siblings, however, should be carefully coordinated between therapists. Additionally, each therapist needs to determine whether conjoint family sessions would be in the best interests of each of the children.

The preparation for conjoint sessions including siblings would be essentially the same as the preparation for the above described conjoint parent-child sessions. After deciding on the specific topics to be addressed, the identified client and the parent may prepare and/or participate in role-plays with the therapist designed to increase their skills and their comfort level in discussions with the sibling.

The exact contents of the conjoint sessions involving siblings will vary from case to case. Of course, in cases in which siblings are unaware of the abuse, the therapist should carefully plan a session in which the parent shares that information with the sibling (without the client's involvement) with the therapist's support and guidance. Many parents require careful practice and preparation for this session especially if they have attempted to spare the sibling pain by making up stories about the offender's whereabouts. Next, conjoint or family sessions can be used effectively to practice skills to enhance the sibling relationships (e.g., relaxation and affective expression and regulation skills) and address problems that have arisen as a consequence of the abusive experience.

The TF-CBT therapist might also engage the family in a psychoeducational discussion or game regarding CSA in general. This often creates a more relaxed atmosphere in which children and parents get comfortable with the language needed to discuss what has occurred in the family. In fact, it has been the experience of the authors that playing an educational game with the entire family can alleviate a great deal of tension. When several children in the same family participate together in the *What Do You Know?* card game (Deblinger, Neubauer, et al., 2006), for example, they often like to create teams and compete for points. In fact, some families have enjoyed having the parent(s) compete against the kids and they have chosen team names (e.g., kid power, parents unite, sisters strong, team awesome, etc.) that are empowering. The therapist then plays the role of the game host in charge of asking the questions and keeping close track of the score. This competitive therapeutic game often leads to enthusiastic responses and laughter, creating positive associations with abuse reminders that previously triggered only negative emotions.

Once the family has demonstrated some comfort in discussing sexual abuse in general, the focus can then turn to discussing their personal experiences associated with CSA and/or other traumatic experiences that occurred. When clinically appropriate, given the extreme secrecy often associated with CSA, it can be healing for the therapist to help families to create a sense of open family communication about CSA and its impact of the child and other family members. Most parents and children prepare to discuss at least some basic information about the CSA with siblings.

Sometimes children inquire about sharing their narratives with siblings. It is important to acknowledge to both parents and children that such desires often reflect feelings of increased strength and the shedding of any shame associated with the abuse. However, in most cases, it is best to avoid disrupting the integrity of the therapy relationship and risking that a sibling might share something in the narrative with other children potentially embarrassing the client. However, in some situations, the therapist may be responsive to such requests by suggesting that siblings engage in a structured general discussion about the abusive experiences and/or the sharing of information from the child's final chapter(s) that might be of therapeutic value. As always, it is important to carefully collaborate and review with the parent whatever might be shared with siblings so the parent can be fully prepared for the questions and concerns that siblings may raise.

14

Enhancing Safety and Future Development

The final therapeutic component for children and their caregivers focuses on the provision of education and skills that will support the child's future development, including sex education, personal safety skills training, and/or other additional skills training specific to the needs of the child and family. Again, at this stage of treatment, it is important to help parents and children consolidate all the skills they have learned. Thus, for example, some children may benefit from additional training with respect to problem solving with skills practice activities focused on issues that may be particularly relevant to their individual circumstances. Practice activities, for example, might be designed to help clients integrate the use of relaxation, affect expression/modulation, cognitive coping, and problem-solving skills to manage conflicts and avoid violence. Educational handouts that may be used during this component are available in Appendix B, as well as through the websites listed in the appendix.

Education about the names of private parts and other basic facts about healthy sexuality may have been provided earlier in the child's treatment depending on the age of the child. However, during this component, it is important to integrate more comprehensive sex education that is developmentally appropriate and consistent with parents' values and views. This education enhances the safety of children by reducing their risk of premature sexual involvement, teen pregnancy, and exposure to sexually transmitted infections (STIs; Handelsman, Cabral, & Weisfeld, 1987; Kastner, 1984; Kirby, Laris, & Rolleri, 2007; Kohler, Manhart, & Lafferty, 2008). Moreover, sex education will help children to appreciate that sexual experiences can be positive and healthy in the context of loving, respectful relationships. This is important because it has been found that survivors of child sexual abuse (CSA) may develop sexual dysfunctions and/or problematic sexual behaviors (Deblinger et al., 1989; Finkelhor et al., 1989; Lacelle, Hébert, Lavoie, Vitaro, & Tremblay, 2012). The findings of recent research, however, suggests that the development of such adaptive coping strategies and optimism about the future may reduce CSA survivors' risk of developing negative sexual self-concepts and/or high-risk sexual behaviors (Lacelle et al., 2012). The earlier components of trauma-focused cognitive-behavioral therapy (TF-CBT) directly support the development of such adaptive coping skills and optimism and the focus in this component on providing education about healthy sexual behavior and interactions may also reduce children's risk of sexual problems. Providing information about sex in an educational and positive manner in individual sessions with the child and later in conjoint parent-child sessions will help children learn to associate sexuality with positive emotions, as opposed to the negative or confusing emotions that were experienced at the time of the abuse. The issue of sexuality is important to discuss with all clients impacted by CSA including LGBTQ (lesbian, gay, bisexual, transgender, questioning) youth. Valuable guides and tools for working sensitively to address sexual abuse and sexuality issues with this population are available through the National Children Traumatic Stress Network website (www.nctsn.org). In general, encouraging positive feelings help children and adolescents who have been sexually abused feel more comfortable with their sexuality, while also feeling more optimistic about the potential for positive sexual interactions with others in the future.

Personal safety information and skill building is also provided during this component. Children initially learn body safety skills with the therapist individually and later practice them with parents in conjoint parent-child sessions. The development of effective body safety skills is essential for children who have been sexually abused given they have an increased risk of re-victimization during adolescence and adulthood as compared to children without a history of abuse (Finkelhor, Asdigian, & Dziuba-Leatherman, 1995; Finkelhor et al., 1989; Widom, Czaja, & Dutton, 2008). Research findings suggest that behavior rehearsal, role-plays, and skills practice in session and at home are important to incorporate, as these methods have been associated with increased knowledge, retention, and potential use of these important skills to avert re-victimization experiences (Deblinger, Thakkar-Kolar, Berry, & Schroeder, 2010; Finkelhor et al., 1995; Wurtele, Marrs, & Miller-Perrin, 1987). The involvement of the parent in practicing personal safety skills is particularly important given the recent research documenting that children are more likely to disclose sexual abuse experiences to their mothers as opposed to other adults (Malloy et al., 2013). During the enhancing safety sessions, the therapist continues to reference the sexual abuse by highlighting the strength and courage the child had in discussing and processing the abuse experience(s). Finally, during this component, the therapist assesses the child's and parent's progress and preparedness for ending treatment and, when appropriate, the planning of an end of therapy celebration is encouraged.

PARENT SESSION(S)

The therapist may introduce this component by reviewing and linking the child's treatment progress to the strengths the child demonstrated, as well as the crucial support the parent provided during the trauma-focused conjoint sessions.

Constructive feedback can also be provided by the therapist in the form of compliment sandwiches if parental reactions were less than optimal during the conjoint sessions. In the context of this final treatment component, it is important to (1) assess the parents' attitudes and values with respect to sexual issues and personal boundaries, (2) obtain parental permission to provide sex education information and/or share selected sex education books with the child, (3) collaborate with parents on the presentation and practicing of personal safety skills, and (4) prepare parents for conjoint session work with regard to sex education and safety issues. These steps are important given the divergent views parents have regarding sex education and personal boundaries. The importance of involving parents in the personal safety skills training is underscored by research suggesting that such involvement enhances children's retention and/or use of personal safety skills (Finkelhor et al., 1995; Wurtele, Kast, & Melzer, 1992).

Practice assignment review

The objective of skill-building practice review during the final stage of therapy is to reinforce positive rituals and routines that parents have developed which will support their ongoing efforts to use these skills after therapy ends. By this stage, it is hoped that many skills have become new habits that are reinforced by the positive results they are producing. In addition, if parents were asked to review any books or materials relevant to sex education and/or personal safety, feedback and reactions to those materials may be elicited prior to engaging the child in this work.

Provide rationale for age-appropriate sex education

Given the serious and widespread prevalence of adolescent pregnancy and STIs among youth, sex education appears to be critical for all children. In fact, research has documented that sex education may help to reduce the likelihood of children facing these difficulties as adolescents and young adults. Moreover, research seems to contradict parents' concerns that the provision of sex education will increase teenagers' interest in having sex. Rather it appears that knowledgeable children are less likely to engage in sex, particularly risky sexual behaviors (Handelsman et al., 1987; Kastner, 1984).

The above rationales for including sex education in treatment can be elicited from the parents through Socratic questioning, (e.g., "Why do you think sex education would be particularly important for a child who has experienced sexual abuse?") or provided by the therapist depending on how parents answer the aforementioned question. The therapist may praise parents for their insights as to why sex education might be important for the child. However, many parents are unsure about the appropriateness or necessity of providing sex education, thus it is important to offer clear rationales explaining the particular importance of sex education for children who have experienced sexual abuse. For example, first it may be suggested that it is critical for children to receive accurate sex education to correct any misconceptions they may have developed concerning sex as a result of their abusive experiences. It may be noted for parents that the child unfortunately has had an abusive sexual experience, which may predispose her to experience greater anxiety, confusion, or dissatisfaction around sexual issues (Cohen, 1995; Finkelhor et al., 1989). Thus, positive discussions and education concerning healthy expressions of adult sexuality are important in countering that negative experience. Second, sex education may help to reduce children's vulnerability to further abuse, premature sexual activity, and/or adult sexual difficulties. Third, sex education reinforces the gradual exposure process for children who have been anxious about discussions of any sexual issues because those discussions spark memories of the abusive experience. In the context of a safe therapeutic environment, children will learn that they can, in fact, think about and talk about sex in a positive way that will not precipitate painful, overwhelming emotions. Finally, through discussions of sex education, adults can model for children how sexual issues can be discussed calmly and positively without excessive embarrassment or shame. Children who have effective models to imitate may be much better prepared to manage sexual matters as they face them in adolescence and adulthood and may be more able to discuss sexual issues with their parents as well as in their relationships as adults.

Whenever possible, parents may be involved in providing sex education in conjunction with the therapist during the conjoint parent-child sessions. However, the therapist first may introduce the topic to parents and children individually to prepare them for successful conjoint sessions. Preparation for and practicing discussions of sexual issues during individual sessions and later in conjoint session will provide parents and children with the skills and comfort level to be able to continue to discuss sex education–related issues after therapy ends. This is important because it is preferable for the "sex talk" to occur on more than one occasion so that it becomes an ongoing conversation as children develop and mature and are capable of understanding more complex information about sex. By providing sex education, parents not only give the child needed information regarding sexuality but they are also demonstrating that they are able and willing to communicate about sexual issues. This is critically important given the high degree of exposure children have to sexual images and messages (e.g., media, internet) and the powerful impact of peer pressure. Having the capacity to talk openly about sexuality should serve clients and parents well, particularly during preadolescent, adolescent, and young adult years when youth are often faced with these complex issues and pressures.

The dialogue in Box 14.1 illustrates how a therapist might talk with a hesitant parent about the rationale for providing sex education.

BOX 14.1

Case Example: Rationale for Sex Education

Therapist: *I'd like to talk about sex education today. Sex education can be important for all children but may be particularly important for children who have experienced sexual abuse. How would you feel about our discussing this today?*

Mother: *I think Sally will get sex education in school. Do you think she will need to learn more than she will learn there?*

Therapist: *Unfortunately, Sally has already received some inappropriate and inaccurate information about sexuality as a result of her sexually abusive experiences. So it is important to correct that misinformation and help her to develop a positive view of healthy adult sexuality.*

Mother: *I'm not sure. She seems pretty young to me. I don't want to put any ideas into her head.*

Therapist: *Because of her experience of sexual abuse, we won't be putting thoughts of sex into her head, we'll just be providing her with more accurate information and helping to sort out any misunderstandings she has. It would be appropriate for her to get some sex education even if she hadn't been sexually abused. But she is an 11-year-old now, and that really isn't too young to learn accurate information about sexuality.*

Mother: *But if we talk to her about sex, won't that make her want to go ahead and do it?*

Therapist: *There is no evidence that sex education has that kind of effect. In fact, research suggests that children who receive sex education are more likely to delay having sex, and if they do have sex they are more likely to engage in safe-sex practices if they are educated.*

Mother: *I don't want her to think it is okay to have safe sex at 11 years old just because Tom did that with her.*

Therapist: *I understand, and we can address those concerns. In our conjoint session, it will be important to not only begin to share sex education but it will also be a time to discuss the values that you want to teach Sally. We don't want to give her educational information alone. We want to combine that sex education with information about your values as well.*

Mother: *I feel really nervous and uncomfortable I guess because I never talk about these kinds of things, and my mother didn't teach me about sex. In fact, I don't think I really understood much about sex until I got pregnant, and then I learned a lot very quickly.*

Therapist: *Well, actually girls who don't know a lot about sex are more likely to get pregnant when they are young. I could certainly take the lead in presenting some of the information. In fact, I thought we could play a question-and-answer game using a sex education book I have and see what your daughter already knows. I'll give you the book so you can read it if you like before we review the questions and answers with your daughter so you will feel comfortable with it.*

Mother: *That sounds good. I would love it if you would help me with this. I don't know where to begin.*

Therapist: *I'm glad to do that.*

Explore parents' feelings about providing sex education

Parents often initially feel uncomfortable and ill-prepared to talk to their children about sex, despite their understanding of the importance of doing so. As a result, some parents seek to avoid the subject completely. After presenting the above rationale, the next step in preparing parents to participate in providing sex education to their children is to help them acknowledge and sort through their feelings about discussing sexual issues with children. The therapist might begin that work by asking parents to recall any sex education they received as a child from their parents. Parents may be asked how they felt as a child at that time. If parents express dissatisfaction with the sex education that was provided to them, the therapist can brainstorm with the parent more effective means of providing the child with sex education. Subsequently, parents may be asked how they feel now when contemplating providing sex education to their children.

When working with parents who acknowledge anxiety or other distress when anticipating providing sex education, the therapist might explain the issues as follows:

> ***Therapist:*** *It is very important to deal with your own discomfort regarding sex and sexuality in order to provide the most effective sex education to your child. Children are highly sensitive to gestures, facial expressions, and, most importantly, what you don't say. If you avoid talking about sexual issues, you may inadvertently convey that sex is secretive, wrong, or something that one should be ashamed of. Moreover, you may unintentionally discourage your child's questions about sex. Let's begin to examine the thoughts that are underlying your feelings of anxiety.*

Then the therapist can lead the parent in cognitive coping exercises designed to dispute or replace dysfunctional thoughts underlying the parent's distress regarding sex education. It is important for the therapist to be prepared to respond to parental concerns and distressing thoughts about providing sex education. Some common misconceptions were noted above including the ideas that (1) sex education will lead to promiscuity, (2) sex education will be perceived by children as condoning sex, and (3) sex education is something that only liberal parents provide because their children are out of control. After eliciting any concerns the parent has, it is useful to use Socratic questions to help reflect on the evidence that contradicts such concerns or misconceptions. In addition, it often calms parental fears to emphasize the fact that only information that is developmentally appropriate and responsive to the child's current needs will be provided to the child.

It should be emphasized that although the therapist will try to help a parent understand the importance of sex education, it is ultimately the parent's choice as to whether this will occur. In particular, some parents with strong religious or cultural values may be opposed to sex education for their children, even in the context of therapy. In these instances, the therapist could suggest some books or other resources that the parents could use if they decide to do any sex education with their child on their own.

Collaborate with parents in presenting sex education

Both the topics discussed, as well as the manner in which they are discussed, can be adjusted to the child's developmental level. For example, young children do not need highly technical explanations of conception or sexual functioning. However, simple and accurate explanations for the differences between girls and boys and where babies come from can be offered to children as young as 3 years of age. In addition, when young children have experienced age-inappropriate sexual interactions, it can be helpful for them to understand when and with whom those behaviors are appropriate. Parents often need help in conveying this information to their young children and appreciate the support provided by the therapist. Parents whose children have been sexually abused often need special encouragement to accept certain sexual behaviors as normal and respond to them naturally (see Chapter 16). A natural and appropriate time to talk with young children about sexual behaviors is when parents observe them engaging in behaviors such as touching their genitals. Parents may want to acknowledge to their children that this may feel good and it is okay to do, but it is something they should only do in private. When sexual behaviors are adultlike or problematic because they persist and/or are repetitive, a therapeutic focus on these behaviors may be required as outlined in the chapter on sexual difficulties (see Chapter 16).

Preadolescents are often most interested in information regarding pubertal changes. The therapist and/or parent(s) may provide information about these changes for both sexes so that children understand what will be happening not only to their own bodies but also to the bodies of their opposite sex peers. This age group may also be developing sexual feelings and learning about sex in school and/or from friends but they may still benefit from opportunities to discuss these complex issues on a more personal level with a parent or therapist.

Adolescents may also appreciate information concerning pubertal changes, as well as information about sexual desires and feelings, dating relationships, sexual activity, and birth control. Parents may be surprised to know that several studies suggest that adolescents prefer to receive this information from parents as opposed to teachers or peers (Alexander & Jorgensen, 1983; Handelsman et al., 1987). Some parents may hesitate to provide this sort of information to their children for fear that they may inadvertently encourage premature sexual activity. Open parent-child communication about sexuality does not appear to be associated with either increased or decreased adolescent sexual activity. However, among sexually active adolescents, those who communicate openly with parents are more likely to use contraception, thereby decreasing their risk of experiencing unintentional pregnancy and/or contracting STIs (Handelsman et al., 1987; Kastner, 1984).

Parents may be informed, however, that some children who have experienced CSA may be uncomfortable receiving sex education. Since sex education is critical for children with a history of sexual abuse, it is important for the therapist and parent to work together to help the child overcome any avoidance or distress associated with discussions and/or references to sex. Thus, during the individual parent session, the therapist and parents may work together to formulate a plan to present the sex education material in a gradual and less anxiety-provoking way. The therapist can engage the parent and child in playful activities in which they compete with one another in creating various sex education lists. One such activity involves encouraging the parent and adolescent to separately list as many sexual acts and/or nicknames for private parts as they can in 30 seconds. These types of activities are excellent "ice breakers" and often reveal what youngsters already know about sex. Moreover, such activities can provide a bridge for offering additional educational information (see providing sex education in child session below for more details).

In summary, the type and amount of sex education that is provided depends on the child's age and maturity, the information the child already has from peers and/or from the sexual abuse experience, and the parent's level of comfort. Again, prior to engaging the child in sex education, it is important to share and discuss with parents the information, activities, and specific books that may be presented to the child in both individual and conjoint sessions. Basic sex education may include simply the names and functions of private parts, the differences between boys and girls, information regarding how babies are conceived and delivered, and/or more advanced information about sexuality and related issues.

Guidelines for parents for providing sex education

When the parent is comfortable with the idea of providing sex education to the child, the therapist might offer the following general guidelines for providing sex education on an ongoing basis. This information may be reviewed in session, and it is designed to increase the likelihood that parents will comfortably participate and continue to communicate openly with their children about sex and related issues at home and after therapy ends.

Approach sex education in a positive manner

Too often, parents and educators approach the topic of sexuality in a very serious manner. This tone may communicate that this is a grim topic and one that is difficult and perhaps unpleasant to discuss. Such a presentation will likely serve to discourage further conversations regarding sexuality. Furthermore, discussing sexuality in an overly serious manner may reinforce children's perception of sexuality as a negative, anxiety-laden experience similar to their abusive experiences. Thus, parents are encouraged to discuss healthy adult sexuality in a positive tone. It is appropriate to describe sexual activity as a pleasant, loving, joyful, and/or playful activity that feels good within the context of the right relationship. The "right" relationship (e.g., in terms of age and marital status) may be defined by parents based on their values and attitudes. Often children will giggle with embarrassment when presented with sexual information. Such laughter should not be viewed negatively. Instead, parents may want to laugh as well, sharing in children's humor regarding the information being provided.

Don't wait for questions

There is a widespread but inaccurate belief that children will ask questions when they are ready to learn about sexuality. That belief may hold true for some children who have no anxiety or discomfort in discussing sexual issues. However, many important questions go unasked by children. This is particularly true among children who have experienced CSA and/or who perceive that their parents are uncomfortable or embarrassed with the discussion of sexual issues. Thus, it is best for parents to be proactive and take the initiative in providing sex education and creating a family atmosphere of openness in which questions and discussion regarding sex and sexuality are encouraged.

Be a good listener

Effectively providing sex education to children involves listening as well as teaching. Indeed, children are unlikely to be responsive to lecturing. Sex education may be more effectively provided through interactive discussions. Children as well as parents sometimes have difficulty talking about sex and sexuality. Thus, parents may need to listen carefully in order to identify specific areas of underlying concerns for their children. For example, if a child seems particularly anxious or avoidant of a specific topic (e.g., pregnancy, AIDS), the parent might consider whether that issue is particularly troubling to the child for some reason. Children who have experienced sexual abuse sometimes harbor unexpressed fears regarding their possible exposure to HIV and/or STIs. The therapist and/or parents can elicit and address such fears during these sex education discussions by encouraging children to ask lots of questions and reminding them that there are no "crazy" or "stupid" questions. Parents can also be reminded that they need not know all the answers as there are many resources available (e.g., books, websites, professionals, etc.) that provide the answers to even the most complex questions.

Use available sex education materials

There are some wonderful books listed in the Appendix C that can assist with these sex education conversations in the context of therapy and after therapy ends. These materials can help to increase and improve parents' knowledge base, reduce their anxiety and discomfort, and provide structure for both the in-session and at-home discussions with their children. *Where Did I Come From?* (Mayle, 1995) is a humorous book for young children that describes how babies are conceived and delivered. *Asking About Sex & Growing Up (revised edition): A Question-and-Answer Book for Kids* (Cole, 2009) and *Teen to Teen: Plain Talk from Teens about Sex, Self-Esteem, and Everything in Between* (Gold, Horwitz, Greene,

Taleb, & Hatcher, 2008) are informational books for preadolescents and adolescents respectively that cover topics such as puberty, conception, masturbation, contraceptive methods, and homosexuality. Each of these books have sections organized with questions and answers that create an easy and natural structure for a conjoint parent-child session and/or discussions in session and/or at home. *How to Talk with Your Child About Sexuality* (Planned Parenthood, 1986) and *The Sex-Wise Parent: The Parent's Guide to Protecting Your Child, Strengthening Your Family, and Talking to Kids about Sex, Abuse, and Bullying* (Rosenzweig, 2012) are excellent resources to support parents' efforts to talk with their children and adolescents about sex and other related topics as well.

Encourage parents to continue sex education after therapy ends

Parents can be prepared to continue the sex education process at home during the final stages of therapy by asking them to continue to read an age appropriate book or other materials with the child at home. In addition, the therapist can establish that these conversations are designed to set the stage for ongoing open parent-child communication regarding sexual matters. In fact, by starting this conversation now, it will be easier to discuss other more complex sexual issues that will be important to discuss as the child matures. Parents may also be encouraged to take advantage of natural opportunities to continue the sex education process. For example, the therapist can advise parents of preschool children to continue to encourage the use of the doctor's names for private parts by using those terms at bath time as they help their children learn to wash all the parts of their bodies including their private parts. Parents may also have opportunities to teach children basic information about where babies come from when a family member or friend is pregnant. General information about puberty and menstruation may be provided when children begin to notice changes in the bodies of older siblings, cousins, and friends and/or ask questions about puberty related issues such as menstrual pads or tampons found in a family bathroom. Family television viewing also often provides opportunities to discuss issues related to dating and sex. These are great opportunities for parents to explore children's developing views with open-ended questions and lots of reflective listening as opposed to lectures.

Prepare in advance to address challenging sexual issues

Therapists may help parents feel prepared to deal with difficult sexual questions and/or behaviors during therapy, as well as naturally, gradually, and incidentally over the course of the child's development. As was mentioned previously, the therapist may model for the parent initially how to effectively present sex education material. After the parent becomes more comfortable, the therapist may assume the role of the child or teen. In that role, the therapist may ask the parent increasingly challenging questions that may come up (e.g., "How do babies get inside the mommy?" "When did you first have sex?"). In this way, the parent becomes more comfortable discussing sexual topics and has the opportunity to think through responses to more difficult questions in advance with the support of the therapist.

Parents may also be reminded that children do not necessarily need answers on demand, and it is reasonable for parents to praise children for asking questions while indicating that certain questions they prefer not to answer and/or need to obtain additional information or books to ensure they provide the correct answers.

Another potentially difficult situation may arise if a child engages in sexual exploratory behavior. The therapist may help the parent formulate appropriate immediate responses to those situations and then have the parent role-play those responses if the parent is concerned about that possibility. However, there is no reason to assume that because a child has been sexually abused that he will abuse another child. The vast majority of those who are sexually abused as children do not abuse others. Moreover, the therapist may point to the child's responsiveness to treatment as further evidence that the likelihood of such difficulties is low. More information to assist in evaluating the nature of child sexual behaviors and the need for professional assistance is provided in Chapter 16.

It is important to acknowledge that it is impossible to anticipate every sexual question or scenario. Rather, parents may share potential concerns (e.g., a teenager's possible sexual relationship with a peer) and may practice a general response approach that sets a calm, open, and positive tone for future parent-child interactions around complex sexual issues. Moreover, it is important for the therapist to establish, when possible, that the therapist and/or the agency will remain available in the future for guidance and support even after therapy ends.

Prepare parents for providing personal safety training to child

Children who experience ongoing symptoms of PTSD may overreact to innocuous cues in their environment because of their prior associations with abuse and may underreact to real danger as a result of ongoing avoidant and/or dissociative symptoms. Thus, parents should be reminded that their commitment to their child's treatment and recovery may be the most important step they can take to enhancing their child's safety and success in responding to potential dangers in the future. However, the therapist can also involve the parent in providing training to the child regarding personal safety skills to further reduce the child's risk of revictimization. This training may be incorporated into education regarding sexuality as the child learns to distinguish between healthy appropriate sexuality and sexual abuse. Skill building with respect to body safety may be initiated with the child in individual sessions but may also be presented to parents and practiced in conjoint sessions. Thus, it is good not only to help children practice responding to potential victimization threats but also to practice telling someone they trust like the participating parent about the threats or abusive experiences. The therapist should be particularly careful to prepare the parent for training that focuses specifically on how the child might respond to inappropriate behaviors on the part of an offender with whom the child may have future contact. Such contact may occur in cases of familial sexual abuse as well as when the offender is a juvenile who attends the same school as the child.

Personal safety skills training in the context of TF-CBT is designed to help children identify and respond effectively to inappropriate sexual touches or threats of any kind of violence or abuse. However, it is important to note for parents that personal safety skills cannot be assumed to offer absolute protection from CSA or other violence. Indeed, regardless of children's skills, some offenders may overcome children's resistance through a variety of positive (e.g., gifts) and negative (e.g., verbal threats) inducements. Most importantly, a potential offender is completely responsible for any inappropriate sexual behavior toward a child, and this is true regardless of any personal safety education that the child has received. In spite of the fact that teaching children personal safety skills does not guarantee the prevention of sexual abuse, there is some evidence that when victimized or threatened, children who have received this type of training are more likely to use self-protection strategies and to disclose the victimization attempt (Finkelhor et al., 1995). In addition, these skills may enhance children's feelings of mastery and confidence in facing many types of threatening situations in the future.

As noted earlier, this education might be included at a number of different points in therapy but is most often implemented during the final phase of treatment. For children remaining in high-risk situations as sometimes can be found in cases of sibling abuse and/or complex trauma, personal safety skills can be included fairly early in treatment. However, because of the possibility of increasing a child's feelings of guilt, for most children it is preferable to postpone the teaching of personal safety skills until after the trauma narrative component has given them the opportunity to fully acknowledge what they did and did not do in response to the actual abuse. When personal safety skills are discussed too early, children may feel a need to distort what really happened in order to appear as if they used the personal safety skills. Thus, with most children and adolescents, this education is provided toward the end of TF-CBT in both individual and conjoint parent-child sessions. Even when provided at this stage, parents should be reminded that whatever the child did do at the time of the abuse was best because it kept her safe and allowed her to tell and receive the support and therapy that she is benefiting from now. The therapist should also emphasize that when parents (as opposed to just professionals) are actively involved in encouraging their children to learn and practice these skills, research findings suggest that children appear to retain and use the skills more effectively in response to victimization attempts (Finkelhor et al., 1995; Wurtele et al., 1992). Thus, parents are encouraged to participate in conjoint personal safety skills sessions and review this education with the child at home, using books and/or other resources suggested by the therapist (see personal safety books Appendix C). Many tools are available to assist in providing body safety education to children at a developmentally appropriate level. These include story books, coloring books, DVDs, games, puppets, and dolls. In addition, empirical research suggests that children retain these skills best when shaping, repetition, and, most importantly, behavior rehearsal are used to teach them (Wurtele et al., 1987; Wurtele, Saslawsky, Miller-Perrin, Marrs, & Britcher, 1986). Thus, the child session below outlines the important points to cover with children and suggests helpful role-play exercises to be utilized during these sessions.

As noted earlier, many children who present for counseling with a history of sexual abuse have also been exposed to other traumas. Therapists, therefore, may engage both parents and children in educational activities about other types of violence endured, as well as the potential for danger in various circumstances. Parents may also be engaged in the development of a safety plan that may be introduced to children in conjoint session to identify practical steps that youth can take (e.g., getting down on the floor if there is gunfire heard; getting away from the fighting as opposed to getting in the middle of it in families in which domestic violence has occurred) and specific individuals (i.e., agreed upon neighbors and/or call 911) that children can contact for help when danger is perceived. Though the development of a safety plan (see therapist form in Appendix F) and the practicing of effective response skills do not guarantee safety, these steps can greatly enhance children's feelings of confidence and calm. Role-plays in which children practice leaving dangerous situations and/or calling 911 (on a disconnected phone), while speaking clearly and providing the needed information can go a long way in preparing children to take such steps if necessary. Similarly, children who have endured bullying may also be encouraged to review and practice assertive communication skills in the context of realistic role-play scenarios drawn from children's actual experiences (see conjoint session preparation below).

Practice activities assigned: Skill-building review

Therapists may lend parents an age-appropriate book about healthy sexuality and/or personal safety to read with the child between sessions. This can reinforce the importance of parents taking on this educational role that is particularly important in this final phase of therapy. Parents may also be asked to practice supporting and providing praise to their children in response to personal safety or assertive communication skills that children are encouraged to practice at home.

Review information and role-plays to be shared in conjoint session

To demonstrate respect for their views and to ensure their support, the therapist should review with parents the basic sex education concepts and personal safety skills that will be shared and practiced with the child or adolescent. The following concepts and topics may be briefly outlined: appropriate language for private parts; body ownership; "okay", "not okay", and confusing touches; the difference between secrets and surprises; assertive behavior; and strategies for getting away, disclosing or telling about threats and abuse until someone stops the abuse and helps. Briefly reviewing the above concepts or having parents read a handout or book about personal safety is important given that parents are often actively encouraged to participate in open discussions and/or skill building activities in conjoint sessions and at home. In fact, it can be useful to review in individual parent sessions the specific information and/or the scenarios that the therapist would like to role-play during the conjoint parent-child sessions. See the therapist forms appendix (Appendix F) for some examples of role-play scenarios that parents may review and practice in individual parent session in order to be fully prepared for a successful conjoint session related to this treatment component. In addition, the therapist may remind parents that conjoint sessions regarding sex education and/or personal safety can be anxiety provoking for children, potentially leading to awkward, silly, and/or oppositional behavior. Parents are therefore encouraged to focus on the child's cooperative behavior using selective attention, as well as specific praise to encourage their cooperation. As always, the therapist may encourage parents to be prepared to engage in a brief end-of-session positive ritual (e.g., mutual exchange of specific and/or global praise) to positively reinforce positive behaviors exhibited by the child during the prior week and/or in session as well as offering general acknowledgement of their pride in the child's treatment progress.

Discuss and prepare parent for future challenges related to the abuse

It is also important to discuss with parents any individualized personal safety skills training one might do with the child. For example, when working with children who may have contact with the offender again, it is critical to prepare the child with personal safety skills training specifically focused on potential scenarios that may occur with that person. As noted earlier, the possibility of further contact between the offender and the child is greatest when the offender is a family member and/or attends the same school as the child. It is important to discuss with parents the plans and expectations for how such contact may be handled. The therapist should remind parents that even after receiving treatment, individuals who have sexually abused children remain at risk for reoffending. Thus, it is best for the child not to have any unsupervised contact with an adult offender at any time. It is also preferable to minimize unsupervised contact when the offender is a sibling or other peer. However, this may be less realistic and thus these role-plays are particularly critical in preparing a child who will have ongoing contact with a sibling or a peer in school, for example, who abused him. With these children, personal safety skills training and role-plays may be reviewed with the parents with a plan to engage the child in training and behavior rehearsals that are highly individualized to their circumstances.

In general, parent sessions during this final component continue to be geared toward reviewing the skills children are learning so that parents can support their implementation at home. Moreover, the child's development and maintenance of assertiveness, personal safety and other skills (e.g., problem solving) are enhanced when parents not only reinforce these skills when observed in their children but model the skills themselves. Parents, for example, may be encouraged to be aware of the importance of modeling assertiveness as opposed to passive and/or overly aggressive responses when managing daily conflicts and/or stressors.

CHILD SESSION(S)

By this phase of therapy, it is important to acknowledge the child's responsiveness to treatment and carefully review the plans for the final therapy sessions. It is also important to highlight the benefits of graduating from therapy in the near future. Planning for a positive end to therapy is particularly helpful for children who have experienced a great deal of loss, as the end of therapy may spark feelings associated with prior losses. Although some sex education (e.g., names of private parts) and safety concepts may have been reviewed during earlier components, education about healthy sexuality and personal safety should be expanded upon and continued with a more in-depth focus and role-play exercises during this component. In addition, this is the time to identify any additional skill building that may be particularly helpful given the child's particular therapeutic needs and circumstances and may serve to further integrate prior skills learned (e.g., see problem solving and assertiveness skills training section below).

Provide age-appropriate sex education

Most if not all children who have experienced sexual abuse would benefit from sex education that helps them view sexuality in a positive context. Thus, after obtaining the parent's support, the therapist may utilize an age appropriate sex education book such as one of those listed in Appendix C to begin this process. By this stage of therapy, it is likely that the doctors' names for private parts will have been discussed and utilized by the child in the context of her narrative. However, it is important to continue to reinforce the use of the doctor's terms for private parts at this time. The therapist therefore should model and praise the use of clear and accurate terms for both male and female genitalia, as this will encourage children's use of these terms after therapy ends. As noted earlier, youth who have a history of CSA are at risk for re-victimization; thus, being able to communicate clearly about private parts and possible sexual threats or abusive experiences is critical. When young children use slang terms or nicknames such as "kit kat, hot dog, or pocket book" to refer to their genitalia, adults may not understand them when they attempt to communicate about their private parts and/or disclose abuse-related threats or experiences in the future.

Young children can be taught the doctor's names for private parts using real or paper dolls that are wearing swimsuits to cover their private areas. When teaching young children about more complex aspects of sexuality, it is important to determine the degree of inappropriate sexual knowledge to which the child has been exposed. For example, some children have knowledge of sexual intercourse as a result of the abuse, and it is therefore important to provide sex education about intercourse that presents this sexual act in the context of a healthy adult relationship. For these children, there are several books listed in Appendix C that provide this type of information. *Where Did I Come From?* by Peter Mayle (1995), which was written for children aged 7 years and older, can be particularly helpful in this regard because it provides considerable detail about male and female reproductive systems, intercourse, and orgasm, but the information is presented in a positive manner that incorporates humor. For young children who have had limited exposure to invasive sexual acts but display poor personal boundaries, *Personal Space Camp* by Julia Cook (2007) is a valuable therapeutic book that teaches children about personal space, boundaries, and keeping their hands to themselves.

Again, it is important for children and adolescents who have experienced sexual abuse to experience positive emotions in relation to sex-related matters to counter the negative emotional associations that may have developed as a result of the abuse. With older children, engaging in educational games in the context of discussing healthy sexuality can similarly create more positive associations with healthy sexuality. A simple exercise that can help encourage adolescents to talk openly about sex involves encouraging them to write a list of as many sexual acts as they can, using the appropriate terminology and/or slang terms if necessary within a specified time frame (e.g., 45 to 60 seconds). As noted earlier, sometimes adolescents may be motivated to participate in this activity by suggesting that their parents will be asked to do the same to see who can come up with the longest list. Oftentimes, parents and/or adolescents state that they would not use certain terms because they are "nasty" or "sound bad." This allows the clinician to encourage them to use the proper terminology. In addition, these lists often stimulate discussions and questions in conjoint session that can help parents and children break the ice in terms of talking about healthy sexuality. For example, when adolescents neglect to list affectionate acts such as holding hands, hugging, looking into one another's eyes, and kissing, the therapist can attempt to elicit such behaviors, thereby encouraging a discussion that highlights the loving and sensual nature of these interactions as well.

When children and adolescents have been sexually abused, their perception of healthy relationships may also be skewed. As such, it is important to include education about healthy relationships particularly when working with adolescents. This is especially important when working with adolescents in statutory rape cases or cases where they may have viewed the adult perpetrator as a partner or boyfriend. Similarly, discussions of healthy relationships may be particularly crucial in situations in which a preadolescent or adolescent boy is sexually abused by an adult female, such as a teacher or an aunt. Society and contemporary media often gives boys messages suggesting that sexual encounters with older females are to be admired and that boys who are sexually active at early ages are particularly virile and masculine. Thus, it is not surprising that boys who are abused by older females may be particularly confused about whether the sexually abusive relationship was inappropriate. Given that likely confusion, it is critical to facilitate thoughtful discussions about the characteristics of healthy relationships and personal qualities that would be desired in a friend or partner. In addition, it is important to explore and incorporate the values that parents want to impart regarding relationships and sexuality. Some books that can be valuable in beginning to address sexuality issues with teens are also provided in the resource list in Appendix C.

Creating a dating timeline

The therapist can help adolescents create an optimal timeline that demonstrates how they would most like to see a romantic relationship progress and at what point in the relationship and/or in their lives important milestones would occur. These milestones can include education and career advances, as well as relationship milestones in an effort to help teens think broadly about the desires they have for the future. Relationship milestones might include flirting, holding hands, hugging, first date, first kiss, establishing their relationship status on Facebook, introducing "boyfriend/girlfriend" to family and/or friends, sexual touching over and under clothes, engagement, marriage, oral-genital contact, sexual intercourse, and having children.

In cases in which the adolescent viewed the sexually abusive interactions as consensual, such an idealized timeline can be introduced after the trauma narrative is complete. By engaging in this exercise separate and apart from discussions relating to the offender, the teenager may be able to enjoy imagining the optimal scenario. Often without much prompting, teens will make their own comparisons to the narrative recently completed, thus helping them to recognize that the development of the abusive relationship (that they viewed as consensual) deviated considerably from their preferred or ideal dating timeline without forcefully pointing that out (see Chapter 16 to follow on sexual behaviors).

With all adolescents, it can be valuable to engage in a discussion regarding the characteristics of a healthy relationship with an intimate partner and whether or not the adolescent would disclose the sexual abuse to this partner (which is an excellent assessment of the adolescent's current level of shame associated with the abuse). *The Teen Relationship Workbook* (Moles, 2001), as well as other books listed in Appendix C can be helpful in generating a discussion about intimate relationships that provides the clinician with opportunities to provide additional education about healthy relationships and potential signs of controlling and/or potentially abusive relationships. Another technique involves having the adolescent describe the qualities that he would want in an "ideal partner." Subsequently, this list of characteristics can be compared to those of a current or past partner (or the offender in cases where the abuse was viewed as consensual) to help adolescents determine themselves whether they are making good choices when choosing intimate partners.

Provide personal safety skills education

Personal safety skills are also critical to teach, review, and practice at this stage of therapy first in individual session with the child and then in conjoint session with parents and children together. Below are important concepts to review with children and adolescents either in the context of a game such as the *What Do You Know?* card game (Deblinger, Neubauer, et al., 2006), when reading a personal safety skills book together (see resource list in Appendix C), and/or through discussions and/or behavior rehearsals (see role-play scenario examples in Appendix F). The *What Do You Know?* card game includes questions about healthy sexuality and personal safety that are generally not introduced until after the trauma narrative is completed. The therapist can also create and/or identify sex-related and/or personal safety questions in the *What Do You Know?* card game to review independently with the parents and children during their individual sessions. These same questions can then be incorporated into a game played with parents and children together in conjoint session. Whether in the context of a game, discussion, or role-plays, it is important to cover all of the concepts and skills outlined below with children as well as adolescents.

Body ownership

In conjunction with teaching the child about body parts, the therapist may begin to teach the child basic information about body ownership. Children should learn that their bodies belong to them, that all parts of their bodies are important, and no one has a right to hurt any part of their body. For example, the therapist might say the following:

> *Your body is your very own and you decide how you like or do not like being touched.*

Again, there are a number of books for young children that highlight this concept (see resource list) and there is a wonderful song designed for preschoolers called, "My body" that can be accessed through the songwriter's website at http://www.peteralsop.com. This song helps children internalize the important concept of body ownership. For older children and adolescents, this concept may be best discussed in the context of reading a relevant book together. It is always best for the therapist to avoid lectures and present material that encourages interactive discussions and exercises that require active client participation.

"Okay" versus "not okay" touches

Therapists should review the differences between "okay" touches, "not okay" touches, and confusing touches with even the youngest children. The therapist might initiate this conversation with a focus on "okay" touches, as follows:

> *Today, we are going to talk about "okay" touches, "not okay" touches, and confusing touches. Can you think of some touches that you like?*

The therapist might help the child identify and share examples of touches that the child likes that will later be defined as "okay" touches. "Okay" touches may include appropriate hugs, kisses, handshakes, pats on the back, and so on. To demonstrate an "okay" touch, the therapist might ask the child to shake hands. This will provide the therapist with some insight regarding the child's comfort and/or ongoing avoidance of "okay" touches. The therapist might end this discussion with the agreement that these touches are called "okay" touches. With the parents' support and knowledge, other "okay" touches that can be important to talk about with children who have experienced sexual abuse include: adults touching each other's private parts when that is what they both want to do, touching one's own private parts, and a doctor or parent touching a child's private parts when the child is hurt or needs help in the bathroom. Devoting significant time in the session on the many kinds of touches that are okay is important because when children have experienced CSA there is often a great deal of focus on touches that are not okay.

Next the therapist can turn the discussion to inappropriate touches by asking:

Can you think of some touches that you don't like?

Again, the therapist might encourage children to come up with their own thoughts and ideas about "not okay" touches, including hitting and punching, as well as the sexual touching of a child by an older child or adult. As has been mentioned, with younger children sexual abuse may be referred to as "not okay" touches. The therapist can further clarify the "not okay" touch by explaining that the touches in this category are not okay because they are against the rules (or against the law, when working with older children), and it is also how a child might feel when an adult or older child touches a child's private parts. To continue to discourage avoidance, the therapist should model and reinforce the use of the terms "child sexual abuse," "sexual assault," and/or "child molestation" with older children and teens.

It is important to emphasize that sometimes it is not clear if a touch is okay or not okay, and that can be quite confusing. Thus, it is particularly important for children to talk to adults not only about "not okay" (or abusive) touches but also about confusing touches. The therapist could ask the child something like the following:

Can you think of a time when you were touched in a way that made you feel confused?

Can you think of a touch that felt good to your body, but you weren't sure if the touch was okay or not okay?

In this discussion, it is useful to talk with the child about the fact that sexual touching, including sexual abuse, sometimes may make one's body feel good regardless of how one thinks about it (e.g., thinking that the behavior is not okay or being confused by it). Although this discussion is important for both girls and boys, boys may be particularly confused if they experienced an erection (which felt good) at the time of the abuse while they simultaneously felt scared. It is important for the therapist to normalize this experience, explaining that when either girls' or boys' genitals are touched it may feel good to the body, but this still does not make the adult's or older child's behavior okay. Some touches can feel good to the body but they still may be against the "rules." Then the therapist can initiate a conversation about personal safety skills by discussing ways the child might respond if touched in an inappropriate or confusing way. During this discussion, it is important to avoid making the child feel bad if the child did not respond in the most effective way during his experience of sexual abuse. For example, the therapist might say the following:

> *Most kids aren't really sure what they should do if someone touches them in a not okay way because no one has ever taught them what to do or they were so confused or scared that they didn't know how to respond. Do you have any ideas about things you might try to do if anyone touched you again in a way that is not okay?*

After having elicited the child's ideas about how to respond to inappropriate touches, the therapist can begin providing information regarding personal safety skills. The basics of body safety can be summarized with the term "NO-GO-TELL," which is explained in more detail below.

No—right to say "no"

It is useful to begin a discussion of personal safety skills by teaching children that they have the right to say "no" if they are being touched in a not okay way. Children can be taught that they can say no even to an adult if the adult is doing something that they think is wrong. Then the therapist and the child can practice saying no in a forceful way that communicates that the child means what she is saying. Many children will need encouragement to speak loudly, stand tall, and make eye contact when being assertive in this way.

Go—getting away

The next safety skill to be taught is to leave the situation. Therapists may encourage children to leave the person doing the inappropriate touching and go to an area where there are other people, if that is possible. Often when asked how they would respond to inappropriate touching, children answer with aggressive strategies such as "I'd kick him or I'd punch him." Although those strategies should not be labeled as wrong or inappropriate, therapists might emphasize that the most important thing to do is to get away from the perpetrator and that sometimes more aggressive responses may prolong contact with the perpetrator. Children can be encouraged to leave an uncomfortable situation as soon as possible, but the therapist should acknowledge that it may not always be possible for children to get away. The therapist can emphasize that even if it is not possible to get away immediately, whenever the child has the opportunity, she should try to get away and take the next and most important step of telling someone about the experience.

Tell—telling and continuing to tell until someone helps

An important aspect of personal safety skills training is teaching children to tell someone as soon as possible when something troubling has occurred. Children need to understand that they may not always be able to prevent sexual abuse from occurring but that they can tell someone about what happened. Children can be encouraged to identify individuals whom they can confide in when something troubling happens. In discussing this skill, it is important to help children identify family members as well as nonfamily members with whom they could talk if "not okay" touching and/or other troubling experiences occur in the future. This is particularly important as many instances of CSA and other types of violence occur within the family. The therapist and the child can create a list of all the people the child could tell, including parents, teachers, relatives, neighbors, coaches, and police officers. Finally, the child can be encouraged to keep telling until someone understands and helps. It should be acknowledged that sometimes the first person one tells doesn't understand or doesn't do anything that truly helps. Again it should be strongly emphasized that despite learning these personal safety skills, children must be told directly by the therapist that if they were abused again in the future, it would not be their fault. In this way, they can understand that personal safety skills are important but may not be sufficient to overcome the advances of a stronger, older, and/or persistent offender.

Keeping secrets

Older children generally can understand the difference between appropriate and inappropriate secrets. Thus, the importance of telling inappropriate secrets can be easily stressed. With younger children, it may be preferable to explain the distinction between surprises and secrets. Children can be taught that pleasant surprises such as birthday presents are okay to keep secret temporarily because the person will soon learn what the surprise is. However, secrets the child is asked to never tell are not okay. Furthermore, children can be told that they do not need to keep such secrets, even if someone else says that they should or must, and even if they promised to keep the secret. Again, it is important to emphasize to children that if someone does not believe or understand them when they tell a troubling secret, they should keep telling until someone does believe them and does something to help.

Practicing body safety skills with role-plays

Repetition, role-plays, and behavioral rehearsal are necessary to use to help youth incorporate the above skills into their behavioral repertoire in order to enhance safety. During these role-plays, preschoolers and school-age children are encouraged to learn the body safety term "No-Go-Tell" (similar to stop, drop, and roll for fire safety) as a reminder of what they will need to do in a variety of situations that involve a range of uncomfortable, "not okay" touches and/or inappropriate sexual advances. While practicing these skills, children are encouraged to practice telling their parents. As noted above, parents practice in their individual sessions how to respond to their children in a supportive manner during these practice role-plays. Parents and therapists can then provide positive feedback after conjoint session role-plays to reinforce the child's skills in responding to a "role-played" "not okay" touch or threat.

When enhancing safety with adolescents, it is important to talk about the "uh oh" feeling and assertive communication to refuse unwanted advances, sexual and otherwise. Role-plays with adolescents may not only depict common CSA scenarios but could also include situations in which adolescents might be at risk for date rape or other peer pressure circumstances particularly around drinking and drugs. In fact, teens should be educated about the steps they can take to reduce their risk of sexual assault. Role-play scenarios designed for children and teens at differential developmental stages are provided in the appendix to support the practicing of personal safety and assertiveness skills (see Appendix F).

Practice activities encouraged

Youth should be encouraged to continue to practice what they have learned during this component, as well as over the course of treatment in relation to non-avoidance of abuse reminders and the use of effective coping and assertiveness skills. Teenagers may be encouraged to read an age-appropriate book or handout provided about healthy sexuality and/or other relevant issues (preferably with their parents) at home and to generate questions about what they have read for the next session. These questions can be used by the therapist to prompt a discussion and/or activity that the youth and parent can engage in during the next conjoint session. Younger children may also be encouraged to use the appropriate terms for genitalia, the NO-GO-TELL body safety skills, as well as other coping skills learned in the course of treatment at home with parents.

Problem-solving and assertiveness skills

It is important to continuously review and encourage the integrated use of the skills learned, especially as the child prepares to complete the therapy process. Helping youth to review skills and practice using them in the context of problems that they might face in the future can be particularly helpful. Many times youth react to problems without understanding exactly what the issue is to which they are reacting and this can be particularly true when cues in the environment elicit problematic responses because of associations with earlier trauma(s). By this stage of therapy, most children have demonstrated greater tolerance and more effective responses to innocuous trauma reminders in the environment. However, it can be valuable for youth to continue to practice slowing down (e.g., focused breathing), utilizing their coping skills, and identifying and gathering information about a problem situation before responding. Learning to respond to a problem or interpersonal conflict using effective problem solving and assertiveness skills can be critical to supporting a child's future development. Perhaps the most effective means of helping children learn new ways of responding to challenging situations is via repeated role-plays of past and potential future conflicts.

Identify the problem

To practice problem-solving and assertiveness skills, the therapist might provide a variety of hypothetical situations depicting a child of similar age and circumstances becoming upset. The client should then be asked to define exactly what the problem was to which the child in the scenario was responding. For example, a hypothetical situation might depict a baseball player cursing at the umpire after striking out, throwing his bat, and getting ejected from the game. The clinician then asks the client to elaborate on exactly what aspects of the situation the player perceived as problematic and resulted in him becoming upset. The client might define the problem as an umpire who was making bad calls. Or the client might report that the pitcher was trying to hit the batter with the ball. After identifying the emotion generated by the problem in several such hypothetical scenarios, the client can then be asked to think about a problem he experienced in the past week that made him similarly upset and to define the problem that aroused the emotion. Since perceptions of a problem situation can vary considerably, the child should be encouraged to explore all possible underlying causes for the problem encountered in real life. This effort to explore all possible explanations for a problem encourages the *cognitive flexibility* that helps children break out of old patterns of maladaptive thinking and allows for consideration of more adaptive explanations for the problem. In examining the problem scenario experienced, the client then may be encouraged to describe his physical state (e.g., tension in a particular part of the body), his emotions, and his behavioral responses, as well as what he was saying to himself (i.e., thoughts).

Brainstorm a range of possible responses

In the next step of problem solving, the therapist may ask the youth to generate as many potential responses to the problem as possible without evaluation of their merit. If the client struggles to generate solutions, the therapist may assist by suggesting a variety of responses. One goal of this step in the problem-solving process is to increase the child's *flexibility* in responding. Rather than automatically following a given (and often problematic) response pattern, the therapist is helping the youth develop behavioral flexibility in responding to frustrating situations. In response to the above scenario regarding the baseball player, the youth might respond that the player could turn around and hit the umpire, charge the plate and hit the pitcher, turn around and walk back to the dugout, take a few deep breaths and try again his next turn at bat, etc. After generating responses to several hypothetical scenarios, the youth may be asked to think of a situation he experienced in the previous week that was frustrating and generate a variety of ways he might have responded in terms of his feelings, thoughts, and behaviors.

Evaluate the possible responses generated through brainstorming

In this step, the clinician encourages the child to evaluate the likely effectiveness of the potential responses identified during the brainstorming activity. One way to encourage this evaluation is to ask the youth to think through the likely outcomes of each of the alternative responses. For example, in response to "turn around and hit the umpire," the therapist might ask, "So, what do you think would happen next if you did hit the umpire?" A follow-up question might be, "How do you think that would work out for you?" After evaluating responses to several hypothetical situations, the therapist might ask the youth to evaluate the potential responses he might make to a situation he experiences in real life that is frustrating to him.

Applying the problem-solving steps to a real-life situation

In this step, the clinician will help the client identify a situation he experiences fairly regularly that arouses mild upset or frustration. It is important not to focus initially on an extremely frustrating or upsetting situation as it will be difficult for the child to modulate his affective response to those situations. An example of a regularly occurring, mildly frustrating situation might be when the youth's younger sibling comes into his room without being invited. Once the child and therapist have identified the situation, the child will be asked to identify what it is about that situation that causes frustration. Subsequently, the child will be encouraged to generate a range of potential responses to the situation including feelings, thoughts, and behaviors. After evaluating the potential responses, the child and therapist will work together to identify the response that the child feels will likely produce the best outcome. The child may then be encouraged to practice the planned response to possible scenarios that are likely to occur in the coming week.

When the problem involves an interpersonal conflict, it is helpful to review the communication and assertiveness skills discussed in the Affect Expression/Modulation chapter (Chapter 8). As noted earlier, behavior rehearsal is perhaps the best way to help youth practice their responses and receive positive and constructive feedback. The subtleties of responding assertively as opposed to passively or aggressively can best be addressed by observing a child's attempts to respond to an interpersonal conflict or dilemma in the context of a role-play scenario. When providing children with feedback about body language, tone of voice, and choice of expression, it is important to consider the context in which they will be communicating with others in terms of cultural and family expectations. For example, the manner in which children address adults and even make eye contact with them is often influenced by cultural and familial norms and expectations.

Evaluate the outcome

In the subsequent session, the therapist and youth may review instances during the week in which the agreed upon solutions or responses were attempted and evaluate how well they worked. The therapist should be careful to reinforce the child for efforts at responding to situations effectively, regardless of the outcome. If difficulties were encountered, the therapist and child may work together to identify what the challenges were and revise the planned responses for the subsequent week. It is critical to focus and offer specific praise for even small cognitive and/or behavioral changes that the child reports, while also acknowledging the value of the child's honesty in reporting less than ideal responses.

Prepare for conjoint session

The therapist can help the child practice body safety and/or problem-solving skills and rehearse assertive responses to various high-risk scenarios (provided in Appendix F) that may be reenacted in the conjoint session in role-plays with parent(s). It is not only helpful for children to have repeated opportunities to practice these skills both in individual and conjoint sessions but it is also reassuring to children to experience their parents' supportive responses in the context of these role-plays. In addition, it is comforting to parents to see their children demonstrate strength in asserting themselves in response to challenging situations their children may face in the future.

CONJOINT SESSION(S)

Conjoint parent-child sessions allow parents and children to become comfortable discussing issues of healthy sexuality and personal safety skills together. Having the ability to openly and clearly discuss these issues allows parents to provide accurate information, impart their own values regarding sexual issues, and assist their children in problem solving around sexual concerns or difficulties as they develop. In addition, teaching children to discuss sexual issues and personal safety openly with their parents may increase the likelihood that the children will disclose to parents any experiences of inappropriate or confusing touches and/or openly share sexual questions, pressures, and/or concerns with their parents in the future.

Engage parent and child in healthy sexuality exercises and discussions

The developmentally appropriate reading material(s) regarding sexuality reviewed by the therapist and parent in advance of the conjoint session may be used to structure the provision of sex education, thereby reducing parental anxieties about how to approach the task. The goals of presenting sex education in conjoint sessions include eliminating any confusion children may have regarding sex, helping children to develop a positive view of sexuality, and increasing communication between parent and child regarding the topic of sexuality. In addition to preparing to present developmentally appropriate factual information on specific topics (e.g., how a child is conceived, puberty, dating relationships, healthy sexuality, and contraceptive methods), the therapist may encourage parents to share whatever values they want to communicate to the child about sex. After deciding on appropriate topics for the child, the therapist and parent may choose to interactively read books and/or other materials and engage in question and answer exercises together.

With very young children, a portion of a conjoint session may be devoted to having the parent (or therapist, if parent is too uncomfortable) read the chosen book or other material to the child. With older children, the child may be encouraged to read the material or take turns reading with the adults who are present. This helps everyone get comfortable using the language that is necessary to openly discuss sex and related issues. There are several sex education books that are organized in question-and-answer format (see resource list). Using this format, the child and/or parent can attempt to answer the question and then the written answer in the book may be shared. This makes for an interesting and fun session. To motivate reticent children to participate, points, stickers, praise, and/or other small rewards may be offered for effort, as well as for correct answers in response to sex education questions. In an attempt to encourage open dialogue, the therapist may pause at times during the reading of the materials to solicit comments or questions regarding the material. If conjoint session(s) focused on providing sex education in this way goes well, the therapist can ask the parent and child to continue reading and discussing the material at home. It is preferable for parents and children to read the materials together because independent reading of the books will not serve to enhance communication between the parent and child.

With older children, the presentation of sex education material may serve as a springboard for discussions of issues such as dating, adolescent sexuality, and contraceptive methods. During a conjoint session, the therapist may facilitate such discussions by asking general questions such as the following:

Do many students in your grade have boyfriends or girlfriends?
What does it mean if you are "going together" (or "hanging out, hooking up" or whatever term is typically used)?
What do you look for in a boyfriend or girlfriend?
What happens physically between boyfriends and girlfriends?
How do you know when it is appropriate to have a sexual relationship?
Have any of your friends had sex?

By having the parent and child begin to discuss these issues in session, the therapist is encouraging an open atmosphere in which they can continue discussions of sexual issues on their own. As a therapist, it is important to model acceptance of the child's developing views through reflective listening and open and clear communication about the realities of engaging in sexual activities. In general, it is helpful to use humor to keep the discussions regarding sex education positive and lighthearted. However, the impact of STIs and teenage pregnancy may also be presented in the context of such discussions in a nonjudgmental but realistic manner. When parents are encouraged to discuss sex openly in a positive, non-threatening, and nonjudgemental manner, teens who have a history of CSA have an opportunity to view sex in a positive manner, while also understanding the realistic risks associated with indiscriminate and unprotected sexual behaviors.

Practice personal safety role-plays with parents and children

Personal safety skills are also important to discuss in conjoint sessions. However, even more important than discussions are role-plays during which children can behaviorally practice how they might handle potential threats, peer pressure, and/or victimization experiences in the future. Different scenarios can be presented so that children have repeated opportunities to practice the skills of saying "no," getting away, and telling, while parents similarly practice responding to disclosures in a therapeutic, supportive, and confident manner. With younger children, the discussion and role-plays may focus both on "okay", confusing, and "not okay" touches, as well as the right to say no, getting away, telling someone, and continuing to tell others until someone helps. This means that in some of the role-plays the scene can include one attempt to disclose abuse that is not responded to well by the adult, thus requiring the child to tell someone else. In fact, it may be best for the therapist (instead of the parent) to play the role of a teacher or relative who does not respond well when the child discloses so the parent can consistently respond with encouraging remarks and appropriate actions when the child practices disclosing. With older children whose sex education discussions included a focus on dating relationships, discussions of personal safety skills may incorporate the issue of sexual aggression in dating relationships.

Special considerations when contact with the offender is anticipated

In cases where there is potential for further contact with the offender, the child should be educated about the fact that some individuals who sexually abuse do offend again, although it cannot be predicted whether a particular individual will reoffend. Role-plays with these children may depict realistic situations that could occur in relation to contact they may have with the person(s) who sexually abused them. The child may be prepared to respond effectively to unexpected contact at a family gathering, as well as possible inappropriate interactions or touches by the offender and/or others in relatively supervised settings. The therapist can carefully plan all role-plays to depict as accurately as possible how the known offender might interact with the child. One group of role-plays may focus on confusing touches that might help a child recognize the possible early stages of grooming, evaluate whether the interactions were "okay" or "not okay" touches, and plan an appropriate response with the help and support of the caregiver. In another role-play, the therapist might help the child respond to a re-victimization experience in the context of a role-play by asking the child to respond if the offender was begging her not to tell as illustrated below:

> *Please, please, don't tell about this. Don't tell your mom I touched you. You know if you tell, your mom will be so upset. I'll have to go to jail and I might never get out. You can't tell. I promise I'll never touch you like that again.*

A number of role-plays might be conducted depicting a variety of different high-risk situations involving potential contact at family gatherings, school functions, as well as unexpected meetings in public places. Parents and children may be reminded that anxiety in such situations is normal, as this is the way the body signals that there is, in fact, real danger which is realistic given the behavior of the offending individual in the past. However, with the support of parents, other caregivers, and the skills learned, children's confidence in managing these complex situations may be greatly enhanced by active behavior rehearsals and role-plays.

Practice activities encouraged

Depending on their needs, parents and children may be asked to read a developmentally appropriate sex education book and/or body safety skills book that encourages practice at home. Clients may be loaned such books to read together prior to the following session. It often helps parents and children to plan in session and record on the practice activity form (Appendix B) the specific time they will sit together and review the material including the specific chapters to be read as this increases the chances that they will have the private time needed to follow through on this activity at home.

End-of-session positive ritual

This is a particularly nice session for parents and children to exchange specific praise regarding the sex education discussions and/or the body safety skills practice activities engaged in during the conjoint session. In addition, it is pleasant to end the session with specific praise related to other positive parent-child interactions as well as global praise. The ritual of exchanging praise on a regular basis is one that many parents and children enjoy and plan to continue beyond the end of therapy. The therapist can encourage this by emphasizing that behavior changes are best sustained when they are incorporated into positive rituals or habits (e.g., exchange of praise regularly at bedtime, dinner time, etc.) that are repeated and thus become routine over time.

15

Ending Therapy

Over the course of therapy, the treatment plan and goals of trauma-focused cognitive-behavioral therapy (TF-CBT) are clearly identified, the clients' progress toward those goals is recognized, and the short-term nature of the TF-CBT model is periodically acknowledged. Thus, the completion of therapy is generally experienced as a natural culmination of the treatment process. Client progress in reaching treatment goals should be evaluated periodically through informal questioning, clinical observations, and the administration of standardized measures. This helps to establish the appropriate timing for treatment completion. Such assessments can confirm the therapist's plan for ending therapy, or they can reveal areas in which continued therapeutic work is needed. As noted before, for children who have had many loss experiences in addition to child sexual abuse (CSA), it is important to gradually expose them to positive discussions about the final treatment session so that the end of therapy is not jarring and/or experienced as a betrayal or traumatic loss. The clients' therapeutic progress and strengths should be applauded during these final sessions particularly with respect to skills learned, as well as the parents' and children's comfort in talking about the sexual abuse as this validates their hard work.

The final treatment session is ideally planned shortly before all other components have been completed with considerable success. This means that education and skills have been mastered, the trauma narrative has been completed, reviewed, processed, and (when appropriate) shared in conjoint sessions with caregivers, and the final sessions have addressed sex education and personal safety. The last session may occur after the posttreatment assessment measures have been administered and have documented significant improvements. This does not mean ending treatment should be delayed until children have no symptoms. In fact, while children generally should not be experiencing full-blown PTSD or behavior problems in the clinical range, by the end of treatment, some mild symptoms may remain and often additional improvements are experienced after treatment ends. Parents may, in fact, be reminded that the behavioral improvements they see in their children are in great part a reflection of their support and parenting adjustments. Thus, continued child behavior improvements may be anticipated as long as parents work at continuing to practice the effective parenting and coping strategies learned as they are their children's most important role models. Still, given the many familial and legal stressors associated with CSA cases, it is important to leave the door open for parents to call for some guidance regarding anticipated and/or unanticipated CSA related or unrelated stressors.

During preparation for the final session, parents and children may meet with the therapist individually to help clients prepare for conjoint celebratory activities and for life after therapy ends. These separate individual sessions often include discussing how parents and children will work to continue to use effective coping skills, while continuing to minimize CSA-related avoidance at home. The majority of the final treatment session, however, might be spent in a conjoint or family session that is focused on celebrating treatment progress and success with self-praise (e.g., "What are you most proud of accomplishing in therapy?") and exchanging praise specifically with regard to participation and successful completion of treatment.

The therapist might begin considering concluding treatment when clients are approaching the following goals:

- Children and parents have shown confidence in their knowledge and ability to discuss the facts about CSA and, when appropriate, other trauma(s).
- Children and parents have demonstrated successful acquisition and implementation of adaptive coping skills.
- Parents have demonstrated improved parenting and communication skills.
- Children and parents have exhibited diminished anxiety, avoidance, and distress when confronted with thoughts and memories of the sexual abuse and related experience(s).
- Children and parents have processed their feelings and come to healthier conclusions about their reactions and skills in coping with CSA and other trauma(s).
- Children have exhibited decreased general and/or sexual behavior problems.
- Children and parents have participated in sessions focused on sex education and personal safety skills.
- Parents and children have grown stronger and closer with one another.

In some cases, the identified treatment goals largely have been reached, but the child still has other difficulties unrelated to the sexual abuse experience. Then the therapist must make a decision with the clients as to whether or not further treatment shall be pursued to address those other issues. It is important for the therapist to carefully consider whether the child's additional problems may be more effectively addressed by someone else who has greater expertise in that area. This might be true for a child who continues to struggle in school due to learning disabilities and might be better helped by a learning specialist.

Conversely, long-standing difficulties with childhood obesity might be something the therapist might feel prepared to address in collaboration with a medical doctor. If the decision is reached to continue treatment focused on the other issues, the therapist should clearly communicate that shift in focus and present a new treatment plan to the clients. At this stage, a celebration could be planned to acknowledge the completion of the sexual abuse–focused phase of treatment. If the therapist feels that the clients would be better served by a referral to a different therapist with expertise in the other issues to be addressed, that plan should be presented to the clients at this time as well.

PARENT SESSION(S)

The contents of the final sessions may consist largely of a review of education provided, skills learned, progress made, and when possible, the posttreatment assessment findings. In addition, a final session should be planned that includes celebratory conjoint activities.

Treatment progress and accomplishments

The assessment based on the therapist's observations and standardized measures should be presented to the parent(s) in an individual session allowing for a discussion of both progress and remaining concerns. It should be explained that it is not necessary for parents and children to be completely symptom free to graduate from TF-CBT. Rather, the assessment may demonstrate significant reductions in emotional and behavioral difficulties such that the symptoms are no longer in the clinical range, nor are they disrupting daily functioning. Parents should be reminded that with continued commitment to effective coping and parenting skills, positive emotional and behavioral changes should be maintained and may show improvements over time. Still, life is such that ups and downs can be anticipated that reflect the natural fluctuations of mood and behavior. Emotional and behavioral relapses may be regarded as signals that life stressors may need more attention and/or or skills practice may have fallen off a bit. Thus, simply recommitting to practicing the learned parenting and coping skills may be sufficient to overcome symptom relapses.

Preparing to practice skills after therapy ends

Skills practices at home should continue to be a focus of treatment even in the final therapy sessions with an emphasis on the critical importance of continued parenting skills practice after therapy ends. As noted earlier, research has demonstrated that when children are acknowledged for their positive qualities, for example as a "helper," they may self-identify that way and continue to demonstrate helping behaviors over time in other settings (Bryan et al., 2014; Grusec & Redler, 1980). Thus, parents may be reminded to model adaptive behaviors while also giving children specific praise (e.g., "I like the way you helped to clear off the table"), as well as praise that describes more global attributions (e.g., "You are a helpful person"). In general, praise and other effective parenting practices (e.g., reflective listening, time out, contingency management) should be reviewed and encouraged as their continued use at home can go a long way in maintaining children's positive behavioral and emotional changes after therapy ends.

In addition to inquiring about ongoing coping and parenting efforts, the therapist may also inquire about sex education and/or personal safety books reviewed at home. This review provides parents with an opportunity to share their experiences and receive constructive feedback in the form of compliment sandwiches regarding their efforts to address these sensitive and important issues with their children. Parents also may be instructed in how to continue to provide sex education at home, as noted in the previous chapter. In addition, the therapist may help the parent anticipate and plan how to present sex education information that will be needed later (e.g., providing a sex education books list for use in the future) but is not appropriate at the child's current developmental level. Parents should be reminded that for children who have experienced sexual abuse, sex education that is presented openly and in a positive light is particularly important given the inappropriate way in which sex was introduced to them.

Once again, parents may be reminded of the importance and benefits of positive rituals, reflective listening, and praise particularly when communicating with children and teens about difficult or sensitive issues. Positive daily or weekly rituals (e.g., pleasant morning greetings, encouraging lunch box notes, and relaxing bedtime rituals) can help to maintain a greater ratio of positive to negative interactions which is important to the overall well-being of children and families.

Parents may be given some suggestions as to how to maintain the parenting and coping gains achieved in treatment on their own. For example, clients may be encouraged to think about creating and/or maintaining reminders in their environment that support their efforts to use the skills learned. Some examples of reminders in the home include the use of carefully placed posters and/or refrigerator magnets that encourage praise, positive family rules, adaptive thinking, and/or effective parenting strategies. In addition, parents may choose to frame children's work (e.g., drawings, report cards, awards, certificates) that reminds them of their child's strengths and accomplishments.

In addition to practicing the skills after therapy ends, it is also important to encourage some open discussion about the sexual abuse experience at home when an opportunity arises naturally (i.e., when a TV show is on regarding sexual abuse or personal safety skills are presented at school). Recent TF-CBT research demonstrated that reductions in children's maladaptive overgeneralized beliefs and increases in healthy adaptive beliefs predicted improvements in internalizing and PTSD symptoms at posttreatment and were associated with long-term reductions in externalizing behaviors (Ready et al., 2014). To maintain such improvements it may be valuable for parents to model, revisit, and reinforce adaptive beliefs (e.g., "We have grown stronger and closer as a result of this experience"; "The offender is responsible for the sexual abuse"; "The future is bright") regarding the sexual abuse even after therapy ends. Although discussions about abuse-related issues are not likely to be frequent, parents may also be encouraged to support their children's adaptive beliefs by demonstrating confidence in their abilities to face innocuous trauma reminders and openly discuss the abuse in an adaptive manner when appropriate.

Finally, parents may be provided with suggestions as to how they judge whether additional treatment becomes necessary in the future. In general, if the child is experiencing a mild reoccurrence of previously treated difficulties, parents should be encouraged to utilize the parenting and coping skills they learned in therapy to address the problem. If despite their efforts to fully reinstate these skills, parents do not then see a reduction but rather see problem behaviors escalating, they may be encouraged to contact the therapist. For example, if the child again begins to exhibit inappropriate sexual behaviors, parents should be encouraged to be sure to model the adaptive behaviors they would like to see and apply the same behavior management techniques they successfully used before with those problems. If parents are not able to reduce the behaviors with those strategies, then they should contact the therapist for guidance and/or booster sessions. Furthermore, high-stress events such as court proceedings or possible reunification with an offending sibling may be identified as times when some children benefit from additional treatment. If the therapist continues to be available in the same facility, the clients may benefit from simply knowing that they may call the therapist to discuss issues of concern and for help in deciding whether or not further treatment is required in the future.

Planning the end of therapy celebration

Although the TF-CBT therapist may create a celebration/graduation cap and certificate for the client(s), parents often enjoy taking a leadership role in planning other aspects of the final treatment session that incorporates their family's culture and/or traditions. Thus, in advance of the celebratory session, it is important to elicit parental input and encourage parents' contributions. This may include inviting other family members and/or contributing snacks, music, games, balloons, and/or even sharing their talents (e.g., dancing, singing, etc.). In addition, this is the parents' final opportunity during treatment to openly acknowledge the child's strength in dealing with CSA and coping with the aftermath. Thus, it is valuable for TF-CBT therapists to encourage parents to prepare praise to share in this final session that specifically focuses on the child's response to the CSA and/or other stressors. Again, it helps to encourage parents to use specific CSA-related words that demonstrate once again that the parent is comfortable discussing the CSA and is proud of the child's courage and skill in talking about and/or writing about the abuse. The parents may prepare something to say or may prefer writing out what they want to express. Either way, the TF-CBT therapist should review what the parents are planning to share to ensure that the final session's specific praise is purely positive, with no negative tags, and it specifically describes some of the child's accomplishments in therapy. Finally, some parents naturally engage in hugs or high fives in the context of their celebration while other parents may need some encouragement to share global praise or expressions of affection with their child. This type of acknowledgement of the child and affection from caregivers is important given that the experience of CSA can undermine some children's feelings of worthiness.

CHILD SESSION(S)

As is the case throughout treatment, the child's final individual sessions should parallel the individual parent sessions. Thus, when developmentally appropriate, the TF-CBT therapist may review the child's accomplishments, progress, and posttreatment assessment findings with an emphasis on the progress made and the skills developed. In addition, the therapist may inquire about the child's reactions to the sex education, personal safety, and/or other materials reviewed and/or skills practiced in the final phase of treatment. The therapist may also help the child develop a plan that will support continued use of the coping skills after therapy ends. Again, it helps to review how their newfound coping skills can be incorporated into routines so that the skills become habitual (e.g., waking up in the morning with a personalized positive self-statement). Finally, it is important for the child to contribute to the celebratory session particularly in terms of thinking about how the parent's participation and progress might be acknowledged and celebrated as well.

Treatment progress and accomplishments review

The therapist may review the child's treatment progress and accomplishments based on observed improvements and/or progress revealed by posttreatment assessments. In reviewing treatment progress, the therapist should focus on positive changes revealed by the assessment, as well as by clinical observation. For some children, it is helpful to provide a concrete document in the form of a graph to demonstrate the therapy progress made, while others respond well to simple explanations of how the therapist's observations, as well as the parents' reports, reflect the child's verbal reports of feeling better and coping more effectively. During these final individual child sessions, it is also helpful to acknowledge and review the particular coping skills that seem to be most natural and effective for the particular child.

With older children and adolescents, it can also be useful to acknowledge areas in which some additional work may lead to continued improvements, particularly with respect to mild behavioral difficulties and/or mild avoidance symptoms. This provides another opportunity for the therapist to encourage continued practice of effective coping skills, while reviewing important lessons learned, specifically the value of facing fears as opposed to avoiding non-dangerous reminders of the abuse or other feared social or interpersonal situations. The child may then be asked the following:

> *What usually happens to people's feelings of fear or anxiety when they face a feared circumstance and nothing bad happens?*
> *What happened when you overcame your fear of talking about the sexual abuse?*
> *Did anything bad happen when you wrote about the sexual abuse? Did anything good happen?*
> *What would you say then to a child who was fearful of telling someone about a CSA experience and/or talking to a therapist about it?*
> *What is something that you were a bit fearful of that you can now face?*

The above questions and ensuing discussions may be expanded to include a review of other therapy accomplishments with an emphasis on skills learned and fears overcome including (when appropriate) those fears addressed through in vivo mastery.

It is also important to review children's reactions to sex education and personal safety skills training. These final sessions provide opportunities to elicit any remaining questions that children may have related to sex, personal boundaries, and/or the sexually abusive experiences. With the end of therapy nearing, such a review will sometimes prompt children to ask questions they have been holding back (e.g., "Can I still get pregnant from the sperm that got into my vagina during the abuse?") or they may reveal concerns that they continue to have, for example, regarding the distinction between sexual abuse and healthy sexuality (e.g., "When is it okay for me to kiss someone because I have feelings for that person?"). Moreover, this review may highlight issues that would be important to address in conjoint parent-child session before therapy ends (e.g., the parents' views regarding the appropriate age for dating, etc.). Discussions about birth control, for example, can be particularly important for adolescents who may still benefit from the therapist's skill in setting the stage for a productive parent-child discussion of such topics in conjoint session. However, it is important to note that such sensitive discussions should not be planned for the final treatment session if at all possible. Whenever possible, the final session should be planned primarily as a progress review and celebration.

Preparing to practice skills after therapy ends

The importance of continuing to implement coping skills even after therapy ends should be emphasized. The TF-CBT therapist, in fact, may invite the child to review the coping skills tool kit and/or create new reminders that the child may maintain at home or elsewhere to help him remember to utilize effective coping skills. This can include creating a coping skills poster and/or creating smartphone reminders in the form of positive wallpaper, voice memos, coping apps, etc. To reinforce children's insights regarding PTSD and/or other symptoms, it helps to use Socratic questions to review with children how they have successfully managed these symptoms when they have occurred, especially in response to CSA or other trauma reminders. In addition, it can be useful to introduce the concept of coping reminders and/or positive mood starters as strategies that can help them cope with the natural stressors of childhood, adolescence, and adulthood. Sometimes just remembering how they successfully coped with the CSA and/or remembering something that made the child laugh in the past can be a powerful reminder of how associations impact our moods. Through the course of therapy, children may be reminded that they have created new associations that may make them smile when they think with pride about the courage they have had and their accomplishments in facing the sexual abuse with their parent or other caregiver.

In addition, it may, in fact, be useful to encourage children to share some stressors that they anticipate may occur after therapy ends, including feelings of loss related to missing therapy (which for some children may elicit a chuckle). This allows the TF-CBT therapist to normalize the occurrence of life stressors and loss that all children, adolescents, and adults face. Moreover, this provides an opportunity to use imaginal exposure to potential future stressors so that clients can have some final opportunities to practice adaptive coping skills thereby providing a great review of the psychoeducation and coping skills.

Planning the end of therapy celebration

The final individual sessions with the child also provide important opportunities for the therapist to prepare the child for ending treatment. Once again, this comes naturally for some children, and just one session may be sufficient to discuss and prepare for ending treatment. Other children may need and benefit from more time to emotionally prepare for the end of the positive therapeutic relationship and the regular therapy meetings. For such children, it may be best to space out the final sessions so that the child gets comfortable not seeing the therapist as regularly. An important aspect of preparing for the conclusion of therapy is encouraging the child to discuss what she found most helpful about therapy, while also planning how the child might express appreciation for the parents' participation in treatment one final time during the celebratory party. The final exchange of specific and global praise is often moving. However, with some children, the therapist may need to use carefully developed Socratic questions to help the child prepare specific praise relevant to the therapy experience for the parent. Below are some questions that help children think about how they would like to acknowledge the parents' support and participation in treatment, as well as any positive parenting changes that were made over the course of treatment. The TF-CBT therapist might explain, for example, the following:

During the celebratory party, it is a nice tradition to share praise with your parents specifically related to how they helped you with the sexual abuse. And of course it is nice for them to hear about how you feel about them in general too. But let's start by thinking about and maybe even writing down what your parents said or did after the sexual abuse that helped you feel better.

What other changes has your dad made since the beginning of therapy that you would like to praise?

Is there something your parent does each night that you really like that you would like to praise?

You told me about one time your mom praised you for something you did in school that meant a great deal to you.

How would you like to tell your mom how you feel about her in general?

Finally, at the last or next-to-last therapy session, many children enjoy creating a final art, music, or computer project that can be designed as an educational message for other children and/or adults about CSA (e.g., "It's never too late to tell") or related issues (e.g., "Believe in yourself!") that they can leave with the therapist and/or contribute to the clinic. In addition, an ending treatment hat or graduation cap may be designed and created out of construction paper. This hat can then be decorated with stickers or encouraging sayings or reminders. Even teenagers seem to enjoy wearing a celebratory cap during the family party at the last session.

CONJOINT FINAL SESSION

It is fun and beneficial to structure the final conjoint therapy session largely as a celebration of the client's and parents' achievements in treatment. As noted above, a celebratory atmosphere may be created with snacks, decorations, balloons, music, etc. In addition, many children enjoy an informal ceremony with a playful pomp and circumstance march, a graduation cap, and/or a certificate noting the child's successful completion of treatment. The therapist should focus on ending therapy on a positive note, recognizing the strengths of the parents and child in coping with this experience and applauding their accomplishments with specific and global praise. The most moving aspect of the celebration, however, is often the parent's and child's final exchange of specific praise and global praise that reflects the child's and parent's shared therapy experience, as well as their feelings of love and admiration for one another. This may include the sharing of words of praise, brief letters, poems, artwork, or other creative products children and/or parents prepared in their respective individual sessions. This is an important opportunity for self-praise as well. In fact, some children, for example, enjoy reading or reviewing their final summary chapter of their narrative that acknowledges what they have learned about themselves and their family, what they would like other children to know about sexual abuse, as well as what they are looking forward to in the future. Once again, this is an opportunity for clients to review important adaptive lessons learned about self, others, and the world as part of the conjoint therapy celebration session. Finally, it is helpful to remind families of the importance of engaging in positive interactions by initiating such with acknowledgements of gratitude and appreciation for each member's contributions to the family "in real life" as they have been doing throughout the therapy sessions.

16

Addressing Sexual Difficulties and the Impact of Commercial Sexual Exploitation

Research has documented that although age-inappropriate sexual behaviors and/or other difficulties with respect to sexuality are not exhibited by all children who have been sexually abused, a child sexual abuse (CSA) history does appear to increase the risk of difficulties in this area (Briere & Runtz, 1990; Cohen et al., 1999; Deblinger et al., 1989). Furthermore, nonoffending parents of children who were sexually abused frequently have significant concerns about children's sexualized behaviors; they also lack an understanding of these behaviors and often do not have the knowledge to respond appropriately to normative or problematic sexual behaviors. Thus, it is important to assess for the presence of sexual behavior problems and other dysfunctions with respect to sexuality. These problems range from age-inappropriate sexual behaviors in young children that may reflect their natural tendency to imitate what they have observed or experienced to more extreme difficulties exhibited by adolescents who have been groomed by their offenders to engage in risky sexual behaviors and/or participate in prostitution. This chapter will provide some guidance across the range of these behavioral and emotional difficulties. It should be noted, however, that children's developing sexuality is a complex matter, and there are many books available that can provide further information and are excellent resources for therapists, parents, teens, and children. A list of such resources and websites is provided in Appendix C at the end of this book.

DEVELOPING A TREATMENT PLAN FOR SEXUAL BEHAVIOR DIFFICULTIES

Several studies have documented the value of trauma-focused cognitive-behavioral therapy (TF-CBT) in addressing children's sexual behavior problems (Cohen & Mannarino, 1997; Deblinger et al., 2011; Stauffer & Deblinger,

1996). In fact, a randomized trial conducted by Cohen and Mannarino (1997) demonstrated the superior effectiveness of TF-CBT over a nondirective supportive treatment approach with regard to age-inappropriate sexual behaviors in preschool children. When children who have experienced sexual abuse exhibit sexual behavior problems, TF-CBT, including all the PRACTICE components, has been found to be effective in addressing sexual and general behavior problems as well as PTSD, abuse-related fear, general anxiety, and depressive symptoms in children (Cohen & Mannarino, 1997; Deblinger et al., 2011; Stauffer & Deblinger 1996).

It should be noted, however, that TF-CBT should be individually tailored to address the particular sexual acting-out behaviors exhibited. For milder problematic sexual behaviors, for example, that do not impact others (e.g., compulsive masturbation in private or imitation of nonabusive sexual behavior or language) an initial focus in the child's individual sessions on the child's experiences of sexual abuse as opposed to the child's inappropriate behaviors may be preferable. Mild problem sexual behaviors, in fact, may be addressed in (1) parent sessions that focus on teaching parents behavior management skills that encourage more adaptive coping and affectionate behaviors, and (2) via child sessions that focus on the usual skill building (including social skills when indicated) and narrative development and processing work. This focus may lead to natural increases in healthy affectionate behaviors and reductions in child anxiety that, in turn, result in less reliance on problematic sexual behaviors for attention or anxiety relief. When working with children whose sexual behaviors put them and other children at increased risk for abuse, acknowledgement of the age inappropriate sexual behaviors (e.g., inappropriately touching younger children or engaging in sexually provocative behaviors toward same age or older peers or adults) and review of sexual behavior rules is important to introduce early in treatment. However, it is extremely important to approach this issue in a nonjudgmental manner. Children may minimize and/or deny these behavior problems because of the shame they are experiencing and/or their fears regarding the consequences of their behaviors. Parents may similarly experience shame due to their children's sexual behavior problems. This is natural given the highly punitive societal and stigmatizing response to adult sex offenders. However, children with sexual behavior problems have little in common with adult sex offenders and should not be treated or thought of similarly. In fact, research suggests that treatment programs for children with sexual behavior problems that incorporate ideas from adult sex offender programs and literature may not only be less effective but also may in fact be counterproductive for children (Chaffin et al., 2008). Rather, children with a history of sexual abuse and resulting sexual behavior problems should receive the same thorough assessment, treatment, and compassion that all children with a history of sexual abuse or inappropriate sexual exposure need and deserve. In fact, as noted above, sexual behavior problems ultimately are best addressed the same way one might treat behavior problems of any type.

THE ROLE OF PARENTS IN ADDRESSING CHILDREN'S SEXUAL BEHAVIOR PROBLEMS

When addressing children's sexual behaviors, it is critical to meet with parent(s) first to elicit their views, attitudes, and concerns given the divergent cultural norms and family values regarding sexuality. Parents of children who have experienced sexual abuse frequently find it difficult to cope with children's sexualized behaviors even when the behavior is reflective of normal sexual development. As Friedrich (1990) pointed out, therapists, as well as parents who otherwise appear to be highly skilled in managing children's behaviors, may become quite disoriented and ineffective when it comes to children's normative and/or problematic sexual behaviors. As a society, issues related to adult, adolescent, and childhood sexuality are not openly and comfortably discussed. Thus, it is not surprising that many parents are ill-prepared to respond to their children's sexual behaviors and/or sex-related concerns. To establish whether these behaviors are age inappropriate and/or otherwise problematic in nature, the first step in working with parents involves conducting a careful assessment of the sexual behaviors of concern.

ASSESSING THE INAPPROPRIATENESS OF CHILDREN'S SEXUAL BEHAVIORS

It is important to assess the inappropriateness and the degree of risk associated with a child's sexual behaviors. With the parents' input and the use of standardized measures such as the Child Sexual Behavior Inventory (Friedrich, 1997) or the Adolescent Clinical Sexual Behavior Inventory (Friedrich et al., 2004) (see Chapter 4 and Appendix A) such information can be obtained. Many sexual behaviors exhibited by children and adolescents reflect normal healthy sexual development. In fact, an investigation conducted by Friedrich, Grambsch, Broughton, Kuiper, and Beilke (1991) offered statistics on the rates of specific sexualized behaviors exhibited by nonabused boys and girls of different age groups to assist in identifying normal sexualized behaviors. Therapists may use this information to support their conclusions about sexual behaviors exhibited by their clients. Parents are often surprised to learn that behaviors such as being shy with men, walking around in underwear, scratching one's crotch, touching one's own sex parts at home, walking around nude, and undressing in front of others are exhibited by more than 40% of nonabused children under the age of 12 years (Friedrich et al., 1991). This information is important to help parents differentiate between common expressions of childhood sexuality and age-inappropriate or abusive sexual behaviors. Conversely, it should be noted that adultlike sexual behaviors, such as inserting one's tongue in the mouth of another person, touching another person's sexual body parts, imitating intercourse, engaging in oral-genital contact, and inserting objects in the vagina and/or anus, appear to be rare in nonabused children and are more often associated with experiences of CSA or exposure to adult sexual activities (Friedrich et al., 1991). Other factors to consider when assessing the inappropriateness of sexualized child behaviors include whether the behaviors reflect exposure to adultlike sexual behavior as described above, cause harm or discomfort to the child or others, and/or persist despite limit setting by others (Hall, Gray, et al., 1998; Hall, Mathews, & Pearce, 1998). In addition, when the client engages others in sexual behavior, it is important to assess the mutuality of the interaction, the power differential in terms of age, cognitive capabilities and/or size, the use of force or threats, and the advance planning and extreme secrecy associated with the interactions.

ASSESS PARENTAL ATTITUDES AND KNOWLEDGE ABOUT CHILDHOOD SEXUALITY

Parents exhibit a wide range of responses to the sexualized behavior and talk exhibited by their children. By exploring parental experiences and attitudes regarding sexuality, the therapist will be better equipped to collaborate effectively with parents in the development and implementation of intervention strategies that are consistent with parental views. Depending on the circumstances of the case, the therapist may want to explore the parents' histories of CSA, their understanding of normative sexual development, and their attitudes toward sex education, nudity, masturbation, adolescent sexuality, contraception, premarital sex, and homosexuality.

A parental history of sexual abuse may contribute to the parents' level of comfort or distress regarding a child's sexual abuse and sexualized behaviors. Indeed, empirical evidence indicates that parents who report a personal history of childhood or adult sexual assault experience higher levels of distress upon discovery that their child has been sexually abused than those parents without such a history (Deblinger et al., 1993). Moreover, those parents who use denial and avoidance as primary mechanisms for coping with their own sexual abuse memories may find it particularly difficult to cope with their children's sexualized behaviors as these are blatant reminders of the abuse both they and their children endured. It should be noted, however, that a history of CSA does not preclude parents from being effective therapeutic resources for their children. As noted earlier, enhancing parental awareness of how their personal history may be affecting their responses to their children may be particularly useful in motivating parents to alter their responses and/or later to pursue abuse-focused therapy for themselves.

HELPING PARENTS EFFECTIVELY RESPOND TO NORMATIVE CHILD SEXUAL BEHAVIORS

Parents' understanding of normative sexual development may also significantly influence their responses to their children's sexual behaviors. Not surprisingly, parents of children who have experienced sexual abuse may view any sexual behavior exhibited by their child as a reaction to the abuse. One parent, for example, was convinced that her preschooler's desire to show off her body was a reaction to the abuse and would ultimately lead to promiscuity. Other parents have viewed any type of masturbatory behavior exhibited by their children as a traumatic reaction to the abuse. Sometimes parents assume any sexual interest or behavior their adolescent reveals is a result of their sexual abuse experience. Unfortunately, these types of fears and misconceptions can lead parents to overreact and inadvertently reinforce sexual behaviors with negative parental attention leading to increases in the intensity and frequency of these otherwise normative sexual behaviors. Thus, it is important to identify and correct these unhealthy parent-child interactions around normal sexual behaviors as early as possible.

Parents often need some assistance in modifying their reactions to normal sexual behaviors and questions. As noted earlier, overreacting to normal sexual behaviors may lead to an exaggeration of these behaviors and/or a disruption of normal sexual development. It is therefore important to help parents develop or regain a degree of comfort with their children's emerging sexuality and curiosity. This may start by educating parents about normative sexual development (see Appendix E for possible resources for such education). Parents may then be encouraged to practice calm and accepting reactions to their children's healthy sexual questions and behaviors. Once parents understand that certain behaviors are common and normal given the child's age, they can then be encouraged to accept the behaviors and/or gently distract children when they are engaging in normal behaviors such as touching their genitals in public for example, by giving the child something else do to with his hands such as holding hands or providing a toy to occupy the child when such behavior occurs. Such behaviors will typically drop out as children get older and develop a greater appreciation for social norms. In addition, the therapist may help parents role-play the initiation of open communication about sexual behaviors and related issues.

DEMYSTIFYING DEVELOPMENT AND MAINTENANCE OF SEXUAL BEHAVIOR PROBLEMS

As noted above, some children do exhibit sexualized behaviors that are age inappropriate and/or abusive in nature in the aftermath of sexual abuse (Deblinger et al., 1989; Kolko, Moser, & Weldy, 1988). Parents are often frightened by these seemingly adultlike sexualized behaviors. They may fear that these behaviors reflect a "loss of innocence" experienced by their child as a result of the abuse. Other parents may worry that inappropriate sexual behaviors reflect damage to their child's developing sexual identity and may lead to promiscuity, prostitution, sex-role confusion, and/or sexual offending. Cognitive coping exercises may be used to help parents develop a more optimistic view of their child's future, including the fact that TF-CBT as well as other behavioral interventions have been found to effectively address these behaviors in children. Moreover, one long-term investigation documented that children who received a similar CBT intervention showed no increased rate of sexual behavior problems as compared to children who had no history of sexual behavior problems in the 15-year period after they received therapy (Chaffin et al., 2008). Conversely, young children with sexual behavior problems who participated in a more nondirective treatment approach showed higher rates of sexual behavior problems during the 15-year follow-up as compared to both those who received CBT and children with no history of sexual behavior problems.

Parental concerns may also be addressed by demystifying the development and maintenance of inappropriate sexual behaviors in children. Parents are often surprised to find that social learning principles apply to inappropriate sexual behaviors in the same way that they apply to other child behaviors. By reviewing the basic learning mechanisms, including observation, association, and consequences, parents will begin to see that the process by which most children learn inappropriate sexual behaviors is neither mysterious nor complex.

As noted earlier, many child behaviors are learned through observation. Children essentially imitate much of what they see and hear. Children, particularly young children whose understanding of the meaning of the imitated behaviors may be quite limited, are not selective in the behaviors they imitate. Viewed in this context, the development of inappropriate sexual behaviors may seem less mysterious to parents. Children exposed to or engaged in adult sexual behaviors will sometimes imitate them, just as they repeat many other observed behaviors. In fact, given the extent to which children engage in imitation, it is almost surprising that inappropriate sexual behaviors are not exhibited by all young children with a history of CSA. Moreover, in some cases, it is fortunate that the child imitates the inappropriate sexual interaction as this may have been the only clue provided that the child had experienced sexual abuse.

In addition to observational learning, children may exhibit inappropriate sexual behaviors as a result of the offenders' deliberate efforts to shape and reinforce specific sexual behaviors. This process, referred to as "grooming," has been described from both the victim's and offender's perspective in several articles (Berliner & Conte, 1990; Conte, Wolf, & Smith, 1989). The offender, for example, may first introduce sexual behaviors to children through images of adult sexual activity on the Internet, then the child may be reinforced for simple touching behaviors before encouraging more complex sexual interactions such as oral-genital or genital-genital contact. In order to repeatedly engage the child in increasingly sexual interactions, offenders may use a variety of reinforcers including attention, affection, and play, as well as concrete rewards and bribes. Negative reinforcers are also commonly used in the form of threats (e.g., "I will not kill your mother if you engage in this sexual behavior and keep it a secret"). By developing an understanding of how the child learned the inappropriate sexual behaviors, the parent can begin to view these behaviors as a reflection of basic learning mechanisms rather than frightening symbolic representations of a loss of innocence or disturbed psychosexual development. This understanding also allows the parent to explore the underlying learning mechanisms that may be inadvertently maintaining the inappropriate sexual behaviors even after the abusive episodes have ceased.

It should also be mentioned that for children who have a diagnosis of PTSD, sexualized behaviors may be a reexperiencing symptom associated with this disorder such that these behaviors are elicted by CSA reminders in the environment. For younger children, this may be reflected in their ongoing play activities. Oftentimes, these sexual behaviors decrease as children face and process their CSA memories in the context of trauma narration and processing.

TREATING SEXUAL BEHAVIOR PROBLEMS

It is important for the therapist to help parents examine the patterns associated with their children's inappropriate sexual behaviors, just as they would for any other behavior problems (see Appendix F for functional analysis therapist form). The therapist may elicit from parents a detailed description of the "problematic" behaviors exhibited by their children, including examining the antecedents, behaviors, and consequences (i.e., ABCs) associated with several occurrences of the problematic behaviors. By examining the parent-child interactions associated with problematic sexual behaviors, parents may begin to identify reinforcing consequences their children are experiencing when engaging in these behaviors. As has been seen with other problem behaviors, sexually inappropriate behaviors are often inadvertently reinforced by the consequences they achieve as described in the case example in Box 16.1. Children engage in behaviors for good reasons and the reinforcing consequences of behaviors are often similar across a wide range of behaviors including sexual behaviors. Common reinforcing consequences children seek include but are not limited to attention, control, escape from distress, positive physical sensations, and/or feelings of belonging. With this in mind, it is often helpful to follow the steps below when developing an individually tailored treatment plan for sexually inappropriate behaviors:

Box 16.1

Case example: Decreasing Age-Inappropriate Sexual Behaviors in a Young Child

Six-year-old Jessica was placed in foster care as a result of her parents' neglect due to substance abuse difficulties. During Jessica's initial foster placement, she experienced repeated sexual abuse perpetrated by an older child in the foster home. When Jessica was removed from the foster home, she was placed in kinship care with her maternal aunt, Mary, and her uncle, Jim. Although they were older, Mary and Jim were considering adopting Jessica, but they were concerned about her behavioral difficulties, particularly the inappropriate sexual behaviors she exhibited.

Jessica presented for treatment with moderate PTSD symptoms, as well as significant preoccupation with sexual matters and age inappropriate sexual behaviors. Jessica responded well to individual sessions in which she was provided with psychoeducation about a variety of topics relevant to the traumas she had been exposed to (e.g., exposure to parental substance abuse, traumatic loss, foster placement, and sexual abuse). Jessica also seemed to greatly enjoy coping skill-building activities and implemented many of the skills with relative ease. However, Jessica's behavioral difficulties in relation to her interactions with her aunt and uncle were challenging. In addition to being highly oppositional, Jessica attempted to French kiss her uncle, she grabbed at his genitals on several occasions, and hugged him in a highly sexual manner. Upon examining the patterns of interaction between Jessica and her uncle, it was apparent that after his long work day, Jim rarely gave Jessica much positive attention. However, Jim's responses to Jessica's inappropriate sexual behaviors tended to be highly emotional and long winded. Not only would he yell at Jessica but he would also draw his wife into family discussions with the child about "ladylike behavior", morality, and the dangers of sexual promiscuity.

Jim and Mary were quick to acknowledge that the content of these discussions may have been beyond 6-year-old Jessica's comprehension. In addition, the therapist helped them to recognize that they were probably inadvertently reinforcing Jessica's behavior with lots of highly emotional negative attention. Moreover, they expressed concern that Jessica's sexually aggressive and oppositional behaviors seemed to be escalating. Thus, they were responsive to developing a treatment plan designed to assist Jessica in healing from the CSA experience, while also encouraging cooperative and healthy affectionate behaviors and reducing oppositional and sexually inappropriate behaviors.

Jessica and her aunt and uncle participated in separate but parallel sessions in which the therapist presented basic information about CSA and began to encourage the use of effective coping skills. In addition, Jim and Mary were encouraged to express their fears and concerns about their niece's history and functional analyses of their interactions with Jessica were conducted to better understand the factors that seemed to motivate Jessica's problem behaviors. The therapist then encouraged the effective use of praise and selective attention as well as skills that enhanced their ability to communicate and encourage cooperative child behavior. It was agreed that a conjoint session would be conducted to outline for Jessica those adaptive behaviors that would be encouraged (via parental modeling, praise, and selective attention) while agreeing on the problematic behaviors that would result in a time out. Although Jessica's aunt and uncle were initially hesitant to use time out, they understood that it would require much less energy and effort and would minimize the attention Jessica was receiving for sexual behaviors that were becoming increasingly problematic. However, Mary and Jim found it difficult to identify and agree on healthy affectionate behaviors (i.e., positive replacement behaviors) for which Jessica could receive positive attention as well as feelings of belonging. Jim was concerned about encouraging any affectionate behaviors as he feared Jessica would get "carried away" and inappropriately hug or kiss him and somehow he might be accused of sexual abuse. After some discussion, Jim was able to identify several behaviors (e.g., a kiss on the top of his head and a side hug such as sitting with arms around one another on the couch) that he would be comfortable encouraging and praising.

After much preparation with the caregivers, "okay" and "not okay" touching rules were reviewed with Jessica in a family session (see Chapter 13 on conjoint parent-child sessions). It is important to note that such discussion should not follow a problem episode. Much of the discussion with Jessica revolved around giving and receiving "okay" touches, particularly those that Mary and Jim had agreed to praise on a consistent basis. There was laughter and enthusiasm for developing a long list of touches and verbal expressions of affection that were okay, including saying "I love you" to each other every day. Then the general rules about "okay" and "not okay" touches were reviewed with those "not okay" touches in which Jessica had engaged briefly but explicitly discussed as examples when explaining the rules. These "not okay" behaviors were described clearly and calmly by Jessica's aunt and uncle. In addition, time out was presented as a way of helping Jessica remember which types of touching behaviors were "not okay."

Jessica showed significant improvement in response to treatment and the behavioral plan described. She was clearly very fond of her aunt and uncle and was now learning how to express these feelings in socially appropriate ways. It should be noted, however, that during a particularly stressful period for the family, Jessica got into her uncle's bed and touched him inappropriately. Startled by the sudden reappearance of this behavior, Jim did not respond appropriately with time out. Moreover, the couple began to have second thoughts about adopting Jessica. However, the family was able to recognize that Jessica was probably feeling desperate for attention as they were highly distracted by other family stressors. Thus, they had been giving Jessica little positive attention. After some review of recent parent-child interactions, Jim and Mary were able to view the incident as a temporary and predictable setback and thus agreed to reinstate the outlined program. They were encouraged to refocus their efforts on reinforcing appropriate affectionate and cooperative behaviors while also involving Jessica in age-appropriate discussions about the stressors the family was facing. Over the remaining period of therapy, Jessica exhibited no relapses of the sexually inappropriate behaviors and showed a steady increase in healthy affectionate behavior toward both her aunt and uncle. In addition, Jessica completed a trauma narrative that incorporated her exposure to parental substance abuse as well as traumatic losses and sexual abuse incidents she experienced during her foster placement. Finally, though Jessica was initially hesitant, the therapist gently encouraged her to share her narrative with her aunt and uncle toward the end of treatment. The sharing of the narrative seemed to enhance the aunt's and uncle's understanding of Jessica's behavioral difficulties, as well as their compassion for the traumas she had endured. Treatment ended with a focus on skills (e.g., personal safety skills) designed to enhance Jessica's future safety and development.

- Identify the possible factors or consequences that may be motivating inappropriate sexual behaviors.
- Identify and shape positive replacement behaviors (e.g., focused breathing, healthy affectionate behavior) that will afford the child a means of achieving the desired consequences (i.e., reduced anxiety, attention, affection, etc.) in a socially appropriate ways.
- Help parents and children to communicate more clearly about both appropriate and inappropriate sexual behaviors.
- Help parents and children to establish clear rules and consequences, such as time out, for the inappropriate sexual behaviors.
- Encourage parents to model and praise adaptive replacement behaviors (e.g., effective coping skills, healthy affectionate behaviors).

In the aftermath of CSA, parents often become more aware of and concerned about children's masturbatory behavior. Moreover, when this behavior occurs repeatedly in public and/or is excessive in frequency it can become problematic. In addition, this sexualized behavior can be particularly difficult to treat because it may serve different functions for different children. In most cases, the therapeutic goal in relation to masturbatory behavior should be carefully discussed with parents as generally the goal is not to eliminate the behavior completely. For example, in some instances, an examination of the behavioral pattern suggests that the child is engaging in the behavior simply because it feels good and does so on an occasional basis in private. Such a pattern suggests that there may be no reason to intervene. It is important, however, to recognize that some parents will consider any type of masturbatory behavior morally wrong. Although one needs to respect this view, the therapist may offer parents some information about the lack of relationship with CSA and the normative and widespread nature of the behavior, as well as the potential pitfalls of attempting to eliminate it. In fact, although such parents are not likely to change their views, the therapist can still discuss with them how their responses to the behavior may inadvertently lead to more frequent, secretive, and/or problematic masturbatory behavior. This may motivate these parents to modify their responses to some degree. For example, the therapist may suggest that parents may want to consider an approach in which they neither condemn nor condone the behavior as a compromise in order to avoid inadvertently reinforcing the behavior with their negative attention.

It is important to assess the degree to which a child's masturbatory behavior has become maladaptive. This may be true, for example, when the behavioral pattern suggests that the child not only derives pleasurable sensations through masturbation but seems to engage in the behavior when others are present in order to obtain attention. Clearly, public masturbation is a problem behavior that can create difficulties at home, at school, and in other social settings. Masturbation in private also may be maladaptive if it appears to be compulsive; that is, if it occurs so frequently that it interferes with the child's participation in age-appropriate activities. The sudden appearance of compulsive masturbation may be just as disconcerting to parents as public masturbation. Although both public and compulsive masturbatory behaviors are problematic, they may be maintained by different consequences. Public masturbation is frequently inadvertently reinforced by the negative attention it elicits from parents, teachers, and others. Not knowing how to react, parents and others often provide attention in the form of yelling, lecturing, and/or highly emotional discussions. Conversely, when children engage in compulsive masturbation in private, they may not be seeking attention but rather may be using the behavior to achieve positive physical sensations or to escape from emotional distress. The child may be using this behavior to cope with and/or escape from sexual abuse–related anxieties as well as the stressors associated with the aftermath of disclosure.

The guidelines outlined earlier for inappropriate sexual behaviors may be used to treat public and/or compulsive masturbation as well. It is important to note, however, that parents often need a great deal of practice talking about masturbation in a calm and positive manner before participating in conjoint sessions with their children. In fact, encouraging role-plays of the conjoint session can help parents relax while also allowing the therapist to assess the parents' levels of comfort and skill in discussing this challenging topic with their children. It is often difficult for parents to discuss masturbation in a positive manner because of the stress it has created. Thus, the therapist will need to strongly encourage parents to focus initially on the positive aspects of masturbation while also normalizing the behavior. Parents should be prepared to spend some time in the conjoint session with their child talking about masturbation in a positive, lighthearted manner. After this positive discussion, parents, with the assistance from the therapist, may introduce the rules about masturbation with respect to appropriate times and places. The consequences for breaking these rules also need to be discussed during this session. The negative consequences chosen should be based on the child's age and behavioral patterns associated with the particular inappropriate sexual behavior. For example, although time out may be used effectively to minimize the attention associated with public masturbation, compulsive masturbation may not respond to this procedure because attention is not motivating the behavior in the first place. Rather, compulsive masturbation may be motivated by the antidote it provides to abuse-related anxiety. Thus, with such children, it is particularly important to shape and reinforce other more effective coping strategies while also encouraging the child to participate in trauma narration, which may indirectly address the problematic behaviors by exploring and processing the issues underlying the child's anxieties.

ASSESSING THE INAPPROPRIATENESS OF SEXUAL PEER INTERACTIONS

Another type of sexualized behavior that can be very troubling for parents is sexual activity with peers. Indeed, when a child is discovered to have engaged another child in sexual behaviors in the aftermath of CSA, parents may leap to distressing conclusions linking the behavior to the sexual abuse and worrying that the child may become a sexual abuser himself. Again, it is important to consider the possibility that the child is engaging in normative sexual exploration and play unrelated to the sexual abuse. As noted above, many sexualized behaviors even those involving other children are common and may be relatively benign (e.g., looking at each other's private parts; Friedrich, 2007). More specifically, one study documented that among parents of children ages 3 to 6 years, 25% reported that their children had been observed playing doctor with other peers (Larsson & Svedin, 2001). Moreover, this is likely underestimated, given that in a retrospective survey of college female students, 80% reported some sex play with peers prior to the age of 12 (Lamb & Coakley, 1993). Given the prevalence of this experience, it is important to avoid pathologizing mildly sexual interactions among children that do not appear to be coercive, abusive, or imitative of their abusive experience (e.g., engaging another child in oral-genital contact). When working with a child who is exhibiting these types of normal exploratory behaviors, the therapist may help parents effectively cope with their concerns by providing psychoeducation about normal sexual development and offering basic parenting guidance. For example, parents may be encouraged to satisfy the child's curiosity by providing age-appropriate education regarding sexuality while simultaneously providing education and limits regarding appropriate versus inappropriate touches. Often those two steps are sufficient to address the parent's concerns and minimize the potential for the development of more frequent or problematic sexual behaviors due to parental negative attention.

TREATING SEXUALLY ACTING OUT BEHAVIOR PROBLEMS

When children's sexual interactions with other children go beyond normal exploration and are problematic in terms of their frequency, severity, and/or are abusive or coercive in nature, an individually tailored treatment plan should be developed. In recent years, there appears to be increasing reports of child on child sexual abuse cases that may be associated with increased exposure to adult sexual interactions depicted in the media as well as Internet pornography. Also, it varies widely as to whether children and adolescents who initiated inappropriate sexual behavior remain in the home or are removed from the home. When the children reside in the same home (i.e., siblings), it is important to ensure that caregivers are appropriately supervising the children's interactions. The therapist(s) should assist the children and parent in discussing and establishing ground rules for children's interactions that are comfortable for all parties involved. In some instances, these are similar age peers or siblings who are engaging in inappropriate sexual behaviors that they have been exposed to or experienced themselves.

An assessment (e.g., a functional analysis) that carefully examines the child's sexual behaviors exploring possible consequences that may be reinforcing and maintaining the problematic behaviors can lay the foundation for such a treatment plan. Some young children, due to their sexual abuse experiences, may imitate abusive behaviors experienced and in turn introduce behaviors to other children that are developmentally inappropriate and reflective of adult sexual activities. Without therapy or therapeutic feedback of some kind, such children may have little understanding of the inappropriateness of their behavior. Moreover, children who are struggling on their own to cope with their abusive experiences may attempt to gain mastery over their experiences by reenacting the sexual abuse with other children. Children who are left feeling powerless and out of control by abusive experiences may engage other children in sexual activities in an effort to regain control.

Once it has been established that the child's sexual behaviors toward other children are problematic, it is important to encourage parental confidence in their children's abilities to overcome these concerning behaviors. As noted earlier, it may be helpful to remind parents that research has documented that children with sexual behavior problems that participated in a similar CBT treatment were no different from children who had never had sexual behavior problems in childhood in terms of rates of sexual offenses 15 years later (Chaffin et al., 2008). Thus, even when children's age-inappropriate, problematic sexual behaviors are related to the sexual abuse and directed to other children, they are highly likely to be responsive to treatment.

Based on the assessment and the overall case conceptualization, factors motivating the child's sexual behaviors inform the development of the TF-CBT treatment plan. Though much of the plan will continue to follow the PRACTICE components, greater emphasis may be placed on certain components that may directly address the youth's particular sexual difficulties.

Some children, for example, may lack well-developed social skills and may learn that sexual behaviors are a means of engaging people in interactions and relationships. With such children, it is important to provide appropriate social skills training, as well as to provide the necessary limits regarding inappropriate sexual behaviors. Again, it is important to involve parents so that they can encourage healthy affectionate behaviors and reinforce effective social skills and peer interactions, while establishing firm limits and consistently enforcing the rules regarding appropriate versus inappropriate touches.

The assessment for children with sexual behavior problems may include the above cited additional measures. The therapist may also elicit baseline narratives about the abuse, as well as an episode in which the child engaged in inappropriate sexual behavior. These baseline narratives, however, may not elicit much more than minimal acknowledgment that should be accepted without any pressure to provide additional details. These baselines will likely reveal the degree to which the child is avoidant about the abuse, as well as the sexually inappropriate behavior. With the development of a trusting therapeutic relationship and the increased comfort that comes with skill building and gradual exposure, children are likely to get more comfortable discussing both the abuse and their age-inappropriate sexual behaviors.

Just as in the usual approach to TF-CBT for CSA, sexual abuse education can be introduced after the assessment. However, in addition to discussing the usual facts about CSA and encouraging the use of appropriate language for discussing private parts (e.g., penis, vagina, breasts, and butt or buttocks), as well as "okay" and "not okay" touches, it is important to incorporate an open discussion about the problematic sexual behaviors and their relationship to the experience of sexual abuse. It may be emphasized that children are often confused by sexually abusive experiences and may engage in the very behaviors they experienced. In addition, most children, abused or not, have never learned sexual behavior rules. Moreover, the person who sexually abused them likely directly or indirectly encouraged sexual behaviors that are age inappropriate through playful coaxing, intimidation, coercion, direct threats, or by taking advantage of children's lack of knowledge regarding sexual behavior rules. This is emphasized to reduce the stigma associated with this type of behavior and encourage open discussion, but is not intended to minimize children's responsibility for current or future problematic sexual behavior. Thus, it is important to introduce the rules and explain that the best way to learn new rules is through repetition so each week the rules may be reviewed to help children learn and remember the rules about "okay" and "not okay" touches. Still, it is important to acknowledge with children that learning new rules is a process; thus, together with their parents, they will agree on reasonable consequences they will experience if they forget the rules and behave inappropriately, as this will help them to remember to follow the rules in the future.

The sexual behavior rules outlined below were developed by Bonner, Walker & Berliner (1999a, 1999b) and revised more recently by Silovsky, Swisher, and Widdifield (2010). They may be simplified for younger children, and/or they may incorporate one or two additional general family rules for older children. It is important to keep the number of rules limited, however, as it becomes difficult for children to remember and follow too many rules.

1. It's okay to touch your private parts when you are alone (with parent consent).
2. It's not okay to touch other people's private parts.
3. It's not okay for other people to touch your private parts.
4. It's not okay to show your private parts to other people.
5. It's not okay to make other people uncomfortable with your sexual words or behavior.

Note: Depending on the child's age, with parental input and agreement, be clear about medical exceptions and other exceptions (e.g., consensual adult sexual interactions) to the above rules.

A series of functional analyses conducted with children and the parents may help to assess the function of the problematic sexual behaviors, thereby revealing the most critical coping skills to work on with children (e.g., social skill building if the behavior serves to engage other children; relaxation if the child seems motivated to engage in the sexual behavior to reduce anxiety, etc.). However, for some children the problematic sexual behaviors are so impulsive that learning impulse control skills may best reduce the likelihood of these behavior problems in the future. Bonner and her colleagues (1999a, 1999b), in fact, found the turtle technique was particularly useful for helping children with sexual behavior problems.

The turtle technique was developed to help children manage impulse control problems that can lead to aggressive or other problem behaviors such as inappropriate sexual behaviors (Bonner et al., 1999a, 1999b). With young children, it is very useful to utilize a turtle puppet or model that allows the therapist to demonstrate how a turtle pulls his head into his shell when there is danger. This allows for a concrete demonstration of the importance of taking steps to notice intense or impulsive feelings and manage them by taking time to think and use self-control strategies. With young children, the simple reminder to be a turtle when they feel an impulse that will get them in trouble is often sufficient. When they are turtles, children are instructed to pull their heads in to relax, breathe, and think of a better way to behave. However, in order to identify the most valuable skills to teach youngsters, it is important to conduct functional analyses with both parents and children to best understand what children are attempting to achieve by engaging in the problematic sexual behaviors. Once children's underlying behavioral motivations are understood, it will be easier to identify the optimal replacement behaviors and/or coping skills to encourage.

Older children, for example, whose sexual behaviors may reflect a means of expressing social desires, may also be struggling with social anxiety as well as impulsive tendencies. Again, the CRAFTS acronym here may be used to remind children of important steps they may take to slow down and effectively problem solve:

Cope effectively with negative feelings elicited by problem
Resist responding impulsively by slowing down (e.g., turtle technique)
Acknowledge problem and brainstorm solutions
Find the best solution
Take time to evaluate solution in terms of outcomes for self and others
Stick to the chosen solution or start again

The overall objective is to encourage the slowing down of impulsive responses to feelings and problems. This technique encourages the use of the relaxation, mindfulness, and/or affect regulation skills to help clients slow down, breathe, and problem solve. This slowing down allows for more thoughtful, calm, and potentially effective responses by providing time for optimal problem solving.

An important aspect of problem solving for children to focus on if they have engaged other children in age-inappropriate sexual interactions is empathy for others. This can be done by having children repeatedly examine how others will feel and respond given one problem solution versus another. In addition, role-plays in which relevant at-risk situations are enacted can be valuable in helping children practice and fine tune their skilled responses and process how other children may feel depending on their response. For example:

> **Therapist:** *Let's practice some situations where you tend to get frustrated and angry. First, we can talk about a situation like that and together we can recreate the situation so that we can role-play how you can respond to the situation using the CRAFTS approach.*

It is important to reiterate that the identification and practicing of coping skills should be individually tailored to suit the child's developmental stage, coping style, and therapeutic needs. Moreover, healthy habits take time to take hold, thus it is important to encourage repeated practice of effective interpersonal and coping skills in session and between sessions so that the skills become natural and automatic. As noted above, helping children and adolescents to slow down when faced with difficult choices is important. In addition, the therapist can help clients learn to brainstorm possible problem solutions, while also taking time to evaluate the impact of each of the possible solutions on themselves and on others before choosing a solution to implement. This evaluation step is an important one for adolescents as they may be prone to making less-than-optimal choices. By slowing down their responses to problems, youth can learn to evaluate the impact of their choices with a therapist who reflectively listens, without judgment, as they problem solve. As noted in earlier chapters, parents may be encouraged to take a reflective listening approach as well, although it may be more difficult for them, especially in response to highly charged sexual issues. However, it is important to emphasize how such an approach demonstrates respect and confidence that the adolescent will come to healthy decisions as she thinks through the issues with the supportive ear of a parent or therapist who simply serves as a sounding board.

Oftentimes parents have engaged in repeated emotionally charged lectures about the inappropriateness of children's sexual behaviors that have not successfully produced change. Thus, the overall objectives of conjoint sessions around sexual behaviors is to encourage clearer, more positive parent-child communication that will produce positive change. Thus, therapists may carefully prepare parents during their individual sessions to engage the child in a positive open discussion first about "okay" touches and/or healthy sexuality using role-plays. Throughout these sessions, therapists model clear, comfortable, positive communication about "okay" touches and healthy sexual communication using the doctor's terms for private parts and sexual activities. It is important to utilize as much of the conjoint session as possible to discuss and encourage positive replacement behaviors as opposed to the problem behaviors. However, the conjoint sessions also should include a focus on the problem sexual behaviors that allows for a specific description of the problematic behaviors and a discussion of the possible link to the sexual abuse when appropriate. Parents may then be encouraged to engage the child in a discussion in which the problem behaviors are clearly described and the negative consequences for engaging in those behaviors are agreed upon. The therapist may take the lead in this discussion if parents have difficulty remaining neutral and nonjudgmental when discussing sexual behavior problems. However, when possible parents (after preparation during individual parent sessions) may take the lead and the therapist may coach the parents' efforts to remain positive and clear. However, the therapist must be prepared to jump in if necessary to keep the parent-child communication clear and positive. This is particularly important if the discussion becomes harsh and/or threatening, as children often turn off when parents go into "lecture mode." Before the end of the session, the therapist and/or parents may elicit children's questions to encourage open communication and provide an opportunity to ensure clarity. Periodic review of children's progress, particularly in terms of positive replacement behaviors (e.g., healthy affectionate behaviors), may be emphasized throughout treatment by encouraging parents to praise these behaviors in conjoint sessions. Children can be encouraged to use conjoint sessions to praise parents' increased affection as well during mutual exchange of praise activities. As has been noted earlier, in order to encourage continued healthy sexual development, open communication about sexual issues will likely need to be revisited after therapy ends as the child enters different developmental phases. These discussions are challenging for many parents and can be greatly facilitated by the books and resources suggested in Appendix C.

ADDRESSING RISKY ADOLESCENT SEXUAL BEHAVIORS

Teenagers may pursue risky, unprotected sexual activities in a misguided effort to gain the acceptance of their peers and achieve feelings of self-worth that may have been eroded by the abusive experiences. With these youth, it may be particularly important to provide sex education earlier in treatment. Since there is evidence that children prefer and may benefit the most when parents as opposed to friends or teachers provide education regarding sex and sexuality (Alexander & Jorgensen, 1983; Handelsman et al., 1987), whenever possible it is best to collaborate with parents (see enhancing safety Chapter 14). Moreover, as noted earlier, sex education has been found to be associated with reduced adolescent participation in premature and unprotected sexual activity (Handelsman et al., 1987; Kastner, 1984). However, teens rarely respond well to limit setting that is threatening and/or excessive when compared to social norms. Moreover, parental dictates concerning sexuality may heighten the teen's interest in the "forbidden" activities. Sex education information may be better received if it is provided in a more neutral manner allowing teenagers to just take in the information. In that way, they may utilize the information received when making decisions as to whether or not to be sexually active and/or to use effective birth control. This education may include facts about sexually transmitted infections and pregnancy, as well as information about the emotional risks of sexual activities. With parental input and participation when possible, frank discussions about masturbation and less risky sexual activities can be useful in that it acknowledges safe sexual activities (i.e., hugging, kissing, sexual touching) as an alternative means of satisfying adolescents' growing sexual urges. As noted, there are many books and other resources available to assist parents in having these conversations with children and adolescents in a friendly, nonjudgmental manner. This is important given that ultimately the decisions youth make regarding sexual activities will occur when parents are not present. Finally, with teenagers whose risky sexual behaviors seem to be driven by the troubling thoughts and feelings generated by their abuse experiences, it is anticipated that the narration and processing work will also help them to cope more effectively with those thoughts and emotions. As the skill-building and trauma-focused components of treatment help teens to overcome feelings of shame and cope more successfully, risky sexualized behaviors may diminish as they are replaced by adaptive behaviors that result in positive attention and feelings of belonging. This builds adolescents' feelings of confidence that will contribute positively to their ability to stand strong in the face of peer pressure associated with sex, drugs, and other complex issues.

Still, adolescence can be a challenging time for parents, requiring a great deal of patience, clear communication, and consistent monitoring of teens' whereabouts to minimize exposure to common perils (e.g., substance abuse, car accidents, pregnancy) faced by teenagers. Parents may also be reminded that adolescent brains do not fully develop until youth are in their mid-twenties (Lebel & Beaulieu, 2011). This means they may be more likely to make impulsive, egocentric decisions. The therapist may encourage parents to use reflective listening and supportive problem solving in order to open the door to hearing about teens' sexual questions and missteps, thereby encouraging open communication when the almost inevitable and sometimes quite serious crises of adolescence occur. In fact, teenagers are more likely to consult with their parents when making difficult sexual decisions if their parents have engaged in reflective listening and have served as non-judgmental sounding boards regarding other difficult decisions. When parents resort to anger, lengthy lecturing, and/or saying "I told you so" when teens share personal dilemmas or problems, teenagers are likely to shut down and/or go to less reliable individuals for support.

SPECIAL CONSIDERATIONS IN TREATING COMMERCIALLY SEXUALLY EXPLOITED CHILDREN

Youth exploited through sex trafficking often have a history of exposure to violence, sexual abuse, and other traumas and appear to be at high risk for developing PTSD and depression, as well as for having other emotional and behavioral difficulties (West Coast Children's Clinic, 2012). Moreover, recent research and clinical experience has demonstrated the value and effectiveness of TF-CBT in addressing the often complex trauma reactions experienced by these youth (Murray, Cohen, & Mannarino, 2013; O'Callaghan et al., 2013). While more detailed discussions concerning complex and ongoing trauma and the treatment of youth who have been commercially exploited may be found elsewhere (Cohen, Mannarino, Kliethermes, et al., 2012; Cohen, Mannarino, & Murray, 2011; Hardy, Compton, & McPhatter, 2013), the case example illustrated below (see Box 16.2) highlights several critical features important to consider when adapting TF-CBT for this population of youth. First, *multidisciplinary collaboration* with other professionals is critical in recovering exploited youth, determining the most appropriate and safe placement, and addressing their medical, educational, and legal needs. Second, *therapeutic engagement* of both the youth and caregiver are important early on to encourage feelings of safety and support, thereby reducing the high risk of dropping out of treatment and/or running away among these youth. Third, *accepting the youth's feelings* (i.e., positive and/or negative) toward the traffickers who engaged them and *mirroring the youth's language* in describing the trafficking experiences (e.g., boyfriend, rescue, the life), while avoiding inaccurate and stigmatizing terms (e.g., prostitute, pimp) can help the youth more openly discuss their experiences. Fourth, given the chronic, continuous nature of the trauma exposure, *trauma narration and processing should focus on themes* underlying youth's complex emotional and behavioral difficulties while also taking an approach that contextualizes the youth's traumatic experiences from standpoint of a broader life perspective (Cohen, Mannarino, & Murray, 2011). Finally, when clinically appropriate, it is important to *carefully prepare both youth and caregivers for the sharing of the narrative* as well as sex education and personal safety in conjoint sessions.

Box 16.2

Case example: Youth Engaged in Domestic Sex Trafficking

Jasmine, the youngest of three children had only vague memories of her mother who died of AIDS when Jasmine was 6 years old. From the time of her mothers' death until she was 14 years of age, Jasmine's stepfather frequently sexually abused her and threatened to kill her if she told. At 14 years old, Jasmine ran away and was picked up by a young adult man at a bus station, and he provided her with a place to stay. When he suggested that they have sex, she expressed concern about having AIDS like her mother because her stepfather sexually abused her. The man then helped her to get an HIV test and when the test came back negative, they celebrated by having sex. Shortly thereafter, Jasmine began having sex for cash with other men as her "boyfriend" (as she referred to him) explained that they needed money to start a life together. When the "boyfriend" revealed that he had other girlfriends, Jasmine began to complain. The "boyfriend" became violent at times in response to Jasmine's complaints, insisting that the other girls were helping him raise money for their life together as well. Jasmine continued having sex with men for cash and experiencing harsh and humiliating treatment; however, she was drawn to the "boyfriend" and fearful of what would happen to her if she left him.

Multidisciplinary collaboration

An acquaintance called the police after Jasmine confided in her that that she was in trouble and that she might be pregnant and feared for her baby's life. When Jasmine would not speak to the policeman, the officer, recognizing how young Jasmine seemed, called a child protection worker experienced in working with girls who had been engaged in trafficking. During the child protection interview, Jasmine reported running away from home because her stepfather had sexually abused her. Although the worker suspected that she was involved in trafficking, Jasmine provided little further details about her whereabouts for the last year. The child protection worker reassured Jasmine that she would support her through the child abuse investigation. Jasmine was placed that evening in a foster home where she felt extremely alone despite the presence of other children in the home. The next morning she promptly returned to her "boyfriend" taking a train back to the downtown area of the city. However, when Jasmine revealed to her "boyfriend" that she might be pregnant, he became violent and insisted that she have an abortion. He threw her to the ground and beat her more severely than ever before. A day later, when Jasmine began to vaginally bleed, she went to an emergency room where she was devastated to learn that she had miscarried. After consulting with a local child abuse pediatrician, the emergency room physician called child protection, and Jasmine asked to speak to the worker she had met previously. The worker placed Jasmine that night with a foster family that was located in a more rural area with less access to public transportation making it more difficult for Jasmine to return to the "boyfriend." Jasmine's foster parents were selected because of their willingness to work closely and collaboratively with child protection and participate in treatment with Jasmine as soon as possible.

Therapeutic engagement

The following week Jasmine was seen by a TF-CBT therapist who conducted an assessment documenting Jasmine's moderate symptoms of PTSD in relation to the sexual abuse by her stepfather, as well as severe depression and significant behavior problems. During the initial meeting, Jasmine, not surprisingly given her history of complex trauma, had difficulty making eye contact and seemed distrusting of the therapist as she frequently asked what the therapist was writing down. Each time Jasmine asked, however, the therapist shared with her what she had written and explained why it was helpful to write things down that they were discussing. When asked why she was concerned, Jasmine reported that it reminded her of the police. Jasmine also reported that she did not like the foster mother who was referring to her "boyfriend" as the "pimp" and was an old lady who would probably die soon. When the therapist inquired about school, Jasmine reported that she hated school and was planning to drop out but that she had met one girl in school who reminded her of her old best friend. The therapist minimized attention to Jasmine's insistence on dropping out and praised Jasmine's effort to make a friend, reminding her how much more pleasant school is when you have a friend to hang around with.

When the TF-CBT therapist met with the foster parents, they were already expressing doubts about keeping Jasmine. They reported that Jasmine was sullen, highly disrespectful, and was wearing skimpy clothes and make up that made her look much older and she engaged in flirtatious and sexualized behaviors toward the foster father. In addition, the foster parents reported that Jasmine refused to attend two out of the last five days of school. The therapist acknowledged the challenges of parenting a teenager with such severe difficulties but expressed that she was told that if any foster parents were up for the challenge they were. The therapist explained that although Jasmine was experiencing significant emotional and behavioral difficulties related to traumas, she would likely be responsive to the treatment model that the therapist planned to utilize given its effectiveness with teenagers similar to Jasmine. The therapist further engaged the foster parents by asking about their prior therapy experiences. When the parents acknowledged some disappointing experiences of therapy with prior foster children who were removed from their home, the therapist pointed out how the TF-CBT treatment plan would be different and potentially more successful. Finally, it was explained that although they probably had excellent parenting skills (having raised three successful adult children), given Jasmine's history of abuse and trauma, the therapist would assist them in sharpening their skills to address Jasmine's special difficulties. The foster parents seemed appreciative of that support, though they were still not able to make a commitment to keep Jasmine in their home. The initial focus of the stabilization and skill-building phase with the foster parents was encouraging Jasmine's school attendance. The therapist praised the foster parents for their success in getting Jasmine to go to school on most days and reviewed the parent-child interactions on both successful and unsuccessful mornings to identify what seemed to motivate Jasmine to go to school. The therapist explained that there are often generalized reminders of children's traumatic experiences that lead to unexplained avoidance behaviors and this might explain Jasmine's refusal to ride the bus. Thus, the foster mom was supported in driving Jasmine to school for the time being given the importance of her attending school. In addition, the foster parents were asked to minimize their attention to their concerns regarding Jasmine's style of dress and makeup, as well as her flirtatious behaviors as the conflicts around these issues seemed to be reinforcing these behaviors. Rather, the foster father was encouraged to increase his efforts to give Jasmine positive attention for age-appropriate behaviors even if they seemed somewhat juvenile (e.g., she seemed to enjoy playing with toys in the home that they maintained for younger foster children). Finally, the therapist asked the foster parents to refrain from referring to the "boyfriend" as a "pimp," as Jasmine had not yet processed that relationship and was still seeing it as a consensual relationship.

Trauma Narration and Processing Should Focus on Themes

During the initial phase, Jasmine repeatedly expressed that though the foster parents were "okay," she doubted that she would be staying there for long and was not sure about therapy either. However, she demonstrated an interest in reading some materials about grief and loss, and she was willing to read about a book about CSA as well. As the therapist got to know Jasmine, she began to conceptualize many of her difficulties as stemming from numerous experiences of loss as well as abuse. The therapist encouraged Jasmine to create a life narrative that incorporated positive as well as negative experiences. Moreover, as Jasmine developed her trauma narrative, the therapist noted themes that seemed to reflect Jasmine's beliefs about herself as well as others. Her thoughts often reflected a fear of rejection and loss and questions about her worthiness. Though initially hesitant to talk about her mother, with gentle encouragement Jasmine was able to tearfully describe some tender positive moments she shared with her mother after she became ill. Jasmine was also surprisingly willing to incorporate several chapters about her stepfather before and after the sexual abuse began. Still, as she dictated the chapter about the first incident of sexual abuse, she broke eye contact and shared only limited details. The therapist reflected back what Jasmine had shared, validating her feelings, and thanking her for helping the therapist to understand what the sexual abuse was like.

Validating feelings by mirroring language used by client

As these sessions proceeded, the therapist encouraged the expansion of the narrative to encompass more of Jasmine's life experiences, including meeting the "boyfriend." Jasmine dictated a chapter about this meeting that initially focused on how her "boyfriend" was misunderstood and her anger toward the foster parents for calling him a "pimp." Jasmine responded quite positively when the therapist asked her to write a chapter about (using Jasmine's words) how her "boyfriend rescued" her from the bus station including all the feelings and thoughts she experienced that night. Over time, the therapist gently encouraged Jasmine to write more about the "boyfriend" and "clients," ultimately encouraging Jasmine to include chapters about the last few painful nights with the "boyfriend." After completing and then processing the narrative, Jasmine slowly began to recognize the "business" relationship she had with her "boyfriend" and when the therapist offered to share information about the business of trafficking, Jasmine seemed more accepting of the term and agreed to read some materials provided. During the processing of several chapters, the therapist noted that Jasmine often reported saying to herself in relation to her interactions with her "boyfriend," "Why does he tell me he loves me and treat me so poorly? I guess my step-father did that too. No one will ever really love me." Much time was spent processing these dysfunctional thoughts utilizing Socratic questions that helped Jasmine to recount loving interactions with her mom, qualities that made her lovable, and ways couples in loving relationships ideally should treat one another. Interestingly, Jasmine used observations of her foster parents' interactions when listing positives.

Carefully prepare youth and caregiver for the sharing of the narrative

By the time Jasmine had completed and processed her narrative, she was reporting fewer PTSD and depressive symptoms, was attending school fairly regularly and receiving additional tutoring, and reporting positive feelings toward her foster mother. Though she still felt less comfortable around the foster father, her overly flirtatious behavior toward him had diminished considerably. Still, Jasmine continued to vacillate about both sharing her narrative with her foster parents and returning to the "life." During the final stages of processing the narrative, the therapist elicited Jasmine's greatest fears about sharing the narrative, and she acknowledged that she feared that her foster parents would be disgusted by her behavior and "would send her packing." The therapist arranged a conjoint session prior to the sharing of the narrative during which Jasmine and the foster mother would review some basic sex education. Despite her extensive sexual experiences, Jasmine had a limited understanding of healthy sexuality. This session was conducted in a playful way that allowed for laughter, as well as for serious discussions about love, romantic relationships, sex, sexually transmitted infections, birth control, conception, pregnancy, babies, etc. Despite prior avoidance, Jasmine agreed to attend the gynecological follow-up appointment her foster mother had scheduled for her. In the context of this session, the foster mother was encouraged to share her feelings about what she had learned about what Jasmine had been through. The foster mother explained to Jasmine that she thought she was the bravest girl she had ever met and that there was nothing in her narrative that could change her thinking. Jasmine hesitatingly agreed to let her foster mother read the narrative with the therapist in their next individual session and asked her foster mother to make the decision about whether her foster father should read it as well. In an effort to support and empower Jasmine, the therapist suggested that after reading the narrative, Jasmine and her foster mother could use their collaborative problem-solving skills to make that decision together. Finally, toward the end of therapy, Jasmine was introduced to a victim witness counselor who was available to assist her in coping with the potential prosecution of her stepfather, while also serving as an advocate for Jasmine if she chose to pursue legal actions in the future relating to her trafficking experiences.

It is worth noting that some adolescents who exhibit signs of complex trauma may not agree to share their narrative, even with a supportive caregiver. This is probably the result of many years and episodes of being hurt by adults who were supposed to take care of them. Though it is reasonable to explore and challenge possible cognitive distortions that may underlie such hesitation, ultimately the wishes of these adolescents should be respected. The creation of the narrative and processing with the therapist will still likely be highly beneficial and therapeutic to these youth even if they choose not to share it with others.

Finally, children and adolescents who exhibit complex trauma reactions may require ongoing therapy beyond the trauma-focused work especially when they are residing in a group home or residential facility. Still, it is important to celebrate their achievements with respect to completing a trauma narrative, mastery of coping and personal safety skills, and learning to integrate these skills into their daily lives. This accomplishment may be acknowledged and celebrated, as described in the previous chapter. When necessary, ongoing therapy may provide additional support for the clients' continued progress, as well as individualized coaching with regard to the mastery of coping skills when facing trauma reminders and more general life stressors.

17

Conclusions

In this text, we have focused specifically on the implementation of trauma-focused cognitive-behavioral therapy (TF-CBT) with youth and their nonoffending caregivers in the aftermath of child sexual abuse (CSA). Due to limitations in the scope and length of this book, we could not thoroughly address a number of relevant issues. However, we would like to draw the reader's attention to certain topics to encourage the pursuit of further information and training in these important areas through related articles, texts, and websites (see Appendix E).

First, we strongly endorse the importance of being sensitive to cultural issues in applying this treatment model. Researchers have suggested that among the most critical factors in effective treatment of minority groups are the therapist's ability to demonstrate cultural sensitivity and cultural competence. In other words, therapists should have knowledge about cultural variables that may affect treatment and then should use that knowledge to provide treatment effectively (Paniagua, 2005). Though we have touched on these issues in the text and other TF-CBT related articles (e.g., Cohen, Deblinger, Mannarino, & DeArrellano, 2001), we urge therapists to develop their skills in this area with additional reading and/or training. This is critically important given that CSA is a problem that affects children and their families across all ethnic groups and social classes. It is worth adding that one of the best ways for therapists to become culturally sensitive and competent is to ask families to educate them about their beliefs and values. Also, one must always remember that because a family is part of a specific racial, ethnic, religious, or other group that they may not always share the values of the larger group. Several excellent up to date books on cultural competency are listed in Appendix E.

Similarly, we want to emphasize the importance of recognizing and responding to developmental issues when applying this treatment model. We believe that the basic principles of the treatment described are applicable to children in a relatively wide age range (i.e., 3–18 years of age). However, there are clearly vast differences in the cognitive abilities of children at various ages, as well as the clinical issues of greatest concern for them. Children across this wide age range will approach the processing of their sexual abuse experiences in dramatically different ways. However, research and clinical experiences have confirmed that youth from preschoolers to adolescents can be successfully engaged in TF-CBT including the trauma narration and processing component. Similarly, the dynamics of involving parents in the child's treatment will vary depending on the child's developmental level. Again, we encourage the pursuit of additional up-to-date knowledge on child development issues to enhance the therapists' overall skills in this area to support their implementation of this model with youth of all ages. Again, several child development texts are recommended and listed in Appendix E.

In addition, given the importance of motivating clients and establishing an effective therapeutic alliance, additional reading in this area is recommended. Motivating clients to fully participate in treatment is important because TF-CBT requires a strong commitment by clients to practice new skills and face difficult memories if it is to be optimally effective. Clients, therefore, need to be motivated to participate in the hard work of therapy as well as to follow through with the practicing of effective skills between sessions. All therapists will at times struggle with the issue of how to engage and motivate clients. Rather than accept the widely held notion that the client is not ready for therapy or did not want to change, it may be more helpful for therapists to understand the basis and function of the client's lack of responsiveness to therapy activities and/or recommendations. Based upon that understanding, therapists can plan appropriate interventions designed to motivate the client's active participation in treatment (Newman, 1994). In particular, the work of Mary McKay (McKay & Bannon, 2004) may be helpful in guiding therapists on how to engage families and overcome both concrete and psychological treatment barriers. Specifically, as noted earlier, recent research demonstrated significant reductions with respect to drop out rates and improvements with regard to completion rates for those families randomly assigned to a TF-CBT treatment condition that incorporated evidence based engagement strategies (Dorsey et al., 2014). Another community-based randomized trial examined the influence of the therapeutic alliance over the course of treatment. The results of this recent community- based randomized trial revealed the establishment of a positive therapeutic alliance by mid-treatment was particularly important for those clients assigned to TF-CBT as compared to those assigned to treatment as usual (Ormhaug, Jensen, Wentzel-Larsen, & Shirk, 2014). More specifically, replicating earlier studies, the overall results indicated that TF-CBT produced significantly greater improvements than treatment as usual. In addition, within the TF-CBT condition, those youth who reported stronger therapeutic alliances at mid-treatment showed greater improvements and needed fewer treatment sessions overall. These relationships with respect to therapeutic alliance and outcomes were not found for those assigned to treatment as usual. The investigators suggest that this somewhat surprising finding may be due to the fact that TF-CBT, much like other more structured behavioral approaches, is more effectively implemented when a positive therapeutic alliance supports the continuous engagement of youth and their caregivers in TF-CBT's active treatment components (Ormhaug et al., 2014).

It is important to emphasize that as an evidence-based practice, TF-CBT continues to evolve as research provides more information about how to optimally treat children and their families. In addition, it should be noted that dissemination research has revealed important information about therapist skill development with respect to this treatment model. A recent TF-CBT dissemination investigation, for example, documented the widespread training and use of this model in child advocacy centers across the United States (Allen & Johnson, 2012). Moreover, the results of this study revealed that among clinicians trained in TF-CBT, almost 94% reported commonly utilizing this approach in their clinical practice (Allen & Johnson, 2012). However, the findings also indicated that the most commonly implemented TF-CBT components were psychoeducation, relaxation, and coping skills. These results were not surprising given that these components are, in fact, incorporated into many therapy models across theoretical orientations and thus may be familiar to many clinicians. Conversely, the components that therapists reported implementing significantly less often included parenting skills and trauma narration and processing. Given the research highlighting the importance of parenting skills in addressing children's acting out behavior problems as well as the value of the trauma narrative component in helping children overcome anxiety and abuse-related fears in the aftermath of CSA, an increased focus on these components in the context of therapist skill development may be warranted (Deblinger et al., 2011). Moreover, it has been found that the utilization of all the TF-CBT components with greater fidelity is associated with improved child outcomes (Amaya-Jackson et al., 2012). Thus, it seems that clinicians interested in optimally implementing TF-CBT may benefit from enhancing their knowledge, skill, and comfort level, particularly with respect to the parenting and trauma narration and processing components. Furthermore, clinicians are encouraged to obtain face-to-face training and consultation as such is likely to enhance TF-CBT implementation skills. More specifically, recent findings suggest that such training enhances clinicians' appreciation for the value of structuring treatment sessions, as well as their confidence in children's abilities to discuss their traumatic experiences (Allen, Wilson, & Armstrong, 2014).

Finally, it is important to acknowledge the stressors associated with working in the field of childhood trauma and the impact these stressors can have on the treating professional. Research findings, in fact, suggest that trauma work can have a significant emotional impact on therapists (Adams, Boscarino, & Figley, 2006; Baird & Kracen, 2006). Moreover, reviews of the research literature have suggested a number of psychosocial factors that may impact the likelihood of experiencing secondary traumatic stress or compassion fatigue (Baird & Kracen, 2006; Sprang, Clark, & Whitt-Woosley, 2007). These factors include, but are not limited to, personal coping style, personal trauma history, supervision adequacy, and percentage of clients with trauma histories and/or significant PTSD symptomatology. Furthermore, it has also been found that clinicians whose caseloads included higher percentages of survivors (particularly child survivors) of human induced trauma or violence may be at particular risk for developing secondary traumatic stress symptoms (Creamer & Liddle, 2005; Cunningham, 2003). Thus, these findings highlight the potential challenges of working in the field of CSA. However, given the opportunities to foster extremely positive changes in children's lives, it should be emphasized that work in this field can be highly rewarding and satisfying. Thus, we urge readers to be attentive to the stressors in their professional and personal lives. As has been mentioned earlier, an important means of combating professional stressors may include working collaboratively with multidisciplinary professionals for the common meaningful goal of supporting the healing of children impacted by CSA. Furthermore, we encourage the practicing of the very coping and communication skills we recommend to clients. Practicing what one preaches in this way may not only help to minimize the impact of personal and work-related stressors, but can also serve to heighten one's appreciation for the challenges clients face in implementing new skills learned in the context of treatment.

In sum, we have attempted to outline in this book a time-limited, evidence-based approach to treating children and their families in the aftermath of CSA. We are well aware that many other modes of treatment are used with this population as well. In fact, we recommend other professional books listed in Appendix E that offer excellent additional reading on the issue of CSA and related topics, as well as several books that further elaborate on the general cognitive behavioral interventions described in this book. This book offers a concise, practical guide to a treatment approach that addresses the diverse needs of children and their families facing the crisis of CSA. We believe this approach has many strengths. First, the therapist engages the clients as partners in this therapeutic process, explaining the process to them and requesting their collaboration. This approach encourages clients to have considerable input and control over the work of therapy and to claim credit for their progress. Second, the therapist using this approach communicates to clients that their thoughts and emotions regarding the abuse are understandable responses to the sexual abuse experience rather than mysterious manifestations of some underlying psychological problems. Such an approach helps to normalize the clients' experience while enhancing clients' self-confidence in their abilities to both cope with the experiences, while simultaneously learning to identify and alter inaccurate and/or unproductive abuse-related beliefs. Third, the fact that it is time limited is an advantage, not only from a cost or insurance perspective but more importantly because TF-CBT is less likely to encourage the client's dependence on the therapist. Fourth, this therapy approach has been rigorously scientifically evaluated and has been documented to be highly effective with a wide range of populations across the United States and the rest of the world. Finally, TF-CBT therapists focus on collaborating with clients to help them develop skills that will enable them to process past abusive experiences, as well as more effectively cope with other life problems in the past, present, and future. In that way, we hope clients will continue to reap the rewards of this therapeutic work long after the formal therapy sessions have ended.

APPENDIX A

Information on How to Obtain Recommended Assessment Measures

UCLA PTSD Reaction Index for DSM-IV (PTSD-RI) is available by contacting:

Alan M. Steinberg, PhD
Associate Director, National Center for Child Traumatic Stress
Department of Psychiatry and Biobehavioral Sciences
University of California, Los Angeles
1150 West Olympic Boulevard, Suite 650
Los Angeles, CA 90064
Ph: 310-235-2633 Ext. 224D
e-mail: ASteinberg@mednet.ucla.edu

Child PTSD Symptom Scale (CPSS) is available by contacting:

Edna Foa, PhD
Department of Psychiatry
University of Pennsylvania
3535 Market Street, 6th Floor
Philadelphia, PA 19104
Phone: (215) 746-3327
Email: foa@mail.med.upenn.edu

Shame Questionnaire is available by contacting:

Candice Feiring, PhD
Center for Youth Relationship Development
The College of New Jersey, Department of Psychology
Social Sciences Building
P.O. Box 7718
2000 Pennington Rd.
Ewing, NJ 08628
Ph: (609) 771-2649
e-mail: feiring@tcnj.edu

Child Sexual Behavior Inventory (CSBI) is available from PAR (www.parinc.com)

Adolescent Clinical Sexual Behavior Inventory (ACSBI) items are listed in the following manuscript:

Friedrich, W. N., Lysne, M., Sim, L., & Shamos, S. (2004). Assessing sexual behavior in high-risk adolescents with the Adolescent Clinical Sexual Behavior Inventory (ACSBI). *Child Maltreatment, 9*(3), 239–250.

Children's Depression Inventory, 2nd Edition (CDI) 2 is available from MHS assessment (www.MHS.com)

The Child Behavior Checklist (CBCL) is available from ASEBA (www.ASEBA.org)

Strengths and Difficulties Questionnaire (SDQ) is available at http://www.sdqinfo.org/

Parent Emotional Reaction Questionnaire (PERQ) items are listed in the following manuscript:

Cohen, J. A., & Mannarino, A. P. (1996). Family-related variables and psychological symptom formation in sexually abused girls. *Journal of Child Sexual Abuse* 5(1), 105–120.

It may also be obtained by contacting:

Judith A. Cohen, M.D.
Department of Psychiatry
Allegheny General Hospital
320 E. North Avenue
Pittsburgh, PA 15212
email: jcohen1@wpahs.org

Beck Depression Inventory-Second Edition (BDI-II) is available from Pearson (www.pearsonassess.com)

Alabama Parenting Questionnaire (APQ) is available by contacting:

Paul J. Frick, Ph.D.
Research Professor Director, Applied Developmental Program, Department of Psychology
University of New Orleans
2001 Geology & Psychology Bldg.
New Orleans, LA 70148
Ph: (504) 280-6012
e-mail: pfrick@uno.edu
web: http://www.uno.edu/~psyc/labpage.html

Parenting Practices Scale (PPS) can be obtained from:

The Western Psychiatric Institute and Clinic
3811 O'Hara Street
Pittsburgh, PA 15213

APPENDIX B

Informational and Parenting Handouts

NCTSN HANDOUTS

The following are brief descriptions of available handouts about child sexual abuse (CSA) and other trauma types. It is recommended that therapists carefully read the handouts in order to select those that would be relevant and helpful for clients to read.
Copies of the handouts/sheets described may be obtained at:
http://www.nctsnet.org/trauma-types

HANDOUTS FOR CAREGIVERS ABOUT CSA

Caring for Kids: What Parents Need to Know about Sexual Abuse is available in both English and Spanish and is comprised of informational handouts for parents/caregivers and adolescents about child sexual abuse and acquaintance rape.

- *Child Sexual Abuse Fact Sheet: For Parents, Teachers, and Other Caregivers*
    - Reviews what child sexual abuse is, who experiences sexual abuse, how to tell if a child may have experienced sexual abuse, why children do not tell about sexual abuse, what to do if a child discloses sexual abuse, myths and facts about sexual abuse, and tips to help protect children from sexual abuse.
- *Questions & Answers about Child Sexual Abuse: Interview with Esther Deblinger, Ph.D.*
    - In a question-and-answer format, reviews the definition of child sexual abuse, the frequency of sexual abuse, who is at risk for sexual abuse, the perpetrators of sexual abuse, keys to preventing sexual abuse, the impact of abuse on children, what to do when it is discovered that a child has experienced sexual abuse, and how children and families recover from the experience of sexual abuse. Additional recommended reading materials are also included.

- *What To Do If Your Child Discloses Sexual Abuse: A Guide for Parents and Caregivers*
  - Reviews what disclosure is, facts about child sexual abuse, information on why children are reluctant to disclose, what parents/caregivers can do if they suspect their child has been sexually abused, what parents/caregivers should do if their child discloses sexual abuse, information regarding why children sometimes recant sexual abuse allegations, and how parents can cope with their own feelings regarding their child's disclosure of sexual abuse. Additional recommended reading materials are also included.
- *Coping with the Shock of Intrafamilial Sexual Abuse: Information for Parents and Caregivers*
  - Reviews the definition of intrafamilial sexual abuse, the effects of intrafamilial sexual abuse on children and the family, how parents can cope with their own reactions to intrafamilial sexual abuse, and how families can move forward in the face of intrafamilial sexual abuse. A story of one family's experience with intrafamilial sexual abuse is also included.
- *Acquaintance Rape: Information for Parents*
  - Reviews the definition of acquaintance rape, how common it is, how parents can help protect their teens from acquaintance rape, and what parents should do if their teen is a victim of acquaintance rape. Information regarding additional resources is provided.
- *Sexual Development and Behavior in Children: Information for Parents and Caregivers*
  - Reviews basic information regarding sexual development and behavior in young children, lists common sexual behaviors in childhood, reviews what sexual behavior problems are and how to respond to them, and briefly reviews how to educate children about sexual issues including what to teach when. Information regarding additional resources is provided.
- *Understanding and Coping with Sexual Behavior Problems in Children: Information for Parents and Caregivers*
  - Reviews characteristics of sexual behavior problems, causes of sexual behavior problems, what to do when a child has sexual behavior problems, the treatment options for children with sexual behavior problems, protecting other children when dealing with children with sexual behavior problems, as well as myths and facts about sexual behavior problems in children. Information regarding additional resources is provided.
- *Child Sexual Abuse: Coping with the Emotional Stress of the Legal System*
  - Reviews the role of the legal system in child sexual abuse cases, lists common concerns about taking legal action, provides a step by step outline of the court process and how to cope with each step,

and provides tips for helping children cope with the stress of a trial. Information regarding additional resources is provided.

HANDOUTS FOR CHILDREN AND TEENS ABOUT CSA

- *Preventing Acquaintance Rape: A Safety Guide For Teens*
  - Provides information on what acquaintance rape is, how common it is, reviews that guys can also experience acquaintance rape, provides information on common acquaintance rape drugs, what teens can do to be safe, and presents myths and facts about acquaintance rape. Information regarding additional resources is provided.
- *What Do I Do Now? A Survival Guide for Victims of Acquaintance Rape*
  - Defines acquaintance rape, outlines steps on what to do if one experiences acquaintance rape (e.g., call 911, get a medical exam, see a counselor), and lists common reactions to acquaintance rape. Information regarding additional resources is provided.

Other resources

- *Sex? Or Sexual Abuse? Respect Yourself—Know the Difference*
  - Reviews the difference between sex and sexual abuse, including the use of physical, emotional, or psychological force; how playful activities can turn into unwanted touches; secrecy; and blaming the victim. Information regarding additional resources is provided.
- *But Who Should I Tell? Questions and Answers About Seeking Help After Sexual Abuse*
  - Provides information on why it is important to tell about sexual abuse, who to tell, what to do if the person does not believe you, what happens after you tell, why it is important to not "take it all back," where to get additional information and further help
- *Staying Safe While Staying Connected: Facts and Tips for Teens*
  - Reviews why sexting is not a good idea and tips for staying safe online.
- *It's Never Your Fault: The Truth About Sexual Abuse*
  - Reviews myths and facts about sexual abuse. Information regarding additional resources is also provided.

HANDOUTS ABOUT OTHER TRAUMA TYPES

Physical Abuse

- *Child Physical Abuse Fact Sheet*
  - Includes a definition of child physical abuse, who experiences physical abuse, how to tell if a child is/has experienced physical abuse, what to do if you suspect physical abuse, reasons children do not tell about physical abuse, and the consequences of physical abuse for families.

- *Physical Punishment: What Parents Should Know*
  - Provides information on the possible risks of utilizing physical punishment, and alternatives to physical punishment.

Traumatic grief

- *Childhood Traumatic Grief Educational Materials for Parents*
  - Includes "Information for Parents on Childhood Traumatic Grief" which reviews what childhood traumatic grief is, how it is different from normal grief, common signs of traumatic grief, and what parents can do to help their children and adolescents.
- *Sibling Death and Childhood Traumatic Grief*
  - Includes a review of the unique challenges families face after sibling death, an overview of how children understand death, and tips for caregivers on how to help themselves and their children manage grief. Additional resources are also provided.

Domestic Violence

- *Children and Domestic Violence*
  - A series of handouts about domestic violence provides information about children's exposure to domestic violence, short and long term effects, developmental considerations, principles for interventions, and additional resources

Community Violence

- *Community Violence: Reactions and Actions in Dangerous Times*
  - Includes information for parents and teens about the prevalence, impact, and ways children may cope with community violence. Additional resources are also provided.

CHILD SEXUAL ABUSE INFORMATION (FOR PARENTS AND ADOLESCENTS)

What is child sexual abuse?

Child sexual abuse is when a person touches or rubs a child's private parts (i.e., penis, testicles, vagina, butt, breasts) or asks the child to touch or rub his/her private parts. The abuser could be an adult, teenager, or another child. It is also sexual abuse if the person makes a child watch something sexual in person or on a computer, a phone, or TV. The abuser might make the child do these things through the use of threats or physical force or that person might pretend it is a special game or give the child a reward. Still it is not okay even if that person makes the abuse seem okay or even fun.

Who sexually abuses children?

Most of the time children and teenagers are sexually abused by someone they know, not a stranger. The abuser may be an acquaintance (e.g., a family friend, a neighbor, a coach, a babysitter, or older peer) or a family member. Most abusers are male, but some are female. You cannot tell if someone might sexually abuse a child by the way that person looks, dresses, or acts. While there are some people who sexually abuse children or teens, most people do not.

Who is sexually abused?

Sexual abuse happens to a lot of children and teenagers. Estimates suggest that at least one of every four girls and one of every six boys may experience some form of sexual abuse by age 18. It can happen to boys and girls of all ages, religions, and races. Children and teens who have experienced sexual abuse come from all kinds of families and all different neighborhoods. Sexual abuse can happen to any child or teenager.

How do children feel when they have been sexually abused?

Children and teens have all kinds of feelings when they are sexually abused. For some, the sexual touching may feel good, and they may still like the person who did it. Others feel angry at the person or afraid of him or her. Other children might feel guilty, scared, or confused about what happened. Sometimes when people have these feelings, the feelings affect the way they behave. A child who is afraid may not want to sleep alone or be alone. Sometimes children and teens get into more arguments, and sometimes they may just feel sad and want to be alone. Some people feel upset for a long time after the abuse has ended, but they often feel better with the help of counseling. Talking with a counselor or a parent can help children and teens who have experienced sexual abuse feel much better.

Why don't children tell?

Children and teens often never tell anyone about sexual abuse. When someone sexually abuses a child, they use tricks and threats to keep children from telling about the abuse. The person might say: "You will get in trouble if you tell" or "Don't tell anyone if you love me" or "If you tell, I will hurt your pet or someone in your family." These are all tricks to keep youngsters from telling. Sometimes children and teens keep it a secret because they feel ashamed, embarrassed, or scared. Because of these threats and confused feelings, many youngsters never tell about their abuse even when they are directly asked about possible sexual abuse. It is difficult for anyone to tell about sexual abuse. It takes a lot of courage to tell. It helps for children and teens to tell and keep telling until they find someone that will help stop the abuse. Some youngsters tell a parent, others don't want to upset their parents so they tell someone else.

Why does sexual abuse happen?

It is hard to know why someone would sexually abuse a child or teen. There may be different reasons for different people. We do know this much: children and teens are not responsible for sexual abuse. The person who engaged the child in the sexual abuse is responsible for the abusive behavior.

When should you suspect abuse?

Some youngsters develop emotional or behavioral problems as a result of sexual abuse, but others show no changes in their emotions or behaviors. You cannot tell by looking at a child or teen that he or she has been abused. Sometimes you can tell by the way they are acting that something is bothering them, but you may not know what it is. Parents cannot usually tell if a child is being abused unless they witness it or someone tells them about it. In fact, most instances of sexual abuse are discovered when a youngster reports the abuse to someone. It helps for parents and children/teens to keep the lines of communication open so they can talk about possible stressors including sexual abuse.

What to do about child sexual abuse?

Children and teens need to know that their bodies belong to them. If they feel uncomfortable or confused about the way they are being touched, they can tell the person "no!" and get away and tell an adult they trust such as a parent, other family member, a teacher, or a counselor. The term NO-GO-TELL can help children remember what to do if they get a "not okay" touch. Sometimes the first person a child tells doesn't know what to do, so it is important for children to keep telling until someone listens and helps.

Coping with child sexual abuse

Research has shown that when children have support from a caregiver and receive effective therapy they can overcome abuse and lead full and productive lives. Learning about sexual abuse and how to cope with it helps children, teens, and their parents heal and recover. In fact, after therapy, parents and children often feel stronger and closer as a family.

When child sexual abuse happens, it is important to get help. There is a special telephone number that children, teenagers, and adults can call to get help for themselves or someone who might be experiencing abuse. By dialing 1-800-4-A-CHILD or 1-800-422-4453 in the United States you can always reach someone who can help connect you to someone who can help with a child abuse problem.

PARENT HANDOUT

HOW CHILDREN LEARN BEHAVIORS

Children learn both positive and negative behaviors from what they experience. They learn from everyday experiences as well as traumatic experiences. Described below are different ways children learn behaviors.

Associations

From an early age, children learn from *associations* they observe in their environment. For example, a very young child may learn to associate Mom putting on her coat with Mom leaving for work. A child who has separation anxiety may become upset each time Mom puts on her coat. Children also develop productive behaviors from learning through associations. For example, a child may touch a hot stove and feel pain. As a result of the association between the stove and pain, the child learns to avoid stoves in the future.

Sometimes children develop problematic fears due to associations learned from abuse. A child who is sexually abused in her bedroom may become fearful of sleeping in that room in the dark. This fear may continue even if the offender is not in the home. The child's fears may also grow and extend to being fearful of other associated things such as the darkness in general.

As parents, you can help identify the associations that your child may have formed as a result of abuse. You can do this by noticing new fears or avoidant behaviors that developed since the abuse. Therapy will help your child overcome unrealistic fears, while also helping her identify and respond effectively to realistic signs of danger.

Consequences

Children also learn a lot from behavioral *consequences*. When parents respond to children's positive behaviors with praise, children are likely to repeat those behaviors. Parents also inadvertently encourage children's negative behaviors. They do this by responding to negative behaviors with consequences that are rewarding. For example, yelling when children engage in problem behaviors provides negative parental attention. For many children, this is better than no attention or unpredictable attention. In fact, behaviors that most *predictably* achieve attention (regardless of whether the attention is positive or negative) are most likely to be repeated. Unfortunately, such behaviors are sometimes negative.

Example: A parent is in the supermarket shopping when her child starts yelling because she wants her favorite cereal. At first the parent says "no" but eventually gives in and buys the cereal. This parent has taught the child if she yells loud and long enough, she will get what she wants. As a result of getting the cereal, the child will likely yell to get things she wants again.

This type of learning can also occur with abuse-related behaviors. Some behaviors may have been initially learned through associations but may be maintained because of the rewarding consequences they achieve.

Example: A teenager becomes easily angered particularly when reminded of the sexual abuse experienced. The parents have tried many different ways to respond to the teen's anger. They spend time discussing why she is angry and often lecture her. The parents again may be inadvertently encouraging the angry behavior by providing rewarding consequences in the form of increased parental attention.

Observations

Observational learning goes on all the time in the lives of children. You may be unaware of how much your child *observes* and imitates you. Think about positive behaviors that your child has learned from observing you. Now, think about negative behaviors that your child may have observed and imitated as well. Children also sometimes observe and imitate behaviors experienced as a result of abuse. This may take the form of language or sexual behavior exhibited by the offender.

Fortunately, children can *unlearn* problem behaviors. And it is important to remember that parents are children's most influential teachers. In fact, children primarily learn to cope with life's challenges by observing their parents. As you learn to cope more effectively, your children will be learning many positive behaviors from observing you!

Practice Assignment

Describe positive and negative behaviors that your child may have learned from observing you.

PRACTICE ASSIGNMENT AND NOTES FORM

This form may be used with any of the practice assignments described in the book or handouts in order to encourage caregivers to follow through with utilizing parenting and/or coping skills.

Record the specific plan for implementing the practice assignment.

____

____

____

____

____

After engaging in the practice assignment above, record your and/or your child's reactions (thoughts, feelings, and behaviors) to the assignment.

____

____

____

____

____

____

____

____

____

PARENT HANDOUT

SELF-CARE: TAKING OF YOURSELF AND YOUR CHILD

Children learn how to manage life's challenges by observing their parents. You are your children's most important teachers and role models, but you are not immune to the negative effects of stress. Although your efforts to put your children's needs first are commendable, it is important to recognize you can more effectively help your children when you are feeling your best. Parents are asked to put their oxygen masks on first before attempting to assist their children during a midair emergency on a plane. Similarly, you will be asked to take care of your own well-being so that you will be in the best position physically, emotionally, and cognitively to help your child(ren).

We recognize that it takes a great deal of effort to restore a sense of emotional balance during times of stress. Thus, we will be asking you to take one small step each week to improve your overall coping while supporting your child's coping efforts as well. You will discover that each of the steps builds on one another. As you practice each of the healthy coping skills that your child will be learning, not only will you benefit personally, but you will also become a better coping role model for your child. Research has demonstrated that the "practice" activities we will review with you and your child over the course of therapy can enhance your well-being and your outlook on life. These activities will positively impact your thoughts, feelings, behaviors, physical well-being and your family functioning.

For the next week, choose one aspect of your personal CARE that you may be neglecting and indicate below what you plan to do to help restore balance in your life. Then record what you did and how you felt when you followed through on your plan.

Practice Assignment and Notes

Choose and circle one activity you can do this week from the list below. During the week, record the step you took and how this self-care activity made you feel. Use the Practice Assignment and Notes form to describe the plan and your experience implementing this practice assignment.

Connect with others who provide positive support
Acknowledge your personal strengths with self-praise
Relax and/or engage in rituals that encourage positive feelings
Enhance eating, sleep, and/or exercise routines

PARENT HANDOUT

POSITIVE RITUALS AND ROUTINES

When families experience a trauma or crisis, it is natural for typical routines to be thrown off and for family members to feel less balanced in their daily functioning. Traumatic experiences are often unpredictable, leaving children fearing the reoccurrence of such experiences and the associated negative emotions. Thus, it is important to initiate or reestablish comforting, positive rituals that restore a sense of balance and calm. Children particularly thrive on predictable positive routines and structure. The establishing of such routines can support children's healing and enhance positive parent-child communication. This is most likely to occur if rituals and routines are designed to increase children's positive behaviors, by providing parents more opportunities to practice effective parenting strategies (e.g., praise, reflective listening). Moreover, such routines also help parents to internalize effective parenting strategies by encouraging the development of new parenting habits in the context of routines that can continue long after therapy ends.

Some examples of positive routines that may be considered include morning rituals (e.g., waking children in a positive manner, sharing breakfast), after-school rituals (e.g., having a snack together after school or after homework is completed; taking a walk), dinnertime rituals (e.g., preparing dinner together), bedtime rituals (e.g., reading a short story, saying a prayer together) and weekend rituals (e.g., attending religious services, special family meals, physical activities engaged in together). Although some rituals may continue throughout a child's development, others may be replaced with more developmentally appropriate ones as the child develops or schedules change. For example, rituals that may be engaged in when children enter adolescence may include special times during which friendly text messages are exchanged and weekly one-on-one times during which parents can provide undivided attention to each child.

Practice Assignment and Notes

You may identify one positive ritual from the list above (or create one of your own) that you can initiate or reestablish in the coming weeks. It is important to identify a ritual that you as well as your child will likely enjoy and that will give you the ability to practice positive parenting. Use the Practice Assignment and Notes form to describe the plan and your experience implementing this practice assignment.

PARENT HANDOUT

PRAISE: THE POWER OF POSITIVE ATTENTION

Parents often are unaware of the powerful influence their attention can have on their children's behaviors. Consistent involvement in youngsters' activities and general attention in the form of global unconditional praise is important for helping children feel loved and secure. Thus, parents are encouraged to express unconditional love generously in global terms (e.g., "I love you", "I am so proud to be your parent"). However, when encouraging particular positive behaviors, it is important to specifically acknowledge those adaptive behaviors with more specific praise. The influence of this type of positive attention can best be appreciated when you begin to provide specific praise for a behavior you would like to see more often. The acronym PRAISE may help you to remember important guidelines for the effective use of specific praise with children and teens. Specific praise describes the behavior. Thus, as opposed to saying "good job," you might say "I really appreciated you clearing off the table, thanks for being a helper." Below are more examples of important qualities of effective praise.

Guidelines for effective specific praise

- **P**urely positive praise works best. Praise should NOT include sarcasm or negative tags (e.g., "I like how you _____; adding why don't you do that all the time?" is an inappropriate negative tag.)
- **R**epeat praise predictably and when possible immediately after the positive behavior occurs. This is particularly important when encouraging a new behavior.
- **A**cknowledge small steps toward achieving positive behaviors with praise (don't wait for perfection) and minimize attention to co-occurring mild negative behaviors.
- **I**ntermittent or occasional praise for positive behaviors is not only sufficient but preferable once the new behavior is established.
- **S**pecifically describe the positive behavior when you praise to increase the effectiveness of praise. "Good job" is often too vague to produce significant behavior change.
- **E**nthusiasm is key to effective praise. Increase enthusiastic reactions to positive behaviors and decrease "enthusiastic" (i.e., emotional yelling) reactions to negative behaviors.

Practice Assignment and Notes

Identify and praise one positive child behavior that you would like to see more often. Work to improve both the quality and frequency of your efforts to use praise. Use the Practice Assignment and Notes form to describe the behaviors to be praised and your experience implementing this practice assignment.

PARENT HANDOUT

REFLECTIVE (ACTIVE) LISTENING

Reflective (active) listening is a very effective way of encouraging and reinforcing a child's healthy sharing of feelings, thoughts, and experiences. This is an important skill for encouraging open parent-child communication and reinforcing effective communication skills.

When engaged in reflective listening, it is important to

1. make eye contact and offer your full attention (e.g., turn off your phone)
2. offer encouraging statements (e.g., "tell me more about that")
3. ask open ended questions (e.g., "how did you feel about that? what happened next?")
4. repeat back what the child expresses
5. summarize and/or paraphrase what the child expresses
6. offer specific praise for simply sharing thoughts, feelings or experiences.

When reflective listening, avoid

1. asking specific, multiple, interrogative questions
2. trying to fix the problems shared
3. criticizing the child and/or his friends
4. offering negative commentary.

Practice Assignment and Notes

Set aside special time to engage in reflective listening (e.g., for a few minutes during dinner, before bed, while having a snack after school, etc.). Younger children respond well to the repeating back of their exact words, whereas it may be preferable to summarize older children's expressed thoughts and feelings. With all children resist the tendency to "fix" problems shared; rather serve as a sounding board for their problem-solving efforts. Use the Practice Assignment and Notes form to describe the plan and your experience implementing this practice assignment.

PARENT HANDOUT

SELECTIVE ATTENTION: PRAISE PLUS ACTIVE IGNORING

Attention is rewarding to your child, even when it is negative. For example, if your child whines and you respond by yelling, your child has gained your *negative* attention which will lead to an increase in the problem behavior. Yelling may *seem* effective because it stops children from misbehaving in the moment, but it does not stop children from repeating the behavior in the future.

Think about it. You probably yell at or lecture your child about the same behaviors over and over again. This suggests that the *yelling is not working.*

To decrease your child's negative behaviors you can learn to *actively ignore* the mild negative behaviors (e.g., whining), while *praising* the positive behaviors you would like to see instead (e.g., asking nicely or accepting a "no" response). We refer to the combination of actively ignoring the problem behavior while praising the positive replacement behavior as *selective attention.*

Active ignoring can be very effective when responding to mild annoying behavior problems such as whining, tantruming, complaining, eye-rolling, etc. However, active ignoring should not be used with behaviors that may cause harm to the child or someone else if they continue or increase (e.g., hitting) which often happens when you begin ignoring the behavior. That increase is referred to an *extinction burst*, which will subside if you continue to use active ignoring in combination with specific praise for the positive replacement behaviors.

Practice Assignment and Notes

Identify one mild problem behavior that you will actively ignore each time it occurs. The negative behavior may increase at first, but continue to ignore it until it subsides. Remember active ignoring does not work alone. It is critical to identify a positive behavior that will replace the problem behavior that you can praise and attend to as often as possible. Use the Practice Assignment and Notes form to describe the plan and your experience implementing this practice assignment.

BEHAVIOR CONTRACT

1. Name: ____________________

2. Job: ____________________

____

Steps:

a. ____________________

b. ____________________

c. ____________________

d. ____________________

e. ____________________

3. When to do the job: ____________________

4. Number of times the job needs to be done for a reward:

____

____

____

____

5. Reward: ____________________

BEHAVIOR CONTRACT: HOW TO USE IT

1. This is a contract between you and your child or teen.
   If you have more than one child, you should make a contract with each child.
2. Choose a behavior you want to encourage.
   We use the word "job" because kids can understand it better than "task" or "behavior." It helps to break a job into smaller steps, as many as you need. For example, instead of saying "Clean you room," break it down into smaller steps such as "Make your bed, put your toys in the toy box, and put your dirty clothes in the hamper."
3. Write down when the job needs to be finished.
   Let kids know when the job needs to be done before they earn a reward. For example, tell the child that when she makes her bed, puts her toys in the toy box, and puts her clothes in the hamper, then she can go ride her bike.
4. Write down the number of times the job needs to be done.
   Decide on a reasonable number of times kids need to do the job to earn their reward. Do not expect 100 percent cooperation. Praise him or her after completion of each part of the task. If he or she makes the bed and puts the dirty clothes in the hamper, but forgets to put the toys in the toy box, do not focus on what the child didn't do; focus on what the child did do. Praise the child for making the bed and putting the clothes in the hamper.
5. Discuss with your child or teen what the reward will be in advance.
   A good reward will motivate your child to complete the job. Children and adolescents can be motivated if they are involved in the process of negotiating the contract and providing input about what the rewards will be. A good time to discuss the behavioral contract and decide on the details is during a family meeting that you may have already set up. You may also have developed a Menu of Fun with your child, so the two of you can decide which rewards from this menu he or she can choose for completing the job. Examples of rewards include a favorite healthy snack, watching a favorite TV show, playing a video game, riding his or her bike, a trip with friends to the mall, an outing with the parent, a video rental, and an overnight stay at a friend's house.
6. Mark success on a chart.
   Make a chart big enough to post somewhere in the house or use a calendar so kids can see it. For younger children, make the chart colorful and use pictures to mark success. Stickers also work well with younger kids. For older children and adolescents, they can be involved in making a poster that has magazine pictures of rewards they are working toward and the jobs expected. This is an activity that parents can engage in with their children and adolescents.

ESTABLISHING HOUSE RULES

House rules outline clear expectations for behavior for the entire family.

Why Is Establishing a Set of House Rules Important?

1. House rules are more likely to be remembered when they are posted
2. House rules reduce potential arguments by:
   a. Making expectations clear
   b. Setting limits
   c. Reducing misunderstandings about their existence and/or meaning
3. House rules specifically state the expectations for privacy and respect

Guidelines for parents

When do you set up or post a rule?

1. When you repeatedly tell your child the same thing
2. When people in the family have difficulty following unposted rules (if everyone follows a rule, then it may not need to be posted)

How do you make it easier for your family to follow the rules?

1. No more than five house rules at a time. With younger children, you may want to start with two or three rules.
2. Be very specific when writing the rules (e.g., "Be home by 10:30" instead of, "Be home at a decent hour," or "Pick up your toys, make your bed, and put your clothes directly in the hamper" instead of "Clean your room").
3. Everyone in the household should agree to live by the rules set. This means adults and children.
4. You gain more cooperation if all family members are involved in negotiating the rules.

Note: Sometimes just writing down the rule helps solve the problem. However, you may need to establish set consequences for breaking specific house rules. Consequences should be applied every time the rule is broken.

Examples of House Rules

1. Everyone is expected to be home and ready to eat at 6:00 PM.
2. If you make a mess, clean it up.
3. All schoolwork must be completed prior to going out, watching TV, etc.

4. Get permission before borrowing things that belong to others. If you break or damage a borrowed item, you need to replace it.
5. Knock and wait for a response before opening someone's closed door.
6. Nights before school days, curfew is 10:30. On nights before days off, curfew is midnight.

Practice Assignment and Notes

1. Negotiate with your family a set of house rules that address specific issues.
2. Set clear consequences for following and breaking house rules.

Use the Practice Assignment and Notes form to describe the plan to develop and use house rules and your experience implementing this practice assignment.

PARENT AND ADOLESCENT HANDOUT

IDENTIFYING AND CHALLENGING YOUR PROBLEMATIC THOUGHTS

It is important to look at the way you think and feel about traumatic experiences. The way you think about these difficult experiences can dramatically affect the way you feel and the way you behave. Negative and pessimistic thinking can cause negative emotions, troubling behaviors, and/or distressing bodily sensations. These emotions can make it difficult for you to heal and function in your daily life.

However, you can learn to identify and change thoughts that cause troubling emotions. When you learn to think about negative experiences (like the sexual abuse) in more accurate and hopeful ways, you will feel less distressed and more able to cope effectively.

Distressing thoughts about traumatic experiences are sometimes *permanent, pervasive*, or *too personalized* and are frequently inaccurate and unproductive. Look at your thoughts related to the sexual abuse to see if they have any of these problem qualities:

- *Permanent*: A *permanent thought* tells you things will *never* change. However, there are few things in life that are permanent. Things constantly change.

  Original thought: "Life will *never* be happy again."
  Replacement thought: "Actually, we do laugh together. Maybe with the help of effective therapy, my family and I will enjoy more happy times in the future."
  Original thought: "Our lives are ruined."
  Replacement thought: "Actually, I think I and our family has gained strength and gotten closer in coping with the sexual abuse."

- *Pervasive*: A *pervasive thought* tells you that something that is true for *one* situation is true for *every* situation. However, most problems are specific, not widespread.

  Original thought: "Men can't be trusted"
  Replacement thought: "Some men sexually abuse children, but most men do not. I know men and boys who are kind and caring and are not abusive."

- *Personal*: A thought that is too *personalized* may lead you to take too much responsibility for something that happened that was not in your control. A thought that is too personalized might also lead you to believe that the problem only happens to you. However, there are many problems that you are not responsible for causing and there are very few problems that only happen to one person or one family.

Original thought: "This happened because there is something wrong with me."
Replacement thought: "Sexual abuse happens to some kids. These things happen because the person who is abusive has a problem. The problem is not with me."

Original thought: "I should have known that man was a sex offender."
Replacement thought: "Even experts in the field cannot identify an adult who might sexually abuse a child by looking at or talking to the person."

If you are still wondering if a thought is problematic, ask yourself:

- "If my best friend was sexually abused or had a child who was sexually abused, would I say to him (or her) what I am saying to myself?"
- "Would I want my friend or child to overhear me making these statements out loud?"

If you would not say this thought out loud or to your best friend, then it may very likely be an unhelpful thought. Be your own best support by catching the things you say to yourself when feeling distressed and replace them with more accurate, kinder, and more hopeful self-talk.

Practice Assignment

Complete the cognitive coping form next time you are feeling distressed about the sexual abuse or other trauma. List the distressing feelings and their intensity using the subjective units of distress scale (SUDS). Record on the form all thoughts you were having when feeling distressed including those that you have not shared with others. First, identify any thoughts that were helpful and repeat them as these encourage a more optimistic outlook. Then, identify distressing, inaccurate, or unhelpful thoughts and replace them with more accurate or hopeful thoughts in the next column. Finally, record feelings and SUDS scores experienced when repeating these helpful replacement thoughts to yourself.

Cognitive Coping Form

Complete this form regarding a recent time you were feeling distressed about the traumatic experience(s)

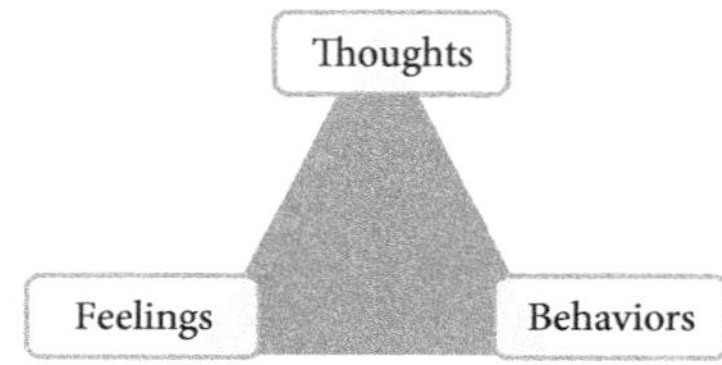

Remember to be your own best friend by replacing distressing thoughts with thoughts that are kind, supportive, accurate, helpful, and hopeful!

What are your feelings?	**SUDS 1–5**	**What are your thoughts? What are you saying to yourself?**	**Are your thoughts accurate & helpful? If not, change them to make them more helpful.**	**What are your feelings now?**	**SUDS 1–5**

SUDS: Subjective Units of Distress Scale 1–5: 1—Not distressed; 3—Moderately distressed; 5—Extremely distressed.

PARENT HANDOUT

ENCOURAGE COOPERATION WITH EFFECTIVE INSTRUCTIONS

Effective instructions can help you get your child to cooperate more:

1. Make eye contact and use a firm but warm tone of voice (e.g., lowering your voice and making eye contact works better than raising your voice).
2. Offer a choice to reduce power struggles (e.g., "choose your black or blue pants").
3. Be specific in your request (e.g., "pick up all the clothes from the floor" vs. "clean up").
4. Give a time frame to respond (e.g., "set the table when the T.V. show is over").
5. Describe positive consequences that will follow compliance with the request (e.g., "after you pack your book bag, you can go ride your bike").
6. Do not use questions, empty threats, or guilt-provoking pleas (e.g., "start your homework" vs. "are you ready to start your homework?").
7. Make no more than one or two requests at a time.
8. Praise and/or reinforce cooperative behavior (e.g., "great job folding the clothes!").

Practice Assignment and Notes

Practice giving effective instructions by following the above guidelines. Take note of errors you make and successes you have in gaining your child's cooperation. Offer specific, enthusiastic, and purely positive praise frequently and generously when your child cooperates in small and big ways. Remember the importance of increasing the ratio of positive to negative exchanges. Use the Practice Assignment and Notes form to describe the plan for using more effective instructions and your experience implementing this practice assignment.

PARENT HANDOUT

TIME OUT GUIDELINES

Time out is a negative consequence that is mild, relatively easy to implement in most places, and can be repeatedly used until the problem behavior diminishes. It is appropriate for children 10 years of age and under. Time out is not effective alone. It must be used in the context of a nurturing "time in" environment in which positive attention and reinforcement is available. Parents also often need some guidance to ensure that time out is being used in the most effective and productive way possible. Below are guidelines for the effective use of time out.

1. Be positive when explaining how time out works. Tell your child it is intended to help him/her remember a particular rule.
2. Role-play or use dolls to show the child how time out works.
3. Start by using time out for one problem behavior or one important rule (e.g., no hitting others).
4. Choose a boring place, free of distractions, for time out.
5. Every time the chosen problem behavior occurs, call a time out for the problem behavior in a calm, unemotional manner.
6. Do not yell or offer additional comments when giving a time out.
7. Set the timer for 5 to 10 minutes depending on the child's age (use shorter intervals for overactive children).
8. Actively ignore and withdraw all privileges from the child until he/she goes to and completes time out. When necessary, repeat a simple phrase like "not until you do your time out."
9. Do not lecture the child during or following time out. Wait one to two minutes after the child completes time out to offer specific purely positive praise for positive behaviors.
10. When the child refuses to do time out, increase the number of minutes or offer a choice of more severe consequences (e.g., "Do your time out or no TV for the evening").

Practice Assignment and Notes

1. Identify one problem behavior that you cannot actively ignore or that you would like your child to stop.
2. Eliminate any reinforcing consequences (e.g., yelling, lectures, etc.) your child may be receiving for that problem behavior.

3. Encourage the positive replacement behavior by offering specific, immediate, and purely positive praise each time the positive replacement behavior occurs.
4. Follow the guidelines to give a time out each and every time the identified problem behavior occurs.

Use the Practice Assignment and Notes form to describe the plan and your experience implementing this practice assignment.

PARENT HANDOUT

USING POSITIVE AND NEGATIVE CONSEQUENCES

Children learn from the consequences following their behaviors, whether those consequences are positive or negative. When parents begin to consciously utilize consequences they can help children develop more adaptive behaviors and minimize problem behaviors.

Using positive consequences

To encourage a positive or cooperative behavior describe a positive consequence that will follow the positive behavior. It is important to express enthusiasm and describe something your child likes to do. It is preferable to use positive consequences to encourage adaptive behavior.

Examples:
"After we finish clearing off the table, you can watch the TV show you wanted."
"If you do your homework now, you'll have time to play outside later."

Using natural consequences

When your child engages in a problem behavior that cannot be actively ignored, you may use a negative consequence to discourage the problem behavior. Natural consequences are negative consequences that occur naturally in a situation. Allowing your child to experience natural negative consequences can often go a long way to resolving a behavior problem. Parents sometimes save children from experiencing the natural consequences of their behaviors, thereby inadvertently undermining natural opportunities children have to learn from their mistakes.

Examples:

Problem Behavior	**Natural Consequence**
Not helping with the laundry	Not having a special shirt to wear
Refuses to eat dinner	Feeling hungry later
Missing school bus	Walking to school (assuming it is safe to do so)

Using logical negative consequences

There may be times when there are not natural negative consequences and, therefore, you may choose to apply a negative consequence that is logically based upon the problem behavior. When logical negative consequences are used, youth should be informed that the problem behavior will lead to a negative consequence with simple *if/then* statements that are stated clearly and calmly or consequences that are agreed upon in advance (e.g., "If you keep playing your IPod that loud, then I'll take it away for the evening.") Logical negative consequences are most successful when they are: (1) in your control, (2) important to your child, and (3) short in duration.

Examples:

Problem Behavior	**Negative consequence**
Coming home late for curfew	Curfew is made earlier
Refusing to get off the phone	No phone use the next night
Fighting with sibling over TV	No TV for one hour

Other negative consequences

For repetitive problem behaviors, it can be helpful to engage in a problem-solving discussion in which the child contributes to the behavioral contract agreement that outlines what will be earned when the positive behavior is exhibited and what will be lost and/or what the negative consequences (e.g., work chores, loss of privileges, etc.) will be for engaging in the problematic behavior. Families may use a behavioral contract that outlines the steps and puts the agreement in writing so that everyone is clear about the agreed-upon positive and negative consequences.

Practice Assignment and Notes

Use the Practice Assignment and Notes form to describe the plan to use positive and negative consequences and your experience implementing this practice assignment.

APPENDIX C

Therapy Resources by PRACTICE Component

All books should be reviewed for their clinical appropriateness before sharing with children and/or caregivers.

PSYCHOEDUCATION

Books: See additional educational books in other components (below)

Your Very Own TF-CBT Workbook
Authors: Alison Hendricks, Judith A. Cohen, Anthony P. Mannarino, & Esther Deblinger
Publisher: Authors (available from https://tfcbt.org/tf-cbt-workbook/)

Dealing With Trauma: A TF-CBT Workbook for Teens
Authors: Alison Hendricks, Judith A. Cohen, Anthony P. Mannarino, & Esther Deblinger
Publisher: Authors (available from https://tfcbt.org/dealing-trauma-workbook-teens/)

The Me Nobody Knows: A Guide for Teen Survivors
Authors: Barbara Bean & Shari Bennett
Publisher: Jossey-Bass

Games

What Do You Know? A Therapeutic Card Game
Authors/Developers: Esther Deblinger, Felicia Neubauer, Melissa Runyon, & Donyale Baker
Publisher: CARES Institute

PARENTING SKILLS

Books for parents: Behavior management

1-2-3 Magic: Effective Discipline for Children 2–12
Author: Thomas W. Phelan
Publisher: ParentMagic, Inc.

Helping School Refusing Children and Their Parents: A Guide for School-based Professionals.
Author: Chris A. Kearney

Publisher: Oxford University Press

Off Road Parenting: Practical Solutions for Difficult Behavior
Authors: Caesar Pacifici, Patricia Chamberlain, & Lee White
Publisher: Northwest Media, Inc.

Parents and Adolescents Living Together Part 1: The Basics
Authors: Gerald Patterson & Marion Forgatch
Publisher: Research Press

Solve Your Child's Sleep Problem
Author: Richard Ferber
Publisher: Simon & Schuster

SOS! Help for Parents: A Practical Guide for Handling Common Everyday Behavior Problems
Author: Lynn Clark
Publisher: SOS Programs and Parents Press

Stickin' To, Watchin' Over, and Getting' With: An African American Parent's Guide to Discipline
Authors: Howard C. Stevenson, Gwendolyn Davis, & Saburah Abdul-Kabir
Publisher: Jossey-Bass

Take Charge of Your Child's Sleep: The All-In-One Resource for Solving Sleep Problems in Kids and Teens
Authors: Judith A. Owens & Jodi A. Mindell
Publisher: Marlowe & Company

The Incredible Years: A Trouble-Shooting Guide for Parents of Children Aged 3–8
Author: Carolyn Webster-Stratton
Publisher: Umbrella Press

Win the Whining War and Other Skirmishes: A Family Peace Plan (for school age children)
Author: Cynthia Whitham
Publisher: Perspective Publishing

RELAXATION

Books

Angry Octopus: A Relaxation Story
Author: Lori Lite
Publisher: Stress Free Kids

Breathe: Yoga for Teens
Author: Mary Kaye Chryssicas
Publisher: DK Publishing, Inc.

Little Yogis Coloring Book
Author: Wai Lana

Mindful Monkey, Happy Panda
Author: Lauren Alderfer
Publisher: Wisdom Publications

Mindful Movements: Ten Exercises for Well-Being
Author: Thich Nhat Hanh
Publisher: Parallax Press

My Daddy is a Pretzel: Yoga for Parents and Kids
Author: Baron Baptiste
Publisher: Barefoot Books

Once Upon a Pose: A Guide to Yoga Adventure Stories for Children
Author: Donna Freeman
Publisher: Trafford Publishing

Peaceful Piggy Yoga
Author: Kerry Lee Maclean
Publisher: Albert Whitman & Company

Sing Song Yoga
Author: Deb Weiss-Gelmi
Publisher: Childswork/Childsplay

Still Quiet Place: Mindfulness for Young Children
Author: Amy Saltzman
Label: CD Baby (Audio CD or MP3 album)

AFFECTIVE EXPRESSION AND MODULATION

Books

Feelings

All My Feelings at Home: Ellie's Day
Authors: Susan Conlin & Susan Levine Friedman
Publisher: Parenting Press

Double Dip Feelings: Stories to Help Children Understand Feelings.
Author: Barbara S. Cain
Publisher: Magination Press

Feelings: Inside You and Outloud Too
Author: Barbara Kay Polland
Publisher: Celestial Arts

The Way I Feel
Author: Janan Cain
Publisher: Parenting Press

Today I Feel Silly and Other Moods That Make My Day
Author: Jamie Lee Curtis
Publisher: Harper Collins

Affective Regulation

Calm Down Time
Author: Elizabeth Verdick
Publisher: Free Spirit Publishing

Every Time I Blow My Top I Lose My Head: A Kid's Guide to Keeping Cool Under Stress
Authors: Laura Slap-Shelton & Lawrence E. Shapiro
Publisher: Childswork/Childsplay

The Chimp Who Lost Her Chatter: A Story about Overcoming Shyness
Author: Lawrence E. Shapiro
Publisher: Childswork/Childsplay

The Lion Who Lost His Roar: A Story about Facing Your Fears
Author: Marcia. S. Nass
Publisher: Childswork/Childsplay

The Mouse, the Monster and Me: Assertiveness for Young People
Author: Pat Palmer
Publisher: Boulden Publishing

Anger Management

Don't Pop Your Cork on Mondays: The Children's Anti-Stress Book (anger too)
Author: Adolph Moser, Ed.D.
Publisher: Landmark Editions, Inc.

No Hitting
Author: Karen Katz
Publisher: Grosset & Dunlap

Bullying

Blue Cheese Breath and Stinky Feet: How to Deal with Bullies
Author: Catherine DePino
Publisher: Magination Press

Bully on the Bus
Author: Carl W. Bosch
Publisher: Parenting Press

How to Handle Bullies, Teasers and Other Meanies
Author: Kate Cohen-Posey
Publisher: Rainbow Books

Stand Tall, Molly Lou Melon
Author: Patty Lovell
Publisher: G. P. Putnam's Sons

Games

Angry Animals 2 (Anger Management)
Author/Developer: Katelyn Mariah
Publisher: Kidsrights

Emotional Bingo for Children
Author/Developer: Marjorie Mitlin
Publisher: Creative Therapy Store

Emotional Bingo for Teens
Author/Developer: Marjorie Mitlin
Publisher: Western Psychological Services

The Peace Path Game (Anger Management)
Author/Developer: Lisa Marie Barden
Publisher: Creative Therapy Store

COGNITIVE COPING AND PROCESSING

Books

Affirmation Weaver: A Believe in Yourself Story, Designed to Help Children Boost Self-esteem While Decreasing Stress and Anxiety
Author: Lori Lite
Publisher: Stress Free Kids

I Believe in Me
Author: Connie Bowen
Publisher: Unity Books

Ready for Anything
Author: Keiko Kasza
Publisher: Putnam Juvenile

Somebody Loves You, Mr. Hatch
Author: Eileen Spinelli
Publisher: Simon & Schuster Books for Young Readers

The Can Do Duck: A Story about Believing in Yourself
Author: Ducktor Morty
Publisher: Can Do Duck Publishing

The Hyena Who Lost Her Laugh: A Story About Changing Your Negative Thinking
Author: Jessica Lamb-Shapiro
Publisher: Childswork/Childsplay, LLC

The Little Engine That Could
Author: Watty Piper
Publisher: Grosset & Dunlap

TRAUMA NARRATIVE

Books

All Kinds of Separation
Author: Carolyn Cunningham
Publisher: Kidsrights

A Safe Place to Live: A Story for Children Who Have Experienced Domestic Violence
Author: Michelle Harrison
Publisher: Jist Publishing

Finding the Right Spot: When Kids Can't Live with Their Parents
Author: Janice Levy
Publisher: Magination Press

Good Grief, It's Sky Blue Pink! A Musical Book about Loss, Grief, and Memories
Author: Toni Griffith
Publisher: Pa & Publication Assembly Corporation

Helping Families Heal: A Story About Child Physical Abuse
Authors: Melissa Runyon, Beth Cooper, & Alissa Glickman
Publisher: CARES Institute

In Their Own Words: A Sexual Abuse Workbook for Teenage Girls
Authors: Karen Risken & Lulie Munson
Publisher: CWLA Press

The Invisible String
Author: Patrice Karst
Publisher: DeVorss Publications

Kids Helping Kids Break the Silence of Sexual Abuse
Author: Linda Lee Foltz
Publisher: Lighthouse Point Press

Laurie Tells
Author: Linda Lowery
Publisher: Maxbooks

Maybe Days: A Book for Children in Foster Care
Authors: Jennifer Wilgocki, Marcia Kahn Wright, & Alissa Imre Geis
Publisher: American Psychological Association

Please Tell! A Child's Story about Sexual Abuse
Author: Jessie (Sandra Hewitt)
Publisher: Hazelden Foundation

Sad Isn't Bad: A Good-Greif Guidebook for Kids Dealing with Loss
Author: Michaelene Mundy
Publisher: Abbey Press

Samantha Jane's Missing Smile: A Story about Coping with the Loss of a Parent
Authors: Julie Kaplow & Donna Pincus
Publisher: Magination Press

Someone I Love Died by Suicide: A Story for Child Survivors and Those Who Care for Them
Author: Doreen Cammarata
Publisher: Limitless Press

Something is Wrong at My House: A Book about Parent's Fighting
Author: Diane Davis
Publisher: Parenting Press

Strong at the Heart: How It Feels to Heal from Sexual Abuse
Author: Carolyn Lehman
Publisher: Sky Pilot Books

ENHANCING FUTURE SAFETY

Books

Personal Safety Skills

It's My Body
Author: Lory Britain
Publisher: Parenting Press Inc.

Let's Talk About Taking Care of You! An Educational Book about Body Safety
Authors: Lori Stauffer & Esther Deblinger
Publisher: Hope for Families, Inc.

Let's Talk About Taking Care of You! An Educational Book about Body Safety for Young Children
Authors: Lori Stauffer & Esther Deblinger
Publisher: Hope for Families, Inc.

My Body is Private
Author: Linda Walvoord Girard
Publisher: Albert Whitham & Company

Personal Space Camp
Author: Julia Cook
Publisher: National Center for Youth Issues

The Teen Relationship Workbook: For Professionals Helping Teens to Develop Healthy Relationships and Prevent Domestic Violence
Author: Kerry Moles
Publisher: Wellness Reproductions and Publishing, Inc.

Uncle Willy's Tickles: A Child's Right to Say No
Author: Marcie. Aboff
Publisher: Magination Press

Your Body Belongs to You
Author: Cornelia Spelman
Publisher: Albert Whitman & Co.

SEX EDUCATION FOR YOUTH

Books

Asking about Sex and Growing Up: A Question and Answer Book for Kids
Author: Joanna Cole
Publisher: Harper Collins

Sex and Babies: First Facts
Authors: Jane Annunziata & Marc Nemiroff
Publisher: Magination Press

Teen to Teen: Plain Talk about Sex, Self-Esteem & Everything In Between
Authors: Melanie Gold, Mara Horowitz, Ashley Greene, Abe Taleb, & Robert Hatcher
Publisher: Bridging the Gap Communications, Inc.

The Care and Keeping of You: The Body Book for Girls
Author: Valorie Schaefer
Publisher: Pleasant Company Publications

The What's Happening to My Body Book for Boys
Authors: Lynda Madaras & Area Madaras
Publisher: Newmarket Press

Where Did I Come From? The Facts of Life Without Any Nonsense and With Illustrations
Author: Peter Mayle
Publisher: Kensington Publishing Corp.

SEX EDUCATION GUIDES FOR PARENTS

Books

How to Talk with Your Child about Sexuality
Author: Planned Parenthood
Publisher: Doubleday

The Sex-Wise Parent: The Parent's Guide to Protecting Your Child, Strengthening Your Family, and Talking to Kids About Sex, Abuse, and Bullying
Author: Janet Rosenzweig
Publisher: Skyhorse Publishing

APPENDIX D

Glossary of Terms

ABCs of behavior: An assessment process used to evaluate and explore the situational factors influencing a problematic behavior pattern. A = antecedents are the events, actions, or situations that occur before a behavior. B = the behavior that is being studied and targeted for change. C = consequences are the outcomes that follow and may motivate the behavior.

Active listening: The process whereby one individual validates and reflects back what the other individual shares. Active or reflective listening provides nonverbal (e.g., eye contact) and verbal cues (e.g., encouraging remarks, summarizing what was heard, repeating back exactly was said) that the individual speaking has one's full and undivided attention. Active listening may include open ended encouraging questions and remarks (e.g., "What happened then? Tell me more"), but should avoid critical or interrogating questions that are designed to change thoughts and/or fix problems. Rather, the individual engaged in active listening serves as a sounding board helping the child or adult to feel heard, validated, and supported in resolving problems on his/her own. This enhances communication by creating a safe atmosphere for the children, adolescents, and adults to share thoughts and feelings. Nonverbal strategies of active listening include making eye contact with the individual, leaning toward them, and nodding to demonstrate listening. This is also called "reflective" listening.

Active ignoring: An approach used to reduce problematic attention-seeking behaviors by selectively ignoring, or removing all attention from the misbehavior while the replacement positive behavior is praised. Active ignoring may lead to a temporary extinction burst in the problem behavior (see "extinction burst" below).

Cognitive triangle: Refers to a 3-point diagram with the points depicting feelings, thoughts, and behaviors. The triangle is used to illustrate the interrelationships of feelings, thoughts, and behaviors. One's perception or what one thinks about a certain situation is related to how one feels and behaves when faced with that situation. For example, the cognitive triangle can be used to show how dysfunctional thinking can lead to negative moods and highlights how behaviors such as isolating oneself can reinforce dysfunctional thinking (e.g., "I am all alone in the world"), which may lead to negative emotions (e.g., sadness, loneliness) that in turn reinforces the isolative behavior.

Complex trauma: Refers to severe traumatic reactions to chronic, ongoing, and/or multiple traumas resulting in the disruption of attachment relationships and significant problems in multiple domains of functioning, including affective and behavioral regulation, physiological systems, cognitive functioning, and/or interpersonal and attachment relationships.

Compliment sandwiches: Providing feedback in the form of specific praise, followed by constructive feedback, and finally ending with additional praise.

Consequences: Through the learning process of operant conditioning, consequences that follow a behavior influence whether or not the behavior is likely to recur. Positive consequences increase the likelihood of a behavior recurring, whereas negative consequences reduce the likelihood that a behavior will recur.

Coping diamond: Refers to a 4-point diagram with points depicting feelings, thoughts, behaviors, and bodily sensations. The diamond is used to illustrate the interrelationships of feelings, thoughts, bodily sensations, and behaviors. One's perception or what one thinks about a certain situation is related to how one feels, one's bodily sensations, and how one behaves when faced with that situation. The coping diamond adds bodily sensations, as it can be helpful for individuals to identify their visceral/bodily responses that are associated with their emotions. The coping diamond is more complex than the cognitive triangle and can be particularly helpful with individuals who are experiencing physical manifestations of anxiety, depression, or PTSD. Reviewing with them how these symptoms are linked to their thoughts, feelings, and behaviors often helps clients feel less vulnerable and better able to manage somatic symptoms.

Differential attention: Minimizing the amount of attention (i.e., either positive or negative attention) given to problematic behaviors (e.g., noncompliance), while increasing attention to any small step toward the positive replacement behavior (e.g., some small level of compliance). For purposes of this guide, this process is referred to as selective attention as this may be a more meaningful term to parents.

Extinction burst: Refers to the increase in a child's behavior before a behavior is extinguished (stopped) that may occur when differential or selective attention is initially implemented. This generally occurs when a parent is instructed to withdraw his/her negative attention and/or engage in active ignoring while attending to or reinforcing a positive replacement behavior. The extinction burst is when the behavior that is no longer being reinforced becomes worse before the behavior stops. It is critically important to warn parents of the possibility of a temporary extinction burst when initially engaging in selective/differential attention or active ignoring plus praise.

Fight, flight, or freeze response: A normal heightened physiological reaction that people experience when faced with a harmful event or stressor. Specifically, it involves hyperarousal of the parasympathetic nervous system. When hyperarousal is experienced, cortisol levels increase, which in turn is associated with increased blood pressure, increased blood sugar, and decreased immune system. The behavioral responses associated with hyperaroused states are often described as fight, flight, or freeze responses. Once the harmful event has ended, most people's level of arousal decreases to the original level. Those children who are exposed to ongoing stressors may remain in the hyperaroused state and develop PTSD symptoms until these symptoms are addressed and decreased during treatment.

Functional analyses: The examination of a sequence of interactions including the antecedents, behaviors, and consequences of a particular behavior. This allows the therapist to assist the parent in identifying patterns of interactions where the parent may be inadvertently reinforcing inappropriate behaviors. See also ABCs.

Global praise: Global praise refers to praise that demonstrates pride, respect, affection, and/or love for the individual regardless of the behaviors exhibited (e.g., "I love you"; "I am so proud of you"; "I admire you"). This type of praise may encourage feelings of security and importance but may not effectively produce specific behavior change. Specific praise (see definition of specific praise below) is more effective in encouraging increases in specific positive behaviors.

Gradual exposure: The process of gradually exposing a client to anxiety-provoking stimuli that may be either internal, such as thoughts or memories, or external, such as tangible reminders of a traumatic experience, in order to have the client habituate to the stimulus and reduce the client's associated anxiety.

Logical consequences: Negative consequences that are logically linked to the problem behavior. For example, if a boy rides his bicycle outside the area permitted by his parents, a logical consequence would be to prohibit him from riding his bike for the rest of the day (or the next day, if the problem behavior occurs late in the day). Logical consequences can be described as punishment that fits the crime.

Loss of privileges: Parents may use loss of privileges as consequences in situations in which natural and logical consequences are not possible or appropriate. Privileges that may be lost include using the telephone, watching television, listening to music, riding a bike, participating in extracurricular or social activities, using the computer, and so on for a specific period of time.

Modeling: Demonstrating a behavior that another person may imitate. Parents often model behavior for children.

Mutual exchange of praise: A positive end-of-session ritual that may be done in conjoint sessions where parents and children engage in the exchange of specific and/or global praise that they prepared for each other in their respective individual sessions. The parent(s) and child(ren), for example, may identify and share something each one did during the week that the other one liked.

Natural consequences: Consequences experienced naturally following a problem behavior, without the need to artificially create or impose the consequences. For example, the natural consequence of a child not studying is getting a poor grade.

Positive end-of-session ritual: Positive rituals that are done at the end of the session that may motivate children to do the hard work of therapy. These rituals should not require much time. Such rituals may include the brief sharing of a pleasant activity (e.g., listening to a song, discussing the local sports team's latest wins or losses, and/or the mutual exchange of praise between parents and children at the end of a conjoint session).

Practice activities or assignments: Many children have a distaste for school and/or homework assignments, thus in this guide therapy assignments to be completed at home are referred to as *practice* rather than homework.

PRACTICE acronym: Summarizes TF-CBT treatment components. It stands for Psychoeducation and parenting, Relaxation, Affective expression and modulation, Cognitive coping, Trauma narrative and processing, In vivo mastery, Conjoint sessions, and Enhancing safety and future development.

Reflective listening: See active listening.

Reinforcers: Reinforcers are any consequences that lead to increases in the behaviors they follow. Such consequences, for example, may include positive attention and negative parental attention, given either of these forms of attention can lead to increases in the child behaviors that they follow.

Selective attention: Minimizing the amount of attention (i.e., either positive or negative attention) given to problematic behaviors (e.g., noncompliance), while increasing attention to any small step toward the positive replacement behavior (e.g., some small level of compliance). Also called differential attention.

Shape or shaping behavior: The reinforcement of closer and closer approximations of a particular behavior in order to shape the behavior until the child is fully engaging in the desired behavior. For example, when a parent wants the child to clean the entire room (e.g., pick up toys, put clothes in hamper, make bed), the parent enthusiastically praises or rewards the child for picking up the toys and gently encourages the child to complete the other tasks. The child is enthusiastically praised for each task he or she completes until the child completes all tasks that comprise cleaning the room.

Socratic method: The Socratic method refers to using carefully designed questions that lead individuals to whom the questions are posed to particular answer or conclusions. In the context of TF-CBT, this type of questioning is most often used during trauma processing when therapists may pose a series of Socratic questions to assist clients in disputing distorted and/or dysfunctional thoughts associated with their traumatic experiences. This is done in order to encourage more adaptive thoughts and/or beliefs.

Specific praise: Providing verbal praise for a specific behavior that will increase the likelihood of the child engaging in that behavior again. Specific praise helps clients understand what kinds of behavior one wants to see by positively encouraging and specifically describing the desired behaviors when they are exhibited (e.g., "I really like how you took a deep breath when you were feeling frustrated").

Stably unstable: Refers to clients who have shown some improvements in their coping skills such that their extreme affect dysregulation has diminished considerably but their coping improvements have "leveled off." These "stably unstable" clients may benefit from moving on to the trauma narrative and processing component given that complete mastery of the coping skills prior to this component is often unrealistic (Cohen, Mannarino, Kleithermes, et al., 2012).

Subjective units of distress (SUDS): These scores help therapists and clients monitor changes in the degree to which they are experiencing distress in session, in relation to trauma reminders and/or in response to their coping efforts. SUDS are typically based on a scale of 1 to 5 with 5 being the highest level of distress and 1 indicating no distress at all. With children, this scale can be presented as a fear thermometer with the high temperatures depicting more distress and/or it can be presented as a series of faces depicting more or less distress.

Time out (from the opportunity for positive reinforcement): A procedure that is extremely effective for noncompliant behavior, as well as other problem behaviors that cannot be actively ignored. Time out essentially involves placing the child in a designated place where no attention, gratification, or reinforcing consequences may be obtained. Time out is given for a short period of time contingent upon the occurrence of a specified problem behavior. The number of minutes recommended for time out generally corresponds to the child's age (e.g., 3 minutes for a 3 year old).

Trauma reminders: Refers to external cues in the environment (e.g., people, places, or things) or internal cues (e.g., thoughts, feelings, memories, etc.) that remind the client of traumatic event(s) and evoke emotional responses similar to the responses evoked by the initial trauma(s).

APPENDIX E

Professional Resources

BOOKS, WEBSITES, AND OTHER RESOURCES FOR THERAPISTS

Cultural Competency

Assessing and Treating Culturally Diverse Clients: A Practical Guide
Author: Freddy A. Paniagua
Publisher: SAGE Publications

Child Abuse and Culture: Working with Diverse Families
Author: Lisa Aronson Fontes
Publisher: The Guilford Press

NCTSN Culture and Trauma briefs
Available from http://www.nctsn.org/resources/topics/culture-and-trauma

Child development

Child Development (9th ed.)
Author: Laura E. Berk
Publisher: Pearson

Child Development: A Practitioner's Guide (3rd ed.)
Author: Douglas Davies
Publisher: The Guilford Press

Development: Infancy Through Adolescence
Authors: Laurence Steinberg, Deborah Lowe Vandell, & Marc H. Bornstein
Publisher: Wadsworth Cengage Learning

Additional Reading on CSA and Sexual Behavior Problems

Childhood Victimization: Violence, Crime, and Abuse in the Lives of Young People
Author: David Finkelhor
Publisher: Oxford University Press

Children with Sexual Behavior Problems: Family-Based, Attachment-Focused Therapy.
Author: William N. Friedrich
Publisher: W. W. Norton & Company

Interviewing Children about Sexual Abuse: Controversies and Best Practice
Author: Kathleen Coulborn Faller
Publisher: Oxford University Press

Medical Evaluation of Child Sexual Abuse: A Practical Guide
Authors: Martin A. Finkel & Angelo P. Giardino
Publisher: American Academy of Pediatrics

Treatment Exercises for Child Abuse Victims and Children with Sexual Behavior Problems
Author: Toni Cavanagh-Johnson
Publisher: Self-published

General Cognitive Behavioral Principles
Child and Adolescent Therapy: Cognitive-Behavioral Procedures (4th ed.)
Editor: Philip C. Kendall
Publisher: The Guilford Press

Cognitive Behavior Therapy, Second Edition: Basics and Beyond
Authors: Judith S. Beck
Publisher: The Guilford Press

Cognitive-Behavior Therapy for Children and Adolescents
Editors: Eva Szigethy, John R. Weisz, and Robert L. Findling
Publisher: American Psychiatric Publishing

Cognitive Therapy Techniques: A Practitioner's Guide
Author: Robert L. Leahy
Publisher: The Guilford Press

Cognitive Therapy with Children and Adolescents, Second Edition: A Casebook for Clinical Practice
Editors: Mark A. Reinecke, Frank M. Dattilio, & Arthur Freeman
Publisher: The Guilford Press

Parenting
Defiant Children: A Clinician's Manual for Assessment and Parent Training (3rd ed.)
Author: Russell A. Barkley
Publisher: The Guilford Press

Helping School Refusing Children and Their Parents: A Guide for School-based Professionals
Author: Chris A. Kearney
Publisher: Oxford University Press

Parent Management Training: Treatment for Oppositional, Aggressive, and Antisocial Behavior in Children and Adolescents
Author: Alan E. Kazdin
Publisher: Oxford University Press

Solve Your Child's Sleep Problems
Author: Richard Ferber
Publisher: Simon & Schuster

Take Charge of Your Child's Sleep: The All-In-One Resource for Solving Sleep Problems in Kids and Teens.
Authors: Judith A. Owens & Jodi A. Mindell
Publisher: Marlowe & Company

Other books by the authors

Can Do and the Storm: A Story about New Beginnings
Authors: Ducktor Morty & Esther Deblinger
Publisher: Can Do Duck Publishing

Combined Parent-Child Cognitive Behavioral Therapy (CPC-CBT): An Approach to Empower Families At-Risk for Child Physical Abuse
Authors: Melissa K. Runyon & Esther Deblinger
Publisher: Oxford University Press

Effective Treatments for PTSD, Second Edition: Practice Guidelines from the International Society for Traumatic Stress Studies
Editors: Edna B. Foa, Terence M. Keane, Matthew J. Friedman, & Judith A. Cohen
Publisher: The Guilford Press

Let's Talk About Taking Care of You: An Educational Book About Body Safety
Authors: Laurie Stauffer & Esther Deblinger
Publisher: Hope for Families, Inc.

Let's Talk About Taking Care of You! An Educational Book About Body Safety For Young Children
Authors: Laurie Stauffer & Esther Deblinger
Publisher: Hope for Families, Inc.

Trauma-focused CBT for Children and Adolescents: Treatment Applications
Authors: Judith A. Cohen, Anthony P. Mannarino, & Esther Deblinger
Publisher: The Guilford Press

Treating Trauma and Traumatic Grief in Children and Adolescents
Authors: Judith A. Cohen, Anthony P. Mannarino, & Esther Deblinger
Publisher: The Guilford Press

HELPFUL WEBSITES

Child Abuse Research, Education, and Services (CARES) Institute http://www.caresinstitute.org/

The CARES Institute, founded and directed by Martin Finkel, D.O. and Esther Deblinger, PhD provides medical and mental health services for children and adolescents who have experienced sexual abuse, physical abuse,

- Cultural and Family Differences in Children's Sexual Education and Knowledge
  - Reviews how children's knowledge of sex varies across developmental levels, how children learn about sex, the cultural factors that impact children's knowledge of and behavior related to sex, why it's important to take the child's and family's culture into consideration when implementing TF-CBT, and provides tips on how to be sensitive to different cultures when implementing TF-CBT.
- The Promise of Trauma-Focused Therapy for Childhood Sexual Abuse
  - This video provides information about the impact of child sexual abuse on children and their families, reviews the importance of including nonoffending caregivers in treatment, and discusses why it is important in therapy for children to talk about the details of their abusive experiences as well as learn skills to deal with their abusive experiences.
- Transforming Trauma in LGBTQ Youth Speaker Series
  - A free speaker series sponsored by NCTSN Child Sexual Abuse Committee and the Persad Center
  - Topics include:
    - "Developing Clinical Competence in Working with LGBTQ Youth and Families"
    - "Working with Families and Schools"
    - "Health Disparity Implications"
    - "Welcoming Environments for LGBTQ Consumers in Care"
    - "Empowering Therapists to Work with LGBTQ Youth and Families"

APPENDIX F

Therapist Forms

TF-CBT Brief Practice Checklist

Therapist Identifier: ____Record C (child) P (parent) J (joint) in box to indicate session type(s) in which component was implemented.

TF-CBT Treatment Component	**Session #:**	**1**	**2**	**3**	**4**	**5**	**6**	**7**	**8**	**9**	**10**
	Date:	/	/	/	/	/	/	/	/	/	/
A: Assessment measures administered and engagement methods used **GE:** Refer to trauma(s) during assessment/engagement											
P: Psychoeducation about trauma(s), reactions, reminders, and treatment **GE:** Use proper words for trauma(s) and private parts; identify trauma reminders and refer to child's trauma experiences											
P: Provide parenting skills (i.e., praise, active listening, selective attention, etc.) **GE:** Connect youth's symptoms/behaviors to trauma											
R: Provide individualized relaxation skills **GE:** Connect use of relaxation skills to youth's trauma reminders											
A: Provide affect expression, identification, and modulation skills **GE:** Connect use of skills to youth's trauma reminders											
C: Introduce cognitive coping/triangle using neutral examples **GE**: PARENT only may be encouraged to use cognitive coping for trauma-related maladaptive thoughts											
T: Develop youth's trauma narrative (TN) in calibrated increments; cognitively process maladaptive thoughts when TN is completed **GE:** Write, read, and/or review TN											
I: GE: Plan in-vivo mastery to overcome avoidance as needed											
C: Conjoint trauma-focused session activities (i.e., trauma education, sharing TN when clinically appropriate, clarification questions, etc.) **GE**: Share TN or address other trauma-related issues in conjoint											
E: Address personal safety, assertiveness, and other relevant skills **GE:** Address skills related to helping cope with trauma reminders											

Note: GE = Gradual Exposure

Therapist Identifier: ____Record C (child) P (parent) J (joint) in box to indicate session type(s) in which component was implemented.

TF-CBT Treatment Component	**Session #:**	**11**	**12**	**13**	**14**	**15**	**16**	**17**	**18**	**19**	**20**
	Date:	/	/	/	/	/	/	/	/	/	/
A: Assessment measures administered and engagement methods used **GE:** Refer to trauma(s) during assessment/engagement											
P: Psychoeducation about trauma(s), reactions, reminders, and treatment **GE:** Use proper words for trauma(s) and private parts; identify trauma reminders and refer to child's trauma experiences											
P: Provide parenting skills (i.e., praise, active listening, selective attention, etc.) **GE:** Connect youth's symptoms/behaviors to trauma											
R: Provide individualized relaxation skills **GE:** Connect use of relaxation skills to youth's trauma reminders											
A: Provide affect expression, identification, and modulation skills **GE:** Connect use of skills to youth's trauma reminders											
C: Introduce cognitive coping/triangle using neutral examples **GE**: PARENT only may be encouraged to use cognitive coping for trauma-related maladaptive thoughts											
T: Develop youth's trauma narrative (TN) in calibrated increments; cognitively process maladaptive thoughts when TN is completed **GE:** Write, read, and/or review TN											
I: GE: Plan in-vivo mastery to overcome avoidance as needed											
C: Conjoint trauma-focused session activities (i.e., trauma education, sharing TN when clinically appropriate, clarification questions, etc.) **GE**: Share TN or address other trauma-related issues in conjoint											
E: Address personal safety, assertiveness, and other relevant skills **GE:** Address skills related to helping cope with trauma reminders											

Note: GE = Gradual Exposure

THERAPIST FORM

PROCESSING DYSFUNCTIONAL THOUGHTS

This form may be used between sessions to record potential maladaptive thoughts uncovered when reviewing children's narratives, notes, and/or other work products. The therapist may first list an uncovered dysfunctional thought or belief and then formulate more accurate functional replacement thoughts that would be preferable. Next, a series of Socratic questions may be listed that may be posed to the child in the context of trauma processing sessions that will lead to answers that reflect the more adaptive replacement thoughts. After trauma narration work is completed, the therapist may use the formulated Socratic questions to help children generate adaptive thoughts and beliefs that can replace dysfunctional thinking patterns. See below example.

DYSFUNCTIONAL THOUGHT

The sexual abuse happened because I am too sexy and was wearing a sexy nightgown.

Positive Replacement Thoughts

Sexual abuse happens to many kids of different ages, sexes, and body types. It doesn't have to do with what the children or teenagers look like or what they are wearing.

Socratic Questions

Who does sexual abuse happen to? Does it happen to kids of different ages, sexes, and body types?

Does sexual abuse happen when kids are wearing regular clothes?

Did you ever wear that nightgown around other people? Did those people sexually abuse you?

Who is responsible for the abuse? Who made the sexual abuse happen? Was it something about the person that caused the abuse or something about you?

Therapist Worksheet Instructions

Utilize the therapist worksheet to record your client's dysfunctional thought(s) and to formulate possible positive replacement thoughts. Then formulate and list Socratic questions on the worksheet that may be used during processing sessions to elicit those or similar positive replacement thoughts from your client.

THERAPIST WORKSHEET

Dysfunctional Thought(s)

____

____

____

Positive Replacement Thoughts

____

____

____

Socratic Questions

____

____

____

- - - - - - - - - - - - - - - - - - - -

Dysfunctional Thought(s)

____

____

____

Positive Replacement Thoughts

____

____

____

Socratic Questions

____

____

____

THERAPIST FORM

CREATING A SAFETY PLAN

Children who have experienced victimization are at greater risk for re-victimization than children with no such history. Thus, it is particularly important to collaborate with clients in creating safety plans that can help children distinguish between real danger signs and innocuous abuse reminders that feel dangerous but in actuality are not. Although training in personal safety skills and the development of a safety plan occurs after the completion of trauma narration and processing, safety skills training and a safety plan should be developed earlier in treatment with children who remain in high-risk circumstances (e.g., living with an adolescent offender or visiting a father who has battered the mother). It is important to identify with the family the most pertinent safety issues in order to create individualized safety plans specific to the circumstances of the abuse experienced. Below are guidelines to encourage a collaborative discussion about safety planning with parents and children during individual as well as conjoint sessions.

1. Describe high-risk situations or safety concerns (e.g., people, places, and circumstances).
   The first step is identifying potential people, places and circumstances that may increase the risk of danger. This may include specific circumstances such as attending family gatherings that may put the child in the same vicinity as the sex offender, walking in the hallways of school knowing that there may be contact with students who are angry about the disclosure of abuse, and/or living in a household where there has been prior domestic violence.
2. Identify individuals who understand the danger(s) and can provide support
   a. Have child memorize names and phone numbers for key individuals (due to the advent of cell phones, many children don't know important phone numbers by heart).
   b. Maintain safety contacts numbers in cellphone address book as well.
3. Agree on proactive plans and/or actions that can reduce the danger(s).
   a. Agree on route or type of transportation to school that minimizes risk.
   b. Encourage child to walk to school with friends as opposed to walking alone.
   c. Establish advance plans if offender visits home or another site unannounced.
   d. Agree on a code word or phrase that alerts others you need help without making it obvious to an offender (e.g., "Is Charlie okay?"; "Nonsense").

4. Identify safe place(s) to go and other steps to take when children feel they are in danger both in the home and outside the home (including what not to do).
   a. Identify individuals in school that will provide support if needed.
   b. Identify safe rooms at home or at school that have accessible phones if possible.
   c. Avoid getting physically in the middle of angry or violent individuals.
   d. Practice calling 911 by doing role-plays without really calling the number but learning the steps needed to use the phone (especially important with young children).
5. Encourage the family to communicate openly and agree on the safety plan.
   a. When possible, the safety plan should be reviewed with siblings and other family members impacted.
   b. When necessary the safety plan may be reviewed with other support people.
6. Review and adjust the plan as circumstances change and/or child matures.

Family Safety Plan

1. Describe high-risk situations or possible safety concerns.

   ____

   ____

   ____

2. Identify names and phone numbers of individuals who understand the concerns/danger(s) and can provide support.

   ____

   ____

   ____

3. Agree on proactive plans and/or actions that can reduce danger(s) including safe travel routes, plans to manage anticipated concerns, and family code words.

   ____

   ____

   ____

4. Identify safe place(s) to go and other steps to increase safety at home and outside home.

   ____

   ____

   ____

THERAPIST FORM

SAMPLE SCENARIOS TO ROLE-PLAY PRACTICING ASSERTIVE COMMUNICATION AND SAFETY SKILLS

The scenarios below are some examples of possible role-plays that can be used to help children and adolescents practice responding in situations that make them feel uncomfortable and/or may be abusive. The role-plays can be adapted for use with both males and females. Therapists should be open and gender neutral with children and adolescents who may have a same sex orientation, so as not to imply that they should like "boys" instead of "girls" or vice versa. The NCTSN handout described in Appendix B provides additional important suggestions for working with LGBTQ youth impacted by sexual abuse.

In general, role-plays should be selected and individually tailored to create situations that are realistic and relevant for individual clients and their circumstances. The therapist may encourage developmentally appropriate and realistic role-plays. With young children, it helps to remind them of the NO-GO-TELL refrain for remembering how to respond to "not okay" and confusing touches. Teens may enjoy helping to set the stage for role-plays. For example, a teen may suggest creating a party scene by putting two chairs side by side to represent a sofa. In addition, with the adolescent's permission, the therapist may suggest that a touch on the client's arm be a signal in the role-play that the date is starting to give uncomfortable/"not okay" touches. The client may then be encouraged to role-play how he/she would respond verbally and behaviorally to a potentially abusive or unsafe situation. The therapist may participate in the role-plays encouraging the client to engage in assertive behavioral responses and clear communication when telling a parent or other individual about the problem situation. In addition, the therapist may provide feedback in the form of compliment sandwiches (i.e., constructive feedback sandwiched in between praise for assertive responses or behaviors), while also encouraging repeated practice of the same scenario in order to enhance clients' personal safety responses.

Note to clinician: Help children and teens review relevant scenarios (below) and identify all possible steps they could take to optimally respond to threats and/or victimization experiences. Next, role-play the scenarios to provide opportunities for clients to practice the steps identified and skills learned.

Example scenarios for adolescents

You and your best friend are at the mall with your parents' permission. You are walking from your car through the parking lot into the mall. A group of older boys (girls) drive up in a really cool car and ask you to hang out with them. You keep walking, but they keep asking you to take a ride in the car. Your friend wants to go with them. Practice responding to your friend and to the situation.

You are asked to go to a party by a boy (girl) that you really like. Your mother agrees that you can go as long as there are no drugs and alcohol involved. She also asks you to call her immediately if anything is not safe. When you arrive, you see multiple teenagers drinking beer and smoking pot. Someone offers you some pills. You are relieved to see the boy (girl) you like. You happily greet one another and he leads you to the couch. You begin to make out (kissing) and you are really enjoying this. Imagine that this person proceeds to touch your breasts (penis) and begins to unzip your pants and you are very uncomfortable with this. Practice what you would say and do.

Your Uncle Joe comes to your house frequently, and your parents are always saying you should treat him with respect and be nice to him. He hugs you constantly and has occasionally brushed your breasts with his hand and patted your butt while he is hugging you. You are extremely uncomfortable with these interactions. *Note to clinician: Encourage the child to practice what steps to take in response to Uncle Joe and later when he/she feels safe.*

Your adult neighbor often invites you to his house to play videogames, but he touches your back and shoulders a lot and it really creeps you out. You thought about telling your parent(s) about it, but you didn't want to get him in trouble because he has a lot of cool videogames that you enjoy playing with him. On one occasion, he touches your breasts/grabs your penis and begs you not tell. *Note to clinician: This scenario may be practiced with several different endings in which the offender says don't tell because* (e.g., *he loves you; he might have to go to jail; he will hurt you or kill your pet; do the same to your little brother or sister). Encourage the child to practice what he/she would say or do in response to this interaction and then who and how he/she would tell.*

Example scenarios for young children:

You are playing with your older cousin, and he tells you and his little brother that he wants to show you a game. He pulls his pants down and begins to rub his penis. He then asks you to rub his penis like he did because it is fun and tells you that he will give you a prize if you play the game. *Encourage the child to practice what he/she would do and say in that situation.*

You are playing ball and your coach asks you to stay and help clean up. Your mom and dad gave you permission to help the coach and to ride home with him after the game. During the ride home, the coach tells you how special you are and begins to rub your legs and back. He tells you that he can help you become his star player. You like how that sounds, but you are also scared because other kids have said he is a "pervert." *Practice what you would do and say to your parent(s) when you get home.*

You are at a sleepover at your friend's house and your friend's stepfather asks you to play a wrestling game. It's really fun at first and you are giggling and laughing. Then, he gives you a "not okay" touch on your butt and he puts his hand down your pants. He tells you he'll hurt you bad if you tell anyone what he did. *Encourage child to practice what he/she would say and do in that situation. Then have the child identify someone he/she would tell about this experience and practice telling.*

A teenage babysitter you like very much suggests that you watch some cool videos with her. She opens a link on the computer and you see naked people touching each other and having sex in the videos. The babysitter is rubbing your back and asks if you would like to try that with her. You are confused and wonder what she means. *Encourage the child to practice what he/she would say and do during and after this experience.*

THERAPIST FORM

CONDUCTING A FUNCTIONAL ANALYSIS

Problematic behaviors exhibited by children sometimes develop in the aftermath of traumatic experiences and, like all behaviors, they often serve a function. Like adaptive behaviors, many problem behaviors achieve natural goals that children desire such as experiencing positive bodily sensations, avoiding or reducing distress/pain, obtaining social attention, increasing feelings of belonging, and/or achieving feelings of control or mastery. A carefully conducted functional analysis can assist therapists in identifying behaviors' functions or the specific consequences achieved by the particular problem behaviors. Information from functional analyses can help therapists guide parents in creating rituals and/or routines (e.g., giving choices of what to wear in the morning) that will increase the child's ability to achieve the desired consequences (e.g., control) with positive adaptive behaviors. Such changes, typically identified in collaboration with parents, are designed to increase the likelihood of children engaging in more adaptive behaviors that serve the same function and/or achieve the desired goal(s) in healthier ways. More specifically, a functional analysis involves the careful collection of information about environmental circumstances and parent-child interactions before (i.e., antecedents), during, and after (i.e., consequences) the occurrence of a problem behavior. Thus, it helps to conduct a functional analysis of problem behaviors using the ABCs (antecedents, behaviors, consequences) format.

This approach involves examining **ANTECEDENTS** or what was happening before the problem behavior occurred. This can include the environmental circumstances, the child's physical or emotional state, what the parent was feeling, thinking, and doing, and parent-child interactions (if any) before the problem behavior happened.

Next, it is important to collect as much information as possible about the **BEHAVIOR** of concern. A detailed description of the behavior often reveals helpful information in determining the developmental or clinical inappropriateness of the behavior as well as missed opportunities to praise small positive behaviors that may occur alongside problem behaviors (e.g., complaining but simultaneously picking clothes up from the floor).

Finally, it is important to elicit as much detail as possible about the **CONSEQUENCES** or what happened after the identified problem behavior occurred. This means asking parents to be as honest and as detailed as possible in reporting what they were thinking and feeling and exactly what they said or did in response to the problem behaviors, as well as how the child responded. Eliciting the exact words and actions associated with the back and forth parent-child interactions can be particularly helpful in identifying the function of the child's behavior as well as ways in which the parent may be minimizing attention to positive behaviors while inadvertently reinforcing problematic behaviors. The below questions may be helpful in structuring the collection of information regarding **A**ntecedents, **B**ehaviors, and **C**onsequences associated with the identified problem behavior.

- What is the problem behavior?
- What was happening before [the problem behavior] occurred?
- When [the problem behavior] occurred, what were you thinking and feeling?
- What did you say and do in response to the behavior?
- How did your child react to your response?

Repeat the below questions as many times as necessary to get a full picture of the parent-child interaction:

- Then what did you do or say?
- Then what did your child do or say?

It is recommended that a separate blank piece of paper be utilized to record a detailed account of ABCs of the problem interactions based on the above questions. The Functional Analysis Summary Form provides a useful way to summarize the information collected as well as the important next steps for identifying the possible function of the problem behavior and potential adaptive replacement behaviors.

FUNCTIONAL ANALYSIS SUMMARY FORM

Child's (Target) Behavior :

Antecedents: Describe what happened before child's behavior (e.g., environment, parent behavior/mood, child's physiological state/mood, etc.).	Behaviors: Describe child's specific behaviors.	Consequences Describe parent's response (include parental thoughts, feelings, behavioral and verbal responses)	Possible Function: (e.g., feels good, escape, control, attention, belonging, mastery)	Possible replacement behavior:

REFERENCES

Abbey, A. (2002). Alcohol-related sexual assault: A common problem among college students. *Journal of Studies on Alcohol, Supplement 14*, 118–128. doi: 10.15288/jsas.2002.s14.118

Aboff, M. (2003). *Uncle Willy's tickles: A child's right to say no* (2nd ed.). Washington, DC: Magination Press.

Achenbach, T. M., & Rescorla, L. A. (2001). *Manual for the ASEBA school-age forms and profiles*. Burlington, VT: University of Vermont, Research Center for Children, Youth, and Families.

Adams, L. A., & Rickert, V. I. (1989). Reducing bedtime tantrums: Comparison between positive routines and graduated extinction. *Pediatrics, 84*, 756–761.

Adams, R. E., Boscarino, J. A., & Figley, C. R. (2006). Compassion fatigue and psychological distress among social workers: A validation study. *American Journal of Orthopsychiatry, 76*(1), 103–108. doi: 10.1037/0002-9432.76.1.103

Adams-Tucker, C. (1981). A socioclinical overview of 28 sex-abused children. *Child Abuse* & *Neglect*, 5, 361–367. doi: 10.10.16/0145-2134(81)90020-x

Alaggia, R. (2004). Many ways of telling: Expanding conceptualizations of child sexual abuse disclosure. *Child Abuse & Neglect, 28*, 1213–1227. doi: 10.1016/j.chiabu.2004.03.016

Alderfer, L. (2011). *Mindful monkey, happy panda*. Boston: Wisdom Publications.

Alexander, S. J., & Jorgensen, S. R. (1983). Sex education for early adolescents: A study of parents and students. *Journal of Early Adolescence, 3*(4), 315–325. doi: 10.1177/0272431683034004

Allen, B., & Johnson, J. C. (2012). Utilization and implementation of Trauma-focused Cognitive Behavioral Therapy for the treatment of maltreated children. *Child Maltreatment, 17*(1), 80–85. doi: 10.1177/1077559511418220

Allen, B., Wilson, K. L., & Armstrong, N. E. (2014). Changing clinicians' beliefs about treatment for children experiencing trauma: The impact of intensive training in an evidence-based, trauma-focused treatment. *Psychological Trauma: Theory, Research, Practice, and Policy, 6*(4), 384–389. doi: 10.1037/a0036533

Amaya-Jackson, L., & Hagele, D., Murphy, R. A., Potter, D., Keen, L., & Briggs-King, E. (2012). "Doctor, I need a good therapist for my traumatized child!" Why outcomes and fidelity matter in creating a state implementation platform to disseminate trauma EBTs. Honors award presentation at the 2012 American Academy of Child and Adolescent Psychiatry Annual Meeting, San Francisco, CA, October 24, 2012.

American Psychiatric Association. (2000). *Diagnostic and statistical manual of mental disorders* (4th ed., text rev.). Washington, DC: Author.

American Psychiatric Association. (2013). *Diagnostic and statistical manual of mental disorders* (5th ed.). Arlington, VA: American Psychiatric Publishing.

American Psychological Association. (2013). Guidelines for psychological evaluations in child protection matters. *American Psychologist, 68*(1), 20–31.

Anderson, S. C., Bach, C. M., & Griffith, S. (1981). *Psychosocial sequelae in interfamilial victims of sexual assault and abuse.* Paper presented at the Third International Conference on Child Abuse and Neglect, Amsterdam, The Netherlands.

Annunziata, J., & Nemiroff, M. (2003). *Sex and babies: First facts.* Washington, DC: Magination Press.

Arata, C. M. (1998). To tell or not to tell: Current functioning of child sexual abuse survivors who disclosed their victimization. *Child Maltreatment, 3*(1), 63–71. doi: 10.1177/1077559598003001006

Arata, C. M. (2002). Child sexual abuse and sexual revictimization. *Clinical Psychology Science and Practice, 9*, 135–164. doi: 10.1093/clipsy.9.2.135

Baird, K., & Kracen, A. C. (2006). Vicarious traumatization and secondary traumatic stress: A research synthesis. *Counseling Psychology Quarterly, 19*(2), 181–188. doi: 10.1080/09515070600811899

Baker, D. (2006). Fishing for feelings game. Unpublished game.

Bal, S., Crombez, G., De Bourdeaudhuij, I., & Van Oost, I. (2009). Symptomatology in adolescents following initial disclosure of sexual abuse: The roles of crisis support appraisals and coping. *Child Abuse & Neglect, 33*, 717–727. doi: 10-1016/j.chiabu.2008.11.006

Bal, S., Crombez, G., Van Oost, I., & De Bourdeaudhuij, I. (2003). The role of social support in well-being and coping with self-reported stressful events in adolescents. *Child Abuse & Neglect, 27*(12), 1377–1395. doi:10.1016/j.chiabu.2003.06.002

Banyard, V. L., & Rozelle, D., & Englund, D. W. (2001). Parenting the traumatized child: Attending to the needs of nonoffending caregivers of traumatized children. *Psychotherapy: Theory, Research, Practice, and Training, 38*, 74–87. doi: 10.1037/0033-3204.38.1.74

Baptiste, B. (2004). *My daddy is a pretzel: Yoga for parents and kids.* Cambridge, MA: Barefoot Books.

Barden, L. M. (1999). *The peace path.* Torrance, CA: Creative Therapy Store.

Barker-Collo, S. L., Melnyk, W. T., & McDonald-Miszczak, L. (2000). A cognitive-behavioral model of post-traumatic stress for sexually abused females. *Journal of Interpersonal Violence, 15*, 375–392. doi: 10.1177/088656000015004003

Barkley. R. A. (2013). *Defiant children: A clinician's manual for assessment and parent training* (3rd ed.). New York: The Guilford Press.

Barnes, V. A., Bauza, L. B., & Treiber, F. A. (2003). Impact of stress reduction on negative school behavior in adolescents. *Health and Quality of Life Outcomes, 1*, 10. doi:10.1186/1477-7525-1-10

Bean, B., & Bennett, S. (1993). *The me nobody knows: A guide for teen survivors.* San Francisco, CA: Jossey-Bass.

Beck, A. T., Steer, R. A., & Brown, G. (1996). *Manual for the Beck Depression Inventory* (2nd ed.). San Antonio, TX: Psychological Corporation.

Beck, J. S. (2011). *Cognitive behavior therapy: Basics and beyond* (2nd ed.). New York: The Guilford Press.

Beidas, R. S., Crawley, S. A., Mychailyszyn, M. P., Comer, J. S., & Kendall, P. C. (2010). Cognitive-behavioral treatment of anxious youth with comorbid school refusal: Clinical presentation and treatment response. *Psychological Topics, 19*, 255–271.

Beitchman, J. H., Zucker, K. J., Hood, J. E., daCosta, G. A., Akman, D., & Cassavia, E. (1992). A review of the long-term effects of child sexual abuse. *Child Abuse & Neglect, 16*, 101–118. doi: 10.1016/0145-2134(92)90011-F

Berk, L. E. (2012). *Child development* (9th ed.) Upper Saddle River, NJ: Pearson.

Berliner, L., & Conte, J. R. (1990). The process of victimization: The victims' perspective. *Child Abuse & Neglect, 14*, 29–40. doi:10.1016/0145-2134(90)90078-8

Berliner, L., & Wheeler, J. R. (1987). Treating the effects of sexual abuse on children. *Journal of Interpersonal Violence, 2*, 415–434. doi: 10.1177/088626058700200407

BigFoot, D. S., & Schmidt, S. R. (2012). American Indian and Alaska Native children. In J. A. Cohen, A. P. Mannarino, & E. Deblinger (Eds.), *Trauma-focused CBT for children and adolescents: Treatment applications* (pp. 280–300). New York: Guilford Publications.

Black, D. S. (2011). A brief definition of mindfulness. *Mindfulness Research Guide.* Accessed from http://www.mindfulnessexperience.org

Blumenthal, J. A., Babyak, M. A., Doraiswamy, M., Watkins, L., Hoffman, B. M., Barbour, K. A., … Sherwood, A. (2007). Exercise and pharmacotherapy in the treatment of major depression. *Psychosomatic Medicine, 69*, 587–596. doi: 10.1097/psy.0b013e318148c19a

Boney-McCoy, S., & Finkelhor, D. (1995). Prior victimization: A risk factor for child sexual abuse and PTSD-related symptomatology among sexually abused youths. *Child Abuse & Neglect, 19*, 1401–1421. doi: 10.1016/0145-2134(95)00104_9

Bonner, B. L., Walker, C. E., & Berliner, L. (1999a). *Treatment manual for cognitive behavioral group therapy for children with sexual behavior problems.* Washington DC: Administration of Children, Youth, and Families, DHHS.

Bonner, B. L., Walker, C. E., & Berliner, L. (1999b). *Treatment manual for cognitive behavioral group treatment for parents/caregivers of children with sexual behavior problems.* Washington D.C.: Administration of Children, Youth, and Families, DHHS.

Bosch, C. W. (1988). *Bully on the bus.* Seattle, WA: Parenting Press.

Bowen, C. (2007). *I believe in me: A book of affirmations.* Kansas City, MO: Unity.

Brand, B. L., & Alexander, P. C. (2003). Coping with incest: The relationship between recollections of childhood coping and adult functioning in female survivors of incest. *Journal of Traumatic Stress, 16*, 285–293. doi: 10.1023A:1023704309605

Brent, D., Oquendo, M., Birmaher, B., Greenhill, L., Kolko, D., Stanley, B., … Mann, J. (2002). Familial pathways to early-onset suicide attempt: Risk for suicidal behavior in offspring of mood-disordered suicide attempters. *Archives of General Psychiatry, 59*, 801–807.

Brent, D., Oquendo, M., Birmaher, B., Greenhill, L., Kolko, D., Stanley, B., … Mann, J. (2004). Familial transmission of mood disorders: Convergence and divergence with transmission of suicidal behavior. *Journal of the American*

Academy of Child & Adolescent Psychiatry, 43(10), 1259–1266. doi: 10.1097/01.chi.0000135619.38392.78

Briere, J., & Runtz, M. (1990). Differential adult symptomatology associated with three types of child abuse histories. *Child Abuse & Neglect, 14*, 357–364. doi: 10.1016/0145-2134(90)90007-G

Britain, L. (1982). *It's my body.* Seattle, WA: Parenting Press Inc.

Brown, E. J., & Kolko, D. J. (1999). Child victims' attributions about being physically abused: An examination of factors associated with symptom severity. *Journal of Abnormal Child Psychology, 27*, 311–322.

Brown, J., Cohen, P., Johnson, J., & Smailes, E. (1999). Childhood abuse and neglect: Specificity of effects on adolescent and young adult depression and suicidality. *Journal of the American Academy of Child & Adolescent Psychiatry, 38*(12), 1490–1496. doi: 10.1097/00004583-199912000-00009

Browne, A., & Finkelhor, D. (1986). Impact of child sexual abuse: A review of the research. *Psychology Bulletin, 99*, 66–77.

Bryan, C. J., Master, A., & Walton, G. M. (2014). "Helping" versus "Being a helper": Invoking the self to increase helping in young children. *Child Development, 85*(5), 1836–1842.

Cain, B. (2001). *Double-dip feelings: Stories to help children understand emotions* (2nd ed.). Washington, DC: Magination Press.

Cain, J. (2000). *The way I feel.* Seattle, WA: Parenting Press.

Cammarata, D. (2009). *Someone I love died by suicide: A story for child survivors and those who care for them.* Jupiter, FL: Limitless Press.

Canter, D., Hughes, D., & Kirby, S. (1998). Paedophilia: Pathology, criminality, or both? The development of a multivariate model of offence behaviour in child sexual abuse. *The Journal of Forensic Psychiatry, 9*(3), 532–555.

Canton-Cortes, D., & Canton, J. (2010). Coping with child sexual abuse among college students and post-traumatic stress disorder: The role of continuity of abuse and relationship with the perpetrator. *Child Abuse & Neglect, 34*, 496–506. doi: 10.1016/j.chiabu.2009.11.004

Carlson, L. E., Speca, M., Faris, P., & Patel, K. D. (2007). One year pre-post intervention follow-up of psychological, immune, endocrine and blood pressure outcomes of mindfulness-based stress reduction (MBSR) in breast and prostate cancer outpatients. *Brain, Behavior, and Immunity, 21*, 1038–1049.

CATS Consortium. (2010). Implementation of CBT for youth affected by the World Trade Center disaster: Matching need to treatment intensity and reducing trauma symptoms. *Journal of Traumatic Studies, 23*, 699–707.

Cavanagh-Johnson, T. (2013). *Treatment exercises for child abuse victims and children with sexual behavior problems.* South Pasadena, CA: Author.

Cavanaugh, C., & Classen, C. (2009). Intergenerational pathways linking childhood sexual abuse to HIV risk among women. *Journal of Trauma and Dissociation, 10*, 151–169. doi: 10.1080/15299730802624536

Cerezo, M. A., & Frias, D. (1994). Emotional and cognitive adjustment in abused children. *Child Abuse & Neglect, 18*(11), 923–932.

Chadwick Center for Children and Families. (2004). *Closing the quality chasm in child abuse treatment: Identifying and disseminating best practices.* San Diego, CA: Author.

Chaffin, M., Berliner, L., Block, R., Cavanagh Johnson, T., Friedrich, W. N., Garza Louis, D., ... Silovksy, J. F. (2008). Report of the ATSA Task Force on Children with Sexual Behavior Problems. *Child Maltreatment, 13*, 199–218.

Chaffin, M., Wherry, J. N., & Dykman, R. (1997). School age children's coping with sexual abuse: Abuse stresses and symptoms associated with four coping strategies. *Child Abuse & Neglect, 21*, 227–240.

Chamberlain, P., Price, J., Reid, J., Landsverk, J., Fisher, P., & Stoolmiller, M. (2006). Who disrupts from placement in foster and kinship care? *Child Abuse & Neglect, 30*, 409–424.

Child Abuse, Domestic Violence, Adoption, and Family Services Act of 1992, Pub. L. 102–295, 1992.

Child Welfare Information Gateway, Children's Bureau, Administration for Children and Families, U.S. Department of Health and Health and Human Services. (1993). *Definitions, scope, and effects of child sexual abuse.* Retrieved from http://www.childwelfare.gov/pubs/usermanuals/sexabuse/sexabuseb.cfm

Chryssicas, M. K. (2007). *Breathe: Yoga for teens.* New York: DK Publishing.

Clark, L. (2005). *SOS! Help for parents: A practical guide for handling common everyday behavior problems* (3rd ed.). Bowling Green, KY: SOS Programs and Parents Press.

Coffey, P., Leitenberg, H., Henning, K., Turner, T., & Bennett, B. (1996). The relation between methods of coping during adulthood with a history of childhood sexual abuse and current psychological adjustment. *Journal of Consulting and Clinical Psychology, 64*, 1090–1093.

Cohen, J. (1995). *Understanding the thoughts and feelings of sexually abused and nonabused children.* Unpublished manuscript, Yeshiva University, New York.

Cohen, J. A. (1991). Psychotherapy meets fundamentalism in the treatment of a sexually abused adolescent. In W. N. Friedrich, (Ed.), *Casebook of sexual abuse treatment* (pp. 196–213). New York: W. W. Norton.

Cohen, J. A., Berliner, L., & Mannarino, A. (2010). Trauma focused CBT for children with co-occurring trauma and behavior problems. *Child Abuse & Neglect, 34*, 215–224.

Cohen, J. A., Deblinger, E., Mannarino, A. P., & De Arellano, M. A. (2001). The importance of culture in treating abused and neglected children: An empirical review. *Child Maltreatment, 6*(2), 148–157.

Cohen, J. A., Deblinger, E., Mannarino, A. P., & Steer, R. (2004). A multisite randomized controlled trial for children with sexual abuse-related PTSD symptoms. *Journal of the American Academy of Child & Adolescent Psychiatry, 43*, 393–402.

Cohen, J. A., & Mannarino, A. P. (1988). Psychological symptoms in sexually abused girls. *Child Abuse & Neglect, 12*, 571–577.

Cohen, J. A., & Mannarino, A. P. (1992). *Structured parental counseling-child psychotherapy treatment manual for sexually abused preschoolers.* Unpublished manuscript, University of Pittsburgh, Pittsburgh, PA.

Cohen, J. A., & Mannarino, A. P. (1993). A treatment model for sexually abused preschoolers. *Journal of Interpersonal Violence, 8*(1), 115–131.

Cohen, J. A., & Mannarino, A. P. (1994). *Sexual Abuse-Specific Cognitive Behavioral Therapy (SAS-CBT) treatment manual.* Unpublished manuscript, MCP-Hahnemann University School of Medicine, Philadelphia, PA.

Cohen, J. A., & Mannarino, A. P. (1996a). A treatment outcome study for sexually abused preschool children: Initial findings. *Journal of the American Academy of Child & Adolescent Psychiatry, 35*(1), 42–50.

Cohen, J. A., & Mannarino, A. P. (1996b). Family-related variables and psychological symptom formation in sexually abused girls. *Journal of Child Sexual Abuse, 5*(1), 105–120.

Cohen, J. A., & Mannarino, A. P. (1996c). Factors that mediate treatment outcome of sexually abused preschool children. *Journal of the American Academy of Child & Adolescent Psychiatry, 34*(10), 1402–1410.

Cohen, J. A., & Mannarino, A. P. (1997). A treatment study of sexually abused preschool children: Outcome during one-year follow-up. *Journal of the American Academy of Child & Adolescent Psychiatry, 36*(9), 1228–1235.

Cohen, J. A., & Mannarino, A. P. (1998a). Factors that mediate treatment outcome of sexually abused preschool children: Six and twelve month follow-up. *Journal of the American Academy of Child & Adolescent Psychiatry, 37,* 44–51.

Cohen, J. A., & Mannarino, A. P. (1998b). Interventions for sexually abused children: Initial treatment outcome findings. *Child Maltreatment, 3*(1), 17–26.

Cohen, J. A., Mannarino, A. P., & Deblinger, E. (2006). *Treating trauma and traumatic grief in children and adolescents.* New York: The Guilford Press.

Cohen, J. A., Mannarino, A. P., & Deblinger, E. (Eds.). (2012). *Trauma-focused CBT for children and adolescents: Treatment applications.* New York: The Guilford Press.

Cohen, J. A., Mannarino, A. P., & Iyengar, S. (2011). Community treatment of posttraumatic stress disorder for children exposed to intimate partner violence: A randomized controlled trial. *Archives of Pediatrics & Adolescent Medicine, 165*(1), 16–21. doi: 10.1001/archpediatrics.2010.247

Cohen, J. A., Mannarino, A. P., Kliethermes, M., & Murray, L. A. (2012). Trauma-focused CBT for youth with complex trauma. *Child Abuse & Neglect, 36*, 528–541.

Cohen, J. A., Mannarino, A. P., & Knudsen, K. (2004). Treating childhood traumatic grief: A pilot study. *Journal of the American Academy of Child & Adolescent Psychiatry, 43*(10), 1225–1233. doi: 10.1097/01.chi.0000135620.15522.38

Cohen, J. A., Mannarino, A. P., & Knudsen, K. (2005). Treating sexually abused children: 1 year follow-up of a randomized controlled trial. *Child Abuse & Neglect, 29*(2), 135–145.

Cohen, J. A., Mannarino, A. P., & Murray, L. K. (2011). Trauma-focused CBT for youth who experience ongoing traumas. *Child Abuse & Neglect, 35*(8), 637–646. doi: 10.1016/j.chiabu.2011.05.002

Cohen, J. A., Mannarino, A. P., & Navarro, D. (2012). Residential treatment. In J. A. Cohen, A. P. Mannarino, & E. Deblinger (Eds.), *Trauma-focused CBT for children and adolescents: Treatment applications* (pp. 73–93). New York: The Guilford Press.

Cohen, J. A., Mannarino, A. P., Perel, J. M., & Staron, V. (2007). A pilot randomized controlled trial of combined trauma-focused CBT and sertraline for childhood PTSD symptoms. *Journal of the American Academy of Child & Adolescent Psychiatry, 46*(7), 811–819.

Cohen, J. A., Mannarino, A. P., & Staron, V. R. (2006). A pilot study of modified cognitive- behavioral therapy of childhood traumatic grief (CTG-CBT). *Journal of the American Academy of Child & Adolescent Psychiatry, 45*(12), 1465–1473.

Cohen, J. B., Deblinger, E., Maedel, A. B., & Stauffer, L. B. (1999). Examining sex-related thoughts and feelings of sexually abused and nonabused children. *Journal of Interpersonal Violence, 14*(7), 701–712. doi:10.1177/088626099014007002

Cohen-Posey, K. (1995). *How to handle bullies, teasers and other meanies: A book that takes the nuisance out of name calling and other nonsense.* Highland City, FL: Rainbow Books, Inc.

Cole, J. (2009). *Asking about sex & growing up: A question-and-answer book for kids* (revised edition). New York: HarperCollins.

Conlin, S., & Friedman, S. L. (1989). *All my feelings at home: Ellie's day.* Seattle, WA: Parenting Press.

Conte, J. R., & Berliner, L. (1988). The impact of sexual abuse on children: Empirical findings. In L. Walker (Ed.), *Handbook on sexual abuse of children: Assessment and treatment issues* (pp. 72–93). New York: Springer Publishing.

Conte, J. R., & Schuerman, J. R. (1987). The effects of sexual abuse on children: A multidimensional view. *Journal of Interpersonal Violence, 2*(4), 380–390. doi: 10.1177/088626058700200404

Conte, J. R., Wolf, S., & Smith, T. (1989). What sexual offenders tell us about prevention strategies. *Child Abuse & Neglect, 13*(2), 293–301.

Cook, A., Blaustein, M., Spinazzola, J., & van der Kolk, B. (Eds.). (2003). *Complex trauma in children and adolescents.* National Child Traumatic Stress Network, Complex Trauma Taskforce. Retrieved from http://www.nctsnet.org/nctsn_assets/pdfs/edu_materials/ComplexTrauma_All.pdf

Cook, A., Spinazzola, J., Ford, J., Lanktree, C., Blaustein, M., Cloitre, M., . . . van der Kolk, B. (2005). Complex trauma in children and adolescents. *Psychiatric Annals, 35*, 390–398.

Cook, J. (2007). *Personal space camp.* Chattanooga, TN: National Center for Youth Issues.

Copeland, W. E., Keeler, G., Angold, A., & Costello, E. J. (2007). Traumatic events and posttraumatic stress in childhood. *Archives of General Psychiatry, 64*(5), 577–584.

Cormier, B. M., Kennedy, M., & Sangowicz, J. (1962). Psychodynamics of father daughter incest. *Canadian Psychiatric Association Journal, 7*, 203–217.

Craven, S., Brown, S., & Gilchrist, E. (2006). Sexual grooming of children: Review of literature and theoretical considerations. *Journal of Sexual Aggression, 12*, 287–299. doi: 10.1080/13552600601069414

Crawford, S. L. (1999). Intrafamilial sexual abuse: What we think we know about mothers and implications for intervention. *Journal of Child Sexual Abuse, 7*, 55–72.

Creamer, T. L., & Liddle, B. J. (2005). Secondary traumatic stress among disaster mental health workers responding to the September 11 attacks. *Journal of Traumatic Stress, 18*, 89-96.

Cuevas, C. A., Finkelhor, D., Clifford, C., Ormrod, R. K., & Turner, H. A. (2010). Psychological distress as a risk factor for re-victimization in children. *Child Abuse & Neglect, 34*, 235–243.

Cunningham, C. (1992). *All kinds of separation.* Charlotte, NC: Kidsrights.

Cunningham, M. (2003). Impact of trauma work on social work clinicians: Empirical findings. *Social Work, 48*, 451–459.

Curtis, J. L. (2007). *Today I feel silly and other moods that make my day.* New York: HarperCollins.

Cutajar, M., Mullen, P., Ogloff, J., Thomas, S., Wells, D., & Spataro, J. (2010). Psychopathology in a large cohort of sexually abused children followed up to 43 years. *Child Abuse & Neglect, 34*, 813–822. doi: 10.1016/j.chiab.2010.04.004

Dahl, R. E. (1996). The regulation of sleep and arousal: Development and psychopathology. *Development and Psychopathology, 8*(1), 3–27.

Daigneault, K., Hebert, M., & Tourigny, M. (2006). Attributions and coping in sexually abused adolescents referred for group treatment. *Journal of Child Sexual Abuse, 15*(3), 35–59.

Davidson, J. R., Payne, V. M., Connor, K. M., Foa, E. B., Rothbaum, B. O., Hertzberg M. A., & Weisler, R. H. (2005) Trauma, resilience and saliostasis: Effects of treatment in post-traumatic stress disorder. *International Clinical Psychopharmacology, 20*(1), 43–48.

Davies, D. (2010). *Child development: A practitioner's guide* (3rd ed.). New York: The Guilford Press.

Davies, M. (1995). Parental distress and ability to cope following disclosure of extra-familial sexual abuse. *Child Abuse & Neglect, 19*(4), 399–408.

Davis, D. (1984). *Something is wrong at my house: A book about parent's fighting.* Seattle, WA: Parenting Press, Inc.

Davis, D. M., & Hayes, J. A. (2011). What are the benefits of mindfulness? A practice review of psychotherapy-related research. *Psychotherapy, 48*(2), 198–208.

de Arellano, M. A., Danielson, C. K., & Felton, J. W. (2012). Children of Latino descent: Culturally modified TF-CBT. In J. A. Cohen, A. P. Mannarino, & E. Deblinger (Eds.), *Trauma-focused CBT for children and adolescents: Treatment applications* (pp. 253–279). New York: Guilford Publications.

De Bellis, M. D., & Kuchibhatla, M. (2006). Cerebellar volumes in pediatric maltreatment-related posttraumatic stress disorder. *Biological Psychiatry, 60*(7), 697–703.

Deblinger, E., Cohen, J. A., & Mannarino, A. P. (2012). Introduction. In J. A. Cohen, A. P. Mannarino, & E. Deblinger (Eds.), *Trauma-focused CBT for children and adolescents: Treatment applications* (pp. 1–26). New York: The Guilford Press.

Deblinger, E., Hathaway, C. R., Lippmann, J., & Steer, R. (1993). Psychosocial characteristics and correlates of symptom distress in nonoffending mothers of sexually abused children. *Journal of Interpersonal Violence, 8*, 155–168.

Deblinger, E., & Heflin, A. (1994). Child sexual abuse. In F. Dattilio & A. Freeman (Eds.), *Cognitive-behavioral strategies in crisis intervention* (pp. 177–199). New York: The Guilford Press.

Deblinger, E., & Heflin, A. H. (1996). *Treating sexually abused children and their non-offending parents: A cognitive behavioral approach.* Newbury Park, CA: SAGE Publications.

Deblinger, E., Lippmann, J., & Steer, R. (1996). Sexually abused children suffering post-traumatic stress symptoms: Initial treatment outcome findings. *Child Maltreatment, 1*(4), 310–321.

Deblinger, E., Mannarino, A. P., Cohen, J. A., Runyon, M. K., & Steer, R. A. (2011). Trauma-focused cognitive behavioral therapy for children: Impact of the trauma narrative and treatment length. *Depression and Anxiety, 28*(1), 67–75. doi: 10.1002/da.20744

Deblinger, E., Mannarino, A. P., Cohen, J. A., & Steer, R. A. (2006). A follow-up study of a multisite, randomized, controlled trial for children with sexual abuse-related PTSD symptoms. *Journal of the American Academy of Child & Adolescent Psychiatry, 45*(12), 1474–1484.

Deblinger, E., McLeer, S., Atkins, M., Ralphe, D., & Foa, E. (1989). Post-traumatic stress in sexually abused, physically abused, and nonabused children. *Child Abuse & Neglect, 13*(3), 403–408.

Deblinger, E., McLeer, S., & Henry, D. (1990). Cognitive-behavioral treatment for sexually abused children suffering post-traumatic stress: Preliminary findings. *Journal of the American Academy of Child & Adolescent Psychiatry, 29*, 747–752.

Deblinger, E., Neubauer, F., Runyon, M., & Baker, D. (2006). *What do you know? A therapeutic card game about child sexual and physical abuse and domestic violence.* Stratford, NJ: CARES Institute.

Deblinger, E., Pollio, E., & Dorsey, S. (2015). *Adapting trauma-focused cognitive behavioral therapy for implementation in group format.* Manuscript submitted for publication.

Deblinger, E., & Runyon, M. K. (2005). Understanding and treating feelings of shame in children who have experienced maltreatment. *Child Maltreatment, 10*(4), 364–376.

Deblinger, E., Stauffer, L., & Landsberg, C. (1994). The impact of a history of child sexual abuse on maternal response to allegations of sexual abuse concerning her child. *Journal of Child Sexual Abuse, 3*(3), 67–75.

Deblinger, E., Stauffer, L. B., & Steer, R. A. (2001), Comparative efficacies of supportive and cognitive behavioral group therapies for young children who have been sexually abused and their nonoffending mothers. *Child Maltreatment*, 6(4), 332–343.

Deblinger, E., Steer, R., & Lippmann, J. (1999). Maternal factors associated with sexually abused children's psychosocial adjustment. *Child Maltreatment, 4*, 13–20.

Deblinger, E., Taub, B., Maedel, A. B., Lippmann, J., & Stauffer, L. (1997). Psychosocial factors predicting parent reported symptomatology in sexually abused children. *Journal of Child Sexual Abuse*, 6(4), 35–49.

Deblinger, E., Thakkar-Kolar, R. R., Berry, E. J., & Schroeder, C. M. (2010). Caregivers' efforts to educate their children about child sexual abuse: A replication study. *Child Maltreatment, 15*(1), 91–100. doi: 10.1177/1077559509337408

Deci, E. L., & Ryan, R. M. (2000). The "what" and "why" of goal pursuits: Human needs and the self-determination of behavior. *Psychological Inquiry, 11*(4), 227–268.

DePino, C. (2004). *Blue cheese breath and stinky feet: How to deal with bullies.* Washington, DC: Magination Press.

DeVoe, E. R., & Faller, K. C. (1999). The characteristics of disclosure among children who may have been sexually abused. *Child Maltreatment, 4*, 217–227.

Diehl, J., Opmeer, B. C., Boer, F., Mannarino, A. P., & Lindauer, R. J. L. (2015). Trauma-focused cognitive behavioral therapy or eye movement desensitization and reprocessing: What works in children with posttraumatic stress symptoms? A randomized controlled trial. *European Child & Adolescent Psychiatry, 24*, 227–236. doi 10.1007/s00787-014-0572-5

Finkelhor, D. (1990). Early and long-term effects of child sexual abuse: An update. *Professional Psychology: Research and Practice*, *21*, 325–330.

Finkelhor, D. (1994). The international epidemiology of child sexual abuse. *Child Abuse & Neglect*, *18*(5), 409–417.

Finkelhor, D. (2008). *Childhood victimization: Violence, crime, and abuse in the lives of young people.* New York: Oxford University Press.

Finkelhor, D., Asdigian, N., & Dzuiba-Leatherman, J. (1995). The effectiveness of victimization prevention instructions: An evaluation of children's responses to actual threats and assaults. *Child Abuse & Neglect*, *19*(2), 141–153.

Finkelhor, D., Hotaling, G. T., Lewis, I. A., & Smith, C. (1989). Sexual abuse and its relationship to later sexual satisfaction, marital status, religion and attitudes. *Journal of Interpersonal Violence*, *4*, 379–399.

Finkelhor, D., Hotaling, G., Lewis, I. A., & Smith, C. (1990). Sexual abuse in a national survey of adult men and women: Prevalence, characteristics, and risk factors. *Child Abuse & Neglect*, *14*, 19–28.

Finkelhor, D., & Jones, L. (2012). *Have sexual abuse and physical abuse declined since the 1990s?* (NCJ 199298). Durham, NH: Crimes Against Children Research Center.

Finkelhor, D., & Ormrod, R. K. (2000). *Characteristics of crimes against juveniles.* Washington, DC: Office of Juvenile Justice and Delinquency Prevention.

Finkelhor, D., Ormrod, R. K., & Turner, H. A. (2007a). Poly-victimization: A neglected component in child victimization. *Child Abuse & Neglect*, *31*, 7–26.

Finkelhor, D., Ormrod, R. K., & Turner, H. A. (2007b). Re-victimization patterns in a national longitudinal sample of children and youth. *Child Abuse & Neglect*, *31*, 479–502.

Finkelhor, D., & Shattuck, A. (2012). *Characteristics of crimes against juveniles.* (CV26R) Durham, NH: Crimes Against Children Research Center.

Finkelhor, D., Turner, H., Ormrod, R., & Hamby, S. L. (2009). Violence, abuse, and crime exposure in a national sample of children and youth. *Pediatrics*, *124*(5), 1411–1423. doi: 10.1542/peds.2009-0467

Finkelhor, D., Turner, H. A., Shattuck, A., & Hamby, S. L. (2013). Violence, crime, and abuse exposure in a national sample of children and youth: An update. *JAMA Pediatrics* *167*(7), 614–621.

Fleming, J., Mullen, P., Sibthorpe, B., & Bammer, G. (1999). The long-term impact of childhood sexual abuse in Australian women. *Child Abuse & Neglect*, *23*(2), 145–159.

Foa, E. B., Johnson, K. M., Feeny, N. C., & Treadwell, K. R. (2001). The Child PTSD Symptom Scale: A preliminary examination of its psychometric properties. *Journal of Clinical Child Psychology*, *30*(3), 376–384.

Foa, E. B., Keane, T. M., Friedman, M. J., & Cohen, J. A. (2009). *Effective treatments for PTSD: Practice guidelines from the International Society for Traumatic Stress Studies* (2nd ed.). New York: The Guilford Press.

Foa, E., Rothbaum, B. O., & Ette, G. S. (1993). Treatment of rape victims. *Journal of Interpersonal Violence*, *8*, 156–276.

Foa, E. B., Rothbaum, B. O., Riggs, D. S., & Murdock, T. B. (1991). Treatment of posttraumatic stress disorder in rape victims: A comparison between cognitive-behavioral procedures and counseling. *Journal of Consulting and Clinical Psychology*, *59*(5), 715–723.

Foltz, L. L. (2003). *Kids helping kids break the silence of sexual abuse.* Pittsburgh, PA: Lighthouse Point Press.

Fontes, L. A. (2008). *Child abuse and culture: Working with diverse families.* New York: The Guilford Press.

Forehand, R. (1977). Child compliance to parental commands: Behavior analysis and treatment. In M. Herson, R. M. Eisler, & P. M. Miller (Eds.), *Progress in behavior modification* (Vol. 5, pp. 111–147). New York: Academic Press.

Foshee, V., Benefield, T., Suchindran, C., Ennett, S., Bauman, K., Karriker-Jaffe, K., ... Mathias, J. (2009). The development of four types of adolescent dating abuse and selected demographic correlates. *Journal of Research on Adolescence, 19*(3), 380–400.

Freeman, D. (2010). *Once upon a pose: A guide to yoga adventure stories for children.* Bloomington, IN: Trafford Publishing

Frick, P. J. (1991). *The Alabama Parenting Questionnaire.* Unpublished instrument, University of Alabama, Tuscaloosa, AL.

Friedrich, W. N. (1990). *Psychotherapy of sexually abused children and their families.* New York: W. W. Norton.

Friedrich, W. N. (1997). *Child Sexual Behavior Inventory: Professional manual.* Odessa, FL: Psychological Assessment Resources.

Friedrich, W. N. (2007). *Children with sexual behavior problems: Family-based, attachment-focused therapy.* New York: W. W. Norton.

Friedrich, W. N., Fisher, J., Broughton, D., Houston, M., & Shafran, C. R. (1998). Normative sexual behavior in children: A contemporary sample. *Pediatrics, 101*(4), 1–8.

Friedrich, W. N., Grambsch, P., Broughton, D., Kuiper, K., & Beilke, R. L. (1991). Normative sexual behavior in children. *Pediatrics, 88,* 456–464.

Friedrich, W. N., Grambsch, P., Damon, L., Hewitt, S. K., Koverola, C., Lang, R. A., ... Broughton, D. (1992). Child Sexual Behavior Inventory: Normative and clinical comparisons. *Psychological Assessment, 4,* 303–311.

Friedrich, W. N., Lysne, M., Sim, L., & Shamos, S. (2004). Assessing sexual behavior in high-risk adolescents with the Adolescent Clinical Sexual Behavior Inventory (ACSBI). *Child Maltreatment, 9*(3), 239–250.

Friedrich, W. N., Urquiza, A. J., & Beilke, R. (1986). Behavior problems in sexually abused young children. *Journal of Pediatric Psychology, 11,* 47–57.

Friman, P. C., Jones, M., Smith, G., Daly, D. L., & Larzelere, R. (1997). Decreasing disruptive behavior by adolescent boys in residential care by increasing their positive to negative interactional ratios. *Behavior Modification, 21*(4), 470–486. doi:10.1177/01454455970214005

Fromuth, M. E. (1986). The relationship of childhood sexual abuse with later psychological and sexual adjustment in a sample of college women. *Child Abuse & Neglect, 10,* 5–15.

Futa, K., Nash, C., Hansen, D., & Garbin, C. (2003). Adult survivors of childhood abuse: An analysis of coping mechanisms used for stressful childhood memories and current stressors. *Journal of Family Violence, 18,* 227–239.

Ghetti, S., Goodman, G. S., Eisen, M. L., Qin, J., & Davis, S. L. (2002). Consistency in children's reports of sexual and physical abuse. *Child Abuse & Neglect, 26,* 977–995.

Girard, L. W. (1984). *My body is private.* Morton Grove, IL: Albert Whitman & Company.

Gladstone, G., Parker, G., Mitchell, P., Malhi, G., Wilhelm, K., & Austin, M., (2004). Implications of childhood trauma for depressed women: An analysis of pathways from childhood sexual abuse to deliberate self-harm and revictimization. *American Journal of Psychiatry, 161*(8), 1417–1425.

Gold, M. A., Horwitz, M., Greene, A., Taleb, A., & Hatcher, R. A. (2008). *Teen to teen: Plain talk from teens about sex, self-esteem, and everything in between.* Atlanta: Bridging the Gap Communications.

Gonzales, L. S., Waterman, J., Kelly, R., McCord, J., & Oliveri, K. (1993). Children's patterns of disclosures and recantations of sexual and ritualistic abuse allegations in psychotherapy. *Child Abuse & Neglect, 17,* 281–289.

Goodman, R. (1997). The Strengths and Difficulties Questionnaire: A research note. *Journal of Child Psychology and Psychiatry, 38,* 581–586.

Goodman, G. S., Bottoms, B. L., Schwartz-Kenney, B. M., & Rudy, L. (1991). Children's testimony about a stressful event: Improving children's reports. *Journal of Narrative and Life History, 1*(1), 69–99.

Goodman, R., Meltzer, H., & Bailey, V. (1998). The Strengths and Difficulties Questionnaire: A pilot study on the validity of the self-report version. *European Child & Adolescent Psychiatry, 7,* 125–130.

Goodman-Brown, T., Edelstein, R., Goodman, G., Jones, D., & Gordon, D. (2003). Why children tell: A model of children's disclosure of sexual abuse. *Child Abuse & Neglect, 27,* 525–540. doi: 10.1016/S0145-2134(03)00037-1

Gordon, J., King, N., Gullone, E., Muris, P., & Ollendick, T. H. (2007). Nightime fears of children and adolescents: Frequency, content, severity, harm expectations, disclosure, and coping behaviours. *Behaviour Resaerch and Therapy, 45,* 2464–2472.

Greer, D., Grasso, D. J., Cohen, A., & Webb, C. (2014). Trauma-focused treatment in a state system of care: Is it worth the cost? *Administration and Policy in Mental Health and Mental Health Services Research, 41*(3), 317–323.

Gries, L. T., Goh, D. S., Andrews, M. B., Gilbert, J., Praver, F., & Stelzer, D. N. (2000). Positive reaction to disclosure and recovery from child sexual abuse. *Journal of Child Sexual Abuse, 9,* 29–51.

Griffith, T. (2002). *Good grief, it's sky blue pink! (A musical book about loss, grief, and memories).* Medford, NJ: Continuing Support Services.

Grosso, C. A. (2012). Children with developmental disabilities. In J. A. Cohen, A. P. Mannarino, & E. Deblinger (Eds.), *Trauma-focused CBT for children and adolescents: Treatment applications* (pp. 175–196). New York: The Guilford Press.

Grusec, J. E., & Redler, E. (1980). Attribution, reinforcement, and altruism: A developmental analysis. *Developmental Psychology, 16*(5), 525–534.

Gullone, E. (2000). The development of normal fear: A century of research. *Clinical Psychology Review, 20*(4), 429–451.

Hall, D. K., Gray, A., Busconi, A., Houchens, P. K., Mathews, F., & Pearce, J. (1998). Factors associated with sexual behavior problems: Identification of five distinct child types and related treatment considerations. *Child Maltreatment, 3,* 384–406.

Hall, D. K., Mathews, F., & Pearce, J. (1998). Factors associated with sexual behavior problems in young sexually abused children. *Child Abuse & Neglect, 22,* 1045–1063.

Handelsman, C. D., Cabral, R. J., & Weisfeld, G. E., (1987). Sources of information and adolescent sexual knowledge and behavior. *Journal of Adolescent Research, 2*(4), 455–463.

Hanh, T. N. (2008). *Mindful movements: Ten exercises for well-being.* Berkeley, CA: Parallax Press.

Hardy, V. L., Compton, K. D., & McPhatter, V. S. (2013). Domestic minor sex trafficking: Practice implications for mental health professionals. *Affilia: Journal of Women and Social Work, 28*(1), *8–18.*

Harrison, M. A. (2002). *A safe place to live: A story for children who have experienced domestic violence.* St. Paul, MN: JIST Publishing.

Hazzard, A., Celano, M., Gould, J., Lawry, S., & Webb, C. (1995). Predicting symptomatology and self-blame among child sex abuse victims. *Child Abuse & Neglect, 19, 707–714.*

Hendricks, A., Cohen, J. A., Mannarino, A. P., & Deblinger, E. (2007). Your very own TF-CBT workbook. Unpublished manuscript.

Hendricks, A., Cohen, J. A., Mannarino, A. P., & Deblinger, E. (2012). Dealing with trauma: A TF-CBT workbook for teens. Unpublished manuscript.

Heriot, J. (1996). Maternal protectiveness following the disclosure of intrafamilial child sexual abuse. *Journal of Interpersonal Violence, 11*, 181–194.

Hershkowitz, I., Lanes, O., & Lamb, M. E. (2007). Exploring the disclosure of child sexual abuse with alleged victims and their parents. *Child Abuse & Neglect, 31*, 111–123. doi: 10.1016/j.chiabu.2006.09.004

Heyne, D., King, N. J., Tonge, B. J., Rollings, S., Young, D., Pritchard, M., & Ollendick, T. (2002). Evaluation of child therapy and caregiver training in the treatment of school refusal. *Journal of the American Academy of Child & Adolescent Psychiatry, 41*(6), 687–695.

Hiebert-Murphy, D. (1998). Emotional distress among mothers whose children have been sexually abused: The role of a history of child sexual abuse, social support, and coping. *Child Abuse & Neglect, 22*, 423–435.

Hiscock, H., Bayer, J., Gold, L., Hampton, A., Ukoumunne, O. C., & Wake, M. (2007). Improving infant sleep and maternal mental health: A cluster, randomized trial. *Archives of Disease in Childhood, 92*, 952–958.

Hofmann, S. G., Sawyer, A. T., Witt, A. A., & Oh, D. (2010). The effect of mindfulness-based therapy on anxiety and depression: A meta-analytic review. *Journal of Consulting and Clinical Psychology, 78*(2), 169–183. doi:10.1037/a0018555

Holliday, R. E., & Albon, A. J. (2004). Minimizing misinformation effects in young children with cognitive interview mnemonics. *Applied Cognitive Psychology, 18*(3), 263–281.

Horowitz, M. (1986). *Stress response syndromes.* New York: Basic Books.

Janoff-Bulman, R. (1985). The aftermath of victimization: Rebuilding shattered assumptions. In C. R. Figley (Ed.), *Trauma and its wake: The study and treatment of post-traumatic stress disorder* (pp. 15–35). New York: Brunner/Mazel.

Jaycox, L. H., Cohen, J. A., Mannarino, A. P., Walker, D. W., Langley, A. K., Gegenheimer, K. L., ... Schonlau, M. (2010). Children's mental health care following Hurricane Katrina: A field trial of trauma-focused psychotherapies. *Journal of Traumatic Stress, 23*(2), 223–231.

Jensen, T. K., Holt, T., Ormhaug, S. M., Egeland, K., Granly, L., Hoaas, L. C., ... Wentzel -Larsen, T. (2014). A randomized effectiveness study comparing Trauma-focused Cognitive Behavioral Therapy with therapy as usual for youth. *Journal of Clinical Child & Adolescent Psychology, 43*(3), 356–369.

Jessie, (1991). *Please tell! A child's story about sexual abuse.* Center City, MN: Hazeldon.

Jinich, S., & Litrownik, A. J. (1999). Coping with sexual abuse: Development and evaluation of a videotape intervention for nonoffending parents. *Child Abuse & Neglect, 23*(2), 175–190.

Johnson, B. K., & Kenkel, M. B. (1991). Stress, coping, and adjustment in female adolescent incest victims. *Child Abuse & Neglect, 15*, 293–305.

Jonzon, E., & Lindblad, F. (2004). Disclosure, reactions, and social support: Findings from a sample of adult victims of child sexual abuse. *Child Maltreatment, 9*(2), 190–200. doi: 10.1177/1077559504264263

Joyce, P. A. (1997). Mothers of sexually abused children and the concept of collusion: A literature review. *Journal of Child Sexual Abuse, 6*(2), 75–92.

Kaplow, J., & Pincus, D. (2007). *Samantha Jane's missing smile: A story about coping with the loss of a parent.* Washington, DC: Magination Press.

Karst, P. (2000). *The invisible string.* Camarillo, CA: DeVorss & Company.

Kastner, L. S. (1984). Ecological factors predicting adolescent contraceptive use: Implications for intervention. *Journal of Adolescent Health, 5*, 79–86.

Katz, K. (2004). *No hitting!* New York: Grosset & Dunlap.

Kasza, K. (2009). *Ready for anything.* New York: G.P. Putnam's Sons.

Kazdin, A. E. (2005). *Parent management training: Treatment for oppositional, aggressive, and antisocial behavior in children and adolescents.* New York: Oxford University Press.

Kearney, C. A. (2008a). *Helping school refusing children and their parents: A guide for school-based professionals.* New York: Oxford University Press.

Kearney, C. A. (2008b). School absenteeism and school refusal behavior in youth: A contemporary review. *Clinical Psychology Review, 28*, 451–471.

Kearney, C. A., & Albano, A. M. (2004). The functional profiles of school refusal behavior: Diagnostic aspects. *Behavior Modification, 28*, 147–161.

Keller, P., & El-Sheikh, M. (2011). Children's emotional security and sleep: Longitudinal relations and directions of effects. *Journal of Child Psychology and Psychiatry, 52*(1), 64–71. doi: 10.1111/j.1469-7610.2010.02263.x

Kelley, S. J. (1990). Parental stress response to sexual abuse and ritualistic abuse of children in day-care centers. *Nursing Research, 39*, 25–29.

Kendall, P. C. (1985). Toward a cognitive-behavioral model of child psychopathology and a critique of related interventions. *Journal of Abnormal Child Psychology, 13*, 357–372.

Kendall. P. C. (2011). *Child and adolescent therapy: Cognitive-behavioral procedures* (4th ed.). New York: The Guilford Press

Kendall-Tackett, K. A., Williams, L. M., & Finkelhor, D. (1993). Impact of sexual abuse on children: A review and synthesis of recent empirical studies. *Psychological Bulletin, 113*(1), 164–180.

Kim, K., Trickett, P., & Putnam, F. (2010). Childhood experiences of sexual abuse and later parenting practices among non-offending mothers of sexually abused and comparison girls. *Child Abuse & Neglect, 34*, 610–622.

King, N., & Bernstein, G. (2001). School refusal in children and adolescents: A review of the past 10 years. *Journal of the American Academy of Child & Adolescent Psychiatry, 40*, 197–205.

King, N., Tonge, B. J., Heyne, D., & Ollendick, T. H. (2000). Research on the cognitive-behavioral treatment of school refusal: A review and recommendations. *Clinical Psychology Review, 20*, 495–507.

King, N., Tonge, G. J., Mullen, P., Myerson, N., Heyne, D., Rollings, S., … Ollendick, T. H. (2000). Treating sexually abused children with post-traumatic stress symptoms: A randomized clinical trial. *Journal of the American Academy of Child & Adolescent Psychiatry, 39*(11), 1347–1355.

Kirby D. B., Laris, B. A., & Rolleri, L. A. (2007). Sex and HIV programs: Their impact on sexual behaviors of young people throughout the world. *Journal of Adolescent Health, 40*, 206–217.

Kliethermes M., & Wamser, R. (2012). Adolescents with complex trauma. In J. A. Cohen, A. P. Mannarino, & E. Deblinger (Eds.), *Trauma-focused CBT for children and adolescents: Treatment applications* (pp. 175–196). New York: The Guilford Press.

Kohler, P. K., Manhart, L. E., & Lafferty, W. E. (2008). Abstinence-only and comprehensive sex education and the initiation of sexual activity and teen pregnancy. *Journal of Adolescent Health, 42*(4), 344–351.

Kolko, D. J., Moser, J. T., & Weldy, S. R. (1988). Behavioral emotional indicators of sexual abuse in child psychiatric inpatients: A controlled comparison with physical abuse. *Child Abuse & Neglect, 12*, 529–541.

Kopiec, K., Finkelhor, D., & Wolak, J. (2004). Which juvenile crime victims get mental health treatment? *Child Abuse & Neglect, 28*, 45–59.

Kovacs, M. (2011). *Children's Depression Inventory 2nd edition (CDI2): Technical manual.* North Tonawanda, NY: Multi-Health Systems, Inc.

Kuhn, B. R., & Weidinger, D. (2000). Interventions for infant and toddler sleep disturbance: A review. *Child and Family Behavior Therapy, 22*, 33–50.

Kumar, G., Steer, R., & Deblinger, E. (1996). Problems in differentiating sexually from nonsexually abused adolescent psychiatric inpatients by self-reported anxiety, depression, internalization, and externalization. *Child Abuse & Neglect, 20*(11), 1079–1086.

Lacelle, C., Hébert, M., Lavoie, F., Vitaro, F., & Tremblay, R. E. (2012). Sexual health in women reporting a history of child sexual abuse. *Child Abuse & Neglect, 36*(3), 247–259. doi: 10.1016/j.chiabu.2011.10.011

Lamb, S., & Coakley, M. (1993). "Normal" childhood sexual play and games: Differentiating play from abuse. *Child Abuse & Neglect, 17*(4), 515–526.

Lamb, M. E., Hershkowitz, I., Orbach, Y., & Esplin, P. W. (2008). *Tell me what happened: Structured investigative interviews of child victims and witnesses.* Hoboken, NJ: Wiley.

Lamb-Shapiro, J. (2001). *The hyena who lost her laugh.* Plainview, NY: Childswork/Childsplay.

Lana, W. (2004). *Little yogis coloring book.* Sacramento, CA: Wai Lana Productions, LLC.

Lane, B., & Gullone, E. (1999). Common fears: A comparison of adolescents' self-generated and fear survey schedule generated fears. *The Journal of Genetic Psychology: Research and Theory on Human Development, 160*(2), 194–204.

Lanktree, C. B., Briere, J., & Zaidi, L. (1991). Incidence and impact of sexual abuse in child outpatient sample: The role of direct inquiry. *Child Abuse & Neglect, 15*, 447–453.

Larsson, I., & Svedin, C. G. (2001). Sexual behaviour in Swedish preschool children, as observed by their parents. *Acta Paediatrica, 90*(4), 436–444. doi: 10.1111/j.1651-2227.2001.tb00446.x

Latham, G. I. (1992). Interacting with at-risk children: The positive approach. *Principal, 72*(1), 26–30.

Layous, K., Chancellor, J., & Lyubomirsky, S. (2014). Positive activities as protective factors against mental health conditions. *Journal of Abnormal Psychology, 123*(1), 3–12.

Leahy, R. L. (2003). *Cognitive therapy techniques: A practitioner's guide.* New York: The Guilford Press.

Leathers, S. J. (2006). Placement disruption and negative placement outcomes among adolescents in long-term foster care: The role of behavior problems. *Child Abuse & Neglect, 30,* 307–324.

Lebel, C., & Beaulieu, C. (2011). Longitudinal development of human brain wiring continues from childhood into adulthood. *The Journal of Neuroscience, 31*(30), 10937–10947.

Leenarts, L. E. W., Diehle, J., Doreleijers, T. A. H., Jansma, E. P., & Lindauer, R. J. L. (2013). Evidence-based treatments for children with trauma-related psychopathology as a result of childhood maltreatment: A systematic review. *European Child & Adolescent Psychiatry, 22,* 269–283.

Lehman, C. (2014). *Strong at the heart: How it feels to heal from sexual abuse* (2nd ed.). Arcata, CA: Sky Pilot Books.

Leifer, M., Kilbane, T., & Grossman, G. (2001). A three-generational study comparing the families of supportive and unsupportive mothers of sexually abused children. *Child Maltreatment, 6*(4), 353–364. doi: 10.1177/1077559502006004008

Leifer, M., Shapiro, J. P., & Kassem, L. (1993). The impact of maternal history and behavior upon foster placement and adjustment in sexually abused girls. *Child Abuse & Neglect, 17,* 755–766.

Leitenberg, H., Greenwald, E., & Cado, S. (1992). A retrospective study of long-term methods of coping with having been sexually abused during childhood. *Child Abuse & Neglect, 16,* 399–407.

Levy, J. (2004). *Finding the right spot: When kids can't live with their parents.* Washington, DC: Magination Press.

Lipovsky, I. A., Saunders, B. E., & Murphy, S. M. (1989). Depression, anxiety, and behavior problems among victims of father-child sexual assault and nonabused siblings. *Journal of Interpersonal Violence, 4,* 452–468.

Lite, L. (2008). *Angry octopus: A relaxation story.* Marietta, GA: Stress Free Kids.

Lite, L. (2011). *Affirmation weaver: A believe in yourself story, designed to help children boost self-esteem while decreasing stress and anxiety.* Marietta, GA: Stress Free Kids.

Liu, X., Liu, L., Owens, J. A., & Kaplan, D. L. (2005). Sleep patterns and sleep problems among schoolchildren in the United States and China. *Pediatrics, 115*(1 Supplement), 241–249.

London, K., Bruck, M., Ceci, S., & Shuman, D. (2005). Disclosure of child sexual abuse: What does the research tell us about the ways that children tell? *Psychology, Public Policy, and Law, 11*(1), 194–226. doi: 10.1037/1076-8971.11.1.194

London, K., Bruck, M., Wright, D., & Ceci, S. (2008). Review of the contemporary literature on how children report sexual abuse to others: Findings, methodological issues, and implications for forensic interviewers. *Memory, 16*(1), 29–47. doi: 10.1080/09658210701725732

Lovell, P. (2001). *Stand tall, Molly Lou Melon.* New York: G. P. Putnam's Sons.

Lovett, B. B. (1995). Child sexual abuse: The female victim's relationship with her non-offending mother. *Child Abuse & Neglect, 19*, 729–738.

Lowery, L. (2008). *Laurie tells.* Laredo, TX: MaxBooks.

Lyons, J. A. (1987). Post-traumatic stress disorder in children and adolescents: A review of the literature. *Developmental and Behavioral Pediatrics, 8*, 349–356.

Lyons, J. S., Weiner, D. A., & Scheider, A. (2006). *A field trial of three evidence-based practices for trauma with children in state custody.* (Report to the Illinois Department of Children and Family Services). Evanston, IL: Mental Health Resources Services and Policy Program, Northwestern University.

Mackenzie, M. J., Carlson, L. E., Ekkekakis, P., Paskevich, D. M., & Culos-Reed, S. N. (2013). Affect and mindfulness as predictors of change in mood disturbance, stress symptoms, and quality of life in a community-based yoga program for cancer survivors. *Evidence-Based Complementary and Alternative Medicine, 2013*, 1–13. doi: 10.1155/2013/419496

Maclean, K. L. (2008). *Peaceful piggy yoga.* Morton Grove, IL: Albert Whitman & Company.

Madaras, L., & Madaras, A. (2007). *The "what's happening to my body?" book for boys* (3rd ed.). New York: New Market Press.

Malloy, L. C., Brubacher, S. P., & Lamb, M. E. (2011). Expected consequences of disclosure revealed in investigative interviews with suspected victims of child sexual abuse. *Applied Developmental Science, 15*(1), 8–19. doi: 10.1080/10888691.2011.538616

Malloy, L. C., Brubacher, S. P., & Lamb, M. E. (2013). "Because she's one who listens": Children discuss disclosure recipients in forensic interviews. *Child Maltreatment, 18*(4), 245–251. doi: 10.1177/1077559513497250

Malloy, L., Lyon T., & Quas, J. (2007). Filial dependency and recantation of child sexual abuse allegations. *Journal of the American Academy of Child & Adolescent Psychiatry, 46*(2), 162–170. doi: 10.1097/01.chi.0000246067.77953.f7

Manion, G., McIntyre, J., Firestone, P., Ligezinska, M., Ensom, R., & Wells, G. (1996). Secondary traumatization in parents following the disclosure of extrafamilial child sexual abuse: Initial effects. *Child Abuse & Neglect, 20*, 1095–1109.

Mannarino, A. P., & Cohen, J. A. (1986). A clinical-demographic study of sexually abused children. *Child Abuse* & *Neglect, 10*(1), 17–23.

Mannarino, A. P., & Cohen, J. A. (1996a). Abuse-related attributions and perceptions, general attributions, and locus of control in sexually abused girls. *Journal of Interpersonal Violence, 11*(2), 162–180. doi: 10.1177/088626096011002002

Mannarino, A. P., & Cohen, J. A. (1996b). A follow-up study of factors that mediate the development of psychological symptomatology in sexually abused girls. *Child Maltreatment, 1*, 246–260.

Mannarino, A. P., Cohen, J. A., & Berman, S. R. (1994). The Children's Attributions and Perceptions Scale: A new measure of sexual abuse-related factors. *Journal of Clinical Child Psychology, 23*, 204–211.

Mannarino, A. P., Cohen, J. A., Deblinger, E., Runyon, M. K., & Steer, R. A. (2012). Trauma-focused Cognitive-Behavioral Therapy for children: Sustained impact of treatment 6 and 12 months later. *Child Maltreatment, 17*, 231–241.

Mannarino, A. P., Cohen, J. A., & Gregor, M. (1989). Emotional and behavioral difficulties in sexually abused girls. *Journal of Interpersonal Violence, 4*(4), 437–451.

Mannarino, A. P., Cohen, J. A., Smith, J. A., & Moore-Motily, S. (1991). Six and twelve month follow-up of sexually abused girls. *Journal of Interpersonal Violence, 6*(4), 484–511.

Mariah, K. (2004). *Angry animals 2: A board game teaching healthy expression of anger.* Torrance, CA: Creative Therapy Store.

Marx, B. P., & Sloan, D. M. (2002). The role of emotion in the psychological functioning of adult survivors of childhood sexual abuse. *Behavior Therapy, 33*, 563–577.

Mayle, P. (1995). *Where did I come from?* New York: Carol.

McCloskey, K., & Raphael, D. (2005). Adult perpetrator gender asymmetries in child sexual assault victim selection: Results from the 2000 National Incident-Based Reporting System. *Journal of Child Sexual Abuse, 14*(4), 1–24.

McElvaney, R., Greene, S., & Hogan, D. (2012). Containing the secret of child sexual abuse. *Journal of Interpersonal Violence, 27*(6), 1155–1175. doi: 10.1177/0886260511424503

McKay, M., & Bannon, Jr. W. M. (2004). Engaging families in child mental health services. *Child and Adolescent Psychiatric Clinics of North America, 13*, 905–921.

McKay, M., Pennington, J., Lynn, C. J., & McCadam, K. (2001). Understanding urban child mental health service use: Two studies of child, family and environmental correlates. *The Journal of Behavioral Health Services* & *Research, 28*(4), 475–483.

McKay, M., Stoewe, J., McCadam, K., & Gonzales, J. (1998). Increasing access to child mental health services for urban children and their caregivers. *Health and Social Work, 23*, 9–15.

McLeer, S., Callaghan, M., Henry, D., & Wallen, J. (1994). Psychiatric disorders in sexually abused children. *Journal of the American Academy of Child & Adolescent Psychiatry, 33*, 313–319.

McLeer, S., Deblinger, E., Atkins, M., Foa, E., & Ralphe, D. (1988). Post-traumatic stress disorder in sexually abused children. *Journal of the American Academy of Child & Adolescent Psychiatry, 27*, 650–654.

McLeer, S. V., Deblinger, E., Henry, D., & Orvaschel, H. (1992). Sexually abused children at high risk for post-traumatic stress disorder. *Journal of the American Academy of Child & Adolescent Psychiatry, 31*, 875–879.

McMullen, J., O'Callaghan, P., Shannon, C., Black, A., & Eakin, J. (2013). Group trauma-focused cognitive-behavioural therapy with former child soldiers and other war-affected boys in the DR Congo: A randomised controlled trial. *Journal of Child Psychology and Psychiatry, 54*(11), 1231–1241.

McShane, G., Walter, G., & Rey, J. M. (2001). Characteristics of adolescents with school refusal. *Australian and New Zealand Journal of Psychiatry, 35*(6), 822–826.

Meltzer, L. J. (2010). Clinical management of behavioral insomnia of childhood: Treatment of bedtime problems and night wakings in young children. *Behavioral Sleep Medicine, 8*, 172–189. doi: 10.1080/15402002.2010.487464

Merrill, L. L., Thomsen, C. J., Sinclair, B. B., Gold, S. R., & Milner, J. S. (2001). Predicting the impact of child sexual abuse on women: The role of abuse severity, parental support, and coping strategies. *Journal of Consulting and Clinical Psychology, 69*, 992–1006.

Mitlin, M. (2006). *Emotional bingo for teens.* Los Angeles: Western Psychological Services.

Mitlin, M. (2008). *Emotional bingo for children.* Los Angeles: Western Psychological Services.

Moles, K. (2001). *The teen relationship workbook: For professionals helping teens to develop healthy relationships and prevent domestic violence.* Mellville, NY: Wellness Reproductions.

Molnar, B., Buka, S., & Kessler, R. (2001). Child sexual abuse and subsequent psychopathology: Results from the national comorbidity study. *American Journal of Public Health, 19*(5), 753–760.

Morris, A. S., Silk, J. S., Steinberg, L., Myers, S. S., & Robinson, L. R. (2007). The role of the family context in the development of emotion regulation. *Social Development, 16*(2), 361–388.

Morrow, K. B. (1991). Attributions of female adolescent incest victims regarding their molestation. *Child Abuse & Neglect, 15*(4), 477–483.

Morrow, K. B., & Sorrell, G. T. (1989). Factors affecting self-esteem, depression, and negative behaviors in sexually abused female adolescents. *Journal of Marriage and the Family, 51*, 677–686.

Moser, A. J. (1988). *Don't pop your cork on Mondays!: The children's anti-stress book.* Kansas City, MO: Landmark Editions, Inc.

Mowrer, O. H. (1939). A stimulus-response analysis of anxiety and its role as a reinforcing agent. *Psychological Review, 46*, 553–565.

Mundorf, E., & Paivio, S. (2011). Narrative quality and disturbance pre- and post-emotion-focused therapy for child abuse trauma. *Journal of Traumatic Stress, 24*(6), 643–665.

Mundy, M. (1998). *Sad isn't bad: A good-grief guidebook for kids dealing with loss.* St. Meinrad, IN: Abbey Press.

Munson, L., & Riskin, K. (1995). *In their own words: A sexual abuse workbook for teenage girls.* Washington, DC: Child Welfare League of America, Inc.

Murray, L. K., Cohen, J. A., & Mannarino, A. P. (2013). Trauma-focused cognitive behavioral therapy for youth who experience continuous traumatic exposure. *Peace and Conflict: Journal of Peace Psychology, 19*(2), 180–195. doi: 10.1037/a0032533

Murray, L. K., Familiar, I., Skavenski, S., Jere, E., Cohen, J., Imasiku, M., … Bolton, P. (2013). An evaluation of trauma focused cognitive behavioral therapy for children in Zambia. *Child Abuse & Negelct, 37*, 1175–1185.

Murray, L. K., Skavenski, S., Kane, J. C., Mayeya, J., Dorsey, S., Cohen, J. A., ... Bolton, P. A. (2015). Effectiveness of Trauma-Focused Cognitive Behavioral Therapy among trauma-affected children in Lusaka, Zambia: A randomized clinical trial. *JAMA Pediatrics*, E1-E9 doi:10.1001/jamapediatrics.2015.0580

Murray, L. K., & Skavenski, S. A. (2012). International settings. In J. A. Cohen, A. P. Mannarino, & E. Deblinger (Eds.), *Trauma-focused CBT for children and adolescents: Treatment applications* (pp. 225–252). New York: The Guilford Press.

Myers, J., Diedrich, S., Lee, D., Fincher, K. M., & Stern, R. (1999). Professional writing on child sexual abuse from 1900 to 1975: Dominant themes and impact on prosecution. *Child Maltreatment, 4*(3), 201–216.

Nadar, K. (2008). How children and adolescents' brains are affected by trauma. In K. Nader, *Understanding and assessing trauma in children and adolescents: Measures, methods, and youth in context.* (pp. 31–57). New York: Routledge.

Nass, M. S., (2001). *The lion who lost his roar: A story about facing your fears*. Plainview, NY: Childswork/Childsplay.

NCTSN. (2008). Cultural and family differences in children's sexual education and knowledge. *Culture & Trauma Briefs*, *3*(1), 1–6.

Nelson, E., Heath, A. C., Madden, P., Cooper, M., Dinwiddie, S., Bucholz, K., ... Martin, N. (2002). Association between self-reported childhood sexual abuse and adverse psychosocial outcomes: Results from a twin study. *Archives of General Psychiatry*, *59*, 139–145.

Newberger, C. M., Gremy, I. M., Waternaux, C. M., & Newberger, E. H. (1993). Mothers of sexually abused children: Trauma and repair in longitudinal perspective. *American Journal of Orthopsychiatry*, *63*, 92–102.

Newman, C. (1994). Understanding client resistance: Methods for enhancing motivation to change. *Cognitive and Behavioral Practice*, *1*, 47–69.

Nezlek, J. B., & Derks, P. (2001). Use of humor as a coping mechanism, psychological adjustment, and social interaction. *Humor*, *14*(4), 395–413.

Noll, J. (2008). Sexual abuse of children-unique in its effect on development? *Child Abuse & Neglect*, *32*, 603–605. doi: 10.1016/j.chiabu.2007.09.008

Noll, J., Shenk, E., Yeh, M., Ji, J., Putnam, F., & Trickett, P. (2010). Receptive language and educational attainment for sexually abused females. *Pediatrics*, *126*, e615-e622.

Noll, J., Trickett, P., Harris, W., & Putnam, F. (2009). The cumulative burden borne by offspring whose mothers were sexually abused as children: Descriptive results from a multigenerational study. *Journal of Interpersonal Violence*, *24*(3), 424–449. doi: 10.1177/0886260508317194

Noll, J. G., Trickett, P. K., & Putnam, F. W. (2000). Social network constellation and sexuality of sexually abused and comparison girls in childhood and adolescence. *Child Maltreatment*, *5*, 323–337.

Noll, J. G., Zeller, M., Trickett, P., & Putnam, F. (2007). Obesity risk for female victims of childhood sexual abuse: A prospective study. *Pediatrics*, *120*, e61–e67.

O'Callaghan, P., McMullen, J., Shannon, C., Rafferty, H., & Black, A. (2013). A randomized controlled trial of trauma-focused cognitive behavioral therapy for sexually exploited, war-affected Congolese girls. *Journal of the American Academy of Child & Adolescent Psychiatry*, *52*(4), 359–369.

O'Donnell, K., Dorsey, S., Gong, W., Osterman, J., Whetten, R., Cohen, J. A., Itemba, D., ... Whetten, K. (2014). Treating maladaptive grief and posttraumatic stress symptoms in orphaned children in Tanzania: Group-based trauma-focused cognitive-behavioral therapy. *Journal of Traumatic Stress*, *27*, 664–671.

O'Leary, P. J., & Barber, J. (2008). Gender differences in silencing following childhood sexual abuse. *Journal of Child Sexual Abuse*, *17*(2), 133–143.

Ormhaug, S. M., Jensen, T. K., Wentzel-Larsen, T., & Shirk, S. R. (2014). The therapeutic alliance in treatment of traumatized youths: Relation to outcome in a randomized clinical trial. *Journal of Consulting and Clinical Psychology*, *82*(1), 52–64.

Owens, J. A., & Mindell, J. A. (2005). *Take charge of your child's sleep: The all-in-one resource for solving sleep problems in kids and teens*. New York: Marlowe & Company.

Pacifici, C., Chamberlain, P., & White, L. (2007). *Off road parenting: Practical solutions for difficult behavior*. Eugene, OR: Northwest Media, Inc.

Palmer, P. (2011). *The mouse, the monster, and me: Assertiveness for young people*. Weaverville, CA: Boulden Publishing.

Paniagua, F. A. (2005). *Assessing and treating culturally diverse clients* (3rd ed.). Thousand Oaks, CA: SAGE Publications.

Patterson, G. R., & Forgatch, M. S. (2005). *Parents and adolescents living together Part 1: The basics* (2nd ed.). Champaign, IL: Research Press.

Pelcovitz, D., Kaplan, S., Goldenberg, B., Mandel, F., Lehane, J., & Gaurarrera, J. (1994). Post-traumatic stress disorder in physically abused adolescents. *Journal of the American Academy of Child & Adolescent Psychiatry, 33*, 305–312.

Pellegrin, A., & Wagner, W. (1990). Child sexual abuse: Factors affecting victims' removal from home. *Child Abuse & Neglect, 14*, 53–60.

Perez-Fuentes, G., Olfson, M., Villegas, L., Morcillo, C., Wang, S., & Blanco, C. (2013). Prevalence and correlates of child sexual abuse: A national study. *Comprehensive Psychiatry, 54*(1), 16–27. doi: 10.1016/j.comppsych.2012.05.010

Phelan, T. W. (2010). *1-2-3 Magic: Effective discipline for children 2-12* (4th ed.). Glen Ellyn, IL: ParentMagic, Inc.

Pierce, R., & Pierce, L. (1985). The sexually abused child: A comparison of male and female victims. *Child Abuse & Neglect, 9*, 191–199.

Pintello, D., & Zuravin, S. (2001). Intrafamilial child sexual abuse: Predictors of post-disclosure maternal belief and protective action. *Child Maltreatment, 6*(4), *344–352*. doi: 10.1177/1077559501006004007

Piper, W. (2012). *The little engine that could*. New York: Grosset & Dunlap.

Planned Parenthood. (1986). *How to talk with your child about sexuality.* New York: Doubleday.

Plummer, C. A., & Eastin, J. A. (2007). System intervention problems in child sexual abuse investigations: The mother's perspective. *Journal of Interpersonal Violence*, 22(6), 775–787.

Polland, B. K. (1975). *Feelings: Inside you and outloud too.* Berkeley, CA: Tricycle Press.

Pynoos, R., Rodriguez, N., Steinberg, A., Stuber, M., & Frederick, C. (1998). UCLA PTSD Index for DSM-IV. Unpublished manuscript, Los Angeles, CA: UCLA Trauma Psychiatry Service.

Ready, C. B., Hayes, A. M., Yasinski, C. W., Webb, C., Gallop, R., & E. Deblinger. (2014). Overgeneralized beliefs, new learning, and symptom outcome in youth receiving Trauma-Focused Cognitive Behavioral Therapy for childhood trauma. Manuscript submitted for publication.

Reinecke, M. A., Dattilio, F. M., & Freeman, A. (2003). *Cognitive therapy with children and adolescents: A casebook for clinical practice* (2nd ed.). New York: The Guilford Press.

Reyes, C. (2008). Exploring the relations among the nature of the abuse, perceived parental support, and child's self-concept and trauma symptoms among sexually abused children. *Journal of Child Sexual Abuse, 17*(1), 51–70.

Ribbe, D. (1996). Psychometric review of Traumatic Event Screening Instrument for Children (TESI-C). In B. H. Stamm (Ed.), *Measurement of stress, trauma, and adaptation* (pp. 386–387). Lutherville, MD: Sidran Press.

Roberts, K. P., Lamb, M. E., & Sternberg, K. J. (2004). The effects of rapport-building style on children's reports of a staged event. *Applied Cognitive Psychology, 18*(2), 189–202.

Roesler, T. A. (1994). Reactions to disclosure of childhood sexual abuse. The effect on adult symptoms. *Journal of Nervous and Mental Disease, 182*, 618–624.

Roesler, T. A., & Wind, T. (1994). Telling the secret: Adult women describe their disclosures of incest. *Journal of Interpersonal Violence, 9*(3), 327–338.

Rohsenow, D. J., Corbett, R., & Devine, D. (1988). Molested as children: A hidden contribution to substance abuse? *Journal of Substance Abuse Treatment, 5*, 13–18.

Rosenthal, S., Feiring, C., & Taska, L. (2003). Emotional support and adjustment over a year's time following sexual abuse discovery. *Child Abuse & Neglect, 27*, 641–661.

Rosenzweig, J. (2012). *The sex-wise parent: The parent's guide to protecting your child, strengthening your family, and talking to kids about sex, abuse, and bullying.* New York: Skyhorse Publishing.

Rowe, M. B. (1986). Wait time: Slowing down may be a way of speeding up! *Journal of Teacher Education, 37*, 43–50.

Ruggiero, K. J., McLeer, S. V., & Dixon, J. F. (2000). Sexual abuse characteristics associated with survivor psychopathology. *Child Abuse & Neglect*, 24, 951–964.

Rumstein-McKean, O., & Hunsley, J. (2001). Interpersonal and family functioning of female survivors of childhood sexual abuse. *Clinical Psychology Review, 21*, 471–490.

Runtz, M. G., & Schallow, J. R. (1997). Social support and coping strategies as mediators of adult adjustment following childhood maltreatment. *Child Abuse & Neglect, 21*(2), 211–226.

Runyon, M., Basilio, I., Van Hasselt, V. B., & Hersen, M. (1998). Child witnesses of interparental violence: Child and family treatment. In V. B. Van Hasselt & M. Hersen (Eds.), *Handbook of psychological treatment protocols for children and adolescents* (pp. 224–300). Mahwah, NJ: Lawrence Erlbaum Associates, Inc.

Runyon, M. K., Cooper, B., & Glickman, A. R. (2007). *Helping families heal: A story about child physical abuse.* Stratford, NJ: CARES Institute.

Runyon, M. K., & Deblinger, E. (2014). *Combined Parent-Child Cognitive Behavioral Therapy (CPC-CBT): An approach to empower families at-risk for child physical abuse.* New York: Oxford University Press.

Runyon, M. K., Faust, J., & Orvaschel, H. (2002). Differential symptom pattern of post-traumatic stress disorder (PTSD) in maltreated children with and without concurrent depression. *Child Abuse* & *Neglect, 26*(1), 39–53.

Runyon, M. K., Spandorfer, E., & Schroeder, C. (2014). Cognitions and distress in caregivers after their child's sexual abuse disclosure. *Journal of Child Sexual Abuse, 23*, 146–159.

Salloum, A., & Overstreet, S. (2012). Grief and trauma intervention for children after disaster: Exploring copng skills versus trauma narration. *Behaviour Research and Therapy, 50*, 169–179.

Salloum, A., Robst, J., Scheeringa, M. S., Cohen, J. A., Wang, W., Murphy, T. K.,... Storch, E. A. (2014). Step one within stepped care trauma-focused cognitive behavioral therapy for young children: A pilot study. *Child Psychiatry & Human Development, 45*(1), 65–77.

Saltzman, A. (2007). *Still quiet place: Mindfulness for young children* [CD]. Menlo Park, CA: Author.

Sansonnet-Hayden, H., Haley, G., Marriage, K., & Fine, S. (1987). Sexual abuse and psychopathology in hospitalized adolescents. *Journal of American Academy of Child & Adolescent Psychiatry, 26*(5), 753-757.

Santa-Sosa, E. J., Steer, R. A., Deblinger, E., & Runyon, M. K. (2013). Depression and parenting by nonoffending mothers of children who experienced sexual abuse. *Journal of Child Sexual Abuse, 22*(8), 915–930. doi: 10.1080/10538712.2013.841309

Sarles, R. (1975). Incest. *Pediatric Clinics of North America, 22*, 633–641.

Saunders, B. E., & Adams, Z. W. (2014). Epidemiology of traumatic experiences in childhood. *Child and Adolescent Psychiatric Clinics of North America, 23*, 167–184.

Saunders, B. E., Berliner, L., & Hanson, R. F. (2004). *Child physical and sexual abuse. Guidelines for treatment*. Charleston, S.C.: National Crime Victims Research and Treatment Center.

Saunders, B. E., Kilpatrick, D., Hanson, R., Resnick, H., & Walker, M. (1999). Prevalence, case characteristics, and long-term psychological correlates of child rape among women: A national survey. *Child Maltreatment, 4*(3), 187–200.

Saywitz, K. J., Lyon, T. D., & Goodman, G. S. (2011). Interviewing children. In J. E. B. Myers (Ed.), *The APSAC handbook on child maltreatment* (3rd ed.), (pp. 337–360). Newbury Park, CA: SAGE Publications.

Schaefer, V. (1998). *The care and keeping of you: The body book for girls*. Middleton, WI: Pleasant Company Publications.

Schraufnagel, T., Davis, K., George, W., & Norris, J. (2010). Childhood sexual abuse in males and subsequent risky sexual behavior: A potential alcohol-use pathway. *Child Abuse & Neglect, 34*, 369–378. doi: 10.1016/j.chiabu.2009.08.013

Seligman, M. E. P. (2006). *Learned optimism: How to change your mind and your life*. New York: Vintage Books.

Seligman, M. E. P. (2007). *The optimistic child: A proven program to safeguard children against depression and build lifelong resilience*. New York: Houghton Mifflin.

Sgroi, S., & Dana, N. (1982). Individual and group treatment of mothers of incest victims. In S. Sgroi (Ed.), *Handbook of clinical intervention in child sexual abuse* (pp. 191–214). Toronto: Lexington.

Shapiro, L. W. (2004). *The chimp who lost her chatter: A story about overcoming shyness*. Plainview, NY: Childswork/Childsplay.

Sharpley, C. F. (1997). The influence of silence upon client-perceived rapport. *Counseling Psychology Quarterly, 10*(3), 237–246.

Shaw, J., Lewis, J., Loeb, A., Rosado, J., & Rodriguez, R. (2000). Child on child sexual abuse: Psychological perspectives. *Child Abuse & Neglect, 24*(12), 1591–1600.

Shivak, I. M., & Sullivan, C. W. (1989). Use of telephone prompts at an inner-city outpatient clinic. *Hospital and Community Psychiatry, 40*, 851–853.

Sickel, A. E., Noll, J. G., Moore, P. J., Putnam F. W., & Trickett, P. K. (2002). The long-term physical health and healthcare utilization of women who were sexually abused as children. *Journal of Health Psychology, 7*, 583–597.

Silovsky, J. F., Swisher, L., & Widdifield, J. (2010). *Treatment for school-age children with sexual behavior problems and their families* (3rd ed.). Adapted from Bonner, Walker, & Berliner (1999a,b).

Silver, R. L., Boon, C., & Stones, M. H. (1983). Searching for meaning in misfortune: Making sense of incest. *Journal of Social Issues, 39*(2), 81–101.

Silverman, W. K., Ortiz, C. D., Viswesvaran, C., Burns, B. J., Kolko, D. J., Putnam, F. W., & Amaya-Jackson, L. (2008). Evidence-based psychosocial treatments for children and adolescents exposed to traumatic events. *Journal of Clinical Child & Adolescent Psychology, 37*(1), 156–183.

Simon, V. A., Feiring, C., & McElroy, S. K. (2010). Making meaning of traumatic events: Youths' strategies for processing childhood sexual abuse are associated with psychosocial adjustment. *Child Maltreatment, 15*(3), 229–241. doi: 10.1177/1077559510370365

Sin, N. L., & Lyubomirsky, S. (2009). Enhancing well-being and alleviating depressive symptoms with positive psychology interventions: A practice friendly meta-analysis. *Journal of Clinical Psychology, 65*(5), 467–487. doi:10.1002/jclp.20593

Sirles, E. A., & Franke, P. J. (1989). Factors influencing mothers' reactions to intrafamily sexual abuse. *Child Abuse & Neglect, 13*(1), 131–139.

Slap-Shelton, L., & Shapiro, L. E., (1999). *Every time I blow my top I lose my head.* Plainview, NY: Childswork/Childsplay.

Spaccarelli, S. (1995). Measuring abuse stress and negative cognitive appraisals in child sexual abuse: Validity data on two new scales. *Journal of Abnormal Child Psychology, 23*, 703–727.

Spaccarelli, S., & Kim, S. (1995). Resilience criteria and factors associated with resilience in sexually abused girls. *Child Abuse & Neglect, 19*(9), 1171–1182.

Spelman, C. (1997). *Your body belongs to you.* Park Ridge, IL: Albert Whitman & Company.

Spinelli, E. (1996). *Somebody loves you, Mr. Hatch.* New York: Simon & Schuster.

Sprang, G., Clark, J. J., & Whitt-Woosley, A. W. (2007). Compassion fatigue, compassion satisfaction, and burnout: Factors impacting a professional's quality of life. *Journal of Loss and Trauma, 12*, 259–280.

Staller, K. M., & Nelson-Gardell, D. (2005). "A burden in your heart": Lessons of disclosure from female preadolescent and adolescent survivors of sexual abuse. *Child Abuse & Neglect, 29*, 1415–1432.

Stauffer, L. B., & Deblinger, E. (1996). Cognitive behavioral groups for nonoffending mothers and their young sexually abused children: A preliminary treatment outcome study. *Child Maltreatment, 1*, 65–76.

Stauffer, L. B., & Deblinger, E. (2003a). *Let's talk about taking care of you: An educational book about body safety.* Hatfield, PA: Hope for Families, Inc.

Stauffer, L. B., & Deblinger, E. (2003b). *Let's talk about taking care of you! An educational book about body safety for young children.* Hatfield, PA: Hope for Families, Inc.

Steel, J., Sanna, L., Hammond, B., Whipple, J., & Cross, H. (2004). Psychological sequelae of childhood sexual abuse: Abuse-related characteristics, coping strategies, and attributional style. *Child Abuse & Neglect, 28*(7), 785–801.

Stein, R. E., & Nofziger, S, D. (2008). Adolescent sexual victimization: Choice of confidant and the failure of authorities. *Youth Violence and Juvenile Justice, 6*(2),158–177.

Steinberg, L., Vandell, D. L., & Bornstein, M. H. (2010). *Development: Infancy through adolescence.* Belmont, CA: Wadsworth, Cengage Learning.

Sternberg, K. J., Lamb, M. E., Hershkowitz, I., Yudilevitch, L., Orbach, Y., Esplin, P. W., & Hovav, M. (1997). Effects of introductory style on children's abilities to describe experiences of sexual abuse. *Child Abuse & Neglect, 21*(11), 1133–1146.

Stevenson, H. C., Davis, G., & Abdul-Kabir, S. (2001). *Stickin' to, watchin' over, and gettin' with: An African American parent's guide to discipline.* San Francisco: Jossey-Bass.

Stirling, J., & Amaya-Jackson, L. (2008). Understanding the behavioral and emotional consequences of child abuse. *Pediatrics, 122*, 667–673.

Stoltenborgh, M., van IJzendoorn, M., Euser, E., & Bakermans-Kranenburg, M. (2011). A global perspective on child sexual abuse: Meta-analysis of prevalence around the world. *Child Maltreatment, 16*(2), 79–101. doi: 10.1177/1077559511403920

Strayhorn, J. M., & Weidman, C. S. (1988). A Parent Practices Scale and its relation to parent and child mental health. *Journal of the American Academy of Child & Adolescent Psychiatry, 27*, 613–618.

Summit, R. C. (1983). The child sexual abuse accommodation syndrome. *Child Abuse & Neglect, 7*, 177–193.

Suveg, S. C., Sood, E., Barmish, A., Tiwari, S., Hudson, J. L., & Kendall, P. C. (2008). "I'd rather not talk about it": Emotion parenting in families of children with an anxiety disorder. *Journal of Family Psychology, 22*(6), 875–884. doi: 10.1037/a0012861

Suveg, C., Zeman, J., Flannery-Schroeder, E., & Cassano, M. (2005). Emotion socialization in families of children with an anxiety disorder. *Journal of Abnormal Child Psychology, 33*(2), 145–155.

Szigethy, E., Weisz, J. R., & Findling, R. L. (2012). *Cognitive-behavior therapy for children and adolescents*. Arlington, VA: American Psychiatric Publishing.

Tavris, C. (1989). *Anger: The misunderstood emotion*. New York: Simon & Schuster.

Taylor, D. J., & Roane, B. M. (2010). Treatment of insomnia in adults and children: A practice-friendly review of research. *Journal of Clinical Psychology: In Session*, *66*(11), 1137–1147. doi: 10.1002/jclp.20733

Timmons-Mitchell, J., Chandler-Holtz, D., & Semple, W. E. (1996). Post-traumatic stress symptoms in mothers following children's reports of sexual abuse: An exploratory study. *American Journal of Orthopsychiatry, 66*, 463–467.

Timmons-Mitchell, J., Chandler-Holtz, D., & Semple, W. E. (1997). Post-traumatic stress disorder symptoms in child sexual abuse victims and their mothers. *Journal of Child Sexual Abuse, 6*, 1–14.

Tremblay, C., Hebert, M., & Piche, C. (1999). Coping strategies and social support as mediators of consequences in child sexual abuse victims. *Child Abuse & Neglect, 23*(9), 929–945.

Trickett, P., Noll, J., & Putnam, F. (2011). The impact of sexual abuse on female development: Lessons from a multigenerational, longitudinal research study. *Development and Psychopathology, 23*, 453–476. doi: 10.1017/S0954579411000174

Trickett, P., Reiffman, A., Horowitz, L., & Putnam, F. (1997). Characteristics of sexual abuse trauma and the prediction of developmental outcomes. In D. Cicchetti & S. L. Toth (Eds.), *Rochester Symposium on Developmental Psychopathology, Vol VII: The effects of trauma on the developmental process*, (pp. 289–314). Rochester, NY: University of Rochester Press.

Tufts New England Medical Center, Division of Child Psychiatry. (1984). *Sexually exploited children: Service and research project*. Final report for the Office of Juvenile Justice and Delinquency Prevention. Washington, D.C.: U.S. Department of Justice.

Turner, H., Finkelhor, D., & Ormrod, R. (2006). The effect of lifetime victimization on the mental health of children and adolescents. *Social Science & Medicine, 62*, 13–27.

Turner, H. A., Finkelhor, D., & Ormrod, R. (2010). Poly-victimization in a national sample of children and youth. *American Journal of Preventive Medicine, 38*, 323–330.

Ullman, S. E., & Filipas, H. (2001). Predictors of PTSD symptom severity and social reactions in sexual assault victims. *Journal of Traumatic Stress, 14*, 369–389.

van der Kolk, B. A. (1988). The trauma spectrum: The interaction of biological and social events in the genesis of the trauma response. *Journal of Traumatic Stress, 1*, 273–290.

Ventis, W. L., Higbee, G., & Murdock, S. A. (2001). Using humor in systematic desensitization to reduce fear. *Journal of General Psychology, 128*(2), 241–253.

Verdick, E. (2010). *Calm-down time*. Minneapolis, MN: Free Spirit Publishing.

Vilaythong, A. P., Arnau, R. C., Rosen, D. H., & Mascaro, N. (2003). Humor and hope: Can humor increase hope? *Humor, 16*(1), 79–89.

Wahler, R. G., Herring, M., & Edwards, M. (2001). Coregulation of balance between children's prosocial approaches and acts of compliance: A pathway to mother–child cooperation? *Journal of Clinical Child & Adolescent Psychology, 30*(4), 473–478.

Walsh, W. A., Cross, T. P., & Jones, L. M. (2012). Do parents blame or doubt their child more when sexually abused by adolescents versus adults? *Journal of Interpersonal Violence, 27*(3), 453–470.

Webb, C., Hayes, A. M., Grasso, D., Laurenceau, J., & Deblinger, E. (2014). Trauma-focused cognitive behavioral therapy for youth: Effectiveness in a community setting. *Psychologocial Trauma: Theory, Research, Practice, and Policy, 6*(5), 555–562.

Webster-Stratton, C. (1992). *The incredible years: A trouble-shooting guide for parents of children aged 3–8*. Toronto: Umbrella Press.

Weiss-Gelmi, D. (2012). *Sing song yoga*. Plainview, NY: Childswork/Childsplay.

Weisz, J. R., & Hawley, K. M. (2002). Developmental factors in the treatment of adolescents. *Journal of Consulting and Clinical Psychology, 70*(1), 21–43.

West Coast Children's Clinic. (2012). *Research to action: Sexually exploited minors (SEM) needs and strengths*. Oakland, CA: Author.

Whiffen, V., & MacIntosh, H. (2005). Mediators of the link between childhood sexual abuse and emotional distress: A critical review. *Trauma, Violence, & Abuse, 6*(1), 24–39.

Whitham, C. (1991). *Win the whining war & other skirmishes: A family peace plan*. Los Angeles: Perspective Publishing.

Widom, C. (1999). Post-traumatic stress disorder in abused and neglected children grown up. *The American Journal of Psychiatry, 156*(8), 1223–1229.

Widom, C. S., Czaja, S. J., & Dutton, M. A. (2008). Childhood victimization and lifetime revictimization. *Child Abuse & Neglect, 32*(8), 785–796.

Widgery, A., & Winterfield, A. (2013). Mental health professionals' duty to warn. *LegisBrief, 21*(1), 1–2.

Wilgocki, J., & Wright, M. K. (2002). *Maybe days: A book for children in foster care*. Washington, DC: Magination Press.

Williams, J., & Nelson-Gardell, D. (2012). Predicting resilience in sexually abused adolescents. *Child Abuse & Neglect, 36*, 53–63.

Williams, J. E., Paton, C. C., Siegler, I. C., Eigenbrodt, M. L., Nieto, F. J., & Tryoler, H. A. (2000). Anger proneness predicts coronary heart disease risk. *Circulation, 101*, 2034–2039.

Winkler, S. (2013). *The music of World War II: War songs and their stories*. Bennington, VT: Merriam Press.

Worling, J. (1995). Adolescent sibling-incest offenders: Differences in family and individual functioning when compared to adolescent nonsibling sex offenders. *Child Abuse & Neglect, 19*(5), 633–643.

Wright, M. O., Crawford, E., & Sebastian, K. (2007). Positive resolution of childhood sexual abuse experiences: The role of coping, benefit-finding and meaning-making. *Journal of Family Violence, 22*, 597–608.

Wurtele, S. K., Kast, L. A., & Melzer, A. M. (1992). Sexual abuse prevention education for young children: A comparison of teachers and parents as instructors. *Child Abuse & Neglect, 16*(6), 865–876.

Wurtele, S., Marrs, S., & Miller-Perrin, C. (1987). Practice makes perfect: The role of participant modeling in sexual abuse prevention programs. *Journal of Consulting and Clinical Psychology, 55*, 599–602.

Wurtele, S. K., Saslawsky, D. A., Miller-Perrin, C. L., Marrs, S. R., & Britcher, J. C. (1986). Teaching personal safety skills for potential prevention of sexual abuse: A comparison of treatments. *Journal of Consulting and Clinical Psychology, 54*(5), 688–692.

Wyatt, G. E., Loeb, T. B., Solis, B., Carmona, J. V., & Romero, G. (1999). The prevalence and circumstances of child sexual abuse: Changes across a decade. *Child Abuse & Neglect, 23*(1), 45–60.

Yancey, C. T., & Hansen, D. J. (2010). Relationship of personal, familial, and abuse-specific factors with outcome following childhood sexual abuse. *Aggression and Violent Behavior, 15*, 410–421.

ABOUT THE AUTHORS

Esther Deblinger, Ph.D., is co-founder and co-director of the Child Abuse Research Education and Service (CARES) Institute and a professor of psychiatry at Rowan University School of Osteopathic Medicine (RowanSOM). Dr. Deblinger and her colleagues at CARES have conducted extensive research on the impact and treatment of child sexual abuse as well as other childhood traumas. She has received funding for her research and training efforts from the Foundation of UMDNJ, the National Center on Child Abuse and Neglect, the National Institute of Mental Health, the Substance Abuse Mental Health and Services Administration, Robert Wood Johnson Foundation, and Rowan University Foundation. Dr. Deblinger and her collaborators, Drs. Judith Cohen and Anthony Mannarino, developed and extensively tested trauma-focused cognitive-behavioral therapy (TF-CBT), a treatment program that has evolved as the standard of care for children and adolescents who have experienced a wide array of traumatic childhood experiences. Over 25 scientific investigations, including 16 randomized trials, have documented the efficacy of TF-CBT to date. Moreover, introductory training in TF-CBT has been made accessible free of charge to over 200,000 mental health professionals worldwide through an online training site developed in collaboration with professionals from the Medical University of South Carolina (www.musc.edu/tfcbt). Dr. Deblinger also has collaborated with Dr. Melissa Runyon in developing and evaluating another evidence-based treatment approach, Combined-Parent Child Cognitive Behavioral Therapy, which is designed for families at risk for child physical abuse. Dr. Deblinger has co-authored numerous scientific publications, several widely acclaimed professional books on childhood trauma, and several children's books on personal safety. She is also a sought after speaker at national and international conferences. Her work over the past 25 years has been recognized with awards from *Woman's Day* magazine, the state of New Jersey's Office of the Child Advocate, the New Jersey General Assembly, and the American Professional Society on the Abuse of Children (APSAC). In addition, Dr. Deblinger has served two terms on the board of APSAC; she is a founding fellow of the Academy of Cognitive Therapy, and she continues to be an active researcher, teacher, and clinician.

Anthony Mannarino, Ph.D., is director of the Center for Traumatic Stress in Children and Adolescents and vice chair of the Department of Psychiatry at Allegheny General Hospital in Pittsburgh, Pennsylvania. He is also professor of psychiatry at the Drexel University College of Medicine. Dr. Mannarino has been a leader in the field of child traumatic stress for the past 25 years. He has been awarded numerous federal grants from the National Center on Child Abuse and Neglect and the National Institute of Mental Health to investigate the clinical course of traumatic stress symptoms in children and to develop effective treatment approaches for traumatized children and their families. Dr. Mannarino has received many honors for his work including the Betty Elmer Outstanding Professional Award, the Most Outstanding Article Award for papers published in the journal *Child Maltreatment* given by the American Professional Society on the Abuse of Children (APSAC), the Model Program Award from the Substance Abuse and Mental Health Services Administration for "Cognitive Behavioral Therapy for Child Traumatic Stress", and the Legacy Award from the Greater Pittsburgh Psychological Association. Dr. Mannarino has recently completed two-year terms as the president of APSAC and the president of the section on child maltreatment, Division of Child and Family Policy and Practice, American Psychological Association. He is one of the co-developers of trauma-focused cognitive-behavioral therapy (TF-CBT).

Judith A. Cohen, M.D., is professor of psychiatry at Drexel University College of Medicine, and medical director of the Center for Traumatic Stress in Children and Adolescents at Allegheny General Hospital in Pittsburgh, Pennsylvania. With Drs. Tony Mannarino and Esther Deblinger, Dr. Cohen developed and tested trauma-focused cognitive-behavioral therapy (TF-CBT) for traumatized children described in the books *Treating Trauma and Traumatic Grief in Children and Adolescents* and *Trauma-Focused CBT for Children and Adolescents: Treatment Applications*, and the online training course TF-CBT*Web* (www.musc.edu/tfcbt). She has served on the board of directors for the American Professional Society on the Abuse of Children (APSAC) and the International Society for Traumatic Stress Studies (ISTSS). She is on the editorial board of the *Journal of the American Academy of Child and Adolescent Psychiatry* (AACAP) and is chair of the AACAP Child Maltreatment and Violence Committee and the National Child Traumatic Stress Network's Child Sexual Abuse and Traumatic Grief Committees. She consults with Sesame Street and the Tragedy Assistance Program for Survivors to develop resources for traumatically bereaved children.

Melissa K. Runyon, Ph.D., is treatment services director of the Child Abuse Research Education and Service (CARES) Institute and a professor of psychiatry at the Rowan University School of Osteopathic Medicine (RowanSOM). Research and/or service grant funding from the National Institute of Mental Health (NIMH), the Substance Abuse Mental Health and Services Administration, and private foundations has been received to support Dr. Runyon's evaluation and dissemination efforts with Combined Parent-Child Cognitive Behavioral Therapy (CPC-CBT). Dr. Runyon and her colleague, Dr. Esther Deblinger, evaluated CPC-CBT through federal funding from NIMH to examine outcomes associated with child and parent participation in CPC-CBT. CPC-CBT was recently listed on the National Registry of Evidence-Based Programs and Practices, where the model received the highest possible score for readiness for dissemination. Dr. Runyon has also served as a co-investigator on a NIMH-funded study examining trauma-focused cognitive-behavioral therapy (TF-CBT) and is a certified TF-CBT therapist and trainer. Dr. Runyon conducts national and international trainings and provides consultation to disseminate TF-CBT and CPC-CBT to professionals. Dr. Runyon has co-authored numerous journal articles, book chapters, and books in the areas of child abuse and domestic violence, including *Combined*

Parent-Child Cognitive Behavioral Therapy: An Approach to Empower Families At-Risk for Child Physical Abuse.

Anne Heflin, Ph.D., is an associate professor at the American School of Professional Psychology at Argosy University, Washington, DC, where she teaches in the areas of child psychopathology, child psychotherapy, and child maltreatment. She also maintains an active private practice where she treats children, adolescents, and young adults. She was previously a clinical assistant professor of psychiatry within the Center for Children's Support (now the CARES Institute) at the University of Medicine and Dentistry of New Jersey, where she worked on the early randomized control trials evaluating TF-CBT and coauthored *Treatment of Sexually Abused Children and Their Nonoffending Parents: A Cognitive Behavioral Approach* with Esther Deblinger.

INDEX